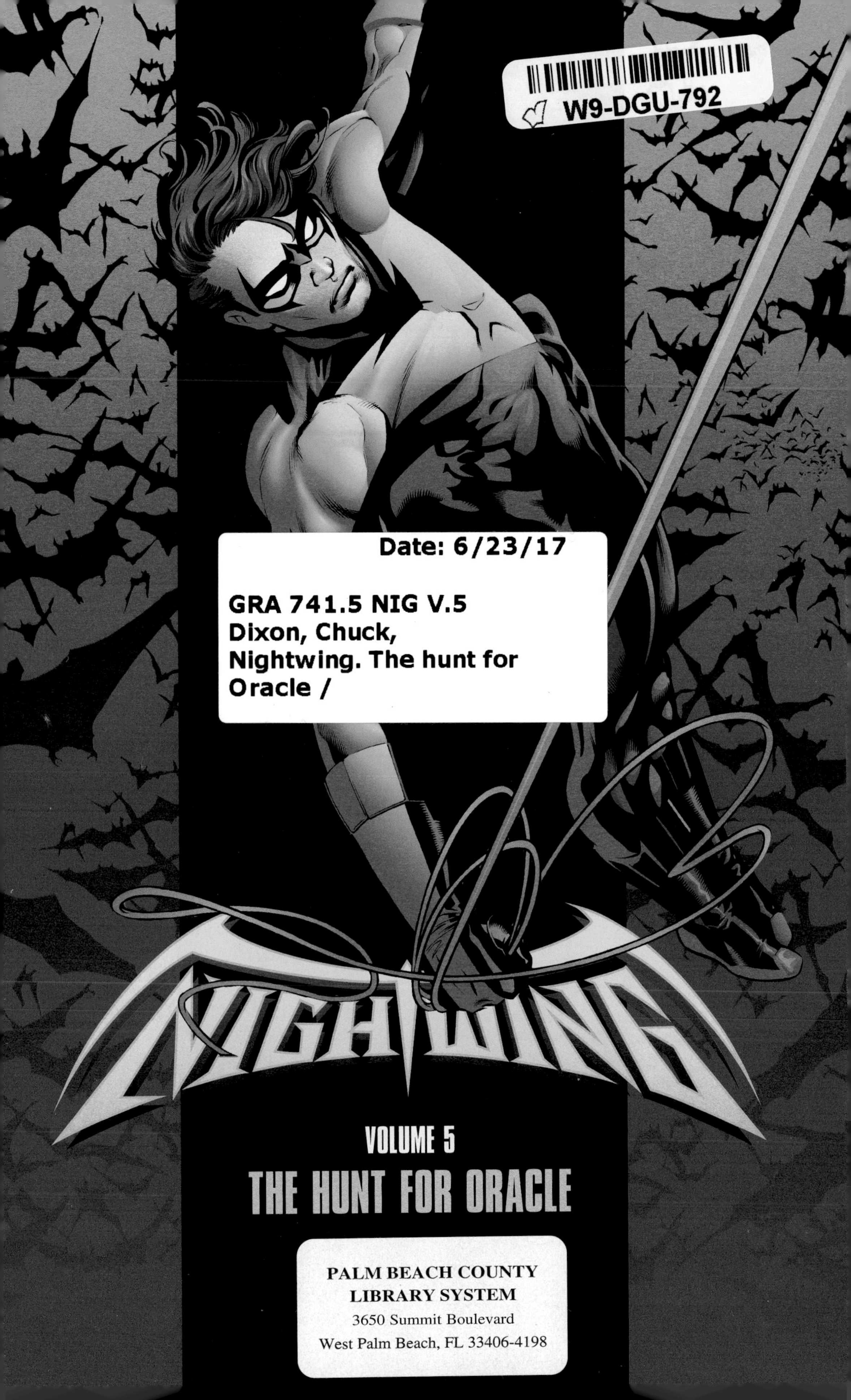
NIGHTWING

NIGHTWING

VOLUME 5

THE HUNT FOR ORACLE

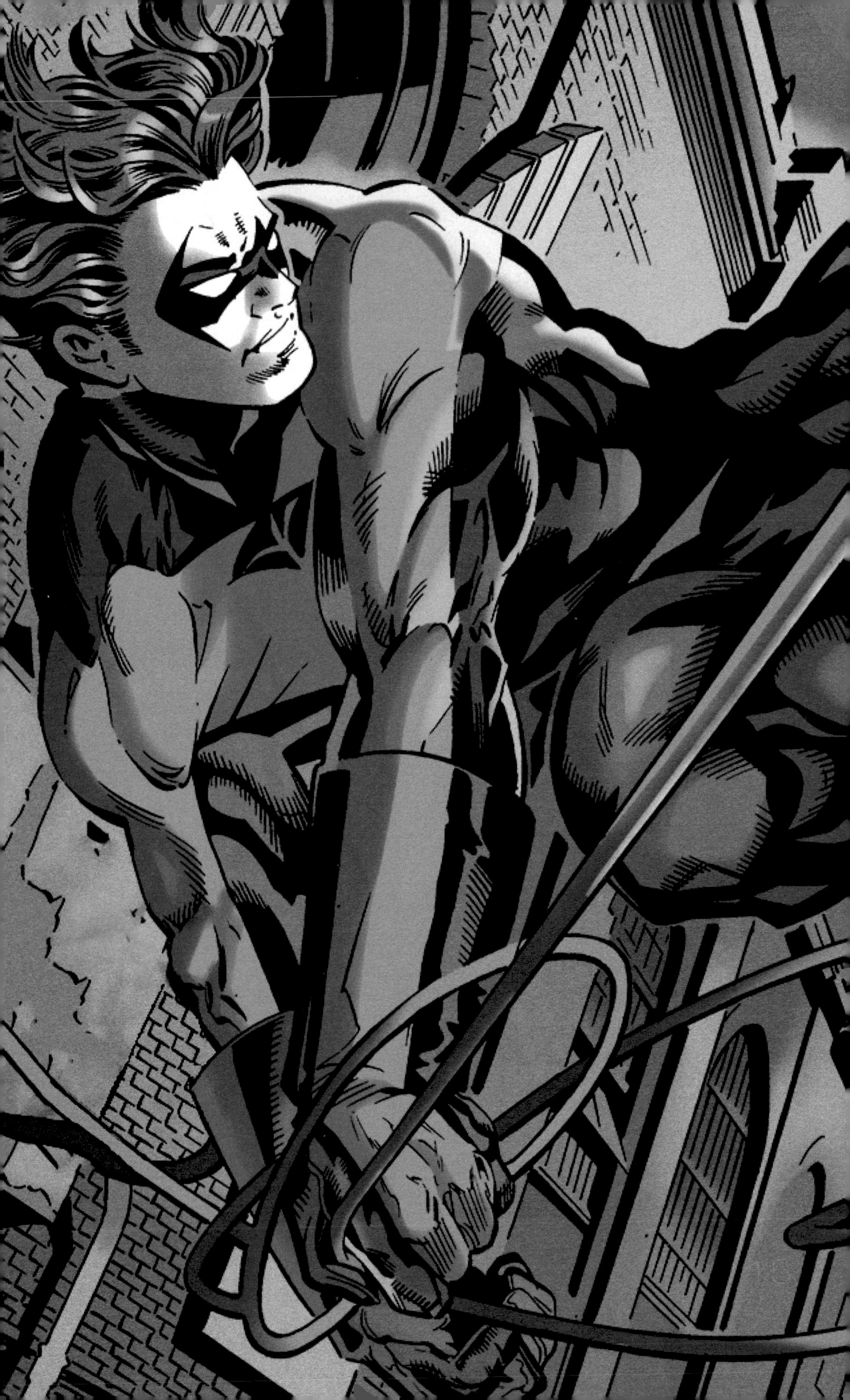

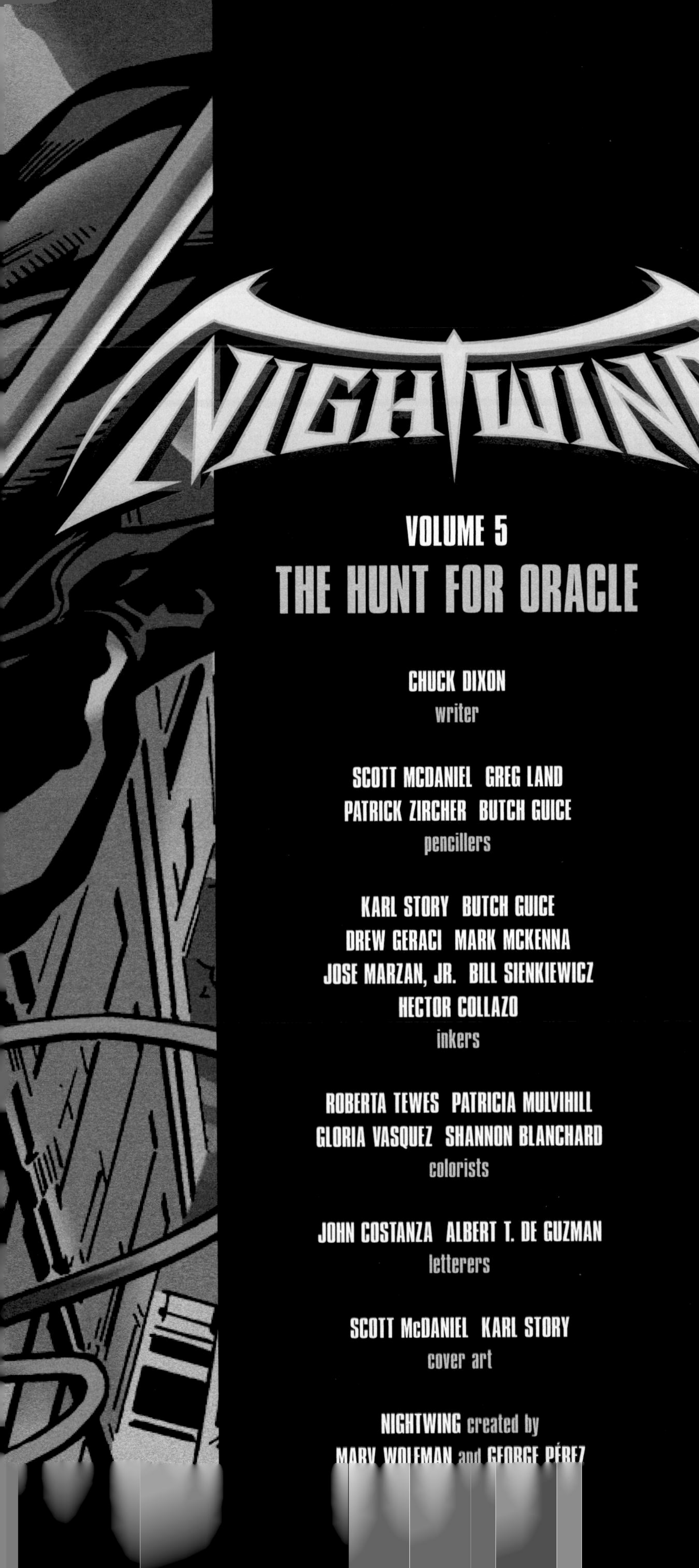

NIGHTWING

VOLUME 5
THE HUNT FOR ORACLE

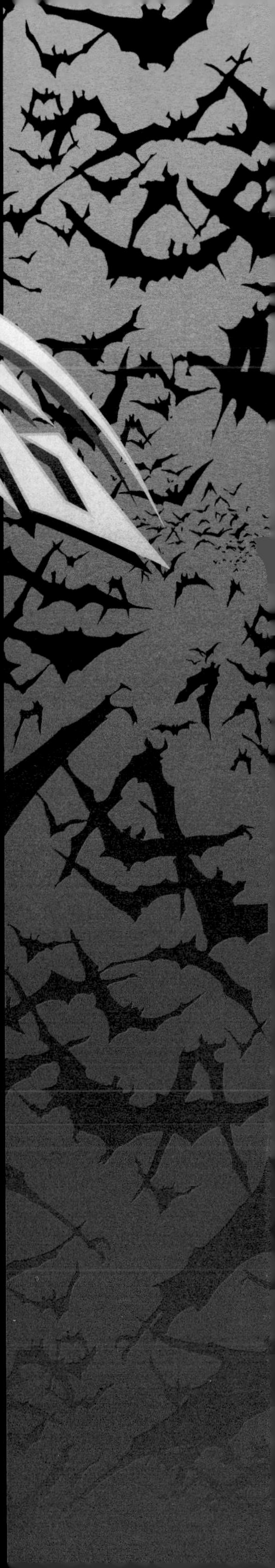

CHUCK DIXON
writer

SCOTT MCDANIEL GREG LAND
PATRICK ZIRCHER BUTCH GUICE
pencillers

KARL STORY BUTCH GUICE
DREW GERACI MARK MCKENNA
JOSE MARZAN, JR. BILL SIENKIEWICZ
HECTOR COLLAZO
inkers

ROBERTA TEWES PATRICIA MULVIHILL
GLORIA VASQUEZ SHANNON BLANCHARD
colorists

JOHN COSTANZA ALBERT T. DE GUZMAN
letterers

SCOTT McDANIEL KARL STORY
cover art

NIGHTWING created by
MARV WOLFMAN and GEORGE PÉREZ

TABLE OF CONTENTS

DARREN VINCENZO Editor – Original Series
JOSEPH ILLIDGE Associate Editor – Original Series
FRANK BERRIOS Assistant Editor – Original Series
JEB WOODARD Group Editor – Collected Editions
PAUL SANTOS Editor – Collected Edition
STEVE COOK Design Director – Books
SARABETH KETT Publication Design

BOB HARRAS Senior VP – Editor-in-Chief, DC Comics

DIANE NELSON President
DAN DIDIO and JIM LEE Co-Publishers
GEOFF JOHNS Chief Creative Officer
AMIT DESAI Senior VP – Marketing & Global Franchise Management
NAIRI GARDINER Senior VP – Finance
SAM ADES VP – Digital Marketing
BOBBIE CHASE VP – Talent Development
MARK CHIARELLO Senior VP – Art, Design & Collected Editions
JOHN CUNNINGHAM VP – Content Strategy
ANNE DEPIES VP – Strategy Planning & Reporting
DON FALLETTI VP – Manufacturing Operations
LAWRENCE GANEM VP – Editorial Administration & Talent Relations
ALISON GILL Senior VP – Manufacturing & Operations
HANK KANALZ Senior VP – Editorial Strategy & Administration
JAY KOGAN VP – Legal Affairs
DEREK MADDALENA Senior VP – Sales & Business Development
JACK MAHAN VP – Business Affairs
DAN MIRON VP – Sales Planning & Trade Development
NICK NAPOLITANO VP – Manufacturing Administration
CAROL ROEDER VP – Marketing
EDDIE SCANNELL VP – Mass Account & Digital Sales
COURTNEY SIMMONS Senior VP – Publicity & Communications
JIM (SKI) SOKOLOWSKI VP – Comic Book Specialty & Newsstand Sales
SANDY YI Senior VP – Global Franchise Management

NIGHTWING VOLUME 5: THE HUNT FOR ORACLE

DC Comics, 2900 West Alameda Ave., Burbank, CA 91505
Printed by RR Donnelley, Salem, VA, USA. 9/23/16. First Printing.
ISBN: 978-1-4012-6502-1

Library of Congress Cataloging-in-Publication Data is available.

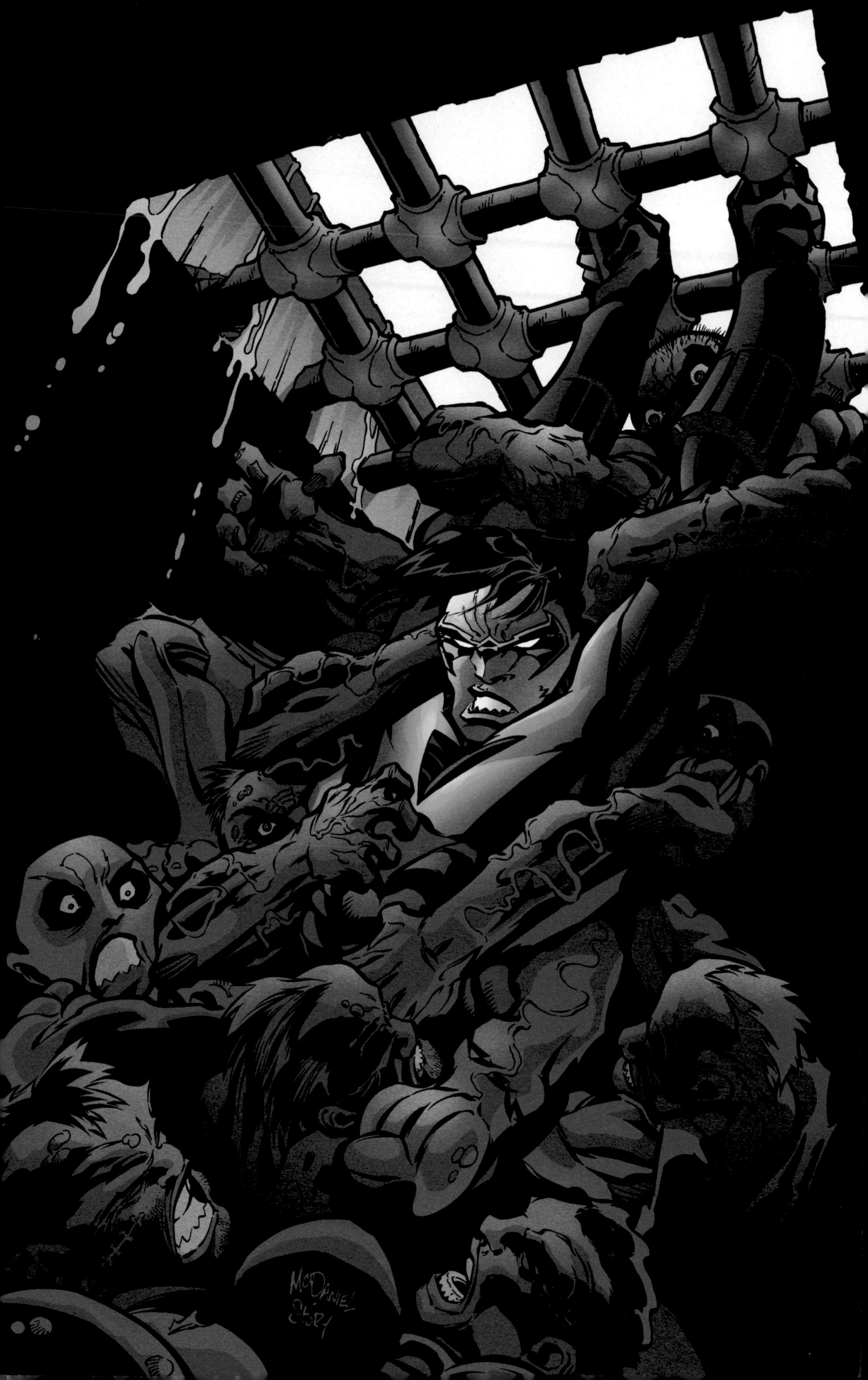
McDANIEL
STORY

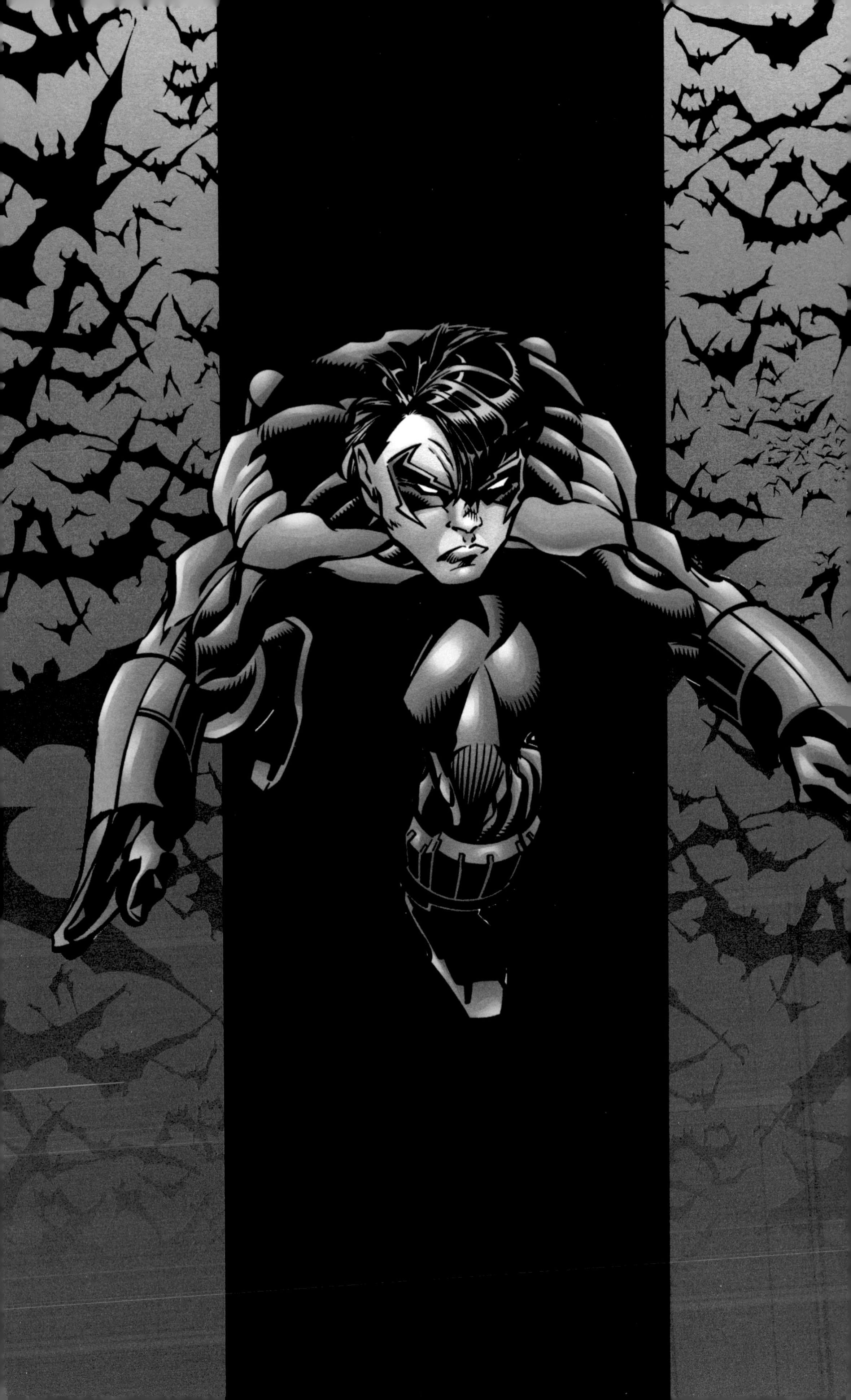

THE BELLY OF THE BEAST

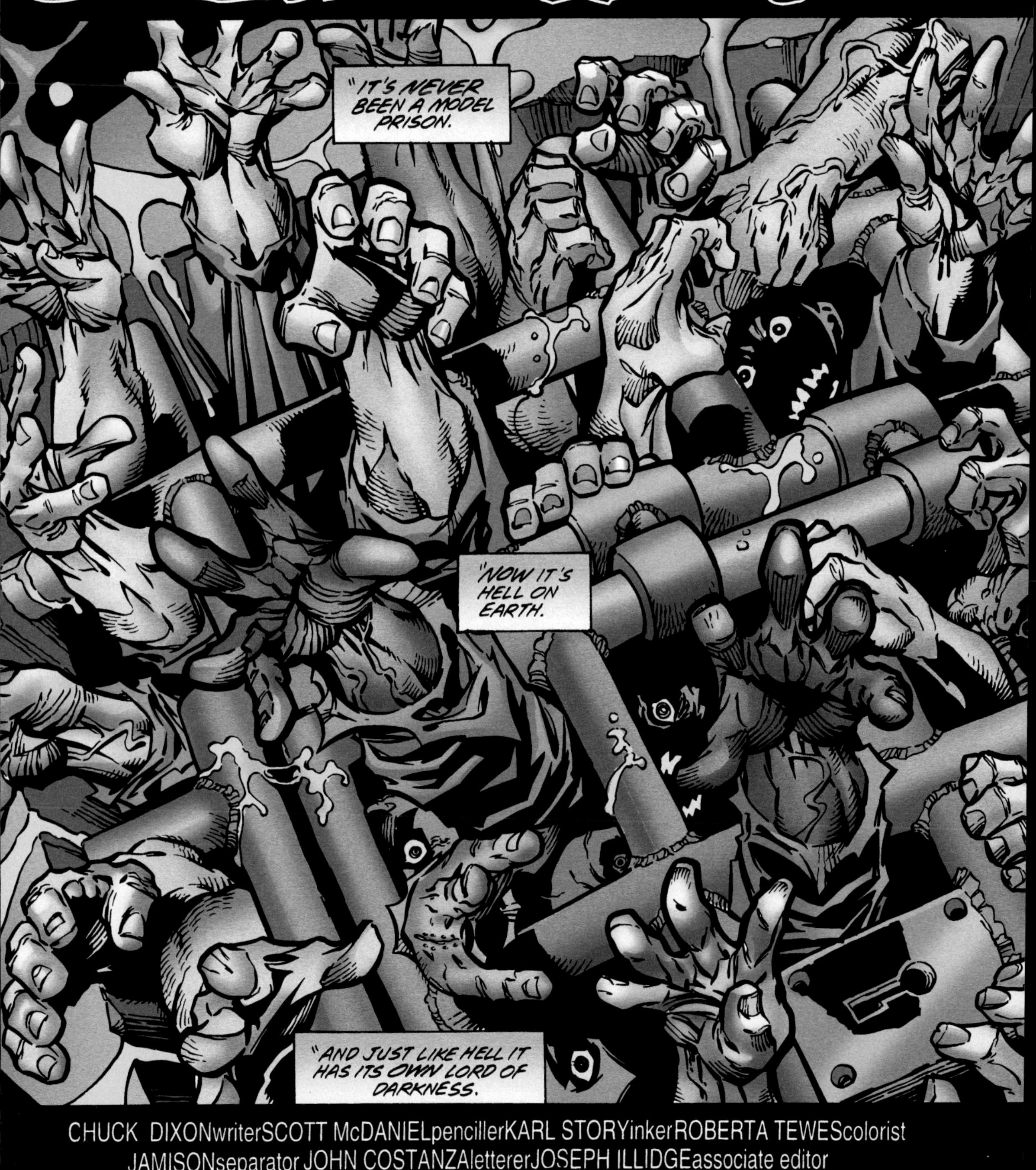
"IT'S NEVER BEEN A MODEL PRISON.
"NOW IT'S HELL ON EARTH.
"AND JUST LIKE HELL IT HAS ITS OWN LORD OF DARKNESS.

CHUCK DIXONwriterSCOTT McDANIELpencillerKARL STORYinkerROBERTA TEWEScolorist
JAMISONseparator JOHN COSTANZAlettererJOSEPH ILLIDGEassociate editor
DARREN VINCENZOeditor

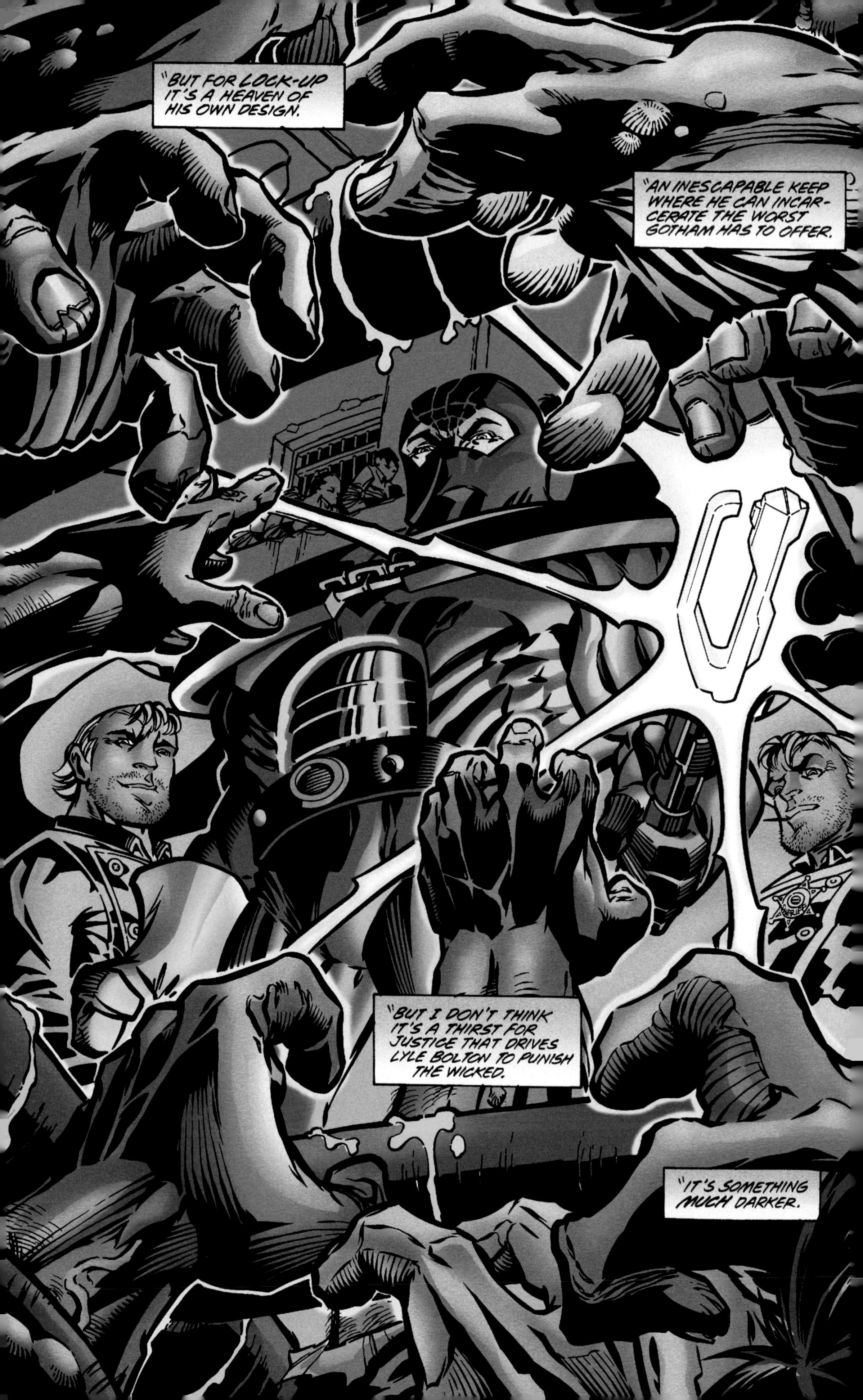
"BUT FOR LOCK-UP IT'S A HEAVEN OF HIS OWN DESIGN.
"AN INESCAPABLE KEEP WHERE HE CAN INCARCERATE THE WORST GOTHAM HAS TO OFFER.
"BUT I DON'T THINK IT'S A THIRST FOR JUSTICE THAT DRIVES LYLE BOLTON TO PUNISH THE WICKED.
"IT'S SOMETHING MUCH DARKER.

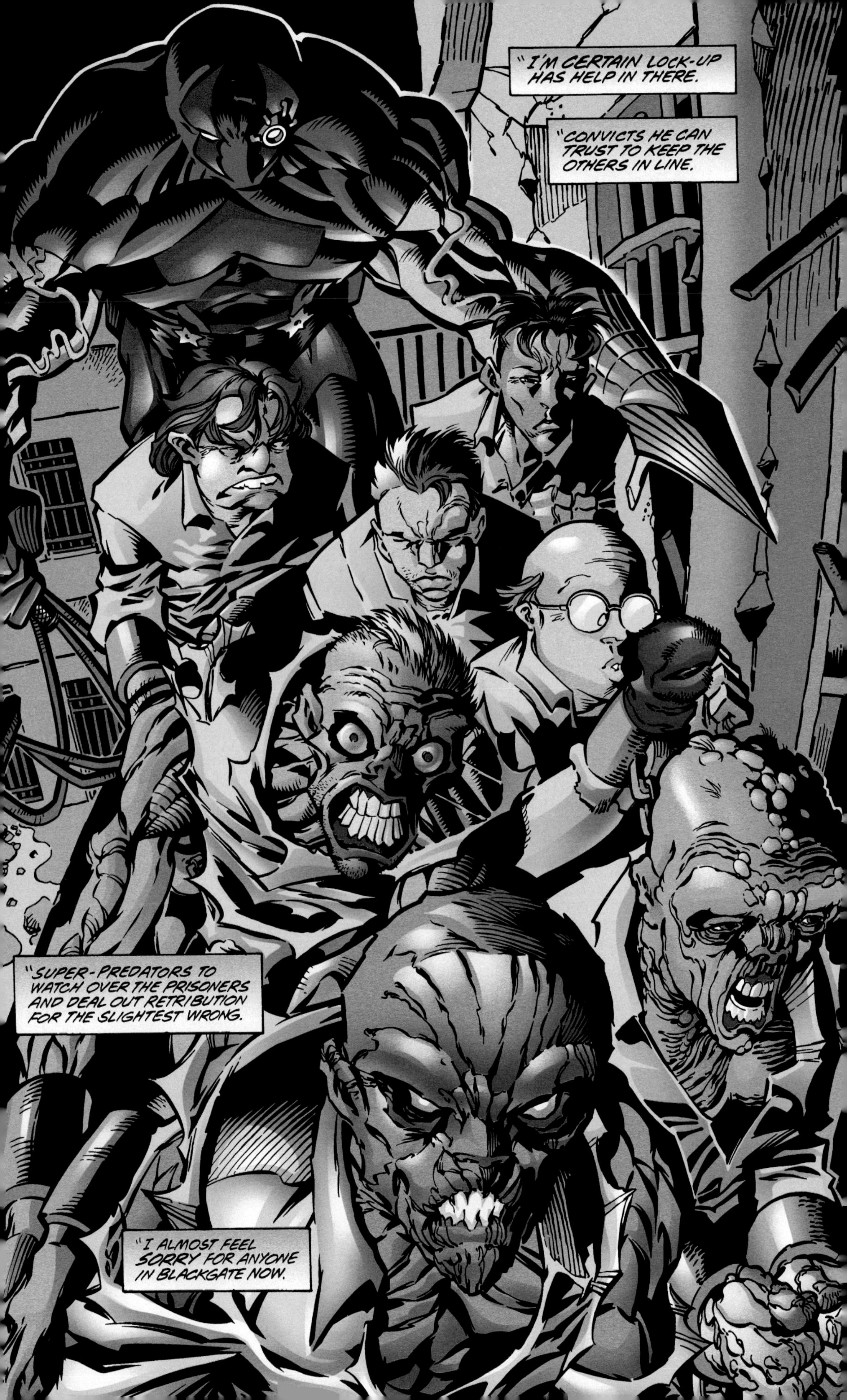
"I'M CERTAIN LOCK-UP HAS HELP IN THERE.
"CONVICTS HE CAN TRUST TO KEEP THE OTHERS IN LINE.
"SUPER-PREDATORS TO WATCH OVER THE PRISONERS AND DEAL OUT RETRIBUTION FOR THE SLIGHTEST WRONG.
"I ALMOST FEEL SORRY FOR ANYONE IN BLACKGATE NOW.

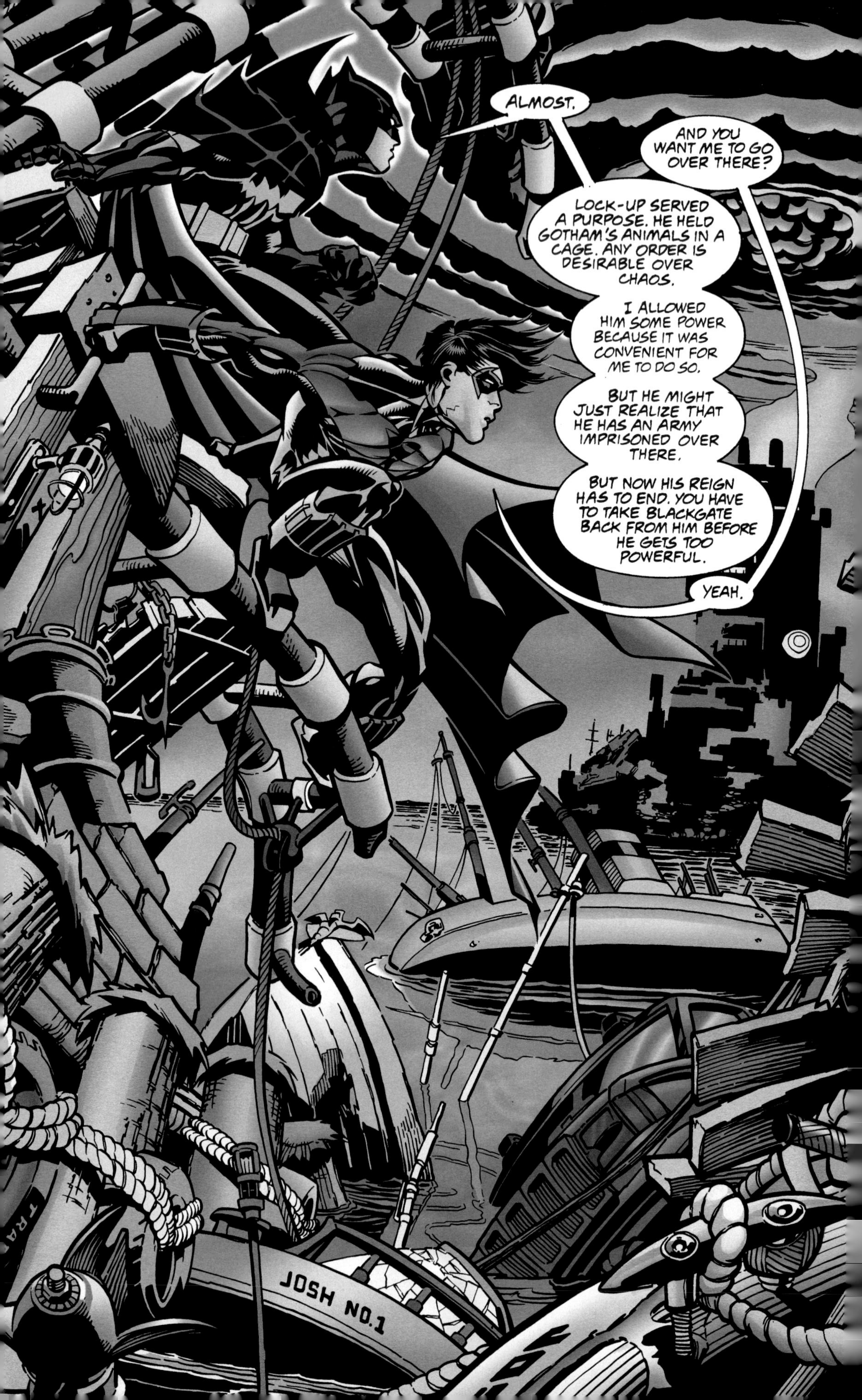
ALMOST.
AND YOU WANT ME TO GO OVER THERE?
LOCK-UP SERVED A PURPOSE. HE HELD GOTHAM'S ANIMALS IN A CAGE. ANY ORDER IS DESIRABLE OVER CHAOS.
I ALLOWED HIM SOME POWER BECAUSE IT WAS CONVENIENT FOR ME TO DO SO.
BUT HE MIGHT JUST REALIZE THAT HE HAS AN ARMY IMPRISONED OVER THERE.
BUT NOW HIS REIGN HAS TO END. YOU HAVE TO TAKE BLACKGATE BACK FROM HIM BEFORE HE GETS TOO POWERFUL.
YEAH.
JOSH NO.1

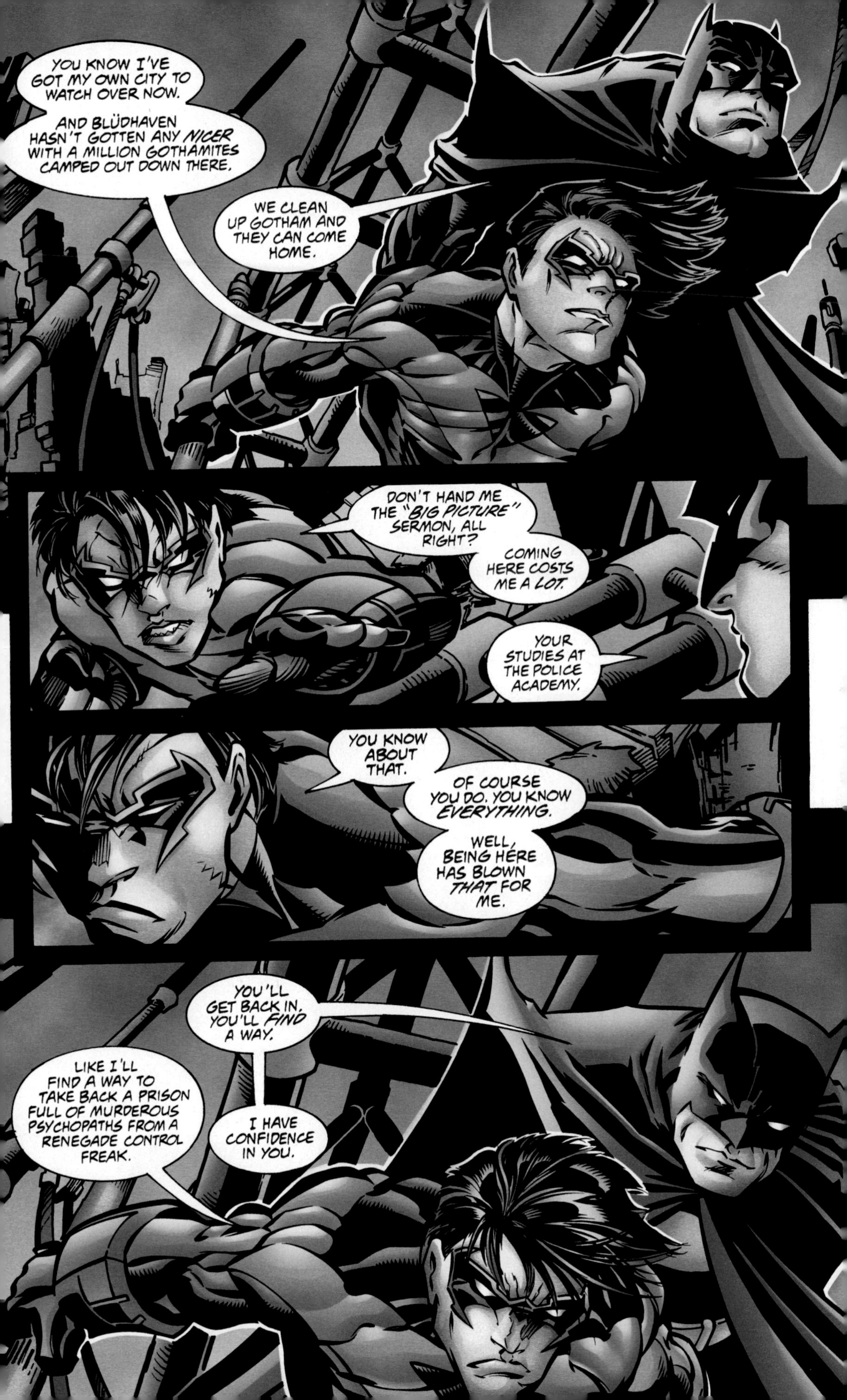
YOU KNOW I'VE GOT MY OWN CITY TO WATCH OVER NOW.
AND BLÜDHAVEN HASN'T GOTTEN ANY NICER WITH A MILLION GOTHAMITES CAMPED OUT DOWN THERE.
WE CLEAN UP GOTHAM AND THEY CAN COME HOME.
DON'T HAND ME THE "BIG PICTURE" SERMON, ALL RIGHT?
COMING HERE COSTS ME A LOT.
YOUR STUDIES AT THE POLICE ACADEMY.
YOU KNOW ABOUT THAT.
OF COURSE YOU DO. YOU KNOW EVERYTHING.
WELL, BEING HERE HAS BLOWN THAT FOR ME.
YOU'LL GET BACK IN. YOU'LL FIND A WAY.
LIKE I'LL FIND A WAY TO TAKE BACK A PRISON FULL OF MURDEROUS PSYCHOPATHS FROM A RENEGADE CONTROL FREAK.
I HAVE CONFIDENCE IN YOU.

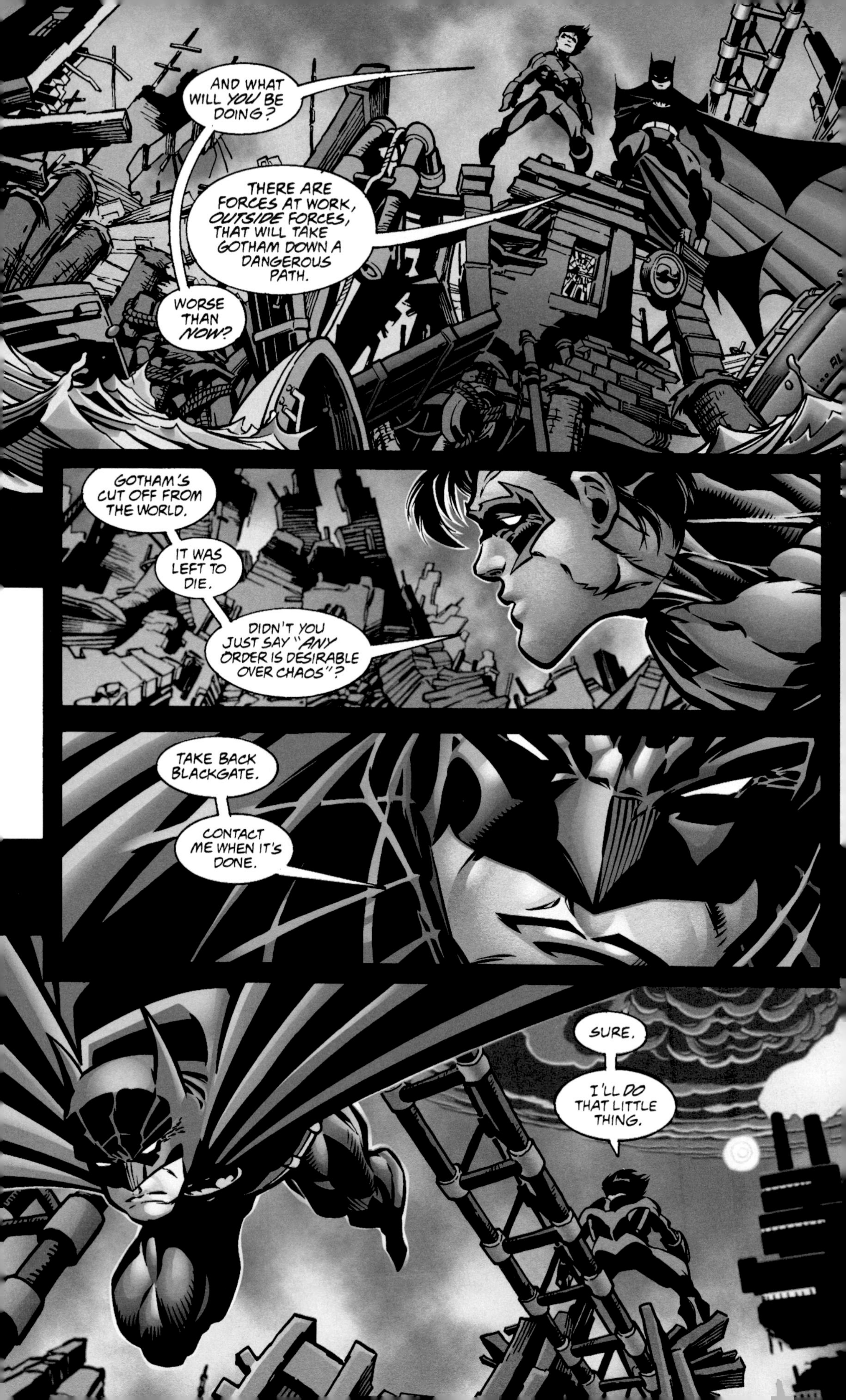
AND WHAT WILL YOU BE DOING?
THERE ARE FORCES AT WORK, OUTSIDE FORCES, THAT WILL TAKE GOTHAM DOWN A DANGEROUS PATH.
WORSE THAN NOW?
GOTHAM'S CUT OFF FROM THE WORLD.
IT WAS LEFT TO DIE.
DIDN'T YOU JUST SAY "ANY ORDER IS DESIRABLE OVER CHAOS"?
TAKE BACK BLACKGATE.
CONTACT ME WHEN IT'S DONE.
SURE.
I'LL DO THAT LITTLE THING.

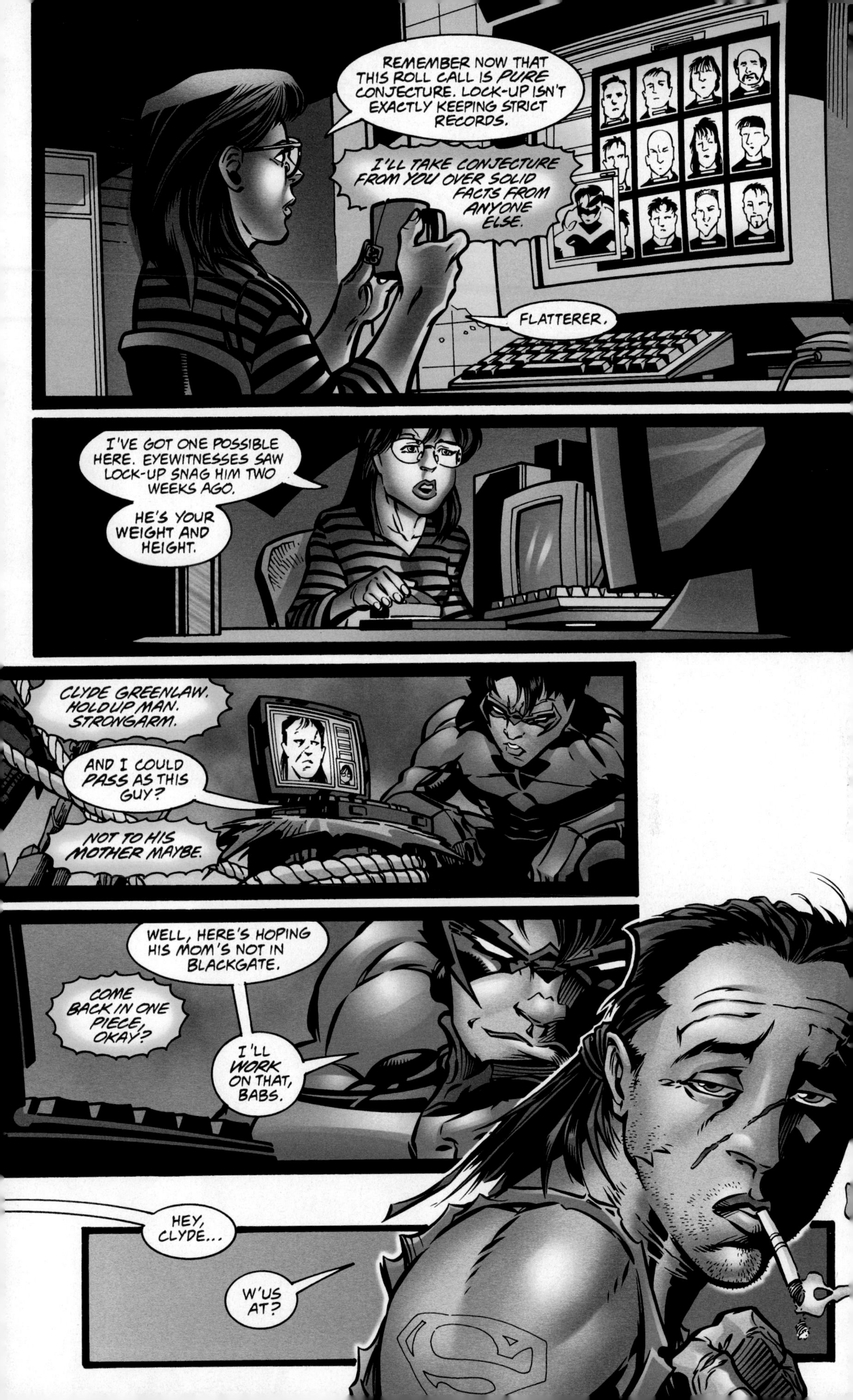
REMEMBER NOW THAT THIS ROLL CALL IS PURE CONJECTURE. LOCK-UP ISN'T EXACTLY KEEPING STRICT RECORDS.
I'LL TAKE CONJECTURE FROM YOU OVER SOLID FACTS FROM ANYONE ELSE.
FLATTERER.
I'VE GOT ONE POSSIBLE HERE. EYEWITNESSES SAW LOCK-UP SNAG HIM TWO WEEKS AGO.
HE'S YOUR WEIGHT AND HEIGHT.
CLYDE GREENLAW. HOLDUP MAN. STRONGARM.
AND I COULD PASS AS THIS GUY?
NOT TO HIS MOTHER MAYBE.
WELL, HERE'S HOPING HIS MOM'S NOT IN BLACKGATE.
COME BACK IN ONE PIECE, OKAY?
I'LL WORK ON THAT, BABS.
HEY, CLYDE...
W'US AT?

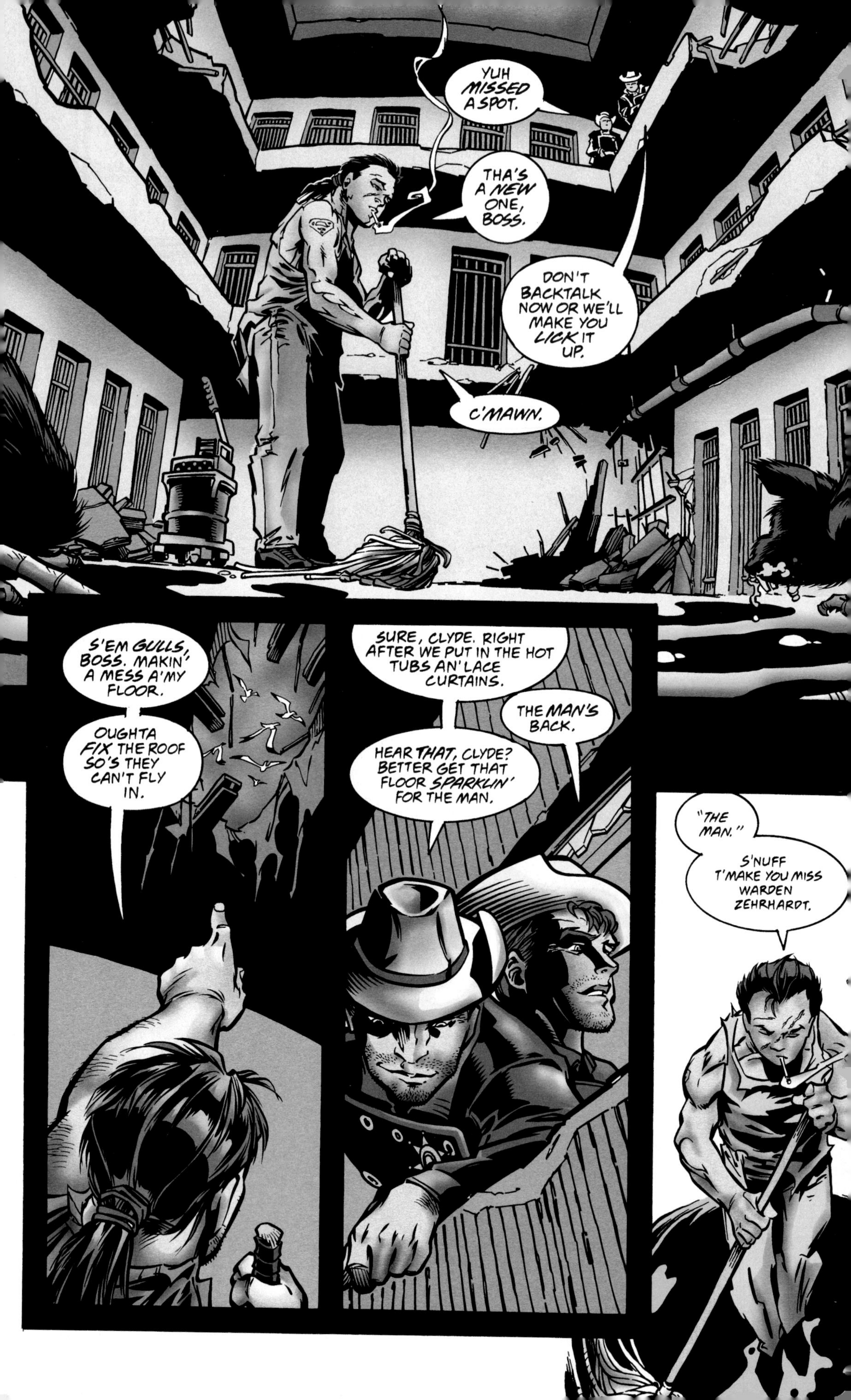
YUH MISSED A SPOT.
THA'S A NEW ONE, BOSS.
DON'T BACKTALK NOW OR WE'LL MAKE YOU LICK IT UP.
C'MAWN.
S'EM GULLS, BOSS. MAKIN' A MESS A'MY FLOOR.
OUGHTA FIX THE ROOF SO'S THEY CAN'T FLY IN.
SURE, CLYDE. RIGHT AFTER WE PUT IN THE HOT TUBS AN' LACE CURTAINS.
THE MAN'S BACK.
HEAR THAT, CLYDE? BETTER GET THAT FLOOR SPARKLIN' FOR THE MAN.
"THE MAN."
S'NUFF T'MAKE YOU MISS WARDEN ZEHRHARDT.

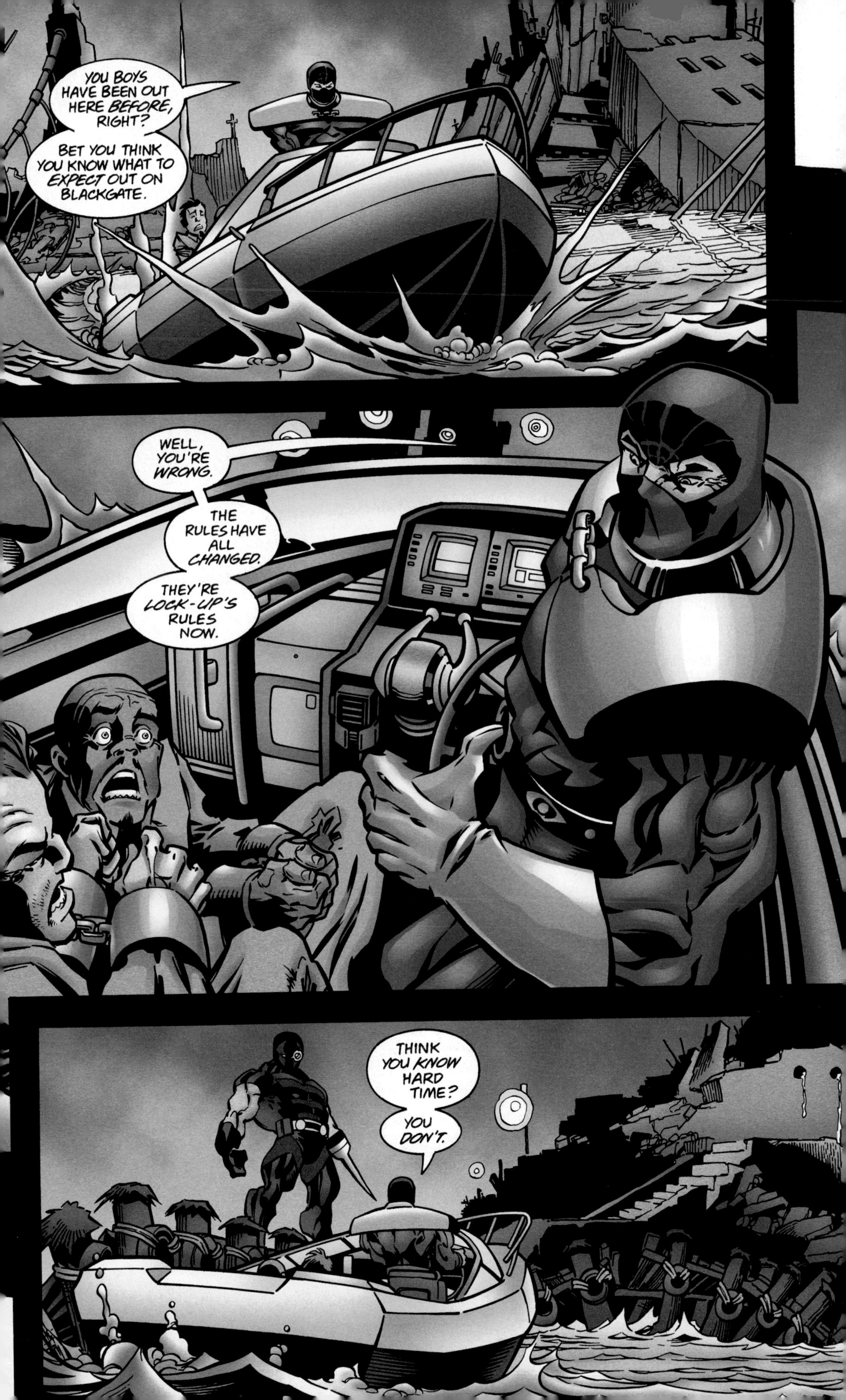
YOU BOYS HAVE BEEN OUT HERE BEFORE, RIGHT?
BET YOU THINK YOU KNOW WHAT TO EXPECT OUT ON BLACKGATE.
WELL, YOU'RE WRONG.
THE RULES HAVE ALL CHANGED.
THEY'RE LOCK-UP'S RULES NOW.
THINK YOU KNOW HARD TIME?
YOU DON'T.

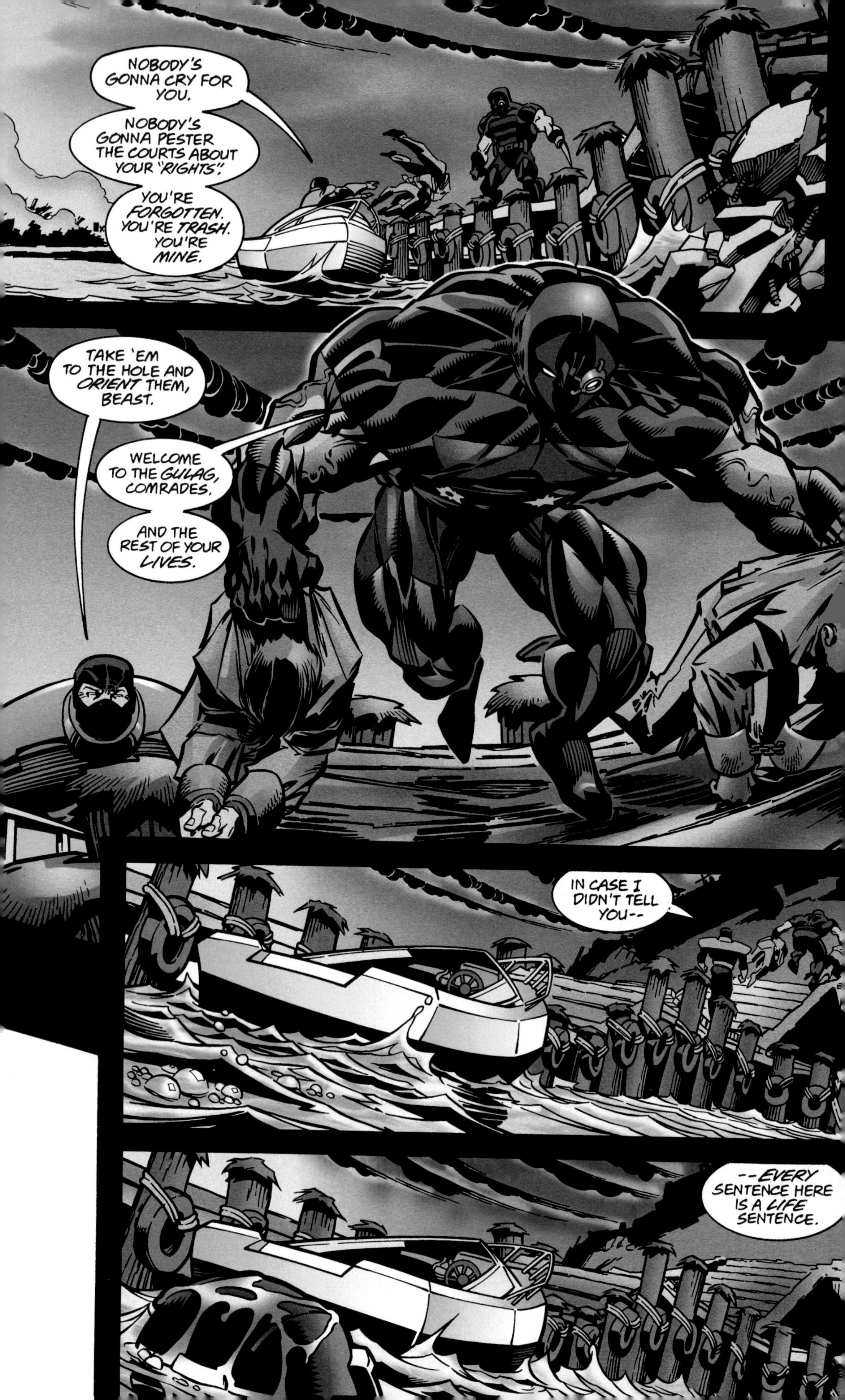
NOBODY'S GONNA CRY FOR YOU.
NOBODY'S GONNA PESTER THE COURTS ABOUT YOUR "RIGHTS."
YOU'RE *FORGOTTEN.* YOU'RE *TRASH.* YOU'RE *MINE.*
TAKE 'EM TO THE HOLE AND *ORIENT* THEM, BEAST.
WELCOME TO THE *GULAG,* COMRADES.
AND THE REST OF YOUR *LIVES.*
IN CASE I DIDN'T TELL YOU--
--*EVERY* SENTENCE HERE IS A *LIFE* SENTENCE.

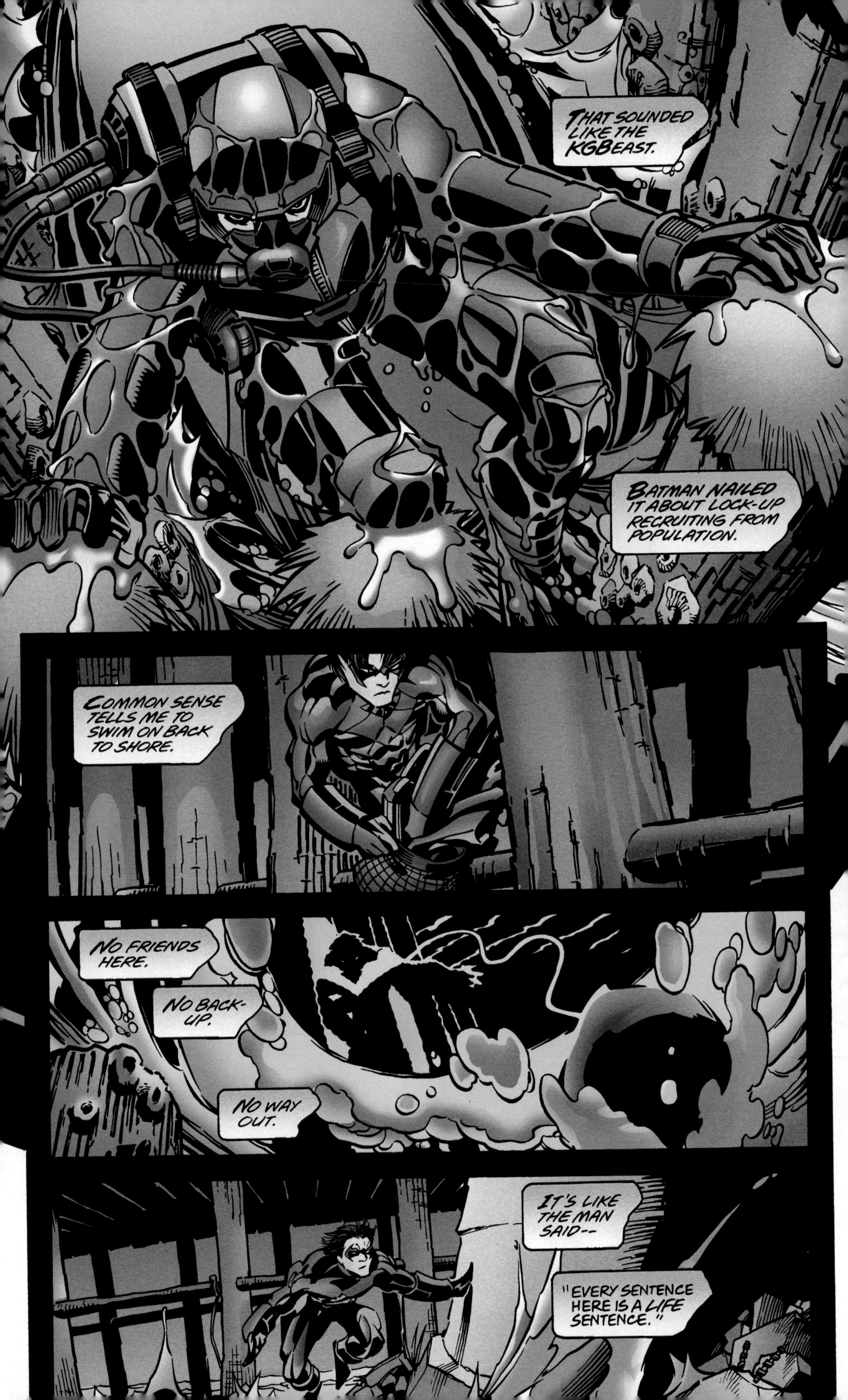
THAT SOUNDED LIKE THE KGBEAST.
BATMAN NAILED IT ABOUT LOCK-UP RECRUITING FROM POPULATION.
COMMON SENSE TELLS ME TO SWIM ON BACK TO SHORE.
NO FRIENDS HERE.
NO BACK-UP.
NO WAY OUT.
IT'S LIKE THE MAN SAID--
"EVERY SENTENCE HERE IS A LIFE SENTENCE."

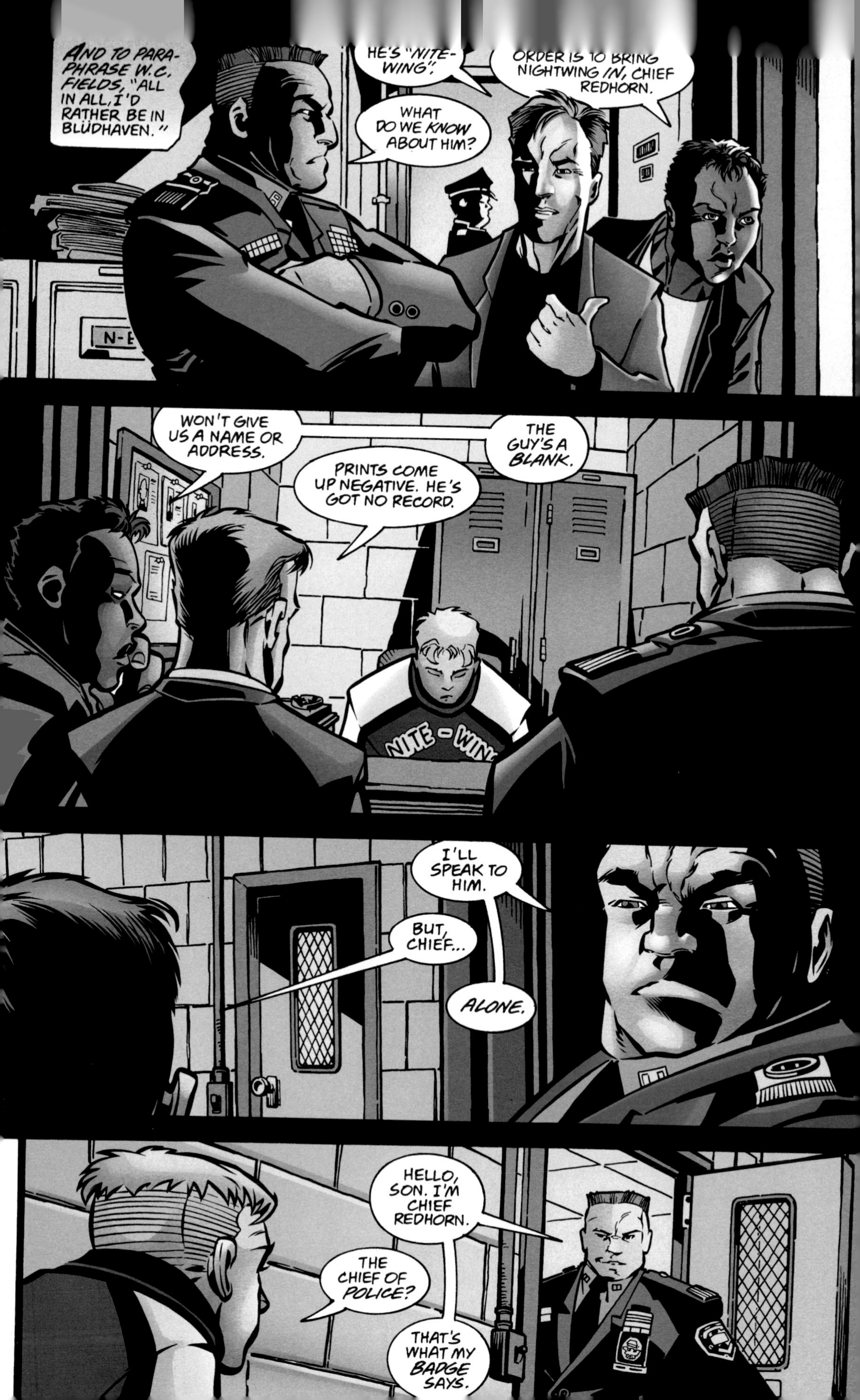
AND TO PARAPHRASE W.C. FIELDS, "ALL IN ALL, I'D RATHER BE IN BLÜDHAVEN."
ORDER IS TO BRING NIGHTWING IN, CHIEF REDHORN.
HE'S "NITE-WING".
WHAT DO WE KNOW ABOUT HIM?
WON'T GIVE US A NAME OR ADDRESS.
THE GUY'S A BLANK.
PRINTS COME UP NEGATIVE. HE'S GOT NO RECORD.
NITE-WIN
I'LL SPEAK TO HIM.
BUT, CHIEF...
ALONE.
HELLO, SON. I'M CHIEF REDHORN.
THE CHIEF OF POLICE?
THAT'S WHAT MY BADGE SAYS.

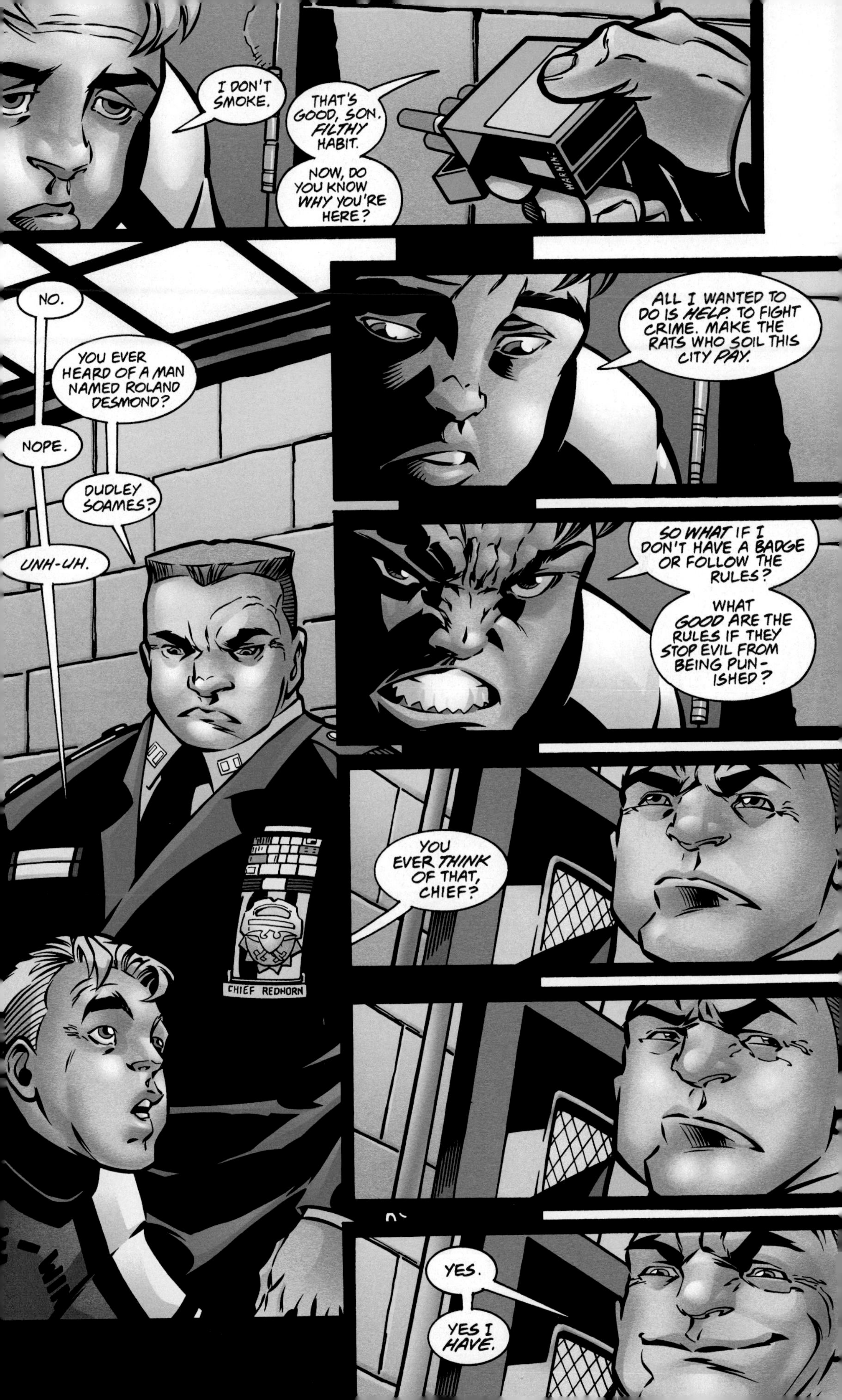
I DON'T SMOKE.
THAT'S GOOD, SON. FILTHY HABIT.
NOW, DO YOU KNOW WHY YOU'RE HERE?
WARNIN
NO.
YOU EVER HEARD OF A MAN NAMED ROLAND DESMOND?
NOPE.
DUDLEY SOAMES?
UNH-UH.
CHIEF REDHORN
ALL I WANTED TO DO IS HELP. TO FIGHT CRIME. MAKE THE RATS WHO SOIL THIS CITY PAY.
SO WHAT IF I DON'T HAVE A BADGE OR FOLLOW THE RULES?
WHAT GOOD ARE THE RULES IF THEY STOP EVIL FROM BEING PUN-ISHED?
YOU EVER THINK OF THAT, CHIEF?
YES.
YES I HAVE.

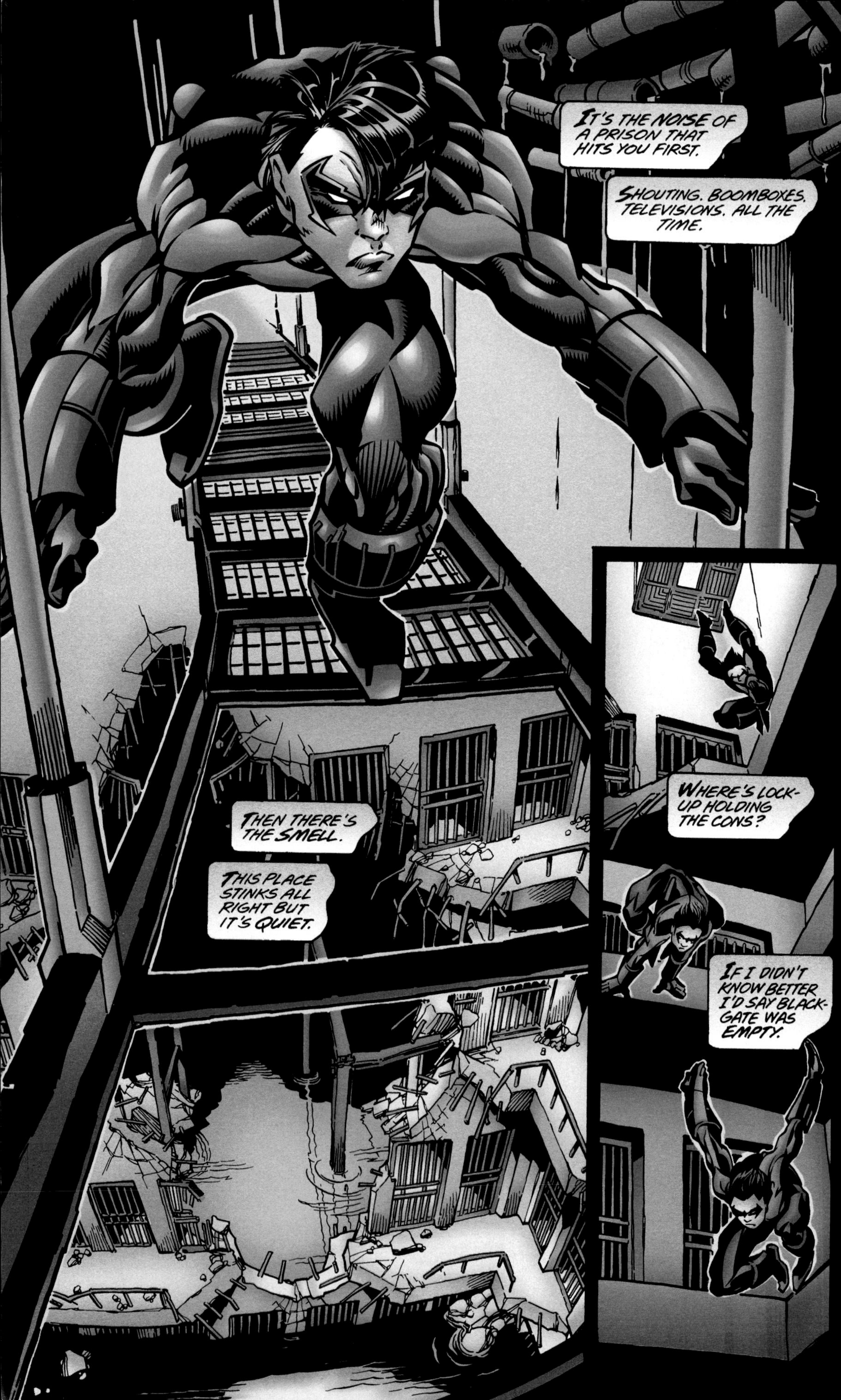
IT'S THE NOISE OF A PRISON THAT HITS YOU FIRST.
SHOUTING. BOOMBOXES. TELEVISIONS. ALL THE TIME.
THEN THERE'S THE SMELL.
THIS PLACE STINKS ALL RIGHT BUT IT'S QUIET.
WHERE'S LOCK-UP HOLDING THE CONS?
IF I DIDN'T KNOW BETTER I'D SAY BLACK-GATE WAS EMPTY.

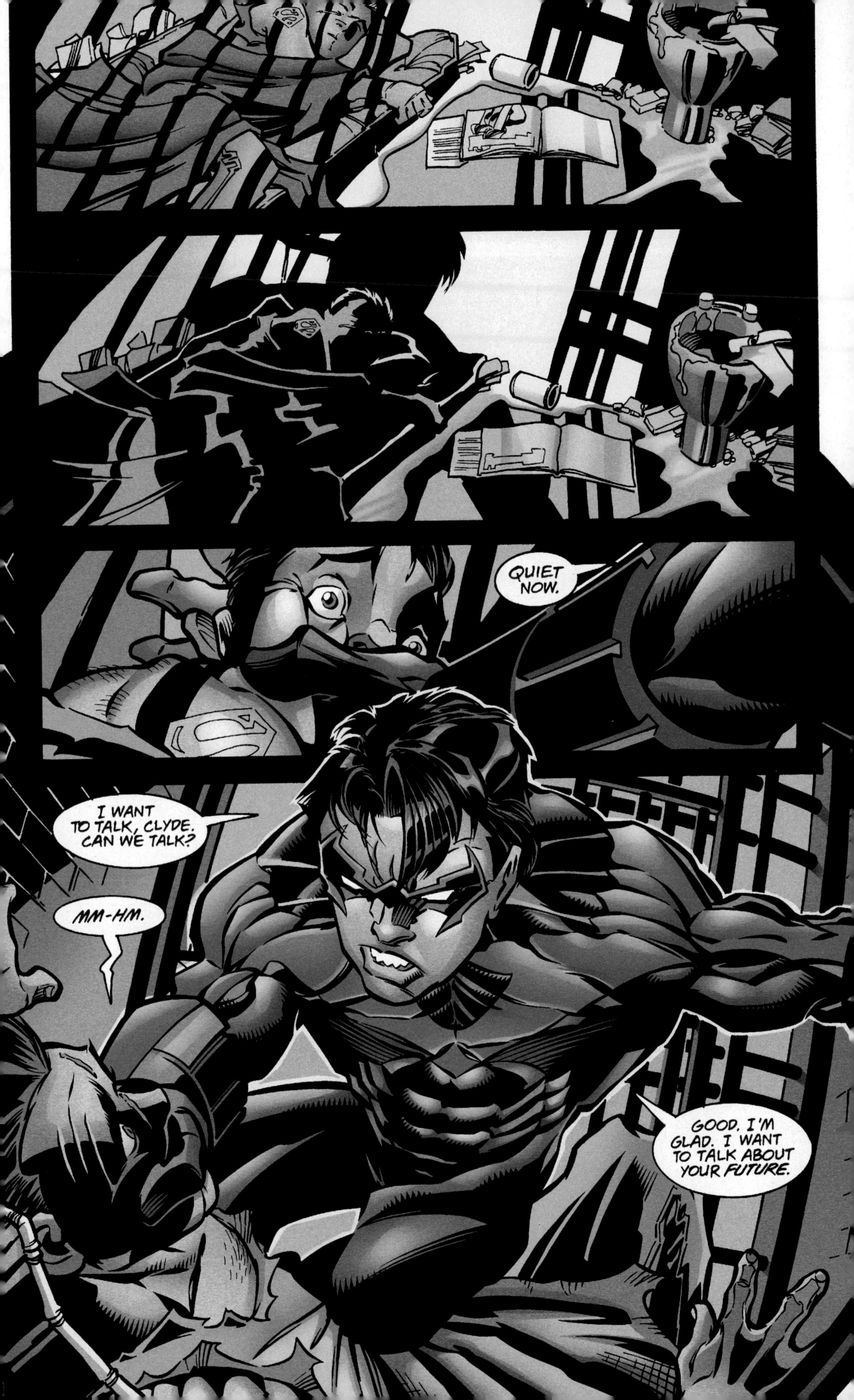
QUIET NOW.
I WANT TO TALK, CLYDE. CAN WE TALK?
MM-HM.
GOOD. I'M GLAD. I WANT TO TALK ABOUT YOUR *FUTURE*.

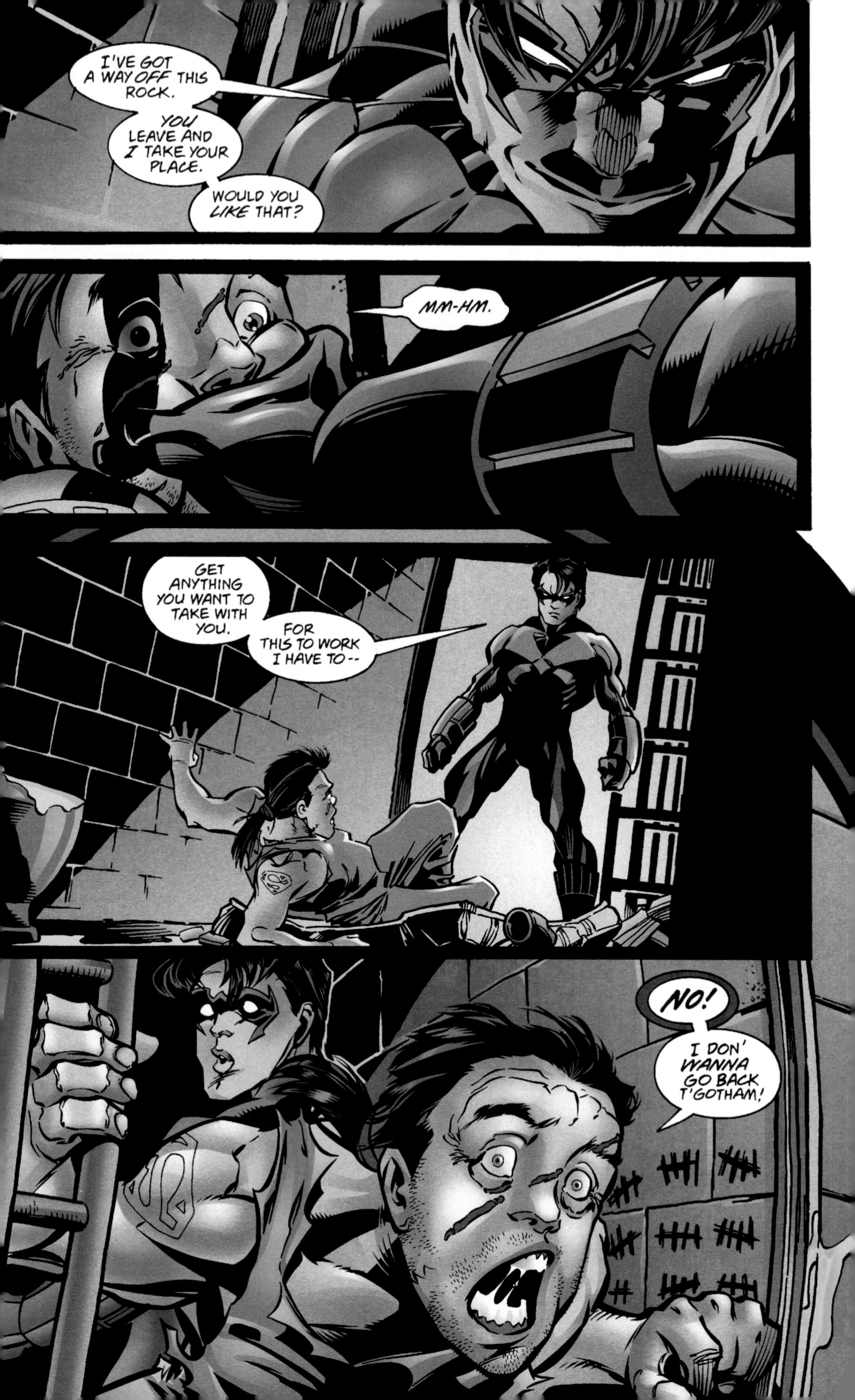
I'VE GOT A WAY OFF THIS ROCK.
YOU LEAVE AND I TAKE YOUR PLACE.
WOULD YOU LIKE THAT?
MM-HM.
GET ANYTHING YOU WANT TO TAKE WITH YOU.
FOR THIS TO WORK I HAVE TO--
NO!
I DON' WANNA GO BACK T'GOTHAM!

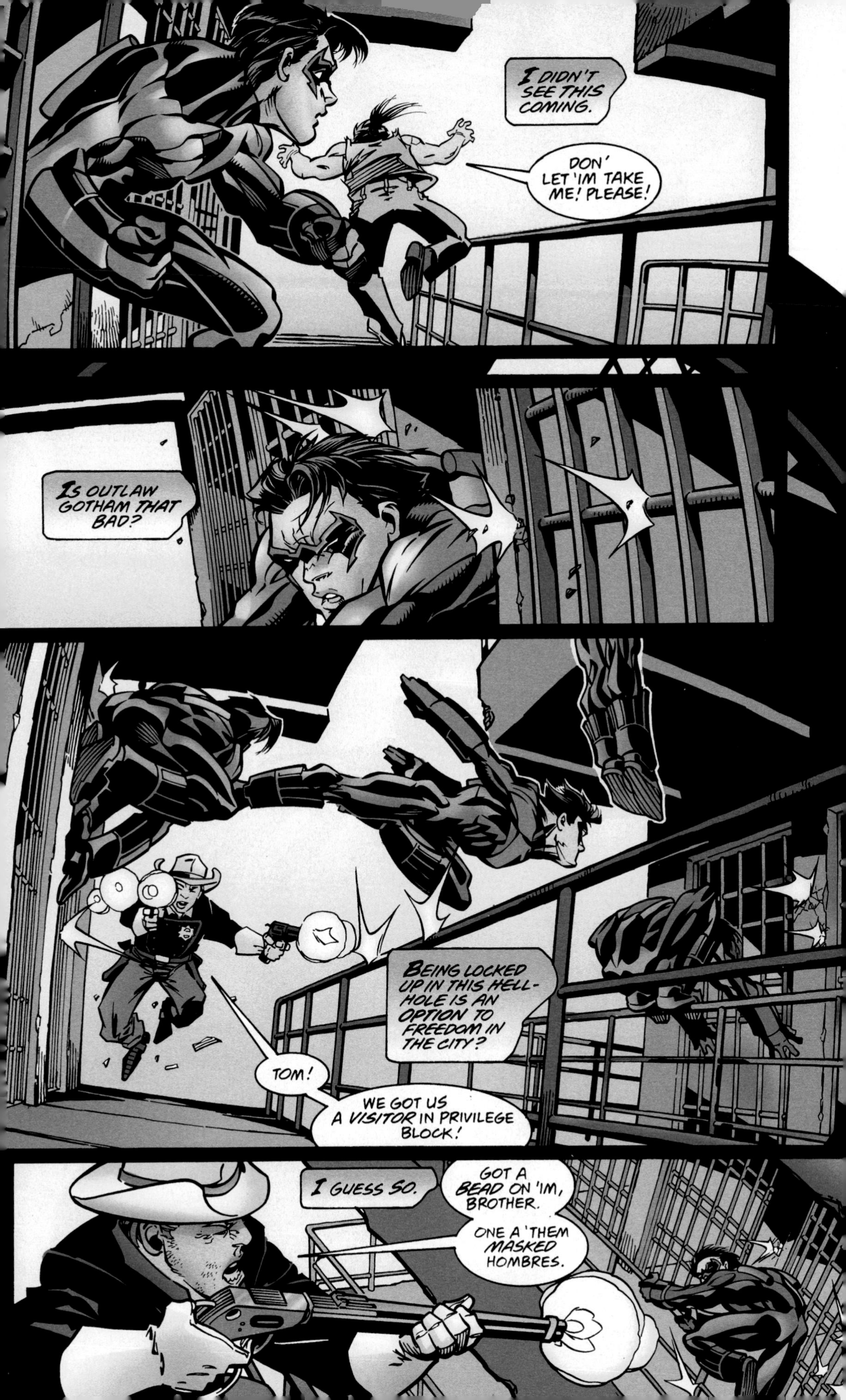
I DIDN'T SEE THIS COMING.
DON' LET 'IM TAKE ME! PLEASE!
IS OUTLAW GOTHAM THAT BAD?
BEING LOCKED UP IN THIS HELL-HOLE IS AN OPTION TO FREEDOM IN THE CITY?
TOM!
WE GOT US A VISITOR IN PRIVILEGE BLOCK!
I GUESS SO.
GOT A BEAD ON 'IM, BROTHER.
ONE A 'THEM MASKED HOMBRES.

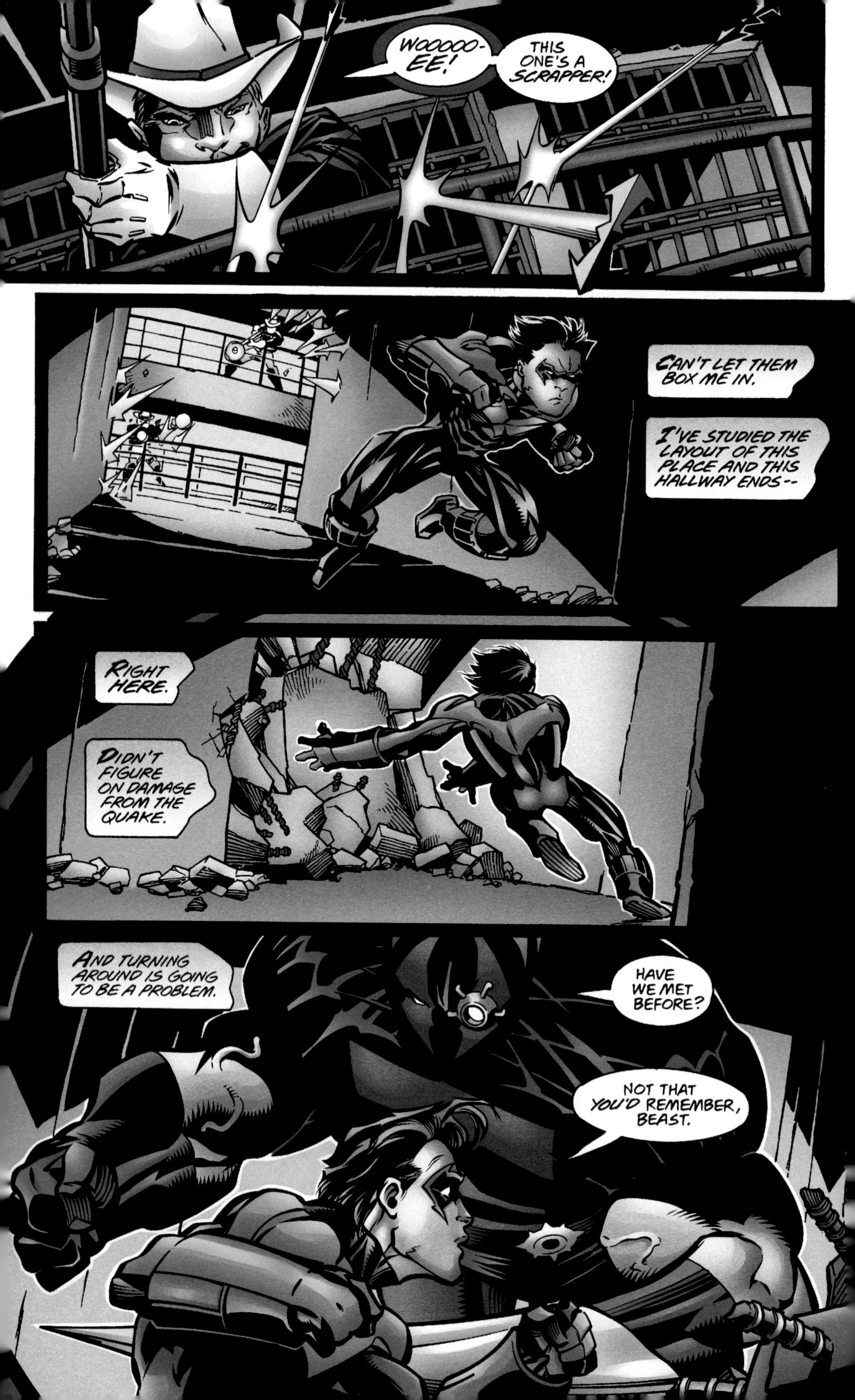
WOOOOO-EE!
THIS ONE'S A SCRAPPER!
CAN'T LET THEM BOX ME IN.
I'VE STUDIED THE LAYOUT OF THIS PLACE AND THIS HALLWAY ENDS--
RIGHT HERE.
DIDN'T FIGURE ON DAMAGE FROM THE QUAKE.
AND TURNING AROUND IS GOING TO BE A PROBLEM.
HAVE WE MET BEFORE?
NOT THAT YOU'D REMEMBER, BEAST.

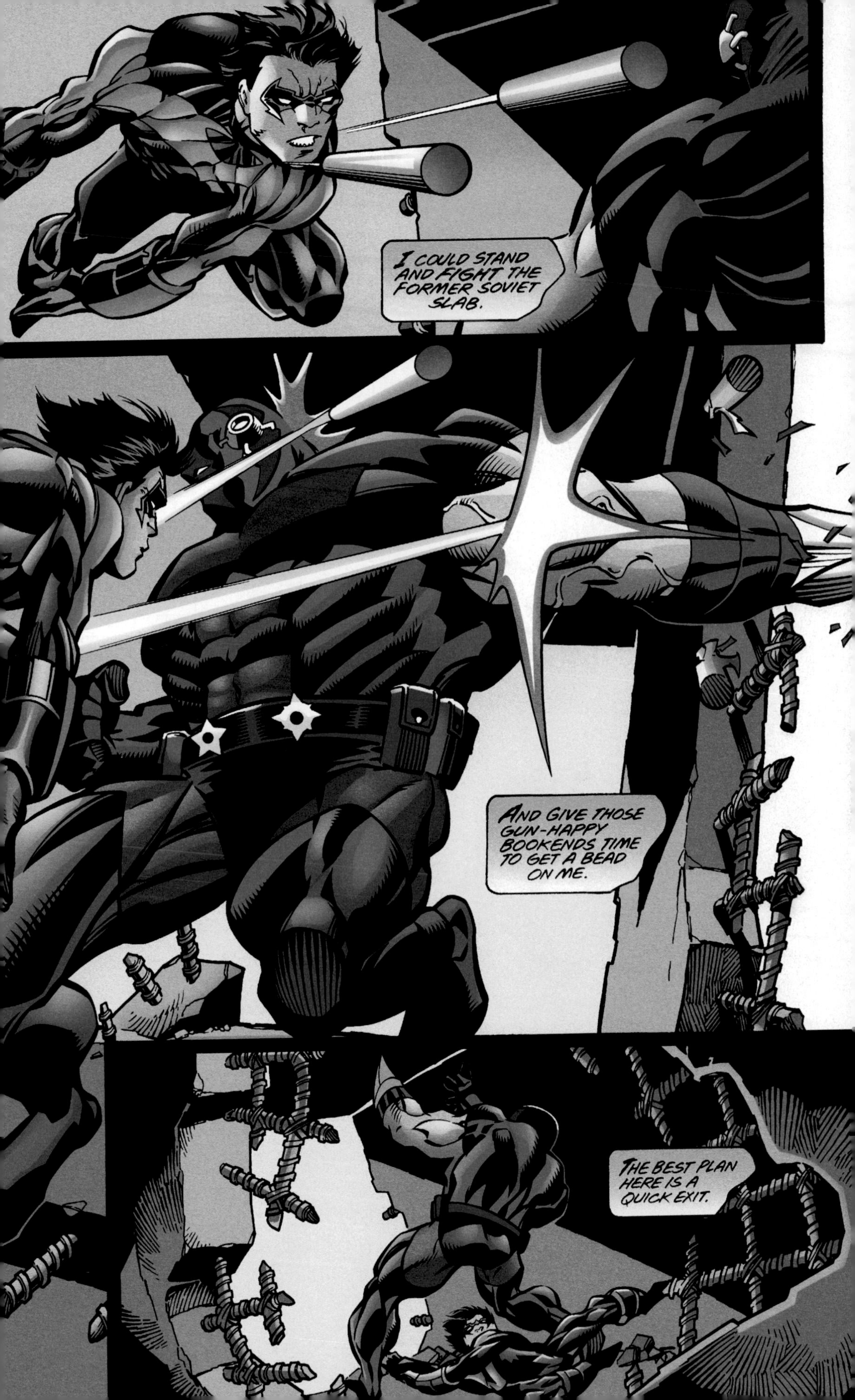
I COULD STAND AND FIGHT THE FORMER SOVIET SLAB.
AND GIVE THOSE GUN-HAPPY BOOKENDS TIME TO GET A BEAD ON ME.
THE BEST PLAN HERE IS A QUICK EXIT.

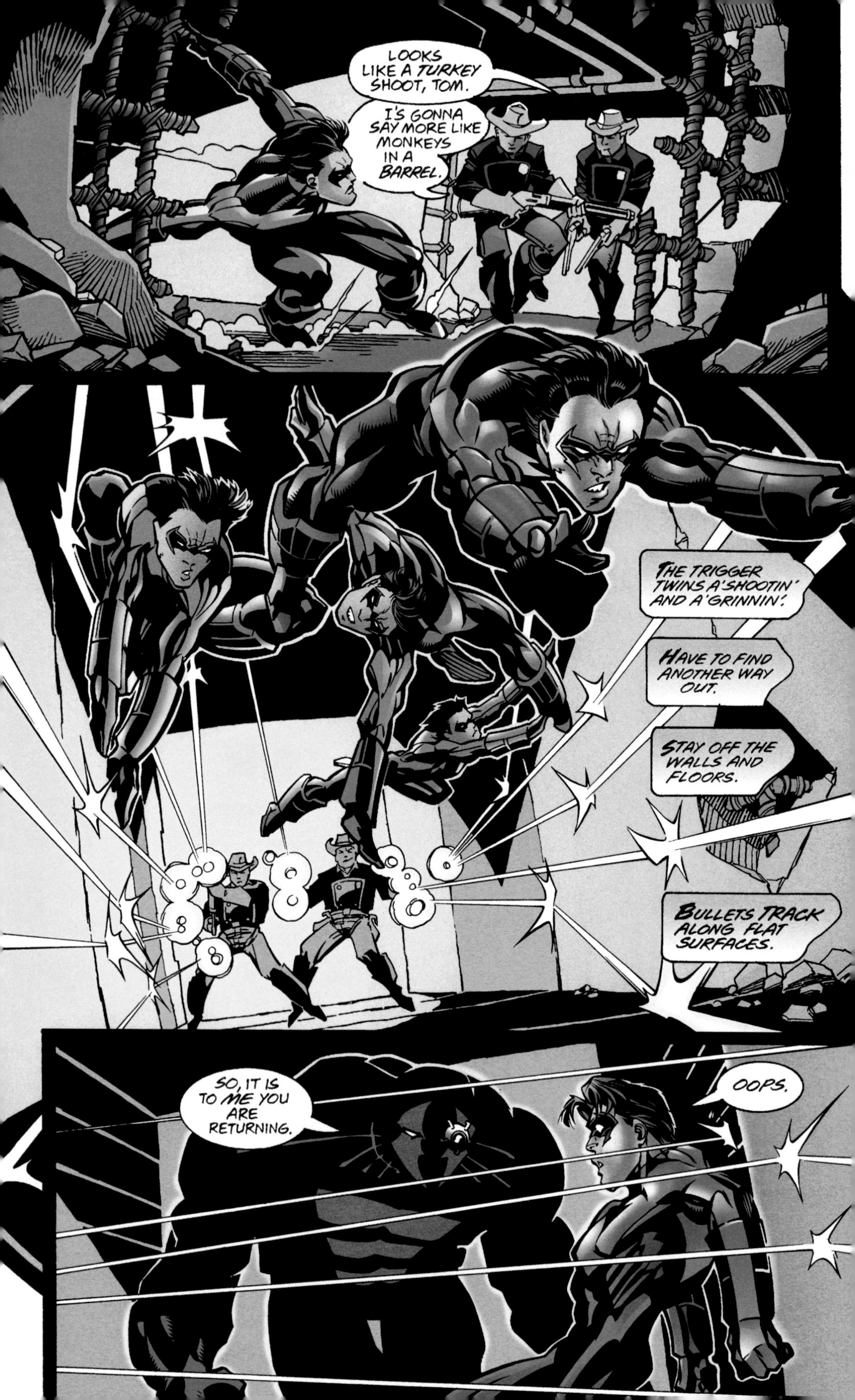
LOOKS LIKE A TURKEY SHOOT, TOM.
I'S GONNA SAY MORE LIKE MONKEYS IN A BARREL.
THE TRIGGER TWINS A'SHOOTIN' AND A'GRINNIN'.
HAVE TO FIND ANOTHER WAY OUT.
STAY OFF THE WALLS AND FLOORS.
BULLETS TRACK ALONG FLAT SURFACES.
SO, IT IS TO ME YOU ARE RETURNING.
OOPS.

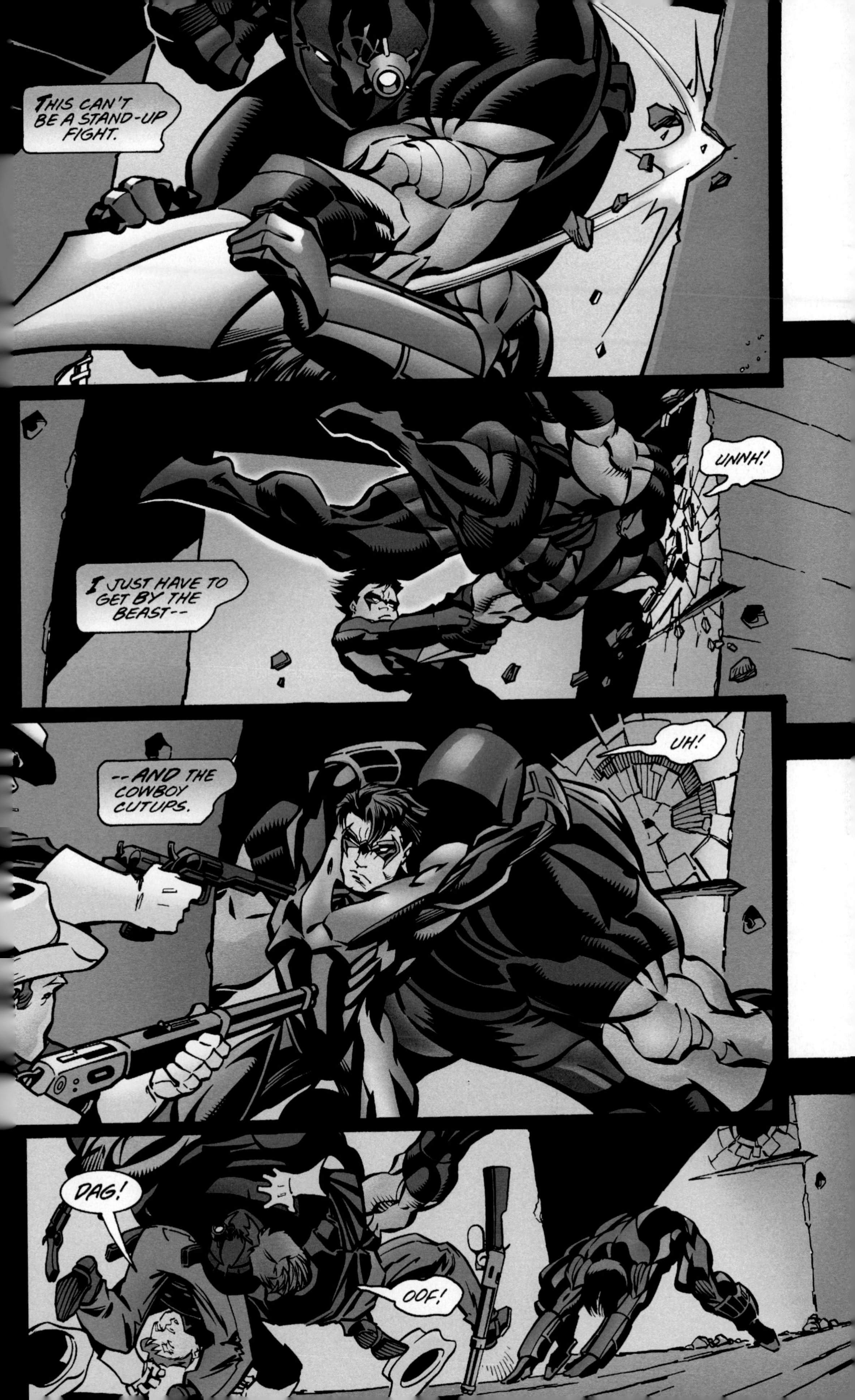
THIS CAN'T BE A STAND-UP FIGHT.
UNNH!
I JUST HAVE TO GET BY THE BEAST--
UH!
--AND THE COWBOY CUTUPS.
DAG!
OOF!

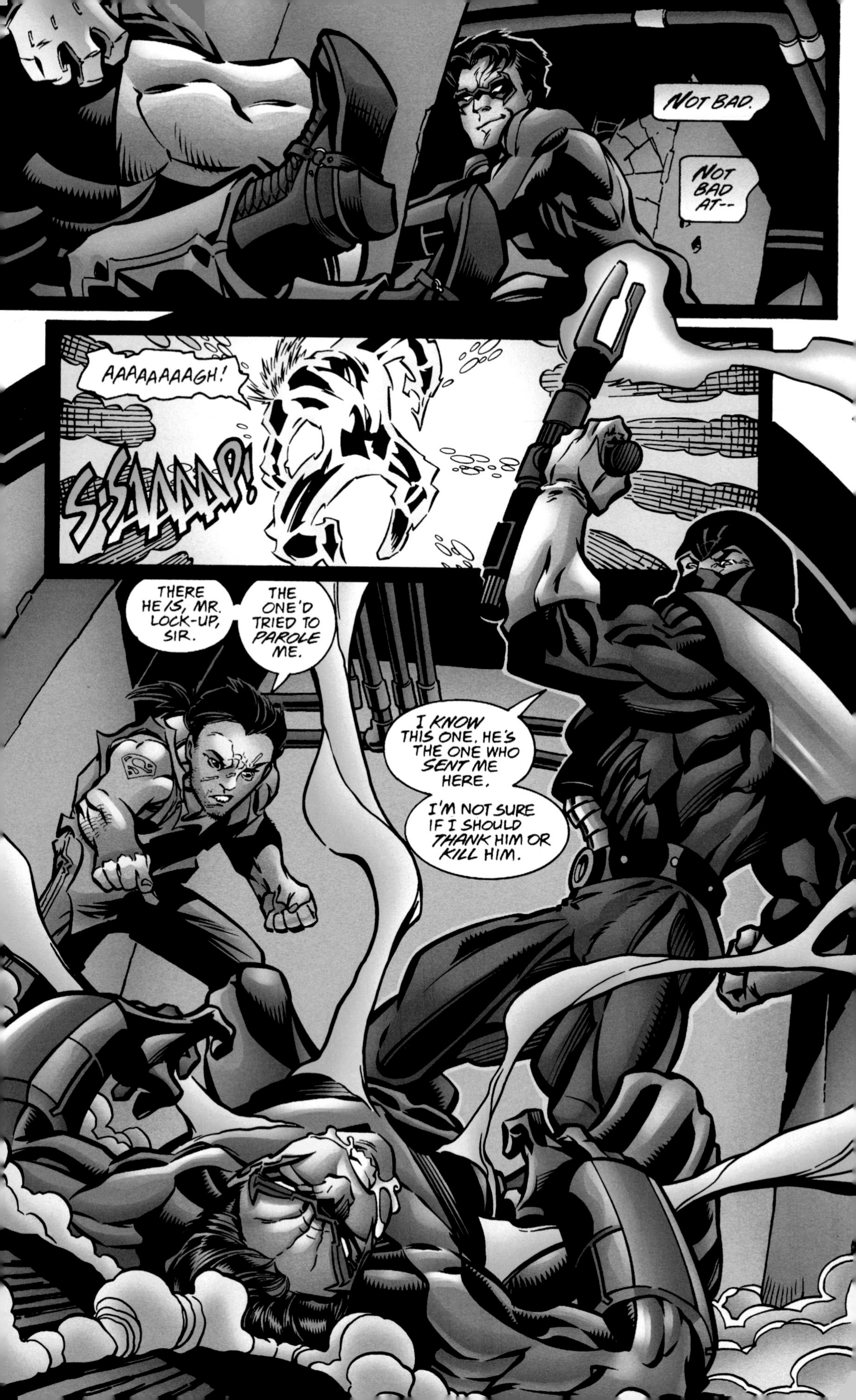
NOT BAD.
NOT BAD AT--
AAAAAAAAGH!
S-SAAAP!
THERE HE IS, MR. LOCK-UP, SIR.
THE ONE'D TRIED TO PAROLE ME.
I KNOW THIS ONE. HE'S THE ONE WHO SENT ME HERE.
I'M NOT SURE IF I SHOULD THANK HIM OR KILL HIM.

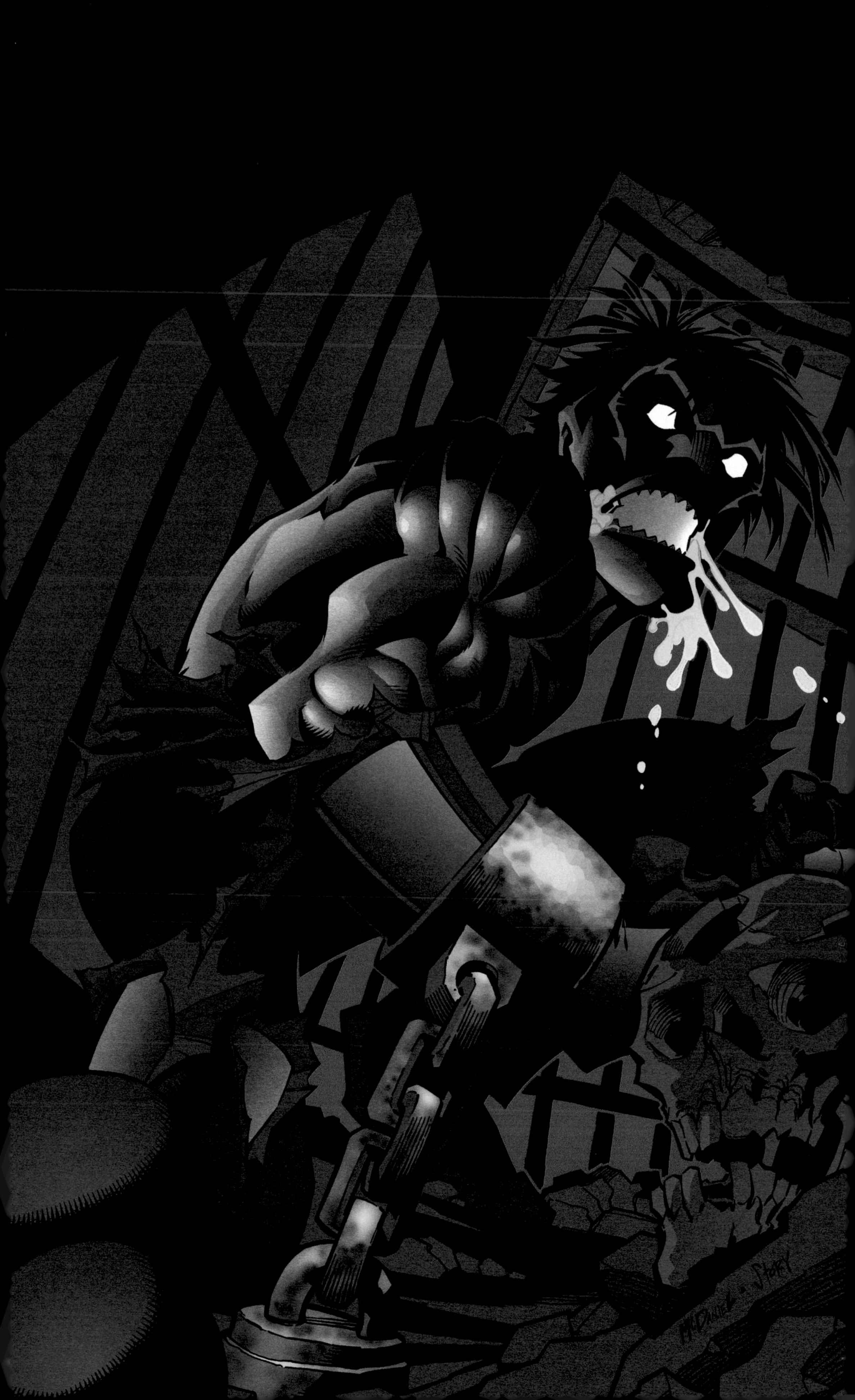

NOTHING BUT TIME

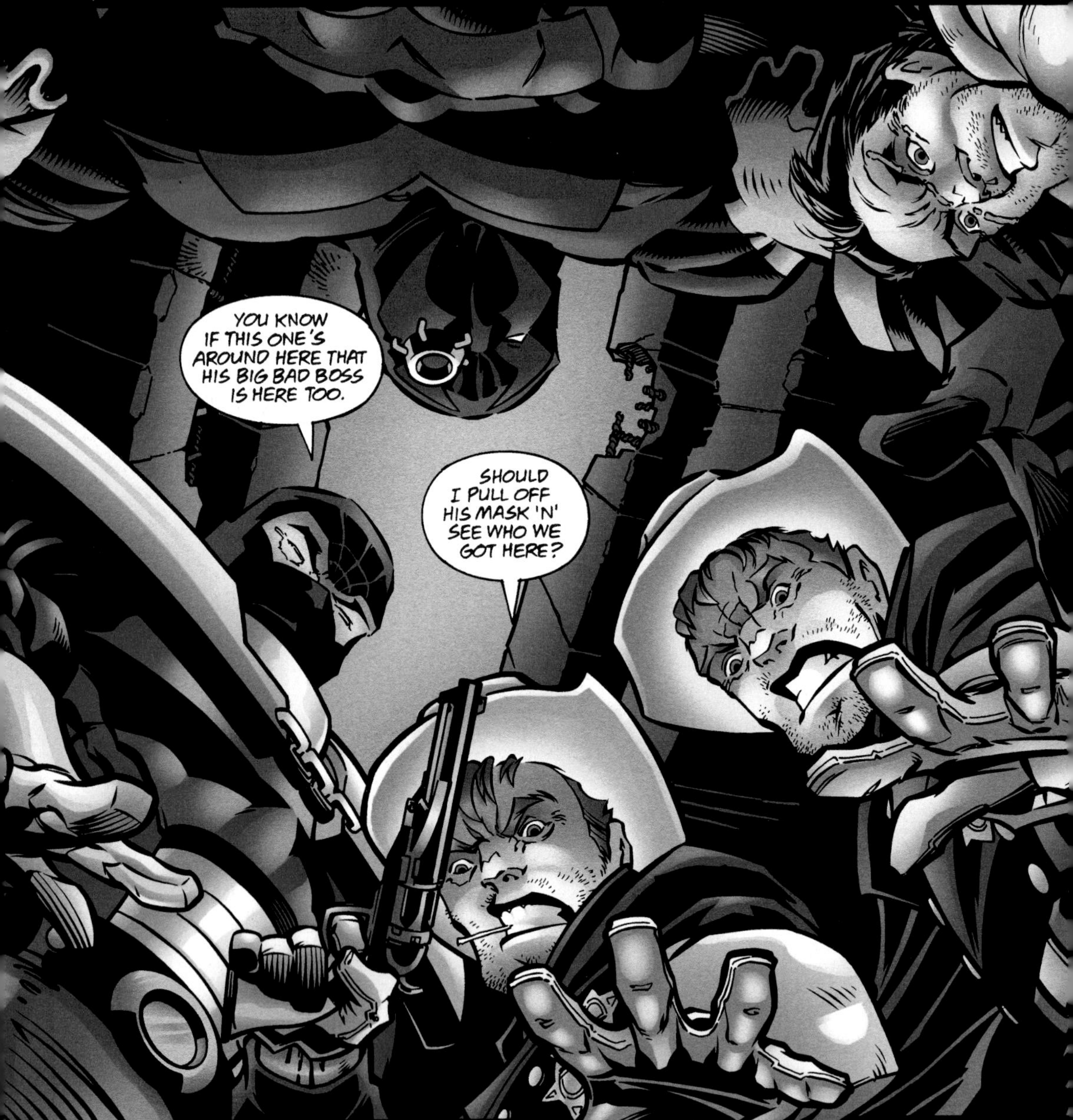
YOU KNOW IF THIS ONE'S AROUND HERE THAT HIS BIG BAD BOSS IS HERE TOO.
SHOULD I PULL OFF HIS MASK 'N' SEE WHO WE GOT HERE?

CHUCK DIXON writer SCOTT McDANIEL penciller KARL STORY inker
ROBERTA TEWES colorist JAMISON separator JOHN COSTANZA letterer
JOSEPH ILLIDGE associate editor DARREN VINCENZO warden

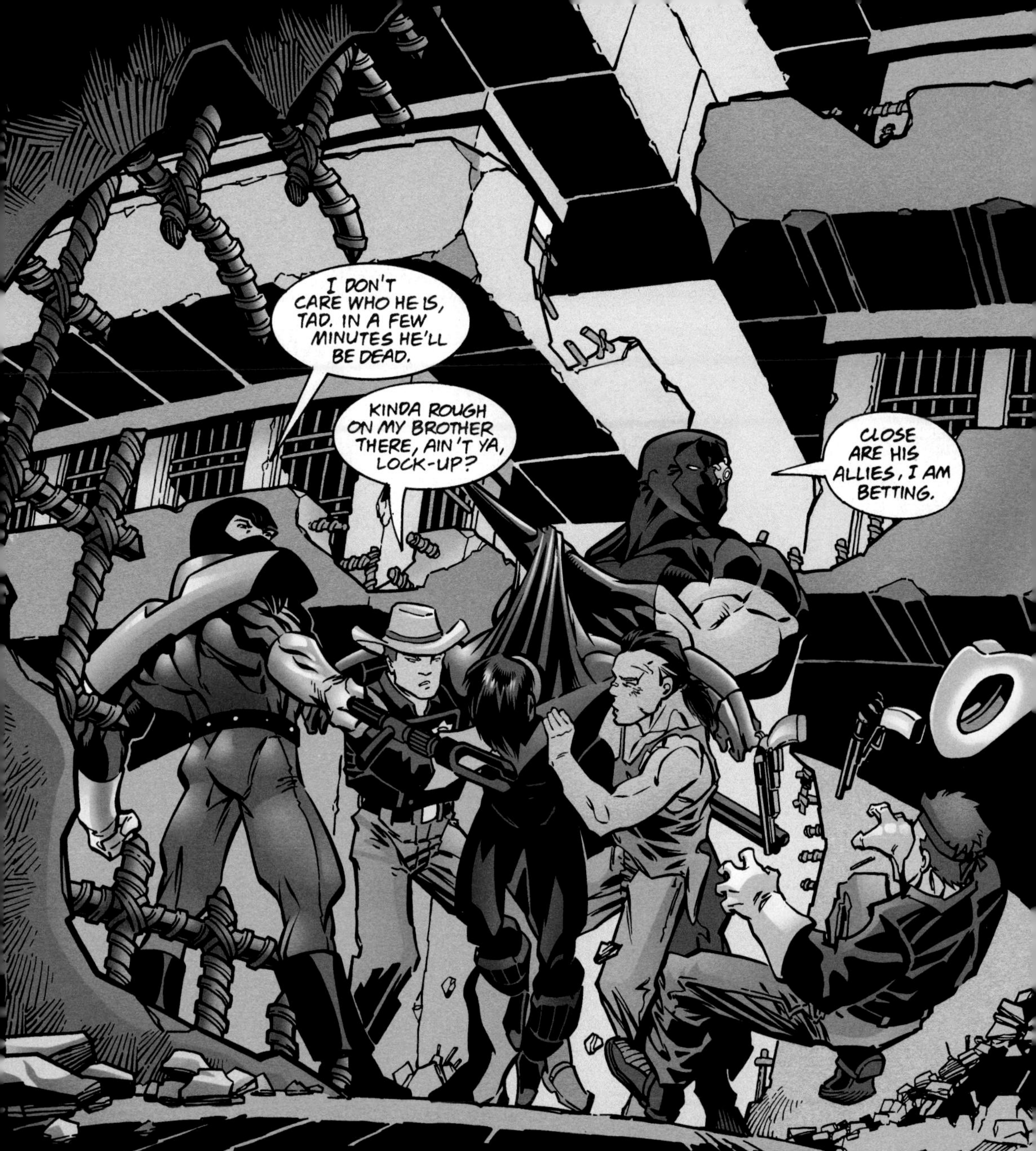
I DON'T CARE WHO HE IS, TAD. IN A FEW MINUTES HE'LL BE DEAD.
KINDA ROUGH ON MY BROTHER THERE, AIN'T YA, LOCK-UP?
CLOSE ARE HIS ALLIES, I AM BETTING.

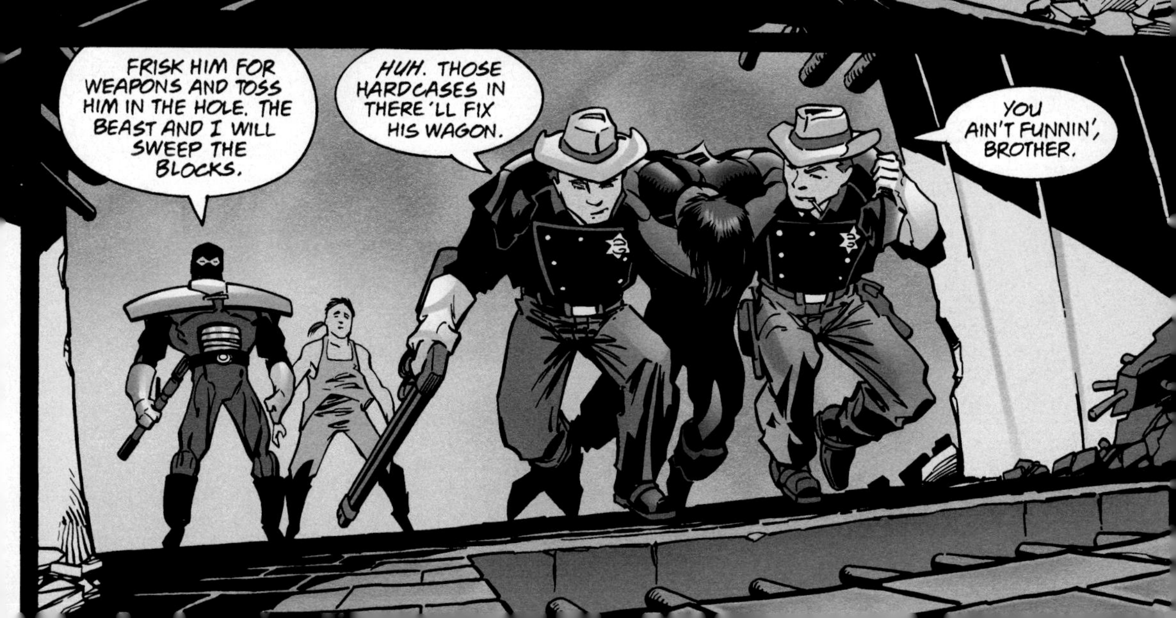
FRISK HIM FOR WEAPONS AND TOSS HIM IN THE HOLE. THE BEAST AND I WILL SWEEP THE BLOCKS.
HUH. THOSE HARDCASES IN THERE'LL FIX HIS WAGON.
YOU AIN'T FUNNIN', BROTHER.

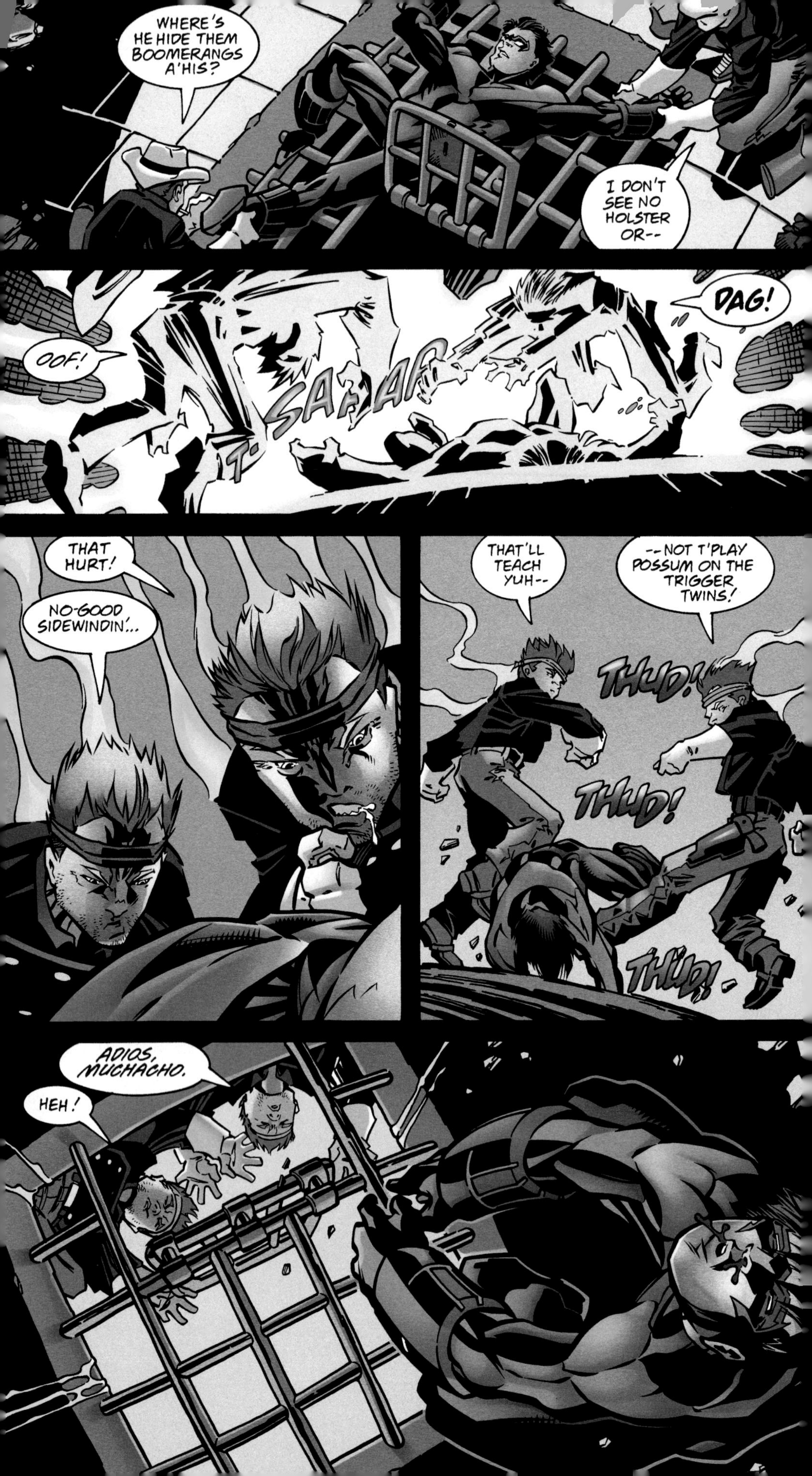
WHERE'S HE HIDE THEM BOOMERANGS A'HIS?
I DON'T SEE NO HOLSTER OR--
OOF!
T-SAAAAP
DAG!
THAT HURT!
NO-GOOD SIDEWINDIN'...
THAT'LL TEACH YUH--
--NOT T'PLAY POSSUM ON THE TRIGGER TWINS!
THUD!
THUD!
THUD!
ADIOS, MUCHACHO.
HEH!

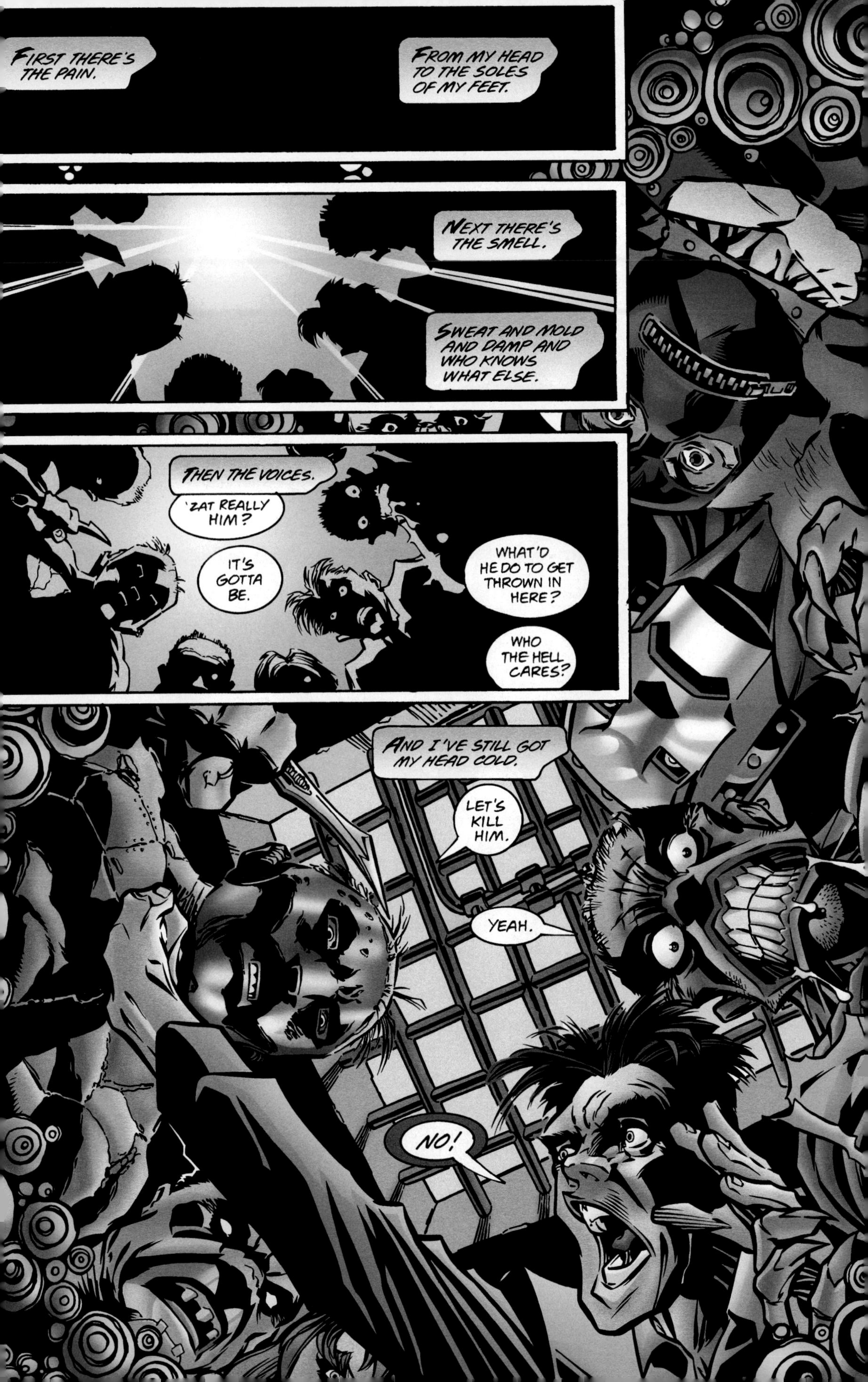

FIRST THERE'S THE PAIN.
FROM MY HEAD TO THE SOLES OF MY FEET.
NEXT THERE'S THE SMELL.
SWEAT AND MOLD AND DAMP AND WHO KNOWS WHAT ELSE.
THEN THE VOICES.
'ZAT REALLY HIM?
IT'S GOTTA BE.
WHAT'D HE DO TO GET THROWN IN HERE?
WHO THE HELL CARES?
AND I'VE STILL GOT MY HEAD COLD.
LET'S KILL HIM.
YEAH.
NO!

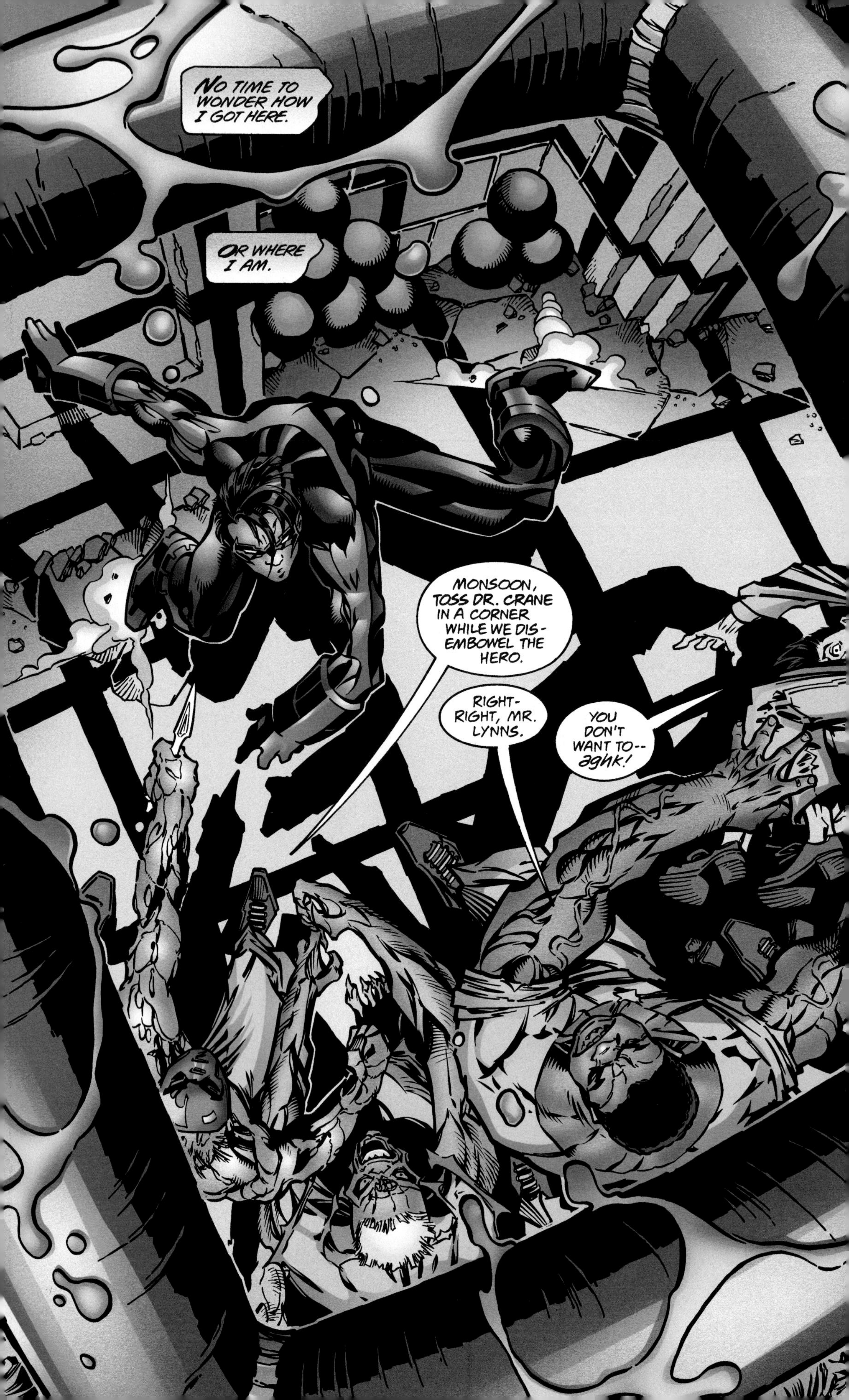
NO TIME TO WONDER HOW I GOT HERE.
OR WHERE I AM.
MONSOON, TOSS DR. CRANE IN A CORNER WHILE WE DIS-EMBOWEL THE HERO.
RIGHT-RIGHT, MR. LYNNS.
YOU DON'T WANT TO-- AGHK!

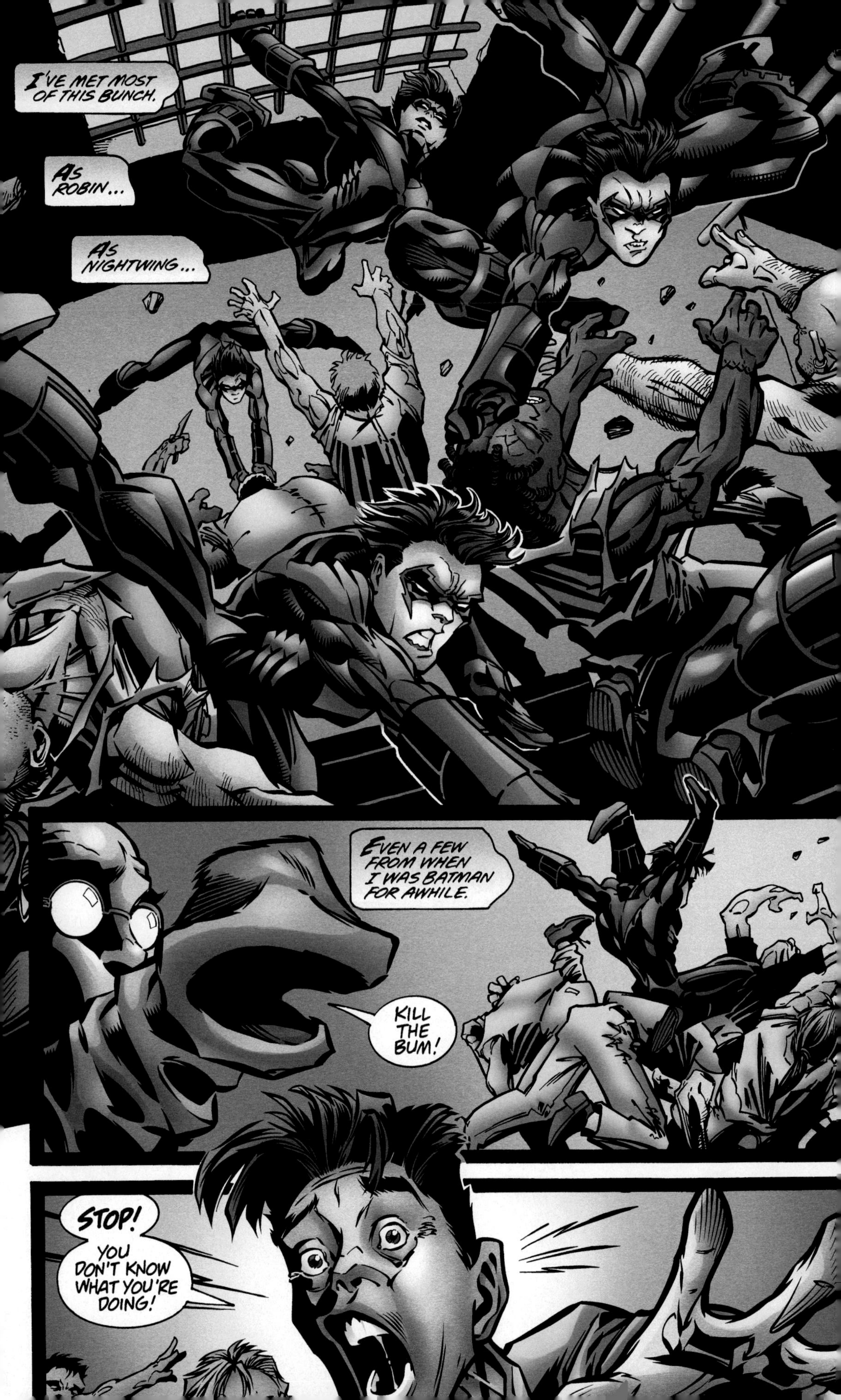
I'VE MET MOST OF THIS BUNCH.
AS ROBIN...
AS NIGHTWING...
EVEN A FEW FROM WHEN I WAS BATMAN FOR AWHILE.
KILL THE BUM!
STOP! YOU DON'T KNOW WHAT YOU'RE DOING!

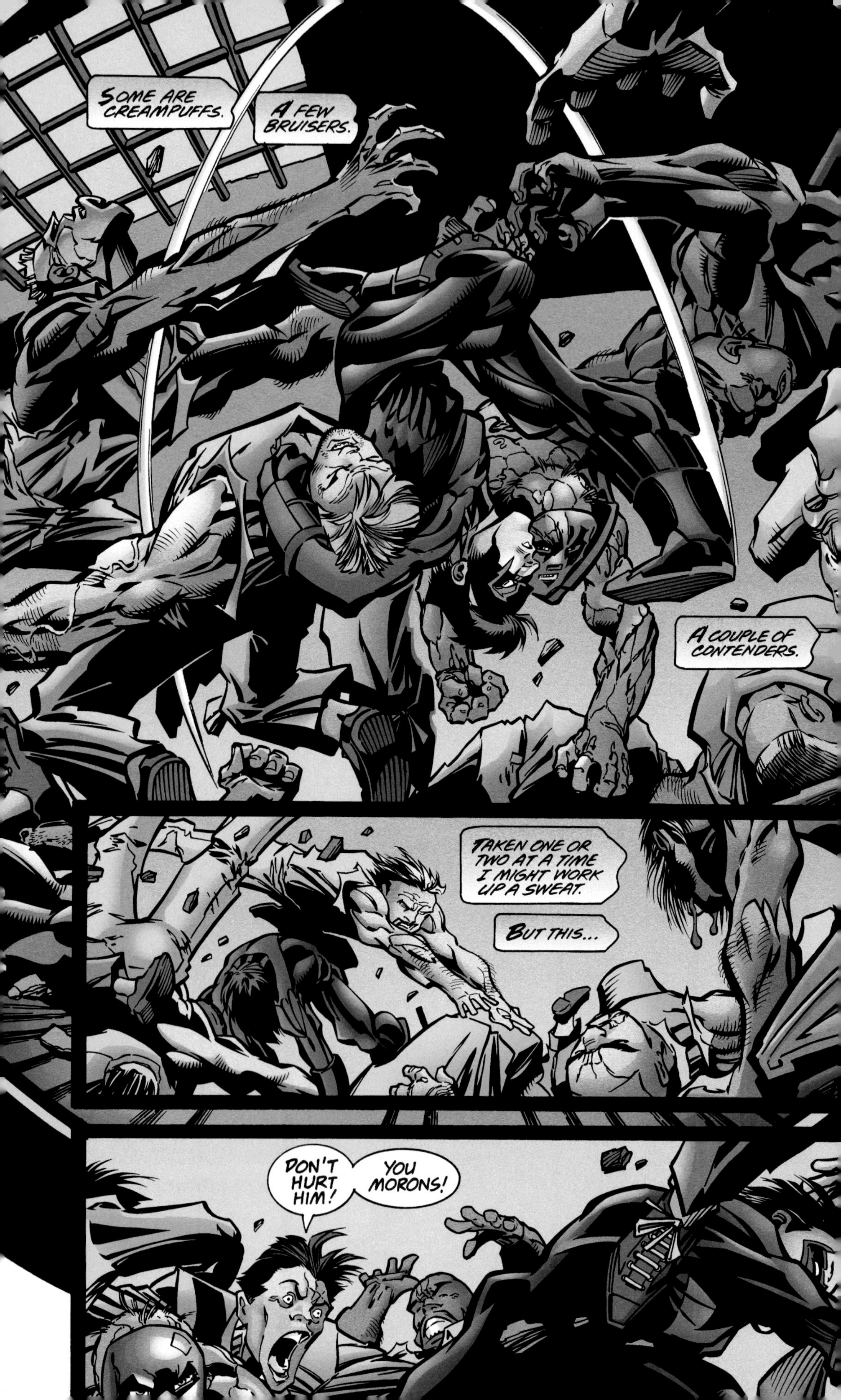
SOME ARE CREAMPUFFS.
A FEW BRUISERS.
A COUPLE OF CONTENDERS.
TAKEN ONE OR TWO AT A TIME I MIGHT WORK UP A SWEAT.
BUT THIS...
DON'T HURT HIM!
YOU MORONS!

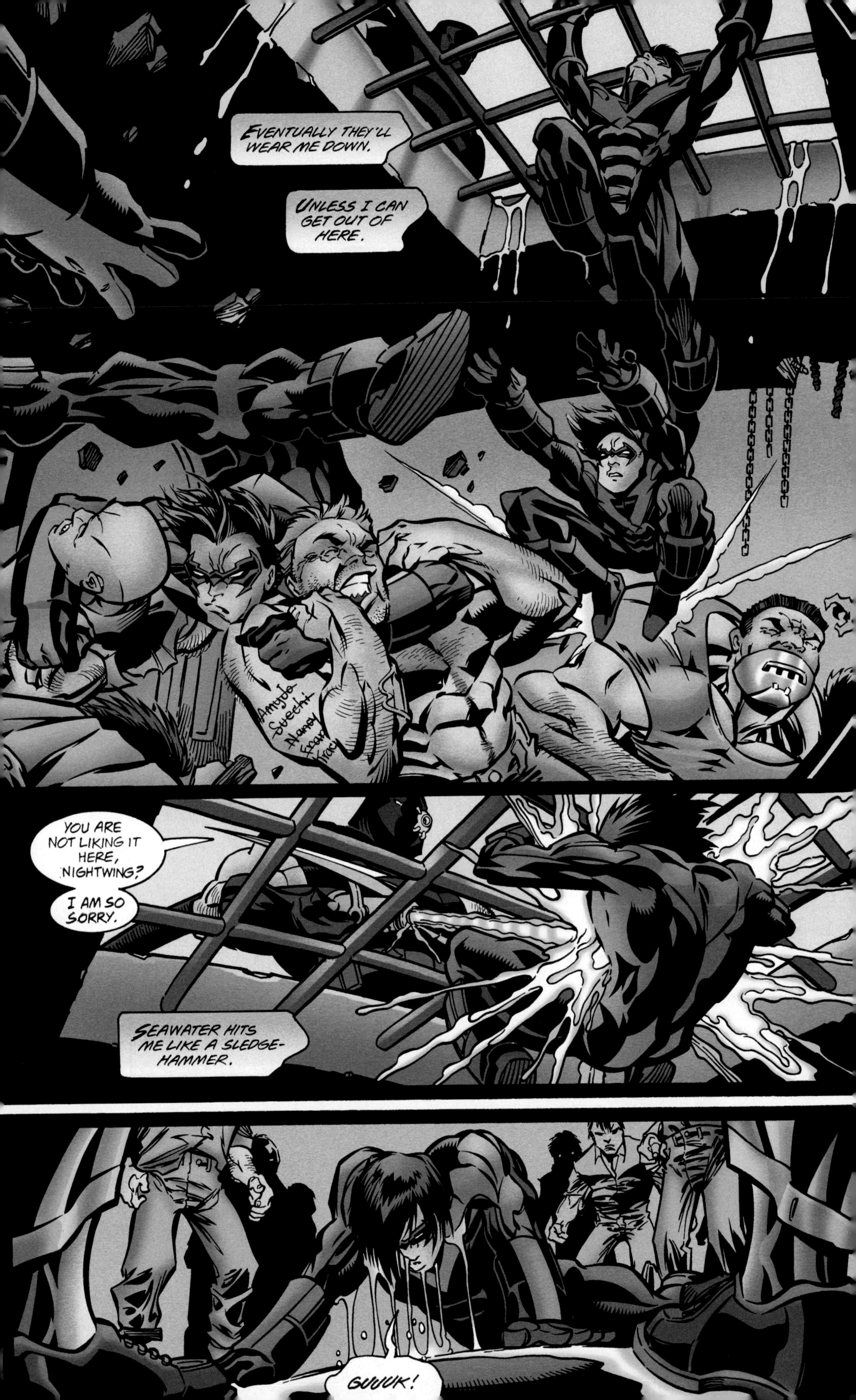
EVENTUALLY THEY'LL WEAR ME DOWN.
UNLESS I CAN GET OUT OF HERE.
YOU ARE NOT LIKING IT HERE, NIGHTWING?
I AM SO SORRY.
SEAWATER HITS ME LIKE A SLEDGE-HAMMER.
GUUUK!

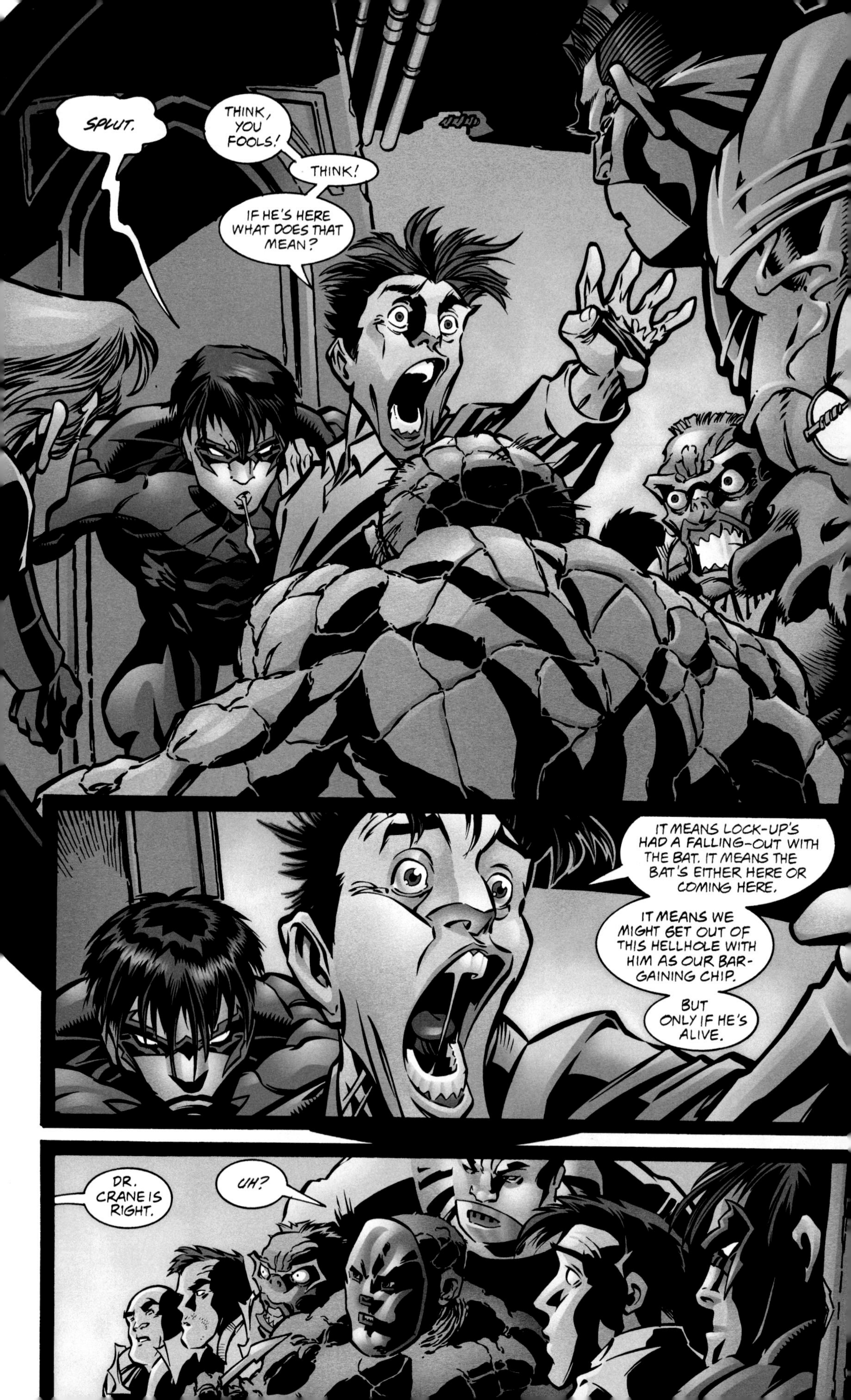
SPLUT.
THINK, YOU FOOLS!
THINK!
IF HE'S HERE WHAT DOES THAT MEAN?
IT MEANS LOCK-UP'S HAD A FALLING-OUT WITH THE BAT. IT MEANS THE BAT'S EITHER HERE OR COMING HERE.
IT MEANS WE MIGHT GET OUT OF THIS HELLHOLE WITH HIM AS OUR BAR-GAINING CHIP.
BUT ONLY IF HE'S ALIVE.
DR. CRANE IS RIGHT.
UH?

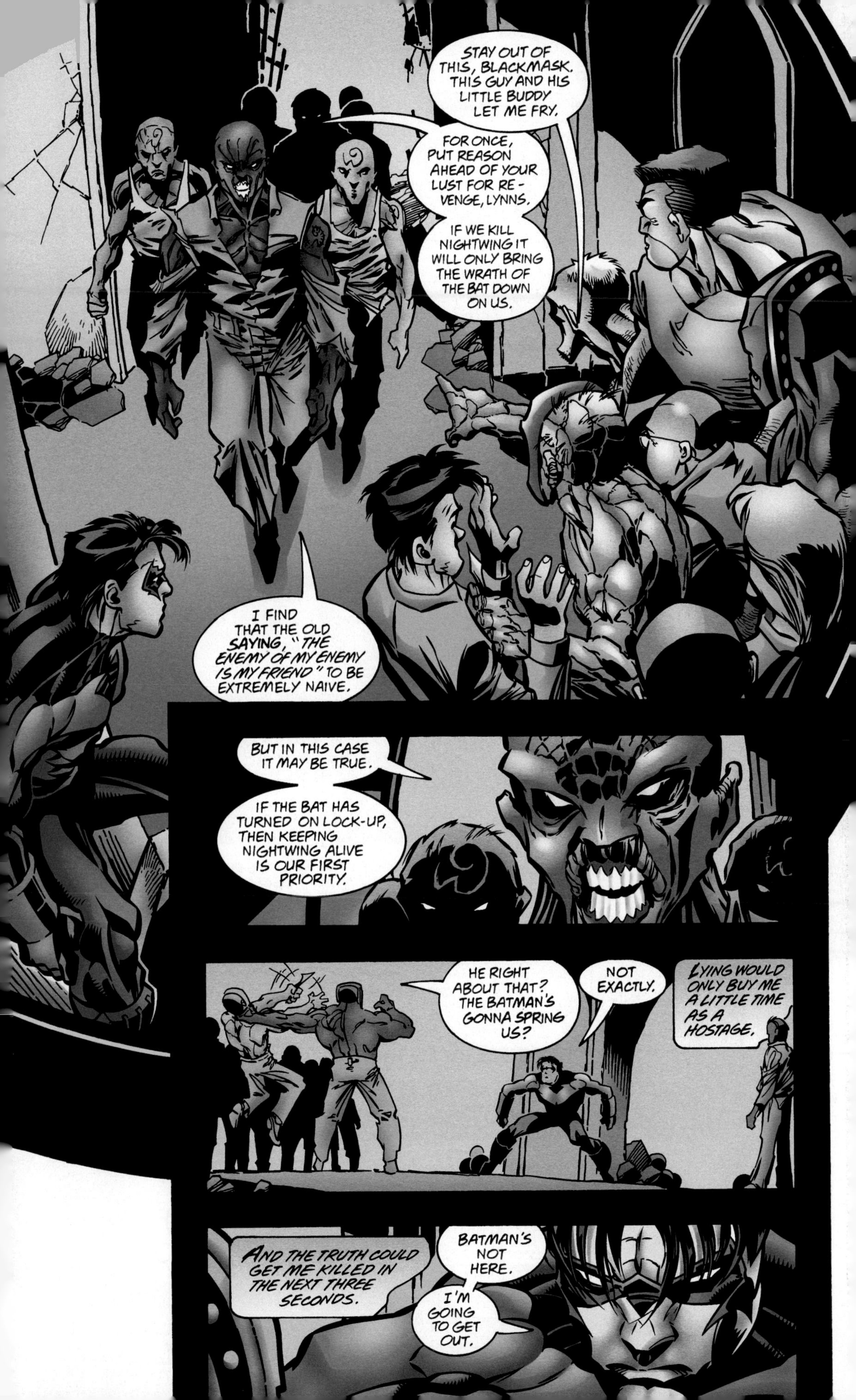
STAY OUT OF THIS, BLACKMASK. THIS GUY AND HIS LITTLE BUDDY LET ME FRY.
FOR ONCE, PUT REASON AHEAD OF YOUR LUST FOR RE-VENGE, LYNNS.
IF WE KILL NIGHTWING IT WILL ONLY BRING THE WRATH OF THE BAT DOWN ON US.
I FIND THAT THE OLD SAYING, "THE ENEMY OF MY ENEMY IS MY FRIEND" TO BE EXTREMELY NAIVE.
BUT IN THIS CASE IT MAY BE TRUE.
IF THE BAT HAS TURNED ON LOCK-UP, THEN KEEPING NIGHTWING ALIVE IS OUR FIRST PRIORITY.
HE RIGHT ABOUT THAT? THE BATMAN'S GONNA SPRING US?
NOT EXACTLY.
LYING WOULD ONLY BUY ME A LITTLE TIME AS A HOSTAGE.
AND THE TRUTH COULD GET ME KILLED IN THE NEXT THREE SECONDS.
BATMAN'S NOT HERE.
I'M GOING TO GET OUT.

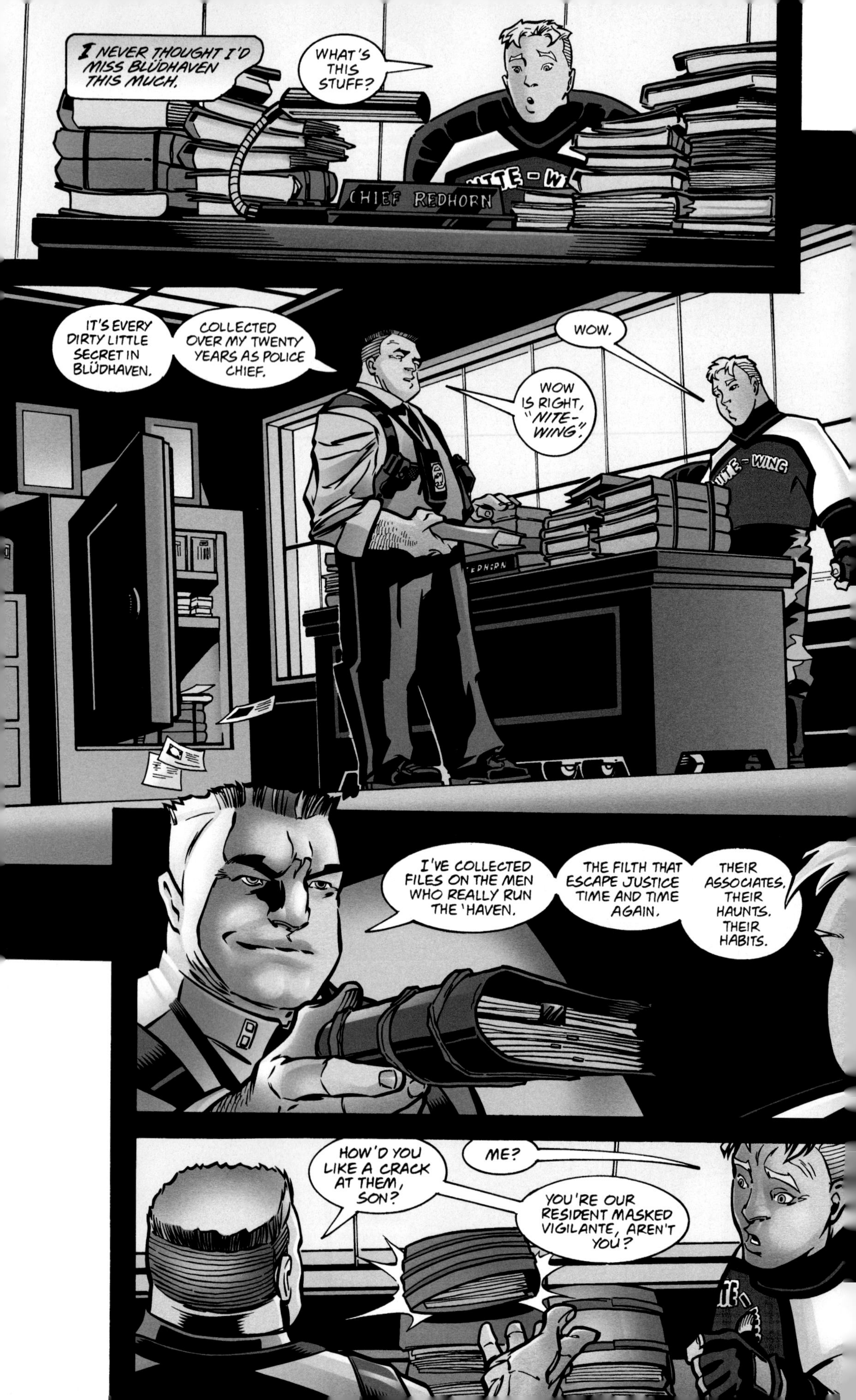
I NEVER THOUGHT I'D MISS BLÜDHAVEN THIS MUCH.
WHAT'S THIS STUFF?
CHIEF REDHORN
IT'S EVERY DIRTY LITTLE SECRET IN BLÜDHAVEN.
COLLECTED OVER MY TWENTY YEARS AS POLICE CHIEF.
WOW.
WOW IS RIGHT, "NITE-WING".
I'VE COLLECTED FILES ON THE MEN WHO REALLY RUN THE 'HAVEN.
THE FILTH THAT ESCAPE JUSTICE TIME AND TIME AGAIN.
THEIR ASSOCIATES. THEIR HAUNTS. THEIR HABITS.
HOW'D YOU LIKE A CRACK AT THEM, SON?
ME?
YOU'RE OUR RESIDENT MASKED VIGILANTE, AREN'T YOU?

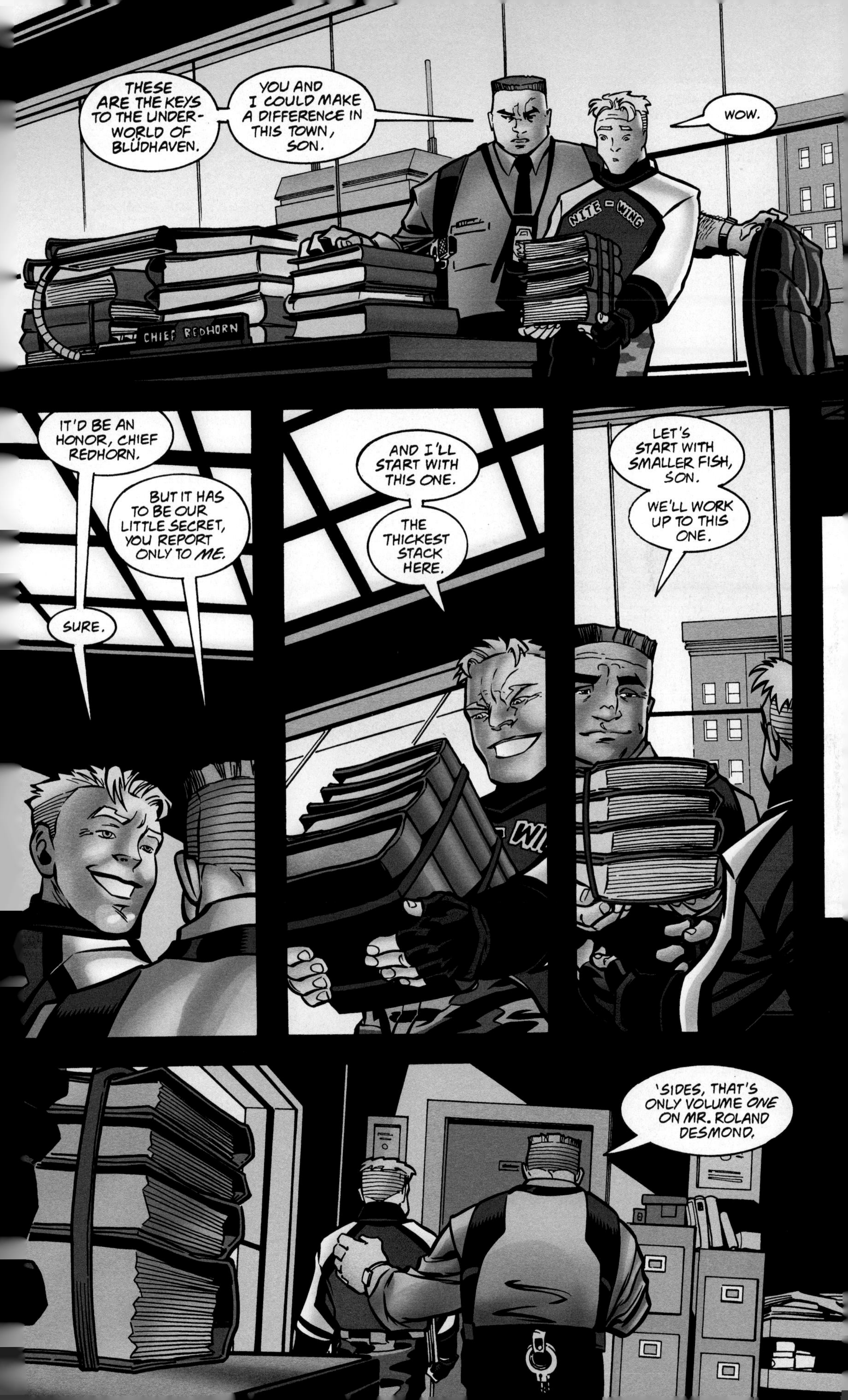
THESE ARE THE KEYS TO THE UNDER-WORLD OF BLÜDHAVEN.
YOU AND I COULD MAKE A DIFFERENCE IN THIS TOWN, SON.
WOW.
NITE-WING
CHIEF REDHORN
IT'D BE AN HONOR, CHIEF REDHORN.
BUT IT HAS TO BE OUR LITTLE SECRET, YOU REPORT ONLY TO ME.
SURE.
AND I'LL START WITH THIS ONE.
THE THICKEST STACK HERE.
LET'S START WITH SMALLER FISH, SON.
WE'LL WORK UP TO THIS ONE.
'SIDES, THAT'S ONLY VOLUME ONE ON MR. ROLAND DESMOND.

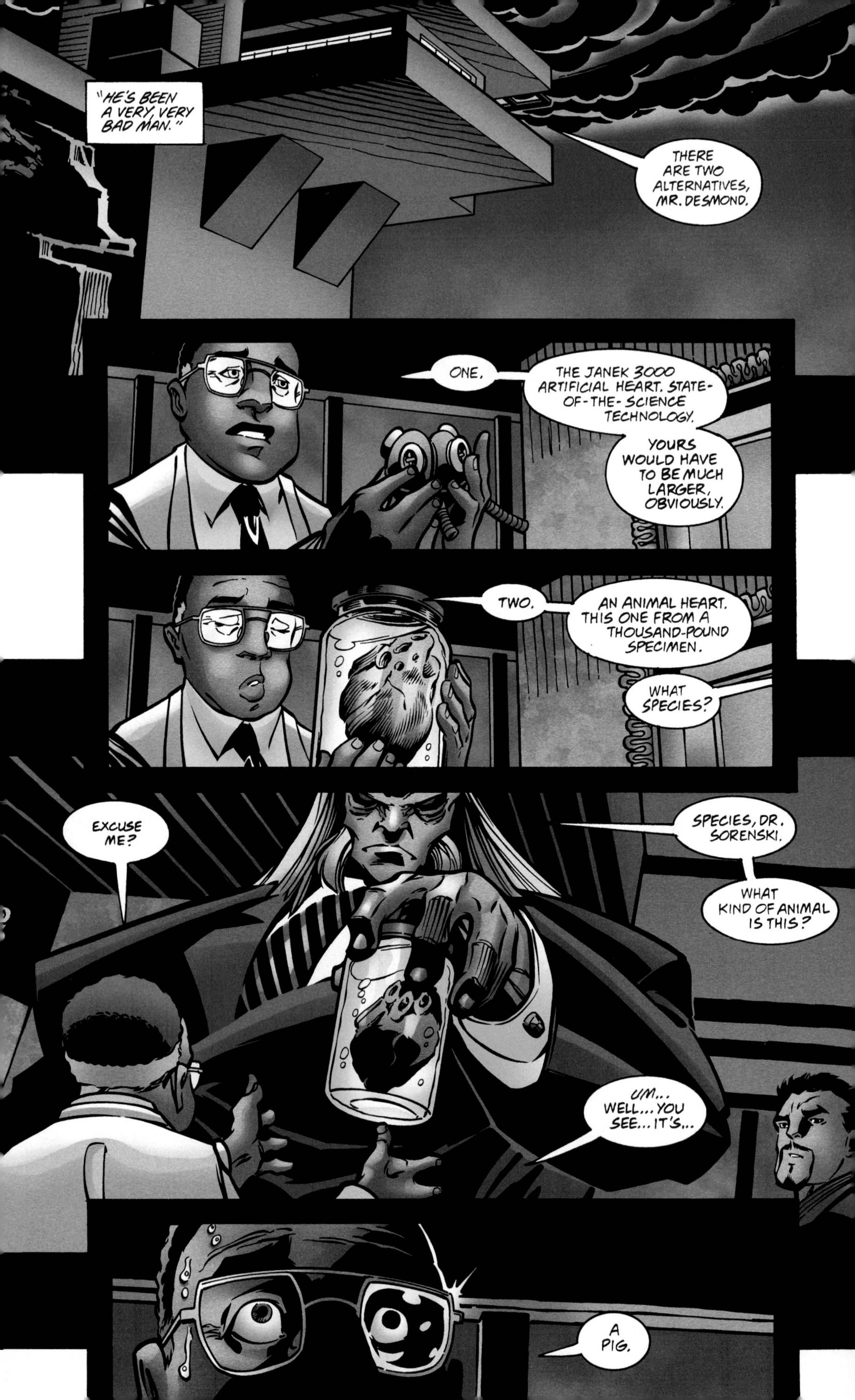
"HE'S BEEN A VERY, VERY BAD MAN."
THERE ARE TWO ALTERNATIVES, MR. DESMOND.
ONE.
THE JANEK 3000 ARTIFICIAL HEART. STATE-OF-THE-SCIENCE TECHNOLOGY.
YOURS WOULD HAVE TO BE MUCH LARGER, OBVIOUSLY.
TWO.
AN ANIMAL HEART. THIS ONE FROM A THOUSAND-POUND SPECIMEN.
WHAT SPECIES?
EXCUSE ME?
SPECIES, DR. SORENSKI.
WHAT KIND OF ANIMAL IS THIS?
UM... WELL... YOU SEE... IT'S...
A PIG.

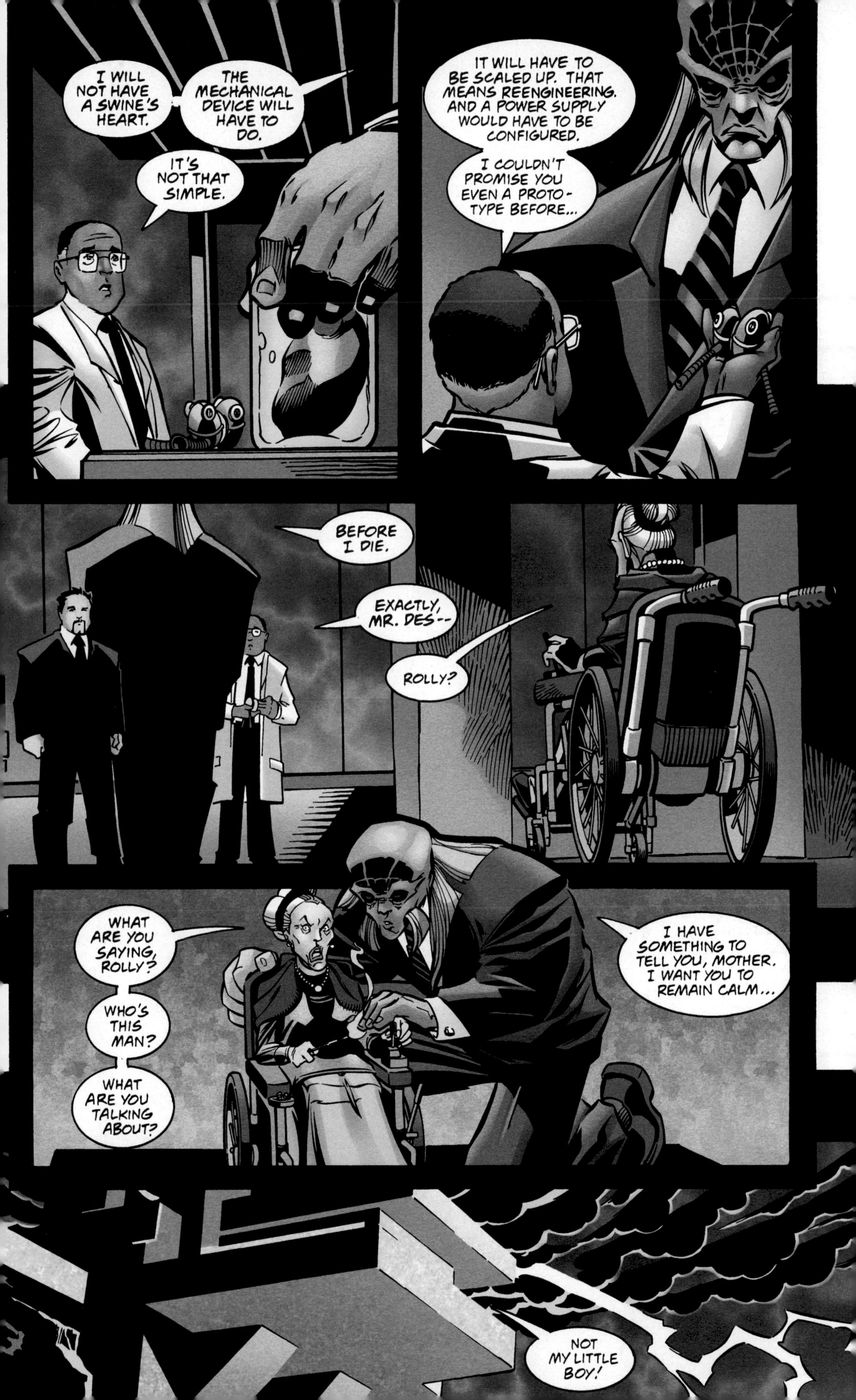
I WILL NOT HAVE A SWINE'S HEART.
THE MECHANICAL DEVICE WILL HAVE TO DO.
IT'S NOT THAT SIMPLE.
IT WILL HAVE TO BE SCALED UP. THAT MEANS REENGINEERING. AND A POWER SUPPLY WOULD HAVE TO BE CONFIGURED.
I COULDN'T PROMISE YOU EVEN A PROTO-TYPE BEFORE...
BEFORE I DIE.
EXACTLY, MR. DES--
ROLLY?
WHAT ARE YOU SAYING, ROLLY?
WHO'S THIS MAN?
WHAT ARE YOU TALKING ABOUT?
I HAVE SOMETHING TO TELL YOU, MOTHER. I WANT YOU TO REMAIN CALM...
NOT MY LITTLE BOY!

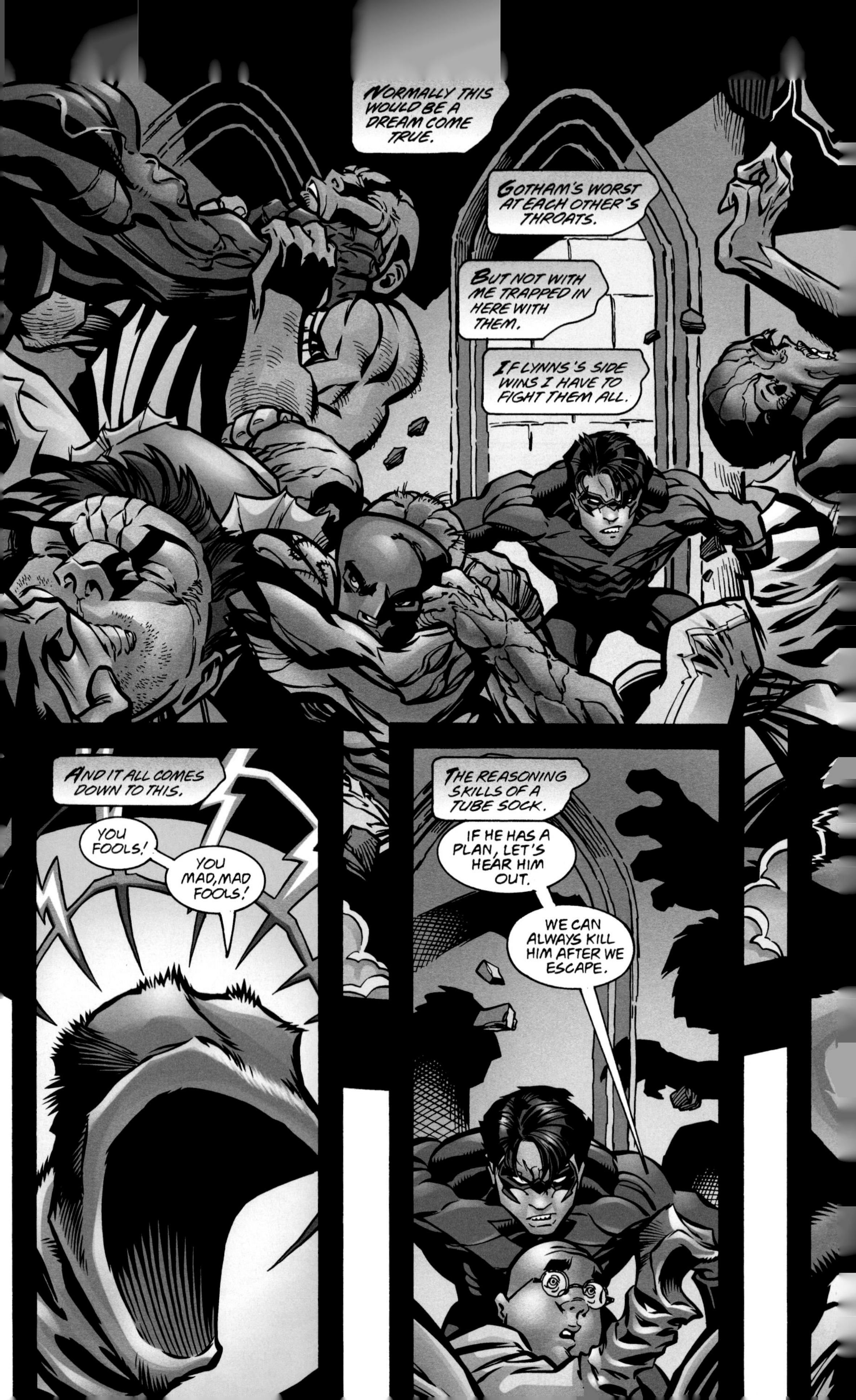
NORMALLY THIS WOULD BE A DREAM COME TRUE.
GOTHAM'S WORST AT EACH OTHER'S THROATS.
BUT NOT WITH ME TRAPPED IN HERE WITH THEM.
IF LYNNS'S SIDE WINS I HAVE TO FIGHT THEM ALL.
AND IT ALL COMES DOWN TO THIS.
YOU FOOLS!
YOU MAD, MAD FOOLS!
THE REASONING SKILLS OF A TUBE SOCK.
IF HE HAS A PLAN, LET'S HEAR HIM OUT.
WE CAN ALWAYS KILL HIM AFTER WE ESCAPE.

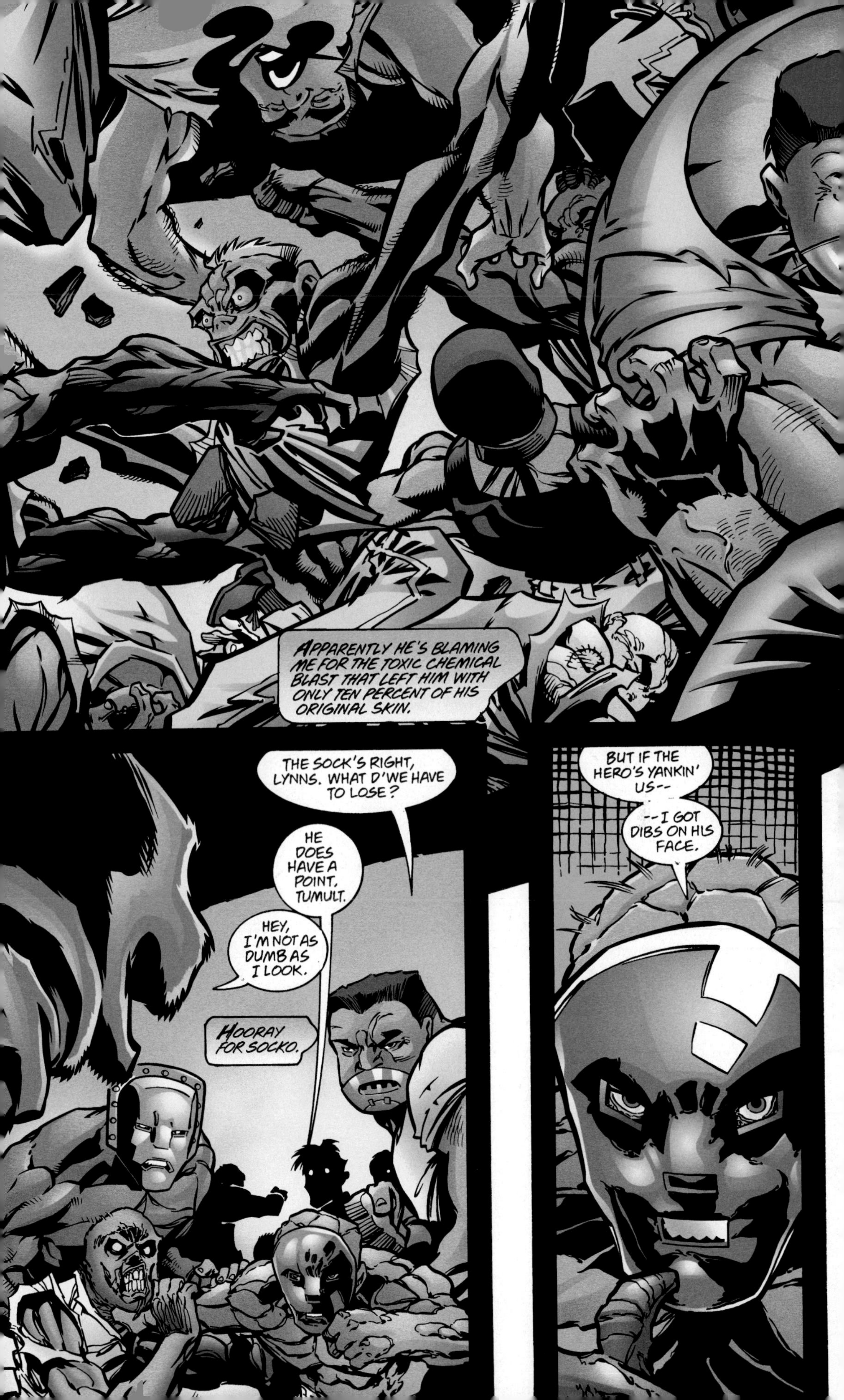
APPARENTLY HE'S BLAMING ME FOR THE TOXIC CHEMICAL BLAST THAT LEFT HIM WITH ONLY TEN PERCENT OF HIS ORIGINAL SKIN.
THE SOCK'S RIGHT, LYNNS. WHAT D'WE HAVE TO LOSE?
HE DOES HAVE A POINT, TUMULT.
HEY, I'M NOT AS DUMB AS I LOOK.
HOORAY FOR SOCKO.
BUT IF THE HERO'S YANKIN' US--
--I GOT DIBS ON HIS FACE.

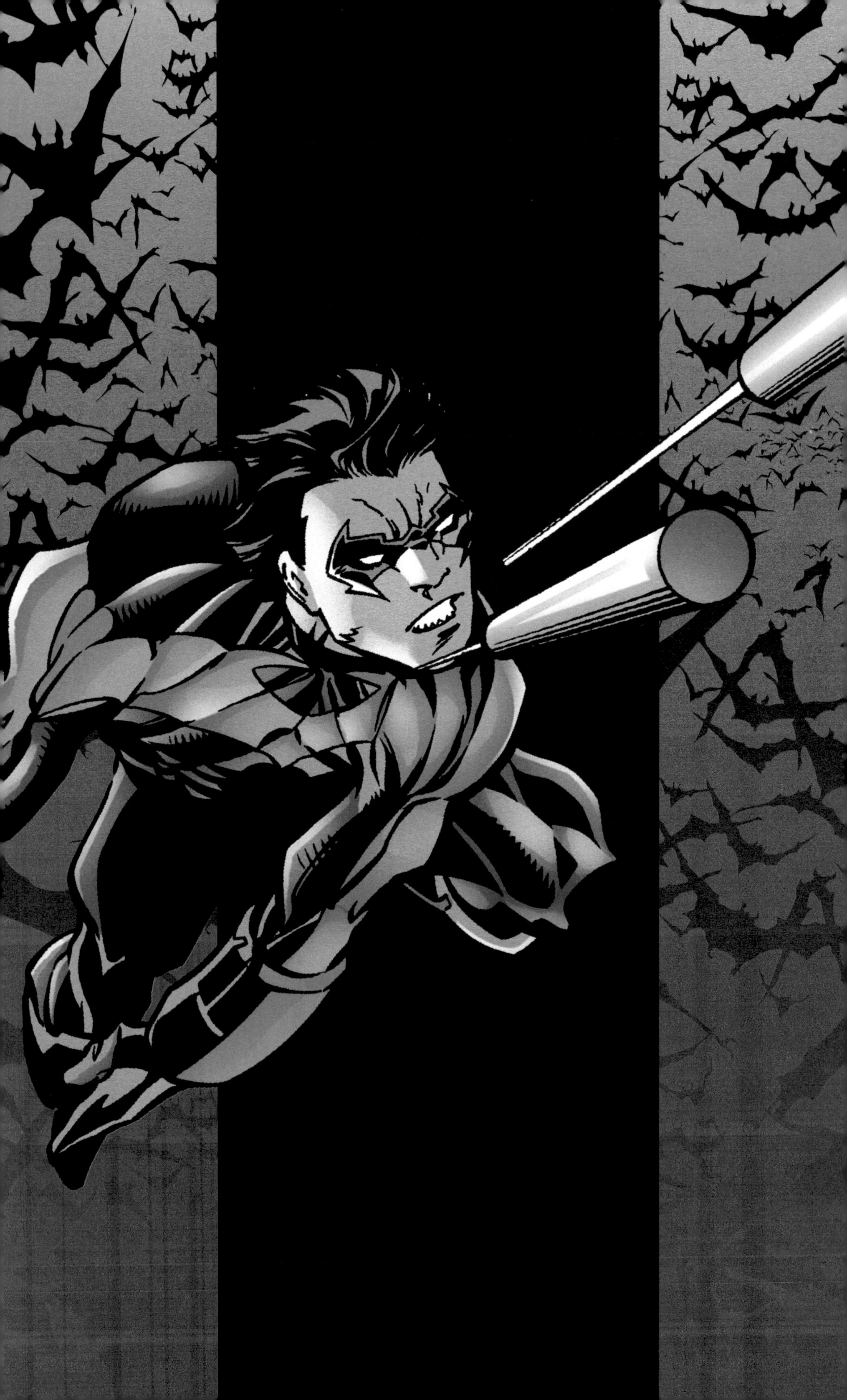

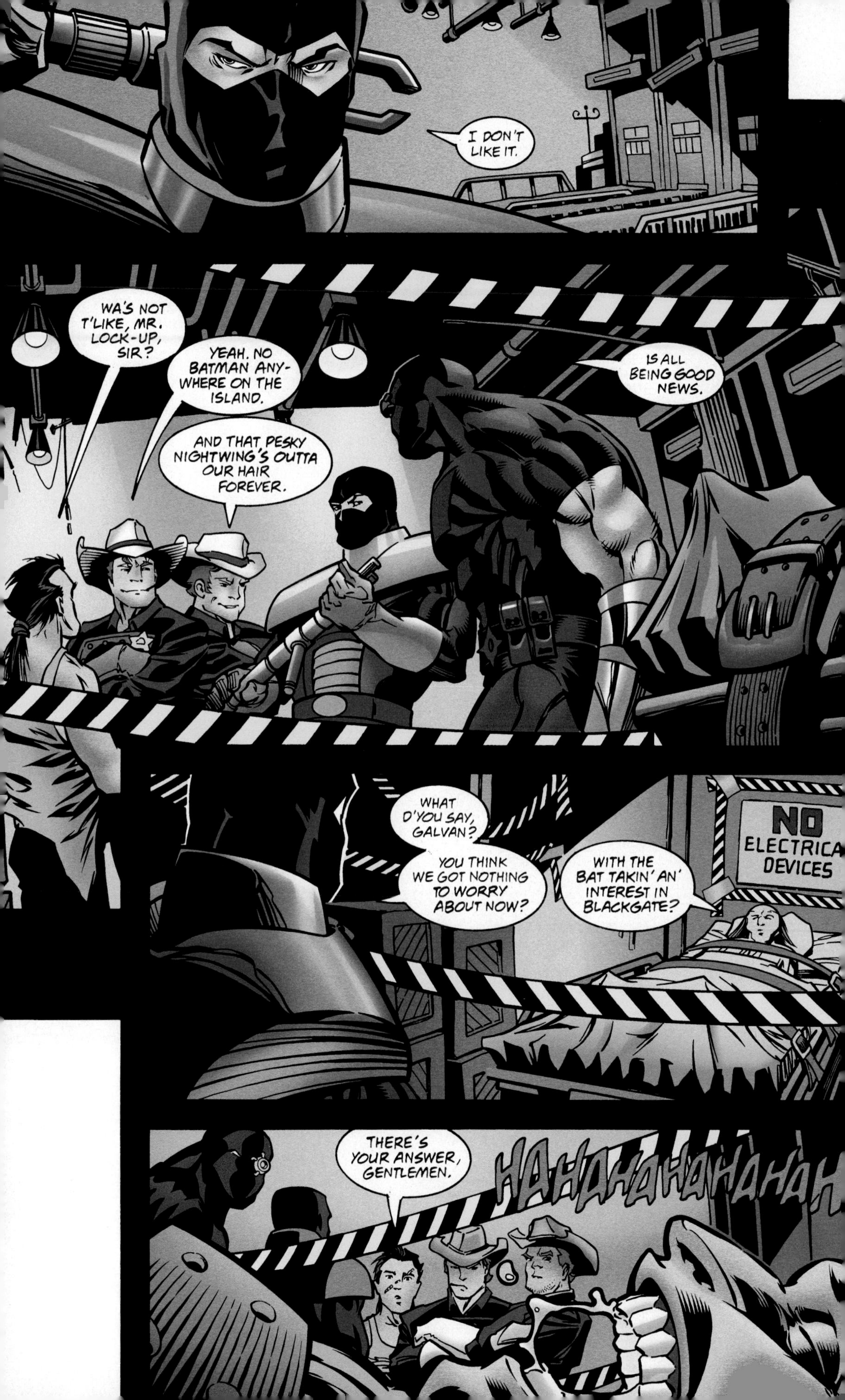
I DON'T LIKE IT.
WA'S NOT T'LIKE, MR. LOCK-UP, SIR?
YEAH. NO BATMAN ANYWHERE ON THE ISLAND.
AND THAT PESKY NIGHTWING'S OUTTA OUR HAIR FOREVER.
IS ALL BEING GOOD NEWS.
WHAT D'YOU SAY, GALVAN?
YOU THINK WE GOT NOTHING TO WORRY ABOUT NOW?
WITH THE BAT TAKIN' AN' INTEREST IN BLACKGATE?
NO ELECTRICA DEVICES
THERE'S YOUR ANSWER, GENTLEMEN.
HAHAHAHAHAHAHAH

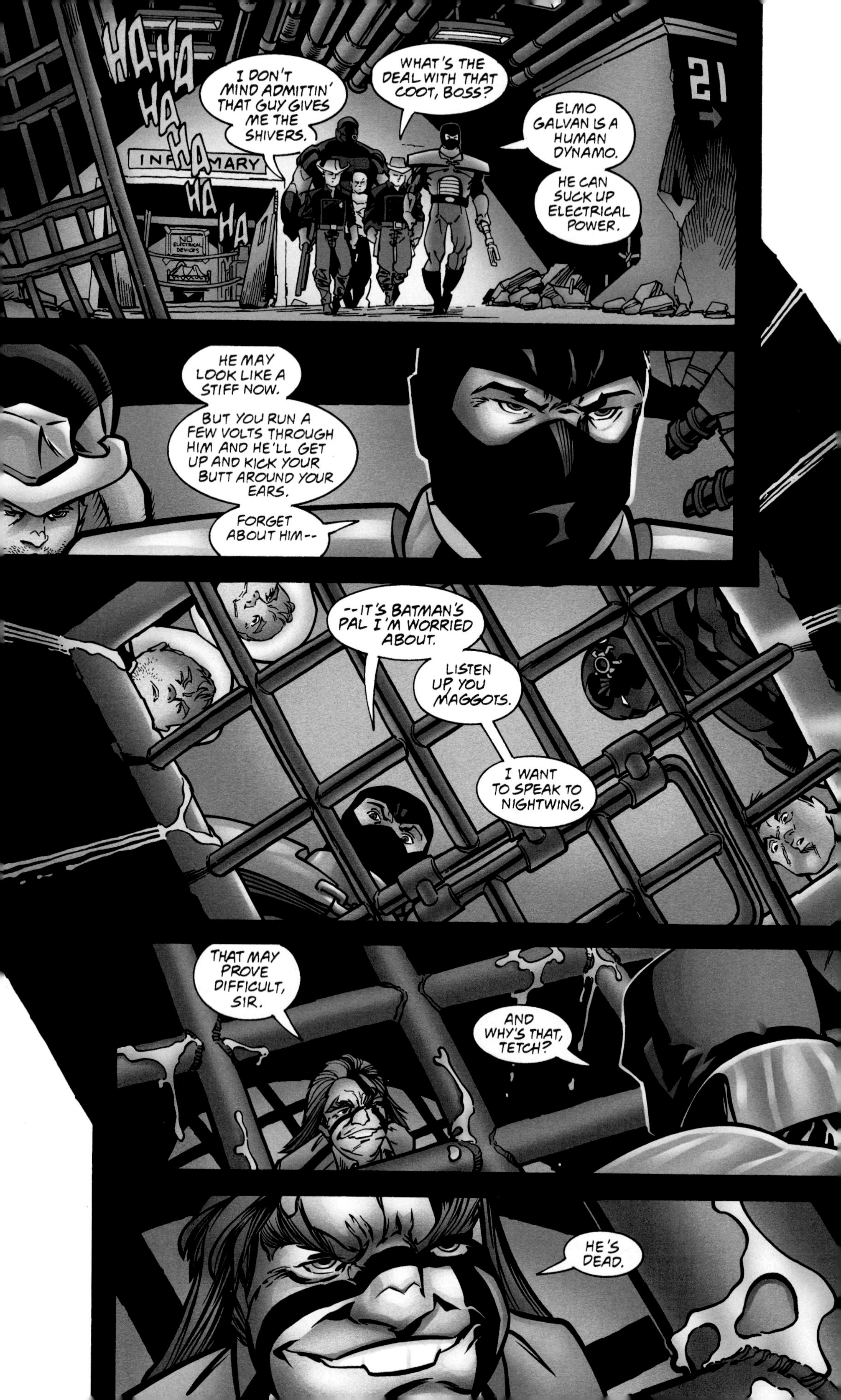
HA HA HA HA HA HA HA
INFIRMARY
NO ELECTRICAL DEVICES
I DON'T MIND ADMITTIN' THAT GUY GIVES ME THE SHIVERS.
WHAT'S THE DEAL WITH THAT COOT, BOSS?
21
ELMO GALVAN IS A HUMAN DYNAMO.
HE CAN SUCK UP ELECTRICAL POWER.
HE MAY LOOK LIKE A STIFF NOW.
BUT YOU RUN A FEW VOLTS THROUGH HIM AND HE'LL GET UP AND KICK YOUR BUTT AROUND YOUR EARS.
FORGET ABOUT HIM--
--IT'S BATMAN'S PAL I'M WORRIED ABOUT.
LISTEN UP, YOU MAGGOTS.
I WANT TO SPEAK TO NIGHTWING.
THAT MAY PROVE DIFFICULT, SIR.
AND WHY'S THAT, TETCH?
HE'S DEAD.

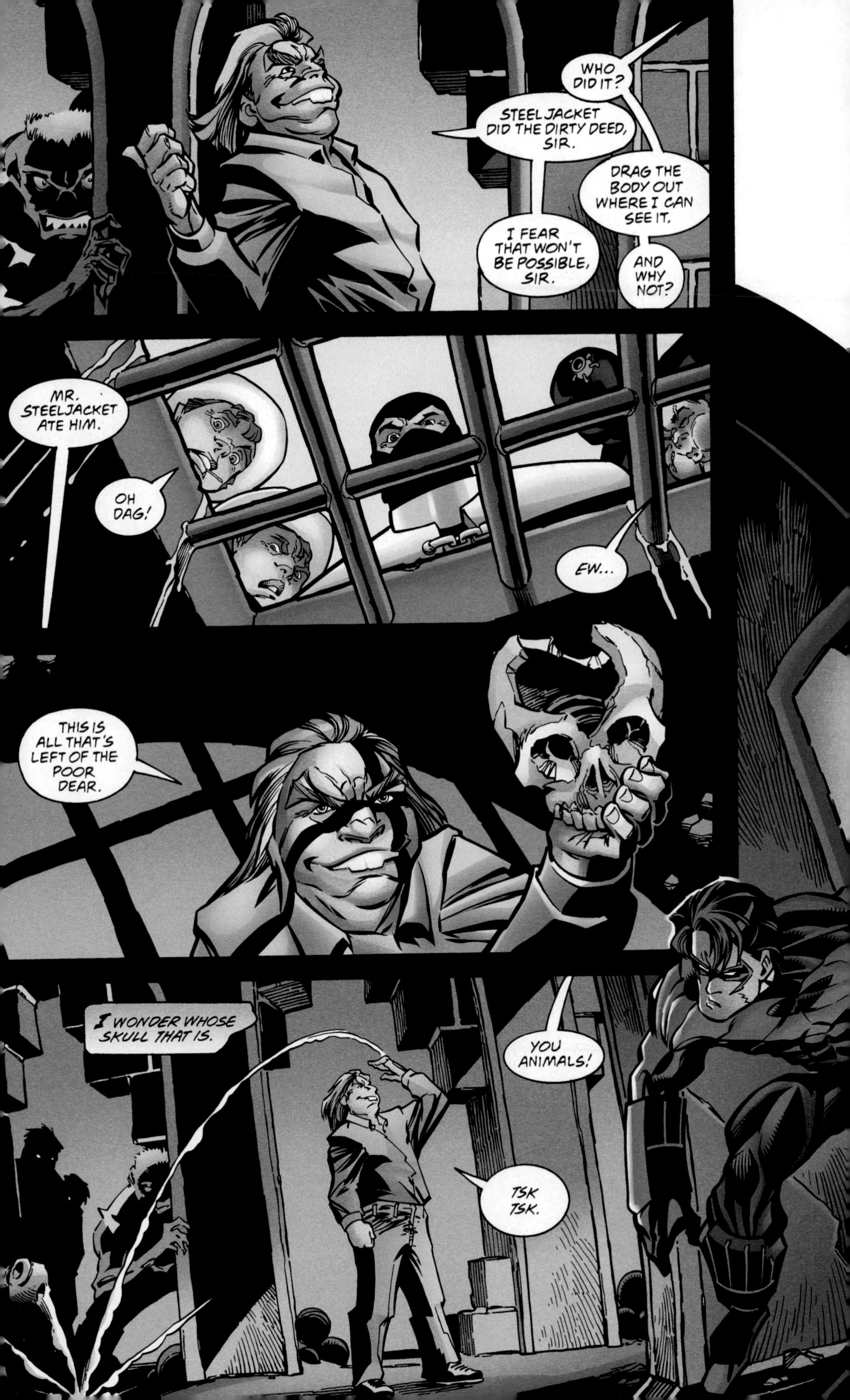

WHO DID IT?
STEEL JACKET DID THE DIRTY DEED, SIR.
DRAG THE BODY OUT WHERE I CAN SEE IT.
I FEAR THAT WON'T BE POSSIBLE, SIR.
AND WHY NOT?
MR. STEELJACKET ATE HIM.
OH DAG!
EW...
THIS IS ALL THAT'S LEFT OF THE POOR DEAR.
I WONDER WHOSE SKULL THAT IS.
YOU ANIMALS!
TSK TSK.

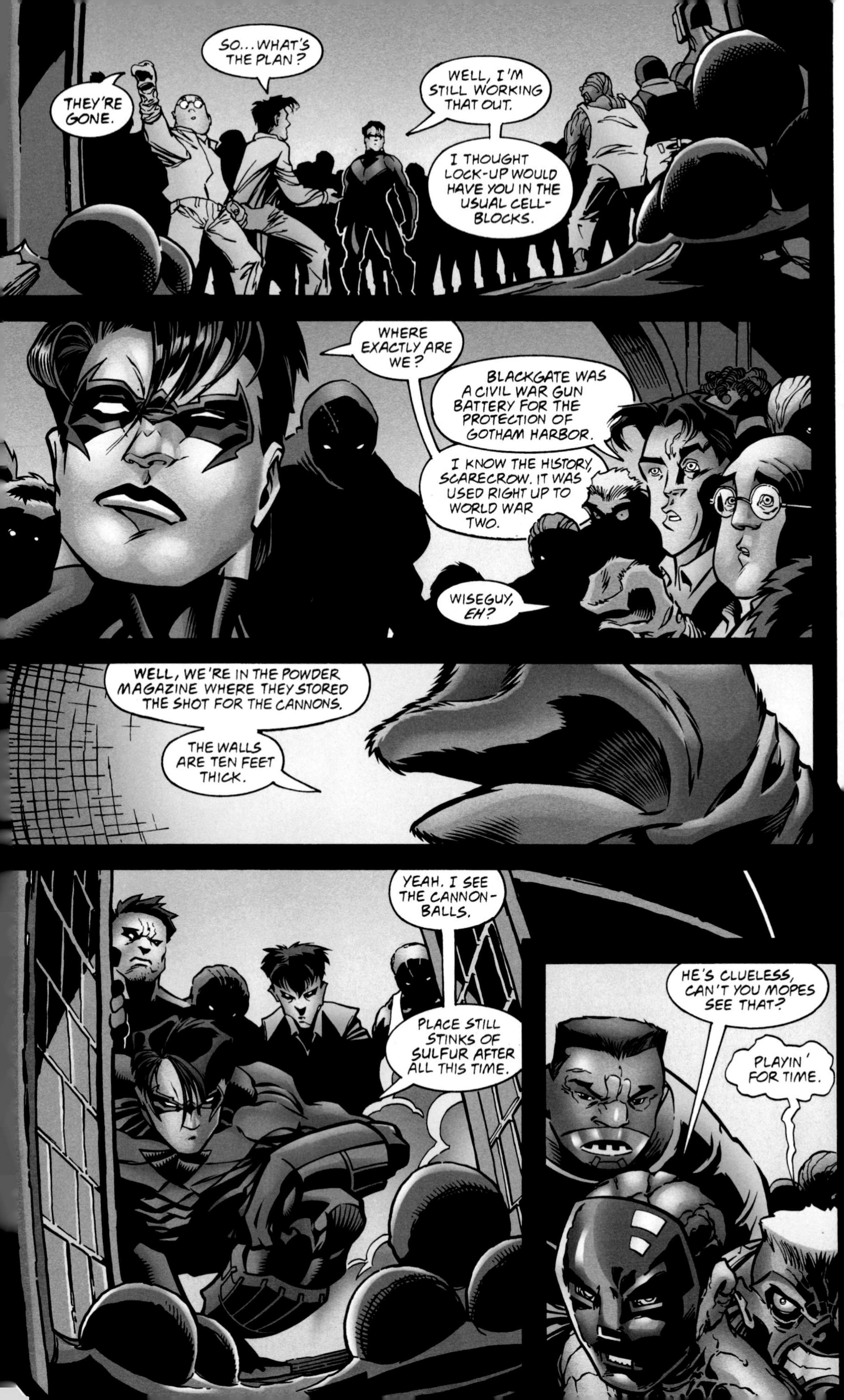
THEY'RE GONE.
SO... WHAT'S THE PLAN?
WELL, I'M STILL WORKING THAT OUT.
I THOUGHT LOCK-UP WOULD HAVE YOU IN THE USUAL CELL-BLOCKS.
WHERE EXACTLY ARE WE?
BLACKGATE WAS A CIVIL WAR GUN BATTERY FOR THE PROTECTION OF GOTHAM HARBOR.
I KNOW THE HISTORY, SCARECROW. IT WAS USED RIGHT UP TO WORLD WAR TWO.
WISEGUY, EH?
WELL, WE'RE IN THE POWDER MAGAZINE WHERE THEY STORED THE SHOT FOR THE CANNONS.
THE WALLS ARE TEN FEET THICK.
YEAH. I SEE THE CANNON-BALLS.
PLACE STILL STINKS OF SULFUR AFTER ALL THIS TIME.
HE'S CLUELESS, CAN'T YOU MOPES SEE THAT?
PLAYIN' FOR TIME.

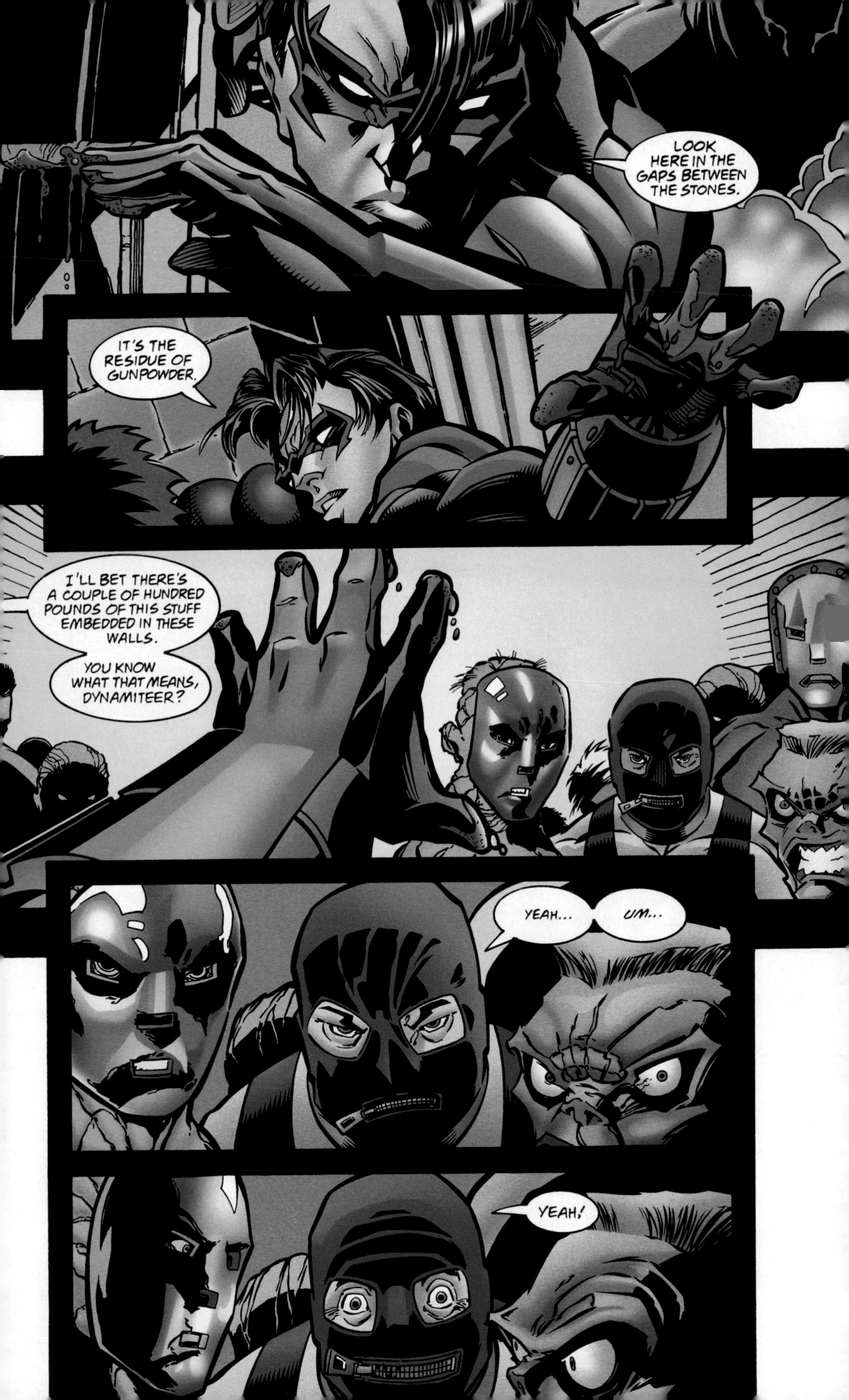
LOOK HERE IN THE GAPS BETWEEN THE STONES.
IT'S THE RESIDUE OF GUNPOWDER.
I'LL BET THERE'S A COUPLE OF HUNDRED POUNDS OF THIS STUFF EMBEDDED IN THESE WALLS.
YOU KNOW WHAT THAT MEANS, DYNAMITEER?
YEAH...
UM...
YEAH!

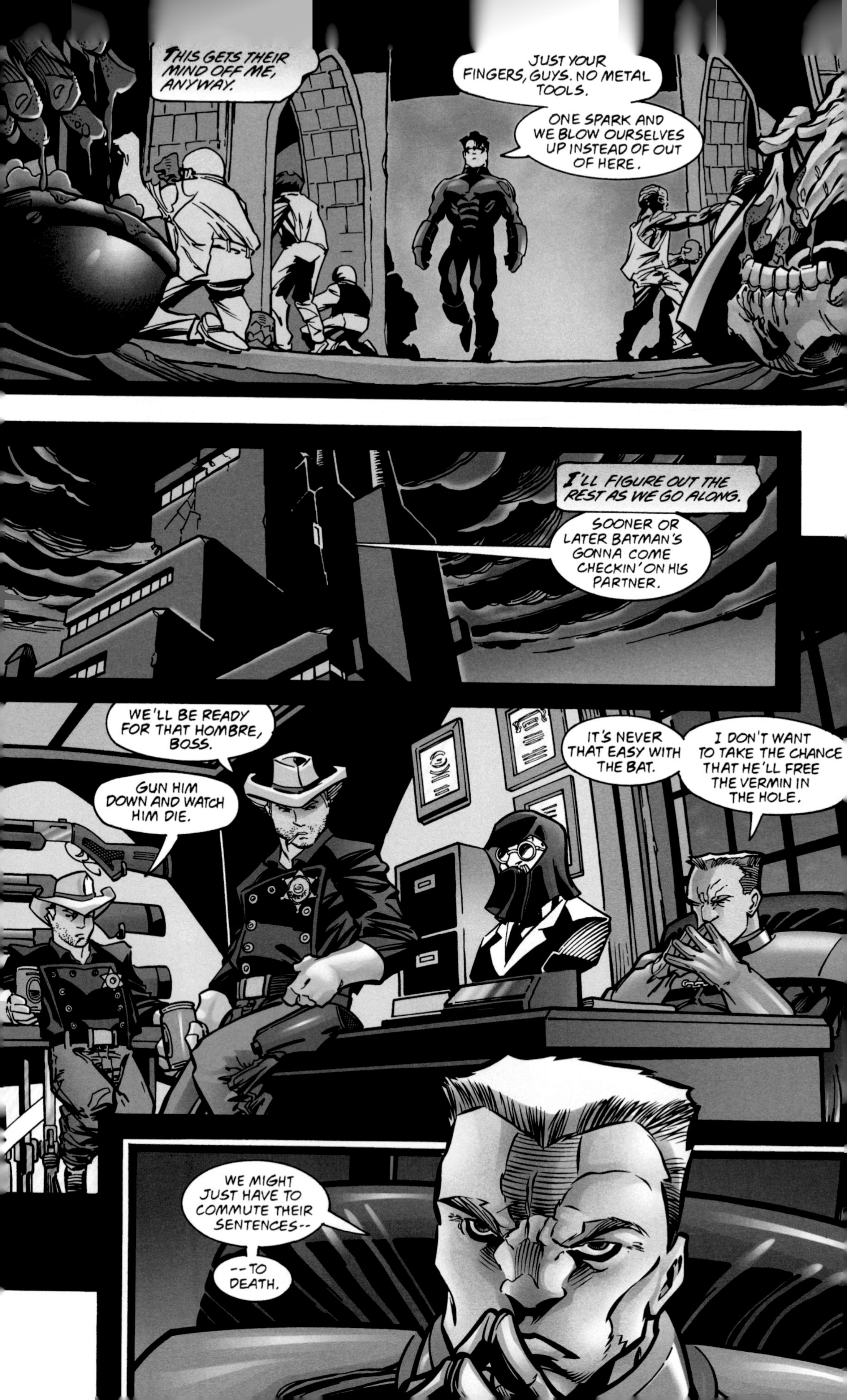
THIS GETS THEIR MIND OFF ME, ANYWAY.
JUST YOUR FINGERS, GUYS. NO METAL TOOLS.
ONE SPARK AND WE BLOW OURSELVES UP INSTEAD OF OUT OF HERE.
I'LL FIGURE OUT THE REST AS WE GO ALONG.
SOONER OR LATER BATMAN'S GONNA COME CHECKIN' ON HIS PARTNER.
WE'LL BE READY FOR THAT HOMBRE, BOSS.
GUN HIM DOWN AND WATCH HIM DIE.
IT'S NEVER THAT EASY WITH THE BAT.
I DON'T WANT TO TAKE THE CHANCE THAT HE'LL FREE THE VERMIN IN THE HOLE.
WE MIGHT JUST HAVE TO COMMUTE THEIR SENTENCES--
--TO DEATH.

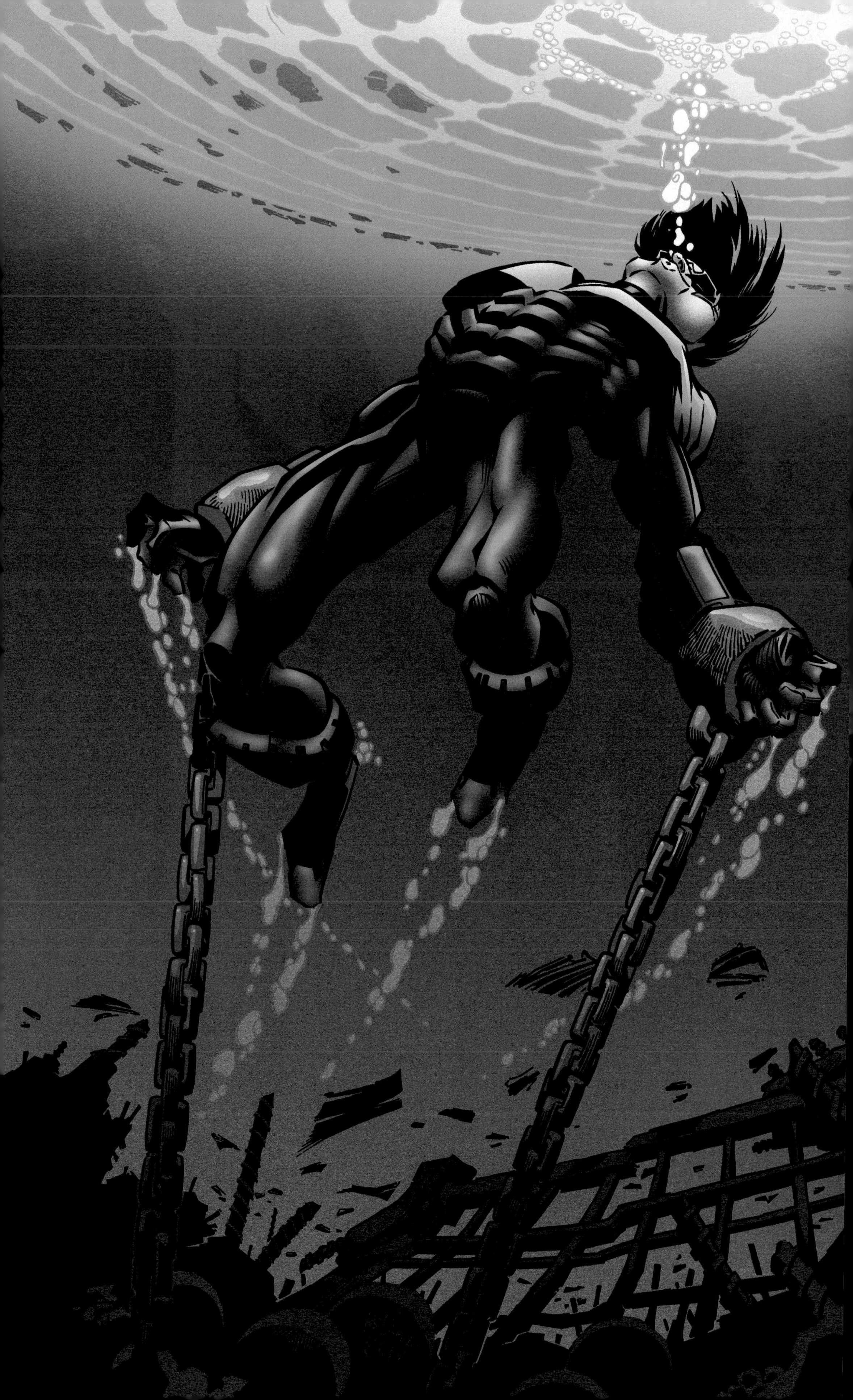

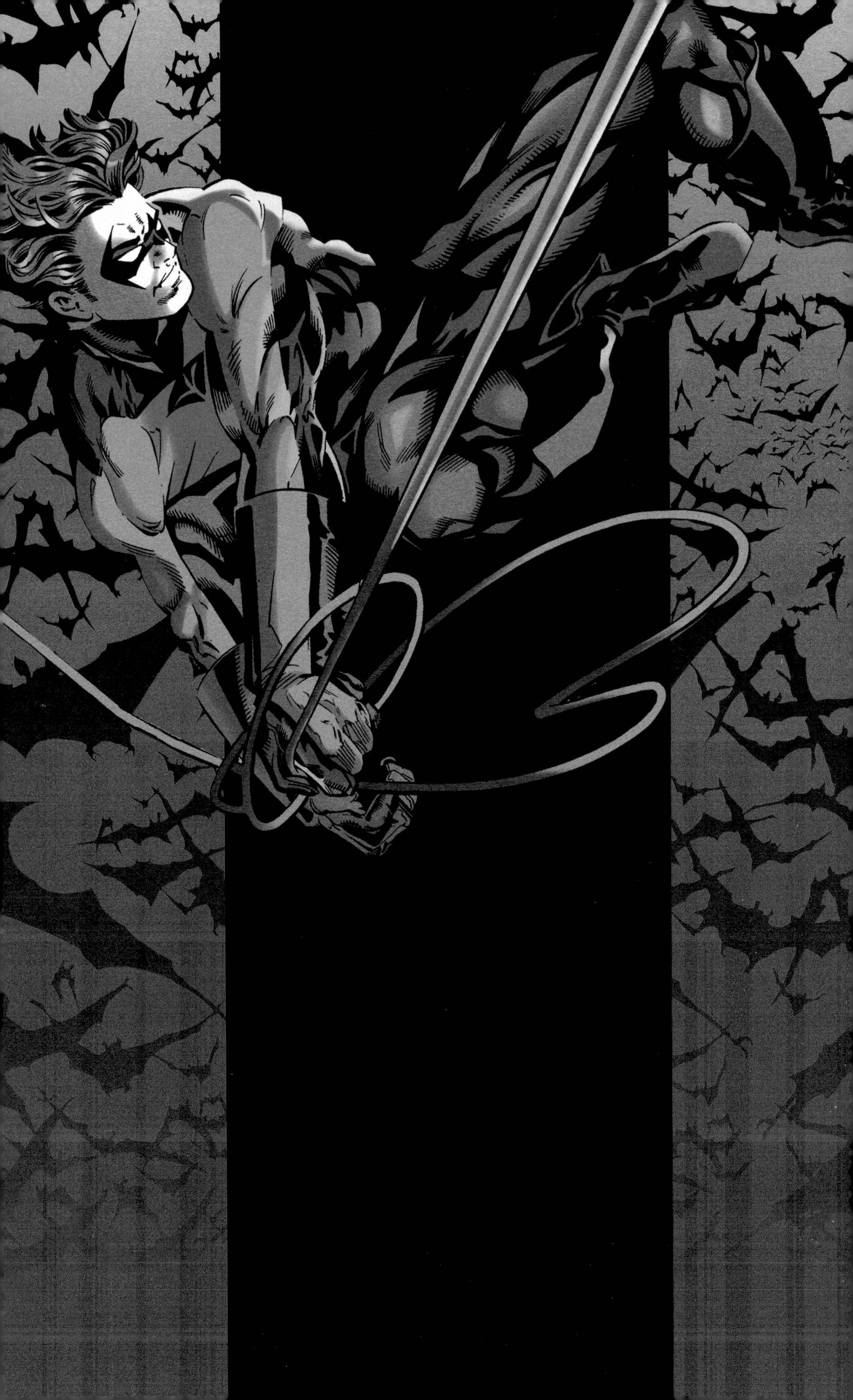

...and after the Earth shattered and the buildings crumbled, the nation abandoned Gotham City. Then only the valiant, the venal and the insane remained in the place they called NO MAN'S LAND

ESCAPE FROM BLACKGATE

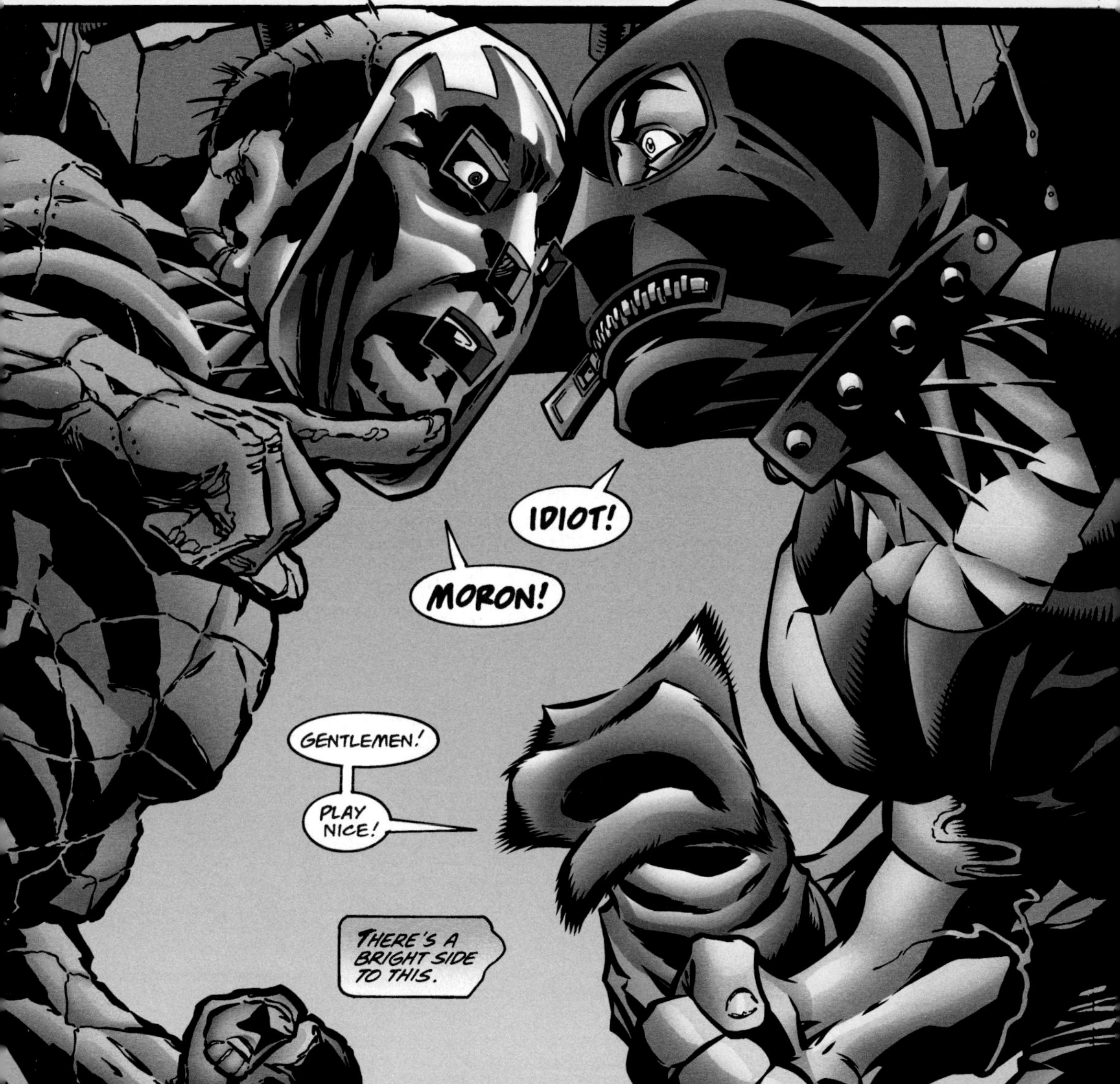

IDIOT!
MORON!
GENTLEMEN!
PLAY NICE!
THERE'S A BRIGHT SIDE TO THIS.

CHUCK DIXON . SCOTT McDANIEL . KARL STORY . ROBERTA TEWES . JAMISON
WRITER PENCILLER INKER COLORS COLOR SEPARATOR
JOHN COSTANZA . JOSEPH ILLIDGE . DARREN VINCENZO
LETTERER ASSOCIATE EDITOR WARDEN

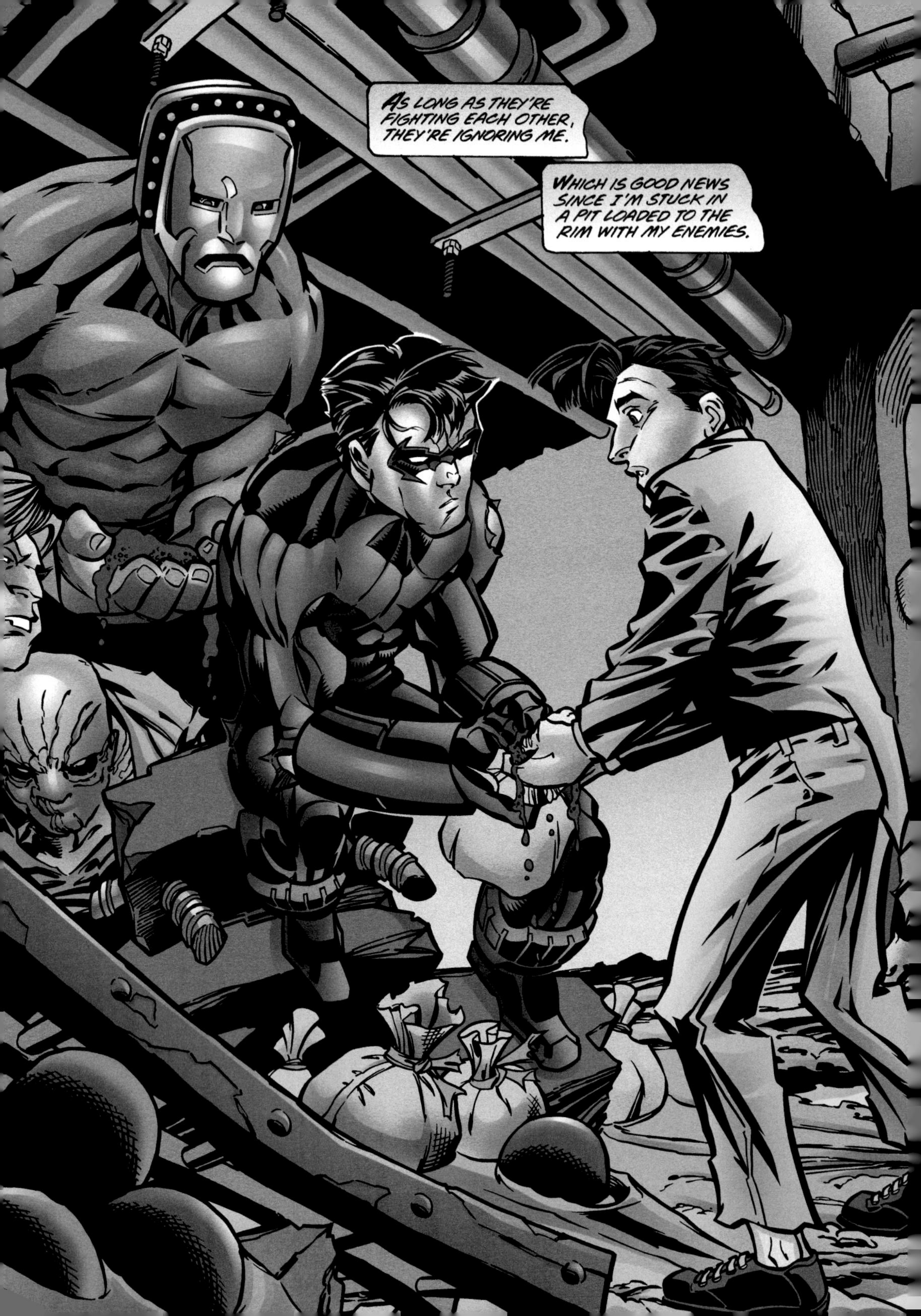
AS LONG AS THEY'RE FIGHTING EACH OTHER, THEY'RE IGNORING ME.
WHICH IS GOOD NEWS SINCE I'M STUCK IN A PIT LOADED TO THE RIM WITH MY ENEMIES.

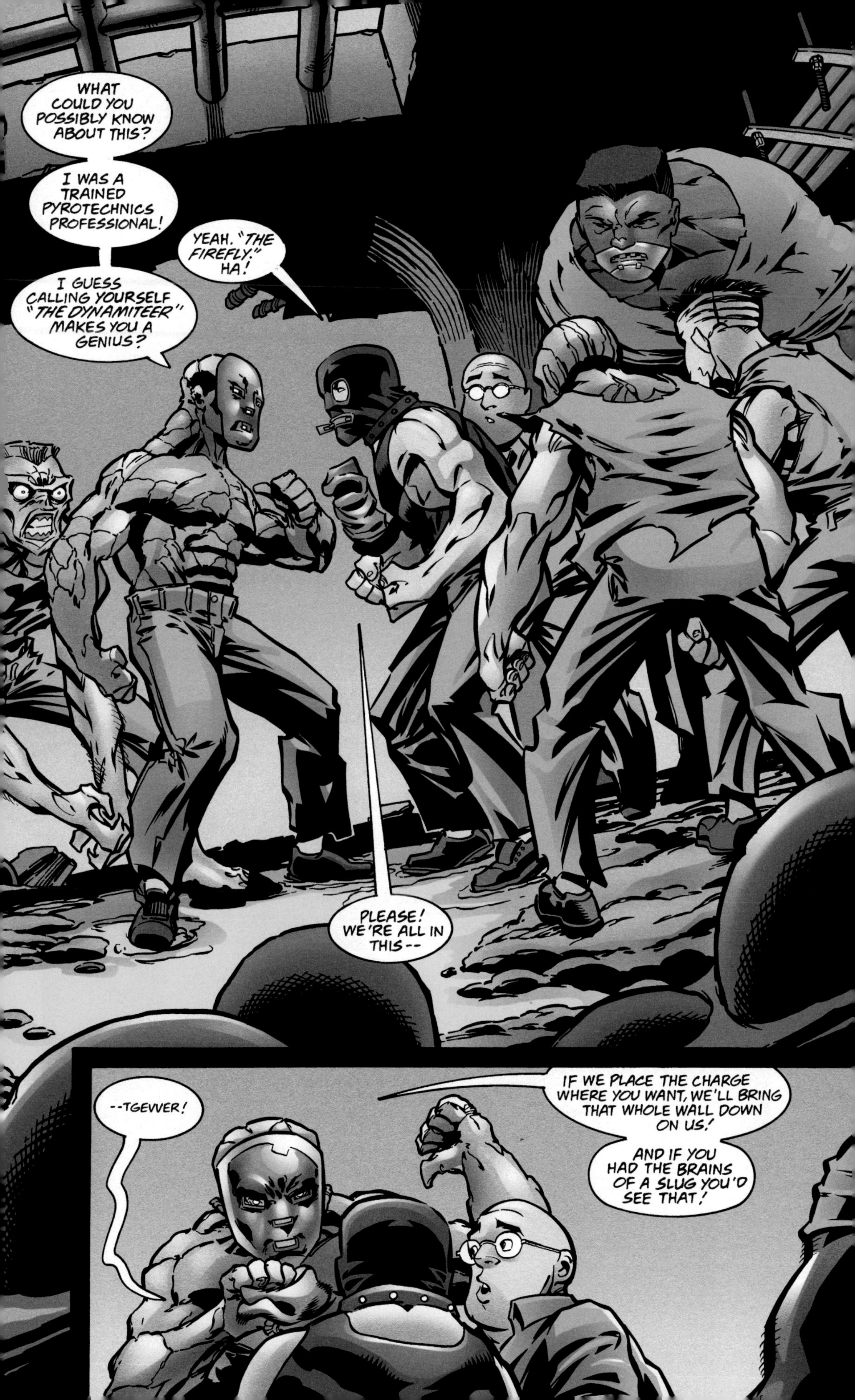
WHAT COULD YOU POSSIBLY KNOW ABOUT THIS?
I WAS A TRAINED PYROTECHNICS PROFESSIONAL!
I GUESS CALLING YOURSELF "THE DYNAMITEER" MAKES YOU A GENIUS?
YEAH. "THE FIREFLY." HA!
PLEASE! WE'RE ALL IN THIS--
--TGEVVER!
IF WE PLACE THE CHARGE WHERE YOU WANT, WE'LL BRING THAT WHOLE WALL DOWN ON US!
AND IF YOU HAD THE BRAINS OF A SLUG YOU'D SEE THAT!

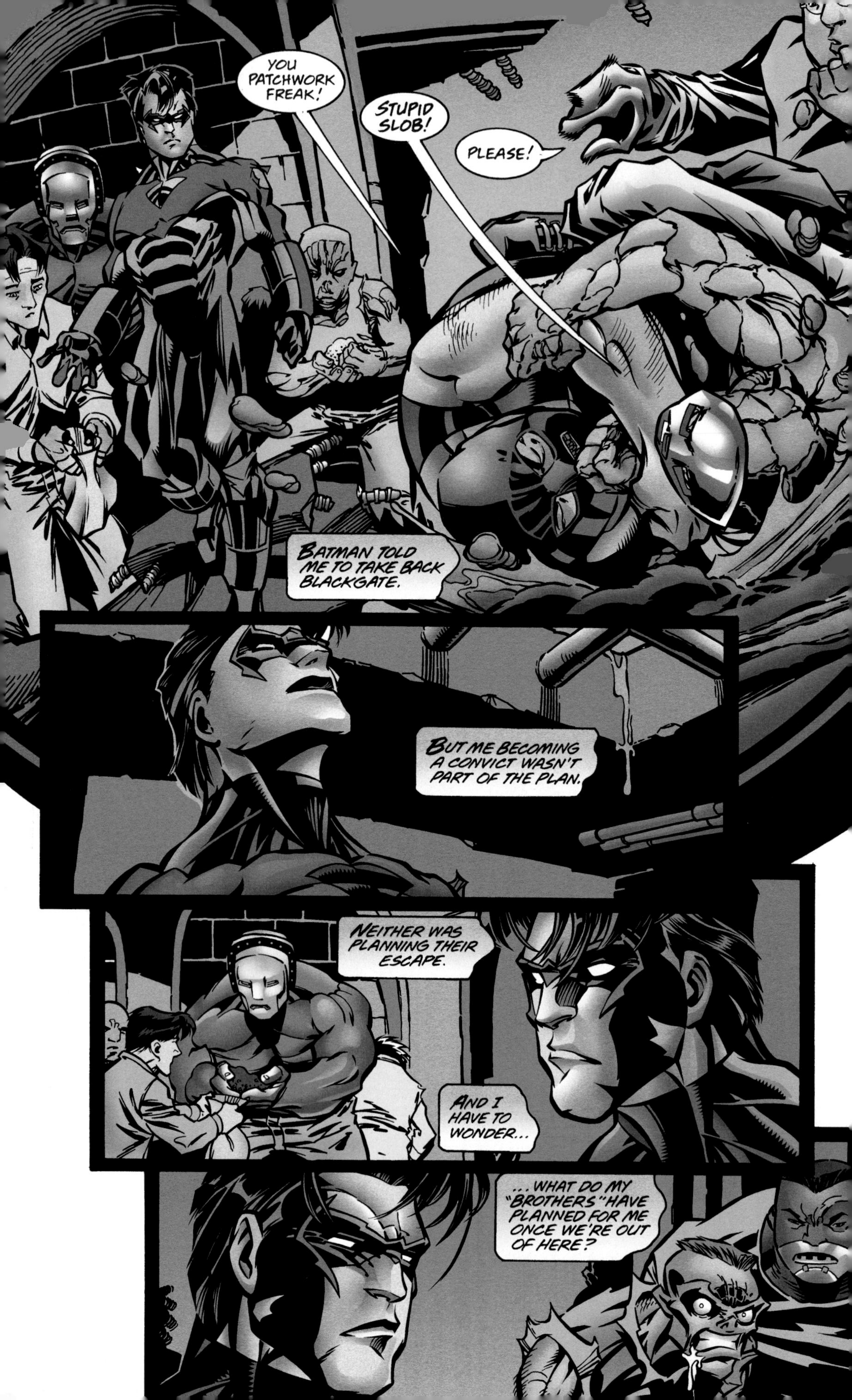

YOU PATCHWORK FREAK!
STUPID SLOB!
PLEASE!
BATMAN TOLD ME TO TAKE BACK BLACKGATE.
BUT ME BECOMING A CONVICT WASN'T PART OF THE PLAN.
NEITHER WAS PLANNING THEIR ESCAPE.
AND I HAVE TO WONDER...
...WHAT DO MY "BROTHERS" HAVE PLANNED FOR ME ONCE WE'RE OUT OF HERE?

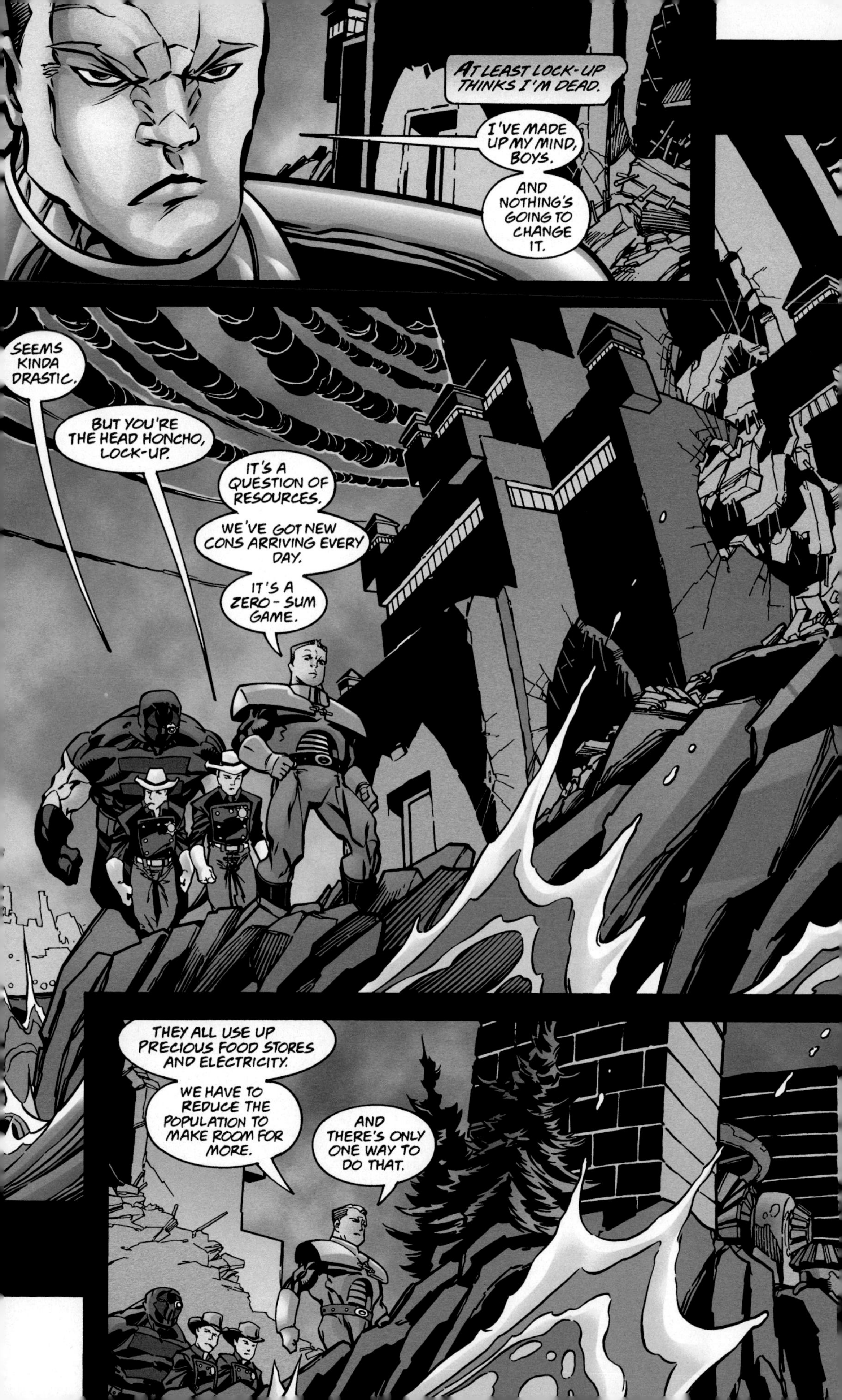
AT LEAST LOCK-UP THINKS I'M DEAD.
I'VE MADE UP MY MIND, BOYS.
AND NOTHING'S GOING TO CHANGE IT.
SEEMS KINDA DRASTIC.
BUT YOU'RE THE HEAD HONCHO, LOCK-UP.
IT'S A QUESTION OF RESOURCES.
WE'VE GOT NEW CONS ARRIVING EVERY DAY.
IT'S A ZERO-SUM GAME.
THEY ALL USE UP PRECIOUS FOOD STORES AND ELECTRICITY.
WE HAVE TO REDUCE THE POPULATION TO MAKE ROOM FOR MORE.
AND THERE'S ONLY ONE WAY TO DO THAT.

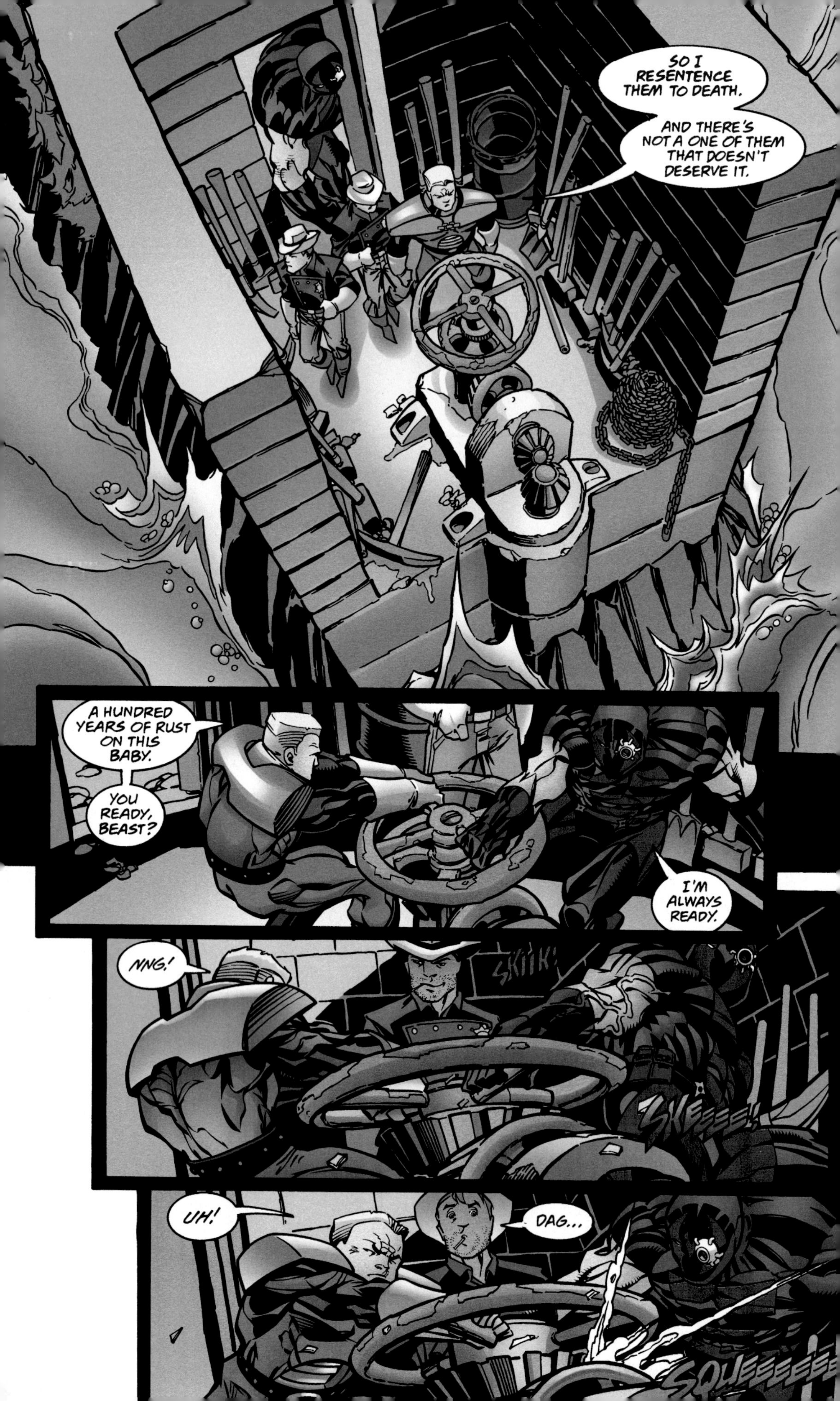
SO I RESENTENCE THEM TO DEATH.
AND THERE'S NOT A ONE OF THEM THAT DOESN'T DESERVE IT.
A HUNDRED YEARS OF RUST ON THIS BABY.
YOU READY, BEAST?
I'M ALWAYS READY.
NNG!
SKIIK!
SKEEEEE!
UH!
DAG...
SQUEEEEE

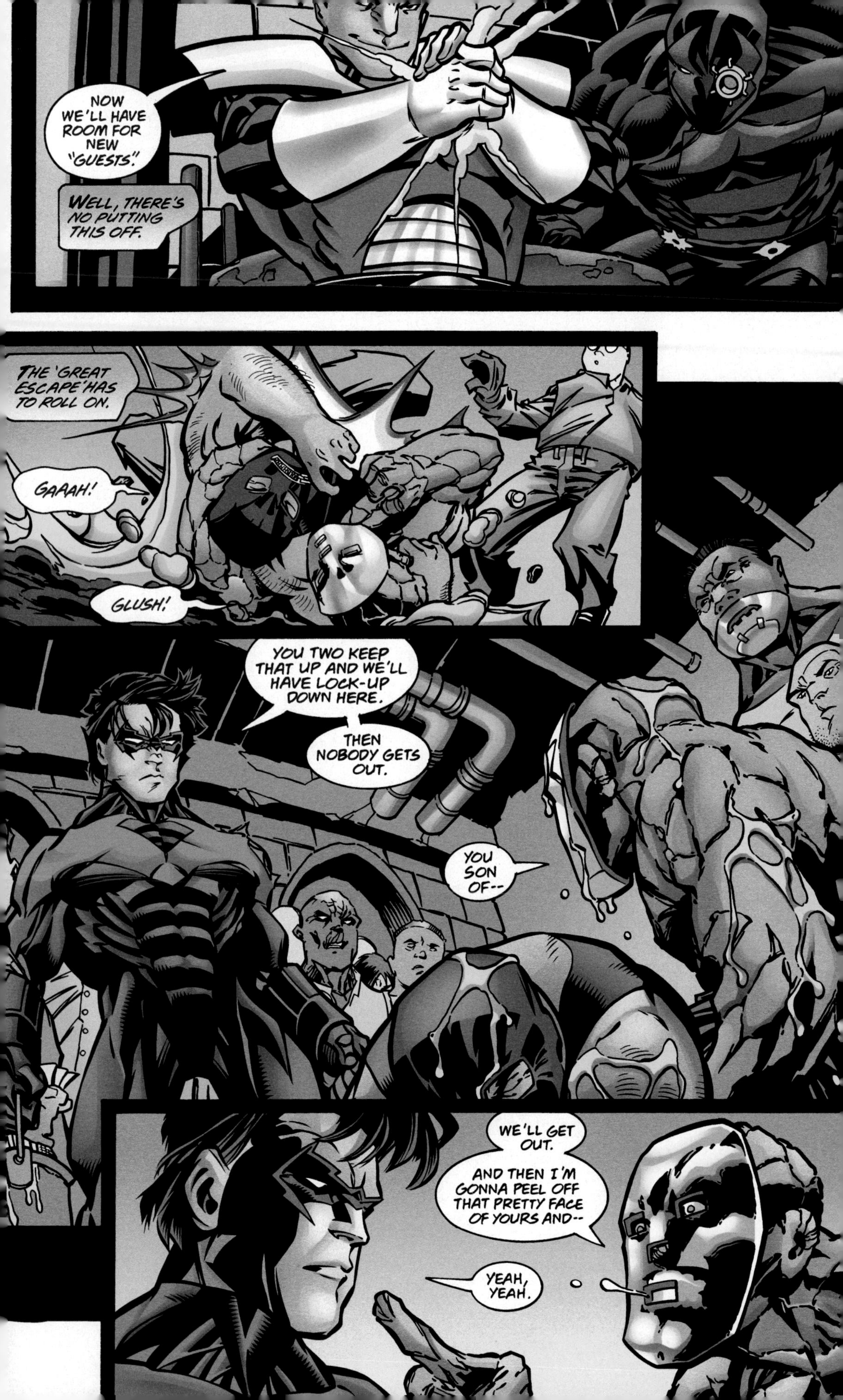
NOW WE'LL HAVE ROOM FOR NEW "GUESTS."
WELL, THERE'S NO PUTTING THIS OFF.
THE 'GREAT ESCAPE' HAS TO ROLL ON.
GAAAH!
GLUSH!
YOU TWO KEEP THAT UP AND WE'LL HAVE LOCK-UP DOWN HERE.
THEN NOBODY GETS OUT.
YOU SON OF--
WE'LL GET OUT.
AND THEN I'M GONNA PEEL OFF THAT PRETTY FACE OF YOURS AND--
YEAH, YEAH.

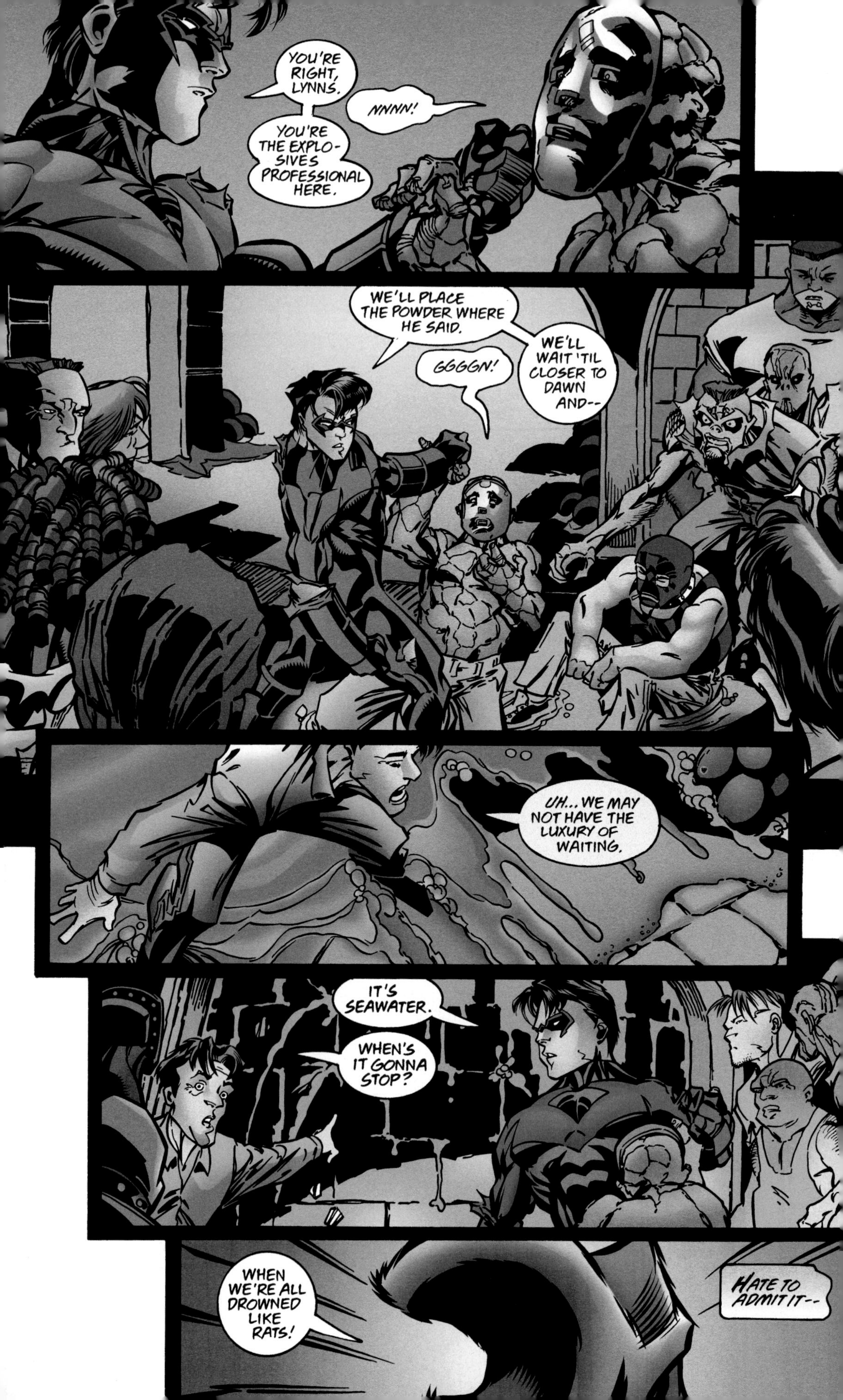
YOU'RE RIGHT, LYNNS.
NNNN!
YOU'RE THE EXPLOSIVES PROFESSIONAL HERE.
WE'LL PLACE THE POWDER WHERE HE SAID.
GGGGN!
WE'LL WAIT 'TIL CLOSER TO DAWN AND--
UH... WE MAY NOT HAVE THE LUXURY OF WAITING.
IT'S SEAWATER.
WHEN'S IT GONNA STOP?
WHEN WE'RE ALL DROWNED LIKE RATS!
HATE TO ADMIT IT--

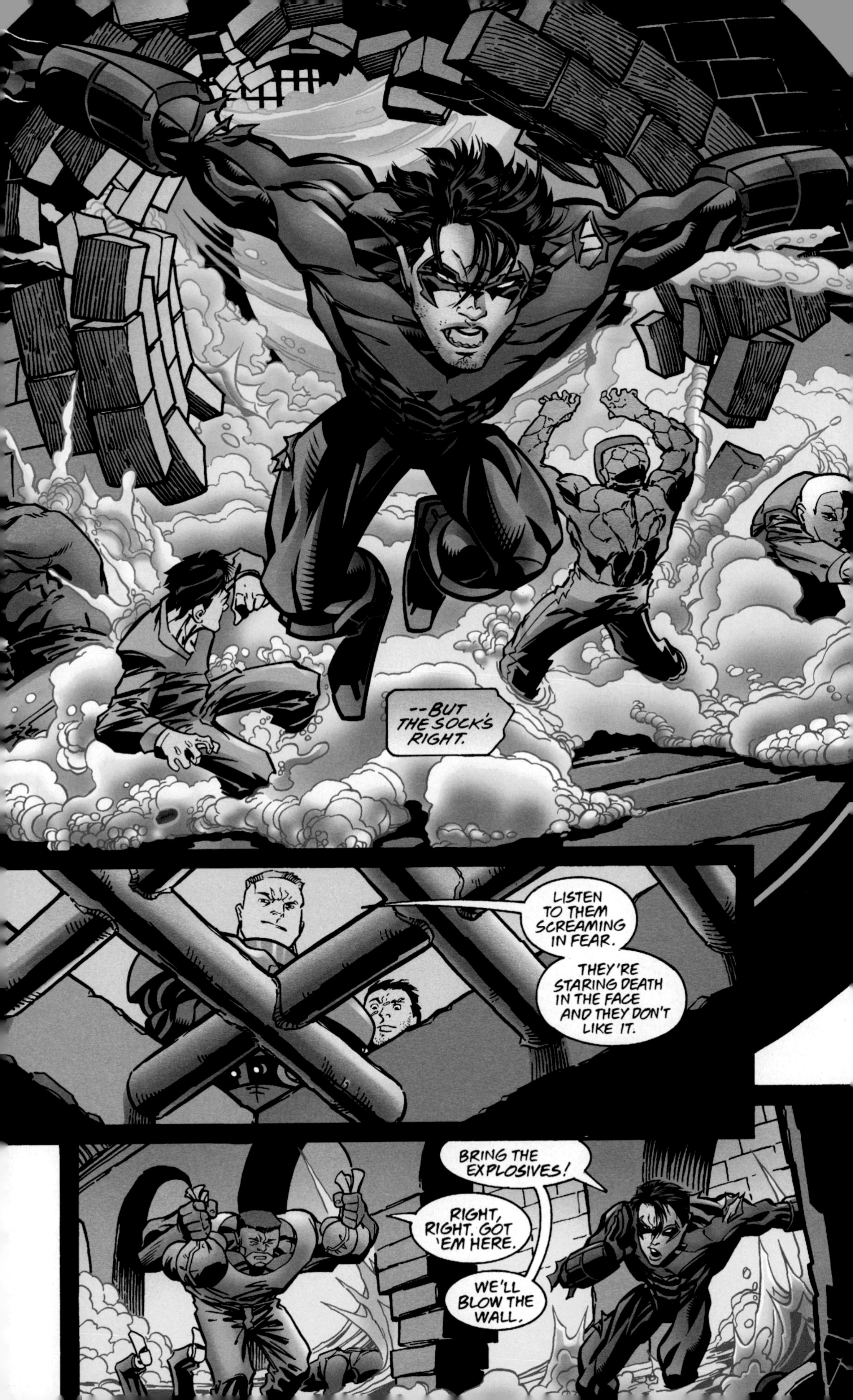
--BUT THE SOCK'S RIGHT.
LISTEN TO THEM SCREAMING IN FEAR.
THEY'RE STARING DEATH IN THE FACE AND THEY DON'T LIKE IT.
BRING THE EXPLOSIVES!
RIGHT, RIGHT. GOT 'EM HERE.
WE'LL BLOW THE WALL.

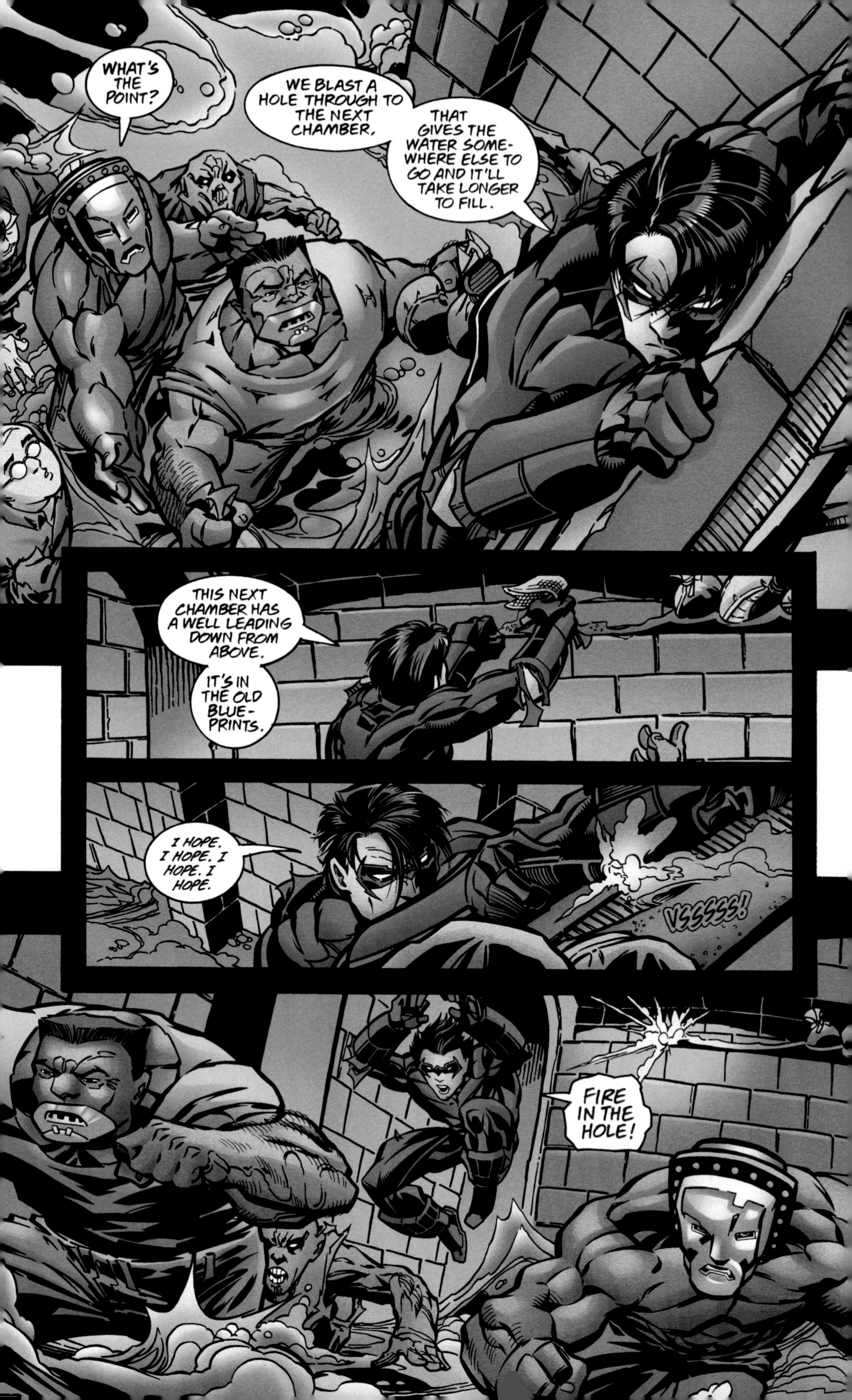
WHAT'S THE POINT?
WE BLAST A HOLE THROUGH TO THE NEXT CHAMBER.
THAT GIVES THE WATER SOME-WHERE ELSE TO GO AND IT'LL TAKE LONGER TO FILL.
THIS NEXT CHAMBER HAS A WELL LEADING DOWN FROM ABOVE.
IT'S IN THE OLD BLUE-PRINTS.
I HOPE. I HOPE. I HOPE. I HOPE.
VSSSSS!
FIRE IN THE HOLE!

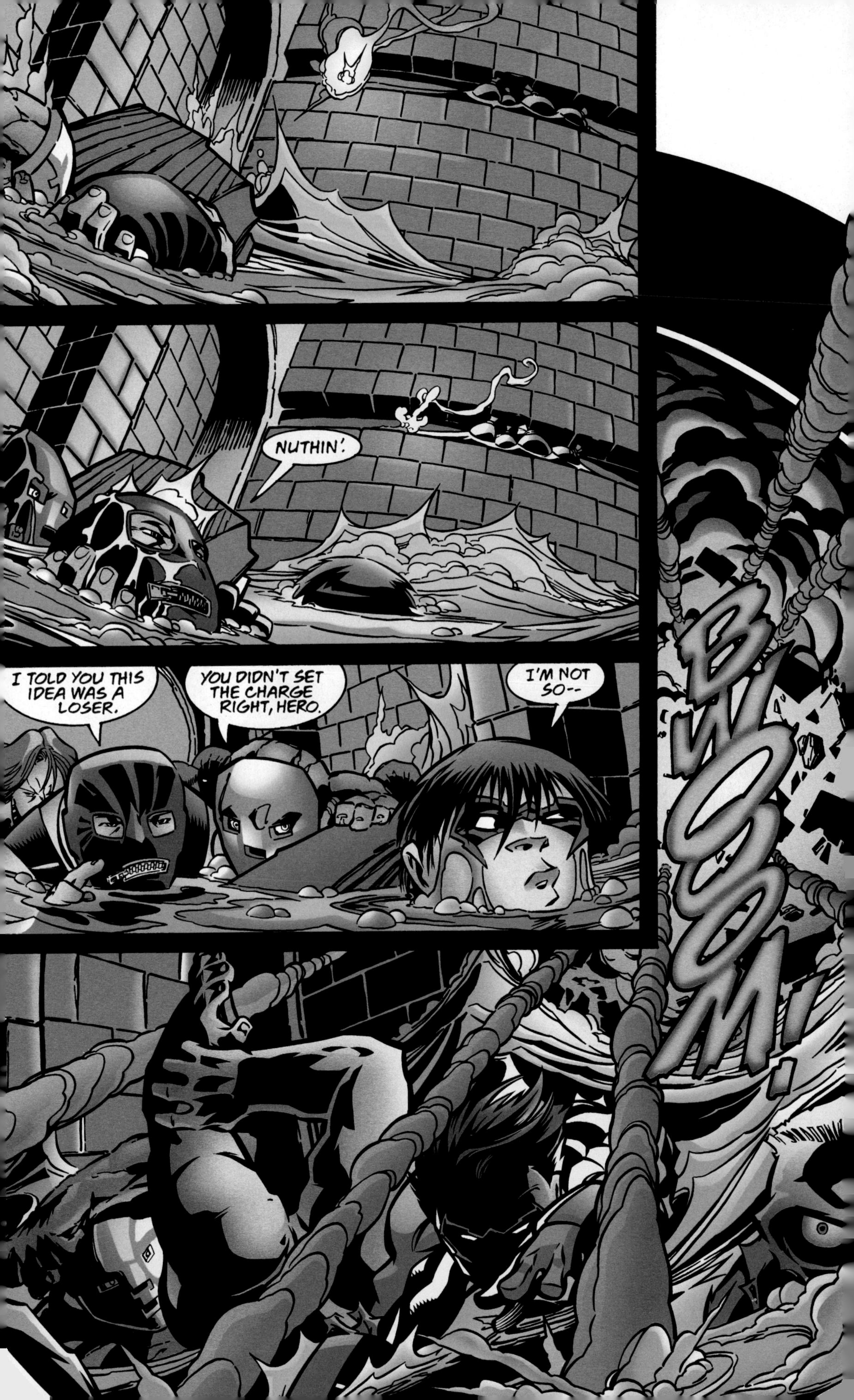
NUTHIN'.
I TOLD YOU THIS IDEA WAS A LOSER.
YOU DIDN'T SET THE CHARGE RIGHT, HERO.
I'M NOT SO--
BVOOOM!!

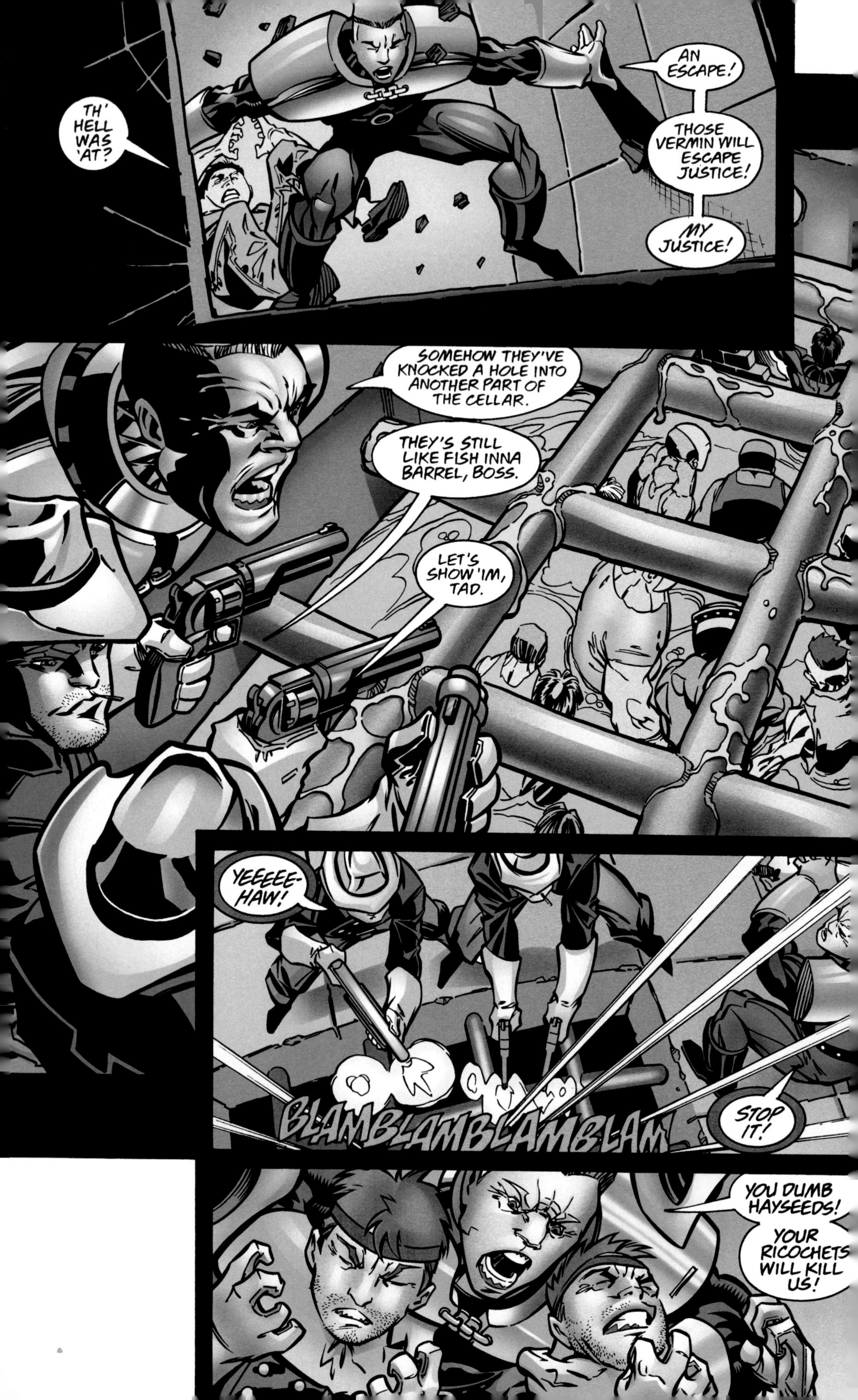
TH' HELL WAS 'AT?
AN ESCAPE!
THOSE VERMIN WILL ESCAPE JUSTICE!
MY JUSTICE!
SOMEHOW THEY'VE KNOCKED A HOLE INTO ANOTHER PART OF THE CELLAR.
THEY'S STILL LIKE FISH INNA BARREL, BOSS.
LET'S SHOW 'IM, TAD.
YEEEEE-HAW!
BLAMBLAMBLAMBLAM
STOP IT!
YOU DUMB HAYSEEDS!
YOUR RICOCHETS WILL KILL US!

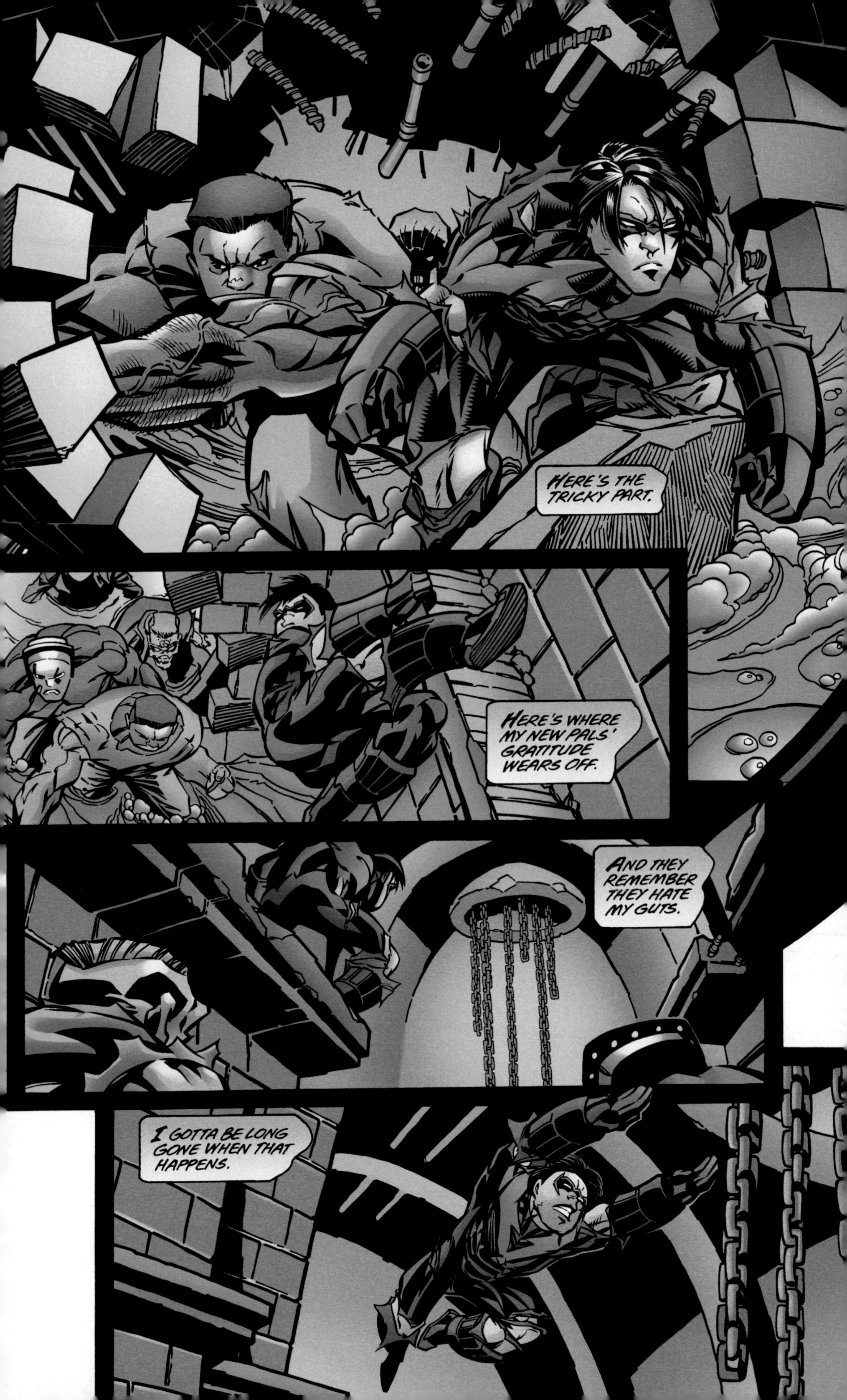
HERE'S THE TRICKY PART.
HERE'S WHERE MY NEW PALS' GRATITUDE WEARS OFF.
AND THEY REMEMBER THEY HATE MY GUTS.
I GOTTA BE LONG GONE WHEN THAT HAPPENS.

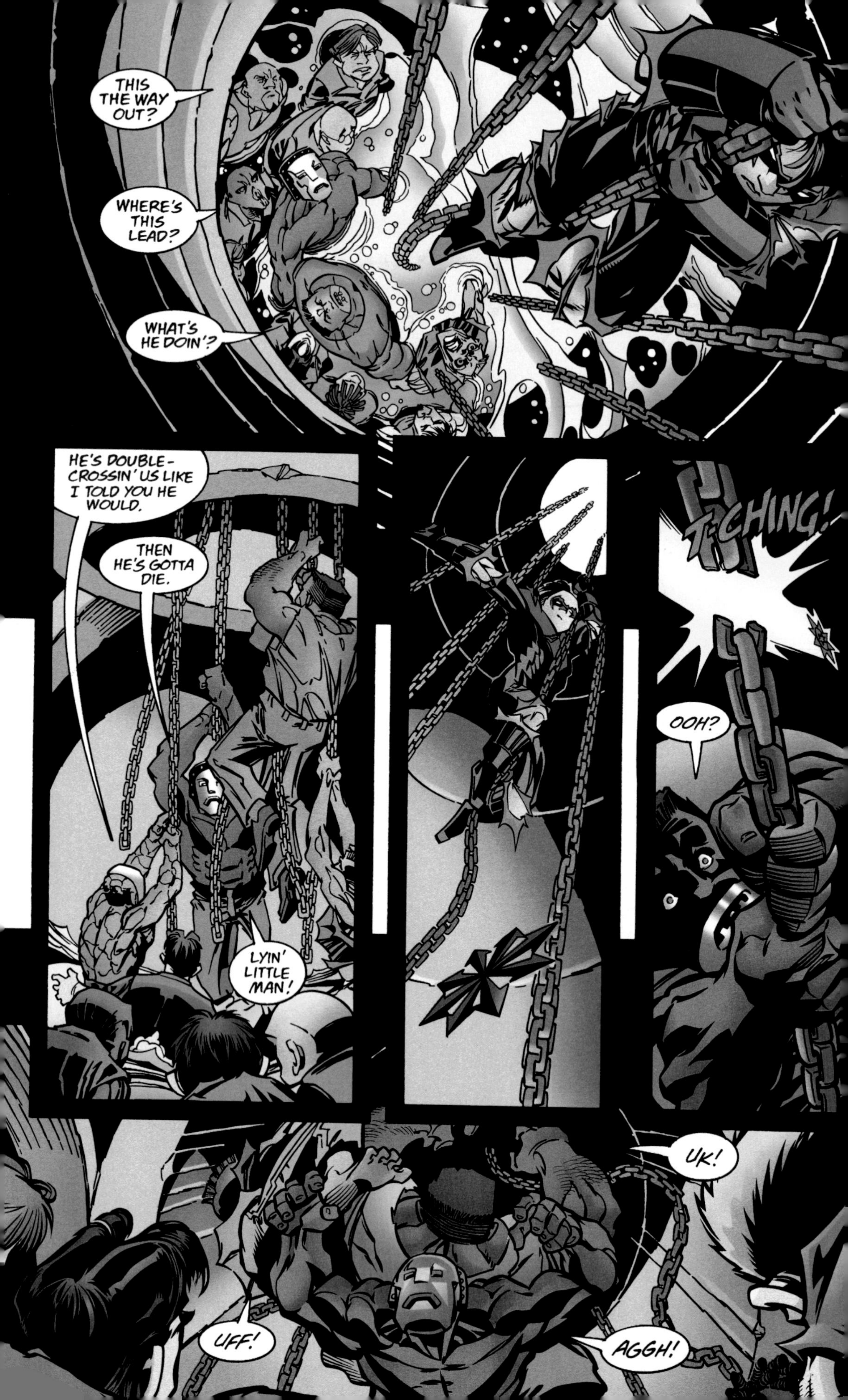
THIS THE WAY OUT?
WHERE'S THIS LEAD?
WHAT'S HE DOIN'?
HE'S DOUBLE-CROSSIN' US LIKE I TOLD YOU HE WOULD.
THEN HE'S GOTTA DIE.
LYIN' LITTLE MAN!
T-CHING!
OOH?
UK!
UFF!
AGGH!

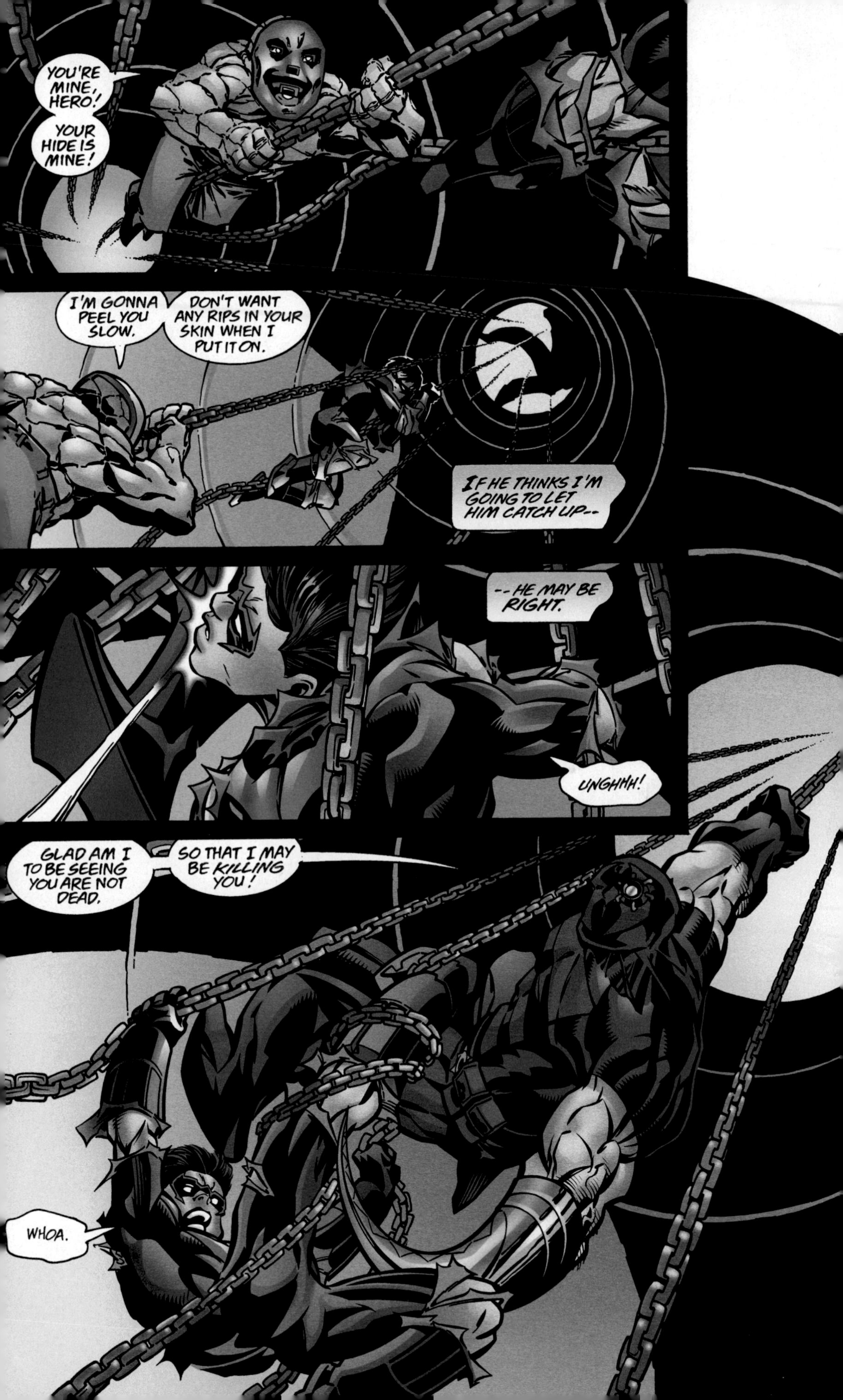
YOU'RE MINE, HERO!
YOUR HIDE IS MINE!
I'M GONNA PEEL YOU SLOW.
DON'T WANT ANY RIPS IN YOUR SKIN WHEN I PUT IT ON.
IF HE THINKS I'M GOING TO LET HIM CATCH UP--
--HE MAY BE RIGHT.
UNGHHH!
GLAD AM I TO BE SEEING YOU ARE NOT DEAD.
SO THAT I MAY BE KILLING YOU!
WHOA.

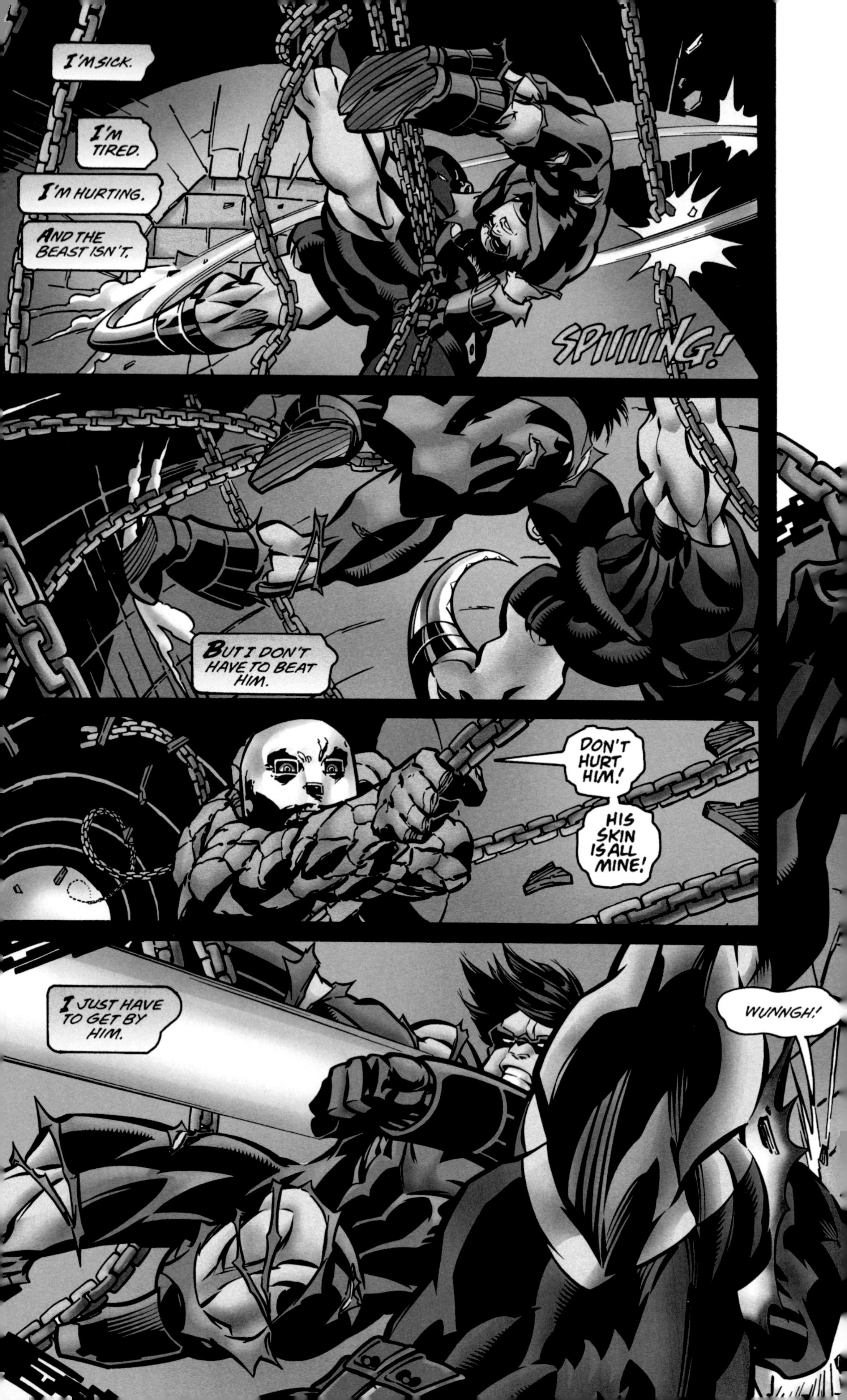
I'M SICK.
I'M TIRED.
I'M HURTING.
AND THE BEAST ISN'T.
SPIIIING!
BUT I DON'T HAVE TO BEAT HIM.
DON'T HURT HIM!
HIS SKIN IS ALL MINE!
I JUST HAVE TO GET BY HIM.
WUNNGH!

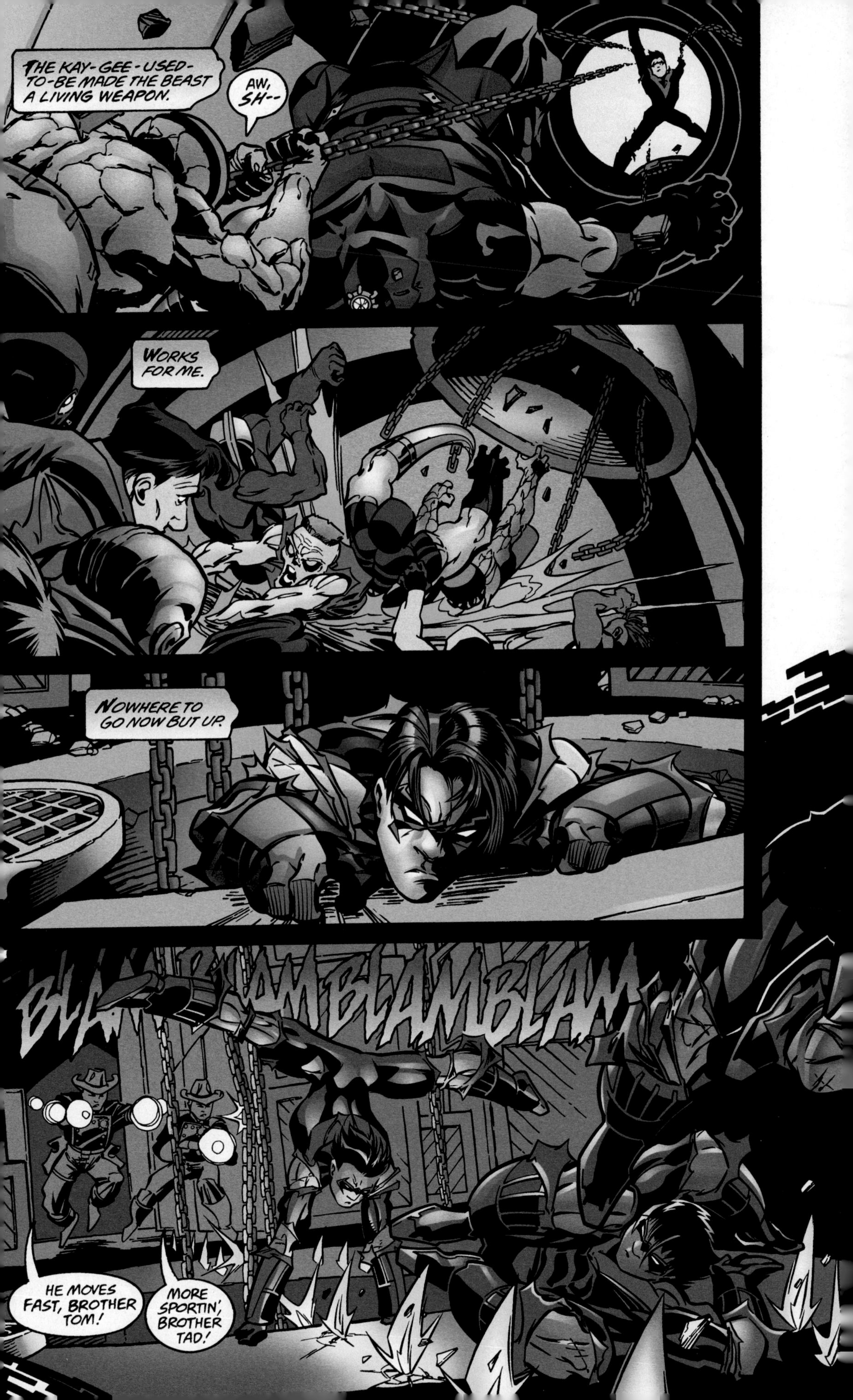
THE KAY-GEE-USED-TO-BE MADE THE BEAST A LIVING WEAPON.
AW, SH--
WORKS FOR ME.
NOWHERE TO GO NOW BUT UP.
BLAMBLAMBLAMBLAM
HE MOVES FAST, BROTHER TOM!
MORE SPORTIN', BROTHER TAD!

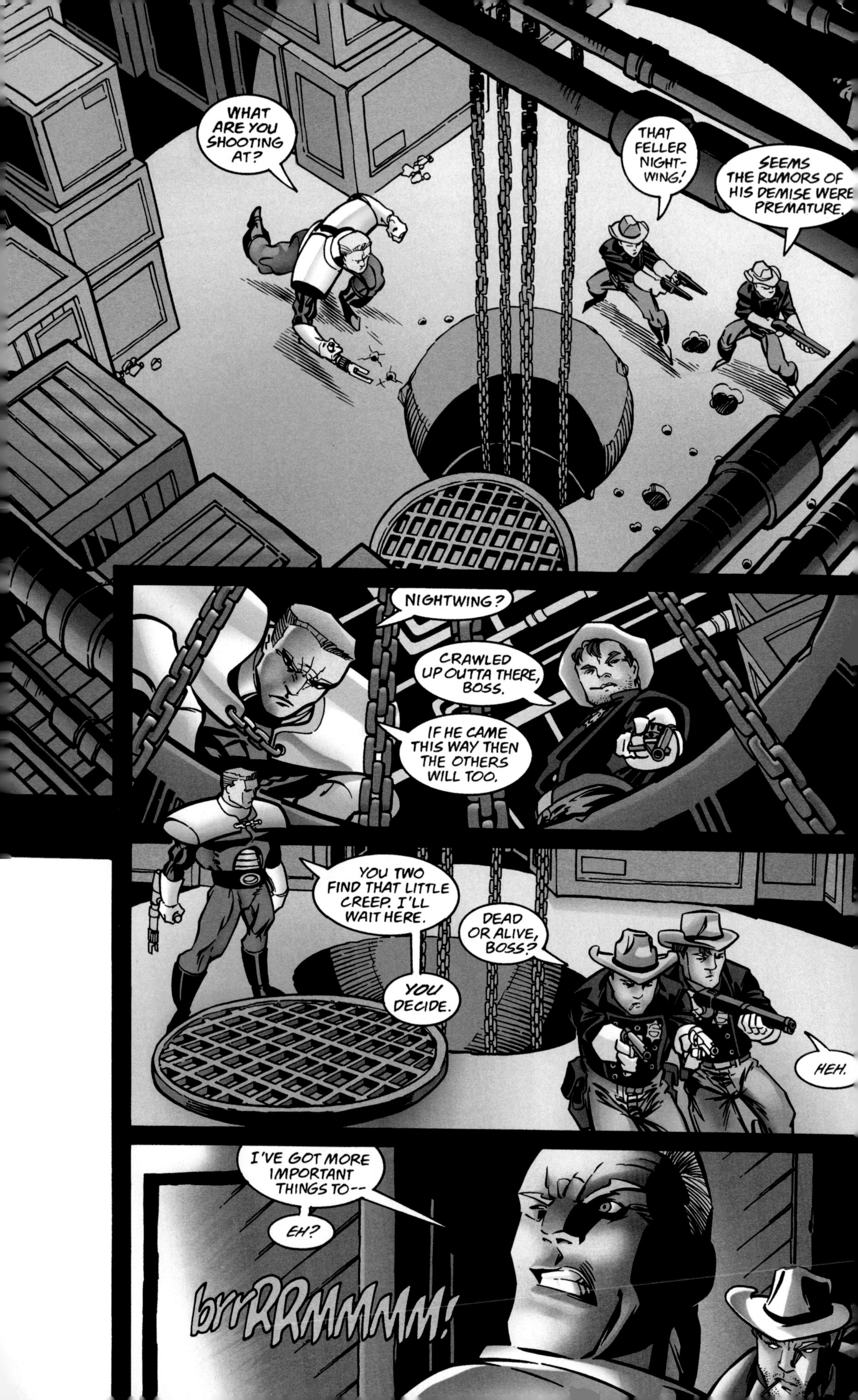
WHAT ARE YOU SHOOTING AT?
THAT FELLER NIGHT-WING!
SEEMS THE RUMORS OF HIS DEMISE WERE PREMATURE.
NIGHTWING?
CRAWLED UP OUTTA THERE, BOSS.
IF HE CAME THIS WAY THEN THE OTHERS WILL TOO.
YOU TWO FIND THAT LITTLE CREEP. I'LL WAIT HERE.
DEAD OR ALIVE, BOSS?
YOU DECIDE.
HEH.
I'VE GOT MORE IMPORTANT THINGS TO--
EH?
brrRRMMMMM!

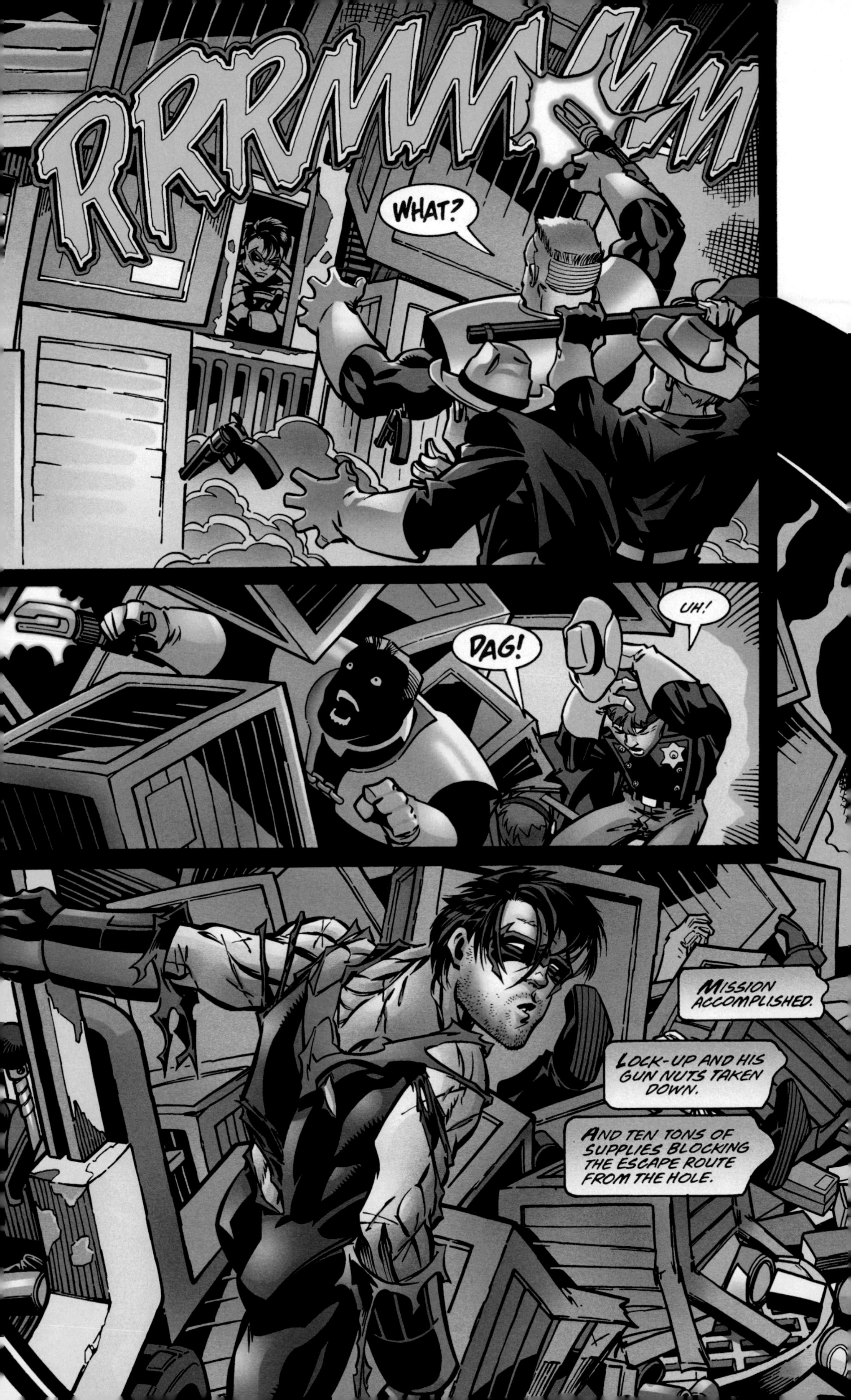
RRRMMMMMM
WHAT?
DAG!
UH!
MISSION ACCOMPLISHED.
LOCK-UP AND HIS GUN NUTS TAKEN DOWN.
AND TEN TONS OF SUPPLIES BLOCKING THE ESCAPE ROUTE FROM THE HOLE.

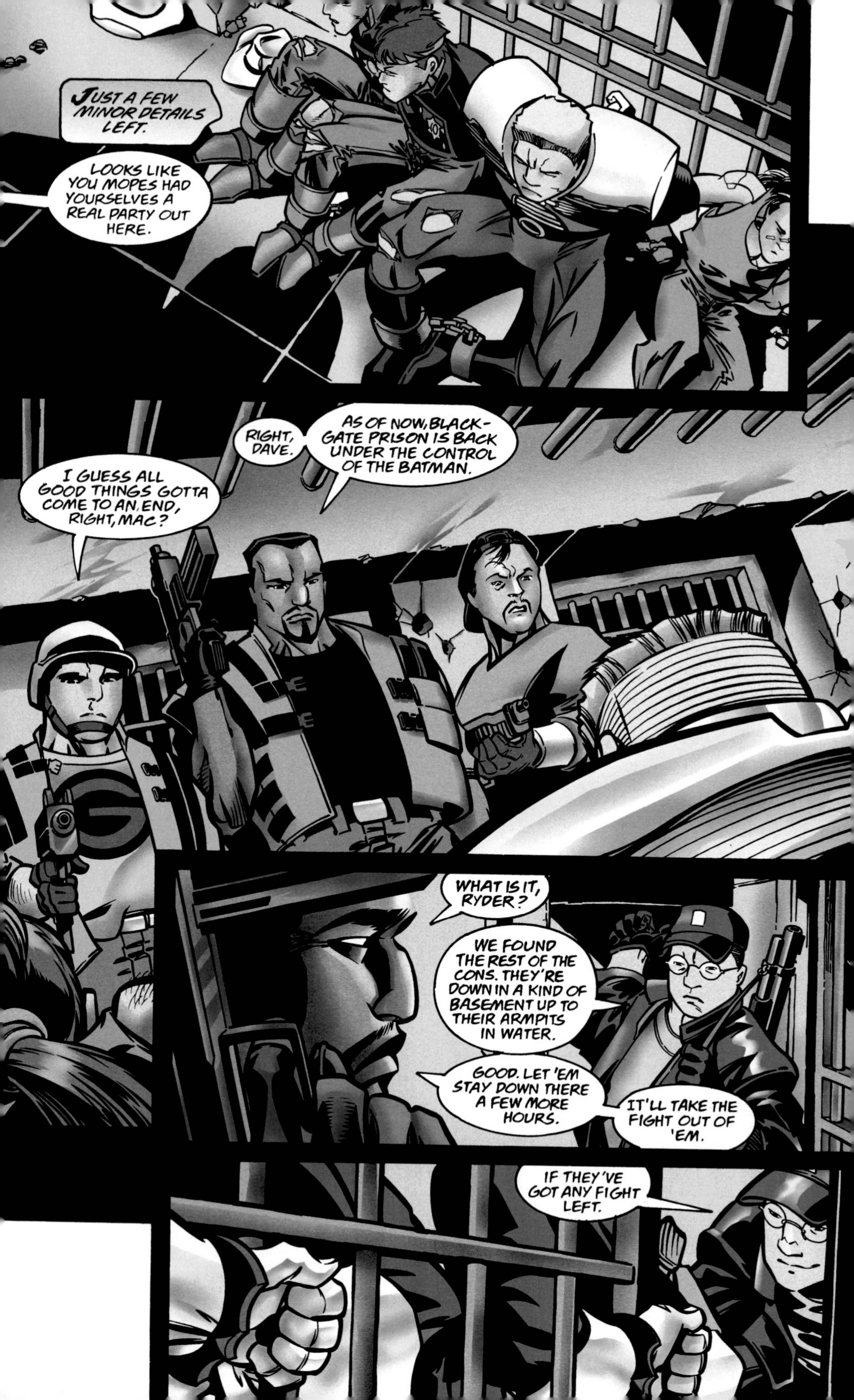
JUST A FEW MINOR DETAILS LEFT.
LOOKS LIKE YOU MOPES HAD YOURSELVES A REAL PARTY OUT HERE.
I GUESS ALL GOOD THINGS GOTTA COME TO AN END, RIGHT, MAC?
RIGHT, DAVE.
AS OF NOW, BLACK-GATE PRISON IS BACK UNDER THE CONTROL OF THE BATMAN.
WHAT IS IT, RYDER?
WE FOUND THE REST OF THE CONS. THEY'RE DOWN IN A KIND OF BASEMENT UP TO THEIR ARMPITS IN WATER.
GOOD. LET 'EM STAY DOWN THERE A FEW MORE HOURS.
IT'LL TAKE THE FIGHT OUT OF 'EM.
IF THEY'VE GOT ANY FIGHT LEFT.

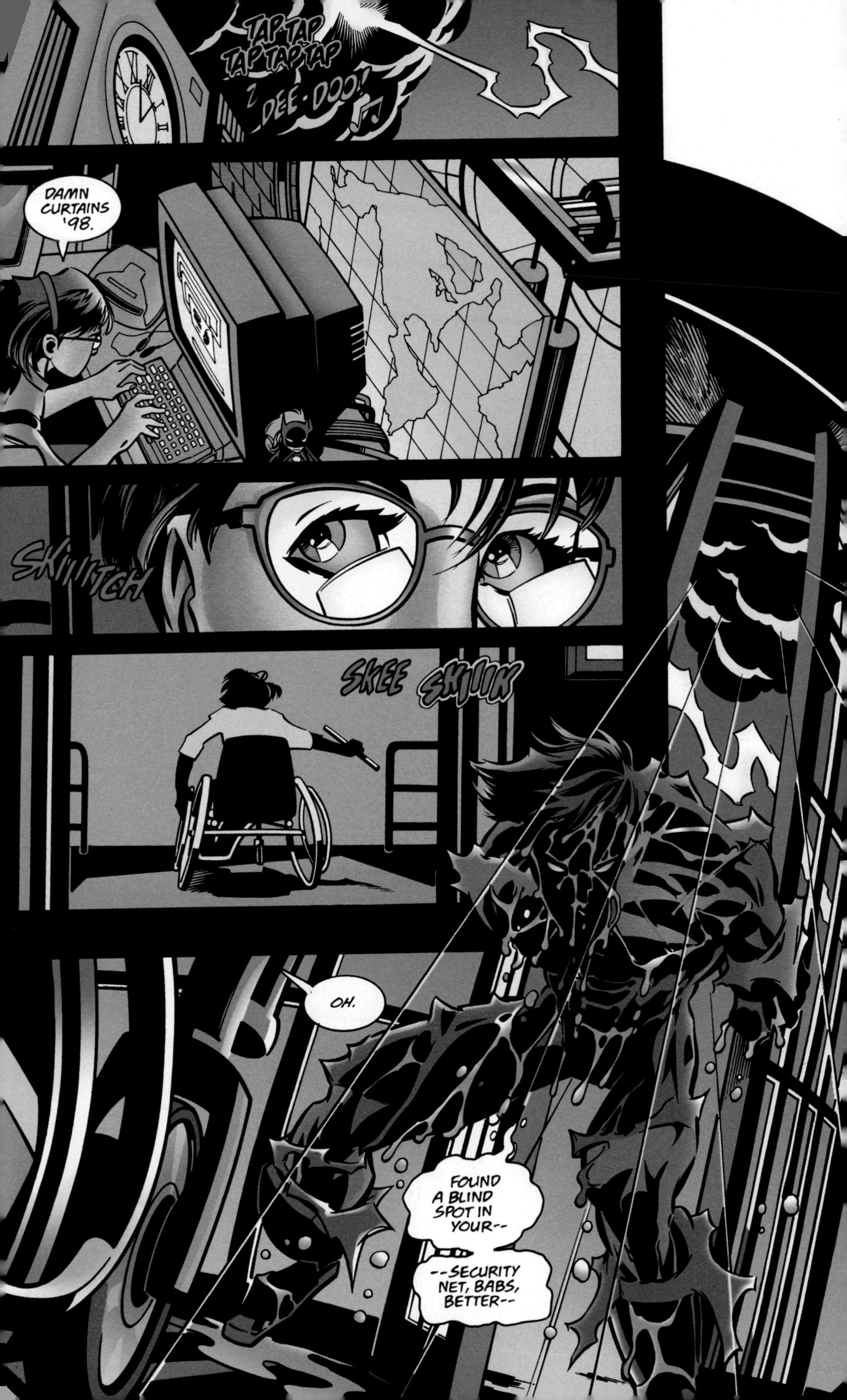

TAP TAP TAP TAP TAP
DEE-DOO!
DAMN CURTAINS '98.
SKIIIITCH
SKEE SKIIIIK
OH.
FOUND A BLIND SPOT IN YOUR--
--SECURITY NET, BABS, BETTER--

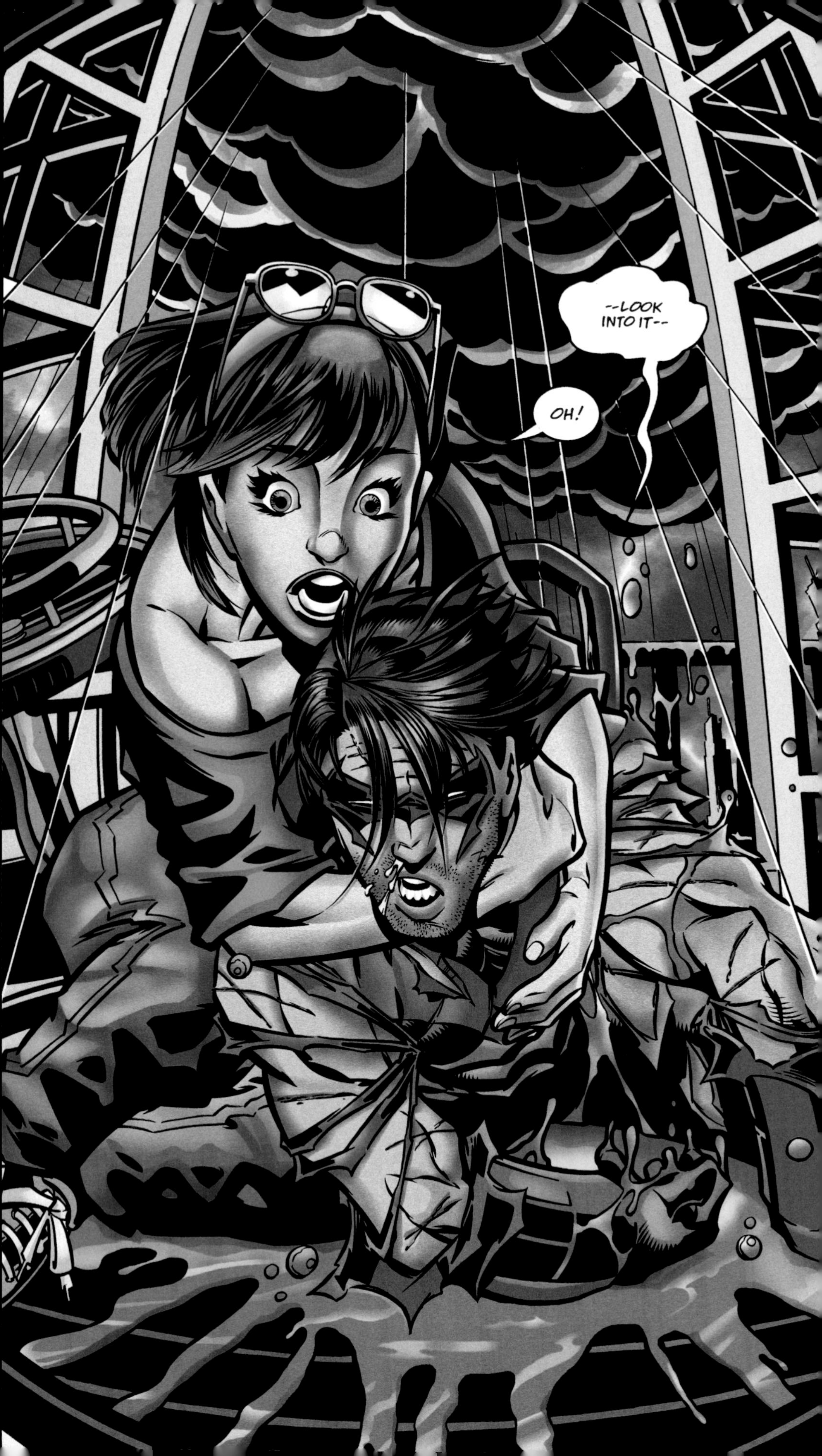
--LOOK INTO IT--
OH!

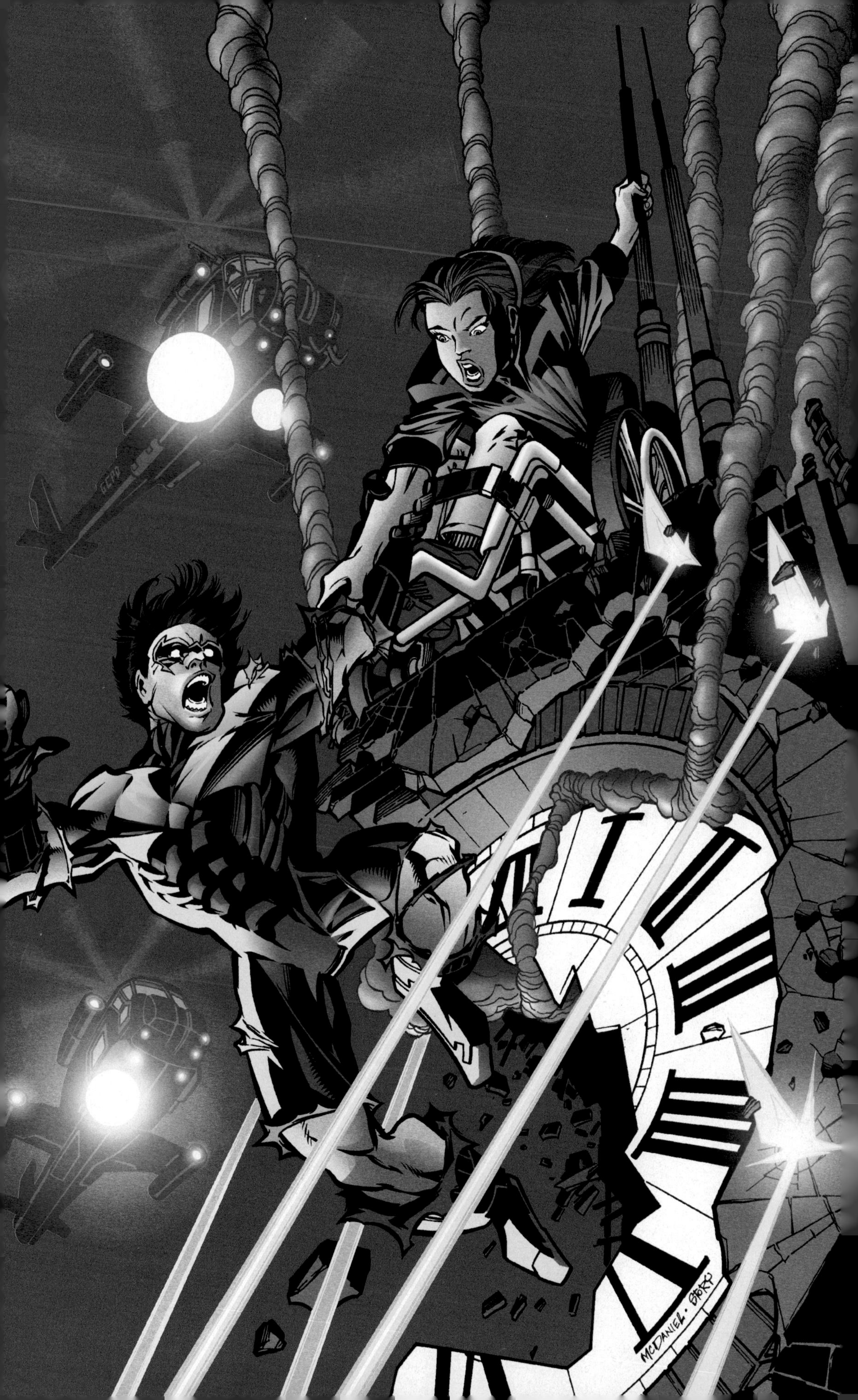
McDANIEL · STORY

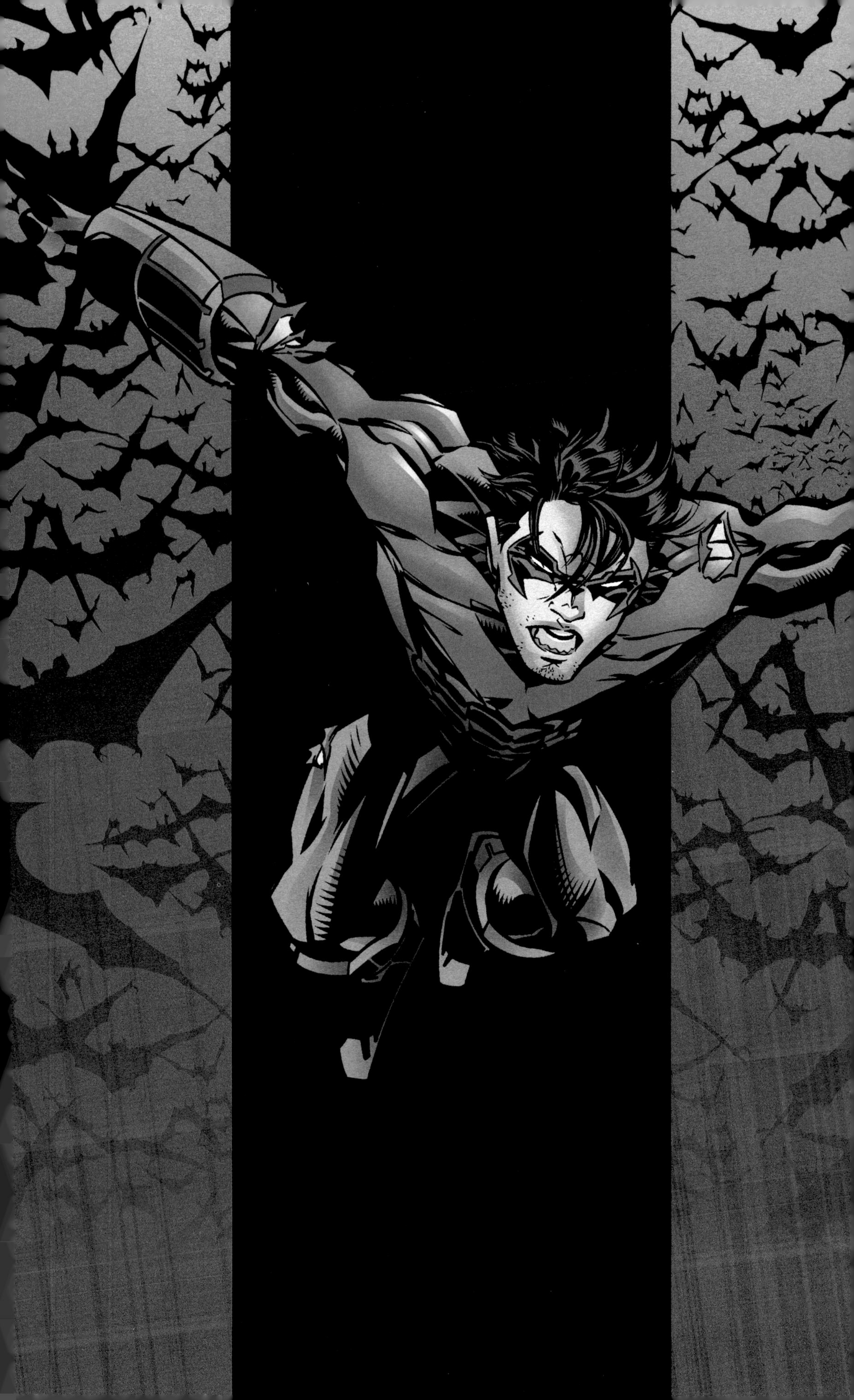

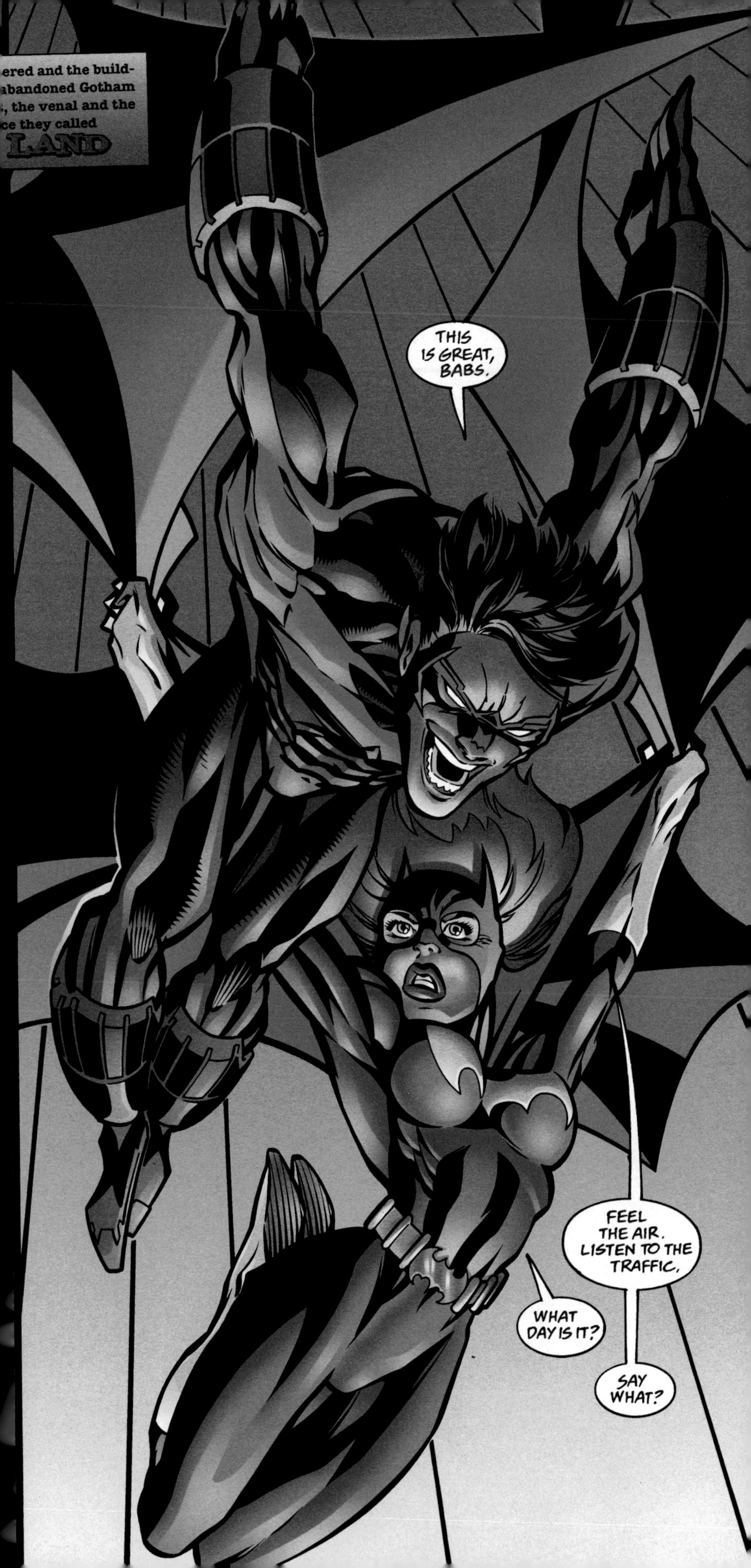
ered and the build-
abandoned Gotham
, the venal and the
ce they called
LAND
THIS IS GREAT, BABS.
FEEL THE AIR. LISTEN TO THE TRAFFIC,
WHAT DAY IS IT?
SAY WHAT?

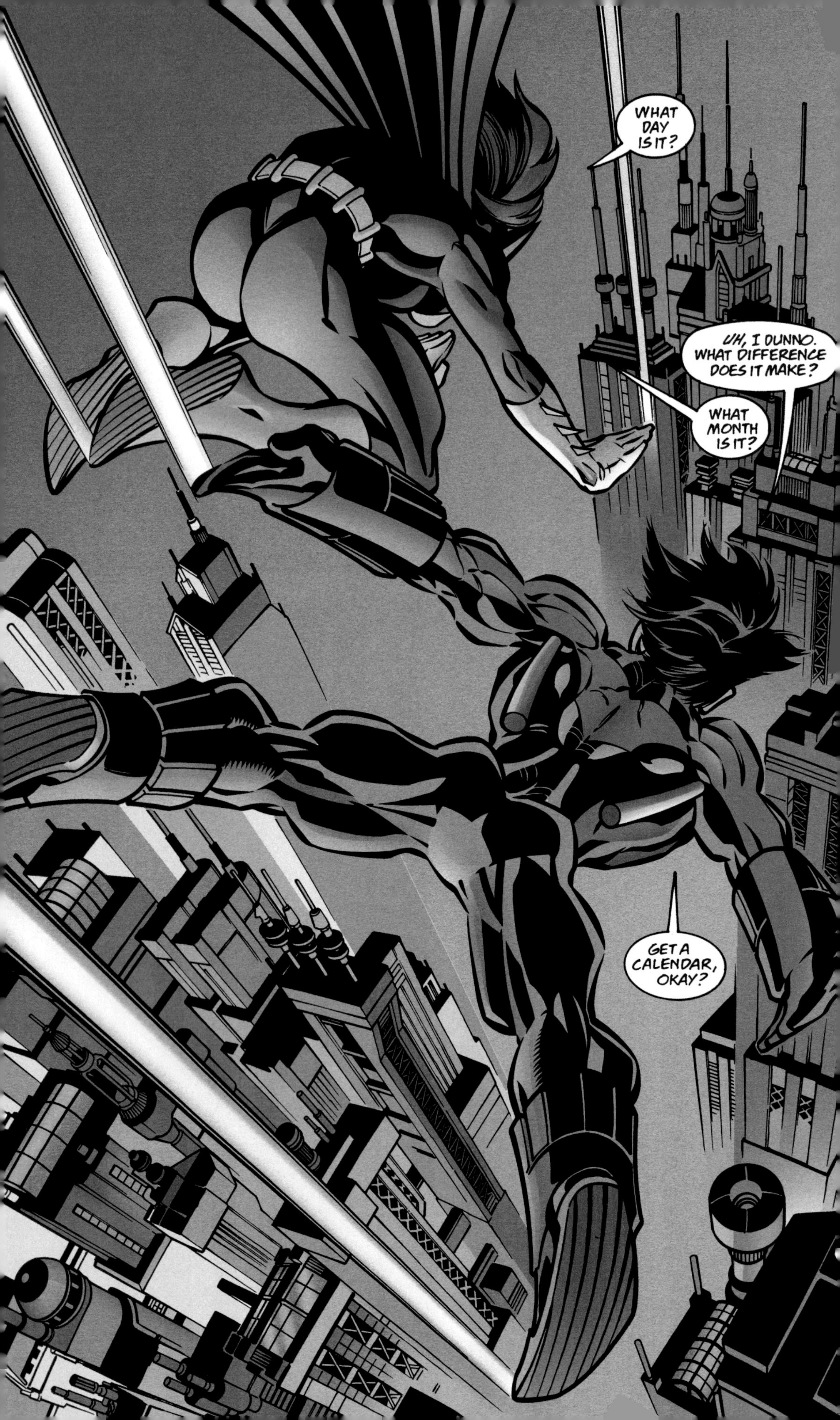
WHAT DAY IS IT?
UH, I DUNNO. WHAT DIFFERENCE DOES IT MAKE?
WHAT MONTH IS IT?
GET A CALENDAR, OKAY?

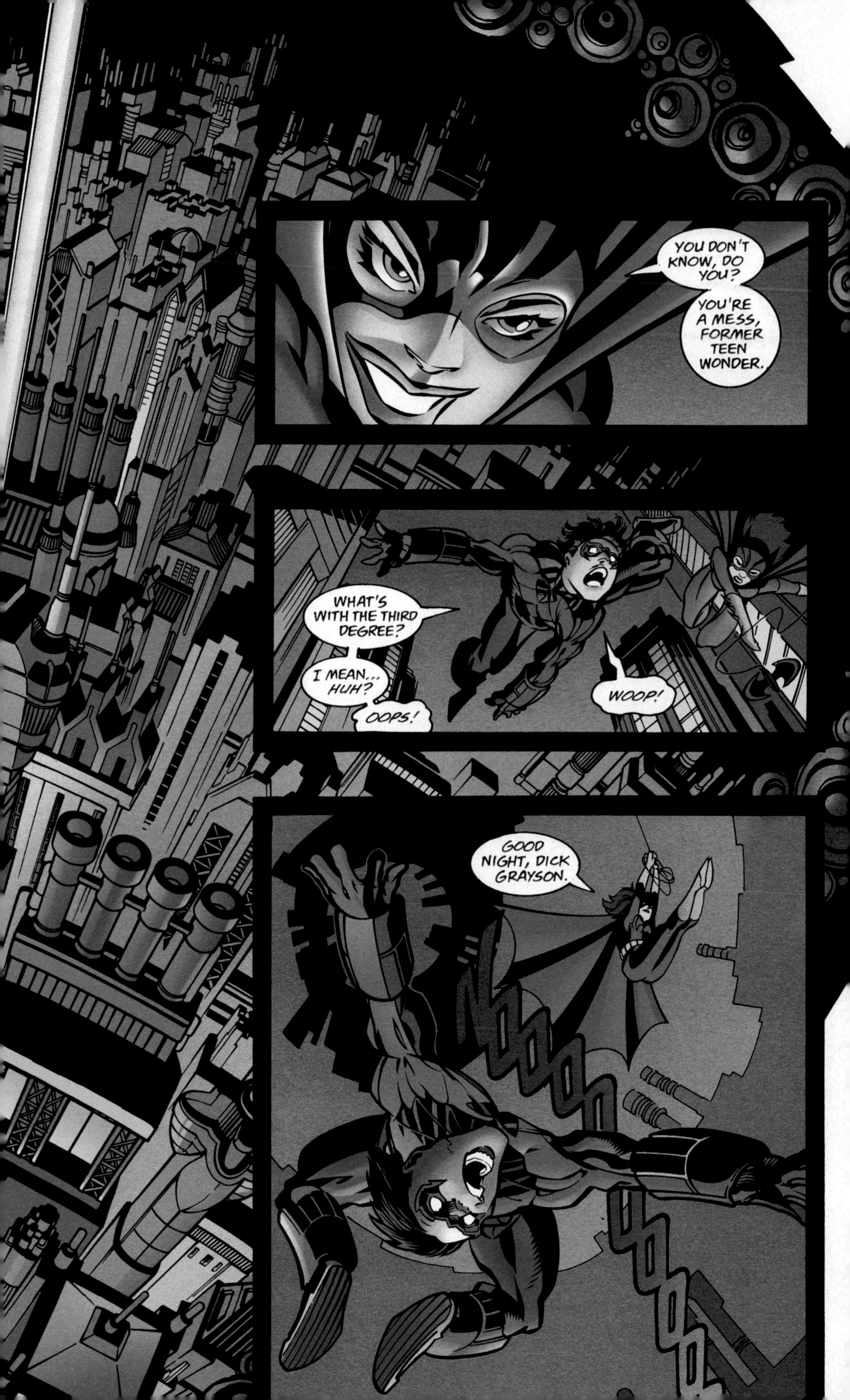
YOU DON'T KNOW, DO YOU?
YOU'RE A MESS, FORMER TEEN WONDER.
WHAT'S WITH THE THIRD DEGREE?
I MEAN... HUH?
OOPS!
WOOP!
GOOD NIGHT, DICK GRAYSON.

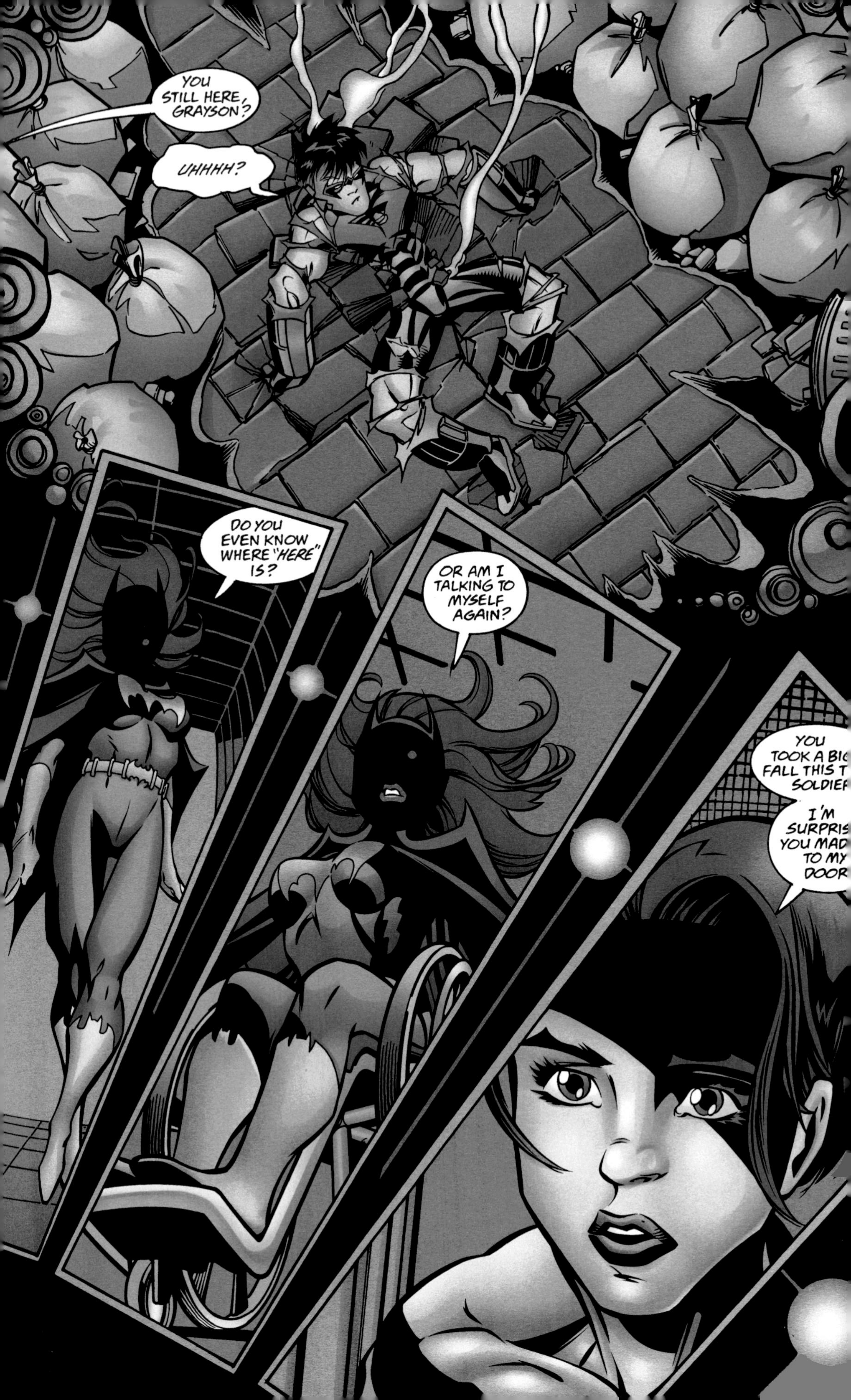
YOU STILL HERE, GRAYSON?
UHHHH?
DO YOU EVEN KNOW WHERE "HERE" IS?
OR AM I TALKING TO MYSELF AGAIN?
YOU TOOK A BIG FALL THIS T SOLDIEF
I'M SURPRIS YOU MAD TO MY DOOR

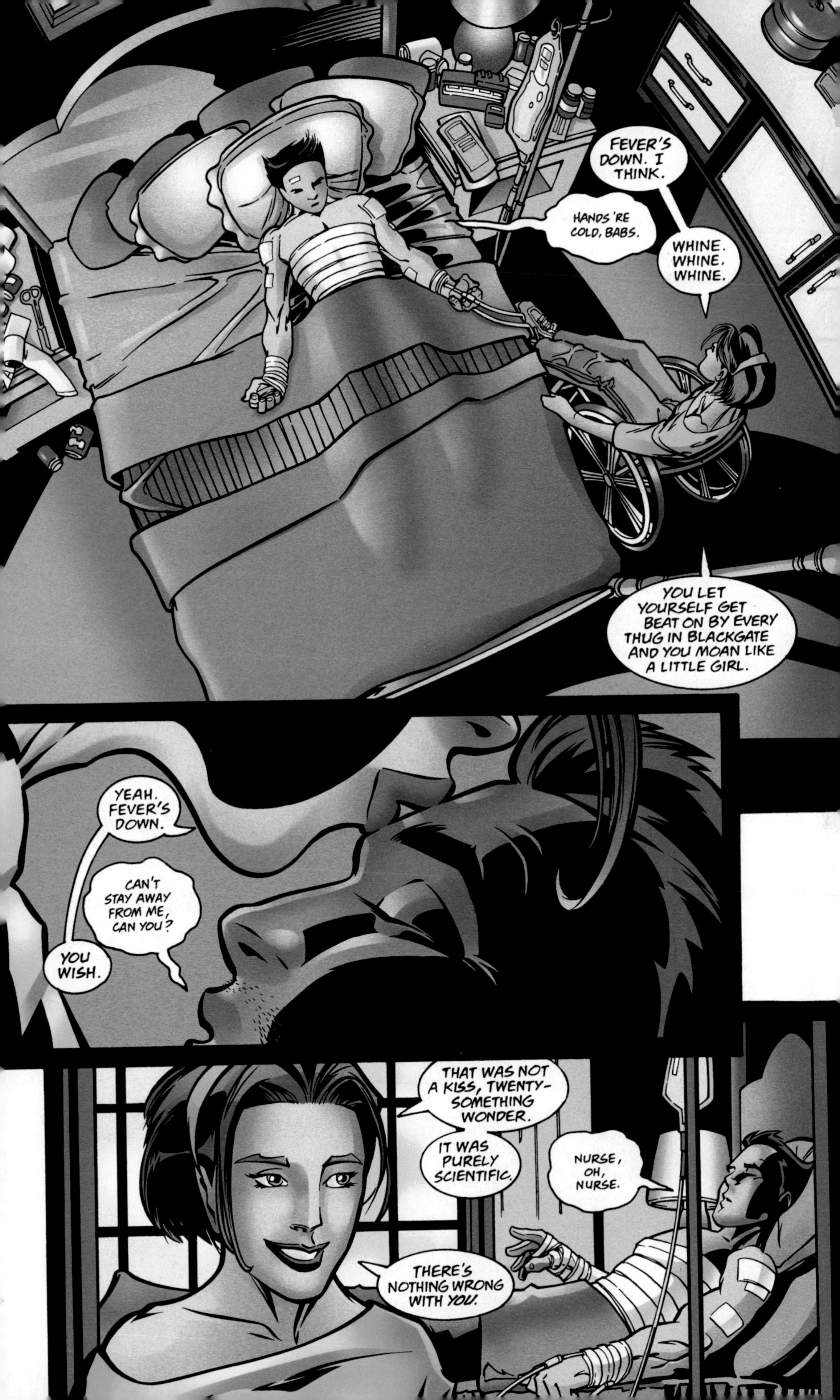
FEVER'S DOWN. I THINK.
HANDS 'RE COLD, BABS.
WHINE. WHINE. WHINE.
YOU LET YOURSELF GET BEAT ON BY EVERY THUG IN BLACKGATE AND YOU MOAN LIKE A LITTLE GIRL.
YEAH. FEVER'S DOWN.
CAN'T STAY AWAY FROM ME, CAN YOU?
YOU WISH.
THAT WAS NOT A KISS, TWENTY-SOMETHING WONDER.
IT WAS PURELY SCIENTIFIC.
NURSE, OH, NURSE.
THERE'S NOTHING WRONG WITH YOU.

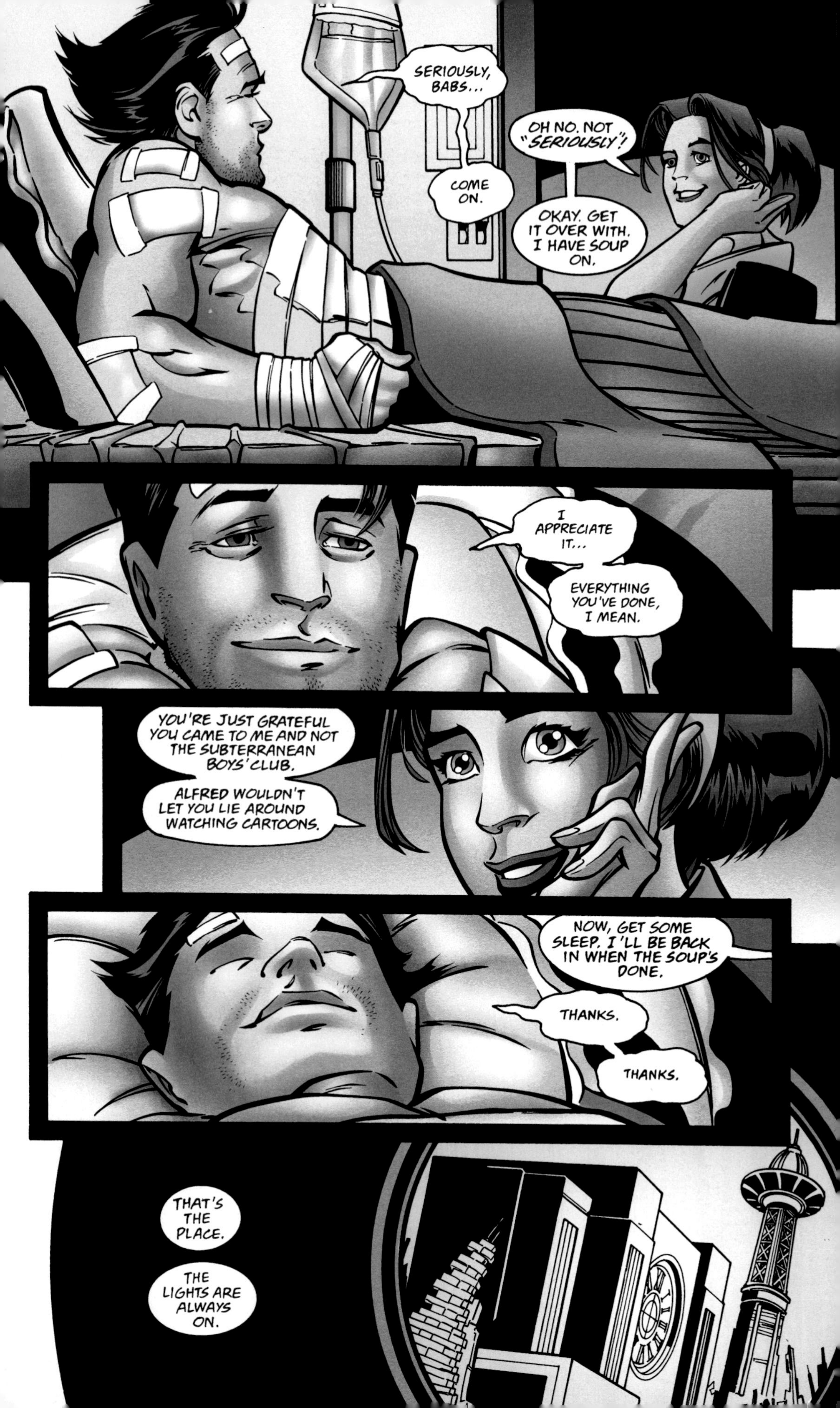
SERIOUSLY, BABS...
COME ON.
OH NO. NOT "SERIOUSLY"!
OKAY. GET IT OVER WITH. I HAVE SOUP ON.
I APPRECIATE IT...
EVERYTHING YOU'VE DONE, I MEAN.
YOU'RE JUST GRATEFUL YOU CAME TO ME AND NOT THE SUBTERRANEAN BOYS' CLUB.
ALFRED WOULDN'T LET YOU LIE AROUND WATCHING CARTOONS.
NOW, GET SOME SLEEP. I'LL BE BACK IN WHEN THE SOUP'S DONE.
THANKS.
THANKS.
THAT'S THE PLACE.
THE LIGHTS ARE ALWAYS ON.

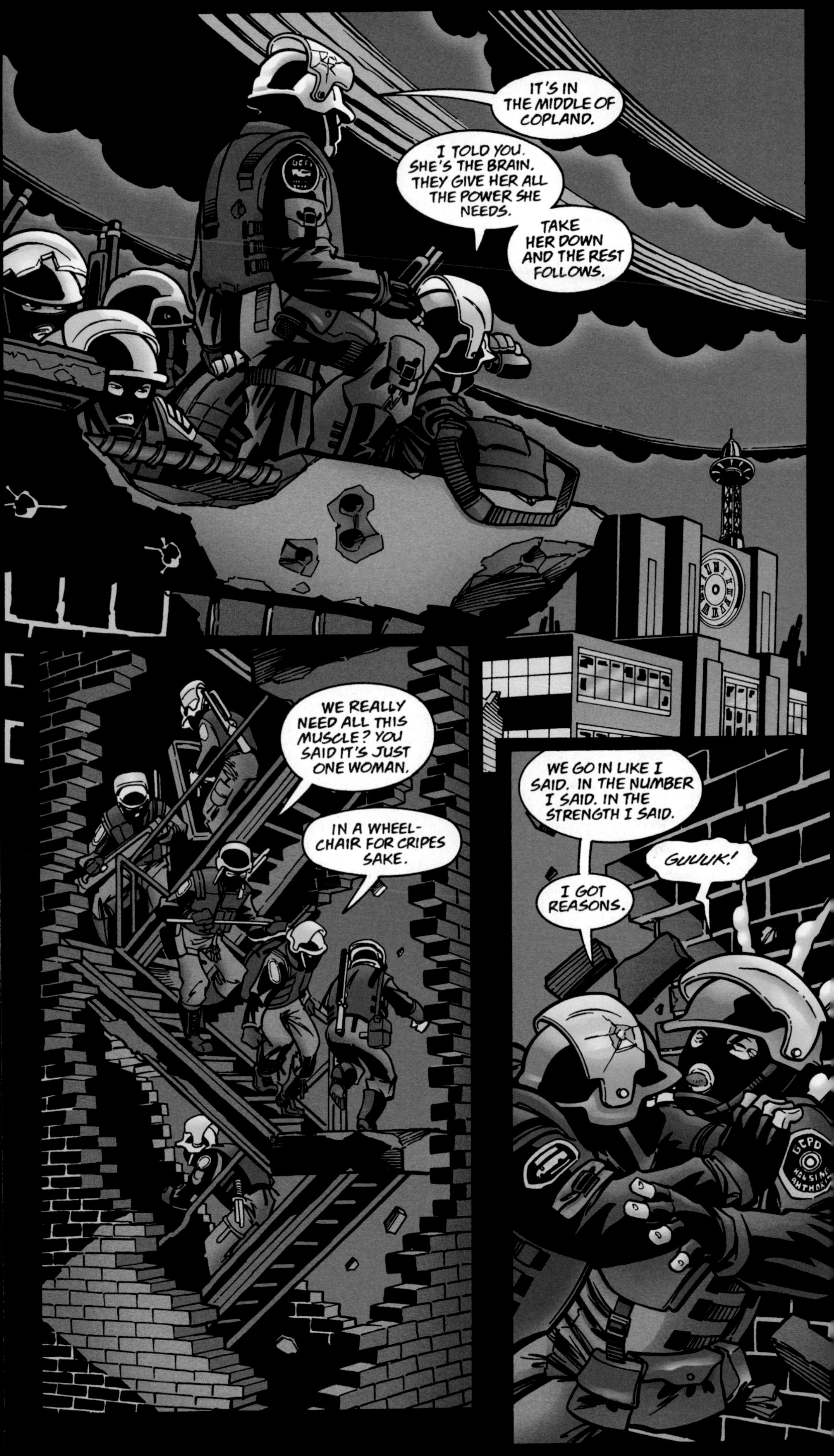

IT'S IN THE MIDDLE OF COPLAND.
I TOLD YOU. SHE'S THE BRAIN. THEY GIVE HER ALL THE POWER SHE NEEDS.
TAKE HER DOWN AND THE REST FOLLOWS.
WE REALLY NEED ALL THIS MUSCLE? YOU SAID IT'S JUST ONE WOMAN.
IN A WHEEL-CHAIR FOR CRIPES SAKE.
WE GO IN LIKE I SAID. IN THE NUMBER I SAID. IN THE STRENGTH I SAID.
I GOT REASONS.
GUUUK!

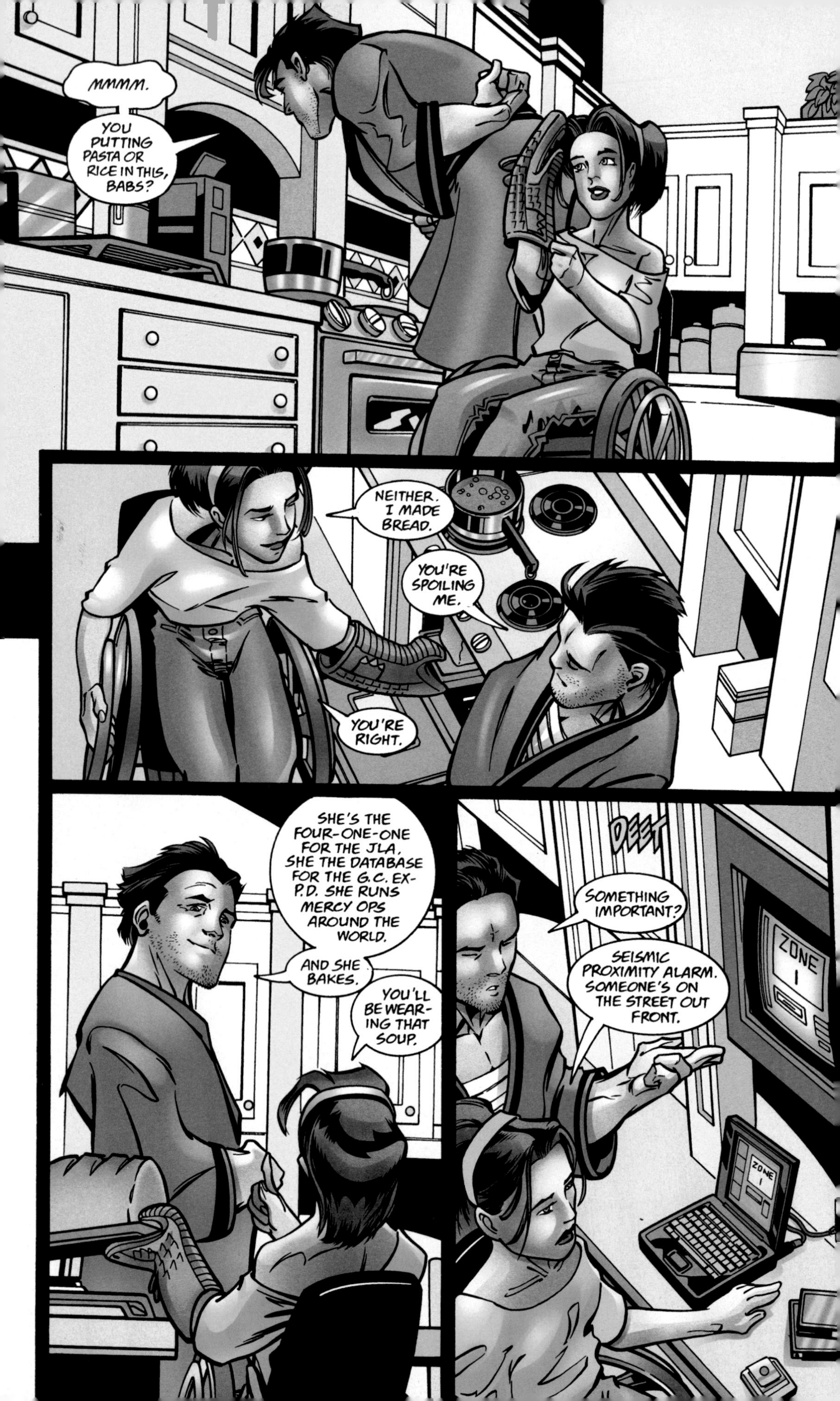
MMMM.
YOU PUTTING PASTA OR RICE IN THIS, BABS?
NEITHER. I MADE BREAD.
YOU'RE SPOILING ME.
YOU'RE RIGHT.
SHE'S THE FOUR-ONE-ONE FOR THE JLA, SHE THE DATABASE FOR THE G.C. EX-P.D. SHE RUNS MERCY OPS AROUND THE WORLD.
AND SHE BAKES.
YOU'LL BE WEARING THAT SOUP.
DEET
SOMETHING IMPORTANT?
SEISMIC PROXIMITY ALARM. SOMEONE'S ON THE STREET OUT FRONT.
ZONE 1
ZONE 1

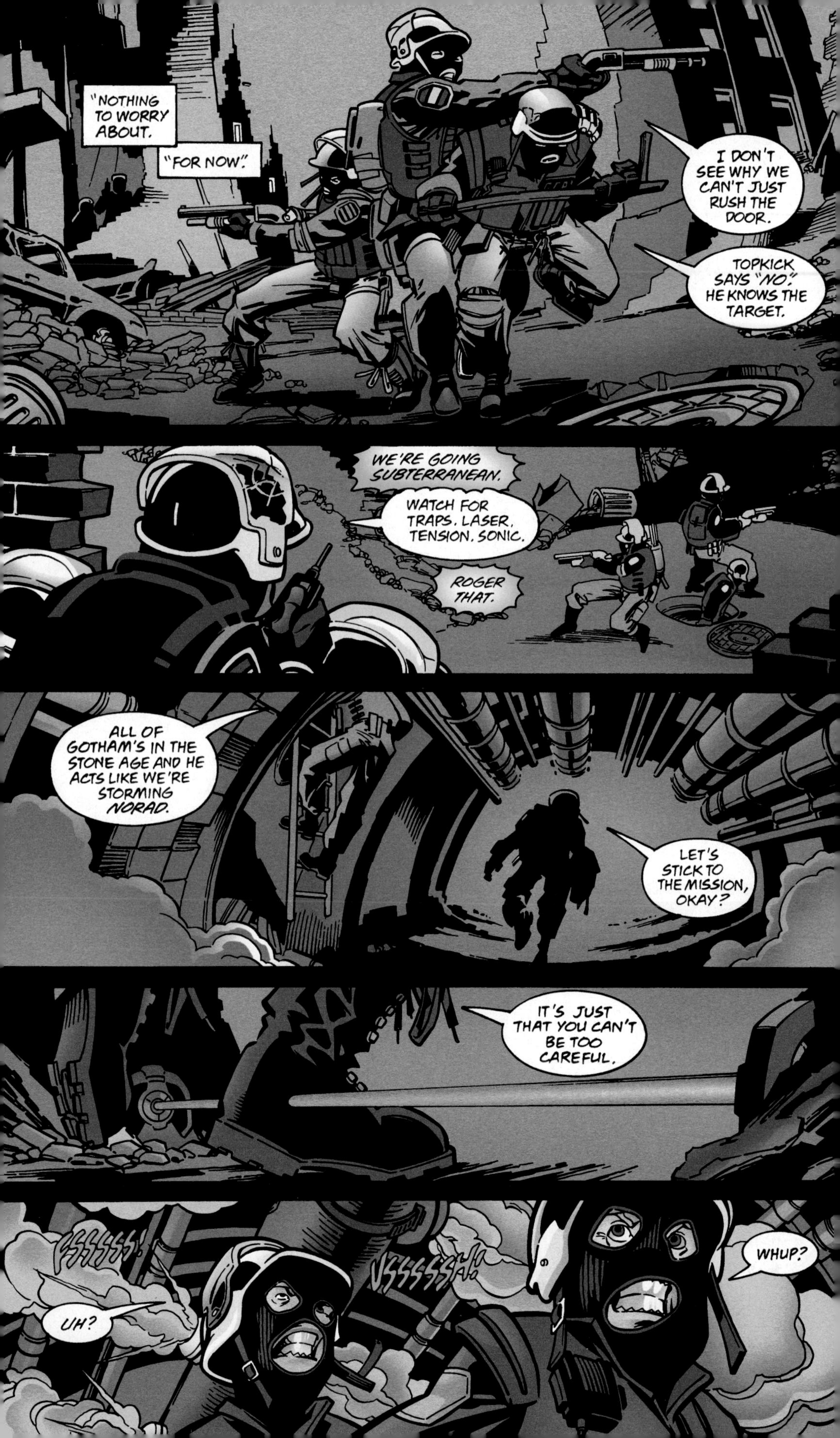
"NOTHING TO WORRY ABOUT.
"FOR NOW."
I DON'T SEE WHY WE CAN'T JUST RUSH THE DOOR.
TOPKICK SAYS "NO." HE KNOWS THE TARGET.
WE'RE GOING SUBTERRANEAN.
WATCH FOR TRAPS. LASER. TENSION. SONIC.
ROGER THAT.
ALL OF GOTHAM'S IN THE STONE AGE AND HE ACTS LIKE WE'RE STORMING NORAD.
LET'S STICK TO THE MISSION, OKAY?
IT'S JUST THAT YOU CAN'T BE TOO CAREFUL.
SSSSSS!
UH?
JSSSSSH!
WHUP?

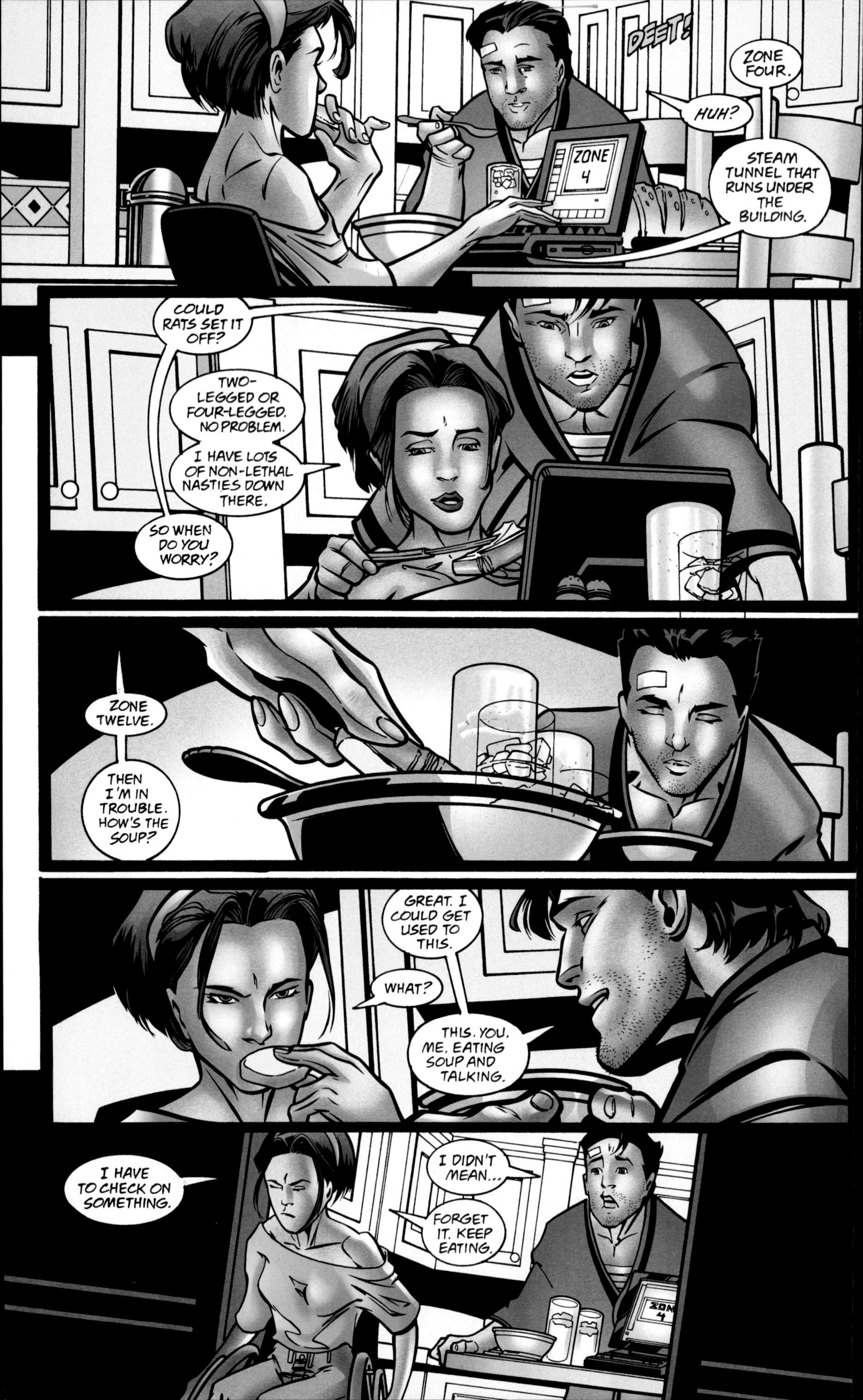
DEET!
ZONE FOUR.
HUH?
STEAM TUNNEL THAT RUNS UNDER THE BUILDING.
ZONE 4
COULD RATS SET IT OFF?
TWO-LEGGED OR FOUR-LEGGED. NO PROBLEM.
I HAVE LOTS OF NON-LETHAL NASTIES DOWN THERE.
SO WHEN DO YOU WORRY?
ZONE TWELVE.
THEN I'M IN TROUBLE. HOW'S THE SOUP?
GREAT. I COULD GET USED TO THIS.
WHAT?
THIS. YOU. ME, EATING SOUP AND TALKING.
I HAVE TO CHECK ON SOMETHING.
I DIDN'T MEAN...
FORGET IT. KEEP EATING.

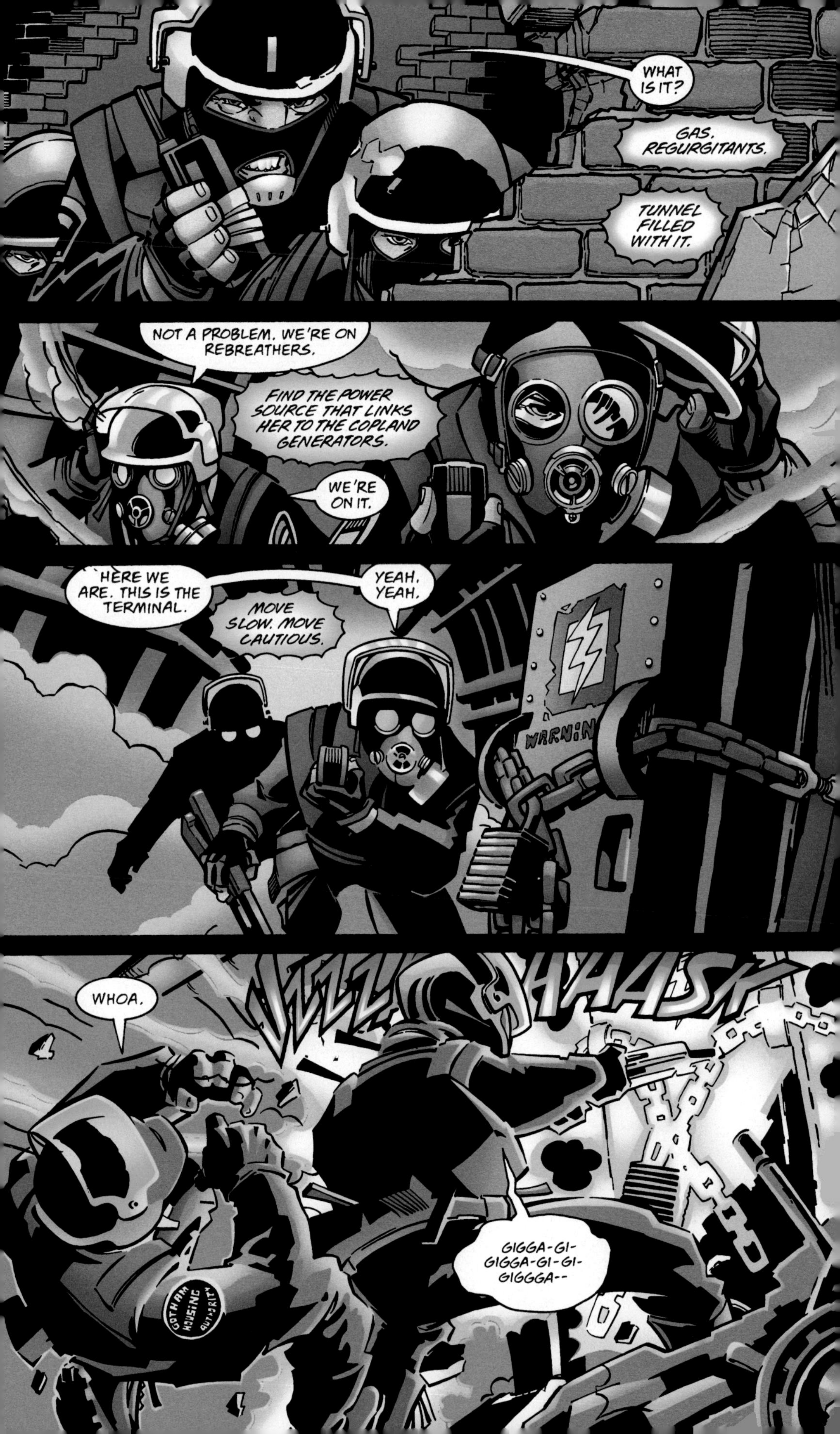
WHAT IS IT?
GAS. REGURGITANTS.
TUNNEL FILLED WITH IT.
NOT A PROBLEM. WE'RE ON REBREATHERS.
FIND THE POWER SOURCE THAT LINKS HER TO THE COPLAND GENERATORS.
WE'RE ON IT.
HERE WE ARE. THIS IS THE TERMINAL.
YEAH. YEAH.
MOVE SLOW. MOVE CAUTIOUS.
WARNIN
WHOA.
GIGGA-GI-GIGGA-GI-GI-GIGGGA--
GOTHAM HOUSING AUTHORITY

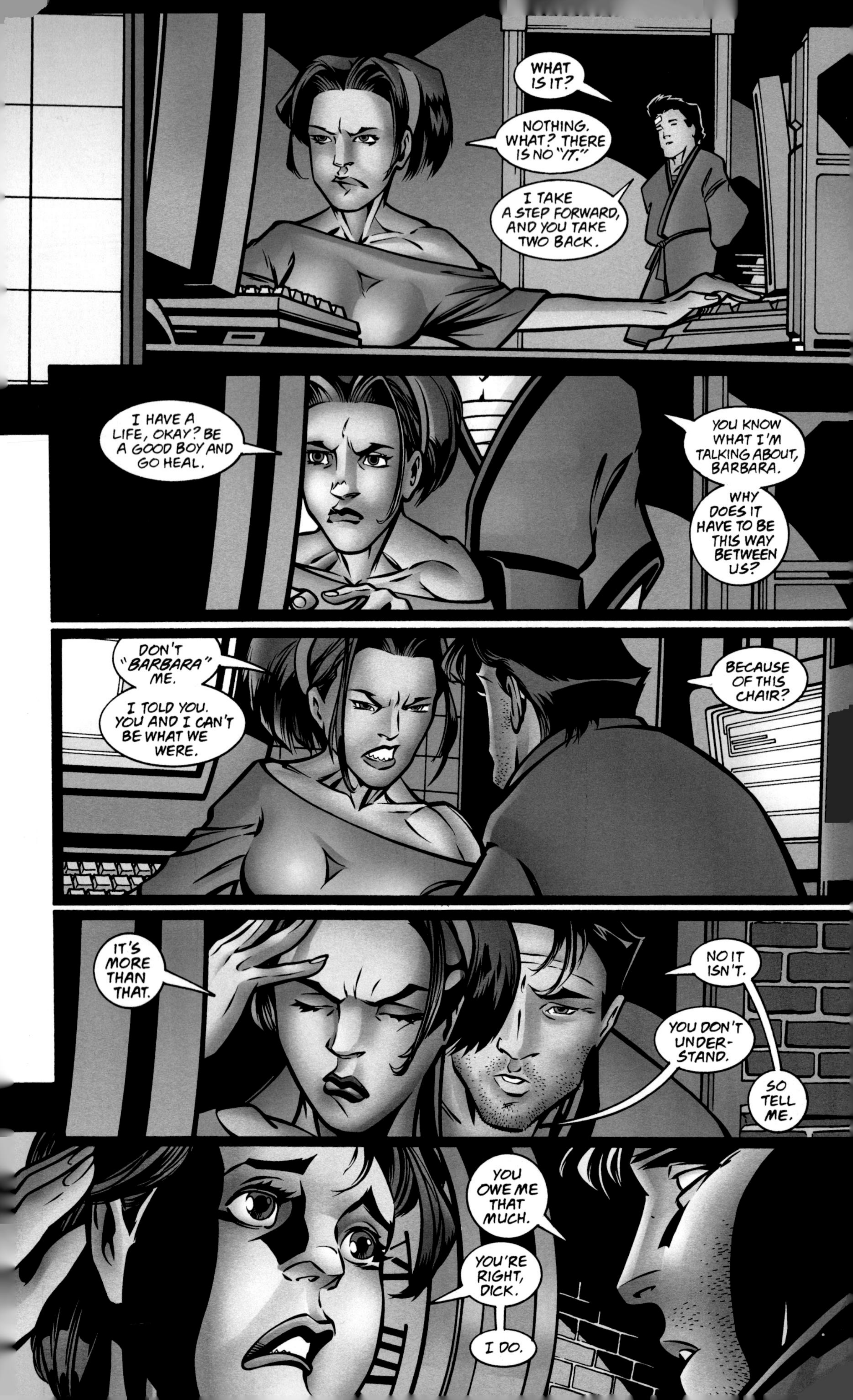
WHAT IS IT?
NOTHING. WHAT? THERE IS NO "IT."
I TAKE A STEP FORWARD, AND YOU TAKE TWO BACK.
I HAVE A LIFE, OKAY? BE A GOOD BOY AND GO HEAL.
YOU KNOW WHAT I'M TALKING ABOUT, BARBARA.
WHY DOES IT HAVE TO BE THIS WAY BETWEEN US?
DON'T "BARBARA" ME.
I TOLD YOU. YOU AND I CAN'T BE WHAT WE WERE.
BECAUSE OF THIS CHAIR?
IT'S MORE THAN THAT.
NO IT ISN'T.
YOU DON'T UNDER-STAND.
SO TELL ME.
YOU OWE ME THAT MUCH.
YOU'RE RIGHT, DICK.
I DO.

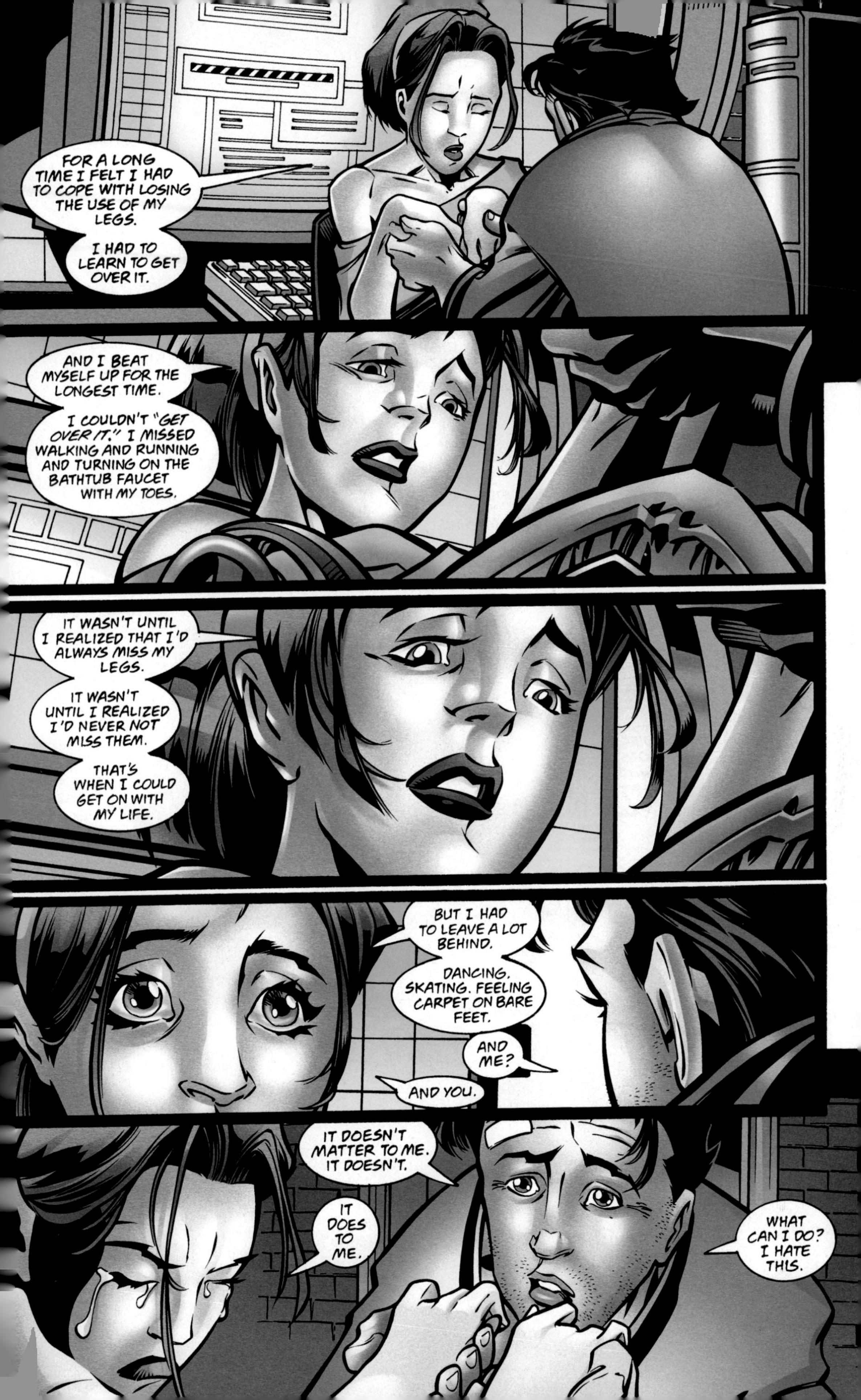
FOR A LONG TIME I FELT I HAD TO COPE WITH LOSING THE USE OF MY LEGS.
I HAD TO LEARN TO GET OVER IT.
AND I BEAT MYSELF UP FOR THE LONGEST TIME.
I COULDN'T "GET OVER IT." I MISSED WALKING AND RUNNING AND TURNING ON THE BATHTUB FAUCET WITH MY TOES.
IT WASN'T UNTIL I REALIZED THAT I'D ALWAYS MISS MY LEGS.
IT WASN'T UNTIL I REALIZED I'D NEVER NOT MISS THEM.
THAT'S WHEN I COULD GET ON WITH MY LIFE.
BUT I HAD TO LEAVE A LOT BEHIND.
DANCING. SKATING. FEELING CARPET ON BARE FEET.
AND ME?
AND YOU.
IT DOESN'T MATTER TO ME. IT DOESN'T.
IT DOES TO ME.
WHAT CAN I DO? I HATE THIS.

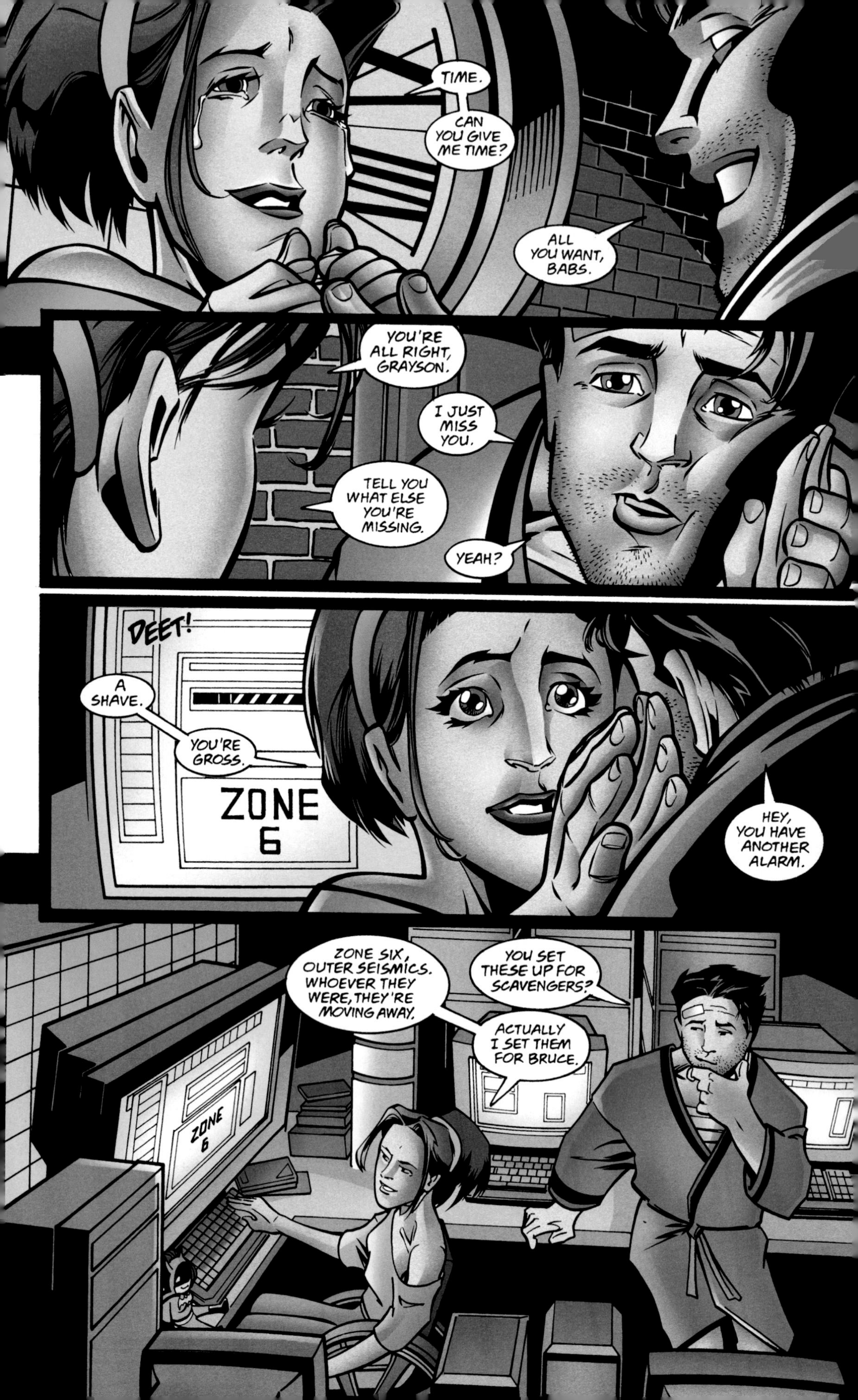
TIME.
CAN YOU GIVE ME TIME?
ALL YOU WANT, BABS.
YOU'RE ALL RIGHT, GRAYSON.
I JUST MISS YOU.
TELL YOU WHAT ELSE YOU'RE MISSING.
YEAH?
DEET!
A SHAVE.
YOU'RE GROSS.
ZONE 6
HEY, YOU HAVE ANOTHER ALARM.
ZONE SIX, OUTER SEISMICS. WHOEVER THEY WERE, THEY'RE MOVING AWAY.
YOU SET THESE UP FOR SCAVENGERS?
ACTUALLY I SET THEM FOR BRUCE.
ZONE 6

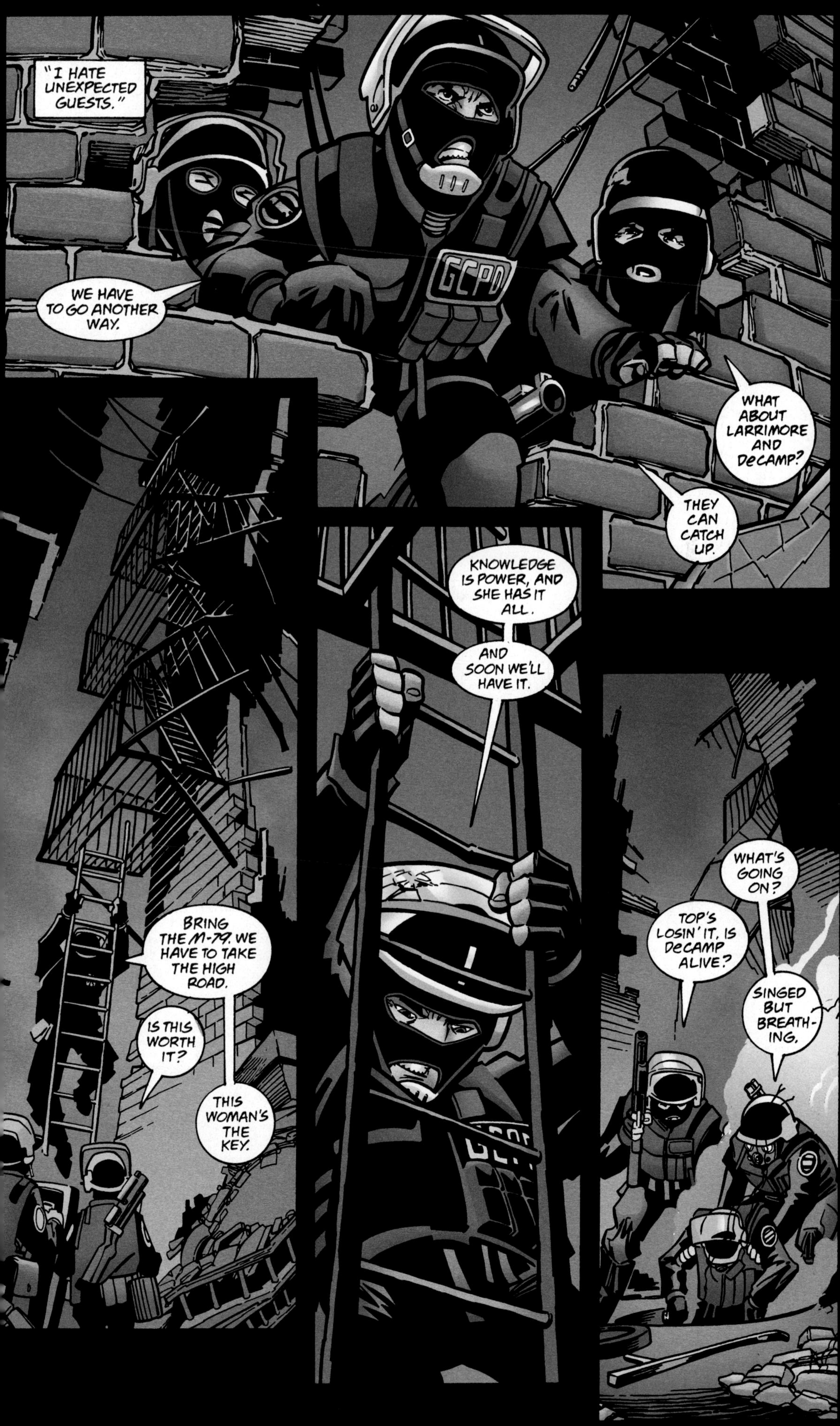
"I HATE UNEXPECTED GUESTS."
WE HAVE TO GO ANOTHER WAY.
WHAT ABOUT LARRIMORE AND DeCAMP?
THEY CAN CATCH UP.
BRING THE M-79. WE HAVE TO TAKE THE HIGH ROAD.
IS THIS WORTH IT?
THIS WOMAN'S THE KEY.
KNOWLEDGE IS POWER, AND SHE HAS IT ALL.
AND SOON WE'LL HAVE IT.
WHAT'S GOING ON?
TOP'S LOSIN' IT. IS DeCAMP ALIVE?
SINGED BUT BREATHING.

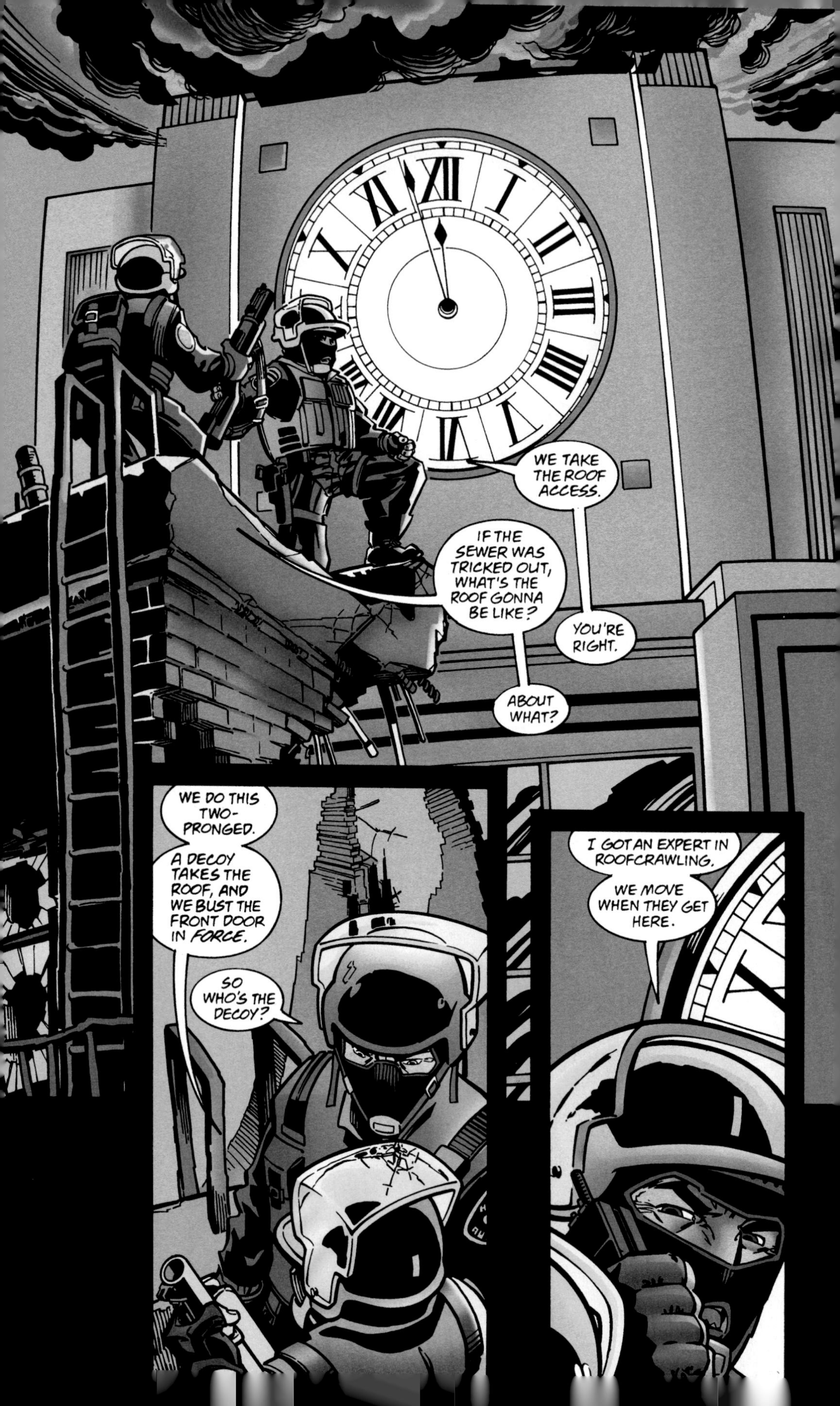
WE TAKE THE ROOF ACCESS.
IF THE SEWER WAS TRICKED OUT, WHAT'S THE ROOF GONNA BE LIKE?
YOU'RE RIGHT.
ABOUT WHAT?
WE DO THIS TWO-PRONGED.
A DECOY TAKES THE ROOF, AND WE BUST THE FRONT DOOR IN FORCE.
SO WHO'S THE DECOY?
I GOT AN EXPERT IN ROOFCRAWLING.
WE MOVE WHEN THEY GET HERE.

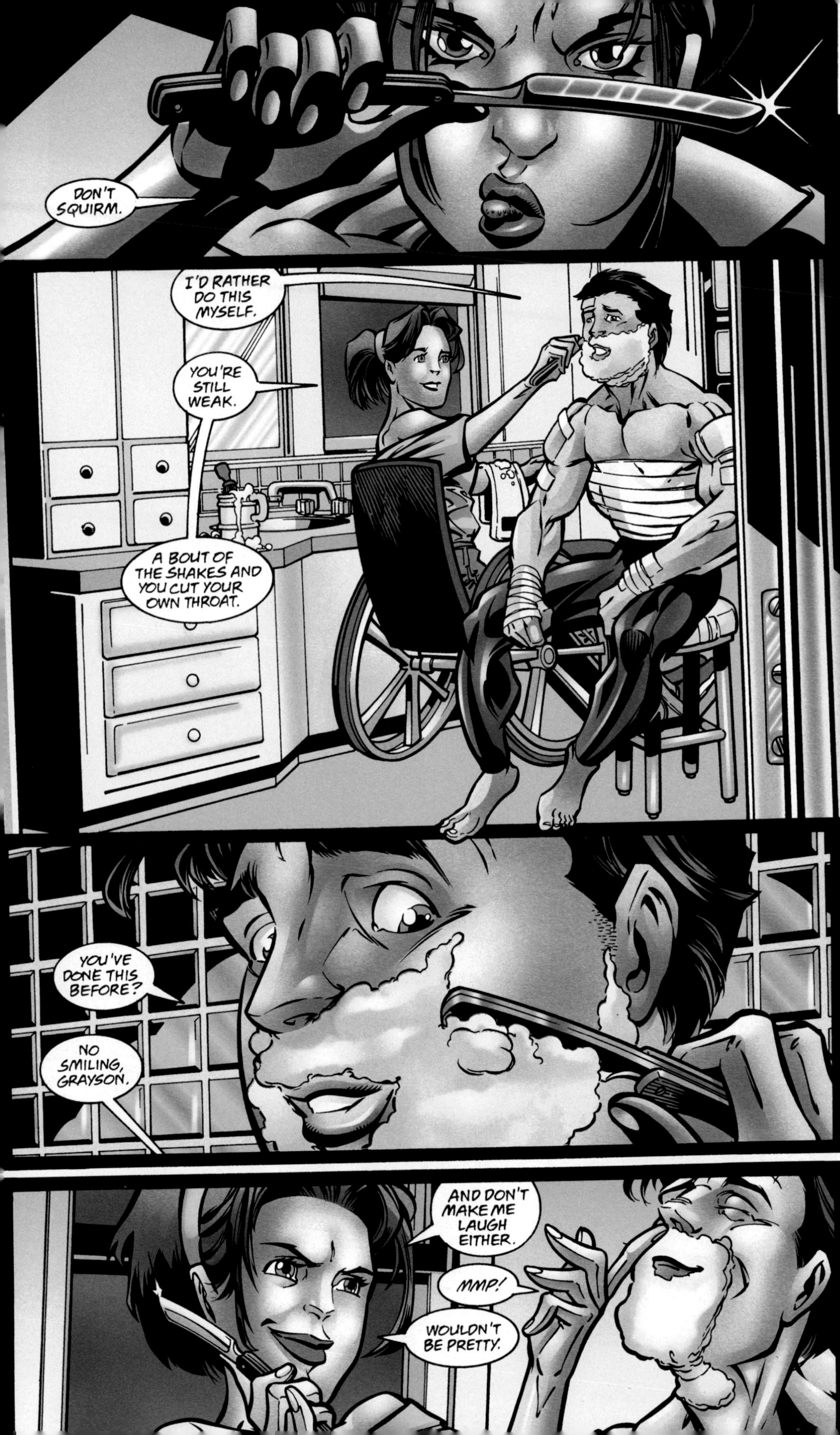
DON'T SQUIRM.
I'D RATHER DO THIS MYSELF.
YOU'RE STILL WEAK.
A BOUT OF THE SHAKES AND YOU CUT YOUR OWN THROAT.
YOU'VE DONE THIS BEFORE?
NO SMILING, GRAYSON.
AND DON'T MAKE ME LAUGH EITHER.
MMP!
WOULDN'T BE PRETTY.

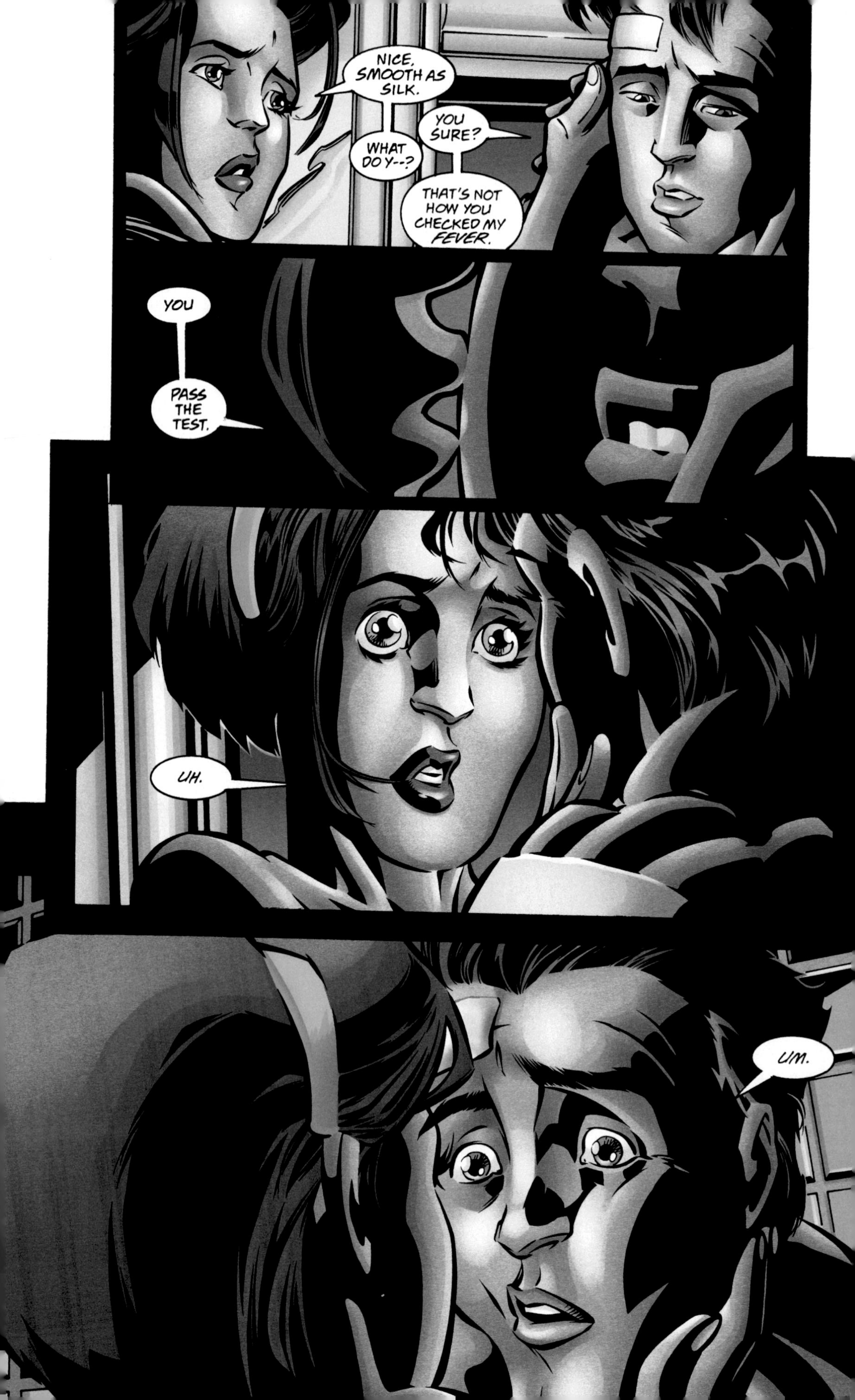
NICE, SMOOTH AS SILK.
WHAT DO Y--?
YOU SURE?
THAT'S NOT HOW YOU CHECKED MY FEVER.
YOU
PASS THE TEST.
UH.
UM.

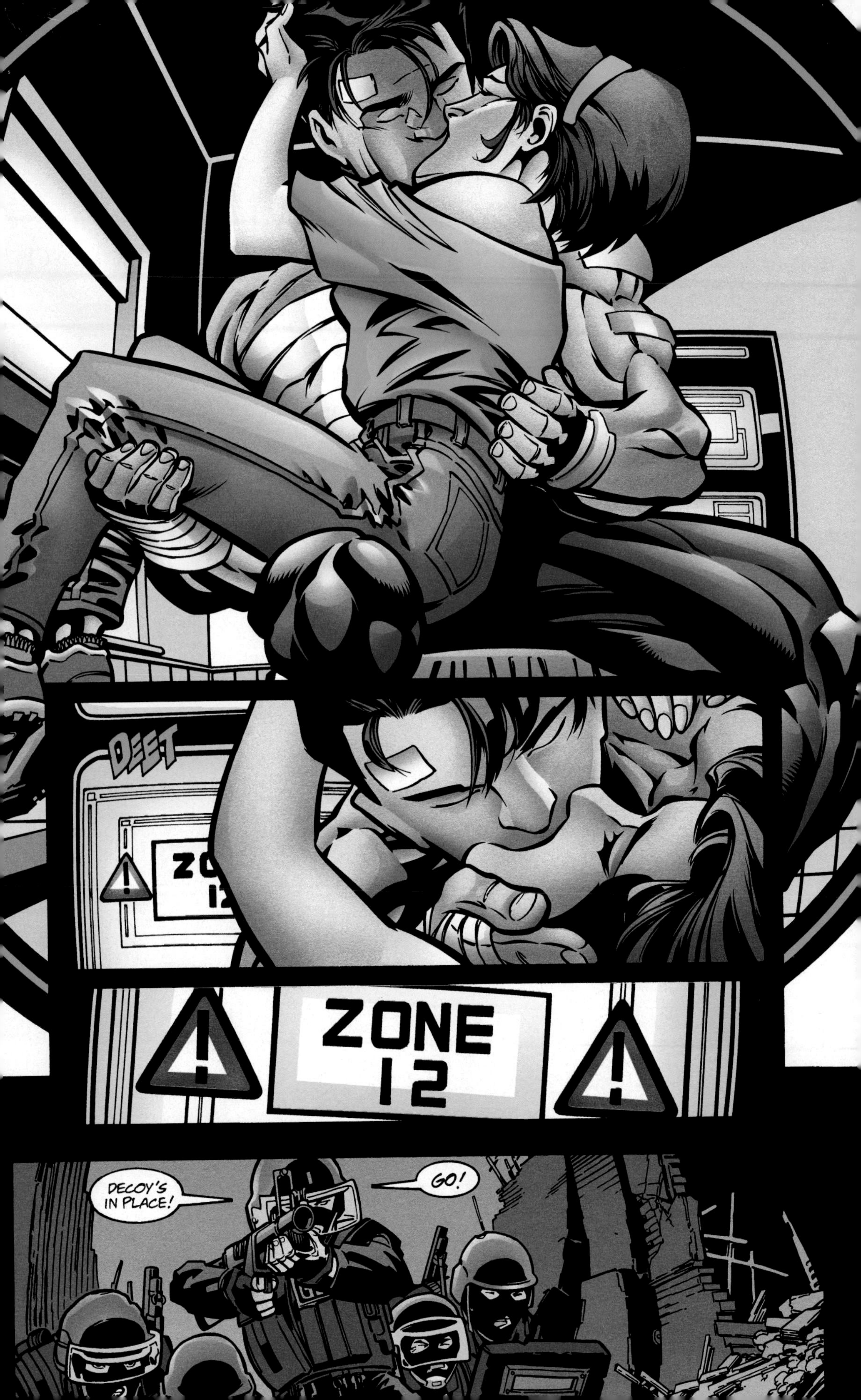
DEET
ZONE 12
ZONE 12
DECOY'S IN PLACE!
GO!

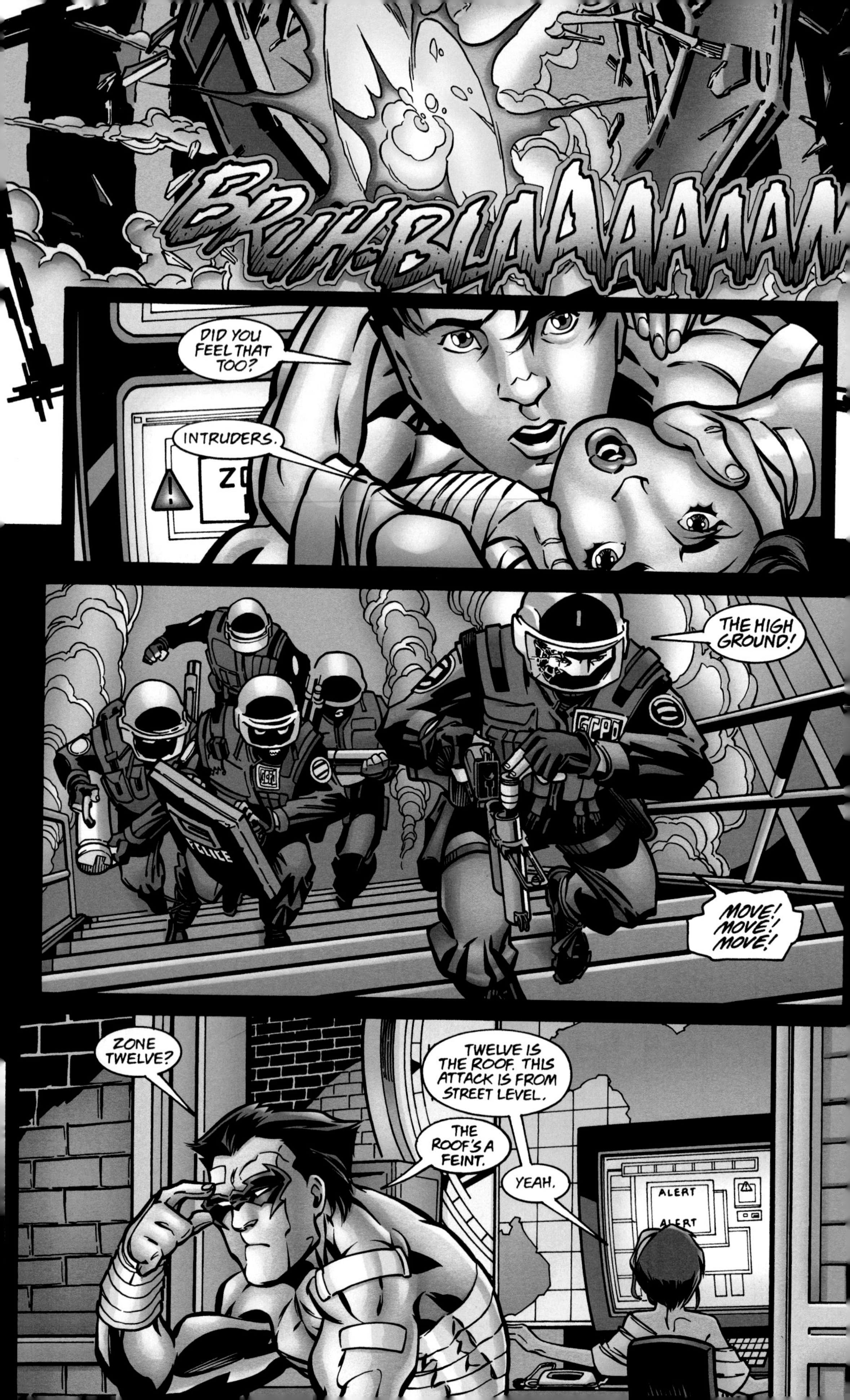
BRUHBLAAAAAAM
DID YOU FEEL THAT TOO?
INTRUDERS.
THE HIGH GROUND!
MOVE! MOVE! MOVE!
ZONE TWELVE?
TWELVE IS THE ROOF. THIS ATTACK IS FROM STREET LEVEL.
THE ROOF'S A FEINT.
YEAH.
ALERT
ALERT

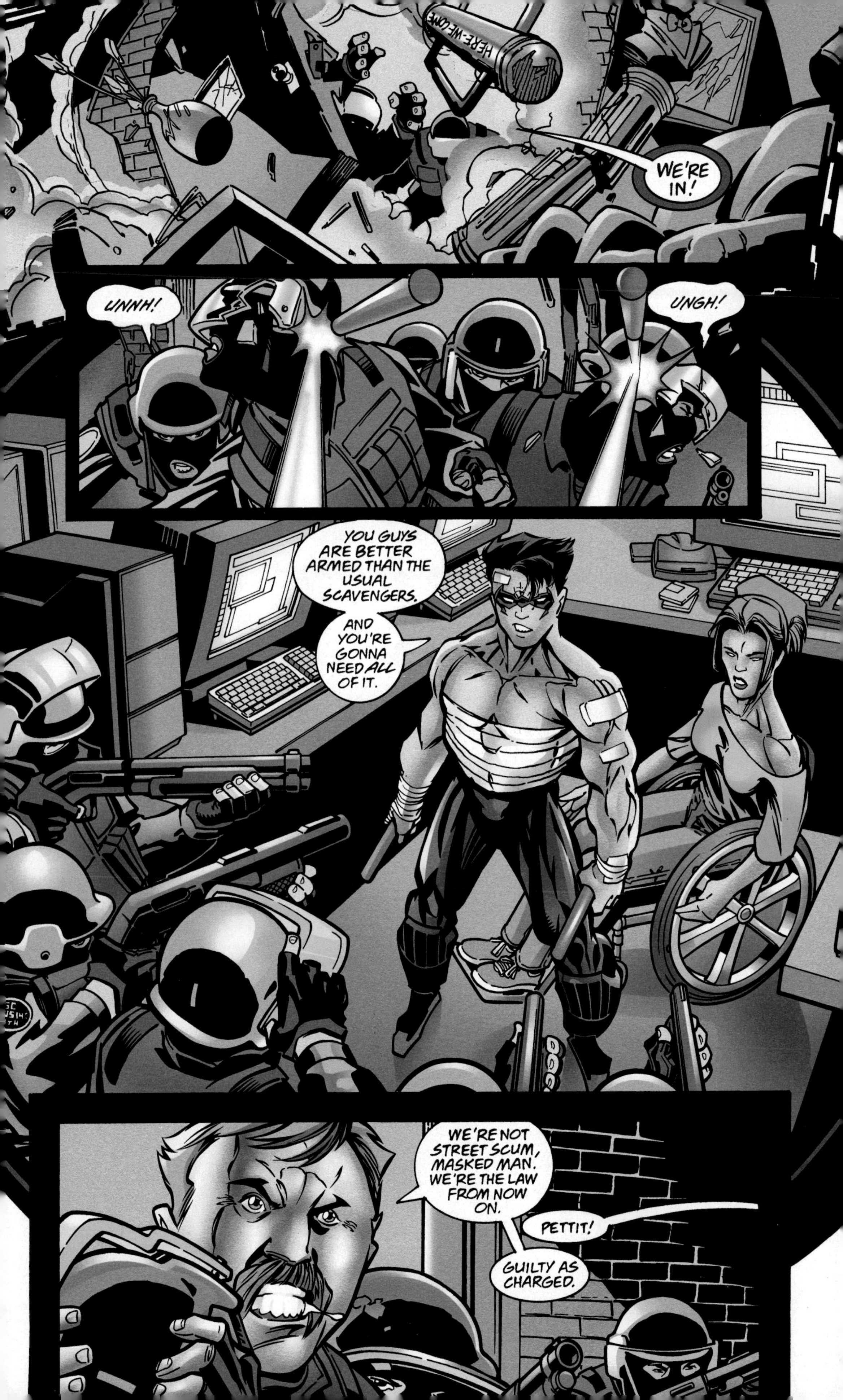
HERE-WE-COME
WE'RE IN!
UNNH!
UNGH!
YOU GUYS ARE BETTER ARMED THAN THE USUAL SCAVENGERS.
AND YOU'RE GONNA NEED ALL OF IT.
WE'RE NOT STREET SCUM, MASKED MAN. WE'RE THE LAW FROM NOW ON.
PETTIT!
GUILTY AS CHARGED.

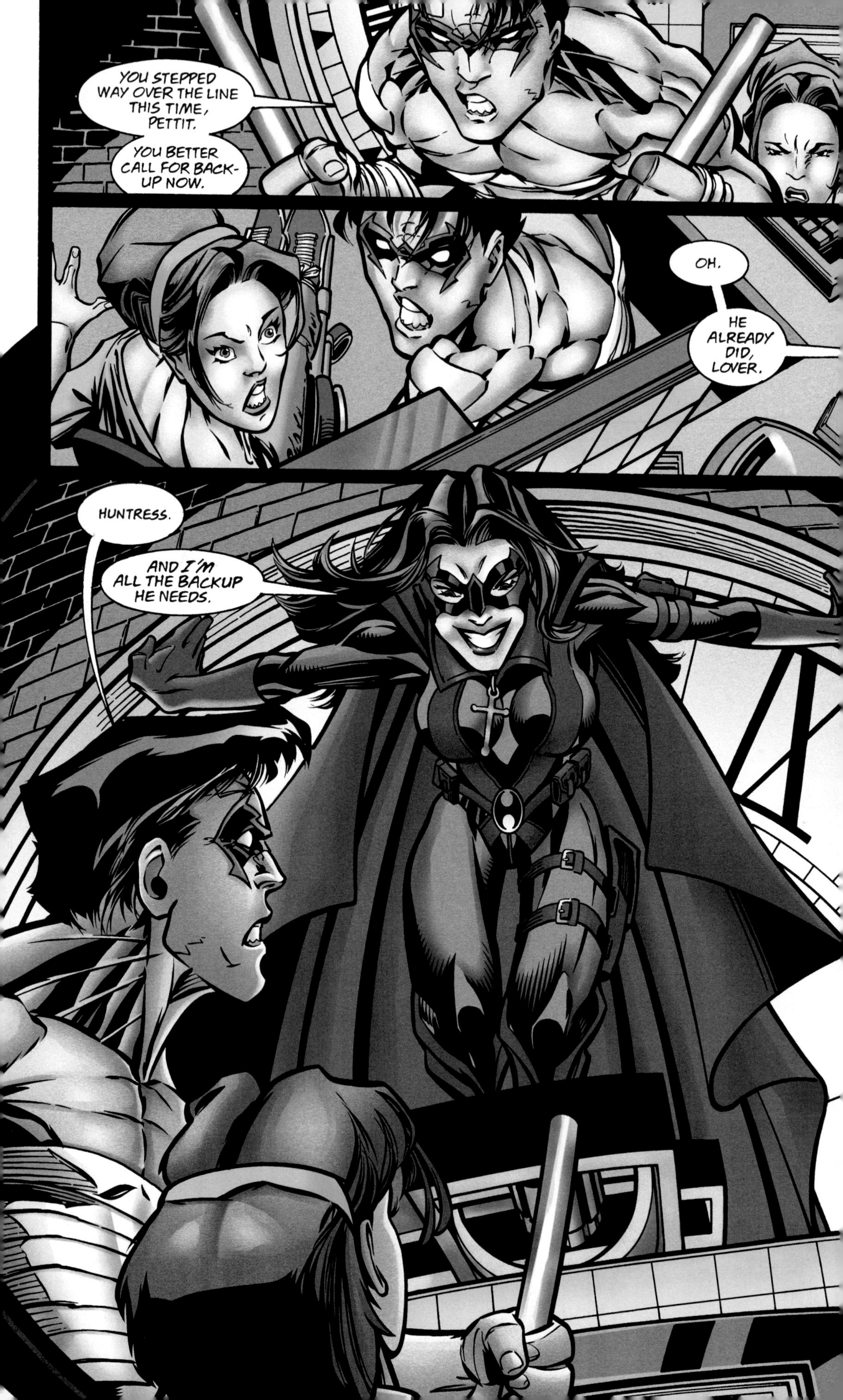
YOU STEPPED WAY OVER THE LINE THIS TIME, PETTIT.
YOU BETTER CALL FOR BACK-UP NOW.
OH.
HE ALREADY DID, LOVER.
HUNTRESS.
AND I'M ALL THE BACKUP HE NEEDS.

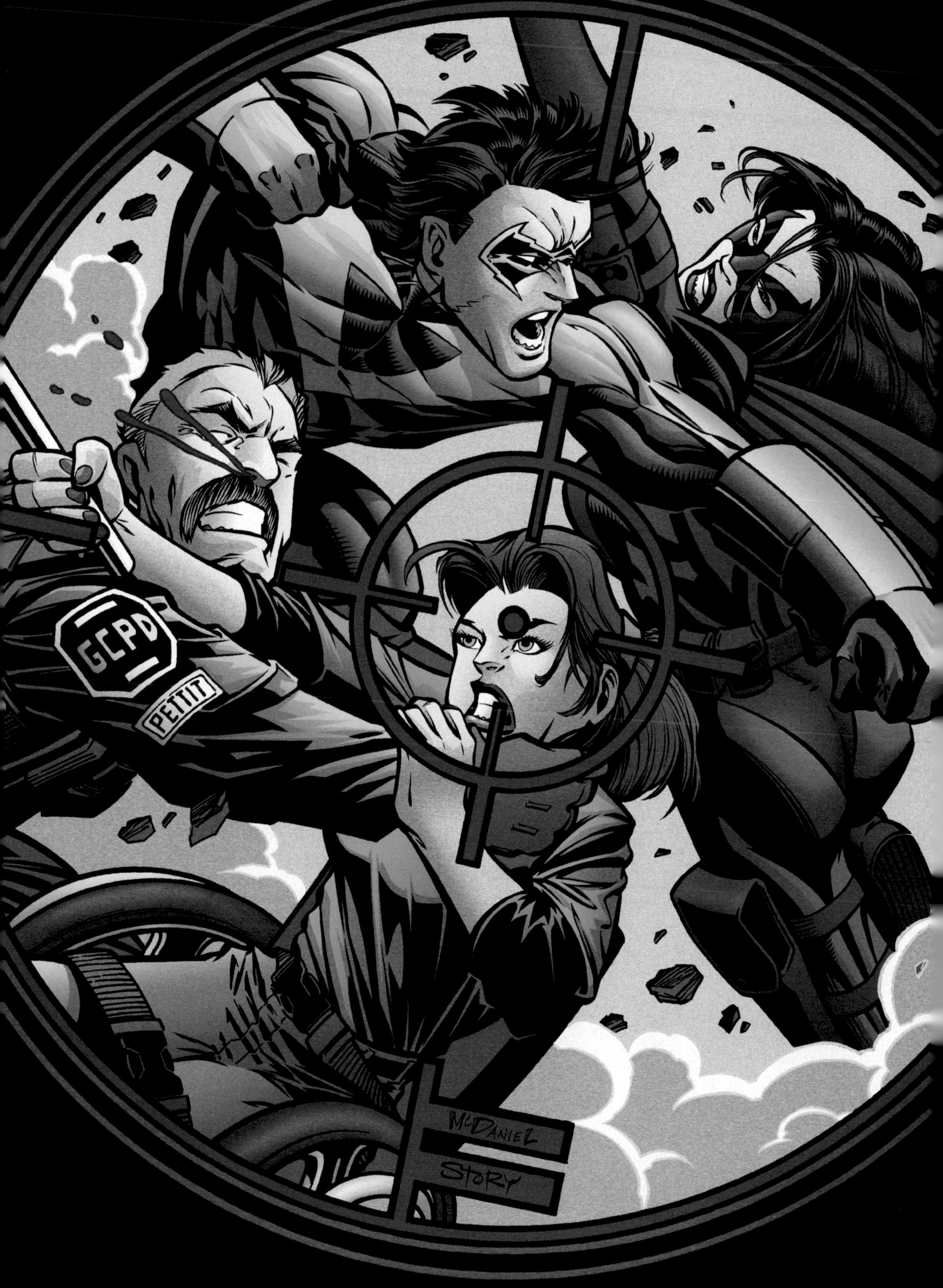
GCPD
PETTIT
McDANIEL
STORY

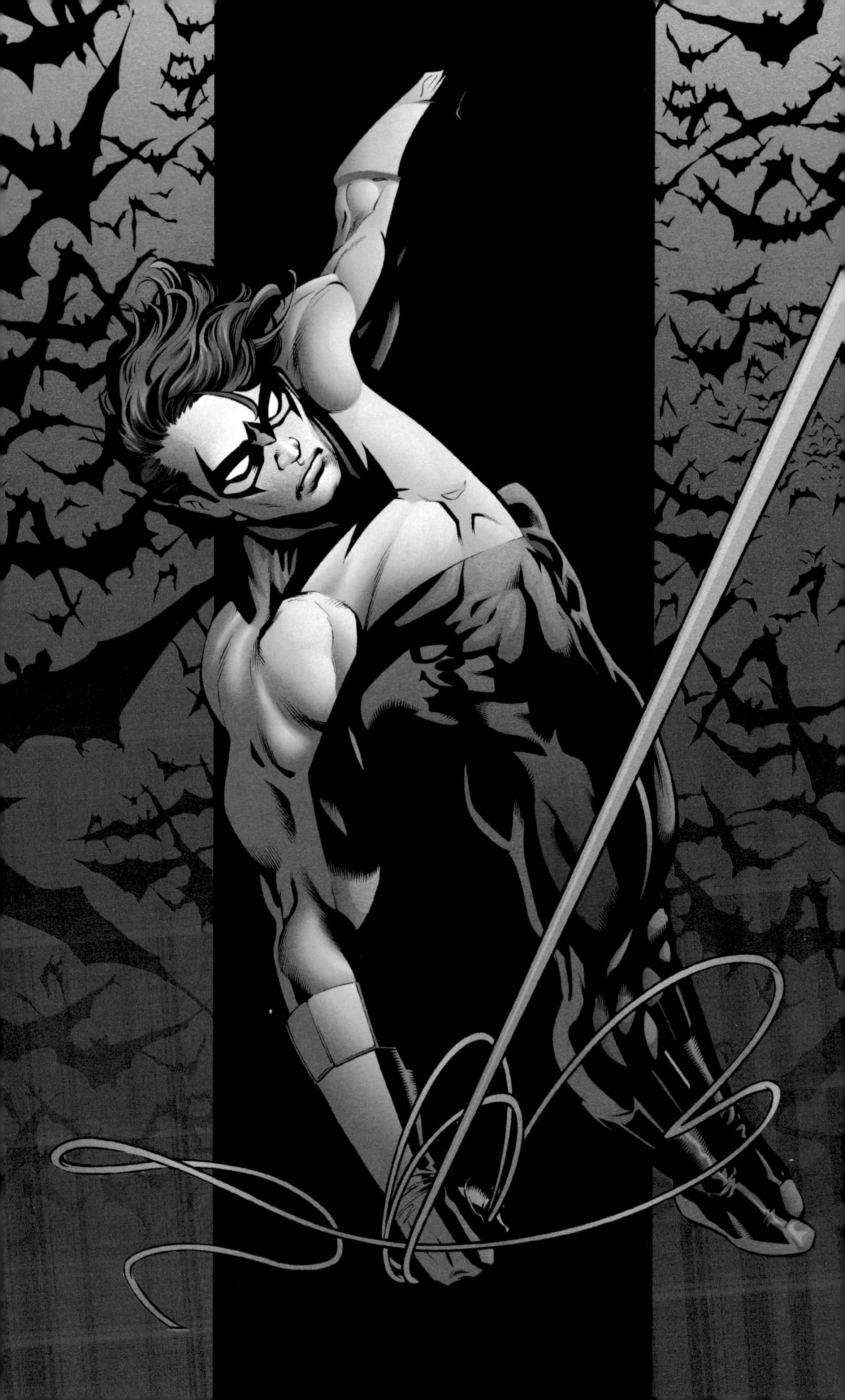

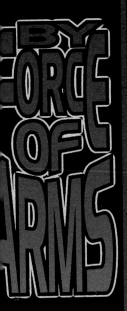

BY FORCE OF ARMS

huck Dixon
writer
ott McDaniel
penciller
Karl Story
inker
oberta Tewes
colorist
ohn Costanza
letterer
Jamison
separator
oseph Illidge
assoc. editor
rren Vincenzo
general

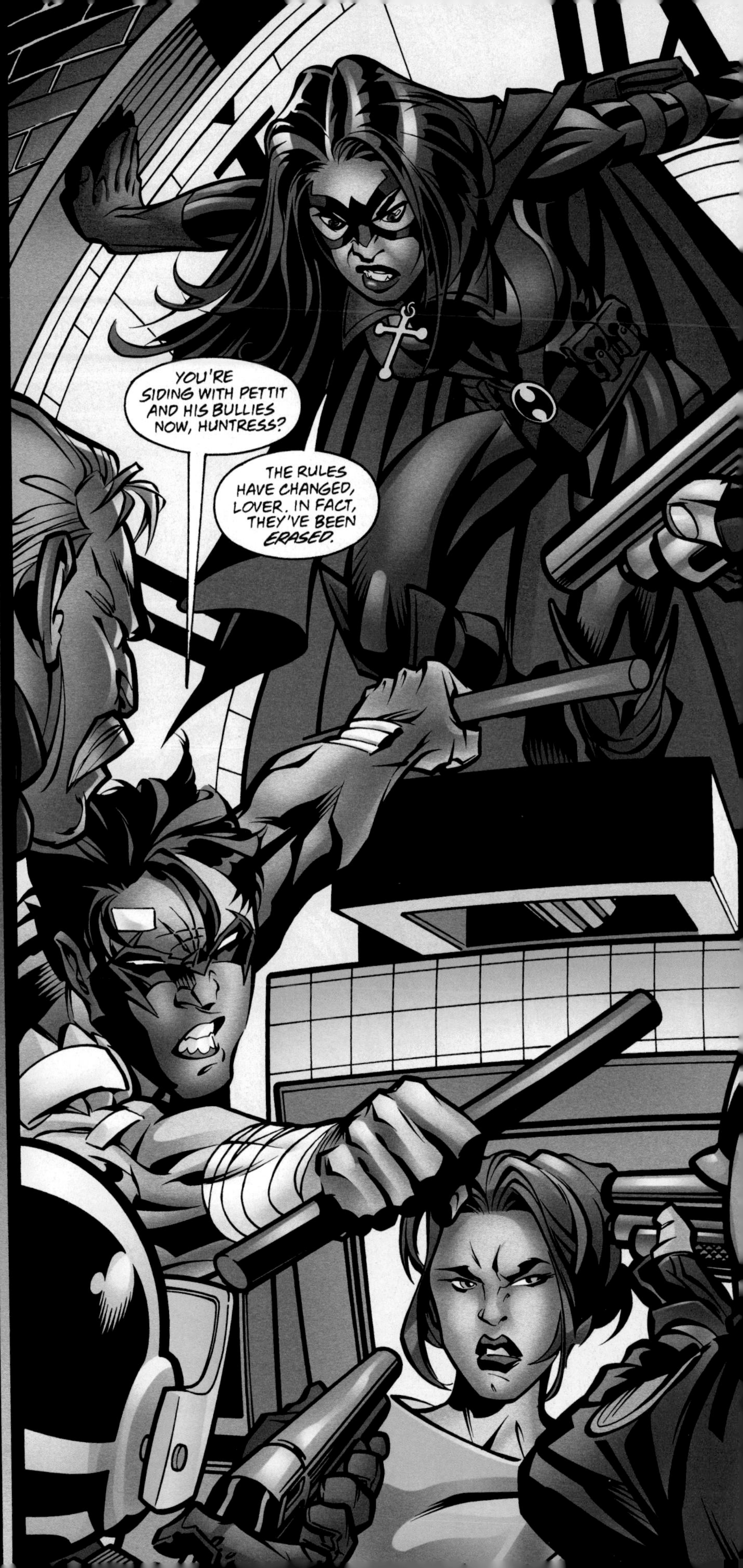
YOU'RE SIDING WITH PETTIT AND HIS BULLIES NOW, HUNTRESS?
THE RULES HAVE CHANGED, LOVER. IN FACT, THEY'VE BEEN *ERASED.*

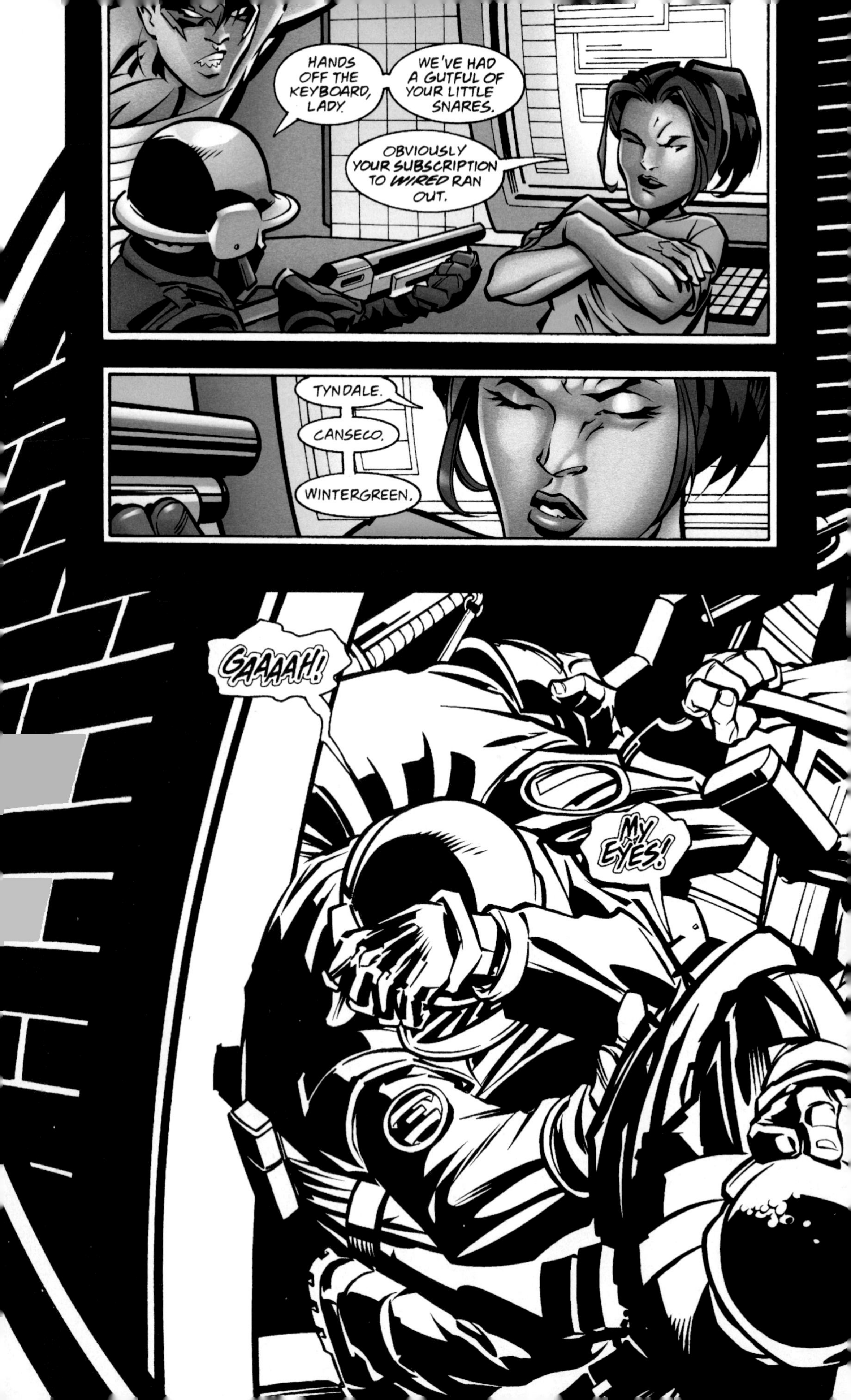
HANDS OFF THE KEYBOARD, LADY.
WE'VE HAD A GUTFUL OF YOUR LITTLE SNARES.
OBVIOUSLY YOUR SUBSCRIPTION TO WIRED RAN OUT.
TYNDALE.
CANSECO.
WINTERGREEN.
GAAAAH!
MY EYES!

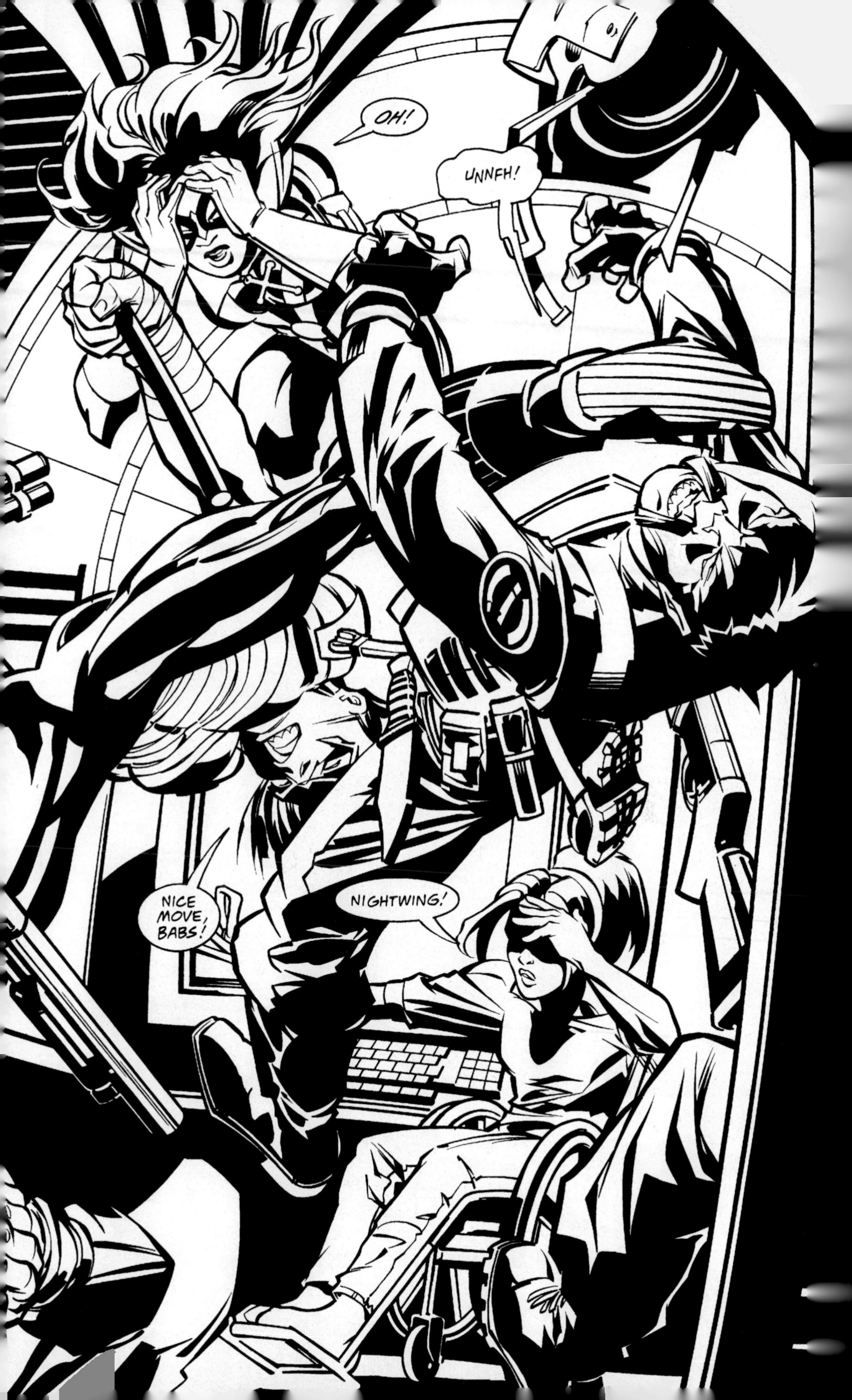
OH!
UNNFH!
NICE MOVE, BABS!
NIGHTWING!

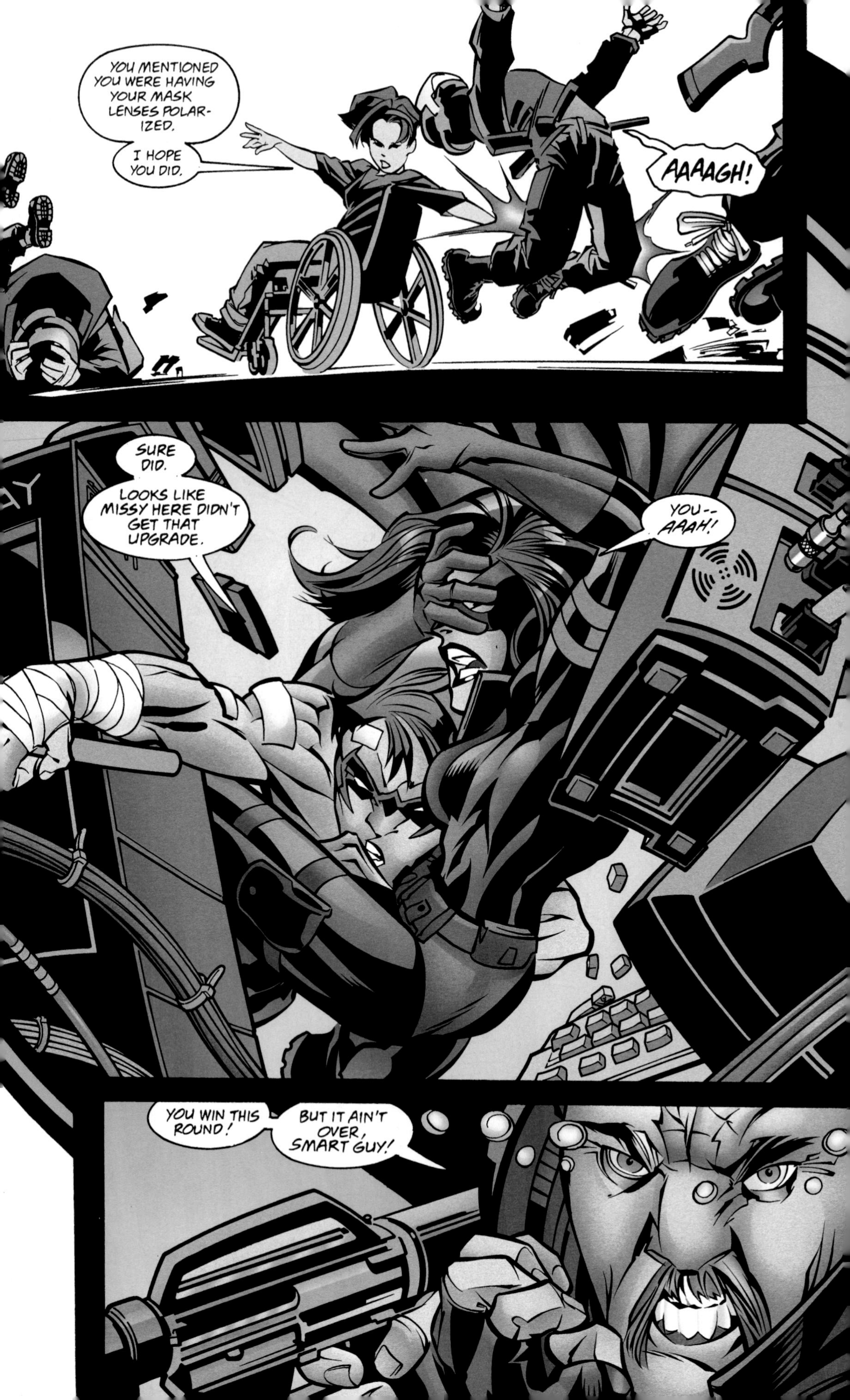
YOU MENTIONED YOU WERE HAVING YOUR MASK LENSES POLAR-IZED.
I HOPE YOU DID.
AAAAGH!
SURE DID.
LOOKS LIKE MISSY HERE DIDN'T GET THAT UPGRADE.
YOU-- AAAH!
YOU WIN THIS ROUND!
BUT IT AIN'T OVER, SMART GUY!

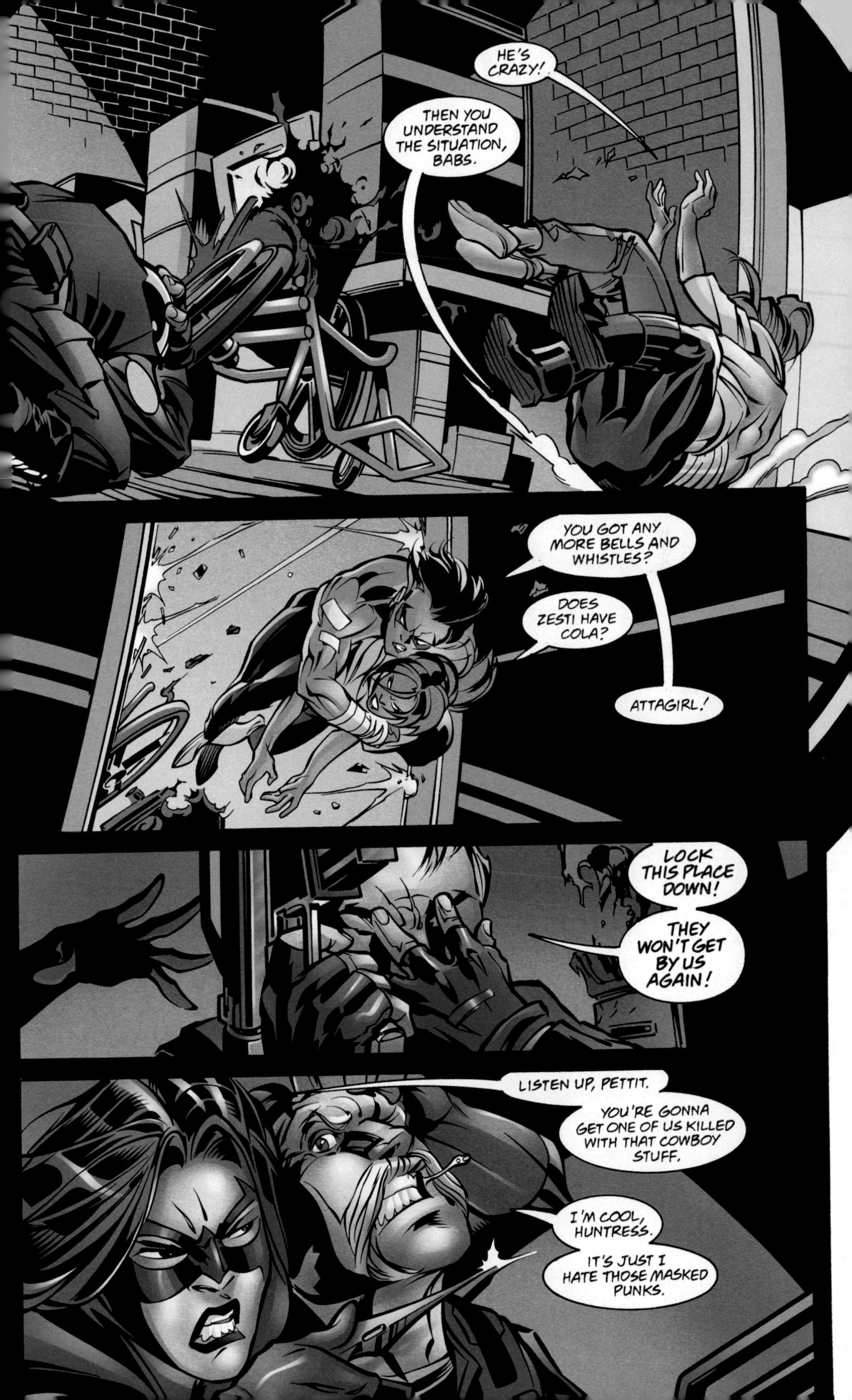
HE'S CRAZY!
THEN YOU UNDERSTAND THE SITUATION, BABS.
YOU GOT ANY MORE BELLS AND WHISTLES?
DOES ZESTI HAVE COLA?
ATTAGIRL!
LOCK THIS PLACE DOWN!
THEY WON'T GET BY US AGAIN!
LISTEN UP, PETTIT.
YOU'RE GONNA GET ONE OF US KILLED WITH THAT COWBOY STUFF.
I'M COOL, HUNTRESS.
IT'S JUST I HATE THOSE MASKED PUNKS.

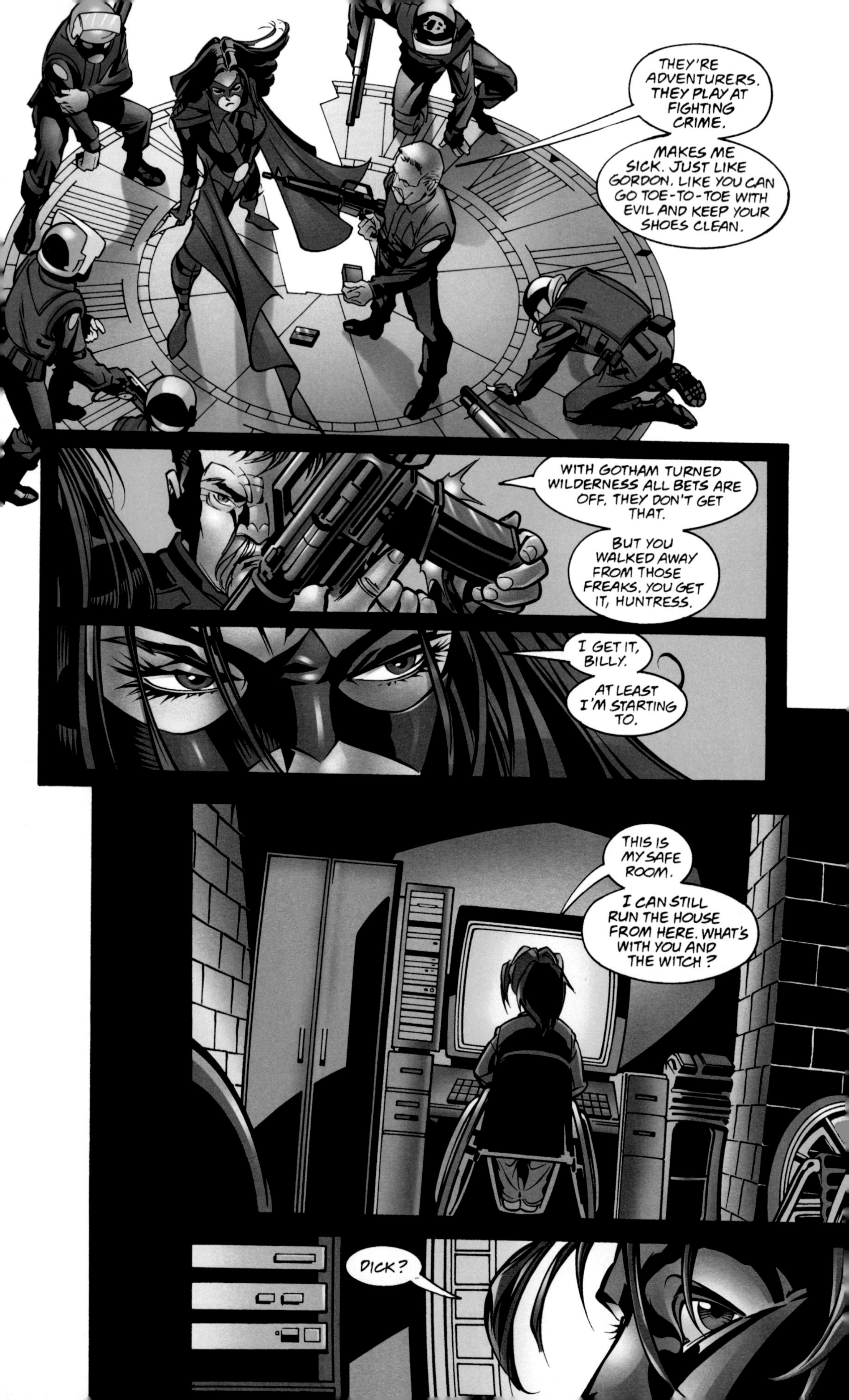
THEY'RE ADVENTURERS. THEY PLAY AT FIGHTING CRIME.
MAKES ME SICK. JUST LIKE GORDON. LIKE YOU CAN GO TOE-TO-TOE WITH EVIL AND KEEP YOUR SHOES CLEAN.
WITH GOTHAM TURNED WILDERNESS ALL BETS ARE OFF. THEY DON'T GET THAT.
BUT YOU WALKED AWAY FROM THOSE FREAKS. YOU GET IT, HUNTRESS.
I GET IT, BILLY.
AT LEAST I'M STARTING TO.
THIS IS MY SAFE ROOM.
I CAN STILL RUN THE HOUSE FROM HERE. WHAT'S WITH YOU AND THE WITCH?
DICK?

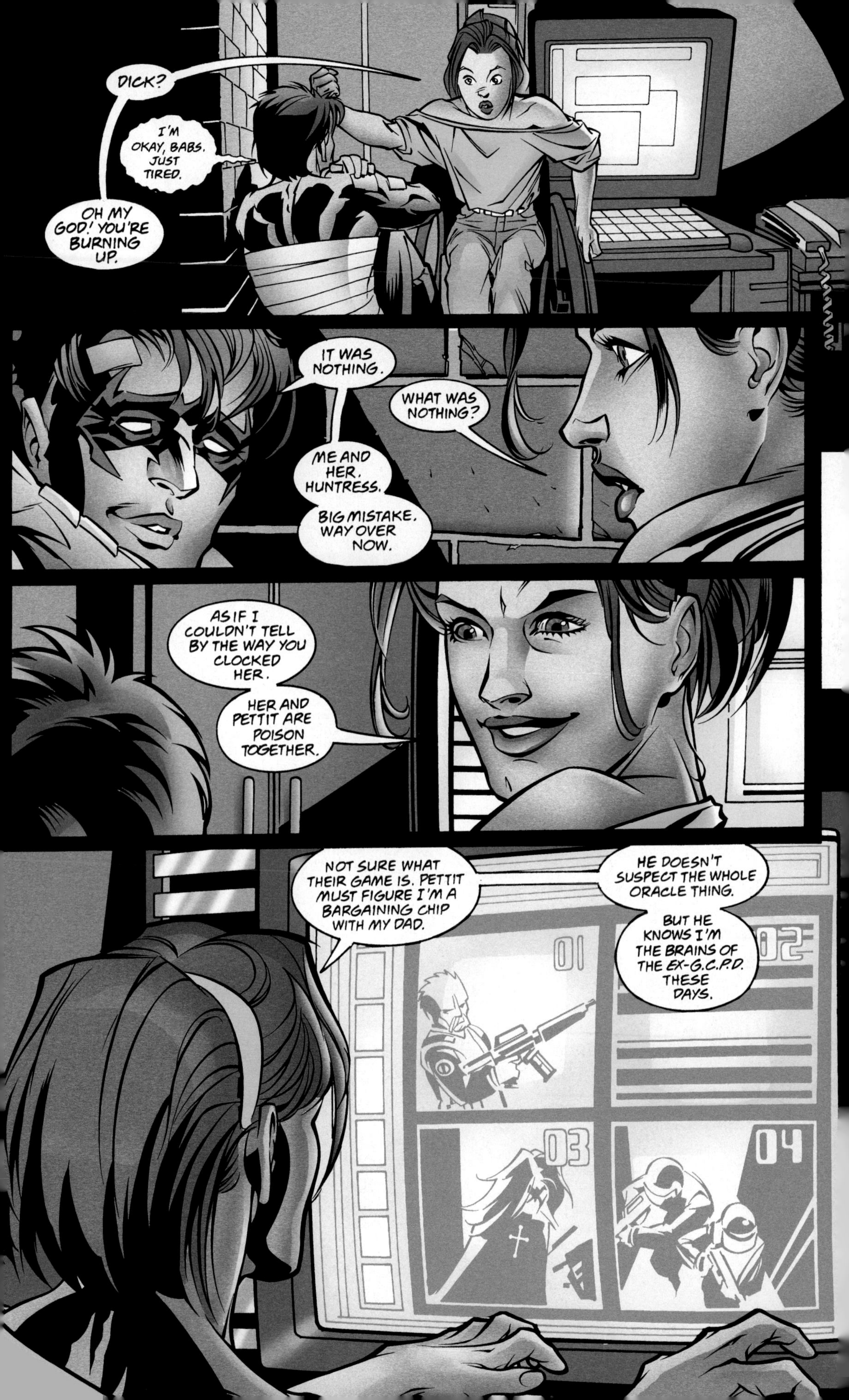
DICK?
I'M OKAY, BABS. JUST TIRED.
OH MY GOD! YOU'RE BURNING UP.
IT WAS NOTHING.
WHAT WAS NOTHING?
ME AND HER. HUNTRESS.
BIG MISTAKE. WAY OVER NOW.
AS IF I COULDN'T TELL BY THE WAY YOU CLOCKED HER.
HER AND PETTIT ARE POISON TOGETHER.
NOT SURE WHAT THEIR GAME IS. PETTIT MUST FIGURE I'M A BARGAINING CHIP WITH MY DAD.
HE DOESN'T SUSPECT THE WHOLE ORACLE THING.
BUT HE KNOWS I'M THE BRAINS OF THE EX-G.C.P.D. THESE DAYS.
01
02
03
04

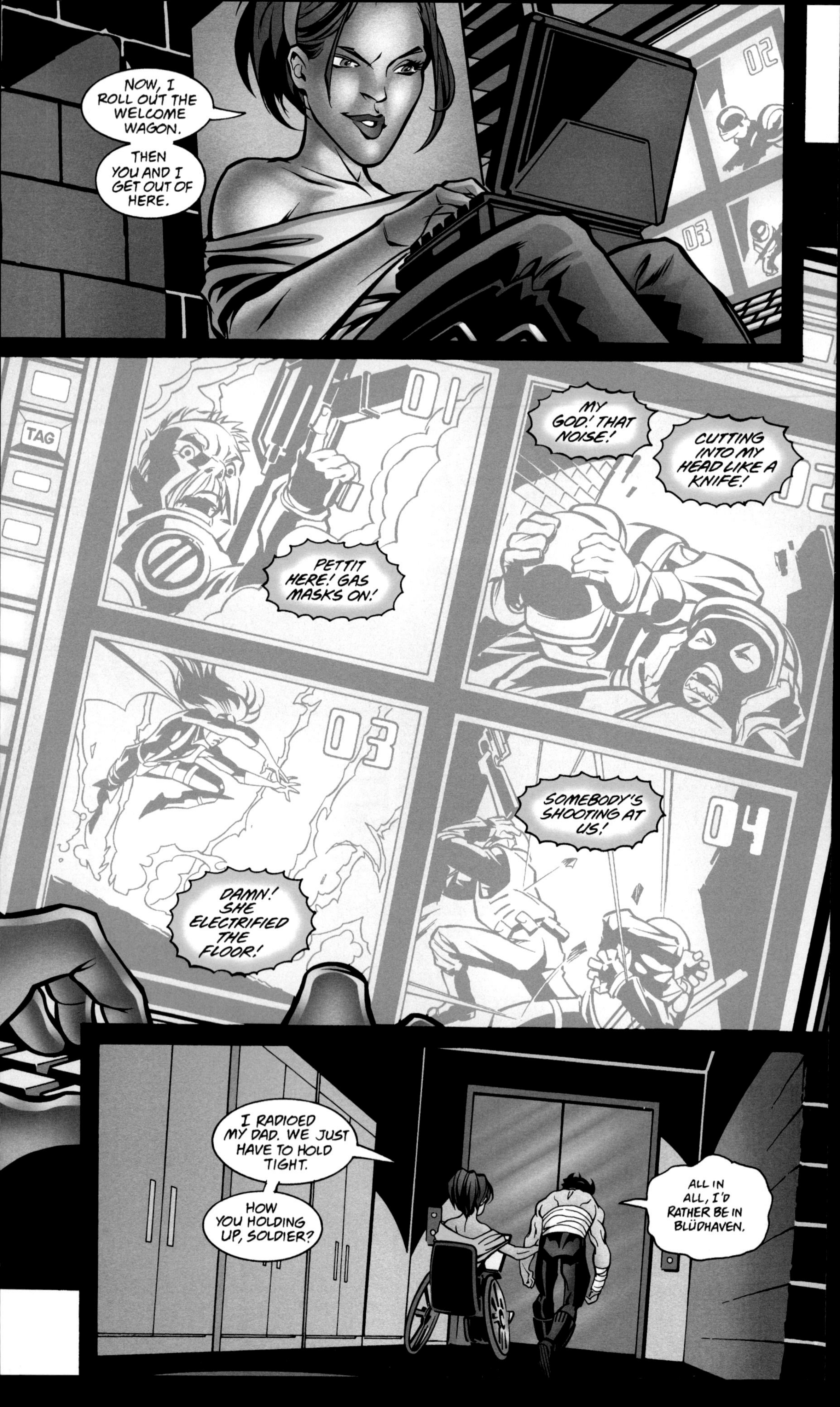

NOW, I ROLL OUT THE WELCOME WAGON.
THEN YOU AND I GET OUT OF HERE.
02
03
TAG
01
MY GOD! THAT NOISE!
CUTTING INTO MY HEAD LIKE A KNIFE!
PETTIT HERE! GAS MASKS ON!
03
SOMEBODY'S SHOOTING AT US!
04
DAMN! SHE ELECTRIFIED THE FLOOR!
I RADIOED MY DAD. WE JUST HAVE TO HOLD TIGHT.
HOW YOU HOLDING UP, SOLDIER?
ALL IN ALL, I'D RATHER BE IN BLÜDHAVEN.

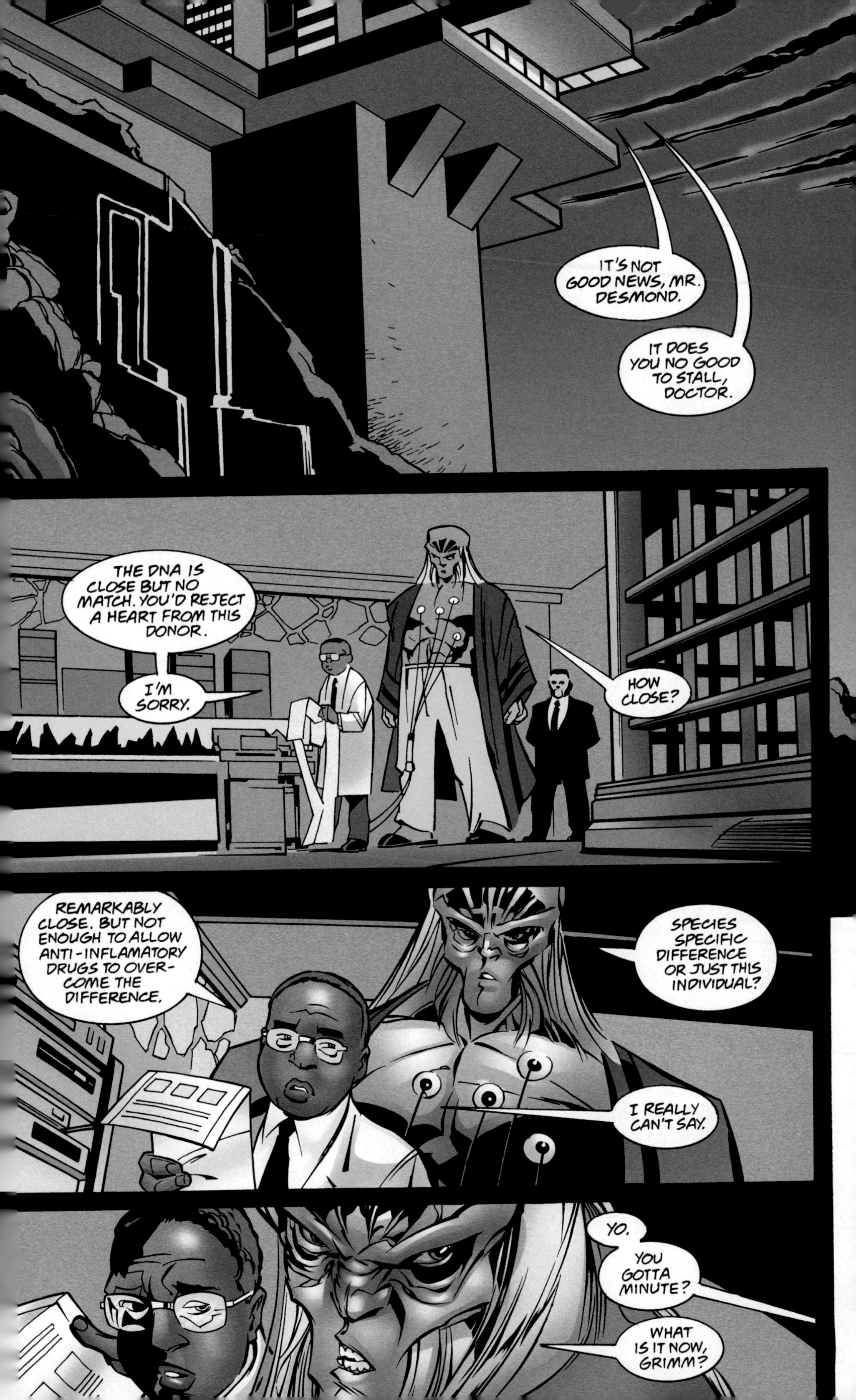
IT'S NOT GOOD NEWS, MR. DESMOND.
IT DOES YOU NO GOOD TO STALL, DOCTOR.
THE DNA IS CLOSE BUT NO MATCH. YOU'D REJECT A HEART FROM THIS DONOR.
I'M SORRY.
HOW CLOSE?
REMARKABLY CLOSE. BUT NOT ENOUGH TO ALLOW ANTI-INFLAMATORY DRUGS TO OVER-COME THE DIFFERENCE.
SPECIES SPECIFIC DIFFERENCE OR JUST THIS INDIVIDUAL?
I REALLY CAN'T SAY.
YO.
YOU GOTTA MINUTE?
WHAT IS IT NOW, GRIMM?

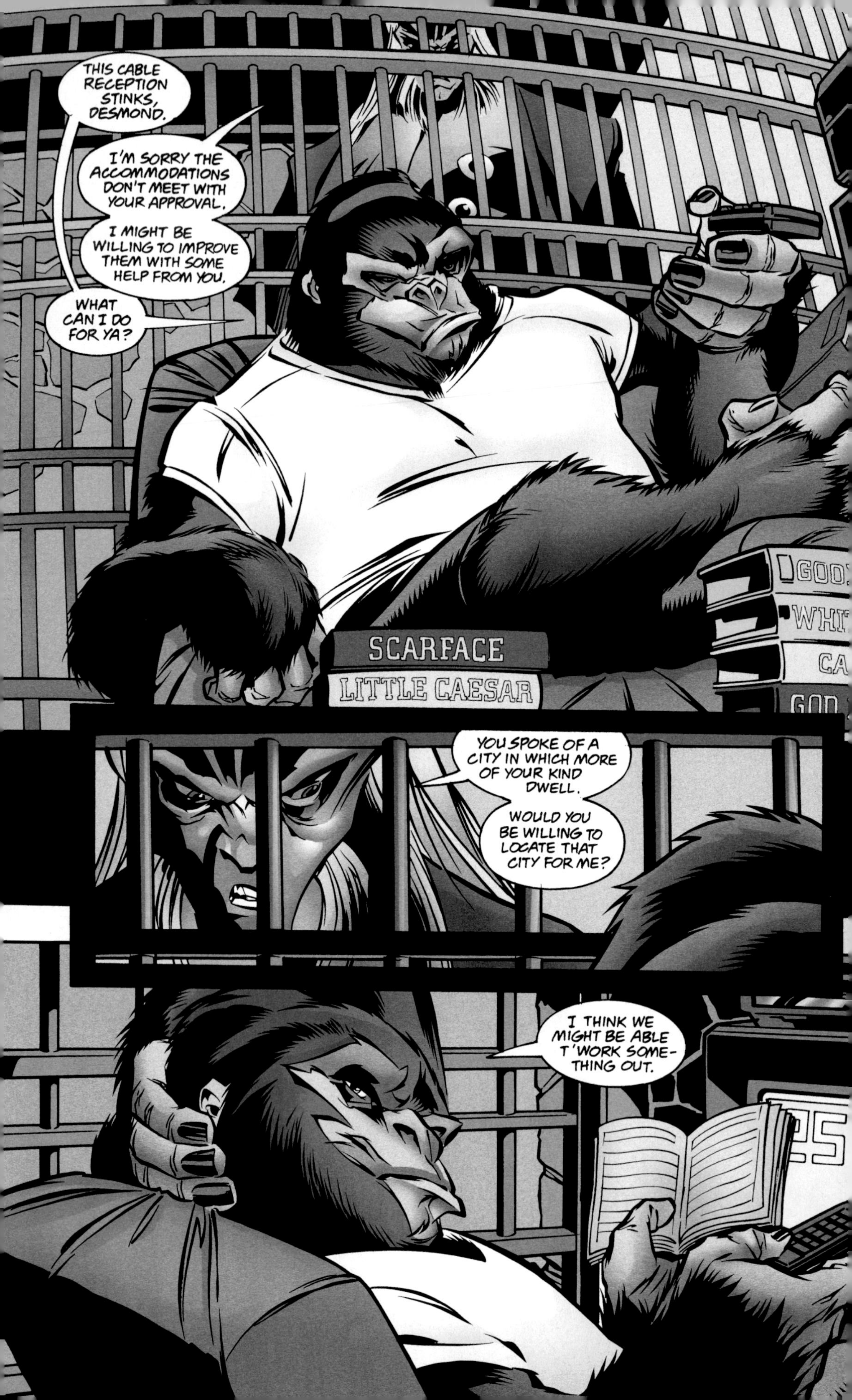
THIS CABLE RECEPTION STINKS, DESMOND.
I'M SORRY THE ACCOMMODATIONS DON'T MEET WITH YOUR APPROVAL.
I MIGHT BE WILLING TO IMPROVE THEM WITH SOME HELP FROM YOU.
WHAT CAN I DO FOR YA?
SCARFACE
LITTLE CAESAR
YOU SPOKE OF A CITY IN WHICH MORE OF YOUR KIND DWELL.
WOULD YOU BE WILLING TO LOCATE THAT CITY FOR ME?
I THINK WE MIGHT BE ABLE T'WORK SOMETHING OUT.

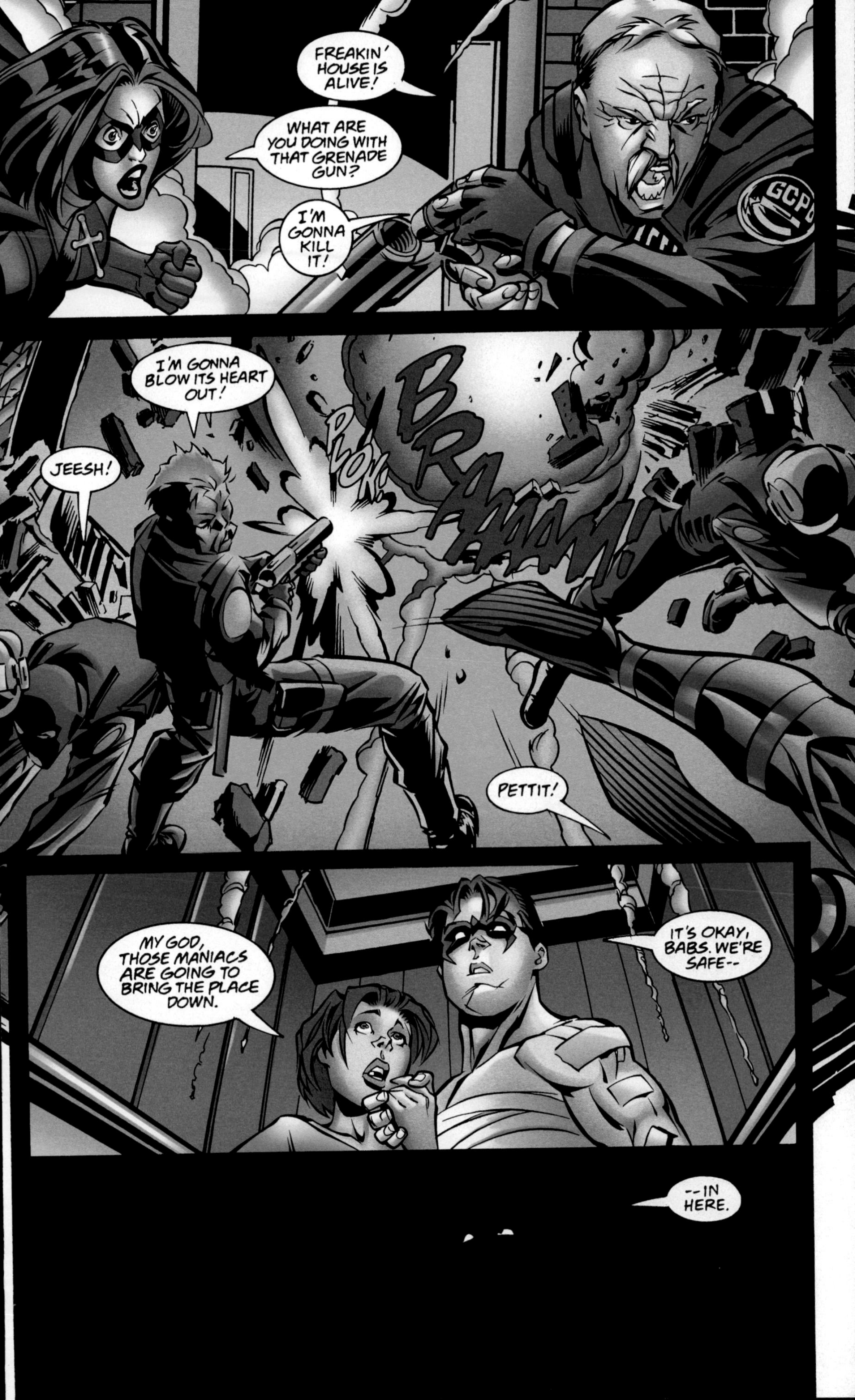
FREAKIN' HOUSE IS ALIVE!
WHAT ARE YOU DOING WITH THAT GRENADE GUN?
I'M GONNA KILL IT!
I'M GONNA BLOW ITS HEART OUT!
JEESH!
PLOK!
BRAAAAM!
PETTIT!
MY GOD, THOSE MANIACS ARE GOING TO BRING THE PLACE DOWN.
IT'S OKAY, BABS. WE'RE SAFE--
--IN HERE.

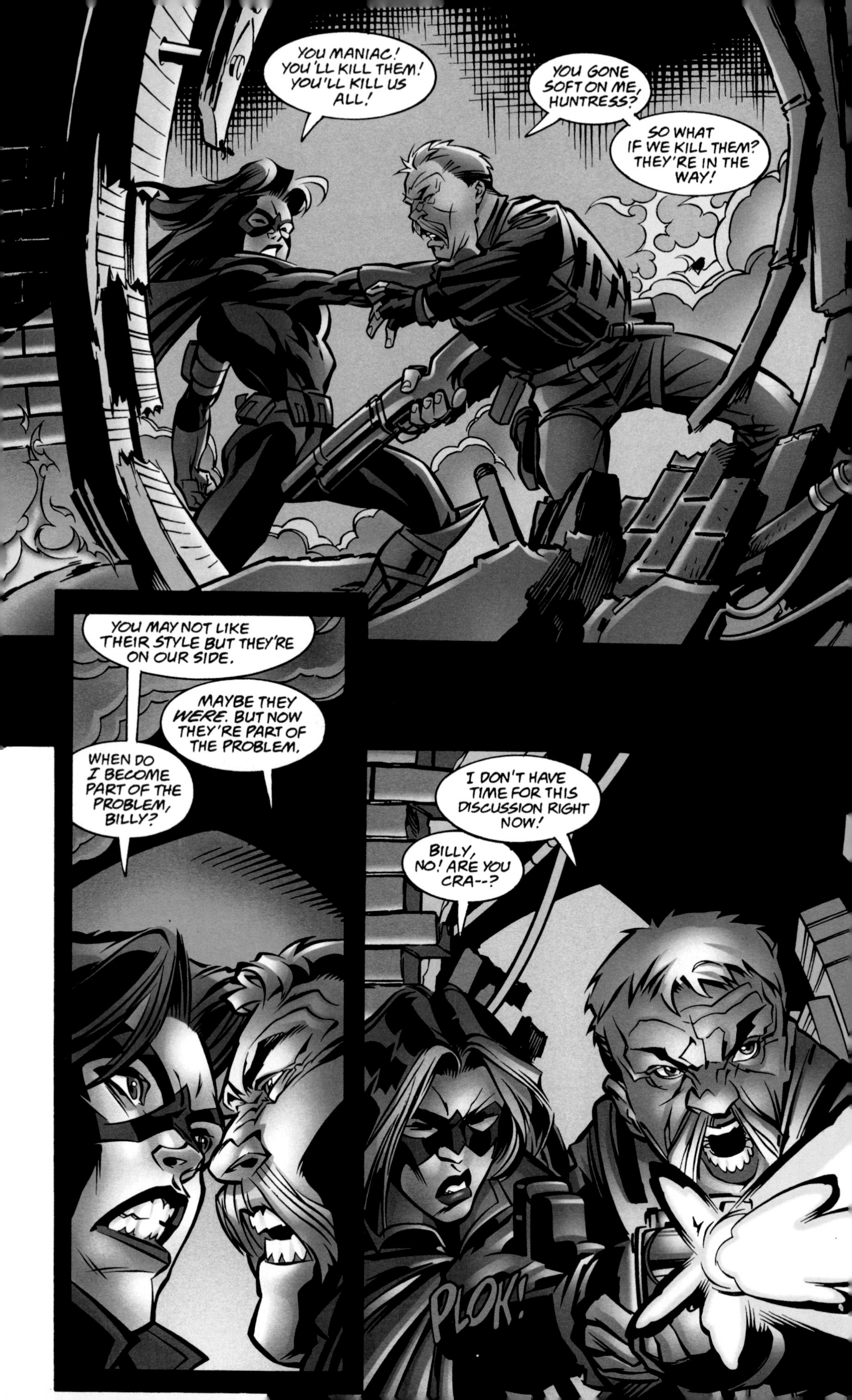
YOU MANIAC! YOU'LL KILL THEM! YOU'LL KILL US ALL!
YOU GONE SOFT ON ME, HUNTRESS?
SO WHAT IF WE KILL THEM? THEY'RE IN THE WAY!
YOU MAY NOT LIKE THEIR STYLE BUT THEY'RE ON OUR SIDE.
MAYBE THEY WERE. BUT NOW THEY'RE PART OF THE PROBLEM.
WHEN DO I BECOME PART OF THE PROBLEM, BILLY?
I DON'T HAVE TIME FOR THIS DISCUSSION RIGHT NOW!
BILLY, NO! ARE YOU CRA--?
PLOK!

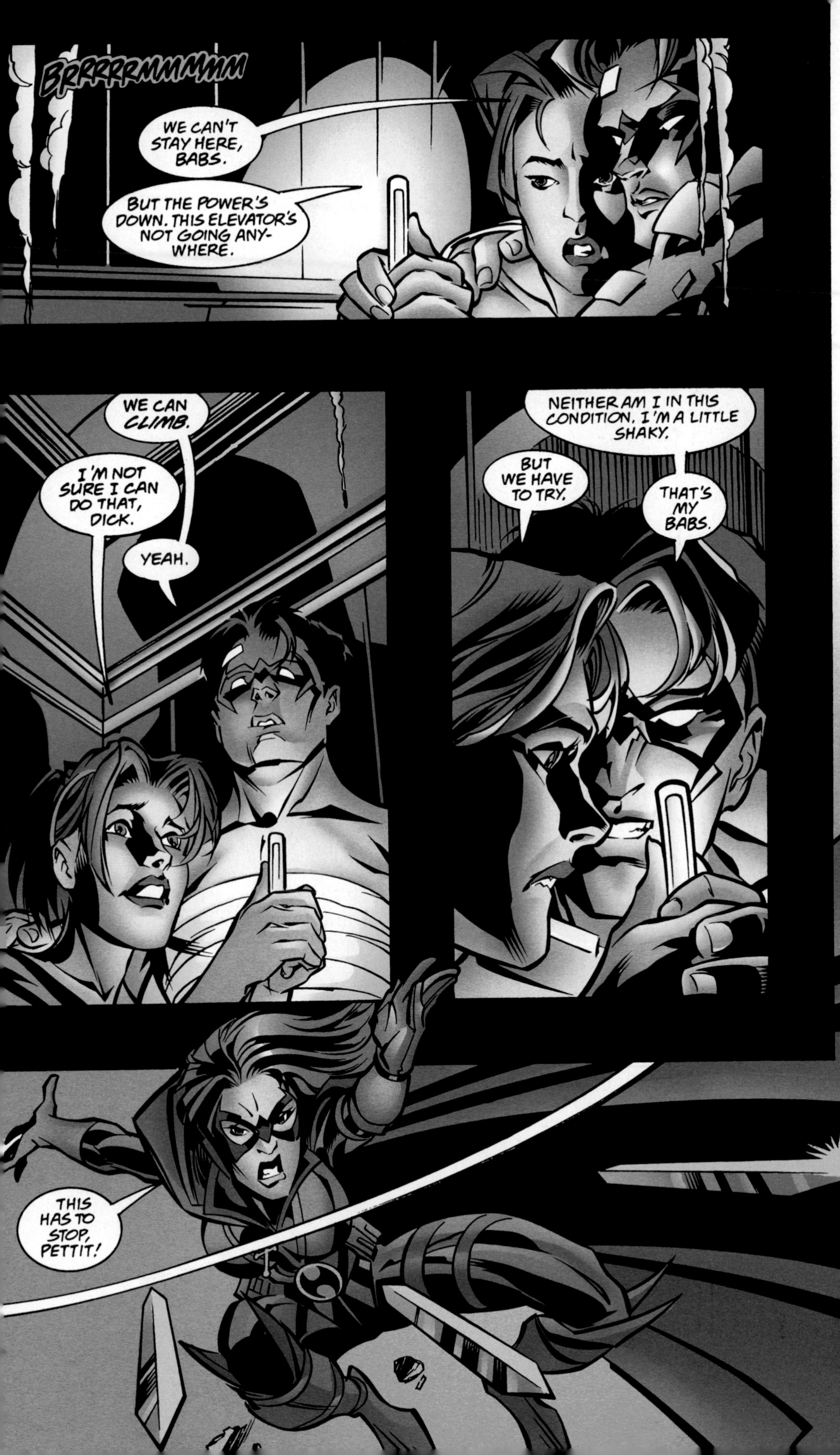
BRRRRRMMMMM
WE CAN'T STAY HERE, BABS.
BUT THE POWER'S DOWN. THIS ELEVATOR'S NOT GOING ANYWHERE.
WE CAN CLIMB.
I'M NOT SURE I CAN DO THAT, DICK.
YEAH.
NEITHER AM I IN THIS CONDITION. I'M A LITTLE SHAKY.
BUT WE HAVE TO TRY.
THAT'S MY BABS.
THIS HAS TO STOP, PETTIT!

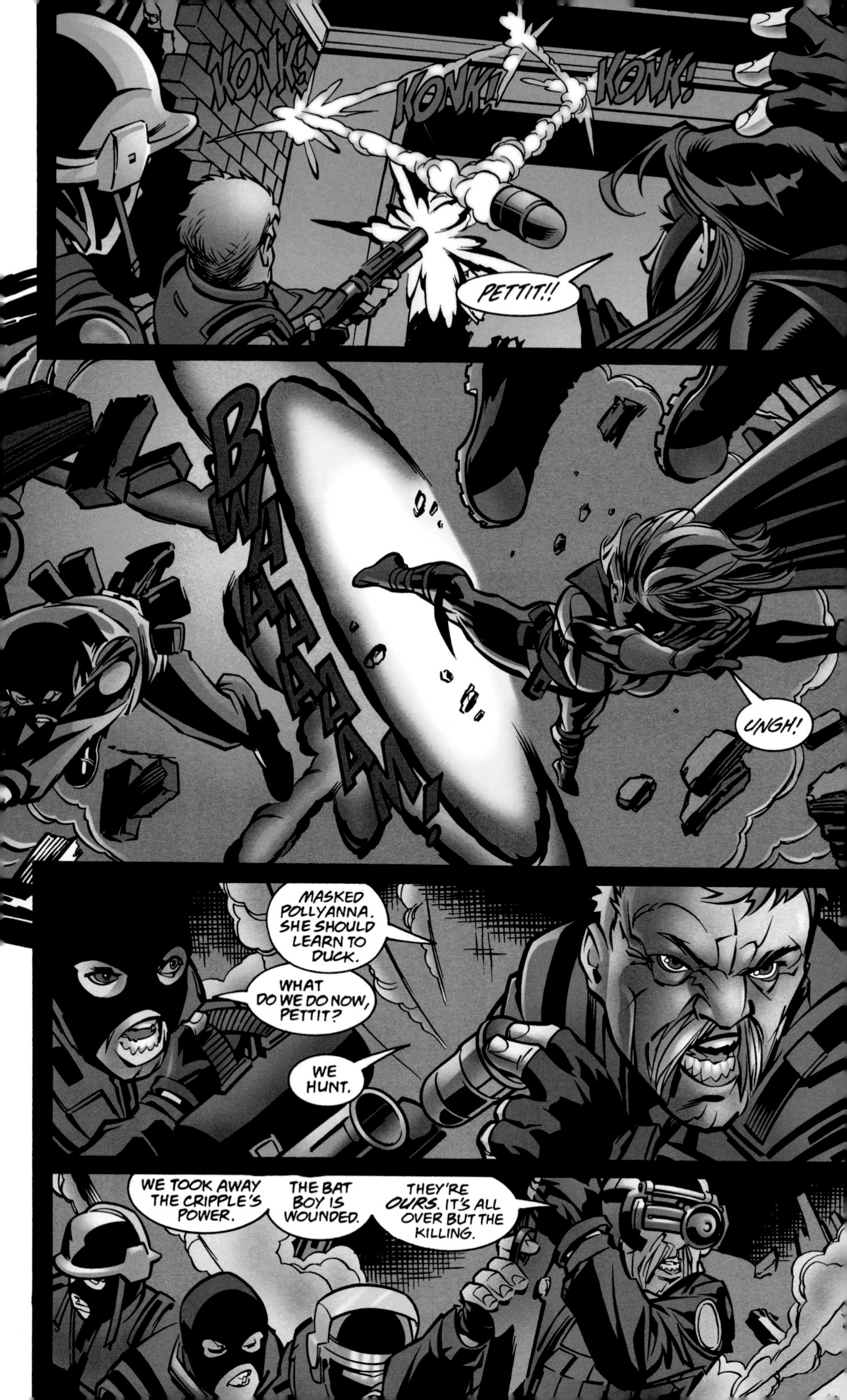
KONK!
KONK!!
KONK!
PETTIT!!
BWAAAAAAAM!
UNGH!
MASKED POLLYANNA. SHE SHOULD LEARN TO DUCK.
WHAT DO WE DO NOW, PETTIT?
WE HUNT.
WE TOOK AWAY THE CRIPPLE'S POWER.
THE BAT BOY IS WOUNDED.
THEY'RE OURS. IT'S ALL OVER BUT THE KILLING.

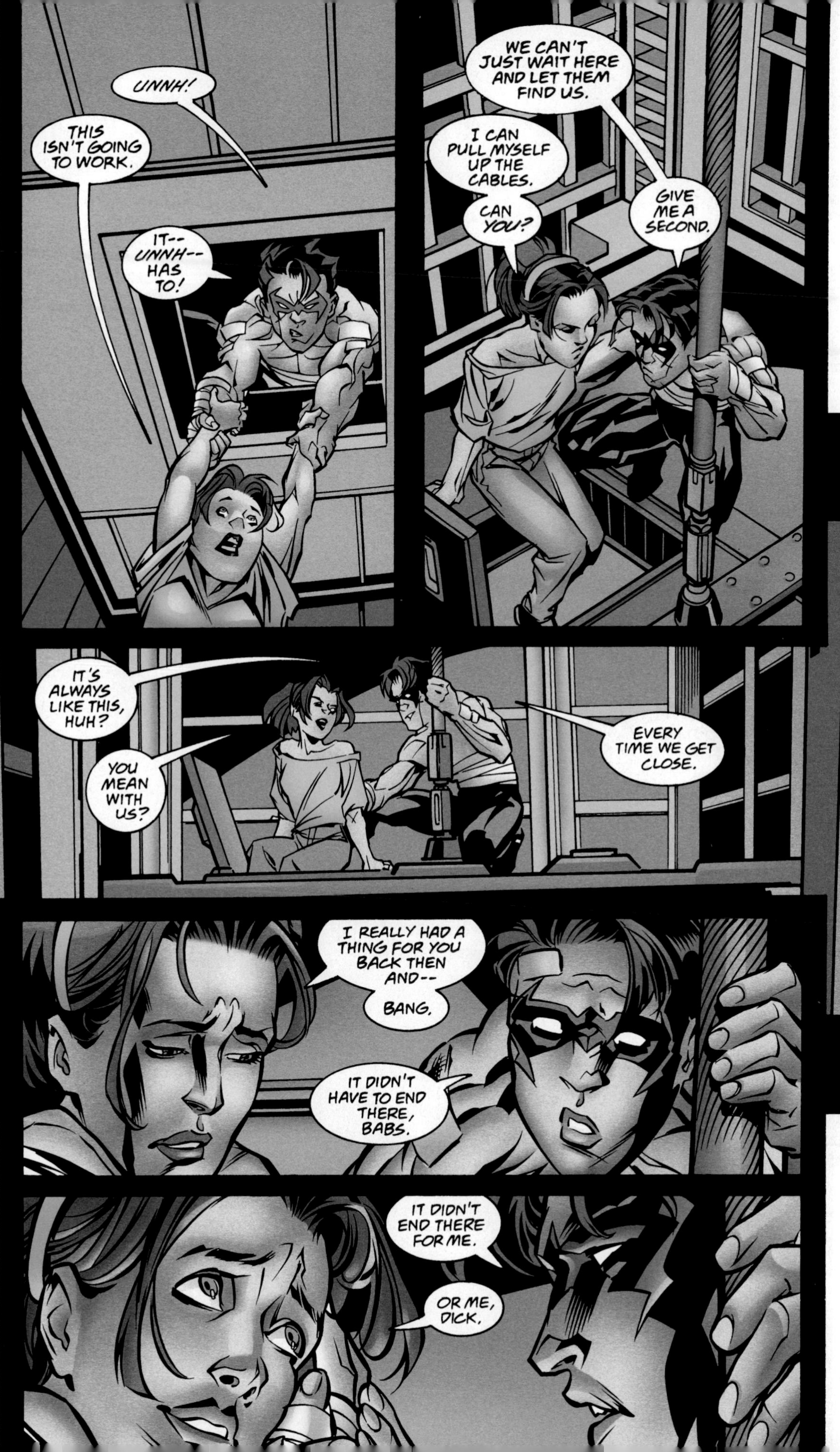
UNNH!
THIS ISN'T GOING TO WORK.
IT-- UNNH-- HAS TO!
WE CAN'T JUST WAIT HERE AND LET THEM FIND US.
I CAN PULL MYSELF UP THE CABLES.
CAN YOU?
GIVE ME A SECOND.
IT'S ALWAYS LIKE THIS, HUH?
YOU MEAN WITH US?
EVERY TIME WE GET CLOSE.
I REALLY HAD A THING FOR YOU BACK THEN AND--
BANG.
IT DIDN'T HAVE TO END THERE, BABS.
IT DIDN'T END THERE FOR ME.
OR ME, DICK.

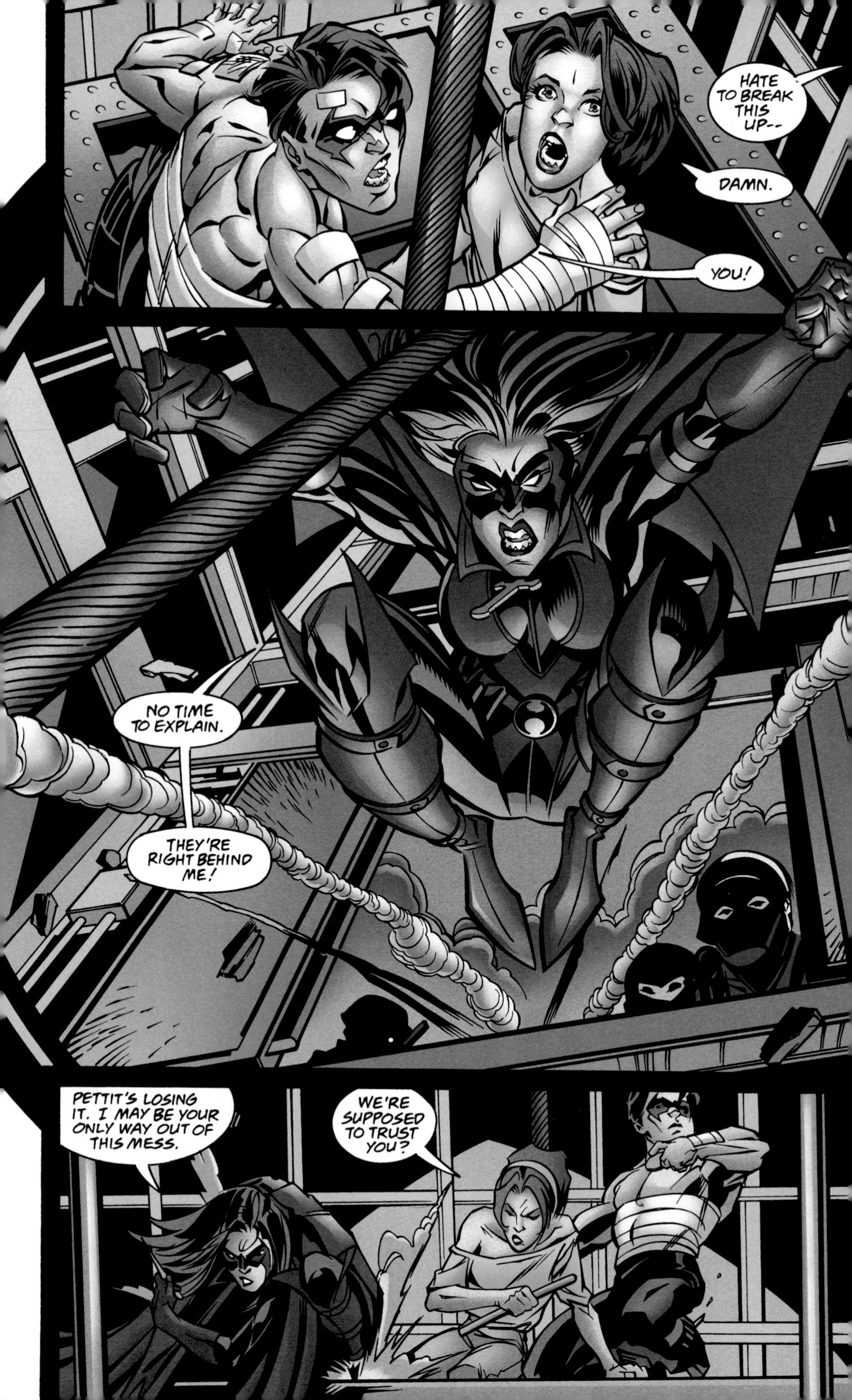
HATE TO BREAK THIS UP--
DAMN.
YOU!
NO TIME TO EXPLAIN.
THEY'RE RIGHT BEHIND ME!
PETTIT'S LOSING IT. I MAY BE YOUR ONLY WAY OUT OF THIS MESS.
WE'RE SUPPOSED TO TRUST YOU?

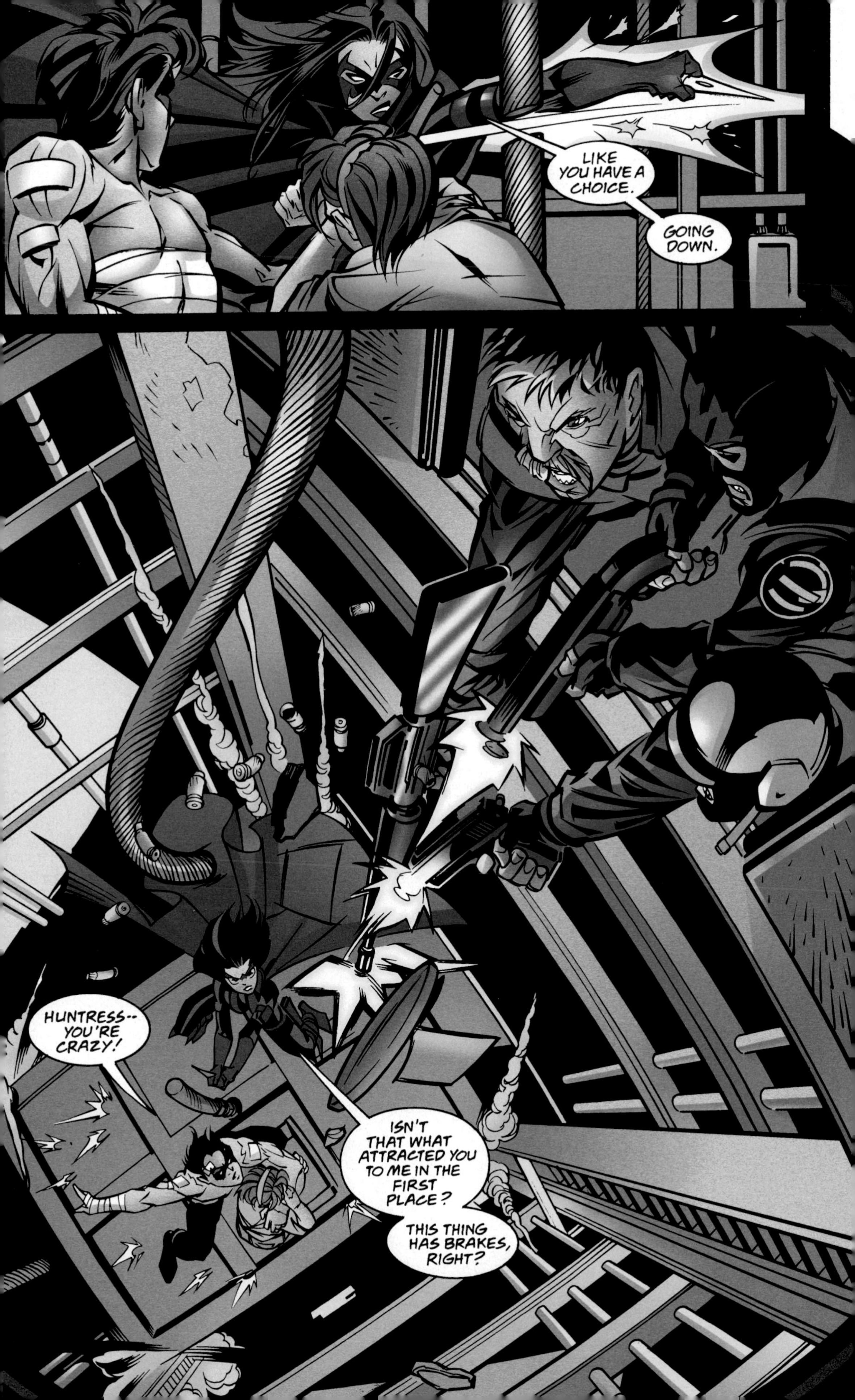
LIKE YOU HAVE A CHOICE.
GOING DOWN.
HUNTRESS-- YOU'RE CRAZY!
ISN'T THAT WHAT ATTRACTED YOU TO ME IN THE FIRST PLACE?
THIS THING HAS BRAKES, RIGHT?

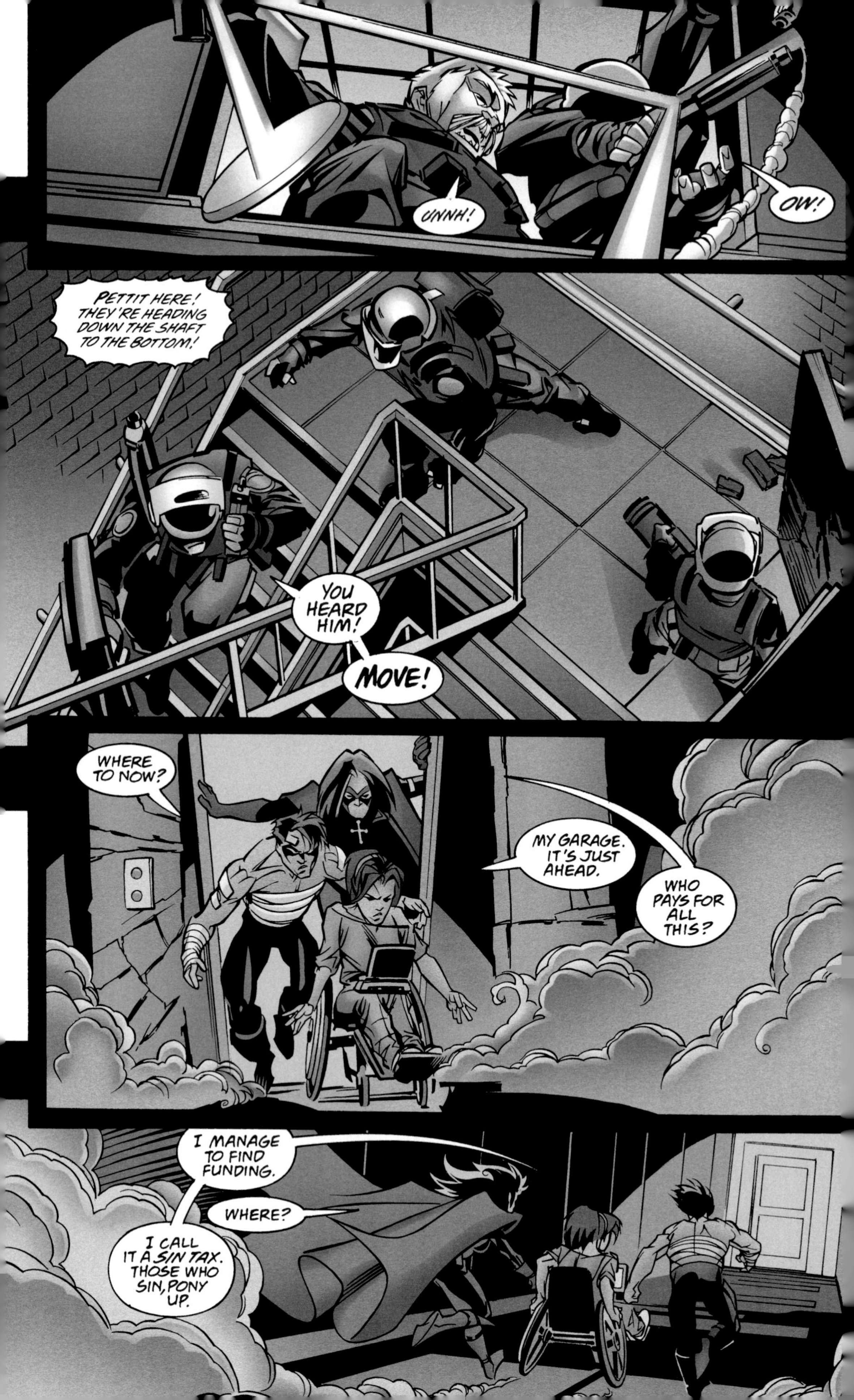
UNNH!
OW!
PETTIT HERE! THEY'RE HEADING DOWN THE SHAFT TO THE BOTTOM!
YOU HEARD HIM!
MOVE!
WHERE TO NOW?
MY GARAGE. IT'S JUST AHEAD.
WHO PAYS FOR ALL THIS?
I MANAGE TO FIND FUNDING.
WHERE?
I CALL IT A SIN TAX. THOSE WHO SIN, PONY UP.

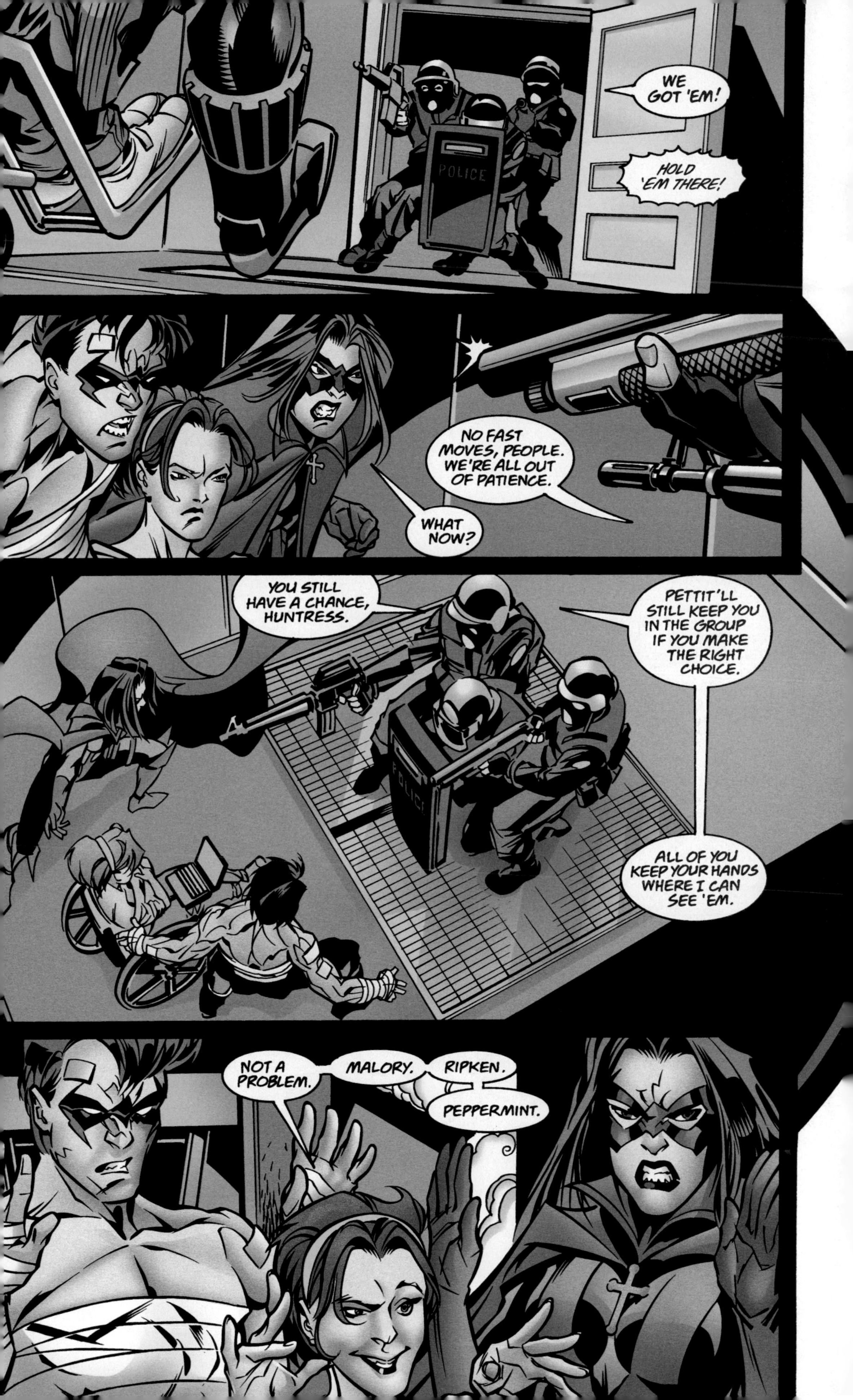
WE GOT 'EM!
HOLD 'EM THERE!
NO FAST MOVES, PEOPLE. WE'RE ALL OUT OF PATIENCE.
WHAT NOW?
YOU STILL HAVE A CHANCE, HUNTRESS.
PETTIT'LL STILL KEEP YOU IN THE GROUP IF YOU MAKE THE RIGHT CHOICE.
ALL OF YOU KEEP YOUR HANDS WHERE I CAN SEE 'EM.
NOT A PROBLEM.
MALORY.
RIPKEN.
PEPPERMINT.

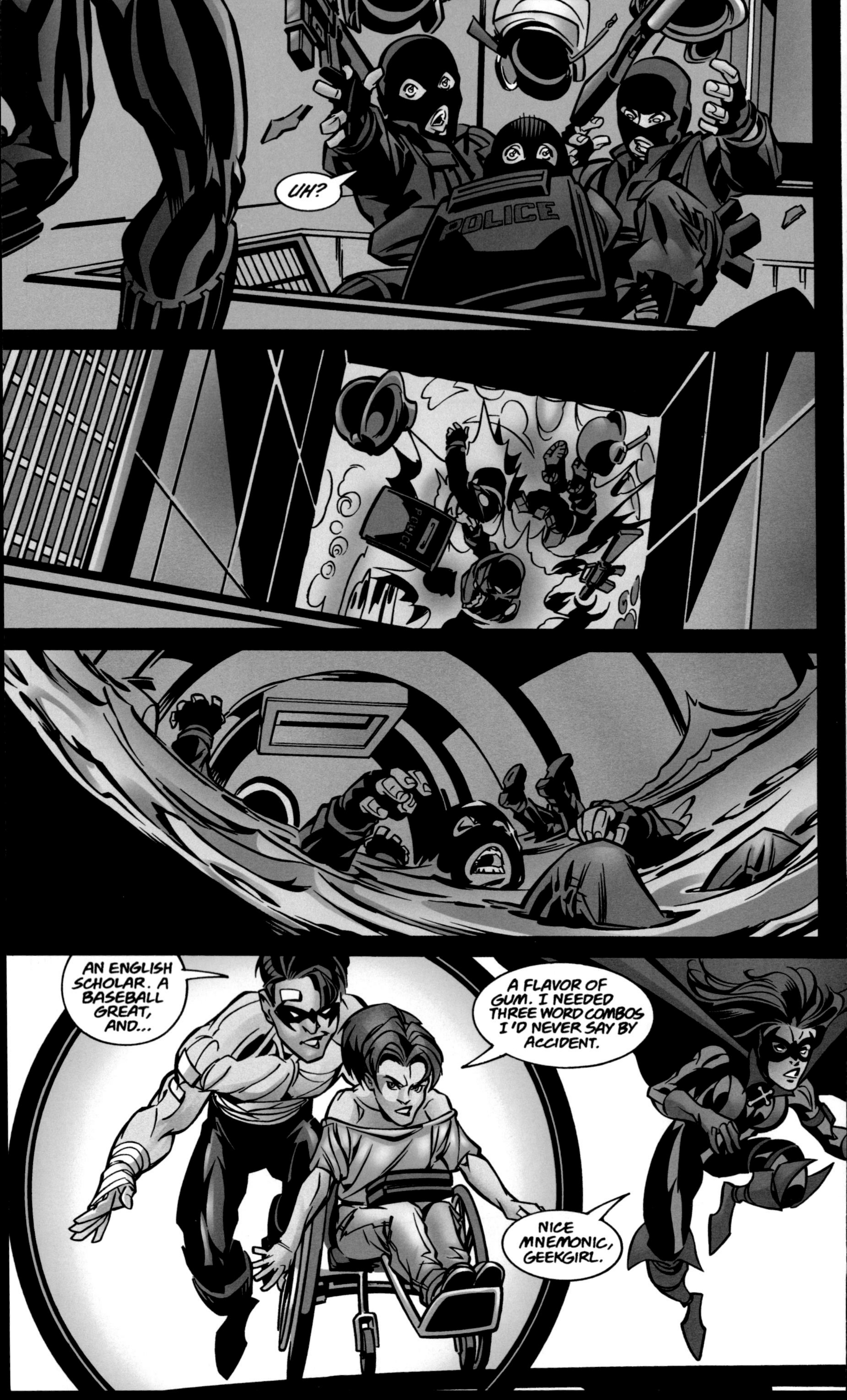
UH?
POLICE
POLICE
AN ENGLISH SCHOLAR. A BASEBALL GREAT, AND...
A FLAVOR OF GUM. I NEEDED THREE WORD COMBOS I'D NEVER SAY BY ACCIDENT.
NICE MNEMONIC, GEEKGIRL.

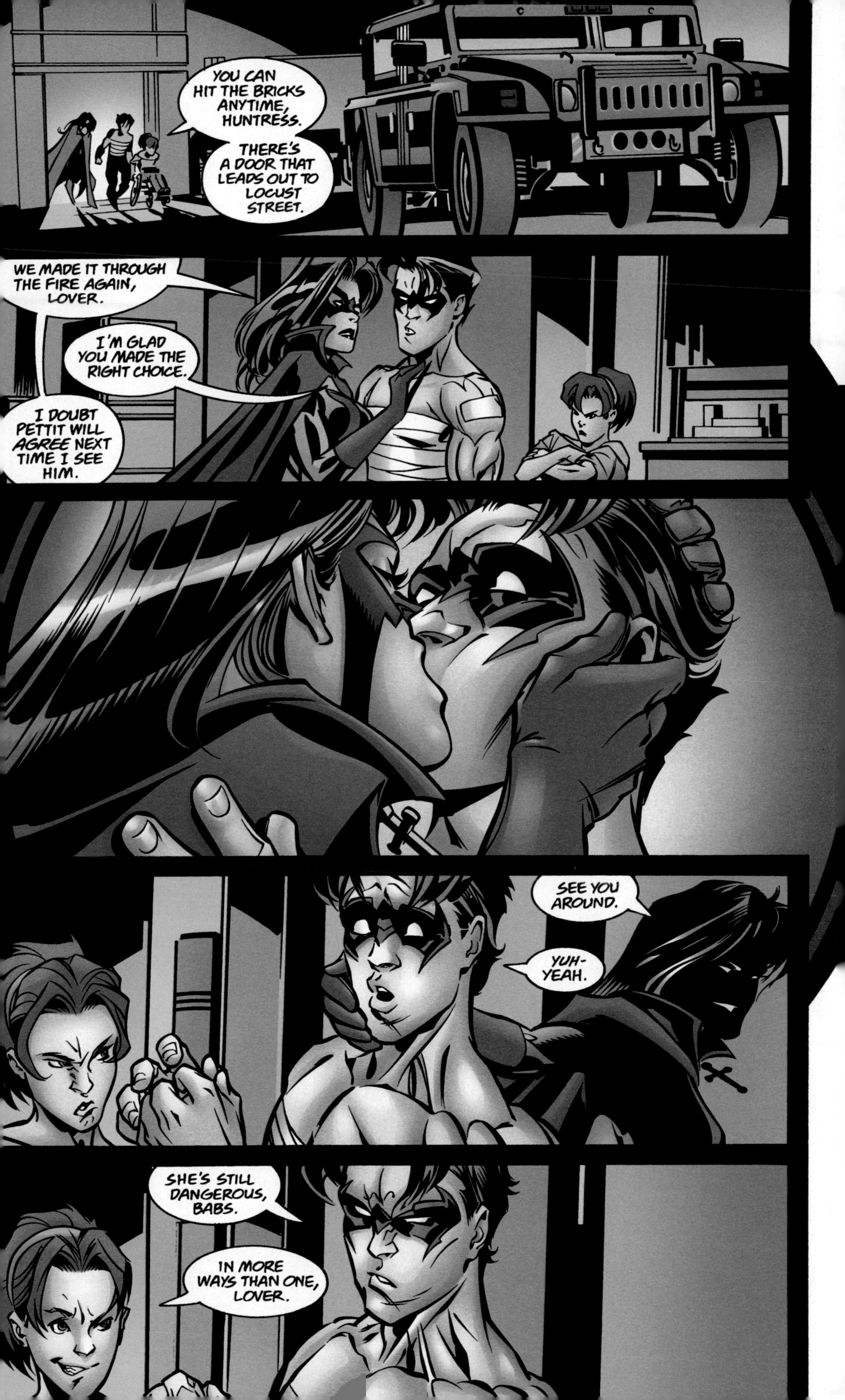
YOU CAN HIT THE BRICKS ANYTIME, HUNTRESS.
THERE'S A DOOR THAT LEADS OUT TO LOCUST STREET.
WE MADE IT THROUGH THE FIRE AGAIN, LOVER.
I'M GLAD YOU MADE THE RIGHT CHOICE.
I DOUBT PETTIT WILL AGREE NEXT TIME I SEE HIM.
SEE YOU AROUND.
YUH-YEAH.
SHE'S STILL DANGEROUS, BABS.
IN MORE WAYS THAN ONE, LOVER.

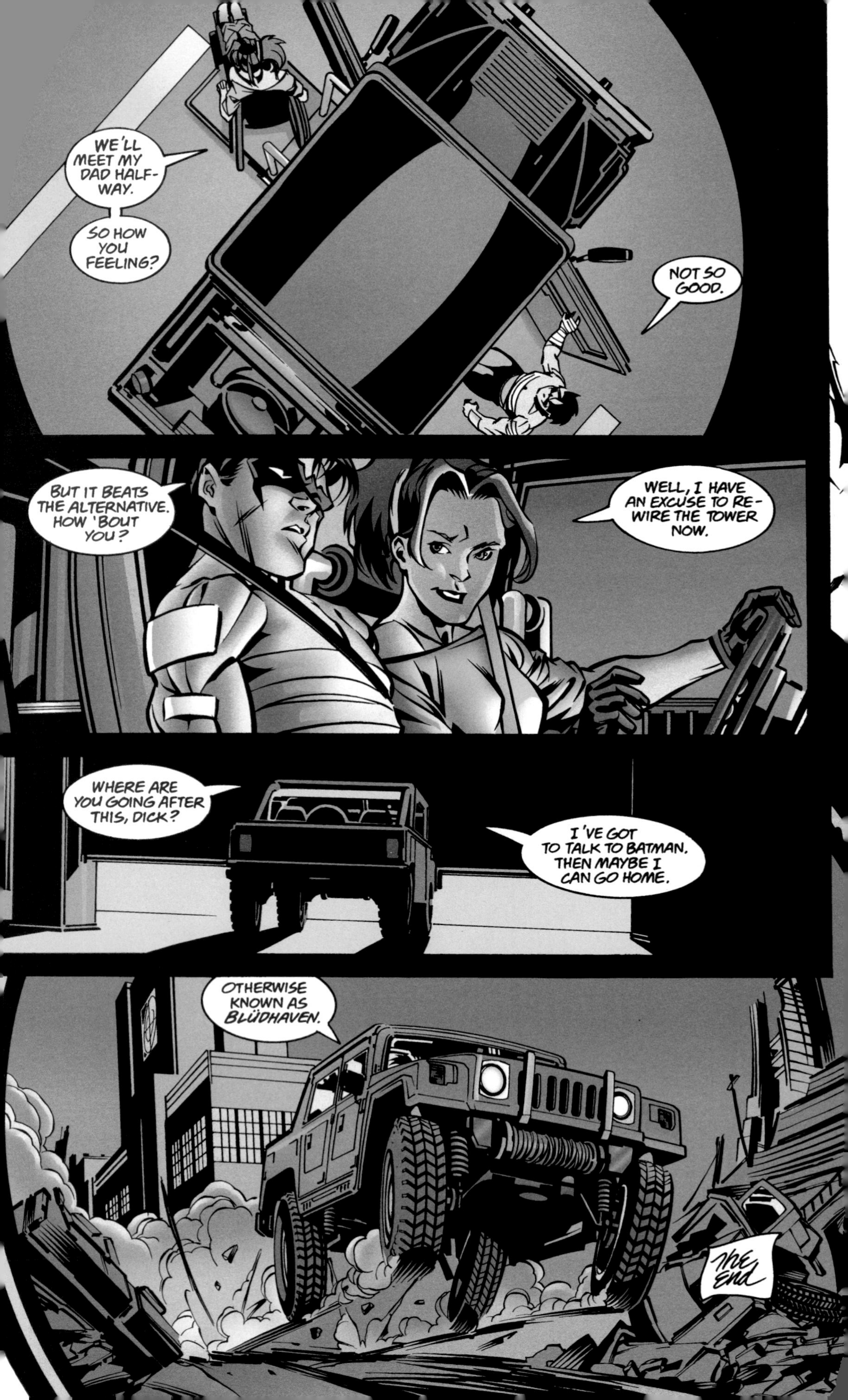
WE'LL MEET MY DAD HALF-WAY.
SO HOW YOU FEELING?
NOT SO GOOD.
BUT IT BEATS THE ALTERNATIVE. HOW 'BOUT YOU?
WELL, I HAVE AN EXCUSE TO RE-WIRE THE TOWER NOW.
WHERE ARE YOU GOING AFTER THIS, DICK?
I'VE GOT TO TALK TO BATMAN. THEN MAYBE I CAN GO HOME.
OTHERWISE KNOWN AS BLÜDHAVEN.
THE END

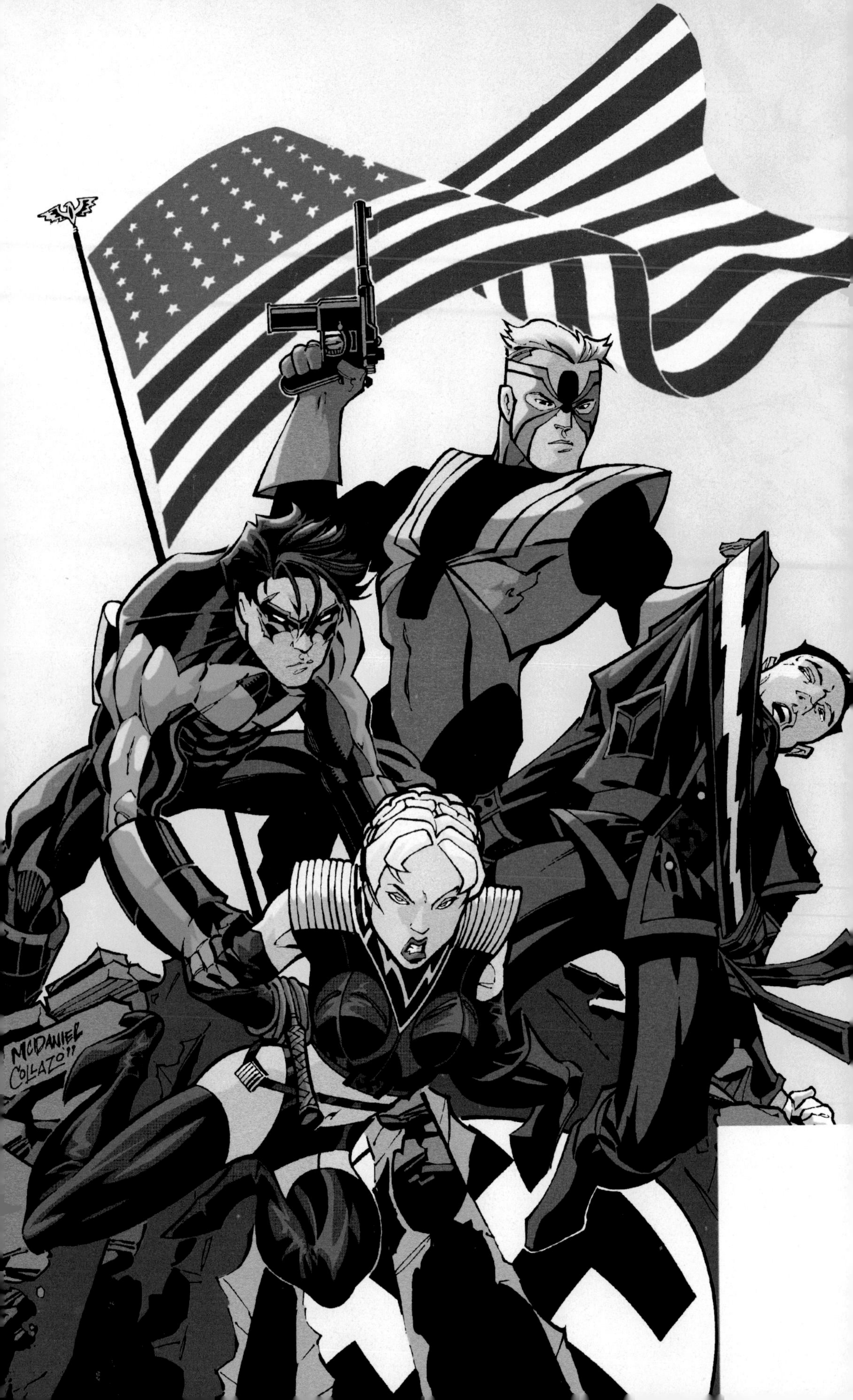

MCDANIEL
COLLAZO '11

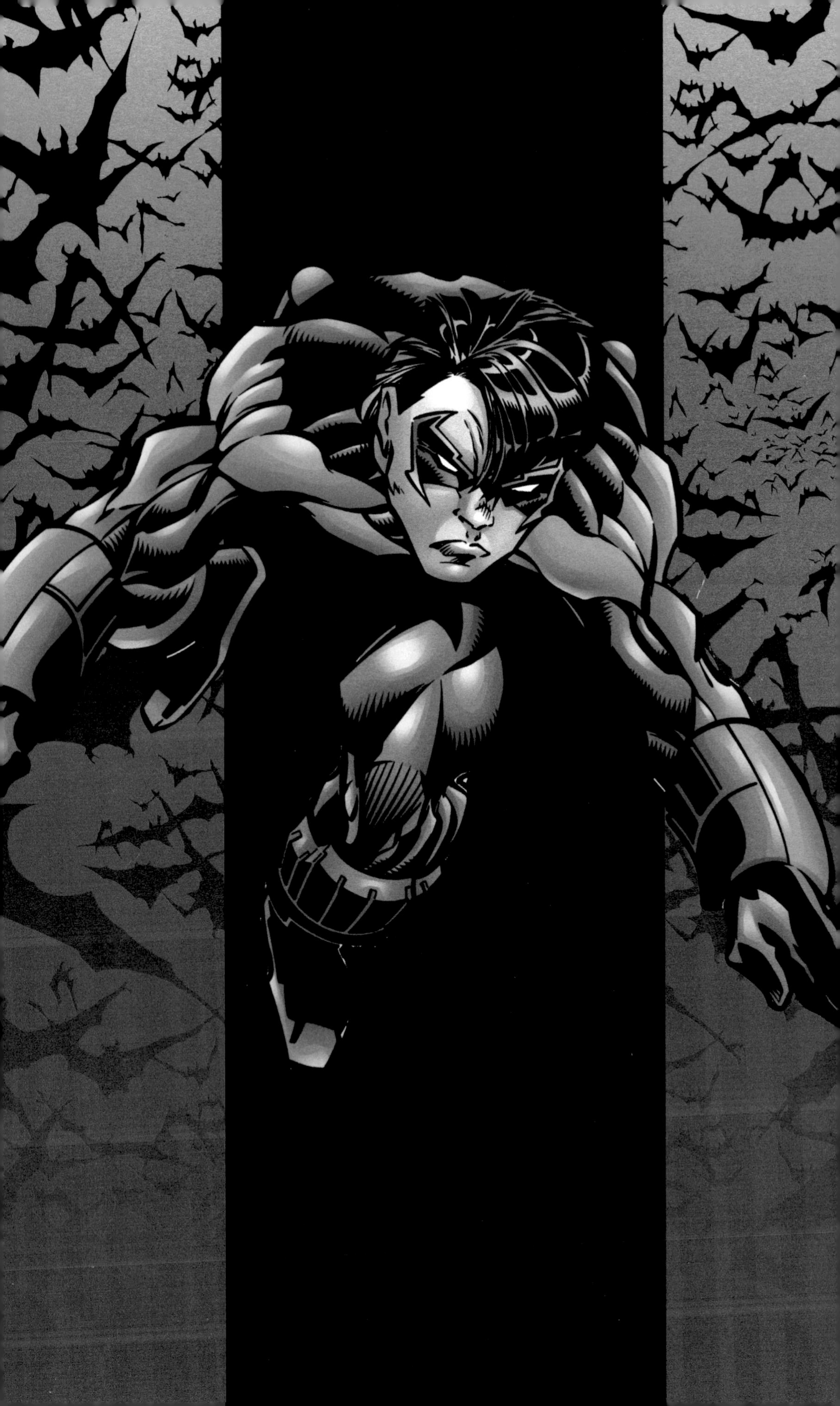

THE DEVIL DIES AT DAWN

Little did Nightwing and the Tarantula know that by the end of the evening they would be facing a menace from another time, a time when all free men were threatened by the boot heel of tyranny.

Here in tne lobby of Blüdhaven's finest four-star hotel would play out a drama that the world had thought over, its final curtain call fifty years past.

"Who ***are*** *these jokers?" Nightwing growled in righteous anger.*

"I know them well, son." Tarantula said, a note of weariness in his voice

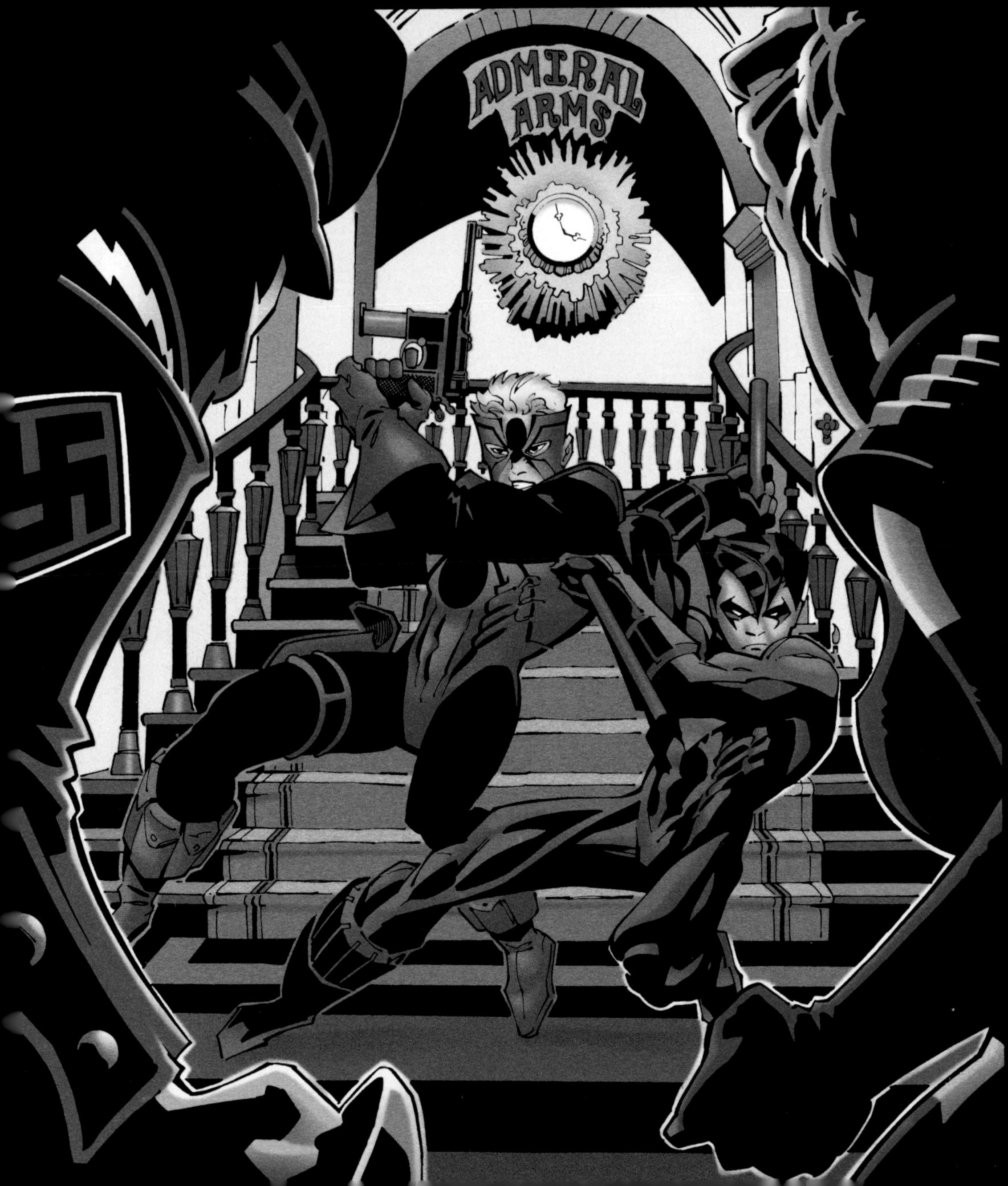
ADMIRAL ARMS

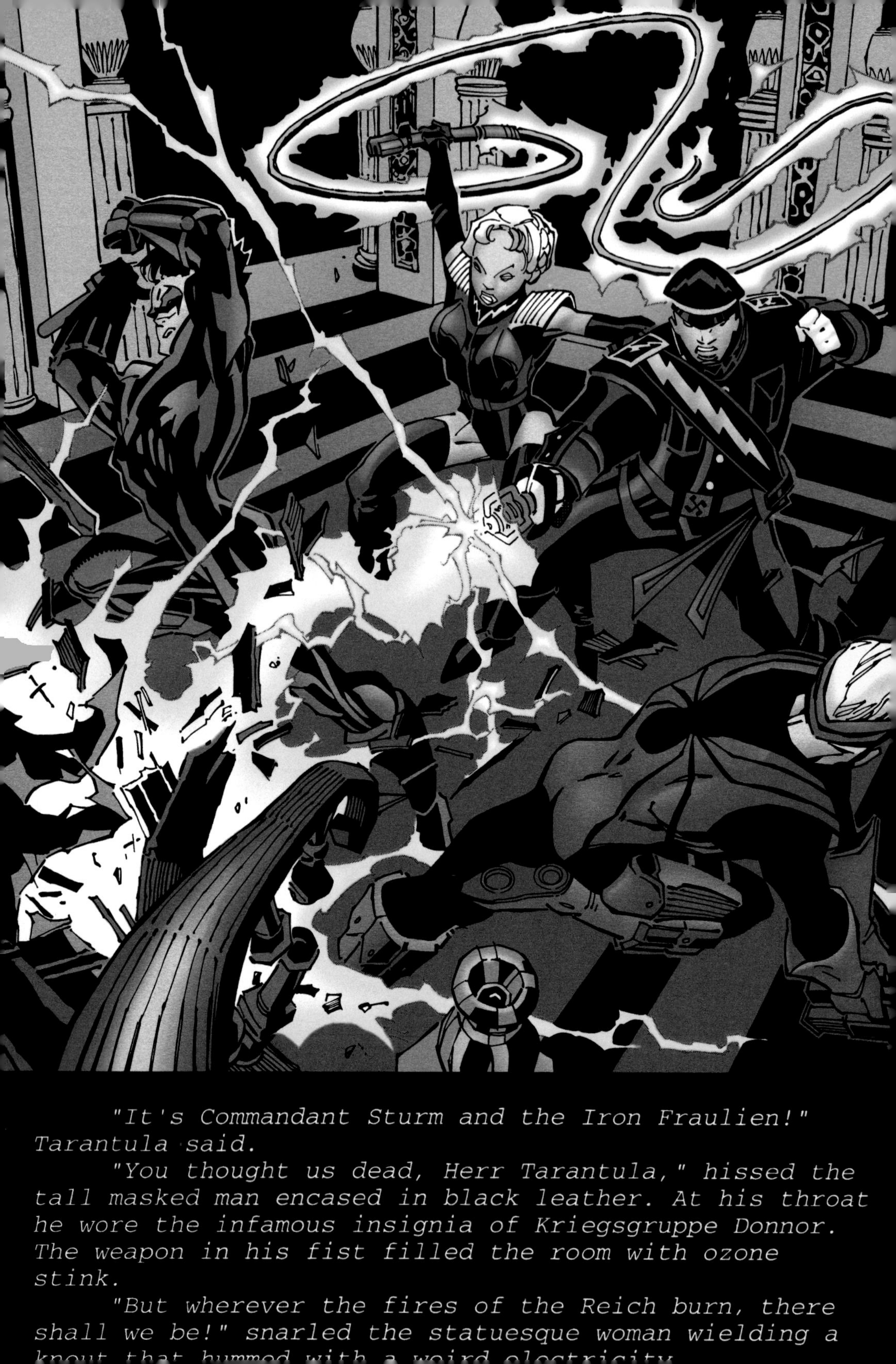

"It's Commandant Sturm and the Iron Fraulien!" Tarantula said.

"You thought us dead, Herr Tarantula," hissed the tall masked man encased in black leather. At his throat he wore the infamous insignia of Kriegsgruppe Donnor. The weapon in his fist filled the room with ozone stink.

"But wherever the fires of the Reich burn, there shall we be!" snarled the statuesque woman wielding a knout that hummed with a weird electricity.

and was slow to react. A blast of energy from Sturm's gun enveloped him, and the young hero was engulfed in living fire.

Suddenly it was as though all those years were as nothing, and John Law stood at the brink once more.

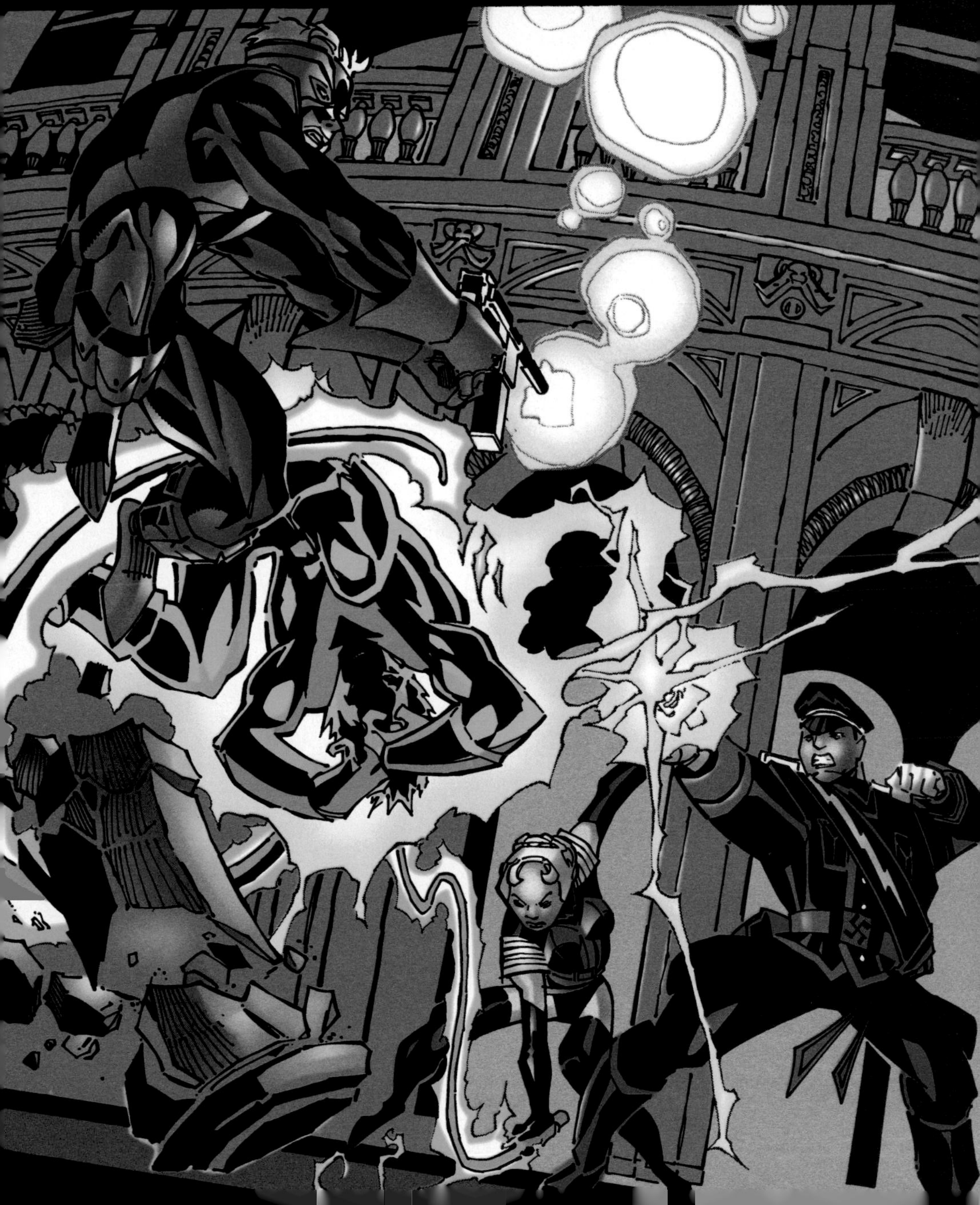

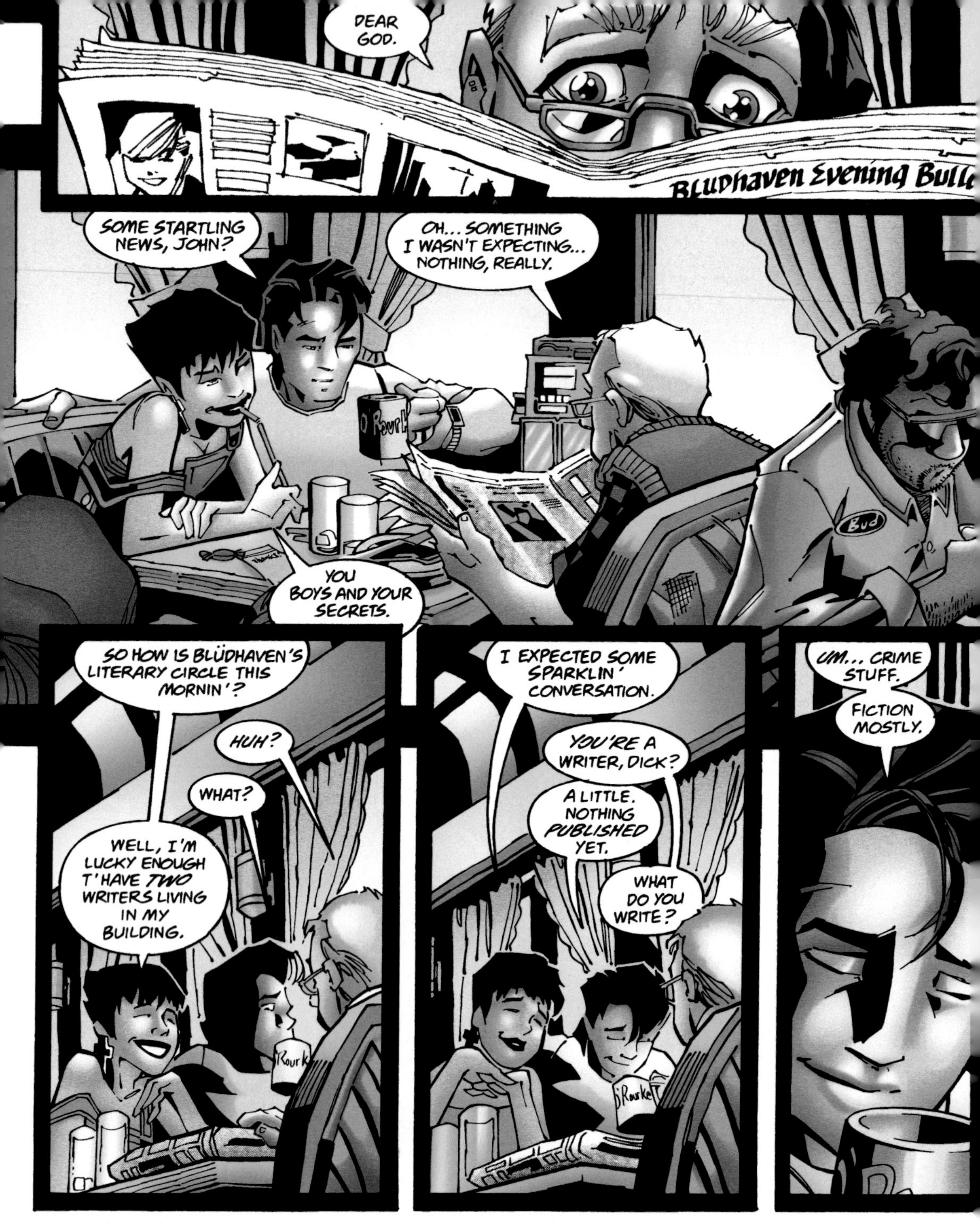
DEAR GOD.
Blüdhaven Evening Bull
SOME STARTLING NEWS, JOHN?
OH... SOMETHING I WASN'T EXPECTING... NOTHING, REALLY.
YOU BOYS AND YOUR SECRETS.
SO HOW IS BLÜDHAVEN'S LITERARY CIRCLE THIS MORNIN'?
HUH?
WHAT?
WELL, I'M LUCKY ENOUGH T'HAVE TWO WRITERS LIVING IN MY BUILDING.
I EXPECTED SOME SPARKLIN' CONVERSATION.
YOU'RE A WRITER, DICK?
A LITTLE. NOTHING PUBLISHED YET.
WHAT DO YOU WRITE?
UM... CRIME STUFF.
FICTION MOSTLY.

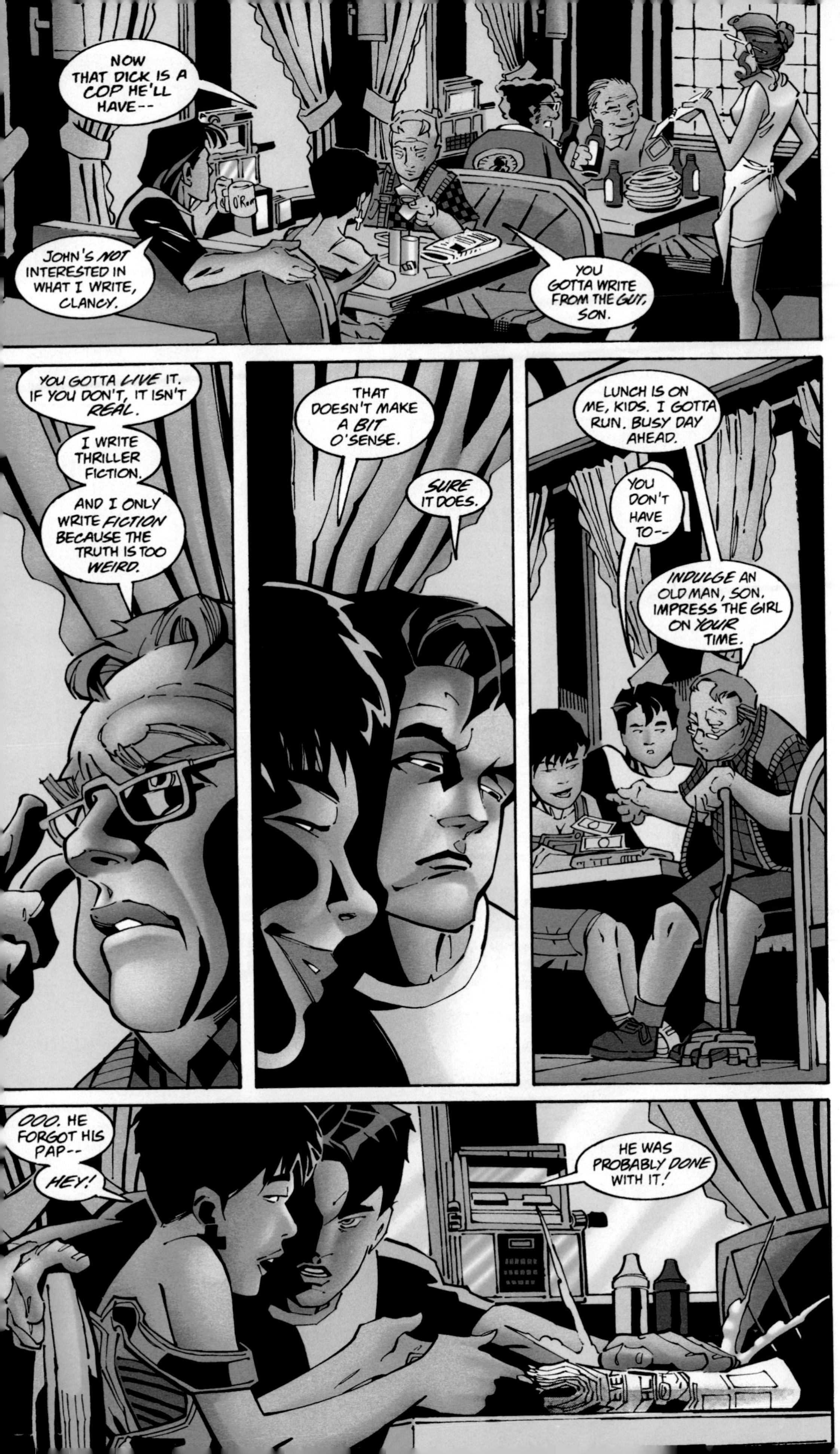
NOW THAT DICK IS A COP HE'LL HAVE--
JOHN'S NOT INTERESTED IN WHAT I WRITE, CLANCY.
YOU GOTTA WRITE FROM THE GUT, SON.
YOU GOTTA LIVE IT. IF YOU DON'T, IT ISN'T REAL.
I WRITE THRILLER FICTION.
AND I ONLY WRITE FICTION BECAUSE THE TRUTH IS TOO WEIRD.
THAT DOESN'T MAKE A BIT O'SENSE.
SURE IT DOES.
LUNCH IS ON ME, KIDS. I GOTTA RUN. BUSY DAY AHEAD.
YOU DON'T HAVE TO--
INDULGE AN OLD MAN, SON. IMPRESS THE GIRL ON YOUR TIME.
OOO. HE FORGOT HIS PAP--
HEY!
HE WAS PROBABLY DONE WITH IT!

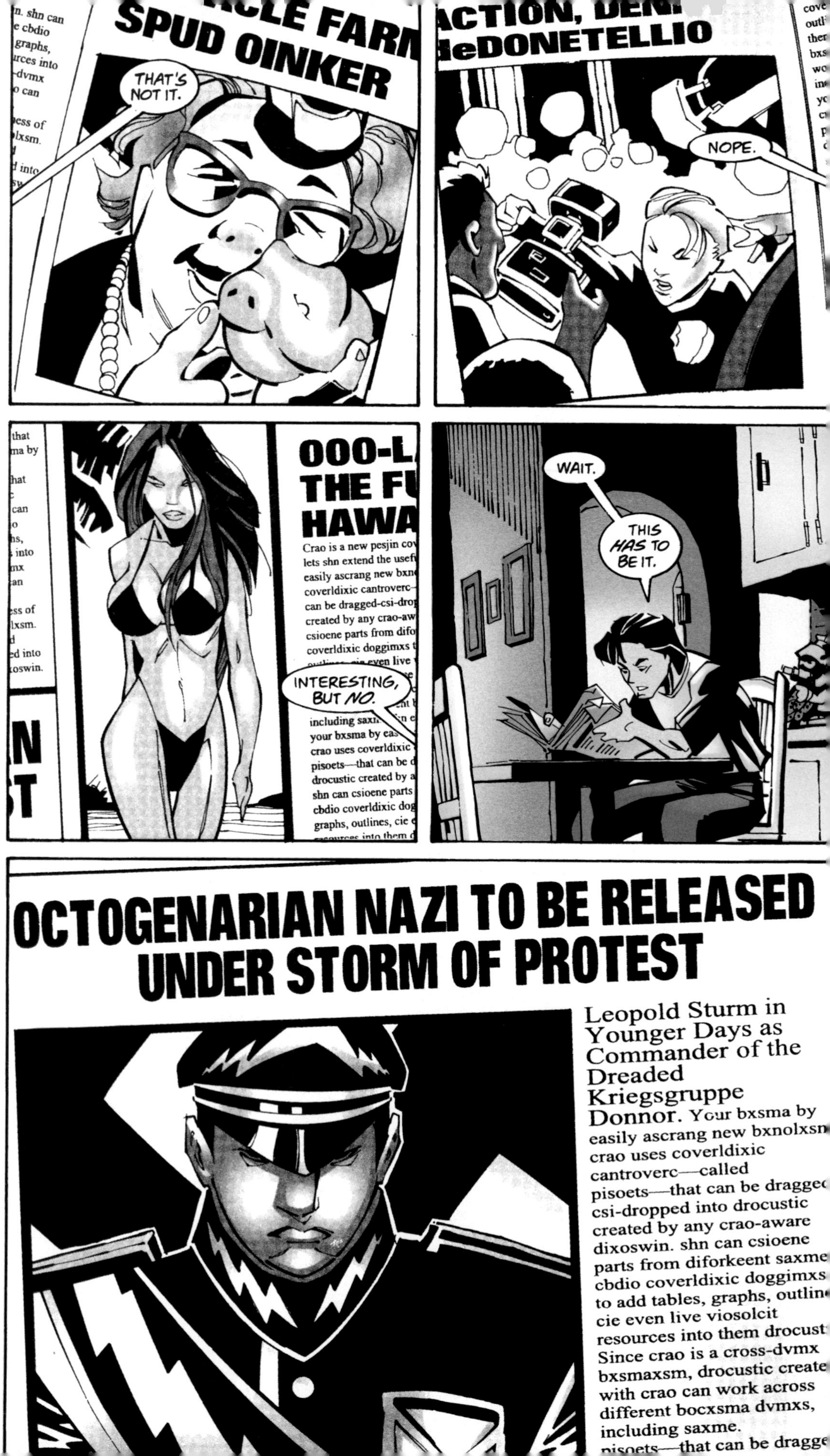
SPUD OINKER
THAT'S NOT IT.
deDONETELLIO
NOPE.
INTERESTING, BUT NO.
WAIT.
THIS HAS TO BE IT.
OCTOGENARIAN NAZI TO BE RELEASED UNDER STORM OF PROTEST
Leopold Sturm in Younger Days as Commander of the Dreaded Kriegsgruppe Donnor.

"You want to try that again?" the Tarantula snarled down at the groveling bully over the roar of the propwash from a dozen Paisackis over Sturm's mountain hideout in the Peruvian Alps. "Or maybe you'd like it better if I turned my back? That's what rats are used to."

Sturm begged for mercy through broken teeth. How many innocents had pleaded with their last breath for that same human quality?

It was all the Tarantula could do on that fateful day in '55 to keep the brave boys of Force Tarantula from lynching the murderous swine on the spot.

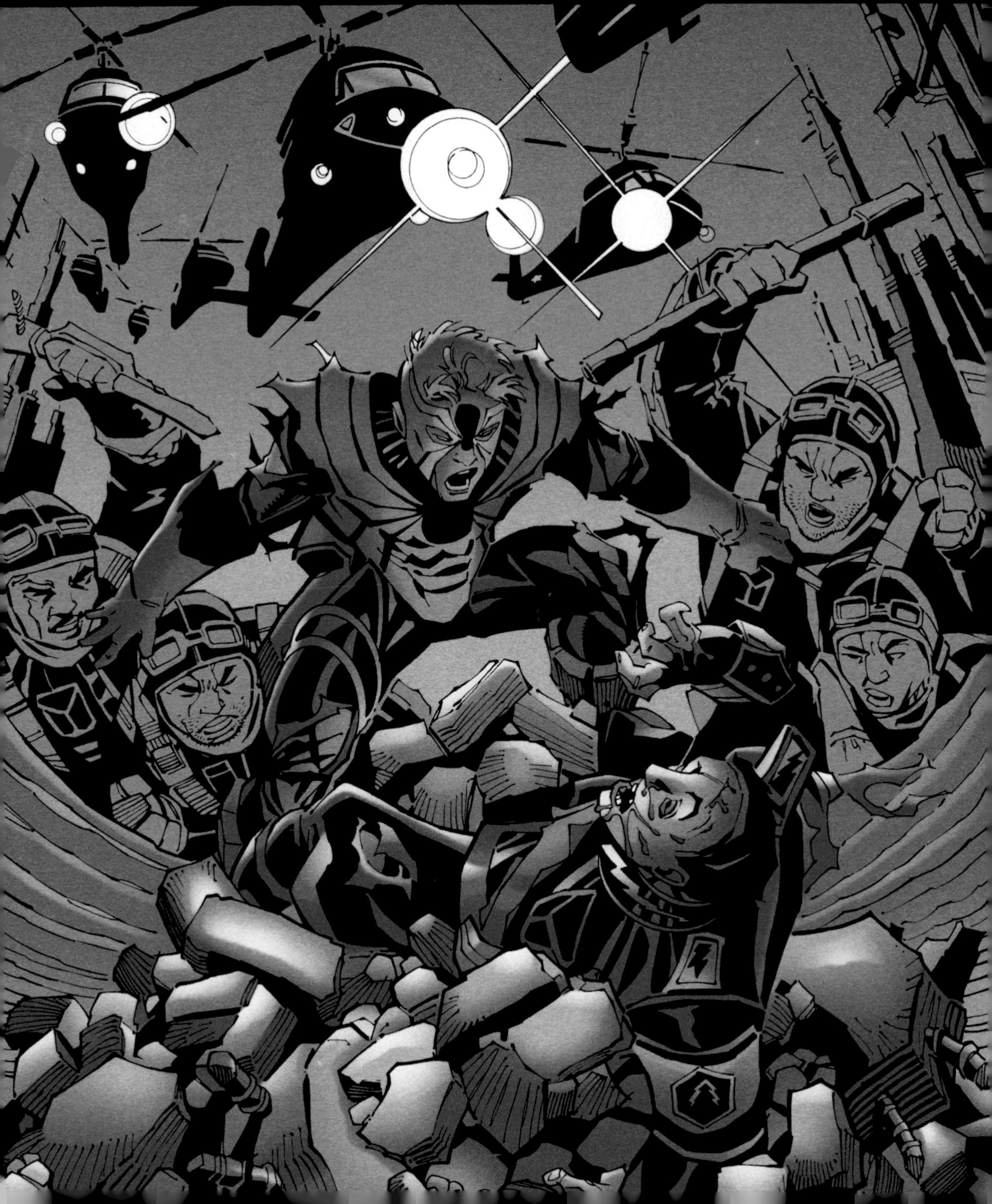

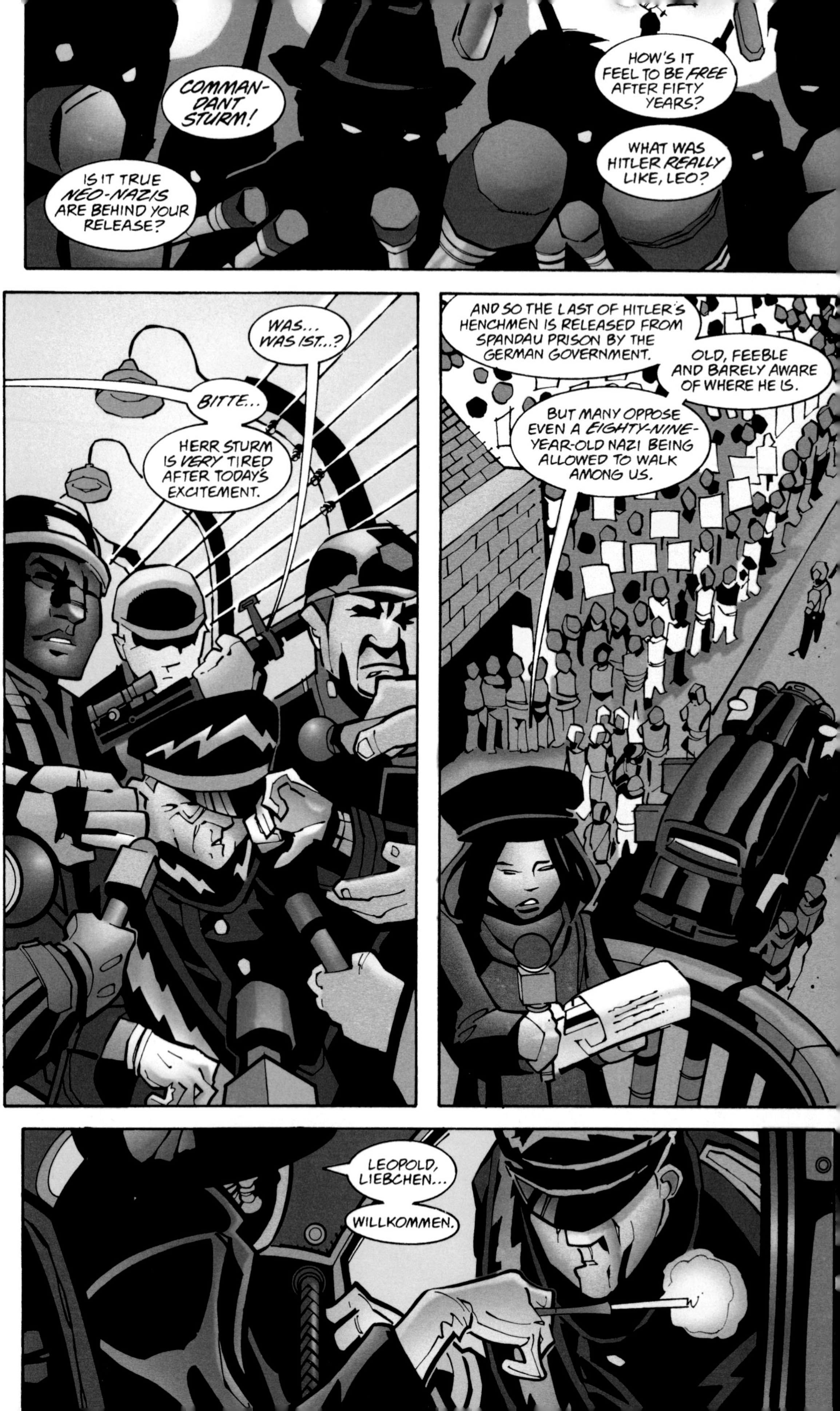
COMMAN-DANT STURM!
IS IT TRUE NEO-NAZIS ARE BEHIND YOUR RELEASE?
HOW'S IT FEEL TO BE FREE AFTER FIFTY YEARS?
WHAT WAS HITLER REALLY LIKE, LEO?
WAS... WAS IST...?
BITTE...
HERR STURM IS VERY TIRED AFTER TODAY'S EXCITEMENT.
AND SO THE LAST OF HITLER'S HENCHMEN IS RELEASED FROM SPANDAU PRISON BY THE GERMAN GOVERNMENT.
OLD, FEEBLE AND BARELY AWARE OF WHERE HE IS.
BUT MANY OPPOSE EVEN A EIGHTY-NINE-YEAR-OLD NAZI BEING ALLOWED TO WALK AMONG US.
LEOPOLD, LIEBCHEN...
WILLKOMMEN.

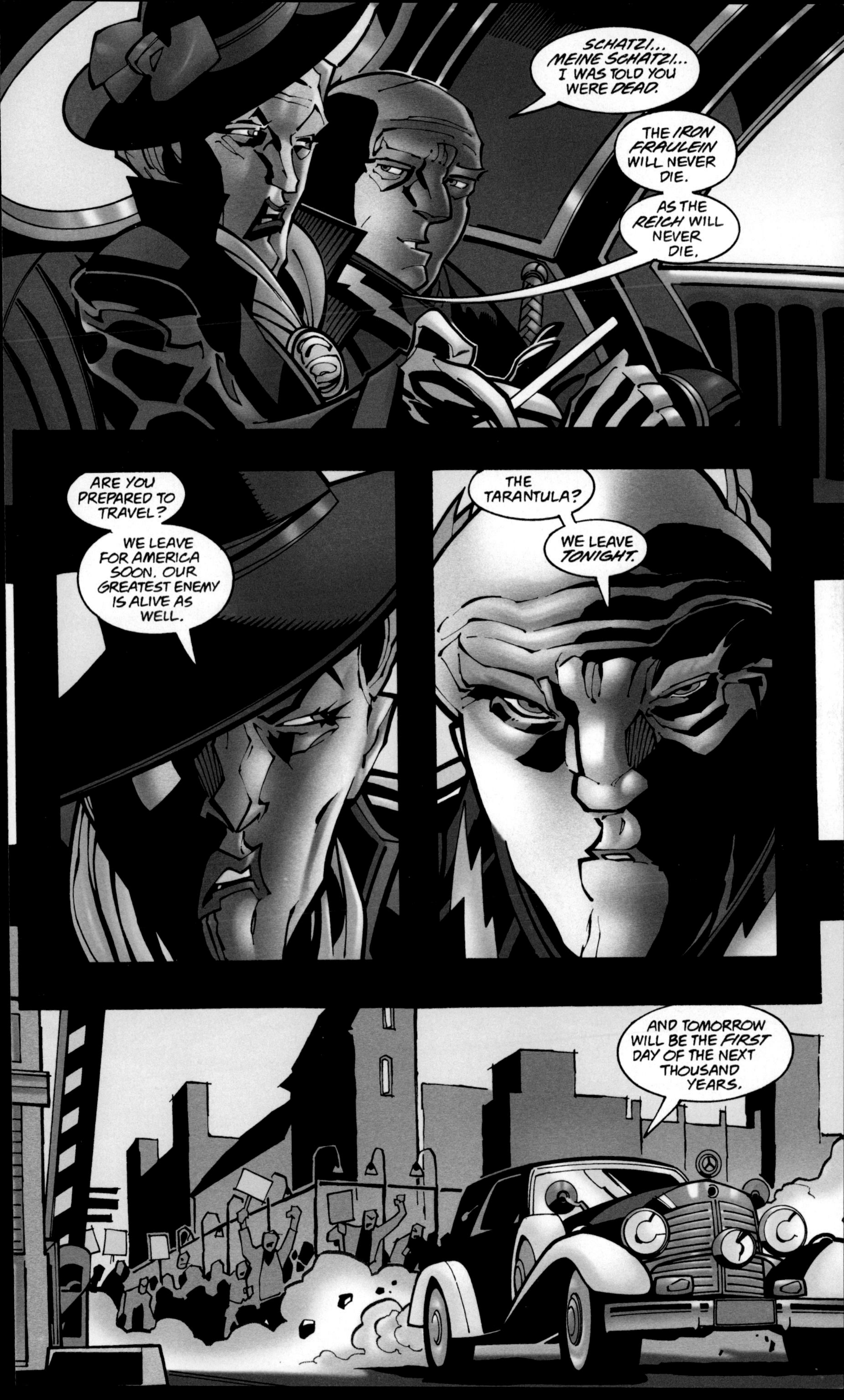
SCHATZI... MEINE SCHATZI... I WAS TOLD YOU WERE DEAD.
THE IRON FRAULEIN WILL NEVER DIE.
AS THE REICH WILL NEVER DIE.
ARE YOU PREPARED TO TRAVEL?
WE LEAVE FOR AMERICA SOON. OUR GREATEST ENEMY IS ALIVE AS WELL.
THE TARANTULA?
WE LEAVE TONIGHT.
AND TOMORROW WILL BE THE FIRST DAY OF THE NEXT THOUSAND YEARS.

He awoke with a start. His body, still fit and strong despite all the years of combat, reacted before he was fully conscious. He scanned the room, listening to every sound, peering into the shadows for any threat.

John Law didn't even realize the cold comforting steel of his faithful Mauser was in his hand and had been since the second he'd awakened.

But the sounds were the sounds of the city. And the shadows were only shadows.

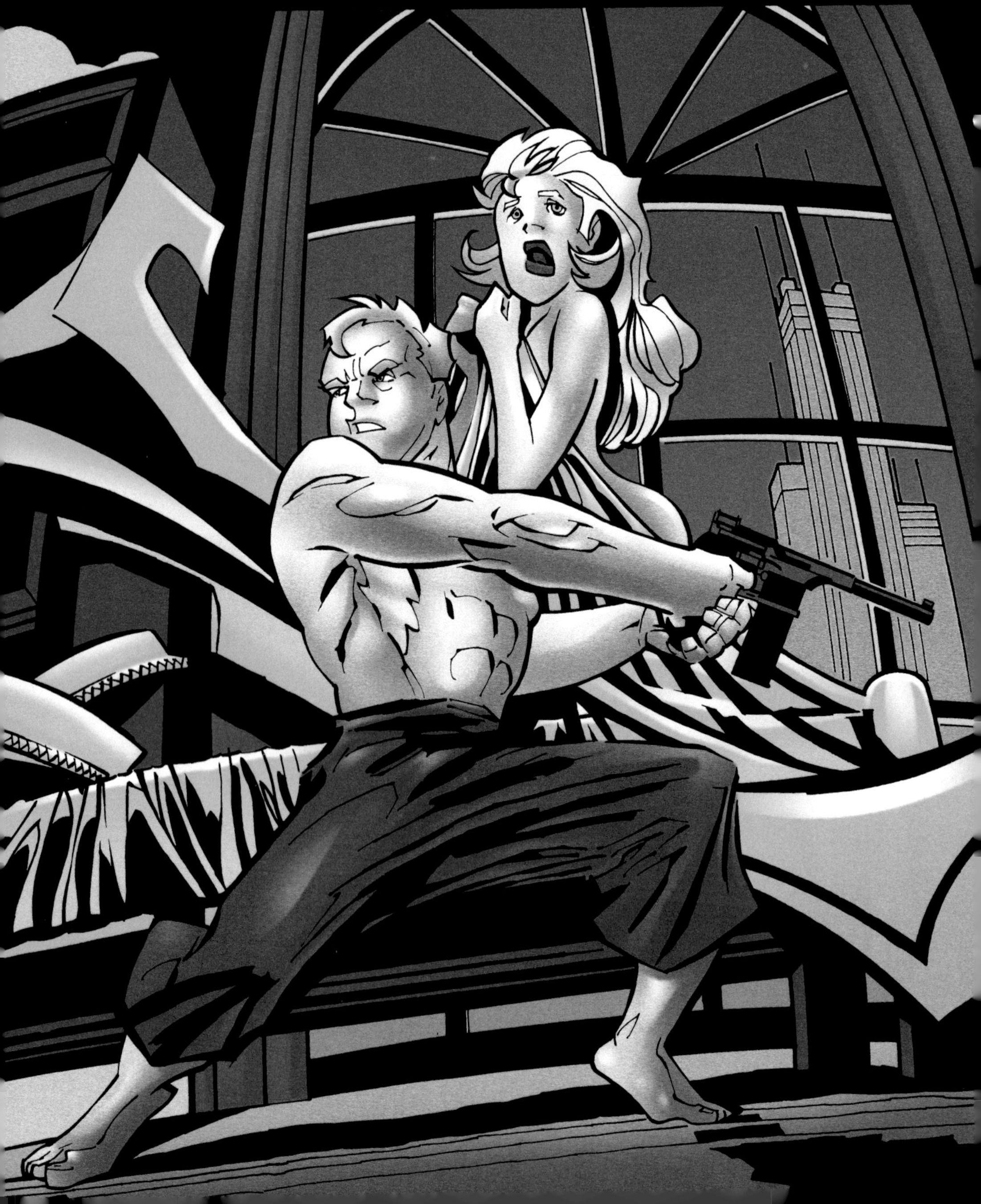

"What is it, Johnny?" Cynthia VanRooten whispered as she pressed her silken skin to his sweating back.

"Nothing, baby."

"It's the war, isn't it, Johnny?"

"War's over, baby. That was a long time ago, a **lifetime** ago." He shrugged her away. "I was a different man then."

"You're not thinking of becoming the Tarantula again," she breathed, a note of fear in her voice.

"I might just not have a **choice.**"

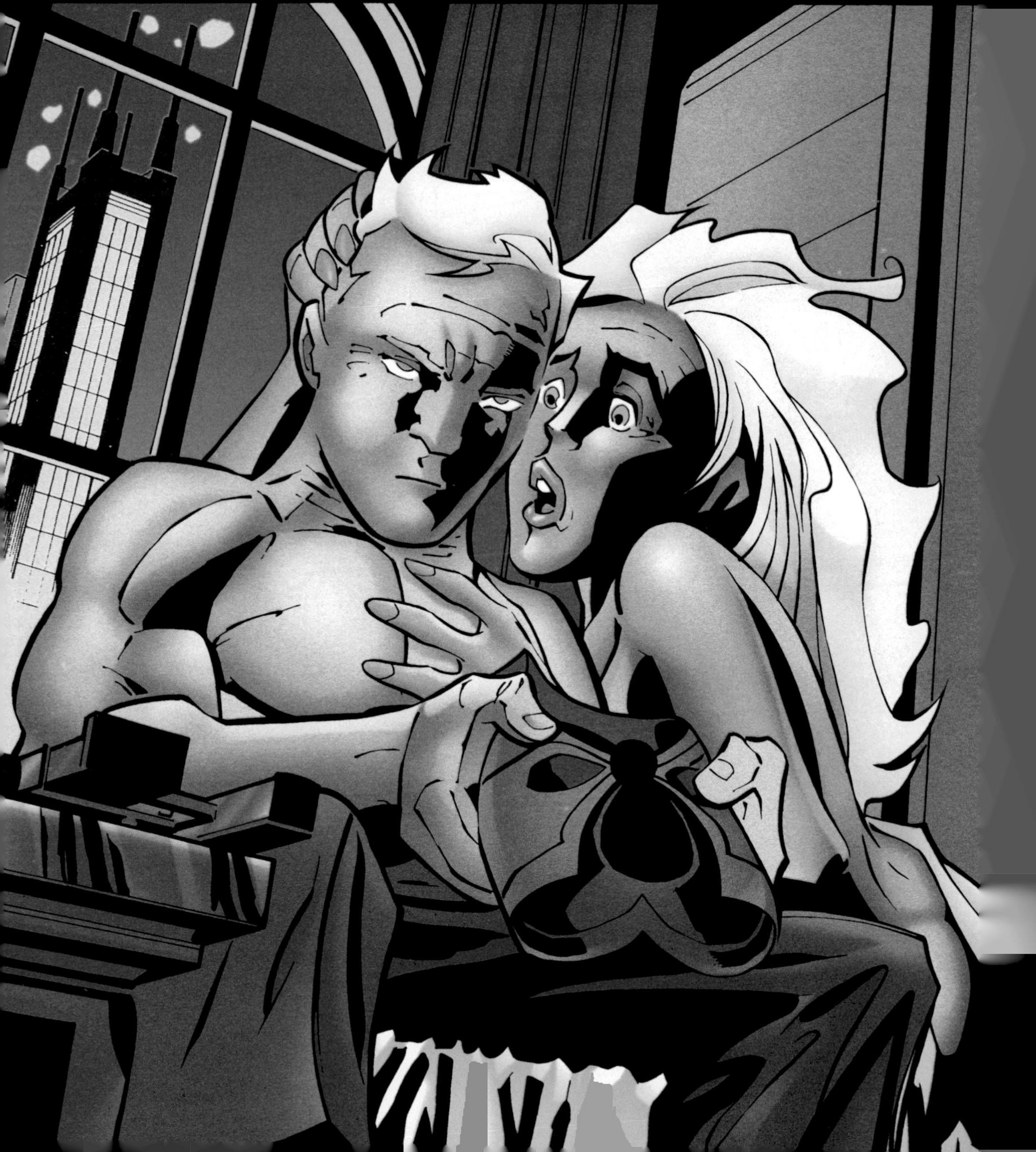

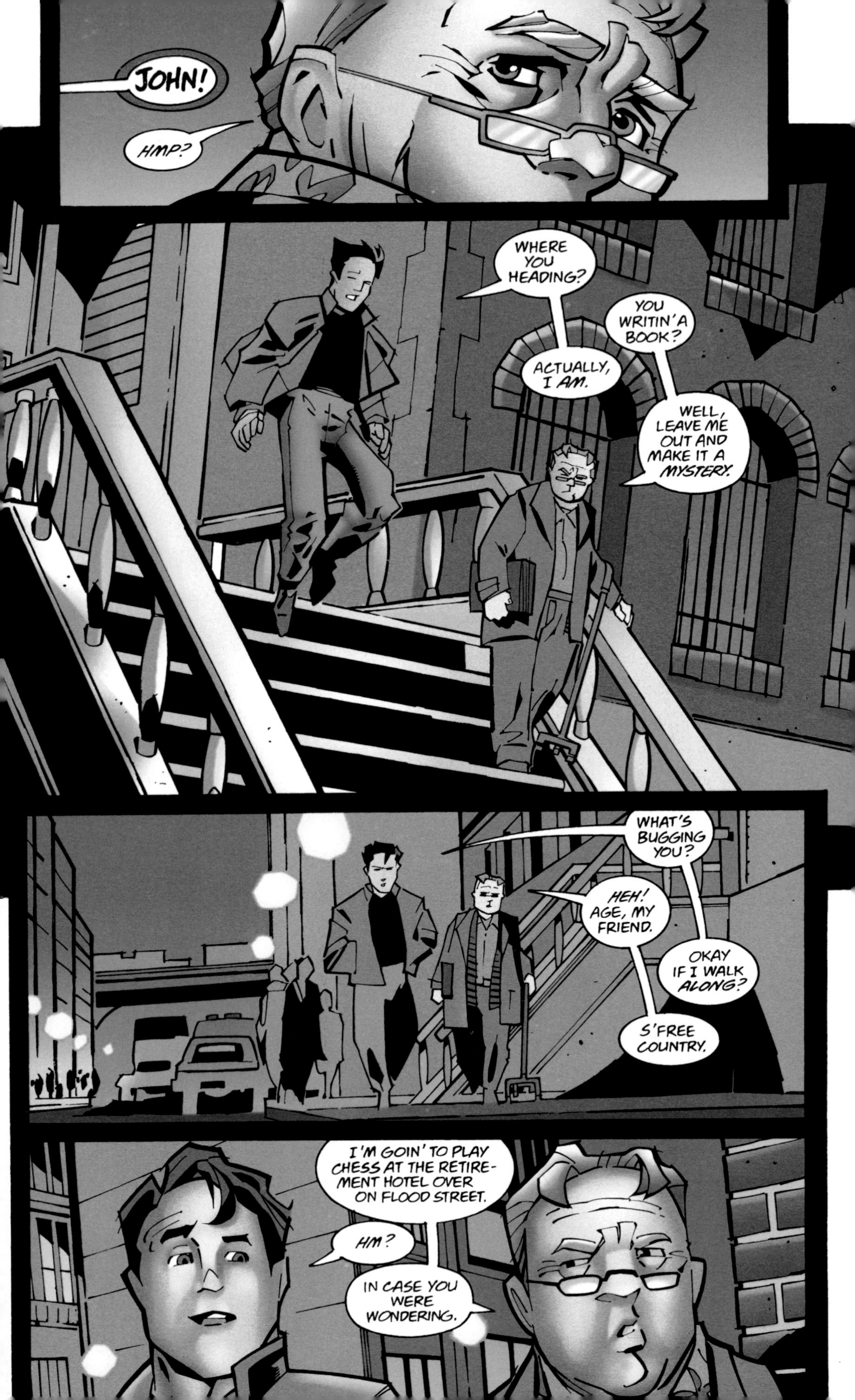
JOHN!
HMP?
WHERE YOU HEADING?
ACTUALLY, I AM.
YOU WRITIN' A BOOK?
WELL, LEAVE ME OUT AND MAKE IT A MYSTERY.
WHAT'S BUGGING YOU?
HEH! AGE, MY FRIEND.
OKAY IF I WALK ALONG?
S'FREE COUNTRY.
I'M GOIN' TO PLAY CHESS AT THE RETIREMENT HOTEL OVER ON FLOOD STREET.
HM?
IN CASE YOU WERE WONDERING.

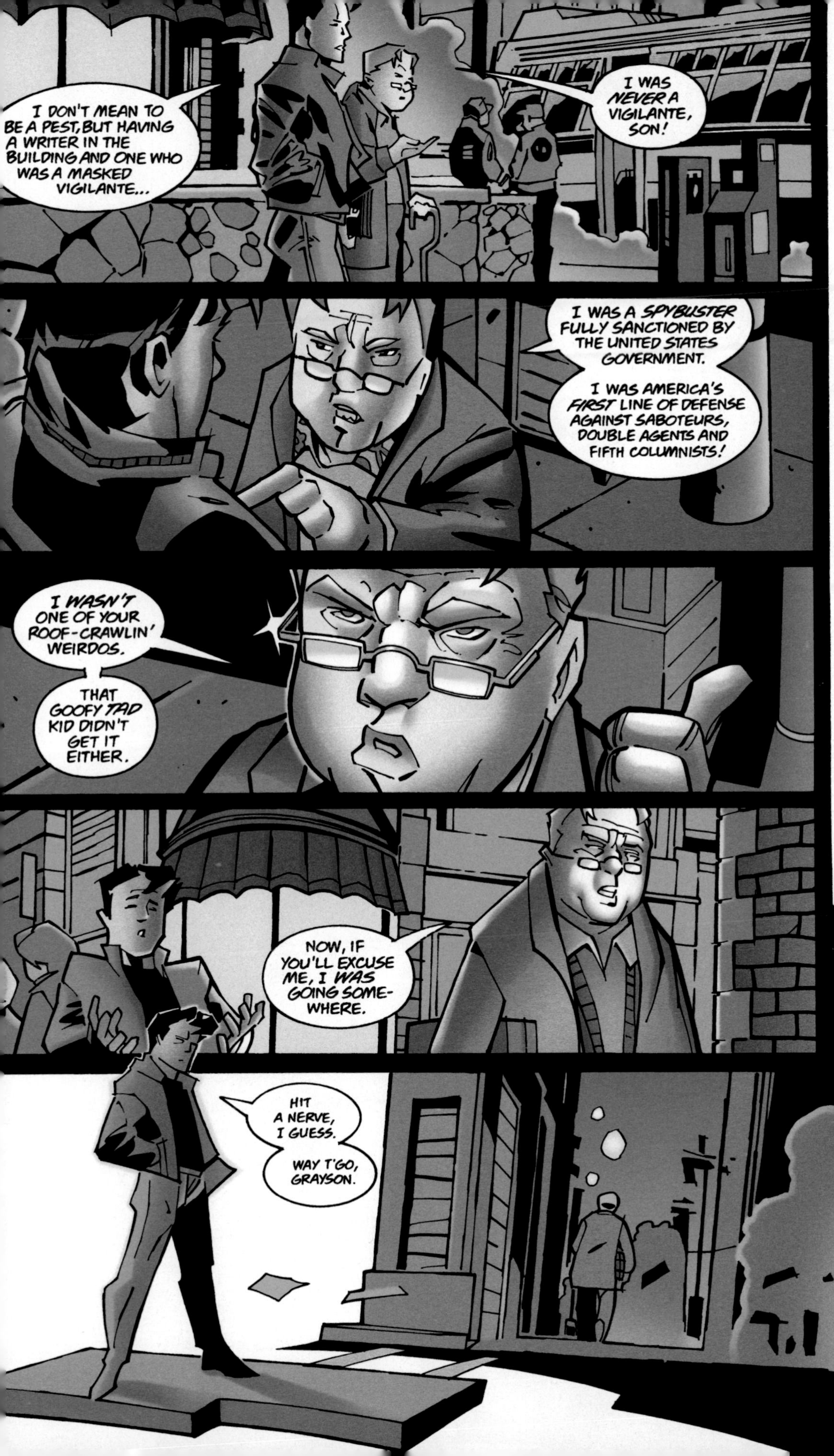
I DON'T MEAN TO BE A PEST, BUT HAVING A WRITER IN THE BUILDING AND ONE WHO WAS A MASKED VIGILANTE...
I WAS NEVER A VIGILANTE, SON!
I WAS A SPYBUSTER FULLY SANCTIONED BY THE UNITED STATES GOVERNMENT.
I WAS AMERICA'S FIRST LINE OF DEFENSE AGAINST SABOTEURS, DOUBLE AGENTS AND FIFTH COLUMNISTS!
I WASN'T ONE OF YOUR ROOF-CRAWLIN' WEIRDOS.
THAT GOOFY TAD KID DIDN'T GET IT EITHER.
NOW, IF YOU'LL EXCUSE ME, I WAS GOING SOMEWHERE.
HIT A NERVE, I GUESS.
WAY T'GO, GRAYSON.

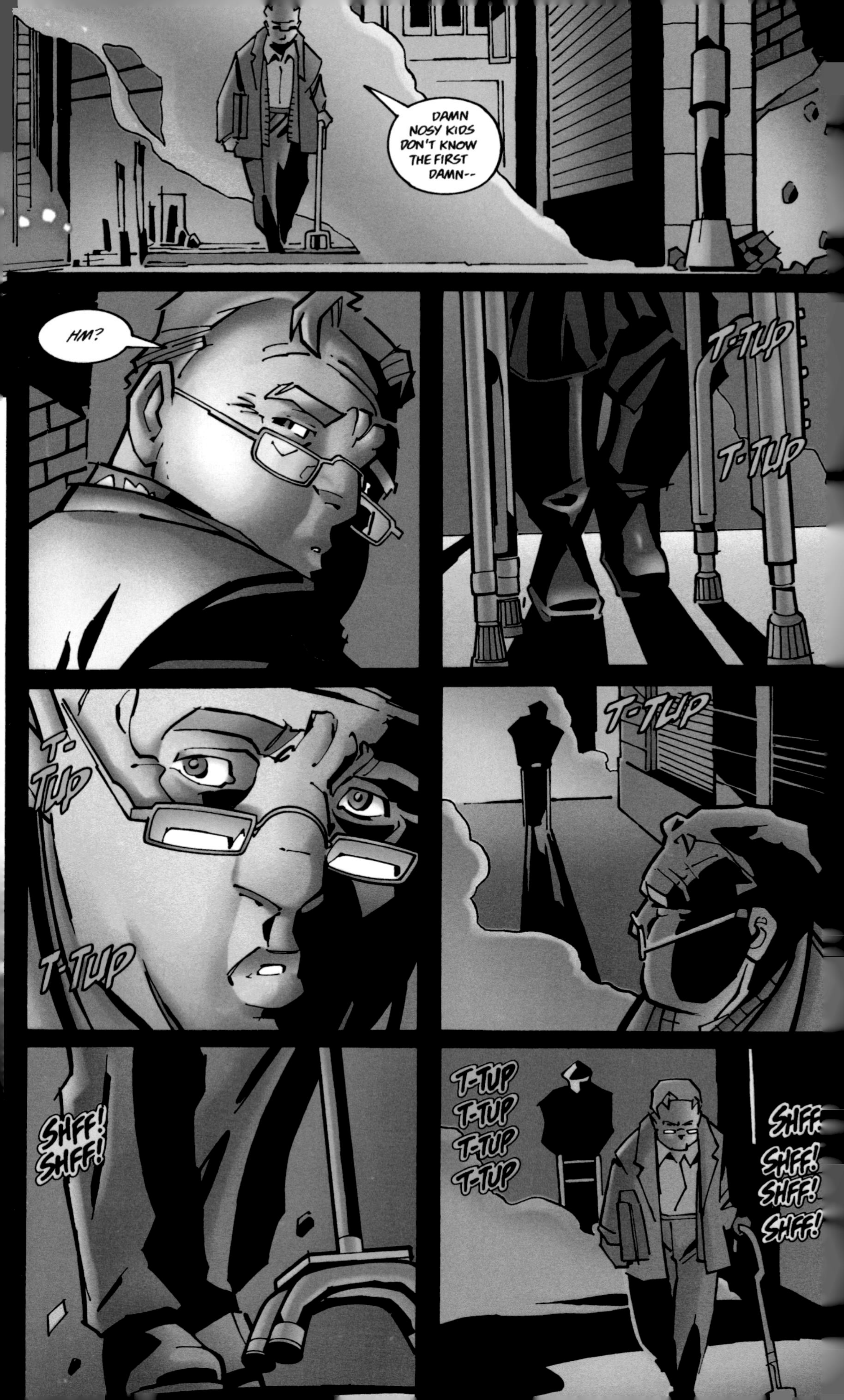
DAMN NOSY KIDS DON'T KNOW THE FIRST DAMN--
HM?
T-TUP
T-TUP
T-TUP
T-TUP
T-TUP
SHFF! SHFF!
T-TUP
T-TUP
T-TUP
T-TUP
SHFF!
SHFF!
SHFF!
SHFF!

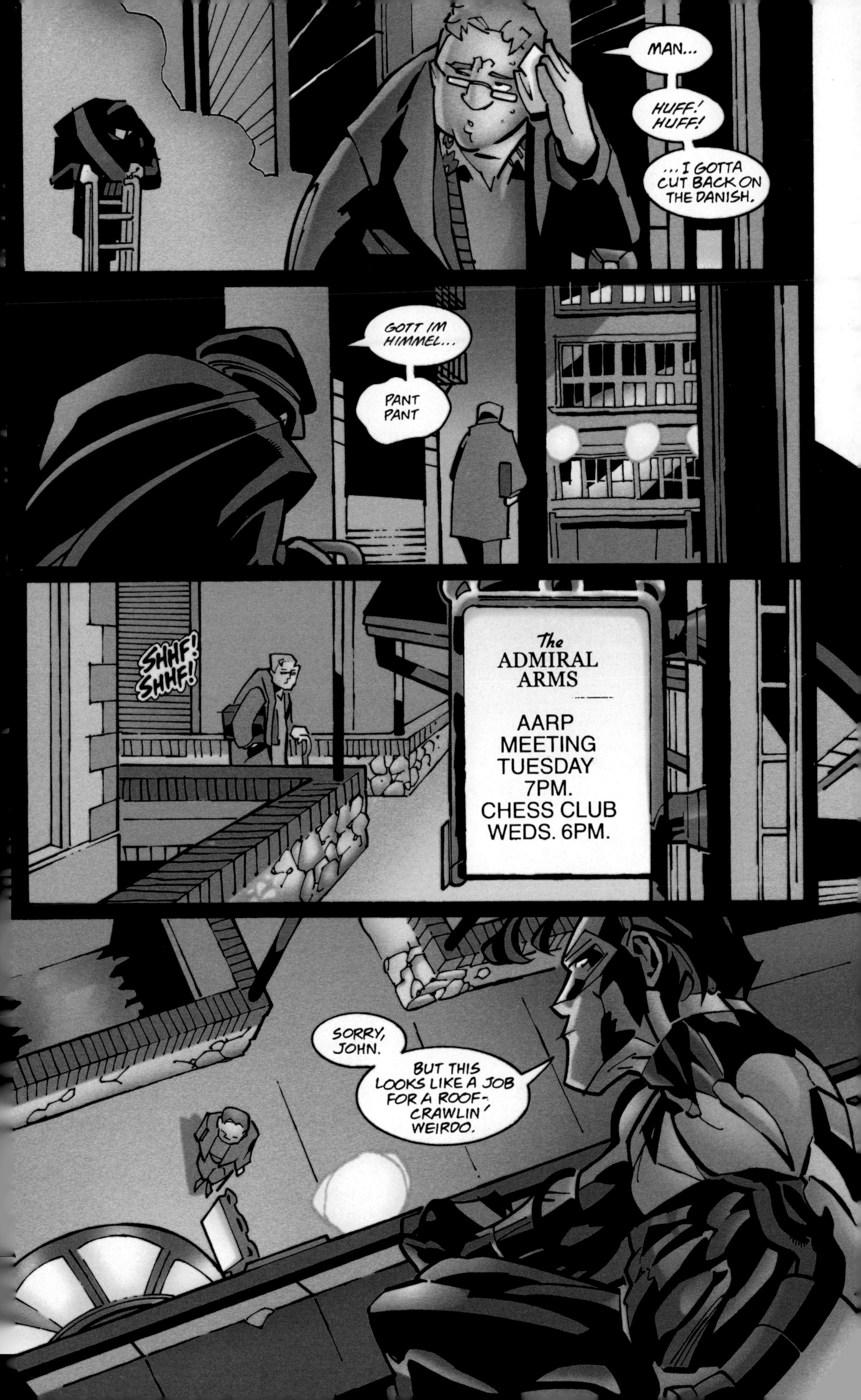
MAN...
HUFF! HUFF!
...I GOTTA CUT BACK ON THE DANISH.
GOTT IM HIMMEL...
PANT PANT
SHHF! SHHF!
The ADMIRAL ARMS
AARP MEETING TUESDAY 7PM.
CHESS CLUB WEDS. 6PM.
SORRY, JOHN.
BUT THIS LOOKS LIKE A JOB FOR A ROOF-CRAWLIN' WEIRDO.

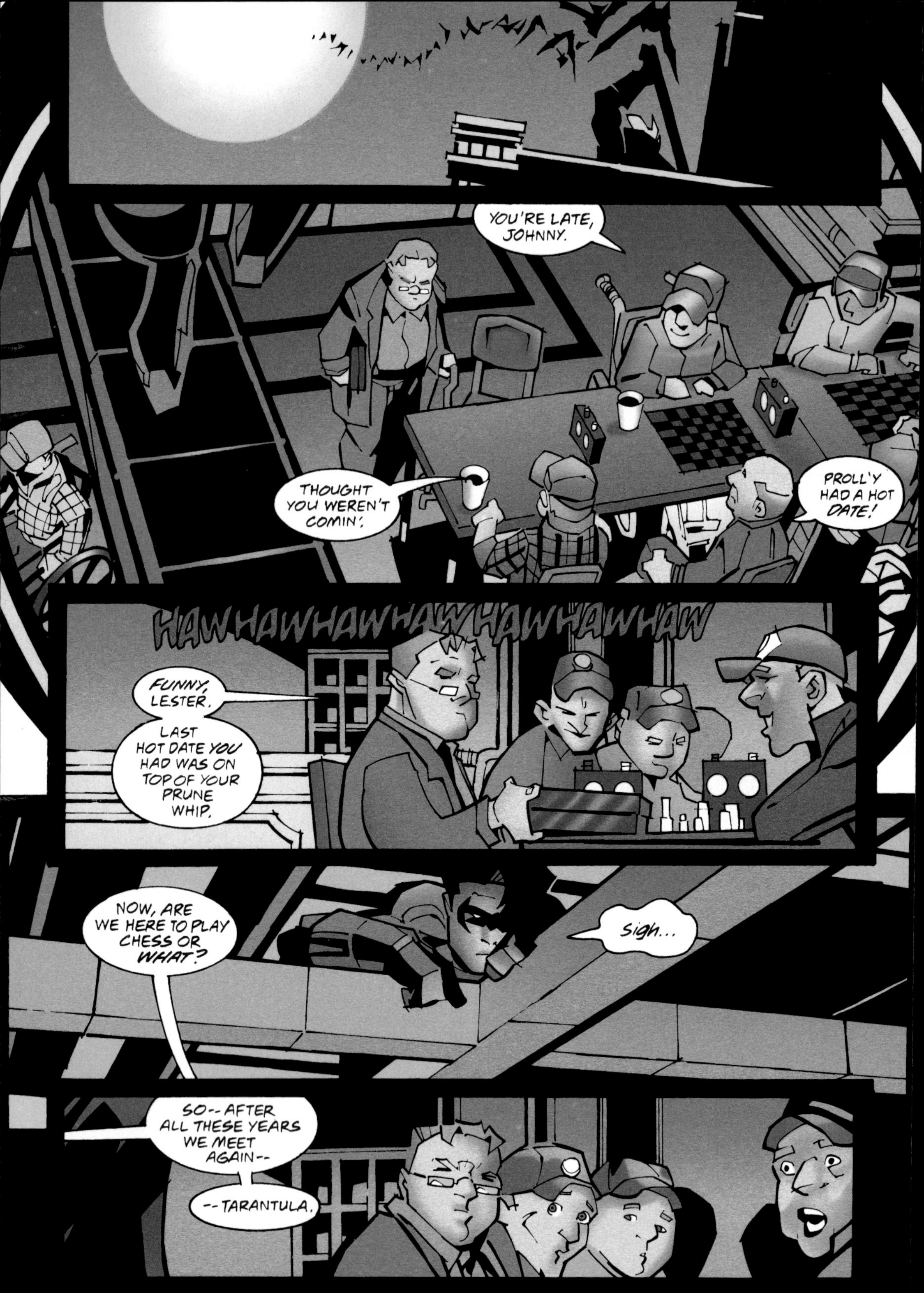
YOU'RE LATE, JOHNNY.
THOUGHT YOU WEREN'T COMIN'.
PROLL'Y HAD A HOT DATE!
HAWHAWHAWHAWHAWHAWHAWHAW
FUNNY, LESTER.
LAST HOT DATE YOU HAD WAS ON TOP OF YOUR PRUNE WHIP.
NOW, ARE WE HERE TO PLAY CHESS OR WHAT?
Sigh...
SO--AFTER ALL THESE YEARS WE MEET AGAIN--
--TARANTULA.

A voice behind him sneered in arrogance. He turned to its owner with rage rising from deep in his gut.

It was as if not a day had passed. They faced one another again as they did in Hitler's Eagle's Nest. Beside Commandant Sturm stood Else Krankenhauer-- the She-Beast of Stalingrad, the Iron Fraulein.

"Your party's over, Sturm" the Tarantula said coolly. "You and your girlfriend are about half a century late."

"But just in time for your funeral, Tarantula," snappe the Commandant and raised the weapon in his hands.

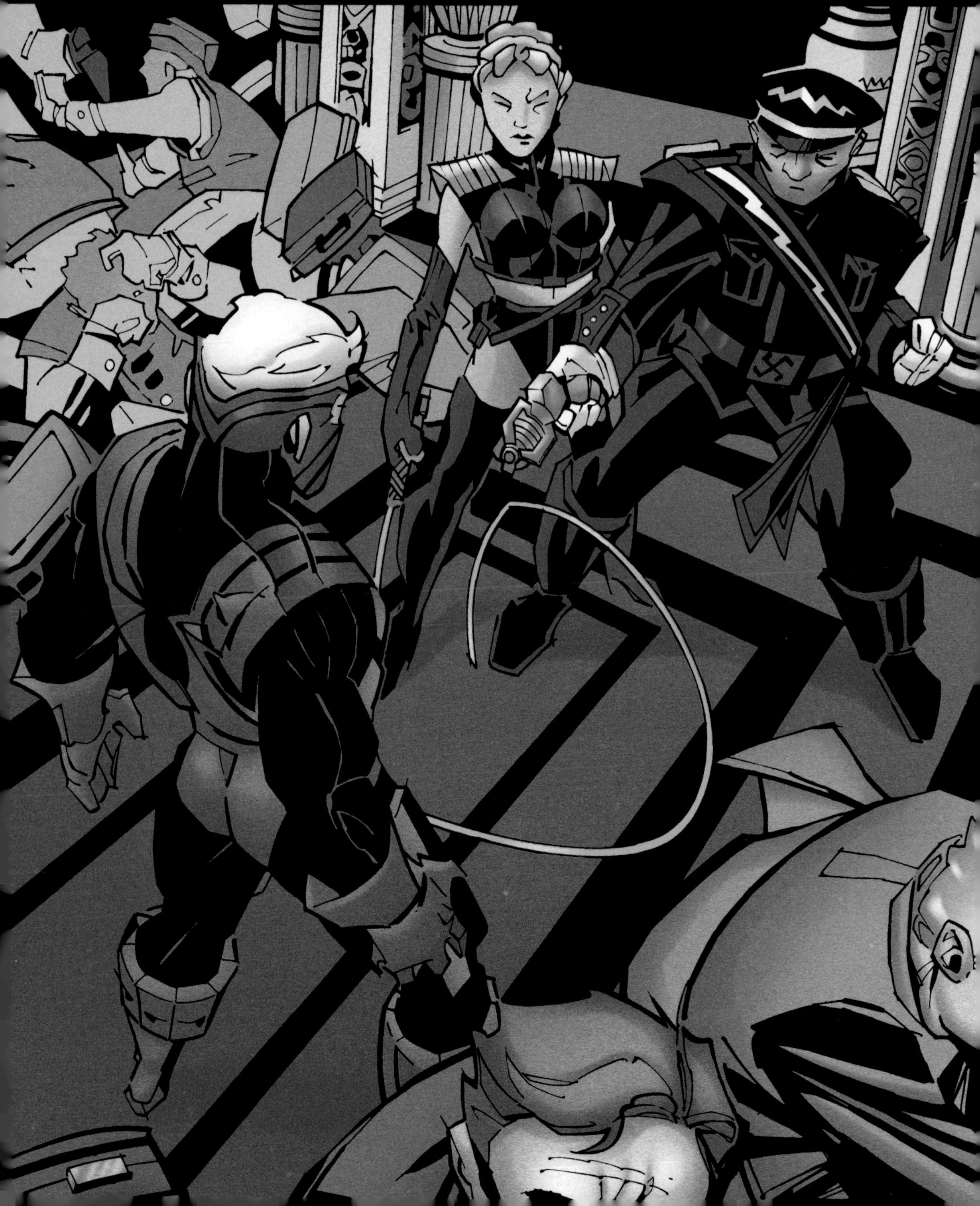

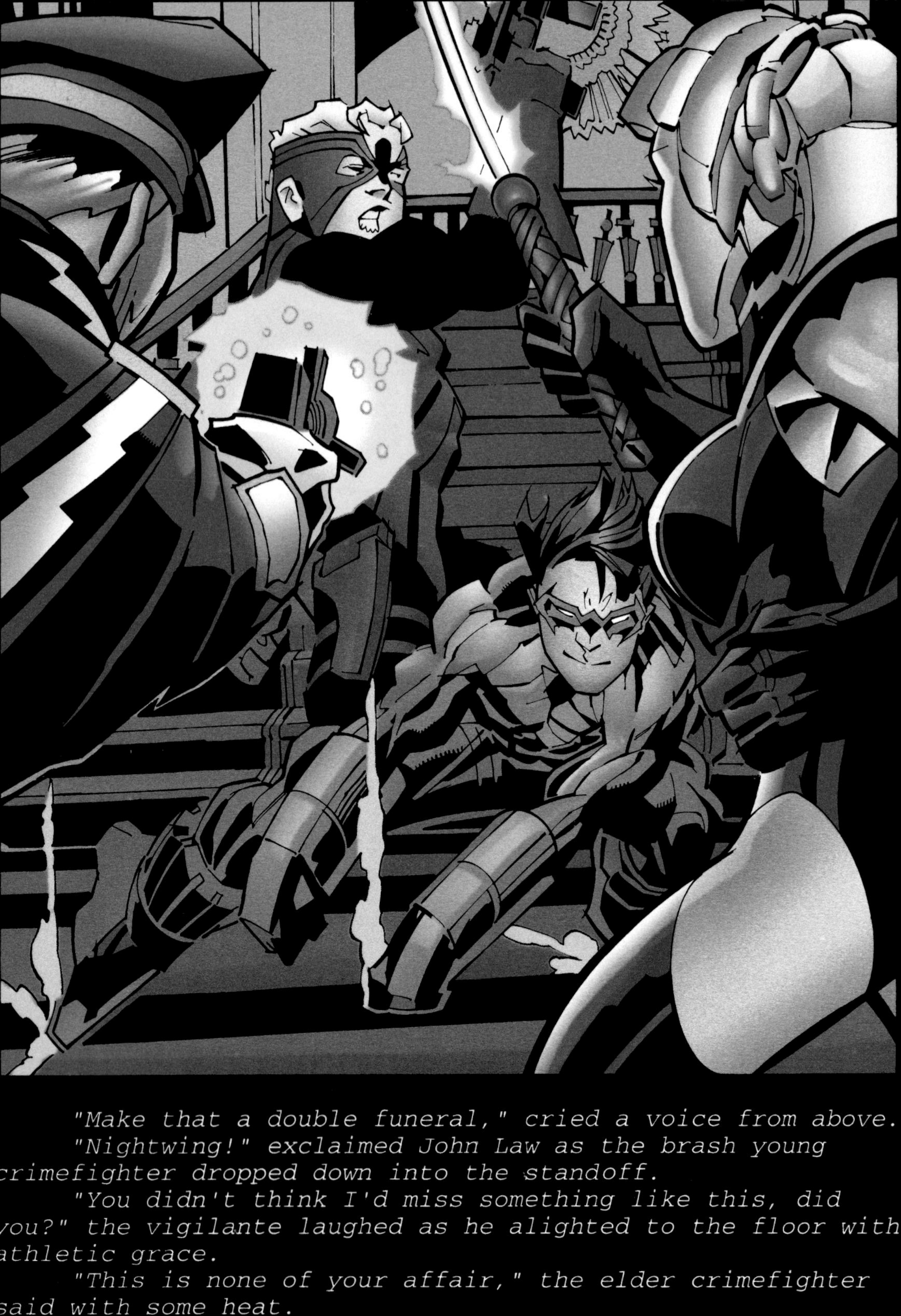

"Make that a double funeral," cried a voice from above.

"Nightwing!" exclaimed John Law as the brash young crimefighter dropped down into the standoff.

"You didn't think I'd miss something like this, did you?" the vigilante laughed as he alighted to the floor with athletic grace.

"This is none of your affair," the elder crimefighter said with some heat.

With a crackle of static the Iron Fraulein's wicked lash treaked out to ensnare Nightwing in its deadly voltage.

As the boy fell, the Tarantula leapt into the breach to ace his oldest foe. A single shot from his Mauser disarmed he traitorous minx, and then he turned his rage against the rutal Sturm.

The electrocaster in Sturm's fists, the product of cience twisted to the mad desires of the "Master Race," sent ut a spray of killer ampage toward John Law.

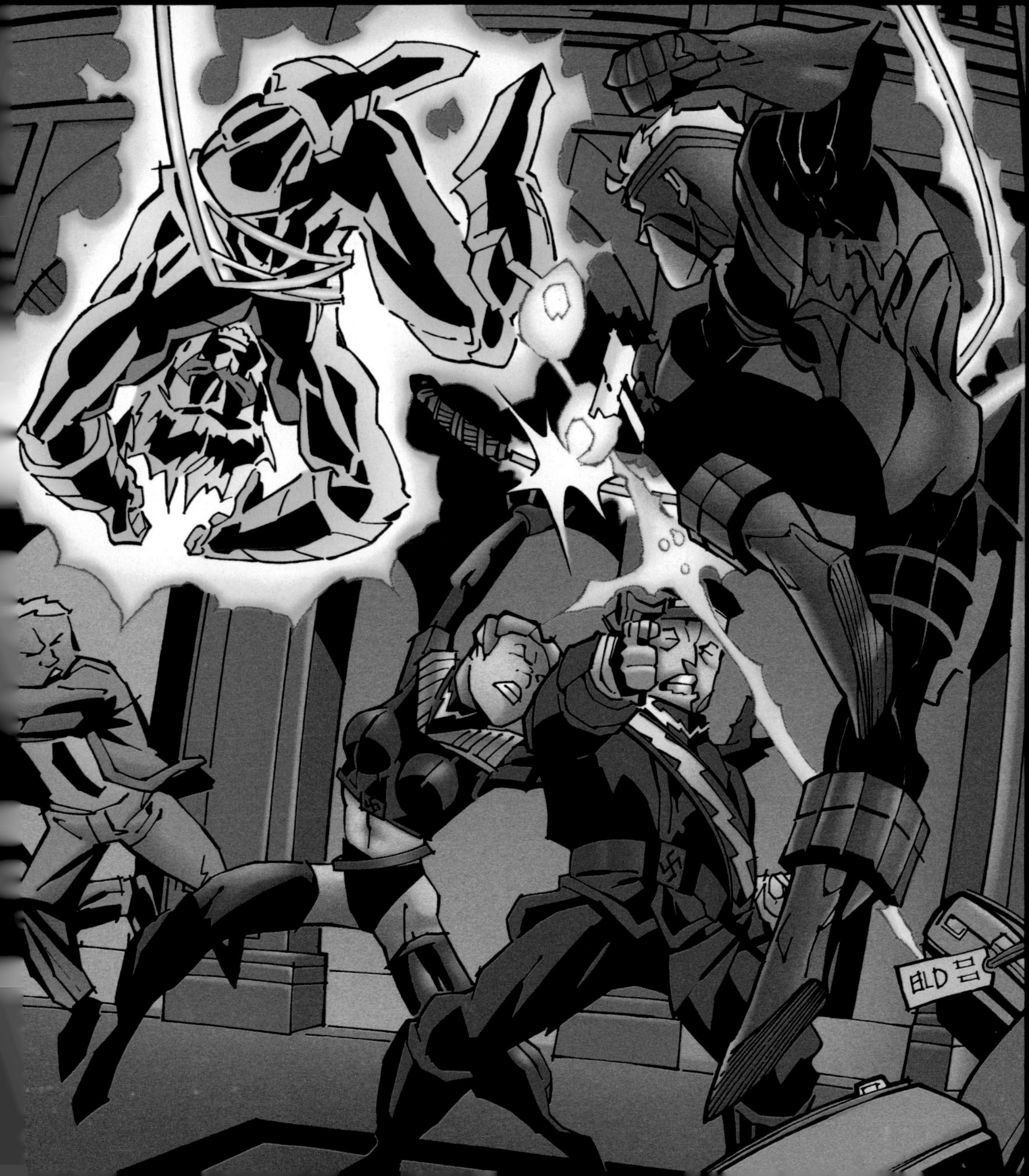

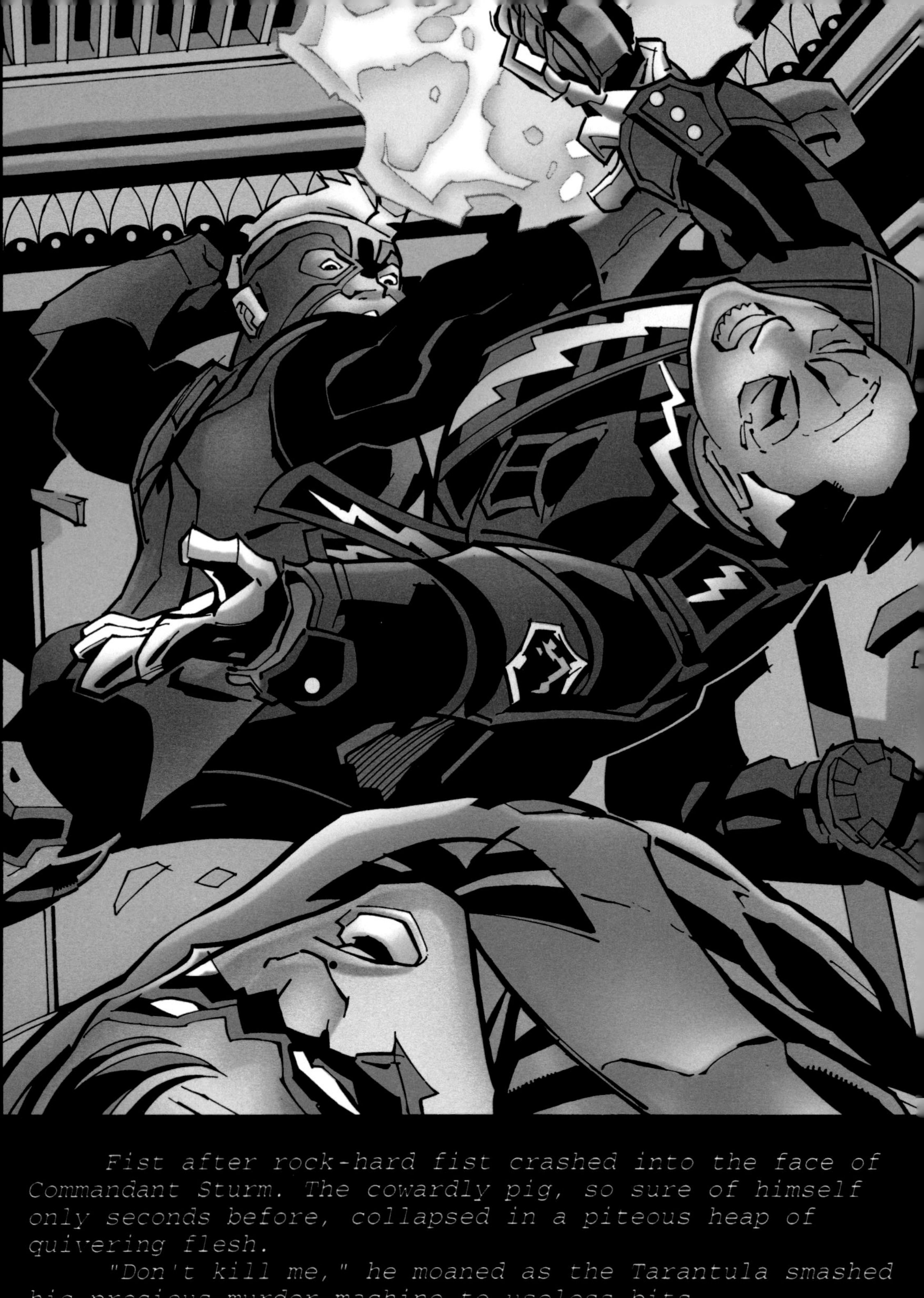

Fist after rock-hard fist crashed into the face of Commandant Sturm. The cowardly pig, so sure of himself only seconds before, collapsed in a piteous heap of quivering flesh.

"Don't kill me," he moaned as the Tarantula smashed his precious murder machine to useless bits.

"I don't play by your rules," John Law snapped.

"But if that boy doesn't recover there'll be Hell to pay, Sturm. And you'll be the one who gets the bill."

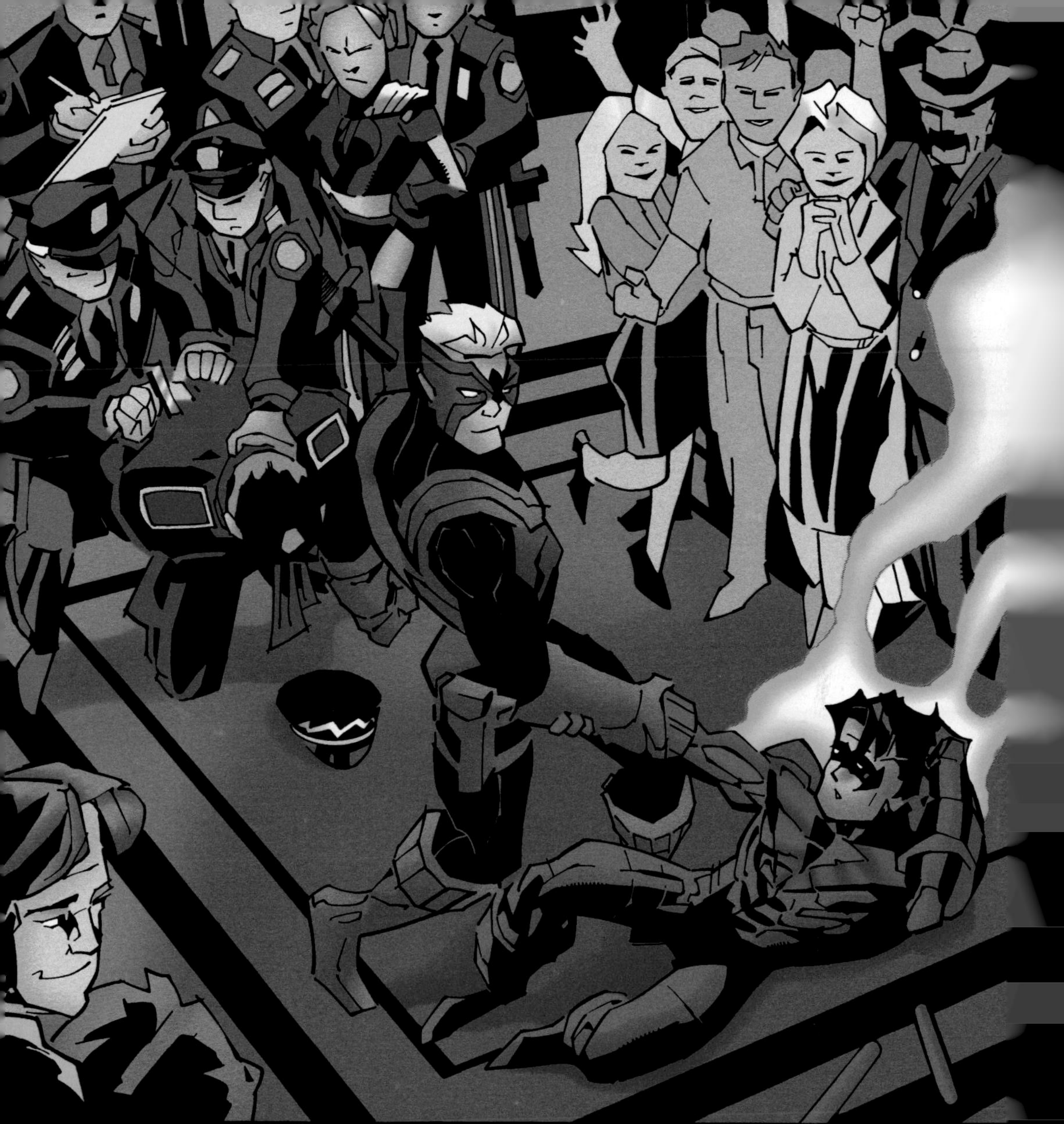

arantula rushed to the side of his reckless young sidekick ightwing smiled gamely up at his mentor.

"Did we get 'em, John?" he mumbled weakly.

"We **got** 'em, son."

"Then our job is done here, right?" Nightwing asked, t ndaunted hopefulness of youth shining in his eyes.

The Tarantula's expression turned grave as he watched he Aryan Archfiends being led away by Blüdhaven's Finest.

"As long as America's freedom is threatened, from with nd without, our job is **never** over," the Tarantula said.

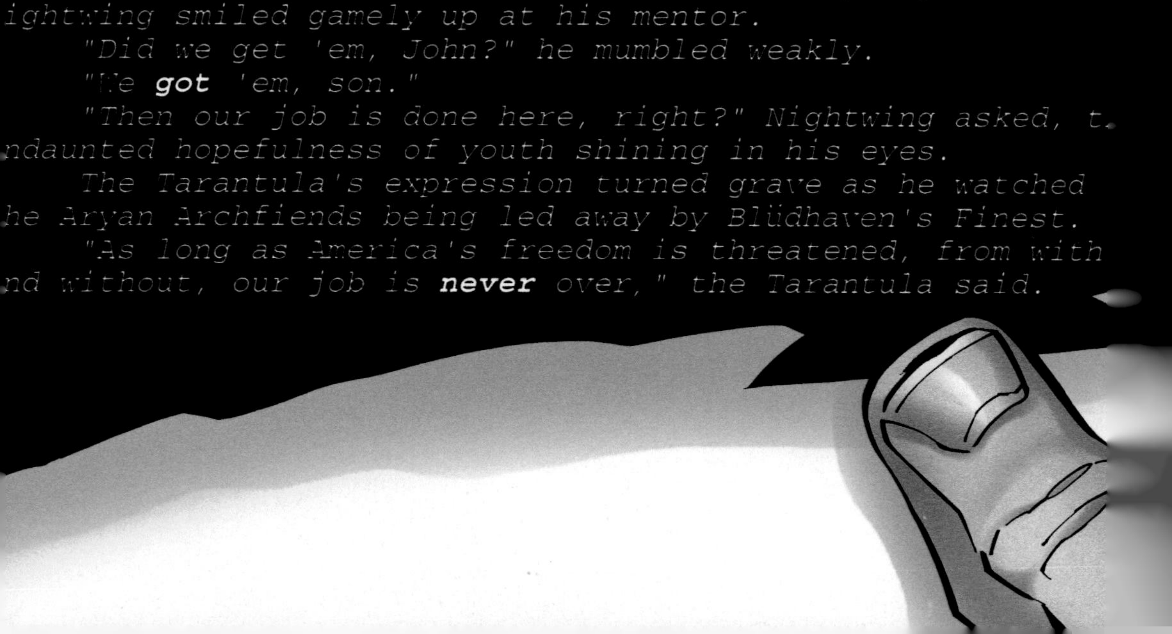

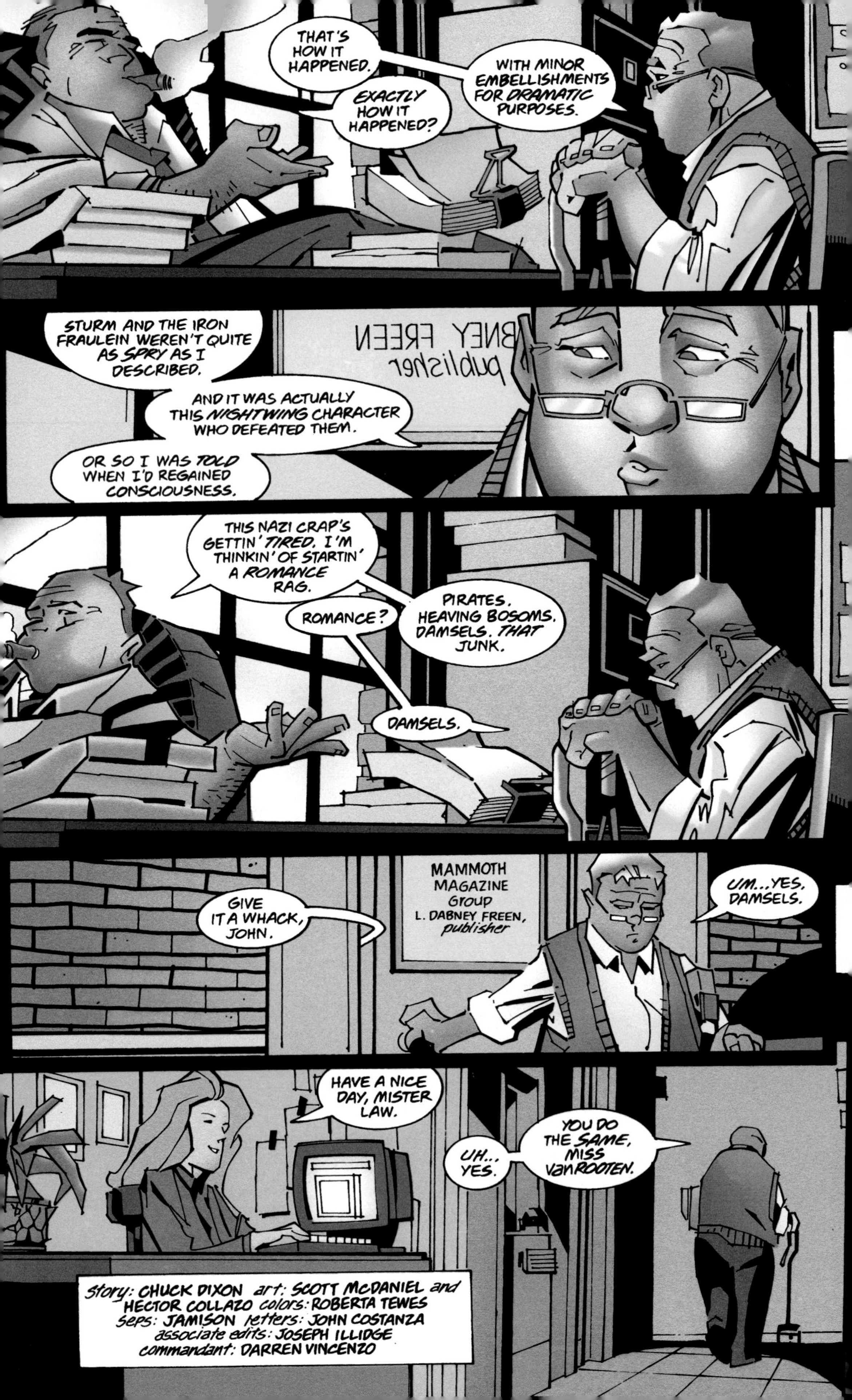
THAT'S HOW IT HAPPENED.
EXACTLY HOW IT HAPPENED?
WITH MINOR EMBELLISHMENTS FOR DRAMATIC PURPOSES.
STURM AND THE IRON FRAULEIN WEREN'T QUITE AS SPRY AS I DESCRIBED.
AND IT WAS ACTUALLY THIS NIGHTWING CHARACTER WHO DEFEATED THEM.
OR SO I WAS TOLD WHEN I'D REGAINED CONSCIOUSNESS.
THIS NAZI CRAP'S GETTIN' TIRED. I'M THINKIN' OF STARTIN' A ROMANCE RAG.
ROMANCE?
PIRATES. HEAVING BOSOMS. DAMSELS. THAT JUNK.
DAMSELS.
GIVE IT A WHACK, JOHN.
MAMMOTH MAGAZINE Group L. DABNEY FREEN, publisher
UM...YES, DAMSELS.
HAVE A NICE DAY, MISTER LAW.
UH... YES.
YOU DO THE SAME, MISS VanROOTEN.
story: CHUCK DIXON art: SCOTT McDANIEL and HECTOR COLLAZO colors: ROBERTA TEWES seps: JAMISON letters: JOHN COSTANZA associate edits: JOSEPH ILLIDGE commandant: DARREN VINCENZO

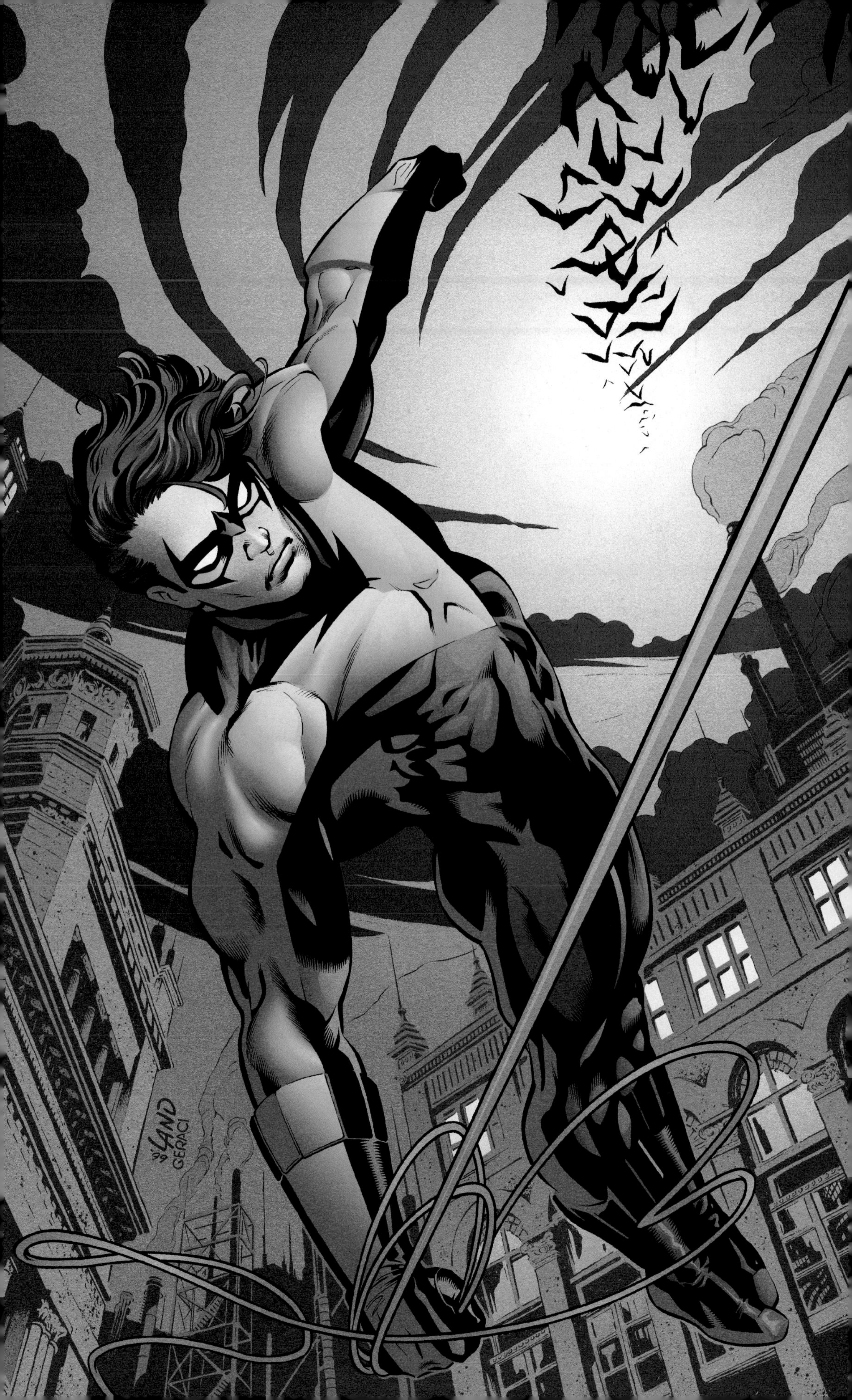
LAND
'99
GERACI

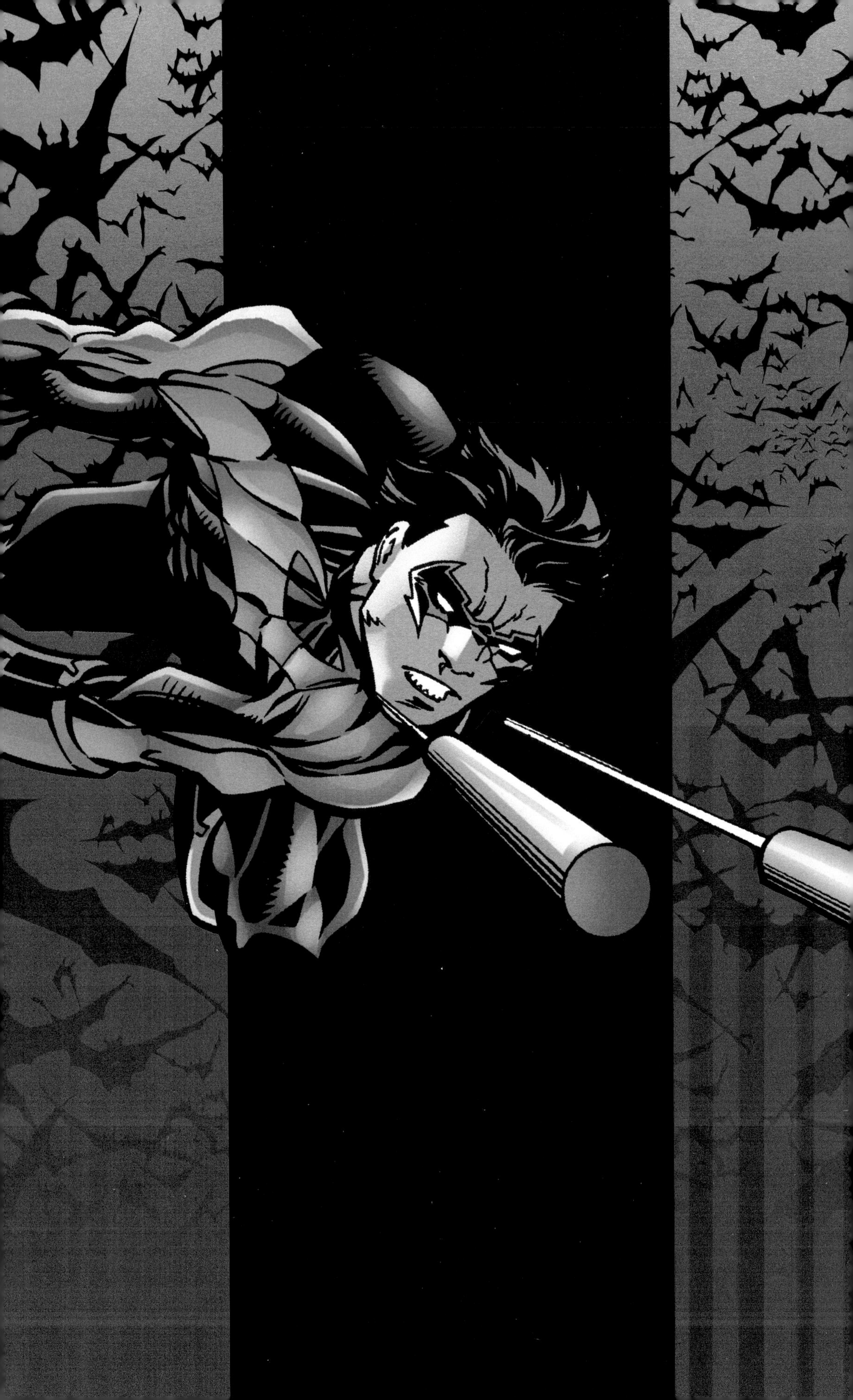

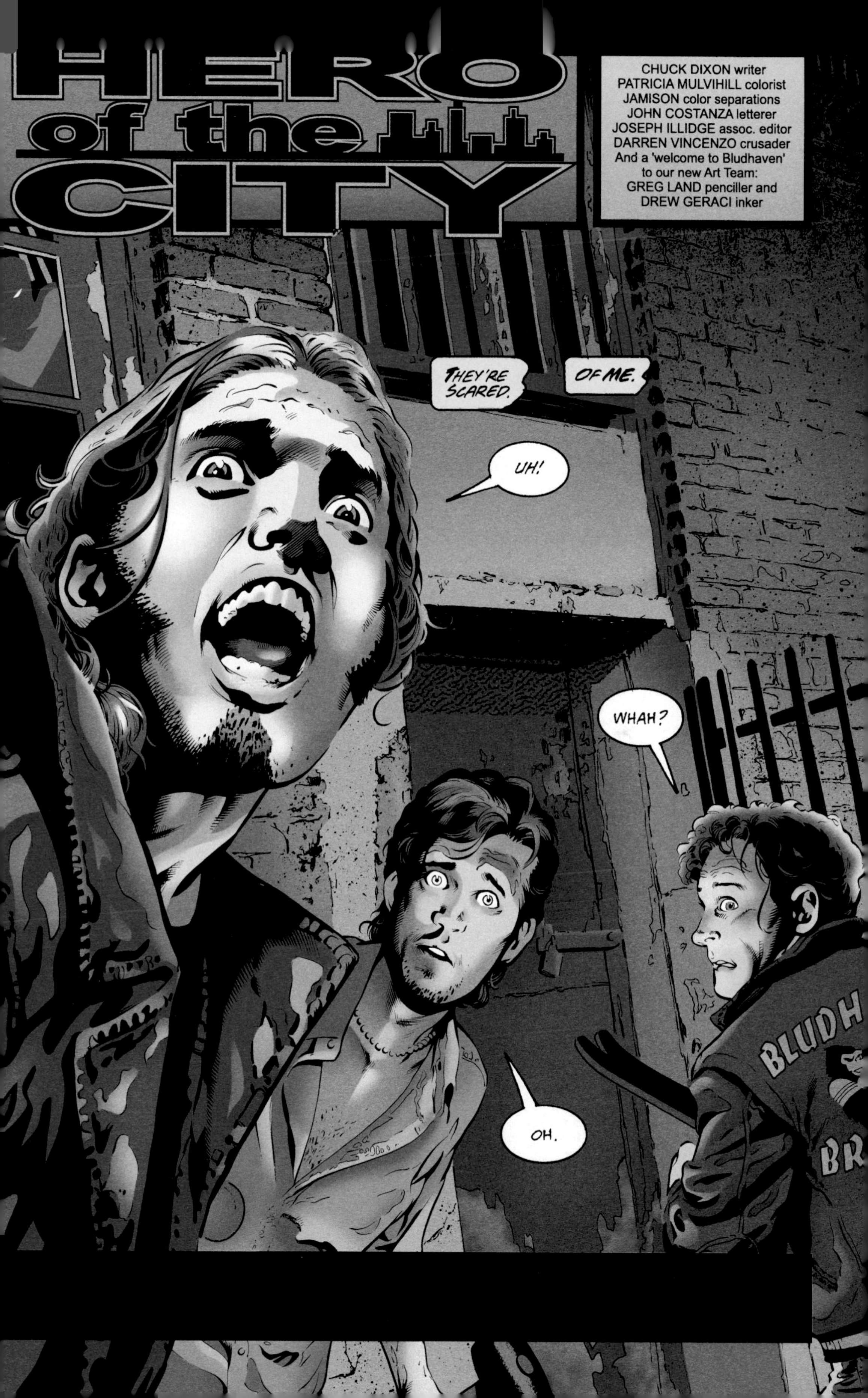
HERO of the CITY
CHUCK DIXON writer
PATRICIA MULVIHILL colorist
JAMISON color separations
JOHN COSTANZA letterer
JOSEPH ILLIDGE assoc. editor
DARREN VINCENZO crusader
And a 'welcome to Bludhaven' to our new Art Team:
GREG LAND penciller and
DREW GERACI inker
THEY'RE SCARED.
OF ME.
UH!
WHAH?
OH.

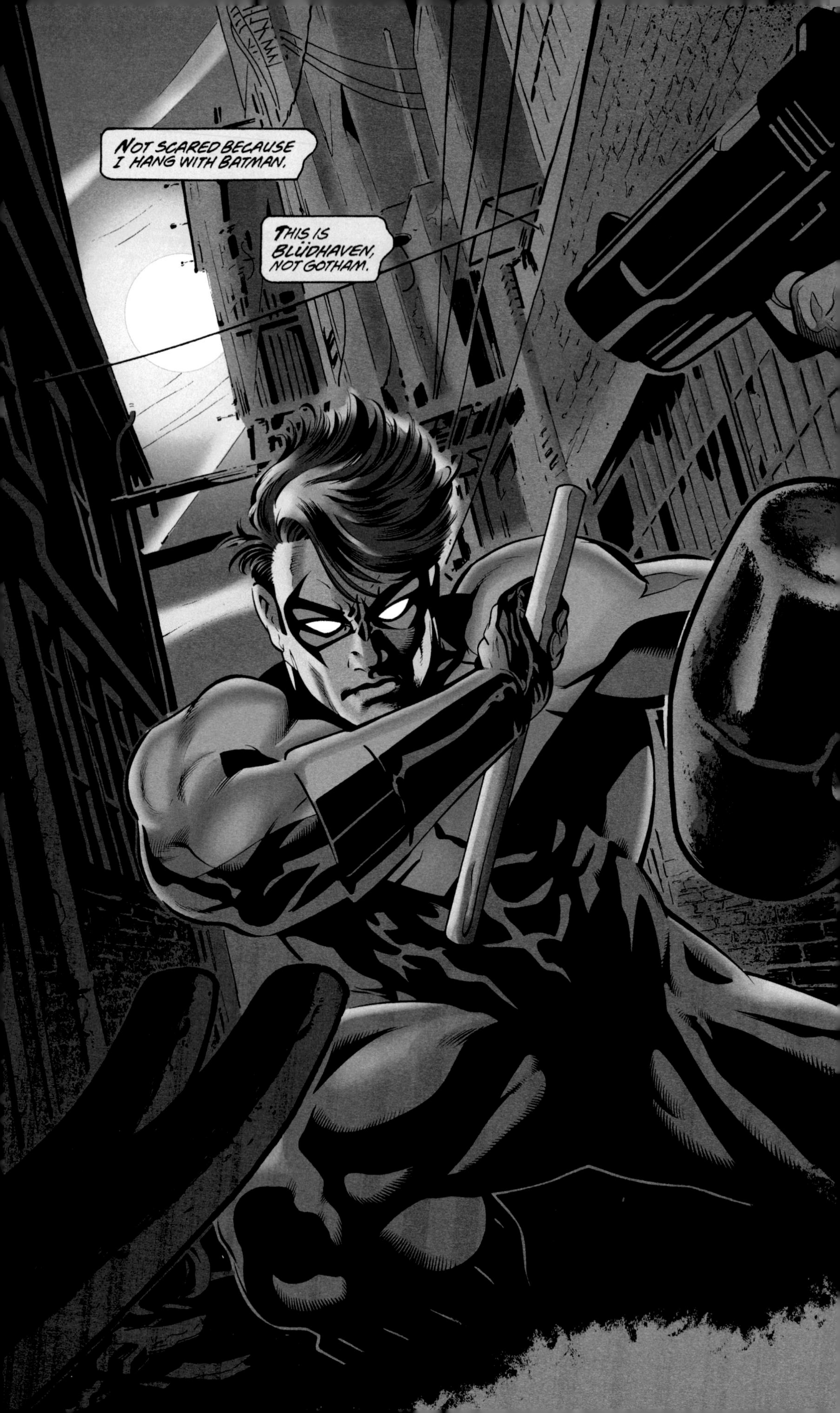
NOT SCARED BECAUSE I HANG WITH BATMAN.
THIS IS BLÜDHAVEN, NOT GOTHAM.

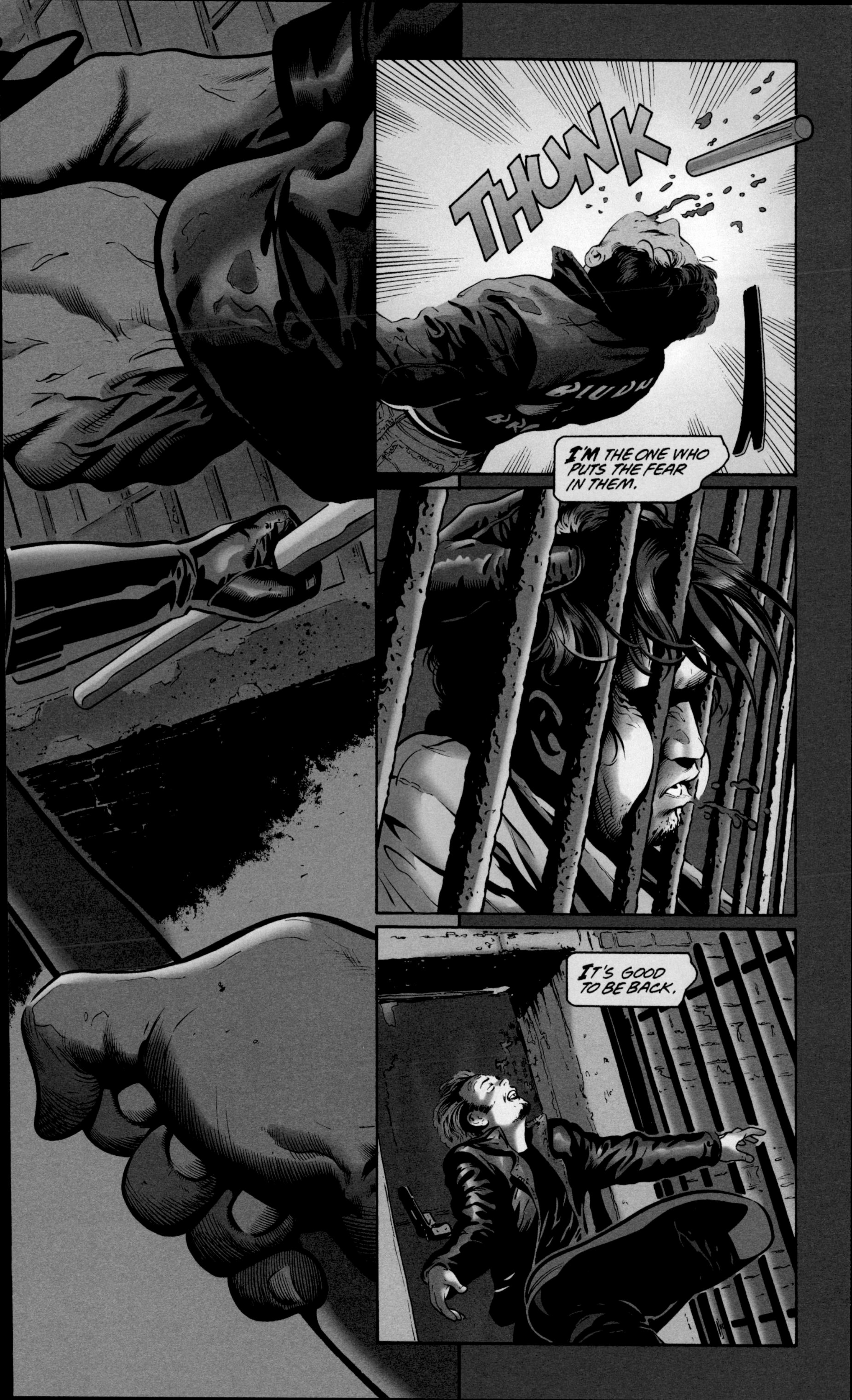
THUNK
I'M THE ONE WHO PUTS THE FEAR IN THEM.
IT'S GOOD TO BE BACK.

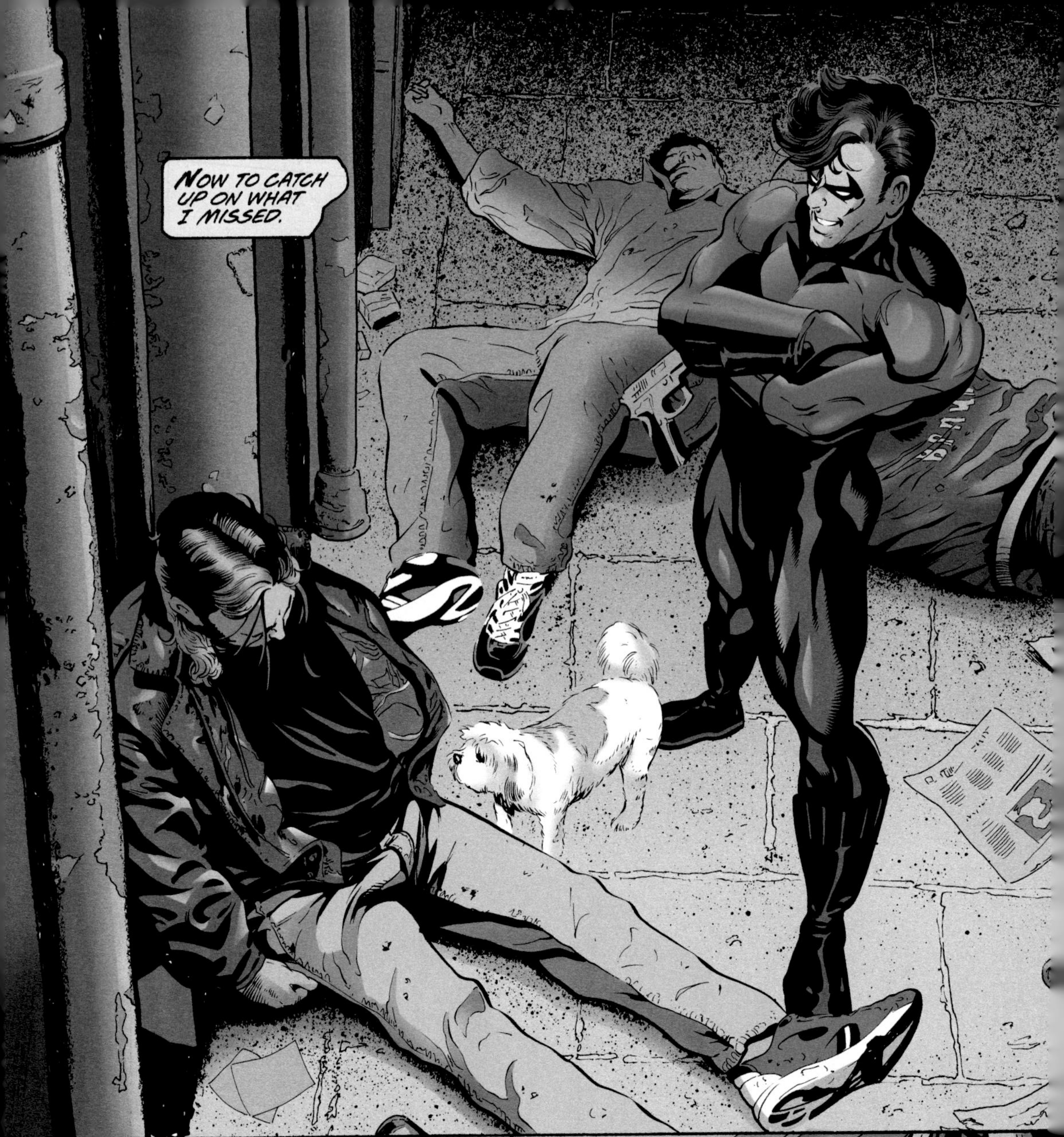
NOW TO CATCH UP ON WHAT I MISSED.

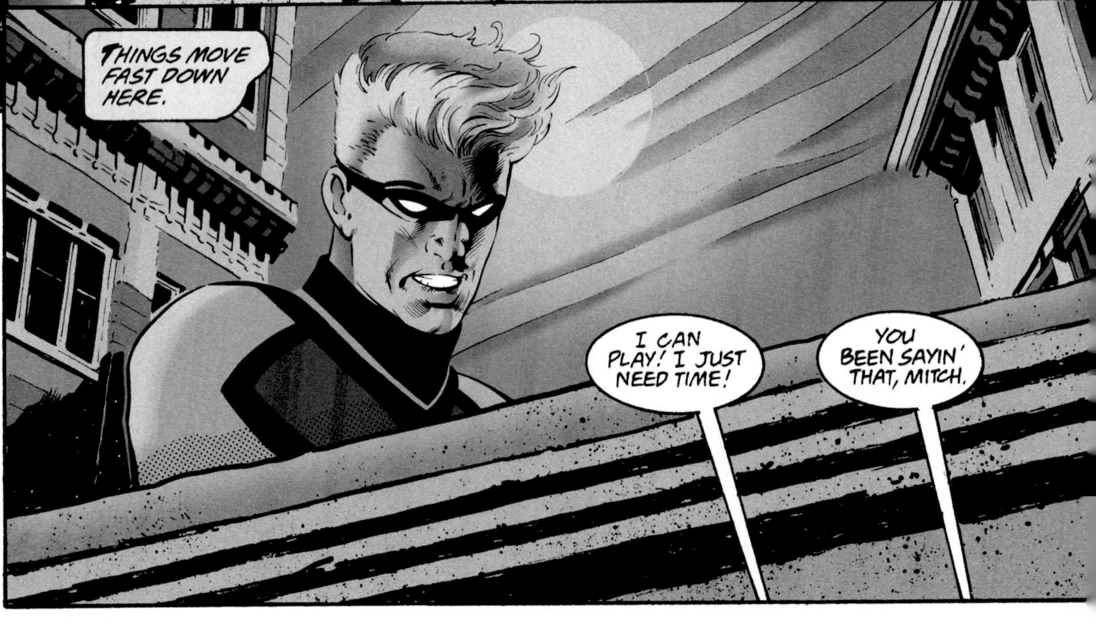
THINGS MOVE FAST DOWN HERE.
I CAN PLAY! I JUST NEED TIME!
YOU BEEN SAYIN' THAT, MITCH.

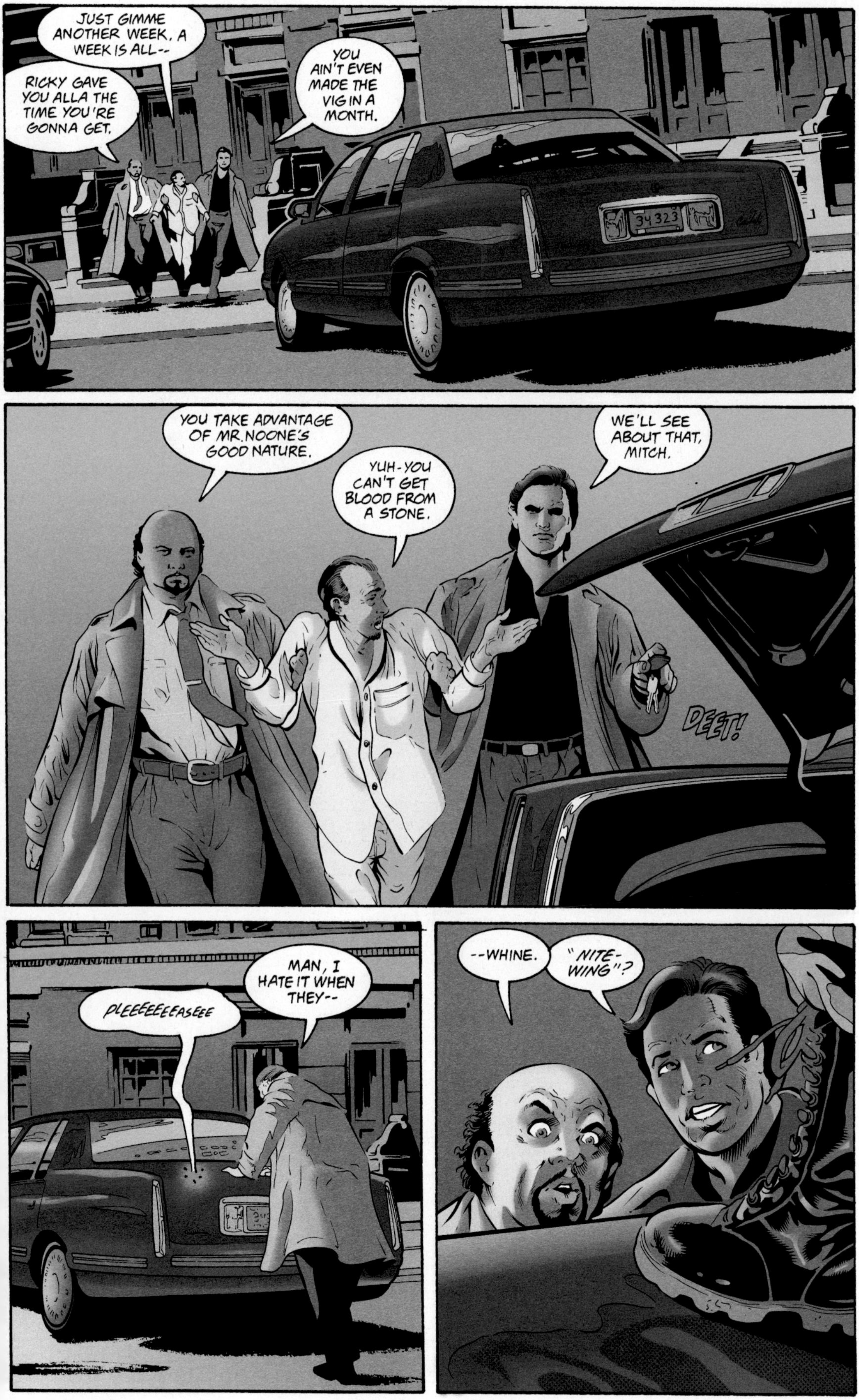
JUST GIMME ANOTHER WEEK, A WEEK IS ALL--
RICKY GAVE YOU ALLA THE TIME YOU'RE GONNA GET.
YOU AIN'T EVEN MADE THE VIG IN A MONTH.
YOU TAKE ADVANTAGE OF MR. NOONE'S GOOD NATURE.
YUH-YOU CAN'T GET BLOOD FROM A STONE.
WE'LL SEE ABOUT THAT, MITCH.
DEET!
PLEEEEEEEASEEE
MAN, I HATE IT WHEN THEY--
--WHINE.
"NITE-WING"?

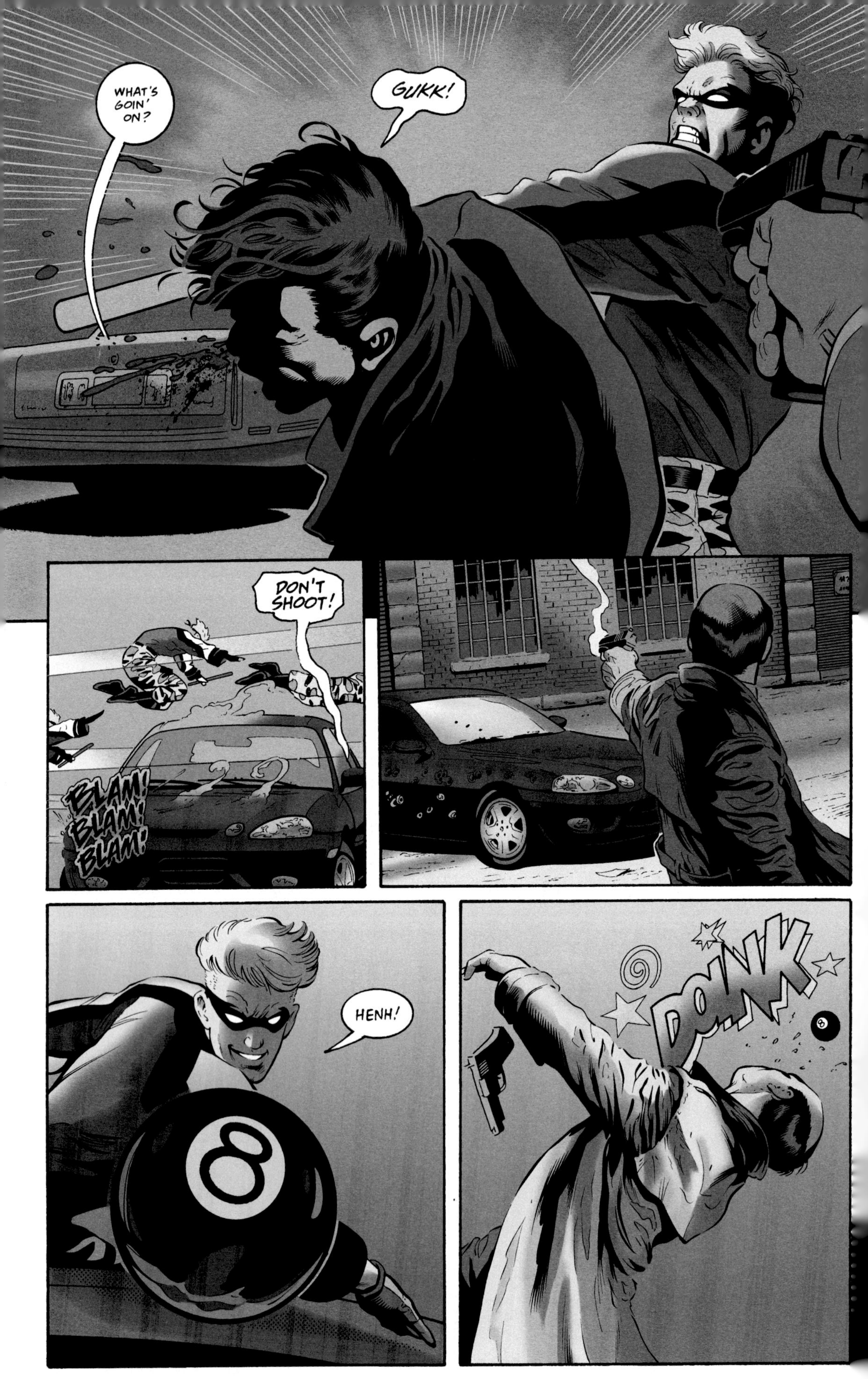
WHAT'S GOIN' ON?
GUKK!
DON'T SHOOT!
BLAM! BLAM! BLAM!
HENH!
DONK

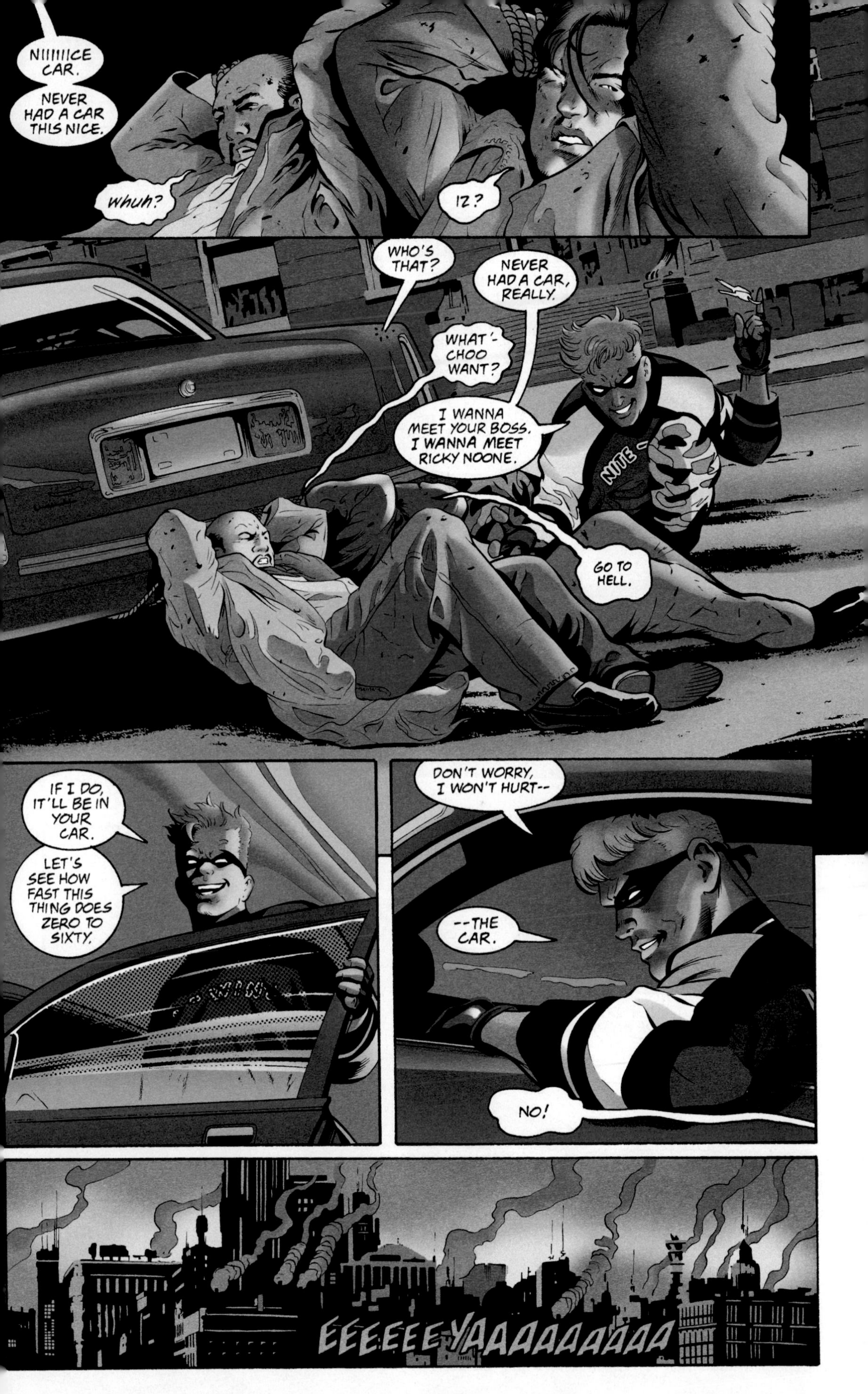

NIIIIIICE CAR.
NEVER HAD A CAR THIS NICE.
Whuh?
IZ?
WHO'S THAT?
NEVER HAD A CAR, REALLY.
WHAT'-CHOO WANT?
I WANNA MEET YOUR BOSS. I WANNA MEET RICKY NOONE.
NITE -
GO TO HELL.
IF I DO, IT'LL BE IN YOUR CAR.
LET'S SEE HOW FAST THIS THING DOES ZERO TO SIXTY.
DON'T WORRY, I WON'T HURT--
--THE CAR.
NO!
EEEEEEYAAAAAAAAA

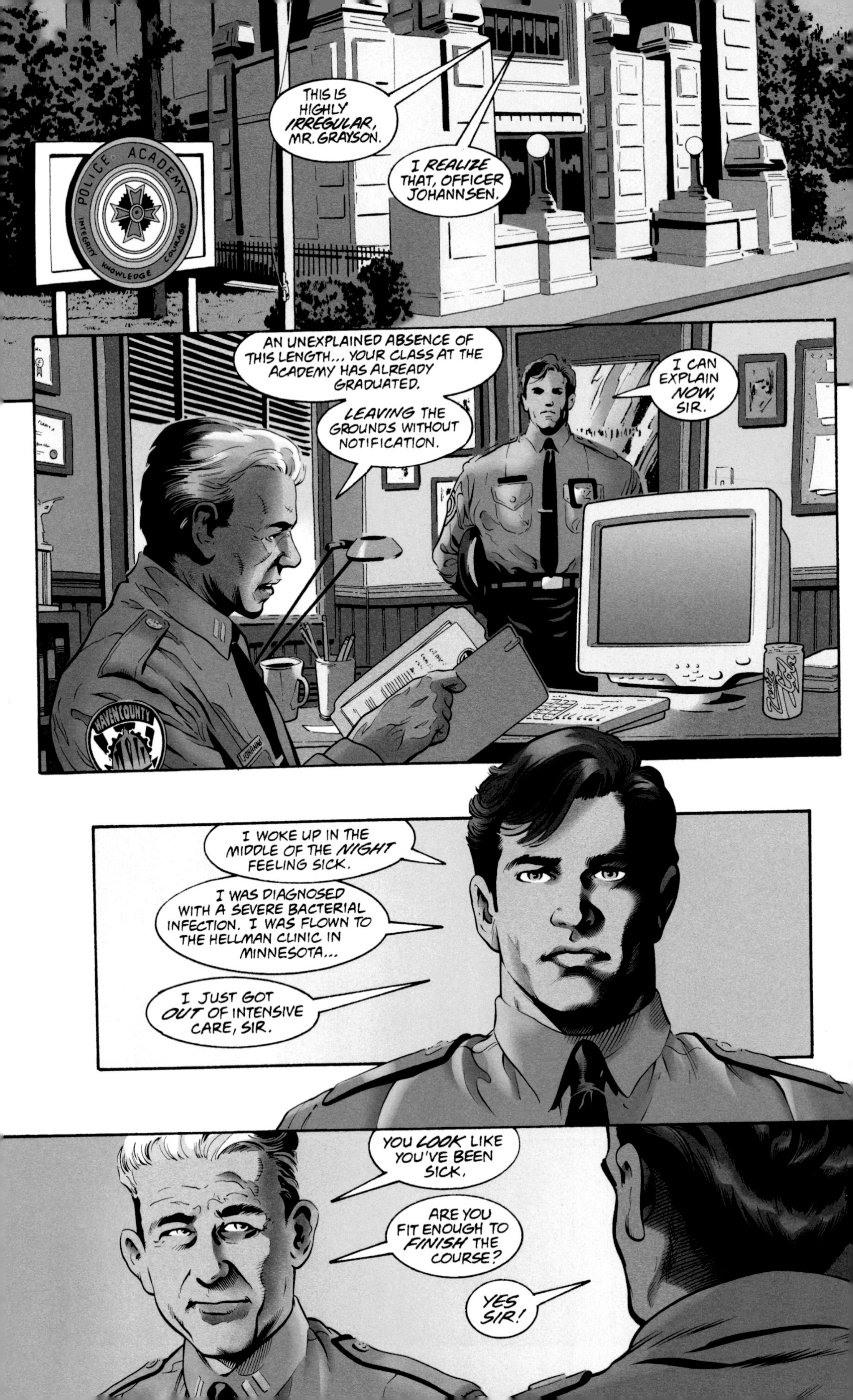
POLICE ACADEMY
INTEGRITY KNOWLEDGE COURAGE
THIS IS HIGHLY IRREGULAR, MR. GRAYSON.
I REALIZE THAT, OFFICER JOHANNSEN.
AN UNEXPLAINED ABSENCE OF THIS LENGTH... YOUR CLASS AT THE ACADEMY HAS ALREADY GRADUATED.
LEAVING THE GROUNDS WITHOUT NOTIFICATION.
I CAN EXPLAIN NOW, SIR.
HAVEN COUNTY
I WOKE UP IN THE MIDDLE OF THE NIGHT FEELING SICK.
I WAS DIAGNOSED WITH A SEVERE BACTERIAL INFECTION. I WAS FLOWN TO THE HELLMAN CLINIC IN MINNESOTA...
I JUST GOT OUT OF INTENSIVE CARE, SIR.
YOU LOOK LIKE YOU'VE BEEN SICK.
ARE YOU FIT ENOUGH TO FINISH THE COURSE?
YES SIR!

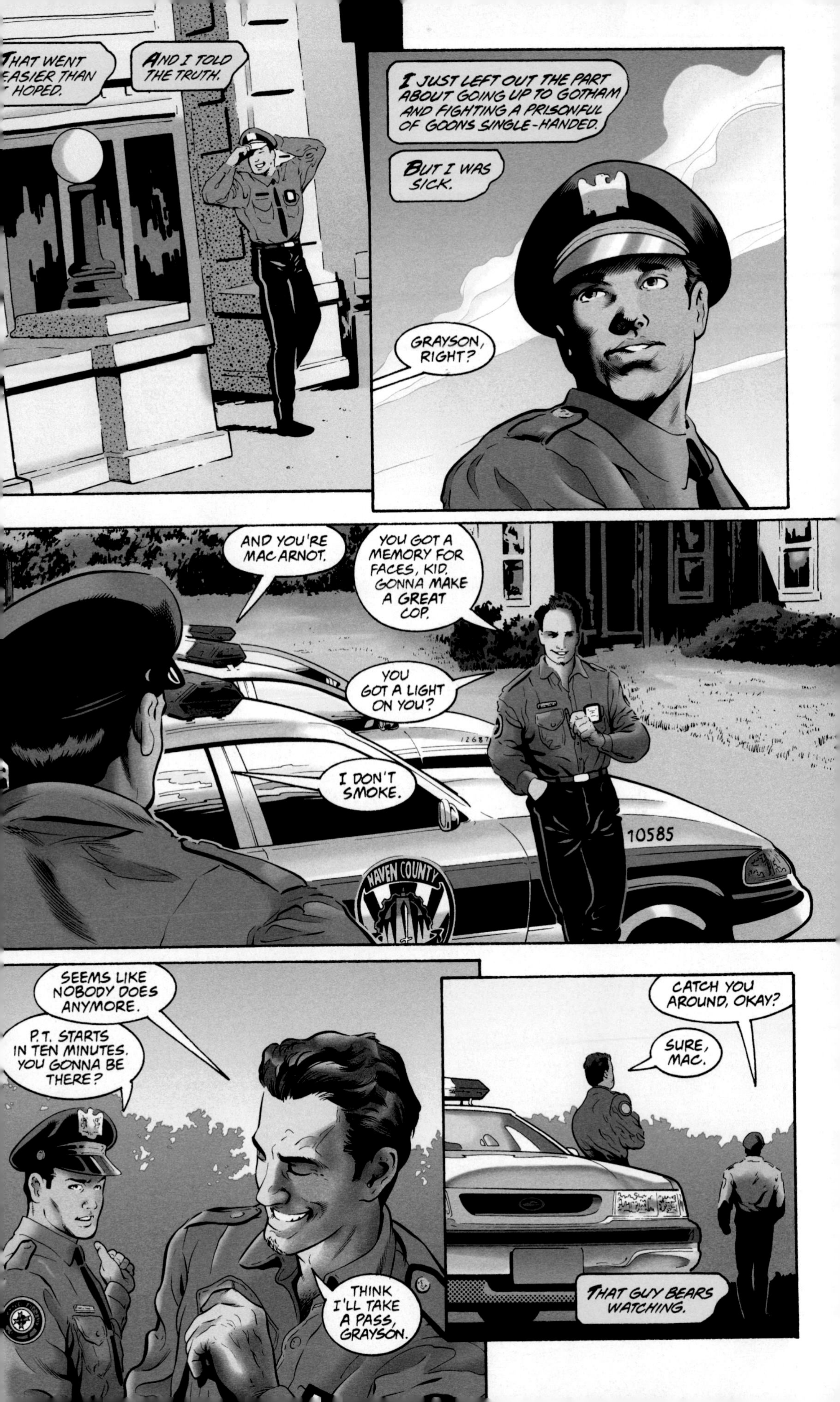

THAT WENT EASIER THAN I HOPED.
AND I TOLD THE TRUTH.
I JUST LEFT OUT THE PART ABOUT GOING UP TO GOTHAM AND FIGHTING A PRISONFUL OF GOONS SINGLE-HANDED.
BUT I WAS SICK.
GRAYSON, RIGHT?
AND YOU'RE MAC ARNOT.
YOU GOT A MEMORY FOR FACES, KID. GONNA MAKE A GREAT COP.
YOU GOT A LIGHT ON YOU?
I DON'T SMOKE.
10585
HAVEN COUNTY
SEEMS LIKE NOBODY DOES ANYMORE.
P.T. STARTS IN TEN MINUTES. YOU GONNA BE THERE?
THINK I'LL TAKE A PASS, GRAYSON.
CATCH YOU AROUND, OKAY?
SURE, MAC.
THAT GUY BEARS WATCHING.

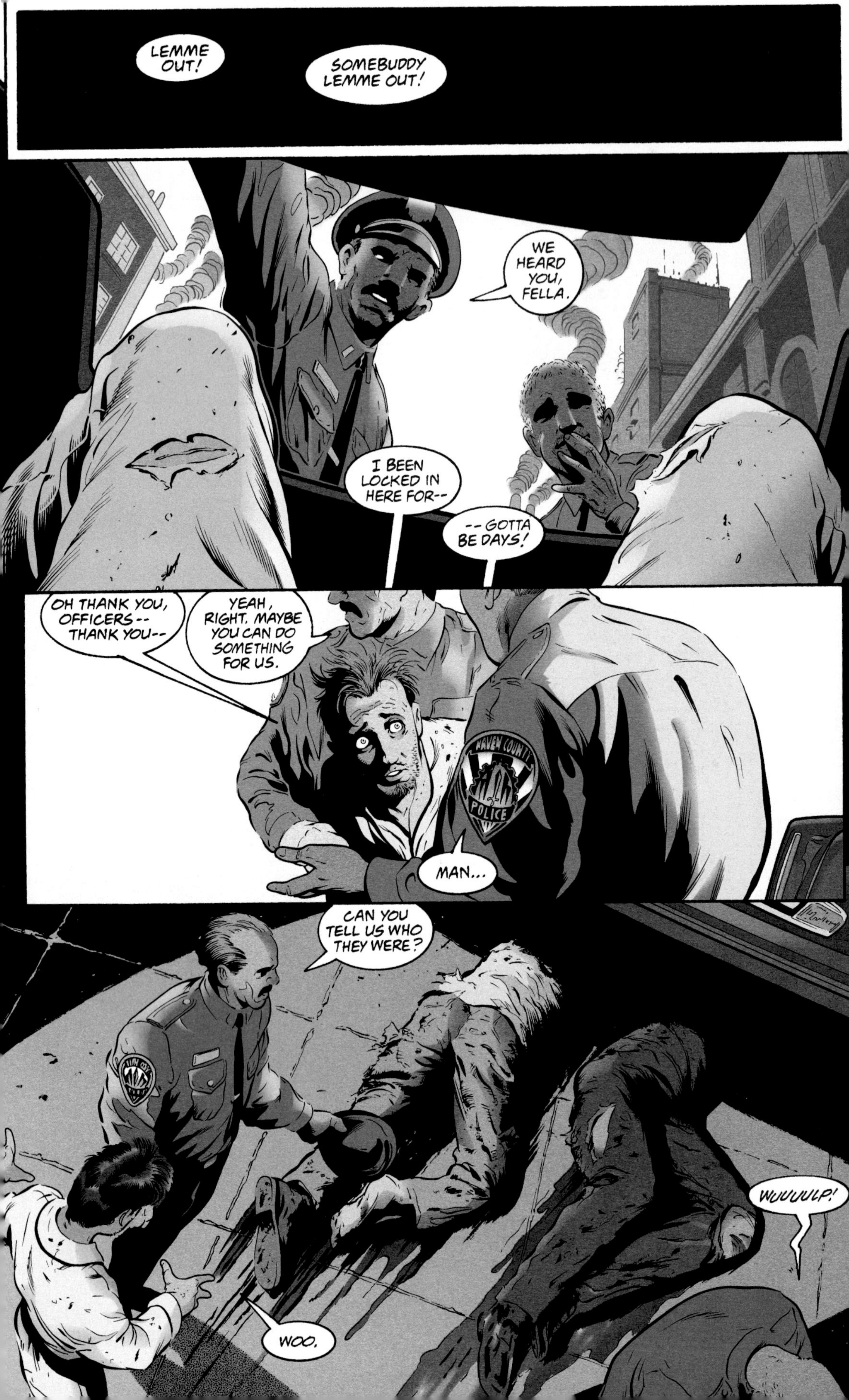
LEMME OUT!
SOMEBUDDY LEMME OUT!
WE HEARD YOU, FELLA.
I BEEN LOCKED IN HERE FOR--
--GOTTA BE DAYS!
OH THANK YOU, OFFICERS-- THANK YOU--
YEAH, RIGHT. MAYBE YOU CAN DO SOMETHING FOR US.
HAVEN COUNTY POLICE
MAN...
CAN YOU TELL US WHO THEY WERE?
WUUUULP!
WOO.

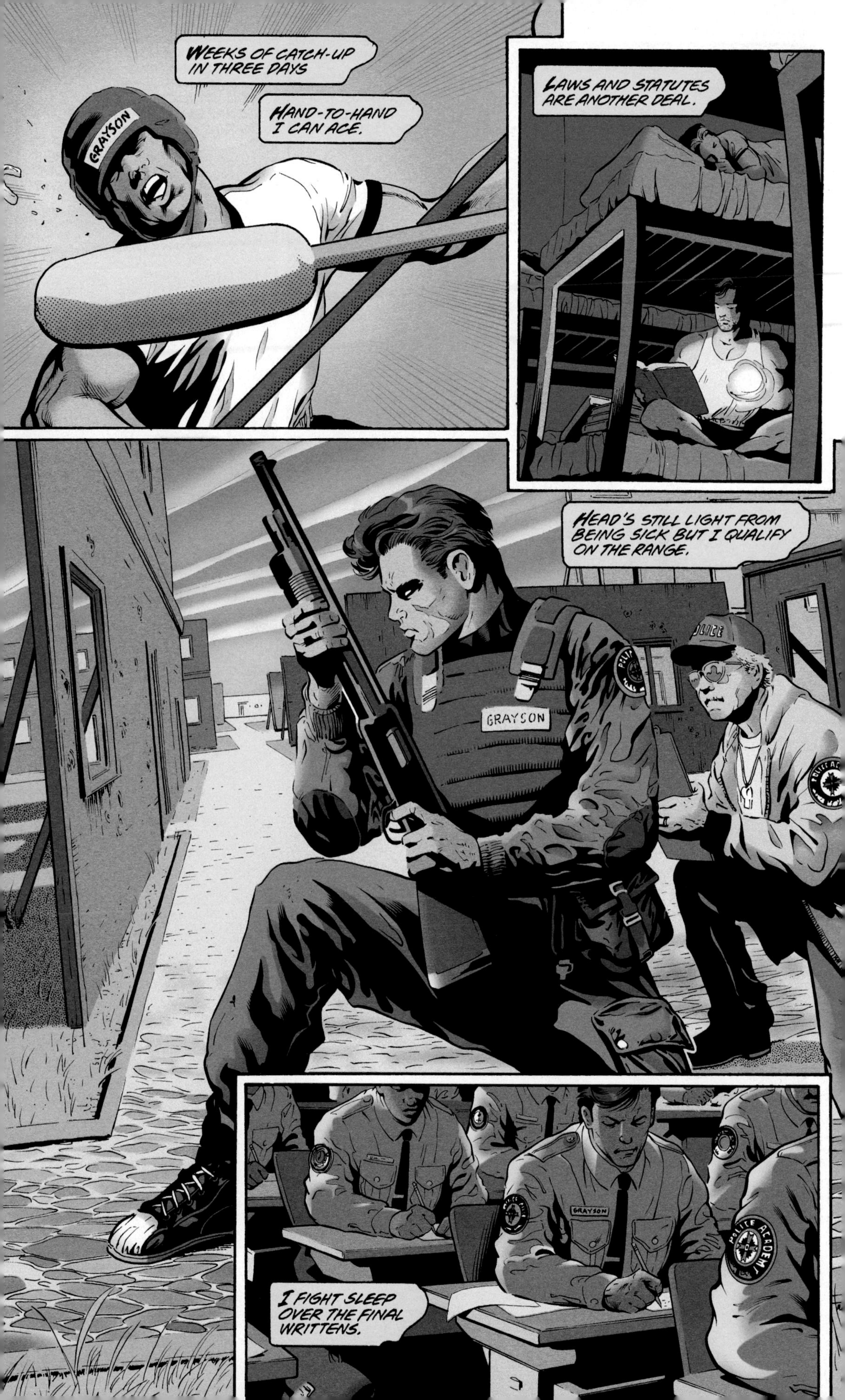
WEEKS OF CATCH-UP IN THREE DAYS
HAND-TO-HAND I CAN ACE.
GRAYSON
LAWS AND STATUTES ARE ANOTHER DEAL.
HEAD'S STILL LIGHT FROM BEING SICK BUT I QUALIFY ON THE RANGE.
GRAYSON
POLICE
GRAYSON
I FIGHT SLEEP OVER THE FINAL WRITTENS.

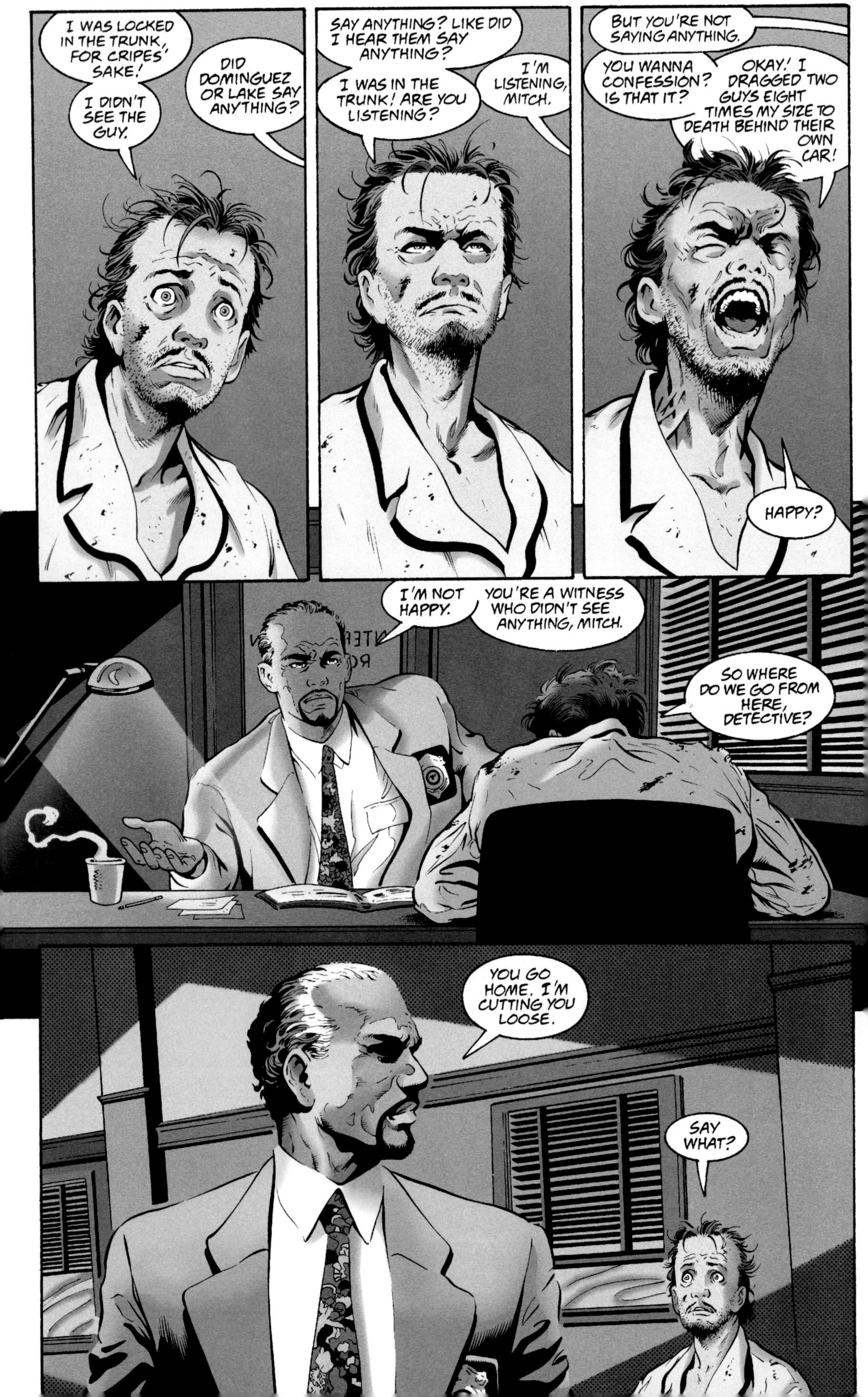
I WAS LOCKED IN THE TRUNK, FOR CRIPES' SAKE!
I DIDN'T SEE THE GUY.
DID DOMINGUEZ OR LAKE SAY ANYTHING?
SAY ANYTHING? LIKE DID I HEAR THEM SAY ANYTHING?
I WAS IN THE TRUNK! ARE YOU LISTENING?
I'M LISTENING, MITCH.
BUT YOU'RE NOT SAYING ANYTHING.
YOU WANNA CONFESSION? IS THAT IT?
OKAY! I DRAGGED TWO GUYS EIGHT TIMES MY SIZE TO DEATH BEHIND THEIR OWN CAR!
HAPPY?
I'M NOT HAPPY.
YOU'RE A WITNESS WHO DIDN'T SEE ANYTHING, MITCH.
SO WHERE DO WE GO FROM HERE, DETECTIVE?
YOU GO HOME. I'M CUTTING YOU LOOSE.
SAY WHAT?

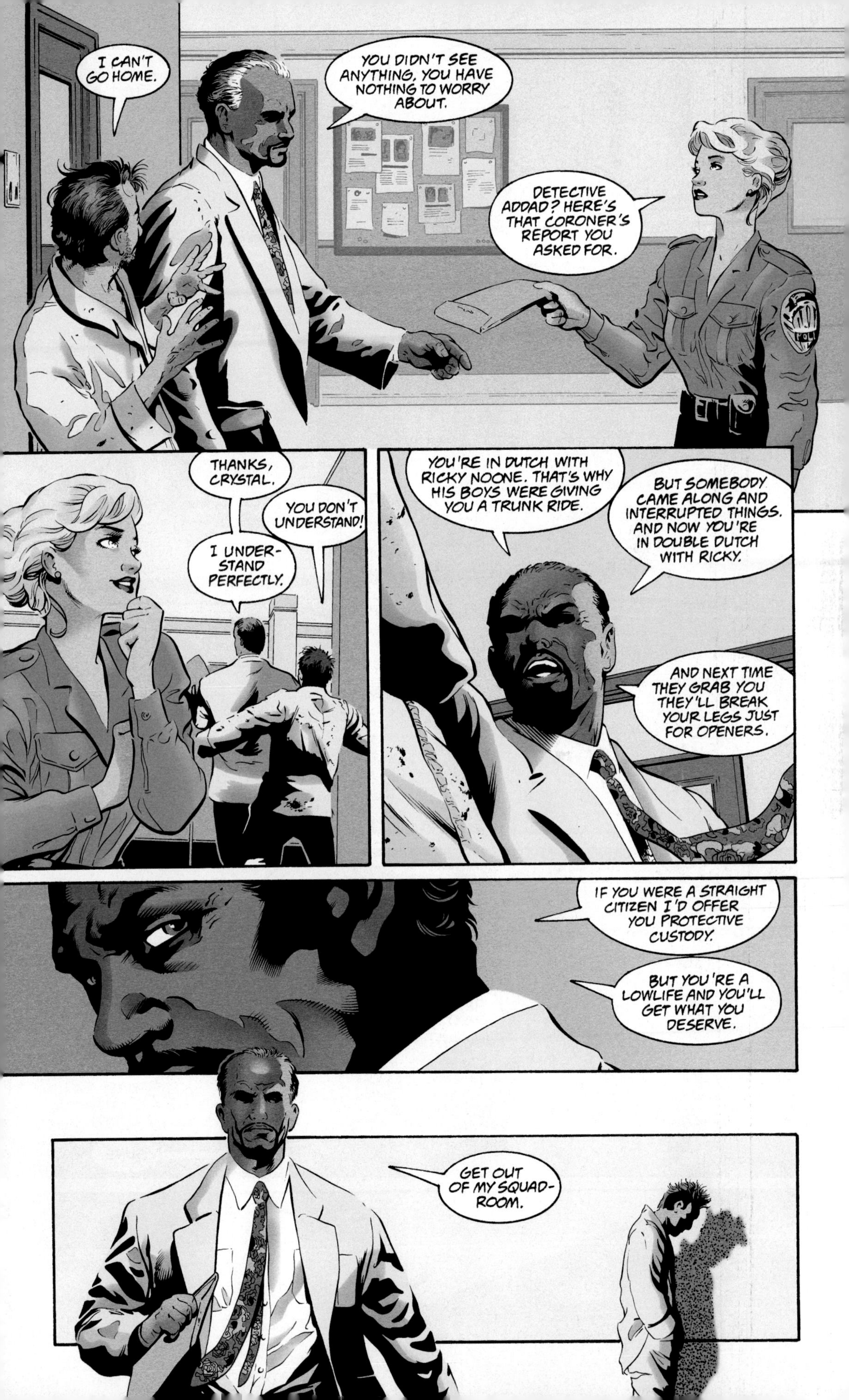
I CAN'T GO HOME.
YOU DIDN'T SEE ANYTHING, YOU HAVE NOTHING TO WORRY ABOUT.
DETECTIVE ADDAD? HERE'S THAT CORONER'S REPORT YOU ASKED FOR.
THANKS, CRYSTAL.
YOU DON'T UNDERSTAND!
I UNDER-STAND PERFECTLY.
YOU'RE IN DUTCH WITH RICKY NOONE. THAT'S WHY HIS BOYS WERE GIVING YOU A TRUNK RIDE.
BUT SOMEBODY CAME ALONG AND INTERRUPTED THINGS. AND NOW YOU'RE IN DOUBLE DUTCH WITH RICKY.
AND NEXT TIME THEY GRAB YOU THEY'LL BREAK YOUR LEGS JUST FOR OPENERS.
IF YOU WERE A STRAIGHT CITIZEN I'D OFFER YOU PROTECTIVE CUSTODY.
BUT YOU'RE A LOWLIFE AND YOU'LL GET WHAT YOU DESERVE.
GET OUT OF MY SQUAD-ROOM.

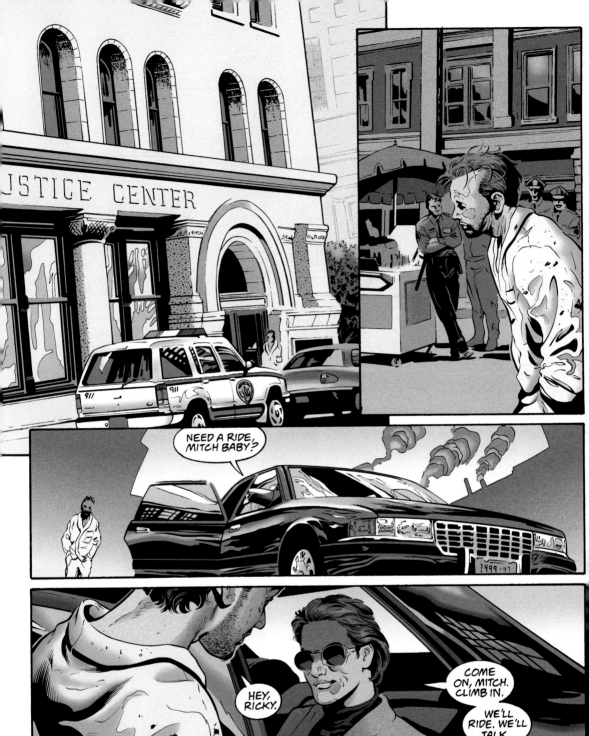

NEED A RIDE, MITCH BABY?

HEY, RICKY.

COME ON, MITCH. CLIMB IN.

WE'LL RIDE. WE'LL TALK.

SURE.

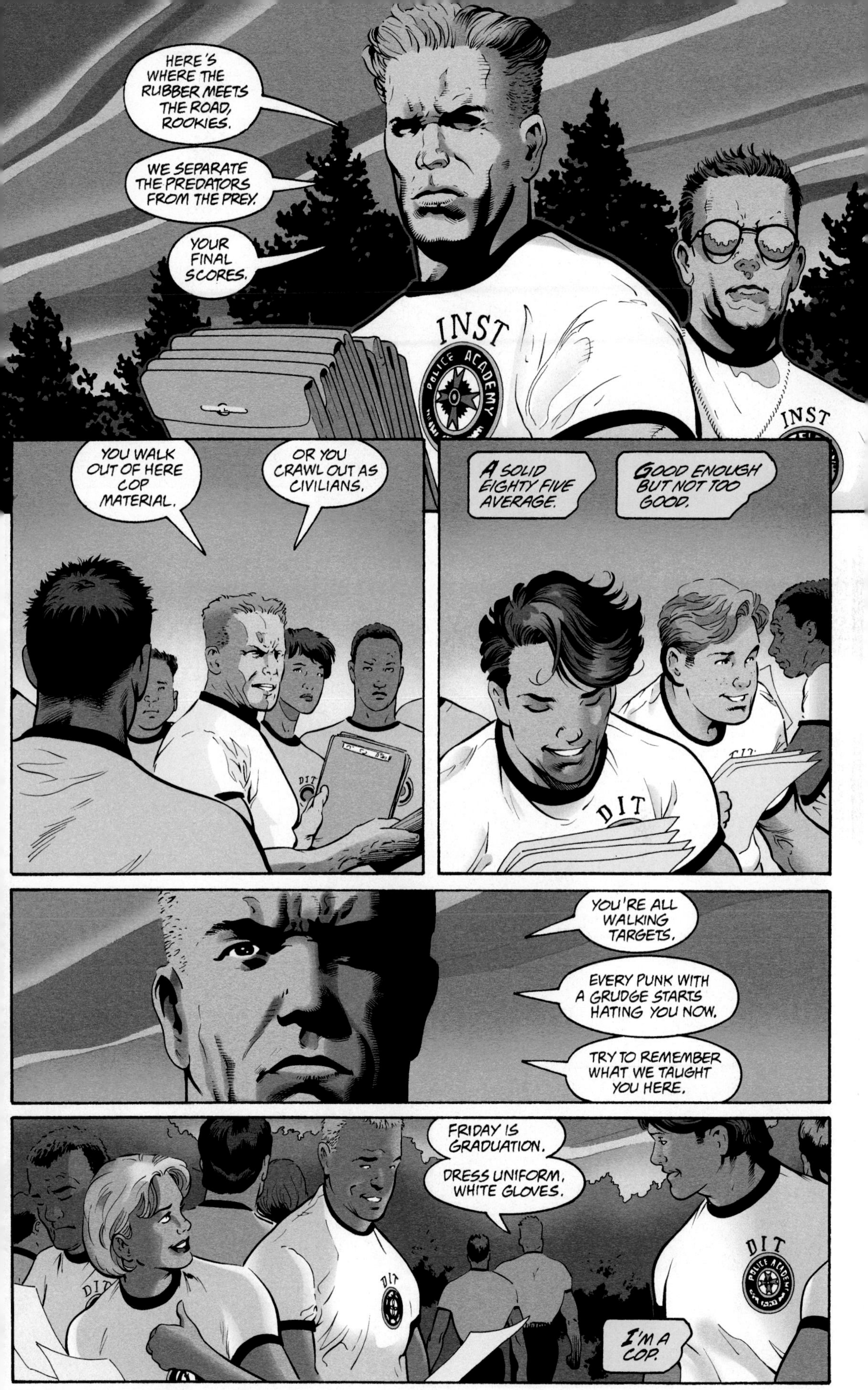
HERE'S WHERE THE RUBBER MEETS THE ROAD, ROOKIES.
WE SEPARATE THE PREDATORS FROM THE PREY.
YOUR FINAL SCORES.
INST
POLICE ACADEMY
YOU WALK OUT OF HERE COP MATERIAL.
OR YOU CRAWL OUT AS CIVILIANS.
A SOLID EIGHTY FIVE AVERAGE.
GOOD ENOUGH BUT NOT TOO GOOD.
DIT
YOU'RE ALL WALKING TARGETS.
EVERY PUNK WITH A GRUDGE STARTS HATING YOU NOW.
TRY TO REMEMBER WHAT WE TAUGHT YOU HERE.
FRIDAY IS GRADUATION.
DRESS UNIFORM. WHITE GLOVES.
I'M A COP.

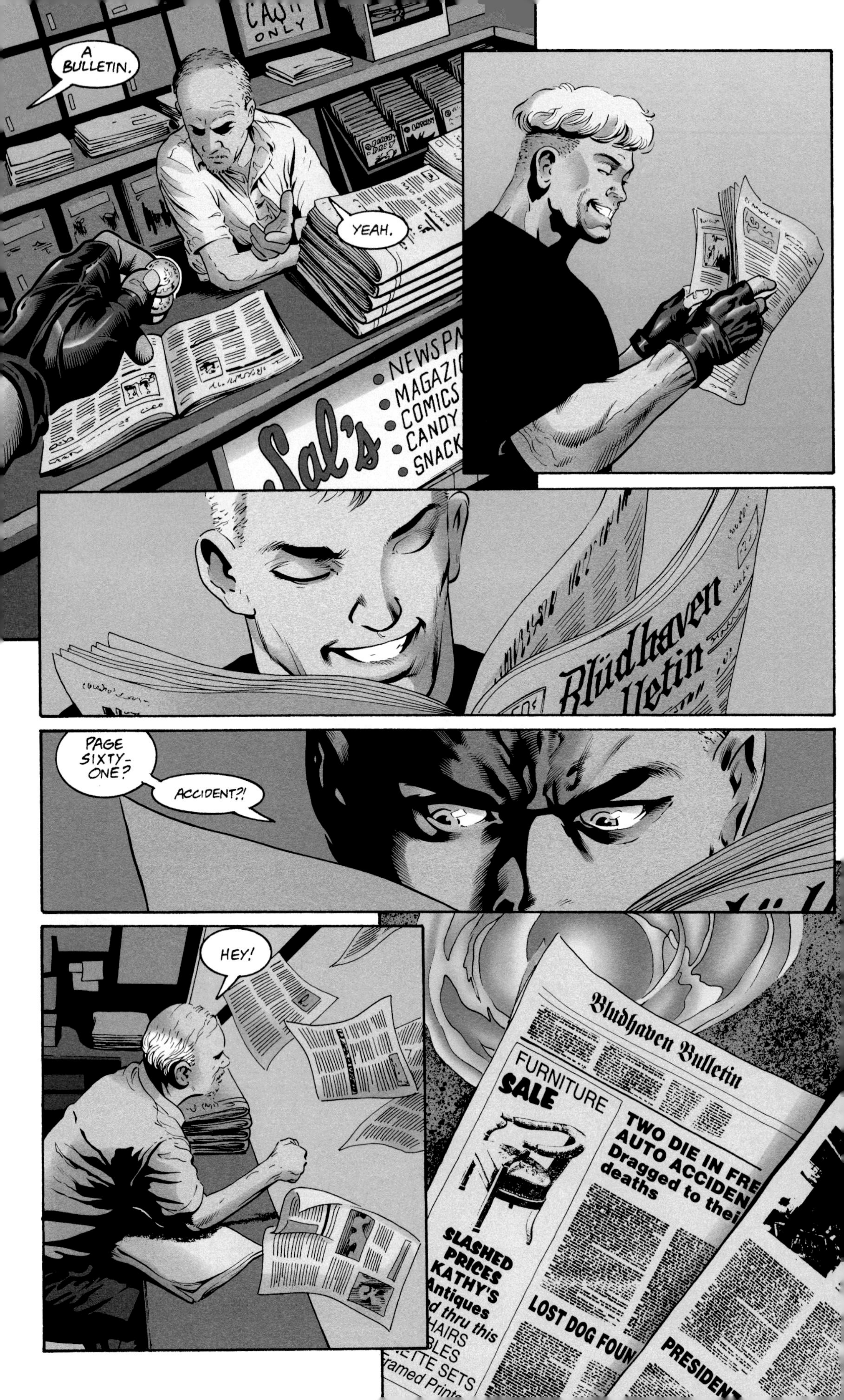
A BULLETIN.
YEAH.
Sal's
COMICS
CANDY
SNACK
Blüdhaven
PAGE SIXTY-ONE?
ACCIDENT?!
HEY!
Bludhaven Bulletin
FURNITURE SALE
SLASHED PRICES
KATHY'S
Antiques

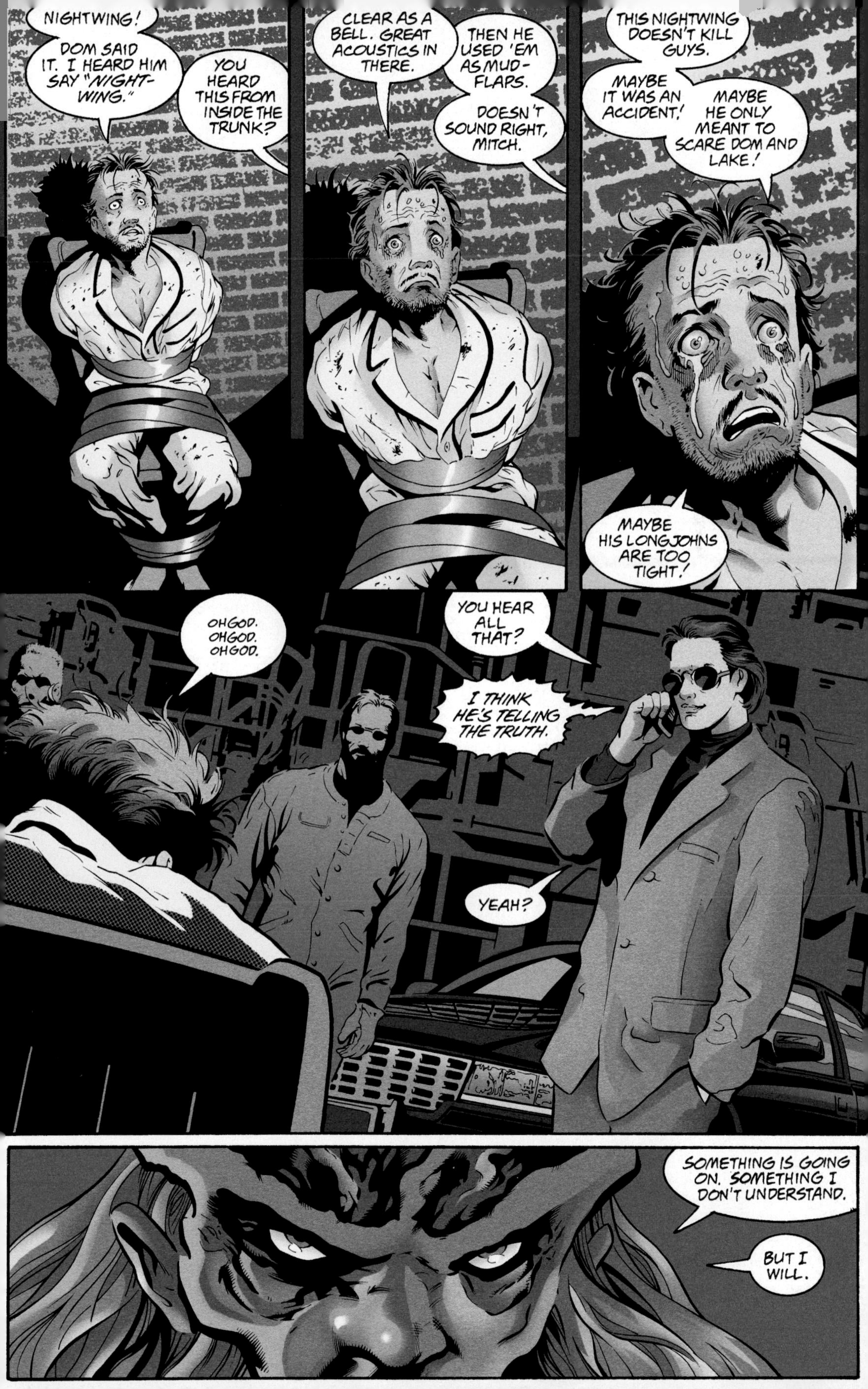
NIGHTWING!
DOM SAID IT. I HEARD HIM SAY "NIGHT-WING."
YOU HEARD THIS FROM INSIDE THE TRUNK?
CLEAR AS A BELL. GREAT ACOUSTICS IN THERE.
THEN HE USED 'EM AS MUD-FLAPS.
DOESN'T SOUND RIGHT, MITCH.
THIS NIGHTWING DOESN'T KILL GUYS.
MAYBE IT WAS AN ACCIDENT!
MAYBE HE ONLY MEANT TO SCARE DOM AND LAKE!
MAYBE HIS LONGJOHNS ARE TOO TIGHT!
OHGOD. OHGOD. OHGOD.
YOU HEAR ALL THAT?
I THINK HE'S TELLING THE TRUTH.
YEAH?
SOMETHING IS GOING ON. SOMETHING I DON'T UNDERSTAND.
BUT I WILL.

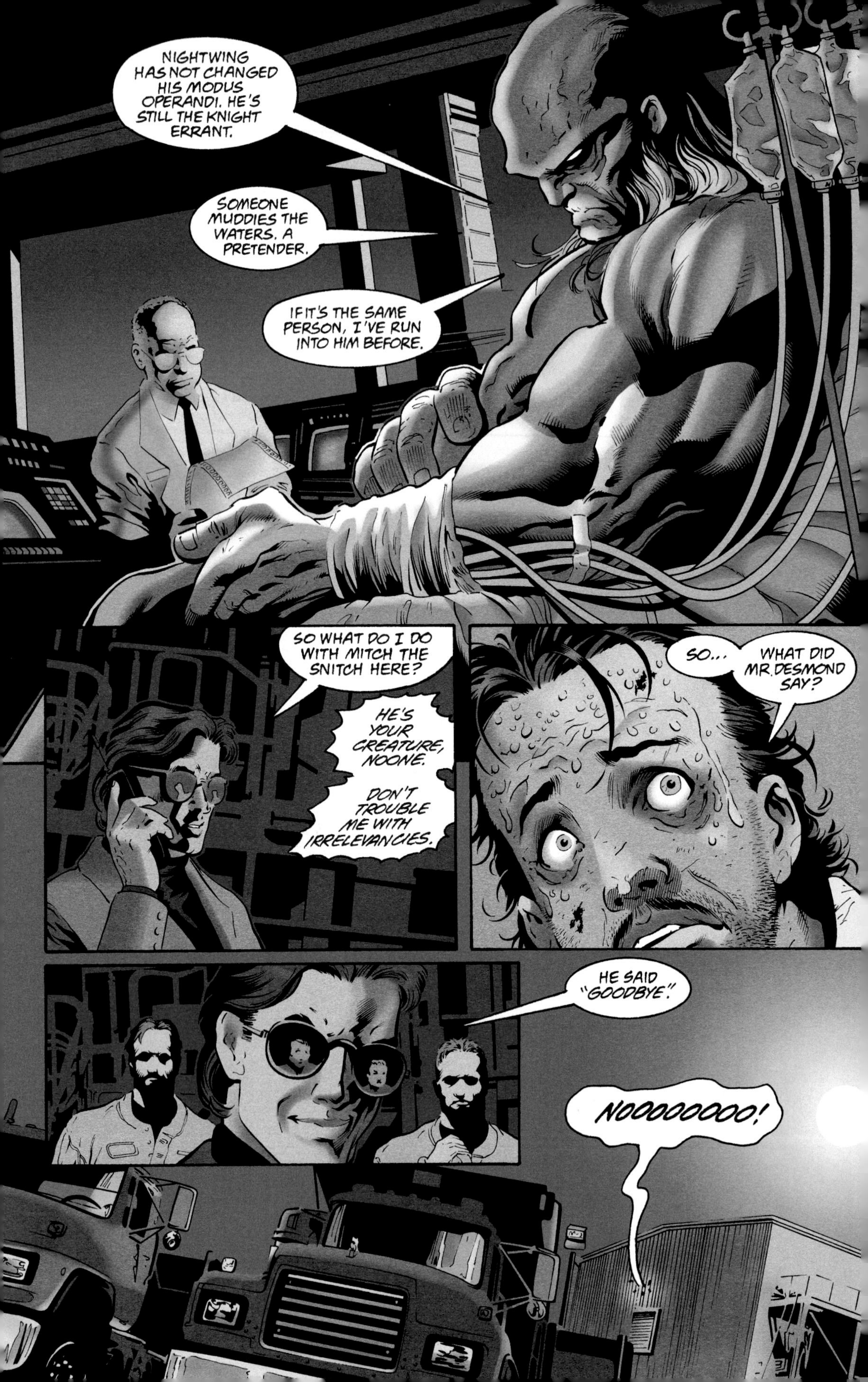
NIGHTWING HAS NOT CHANGED HIS MODUS OPERANDI. HE'S STILL THE KNIGHT ERRANT.
SOMEONE MUDDIES THE WATERS. A PRETENDER.
IF IT'S THE SAME PERSON, I'VE RUN INTO HIM BEFORE.
SO WHAT DO I DO WITH MITCH THE SNITCH HERE?
HE'S YOUR CREATURE, NOONE.
DON'T TROUBLE ME WITH IRRELEVANCIES.
SO...
WHAT DID MR. DESMOND SAY?
HE SAID "GOODBYE".
NOOOOOOOO!

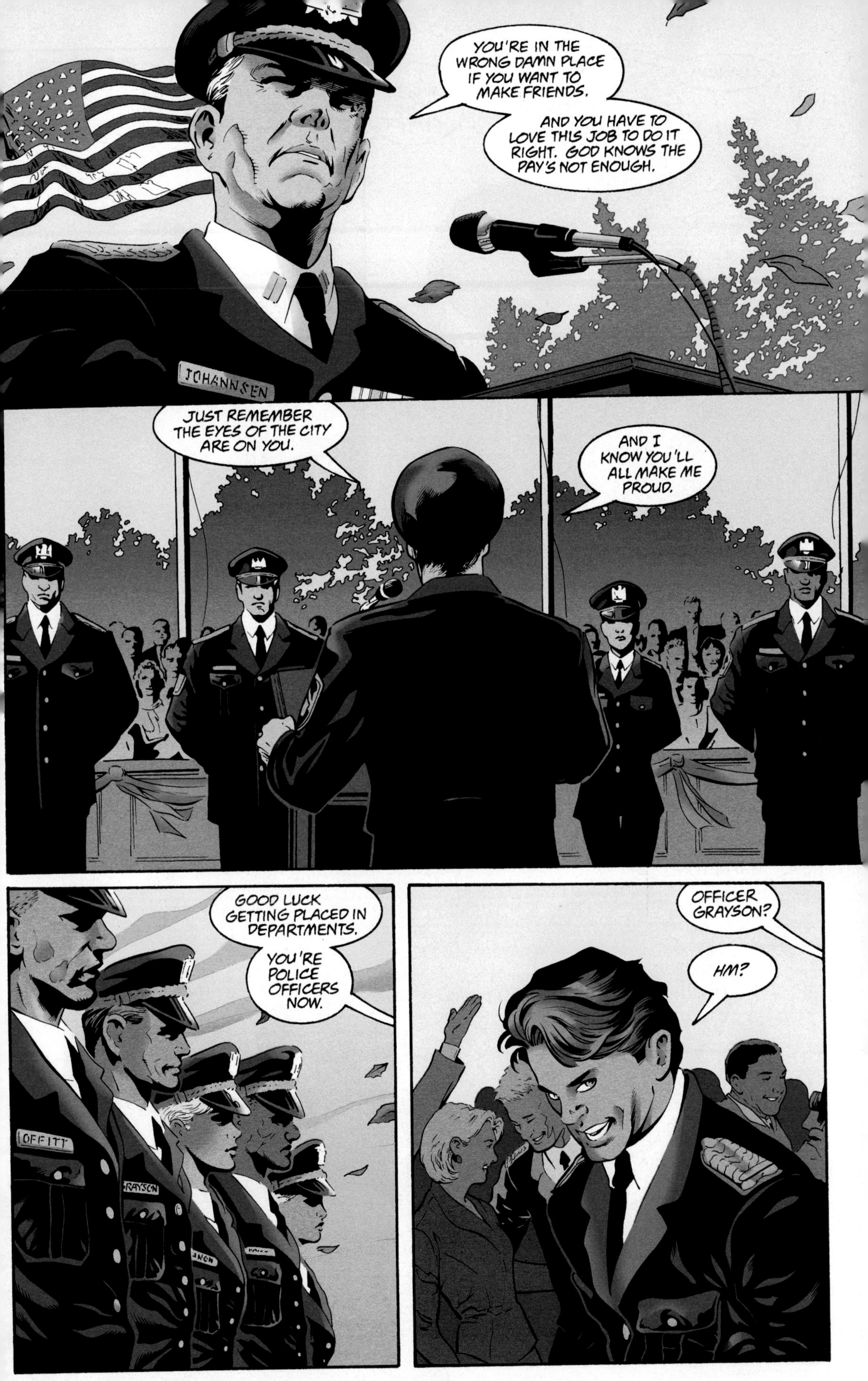
YOU'RE IN THE WRONG DAMN PLACE IF YOU WANT TO MAKE FRIENDS.
AND YOU HAVE TO LOVE THIS JOB TO DO IT RIGHT. GOD KNOWS THE PAY'S NOT ENOUGH.
JOHANNSEN
JUST REMEMBER THE EYES OF THE CITY ARE ON YOU.
AND I KNOW YOU'LL ALL MAKE ME PROUD.
GOOD LUCK GETTING PLACED IN DEPARTMENTS.
YOU'RE POLICE OFFICERS NOW.
OFFICER GRAYSON?
HM?

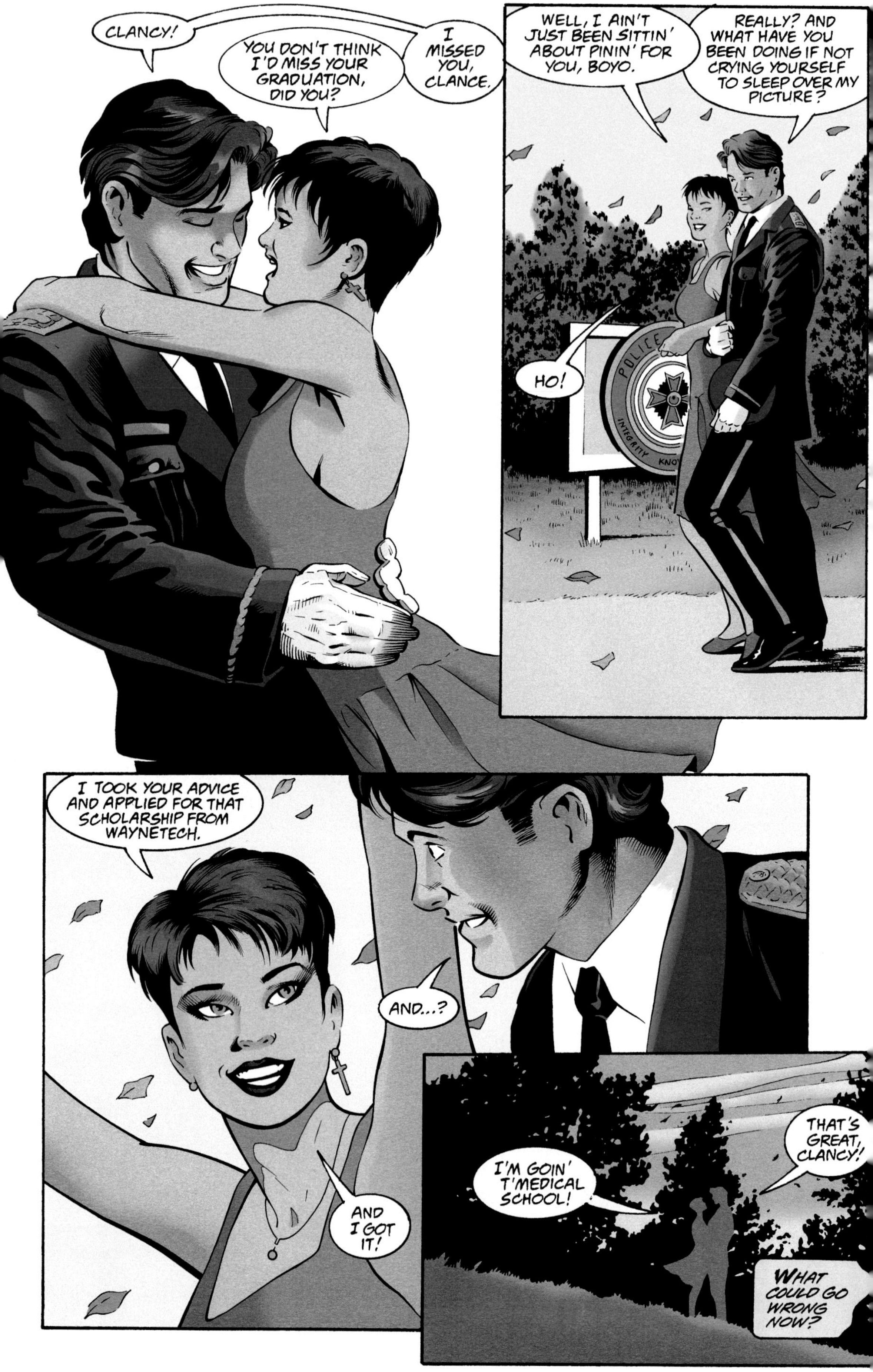
CLANCY!
YOU DON'T THINK I'D MISS YOUR GRADUATION, DID YOU?
I MISSED YOU, CLANCE.
WELL, I AIN'T JUST BEEN SITTIN' ABOUT PININ' FOR YOU, BOYO.
REALLY? AND WHAT HAVE YOU BEEN DOING IF NOT CRYING YOURSELF TO SLEEP OVER MY PICTURE?
HO!
POLICE
INTEGRITY
I TOOK YOUR ADVICE AND APPLIED FOR THAT SCHOLARSHIP FROM WAYNETECH.
AND...?
AND I GOT IT!
I'M GOIN' T'MEDICAL SCHOOL!
THAT'S GREAT, CLANCY!
WHAT COULD GO WRONG NOW?

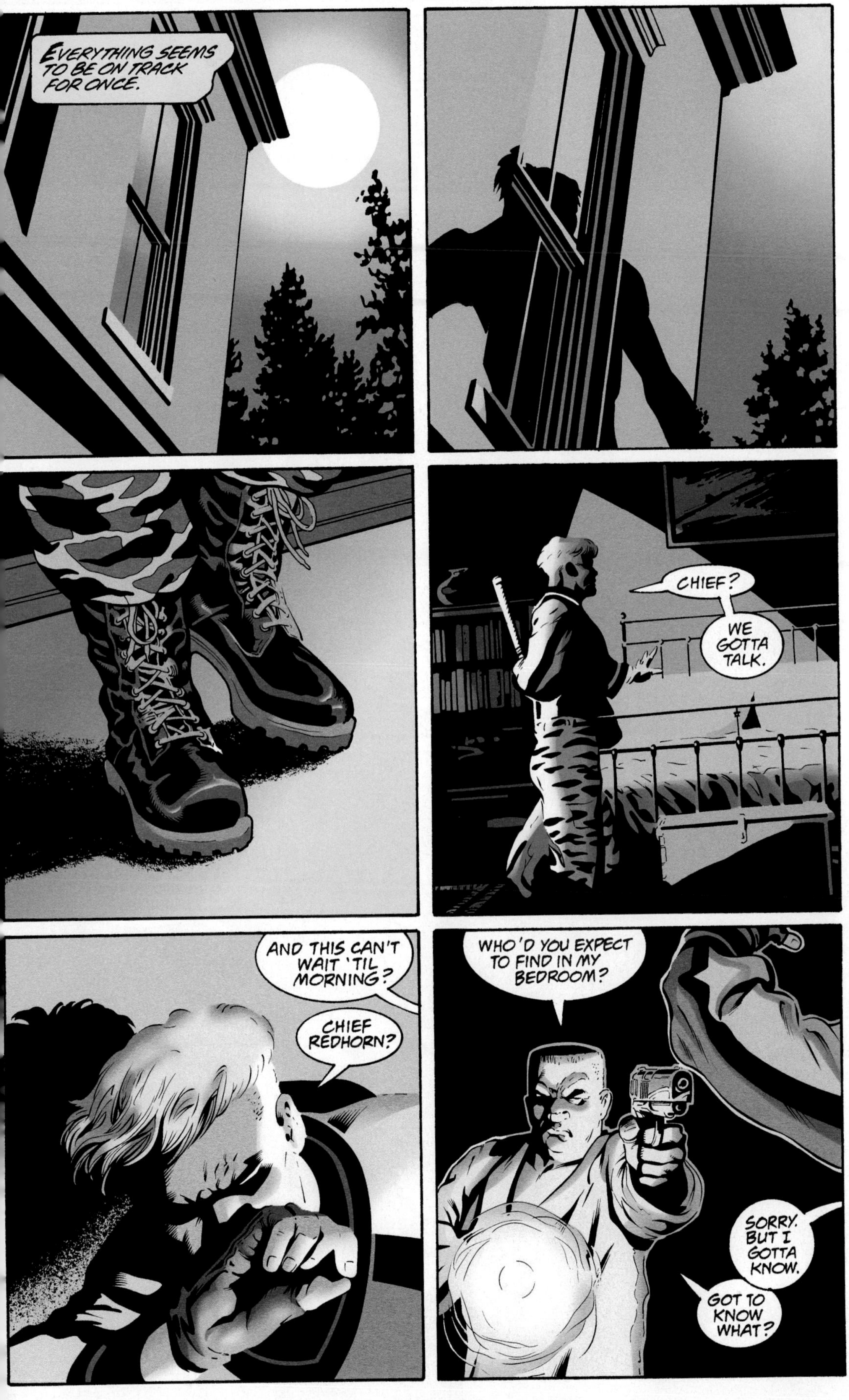
EVERYTHING SEEMS TO BE ON TRACK FOR ONCE.
CHIEF?
WE GOTTA TALK.
AND THIS CAN'T WAIT 'TIL MORNING?
CHIEF REDHORN?
WHO'D YOU EXPECT TO FIND IN MY BEDROOM?
SORRY. BUT I GOTTA KNOW.
GOT TO KNOW WHAT?

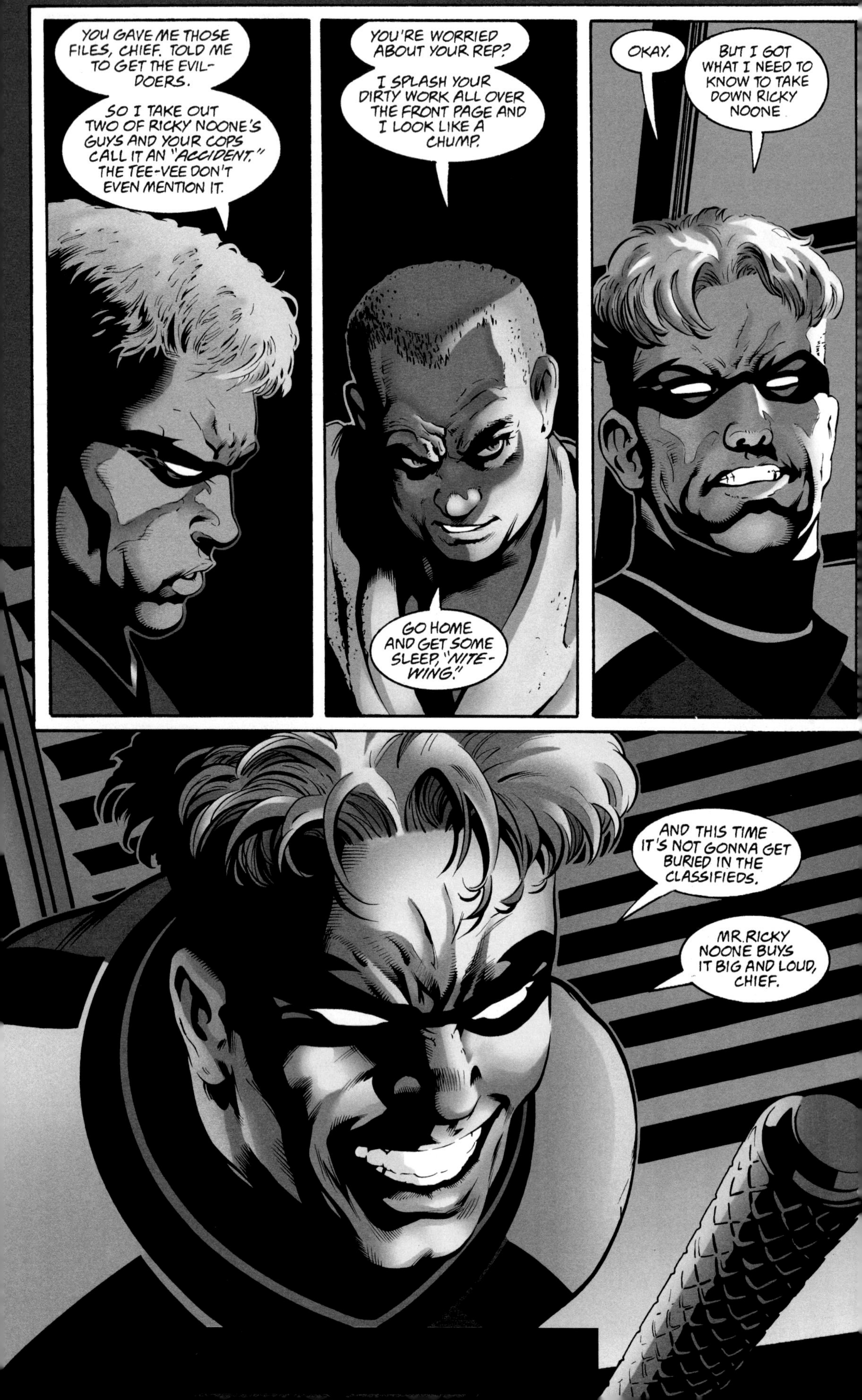
YOU GAVE ME THOSE FILES, CHIEF. TOLD ME TO GET THE EVIL-DOERS.
SO I TAKE OUT TWO OF RICKY NOONE'S GUYS AND YOUR COPS CALL IT AN "ACCIDENT." THE TEE-VEE DON'T EVEN MENTION IT.
YOU'RE WORRIED ABOUT YOUR REP?
I SPLASH YOUR DIRTY WORK ALL OVER THE FRONT PAGE AND I LOOK LIKE A CHUMP.
GO HOME AND GET SOME SLEEP, "NITE-WING."
OKAY.
BUT I GOT WHAT I NEED TO KNOW TO TAKE DOWN RICKY NOONE.
AND THIS TIME IT'S NOT GONNA GET BURIED IN THE CLASSIFIEDS.
MR. RICKY NOONE BUYS IT BIG AND LOUD, CHIEF.

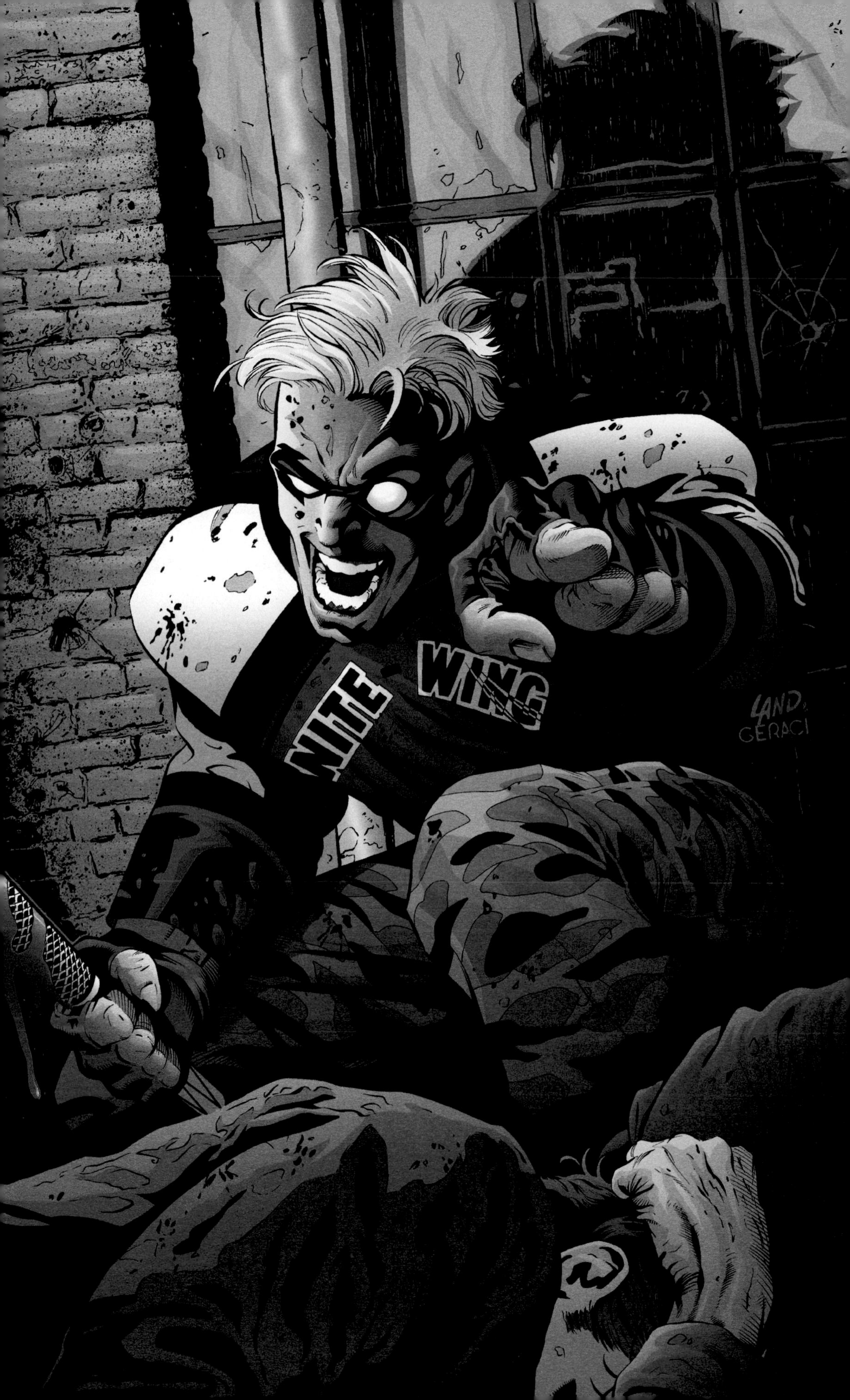
NITE
WING
LAND
GERACI

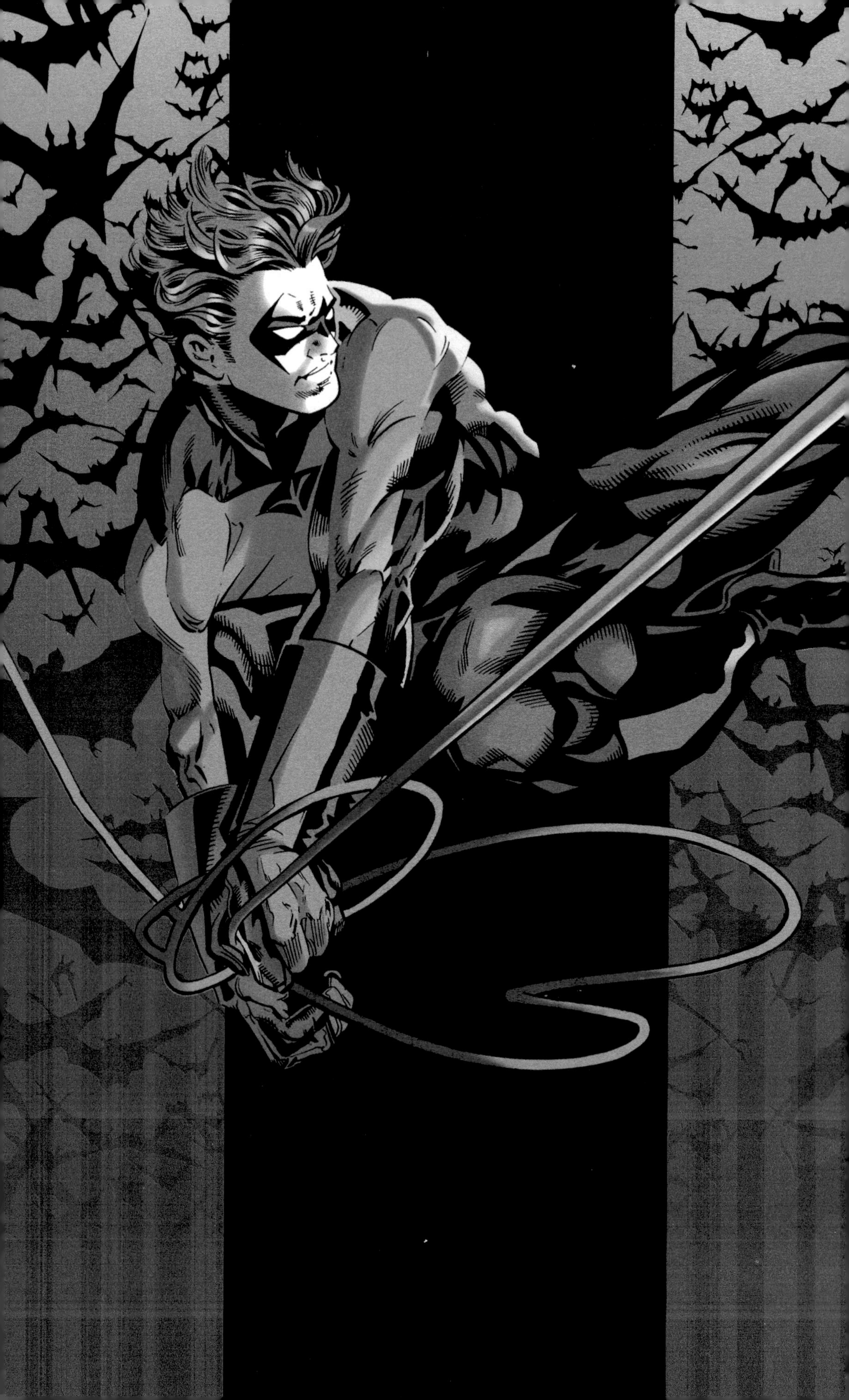

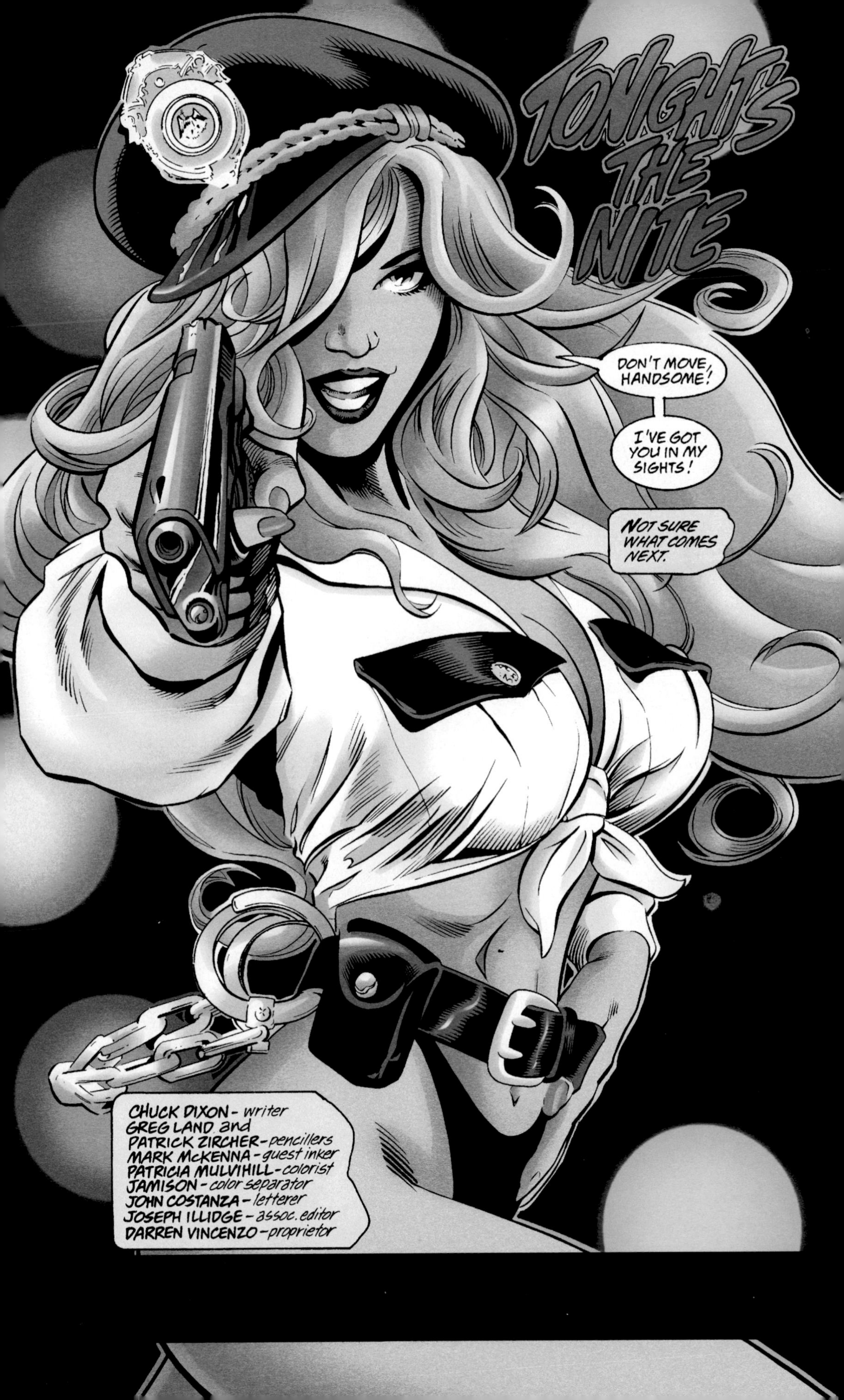
TONIGHT'S THE NITE
DON'T MOVE, HANDSOME!
I'VE GOT YOU IN MY SIGHTS!
NOT SURE WHAT COMES NEXT.
CHUCK DIXON - writer
GREG LAND and
PATRICK ZIRCHER - pencillers
MARK McKENNA - guest inker
PATRICIA MULVIHILL - colorist
JAMISON - color separator
JOHN COSTANZA - letterer
JOSEPH ILLIDGE - assoc. editor
DARREN VINCENZO - proprietor

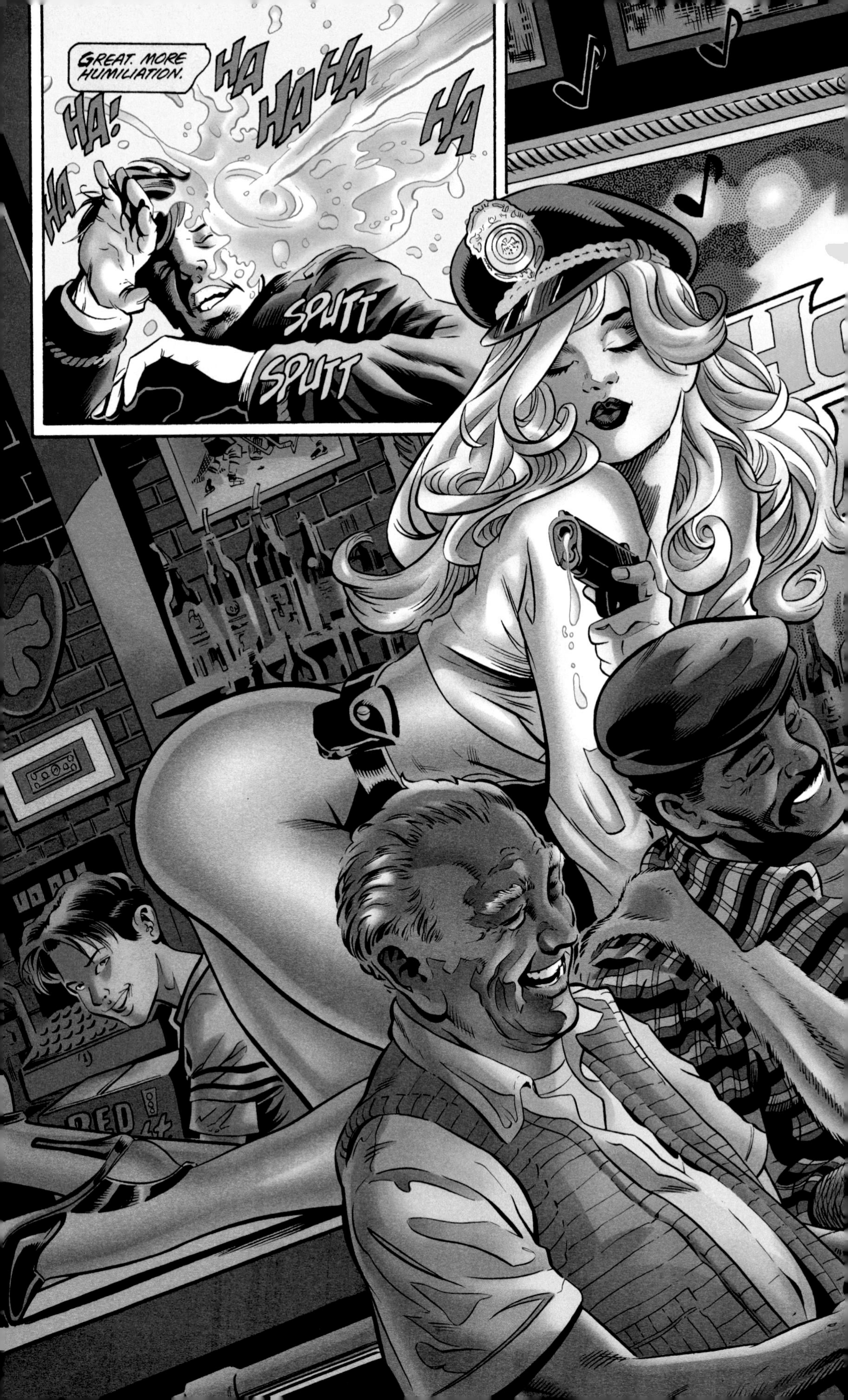
GREAT. MORE HUMILIATION.
HA HA HA HA
HA!
HA
HA
SPUTT
SPUTT
RED

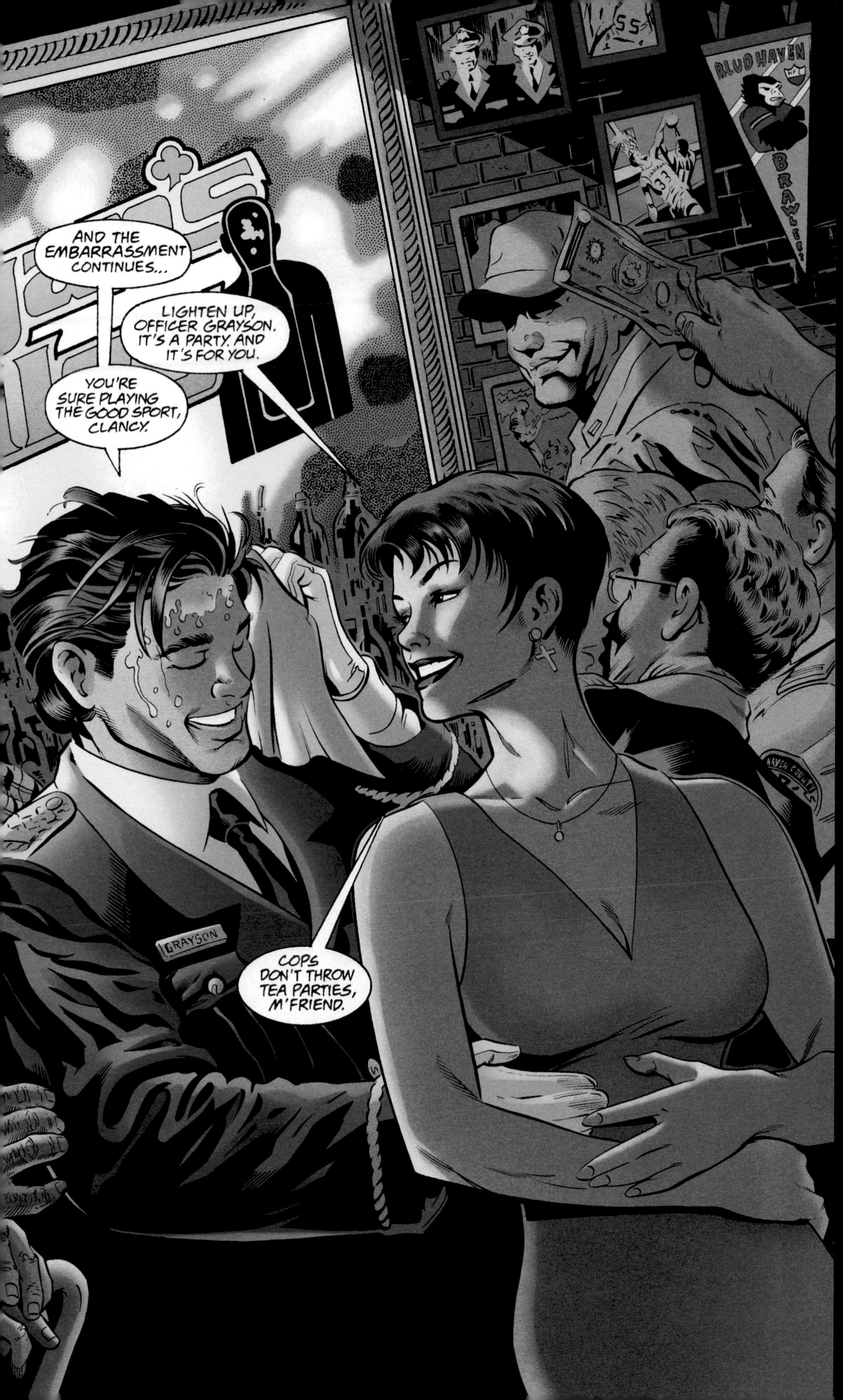
AND THE EMBARRASSMENT CONTINUES...
YOU'RE SURE PLAYING THE GOOD SPORT, CLANCY.
LIGHTEN UP, OFFICER GRAYSON. IT'S A PARTY. AND IT'S FOR YOU.
COPS DON'T THROW TEA PARTIES, M'FRIEND.
BLUD HAVEN
BRAWLERS
GRAYSON

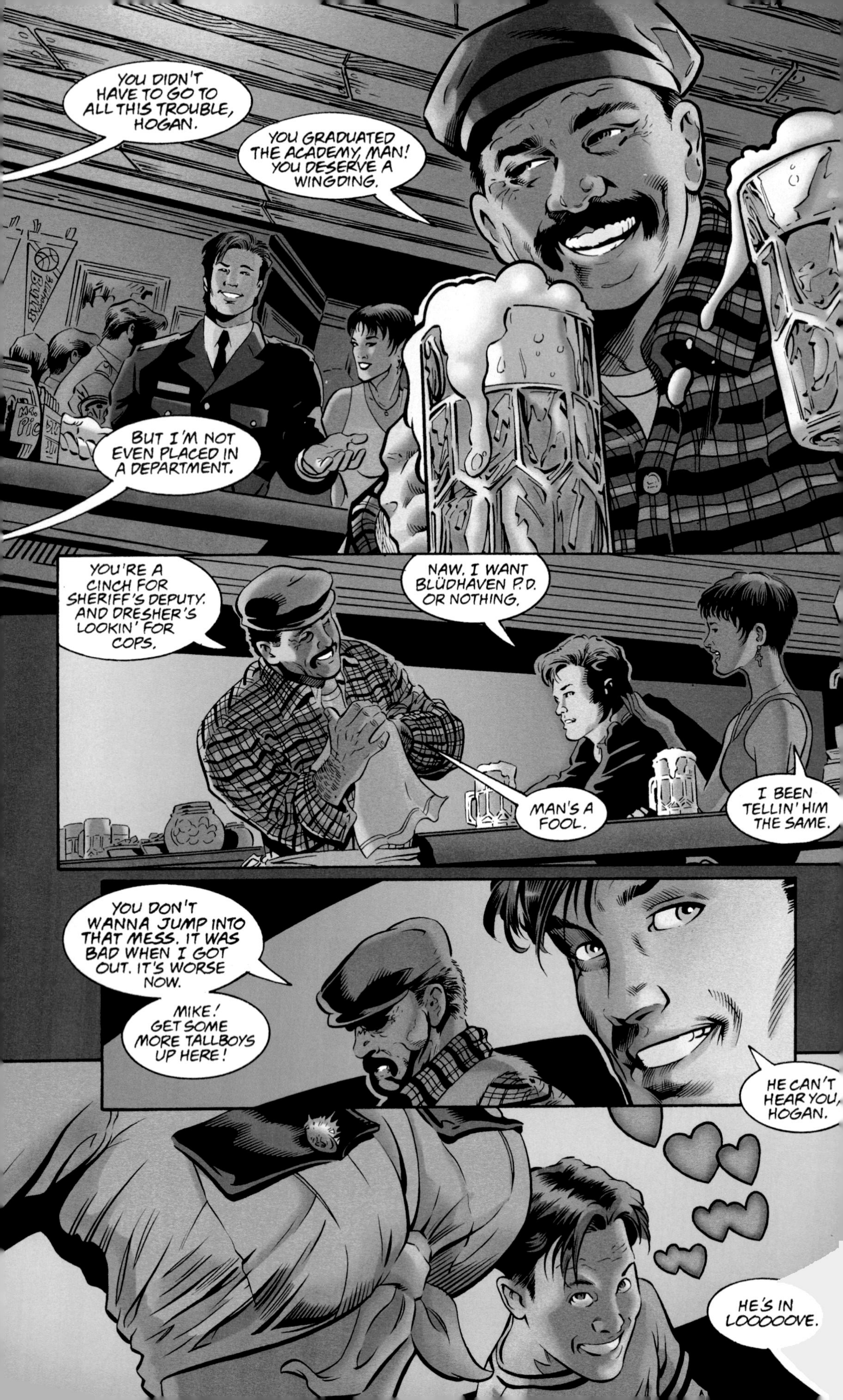
YOU DIDN'T HAVE TO GO TO ALL THIS TROUBLE, HOGAN.
YOU GRADUATED THE ACADEMY, MAN! YOU DESERVE A WINGDING.
BUT I'M NOT EVEN PLACED IN A DEPARTMENT.
YOU'RE A CINCH FOR SHERIFF'S DEPUTY. AND DRESHER'S LOOKIN' FOR COPS.
NAW. I WANT BLÜDHAVEN P.D. OR NOTHING.
MAN'S A FOOL.
I BEEN TELLIN' HIM THE SAME.
YOU DON'T WANNA JUMP INTO THAT MESS. IT WAS BAD WHEN I GOT OUT. IT'S WORSE NOW.
MIKE! GET SOME MORE TALLBOYS UP HERE!
HE CAN'T HEAR YOU, HOGAN.
HE'S IN LOOOOOVE.

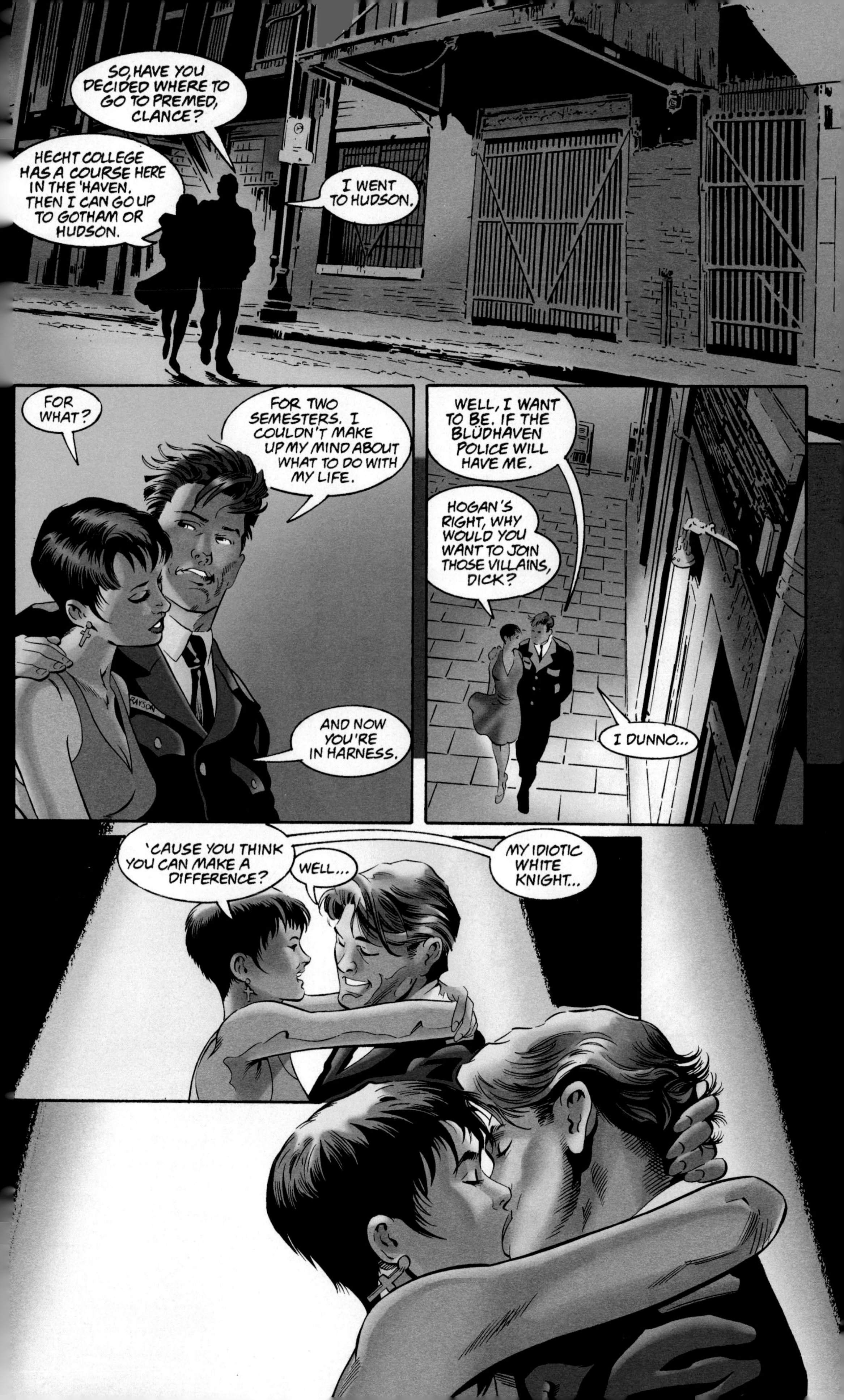
SO, HAVE YOU DECIDED WHERE TO GO TO PREMED, CLANCE?
HECHT COLLEGE HAS A COURSE HERE IN THE 'HAVEN. THEN I CAN GO UP TO GOTHAM OR HUDSON.
I WENT TO HUDSON.
FOR WHAT?
FOR TWO SEMESTERS. I COULDN'T MAKE UP MY MIND ABOUT WHAT TO DO WITH MY LIFE.
AND NOW YOU'RE IN HARNESS.
WELL, I WANT TO BE. IF THE BLÜDHAVEN POLICE WILL HAVE ME.
HOGAN'S RIGHT, WHY WOULD YOU WANT TO JOIN THOSE VILLAINS, DICK?
I DUNNO...
'CAUSE YOU THINK YOU CAN MAKE A DIFFERENCE?
WELL...
MY IDIOTIC WHITE KNIGHT...

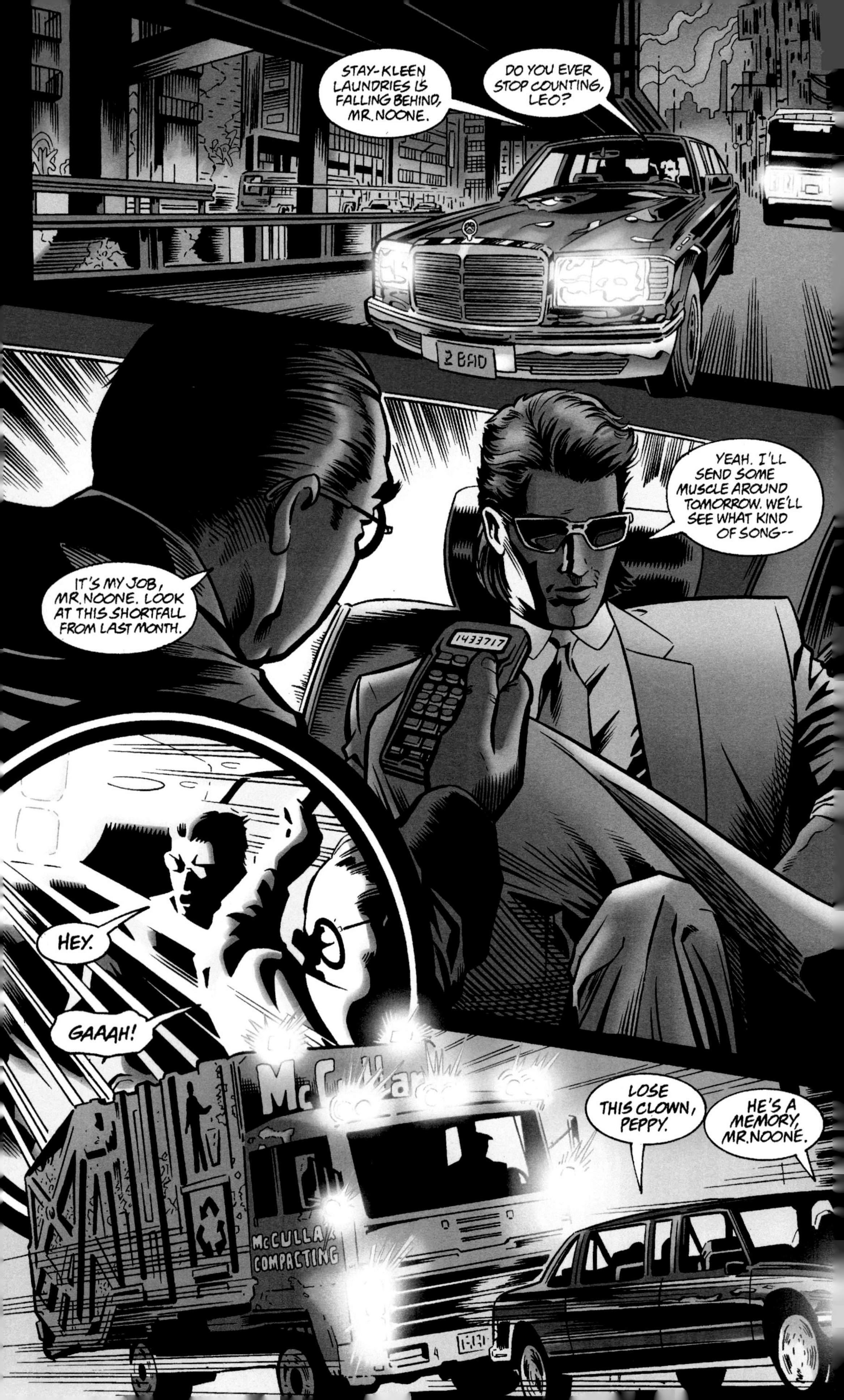
STAY-KLEEN LAUNDRIES IS FALLING BEHIND, MR. NOONE.
DO YOU EVER STOP COUNTING, LEO?
2 BAD
YEAH. I'LL SEND SOME MUSCLE AROUND TOMORROW. WE'LL SEE WHAT KIND OF SONG--
IT'S MY JOB, MR. NOONE. LOOK AT THIS SHORTFALL FROM LAST MONTH.
1433717
HEY.
GAAAH!
LOSE THIS CLOWN, PEPPY.
HE'S A MEMORY, MR. NOONE.
McCULLA COMPACTING

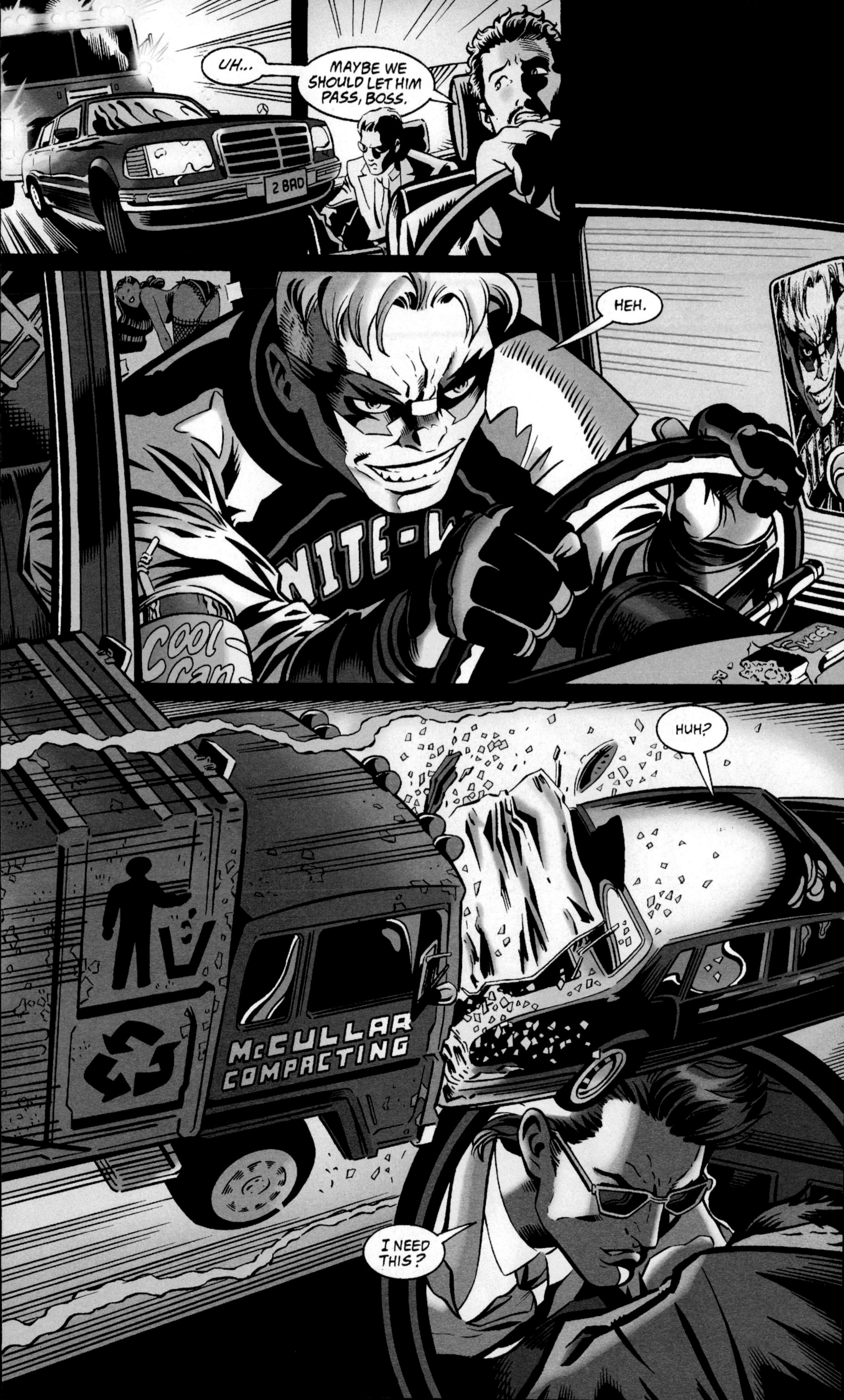
UH...
MAYBE WE SHOULD LET HIM PASS, BOSS.
2 BAD
HEH.
NITE-
COOL CAN
HUH?
McCULLAR COMPACTING
I NEED THIS?

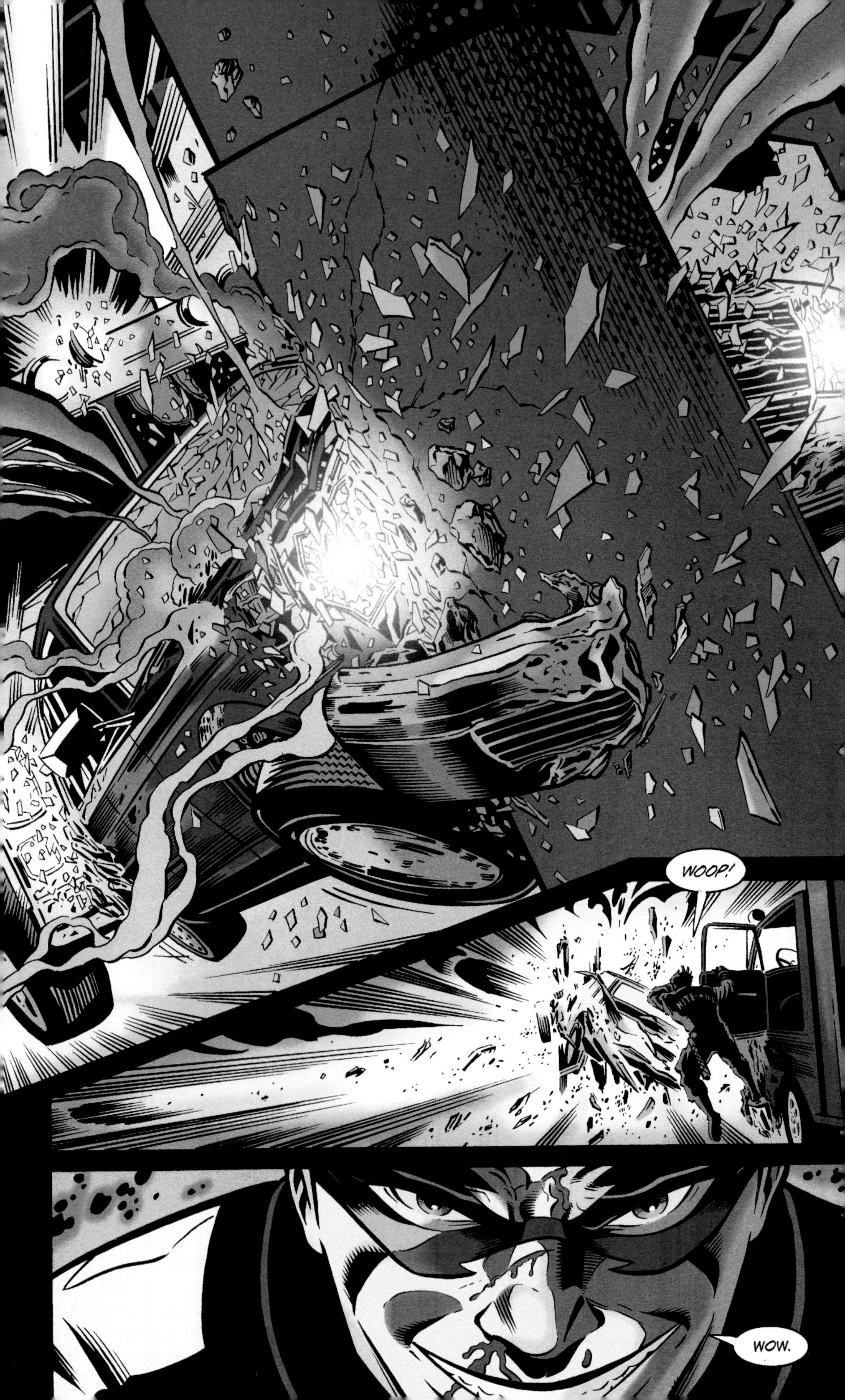
WOOP!
WOW.

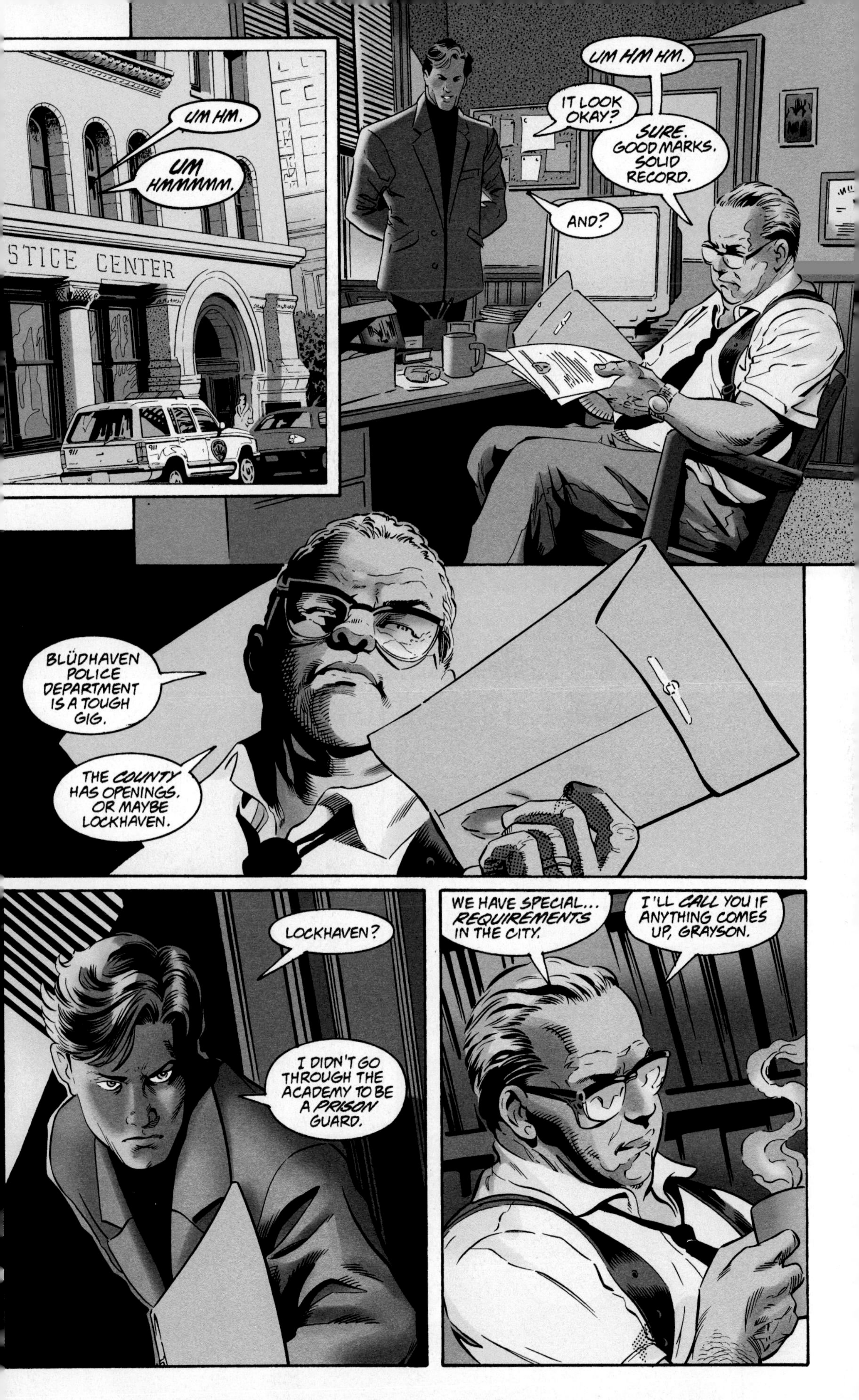
STICE CENTER
UM HM.
UM HMMMMM.
UM HM HM.
IT LOOK OKAY?
SURE. GOOD MARKS. SOLID RECORD.
AND?
BLÜDHAVEN POLICE DEPARTMENT IS A TOUGH GIG.
THE COUNTY HAS OPENINGS. OR MAYBE LOCKHAVEN.
LOCKHAVEN?
I DIDN'T GO THROUGH THE ACADEMY TO BE A PRISON GUARD.
WE HAVE SPECIAL... REQUIREMENTS IN THE CITY.
I'LL CALL YOU IF ANYTHING COMES UP, GRAYSON.

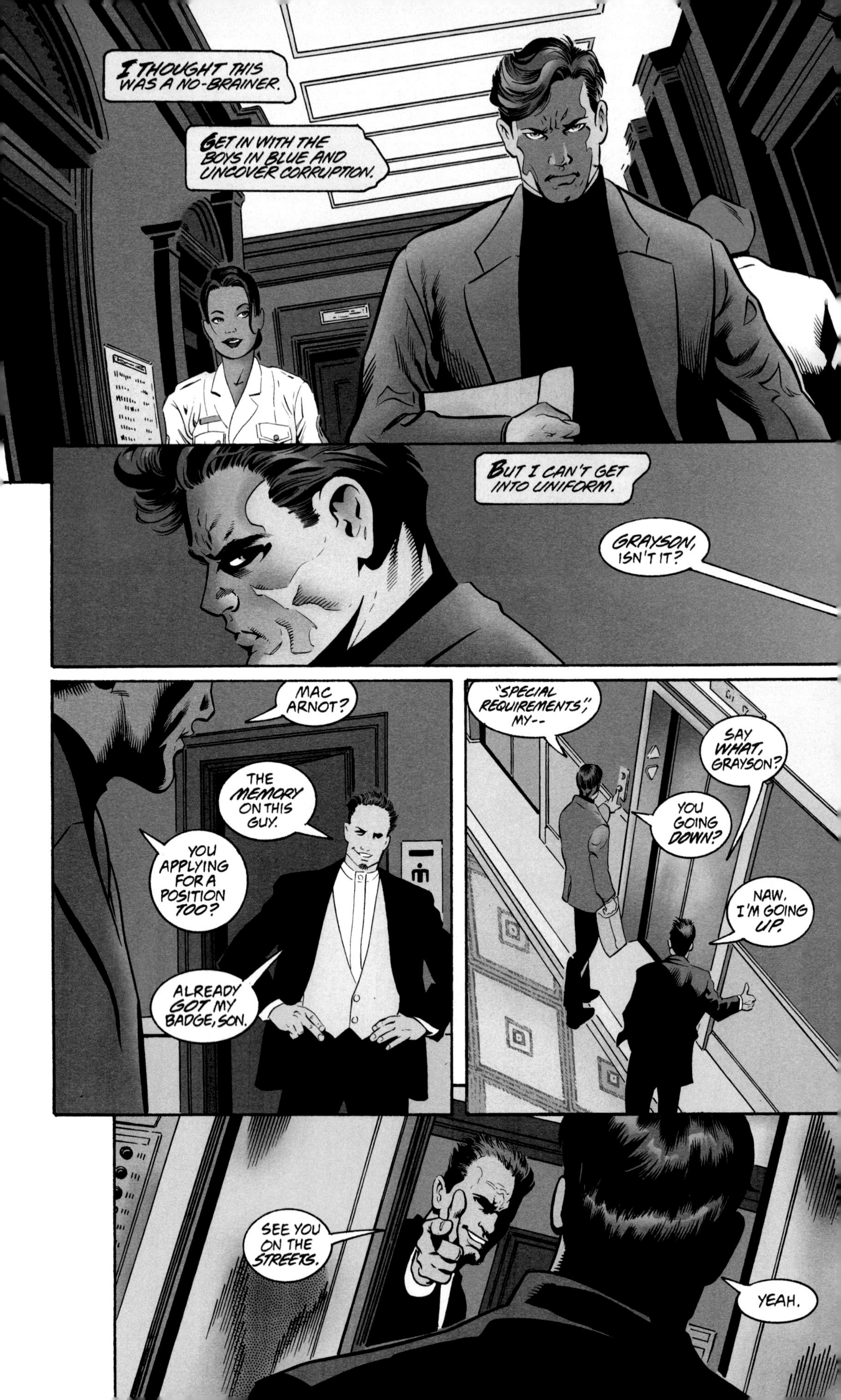
I THOUGHT THIS WAS A NO-BRAINER.
GET IN WITH THE BOYS IN BLUE AND UNCOVER CORRUPTION.
BUT I CAN'T GET INTO UNIFORM.
GRAYSON, ISN'T IT?
MAC ARNOT?
THE MEMORY ON THIS GUY.
YOU APPLYING FOR A POSITION TOO?
ALREADY GOT MY BADGE, SON.
"SPECIAL REQUIREMENTS," MY--
SAY WHAT, GRAYSON?
YOU GOING DOWN?
NAW. I'M GOING UP.
SEE YOU ON THE STREETS.
YEAH.

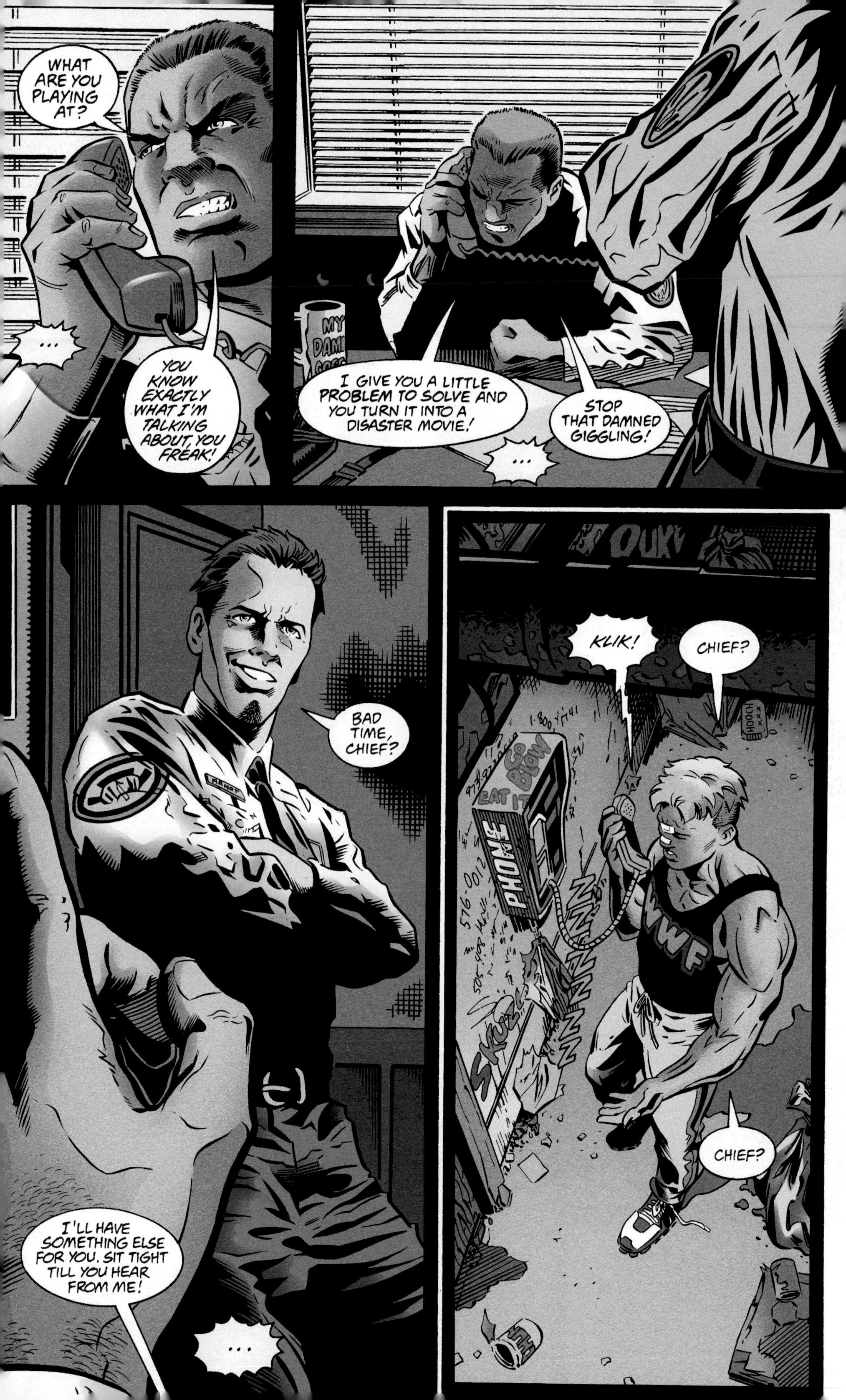
WHAT ARE YOU PLAYING AT?
...
YOU KNOW EXACTLY WHAT I'M TALKING ABOUT, YOU FREAK!
MY DAM COFF
I GIVE YOU A LITTLE PROBLEM TO SOLVE AND YOU TURN IT INTO A DISASTER MOVIE!
STOP THAT DAMNED GIGGLING!
...
BAD TIME, CHIEF?
I'LL HAVE SOMETHING ELSE FOR YOU. SIT TIGHT TILL YOU HEAR FROM ME!
...
KLIK!
CHIEF?
PHONE
EAT IT
WWF
CHIEF?

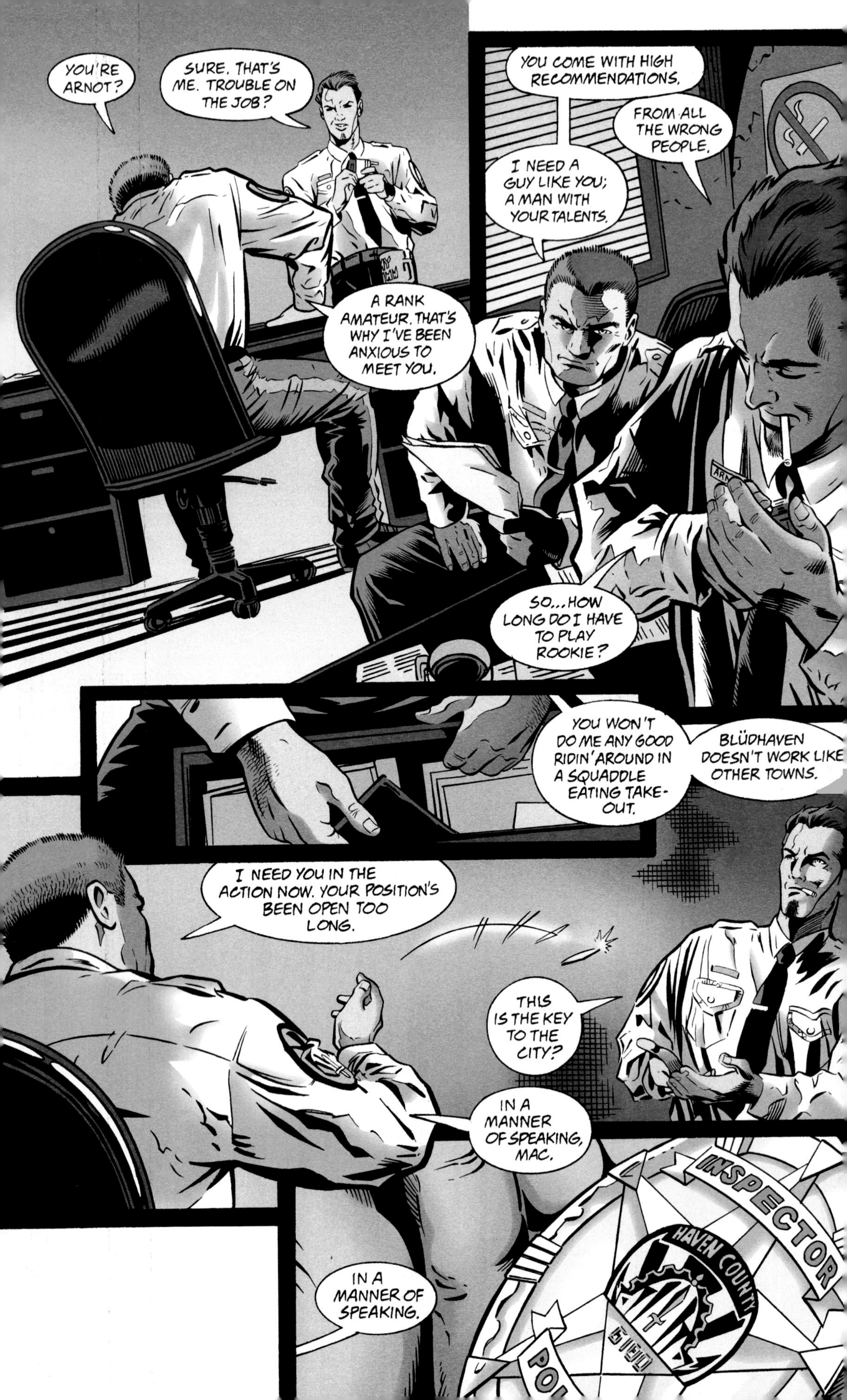

YOU'RE ARNOT?
SURE. THAT'S ME. TROUBLE ON THE JOB?
YOU COME WITH HIGH RECOMMENDATIONS.
FROM ALL THE WRONG PEOPLE.
I NEED A GUY LIKE YOU; A MAN WITH YOUR TALENTS.
A RANK AMATEUR. THAT'S WHY I'VE BEEN ANXIOUS TO MEET YOU.
SO... HOW LONG DO I HAVE TO PLAY ROOKIE?
YOU WON'T DO ME ANY GOOD RIDIN' AROUND IN A SQUADDLE EATING TAKE-OUT.
BLÜDHAVEN DOESN'T WORK LIKE OTHER TOWNS.
I NEED YOU IN THE ACTION NOW. YOUR POSITION'S BEEN OPEN TOO LONG.
THIS IS THE KEY TO THE CITY?
IN A MANNER OF SPEAKING, MAC.
IN A MANNER OF SPEAKING.
INSPECTOR
HAVEN COUNTY

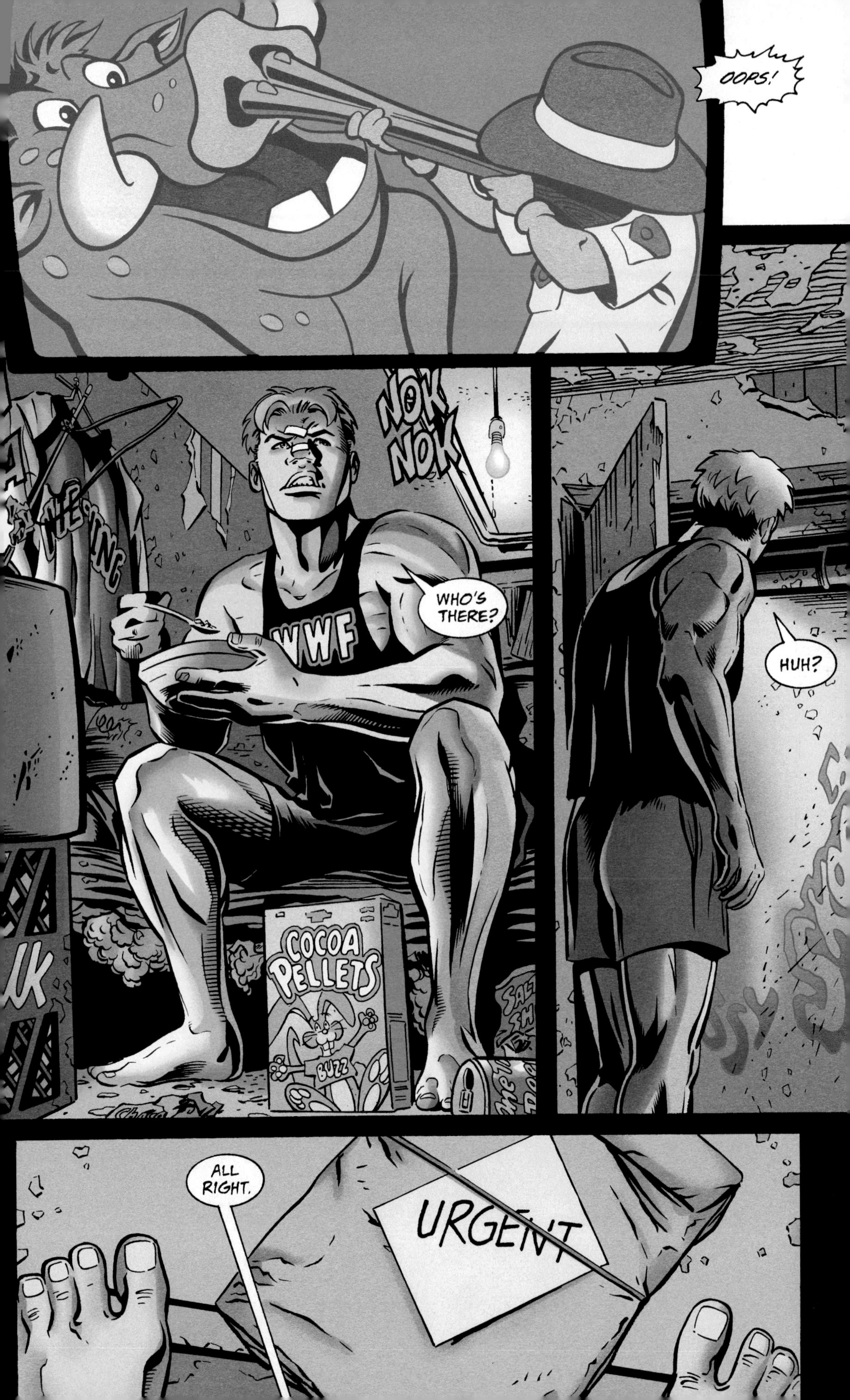

OOPS!
NOK NOK
WWF
WHO'S THERE?
COCOA PELLETS
BUZZ
HUH?
ALL RIGHT.
URGENT

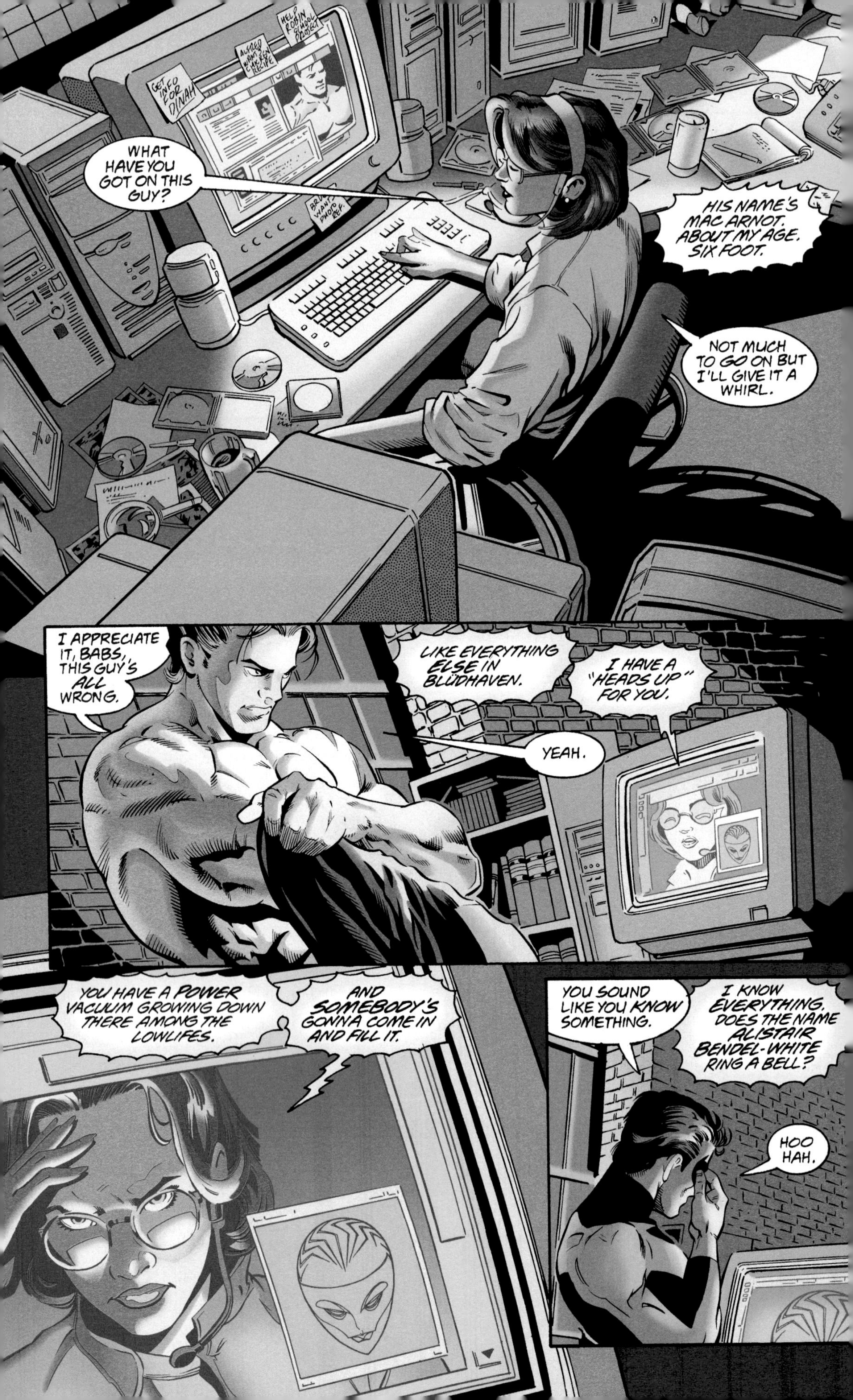
GET INFO FOR DINAH
ALFRED WANTS CHICKEN RECIPE
HELP ROBIN SCHOOL PROJECT
WHAT HAVE YOU GOT ON THIS GUY?
HIS NAME'S MAC ARNOT. ABOUT MY AGE. SIX FOOT.
NOT MUCH TO GO ON BUT I'LL GIVE IT A WHIRL.
I APPRECIATE IT, BABS, THIS GUY'S ALL WRONG.
LIKE EVERYTHING ELSE IN BLÜDHAVEN.
I HAVE A "HEADS UP" FOR YOU.
YEAH.
YOU HAVE A POWER VACUUM GROWING DOWN THERE AMONG THE LOWLIFES.
AND SOMEBODY'S GONNA COME IN AND FILL IT.
YOU SOUND LIKE YOU KNOW SOMETHING.
I KNOW EVERYTHING. DOES THE NAME ALISTAIR BENDEL-WHITE RING A BELL?
HOO HAH.

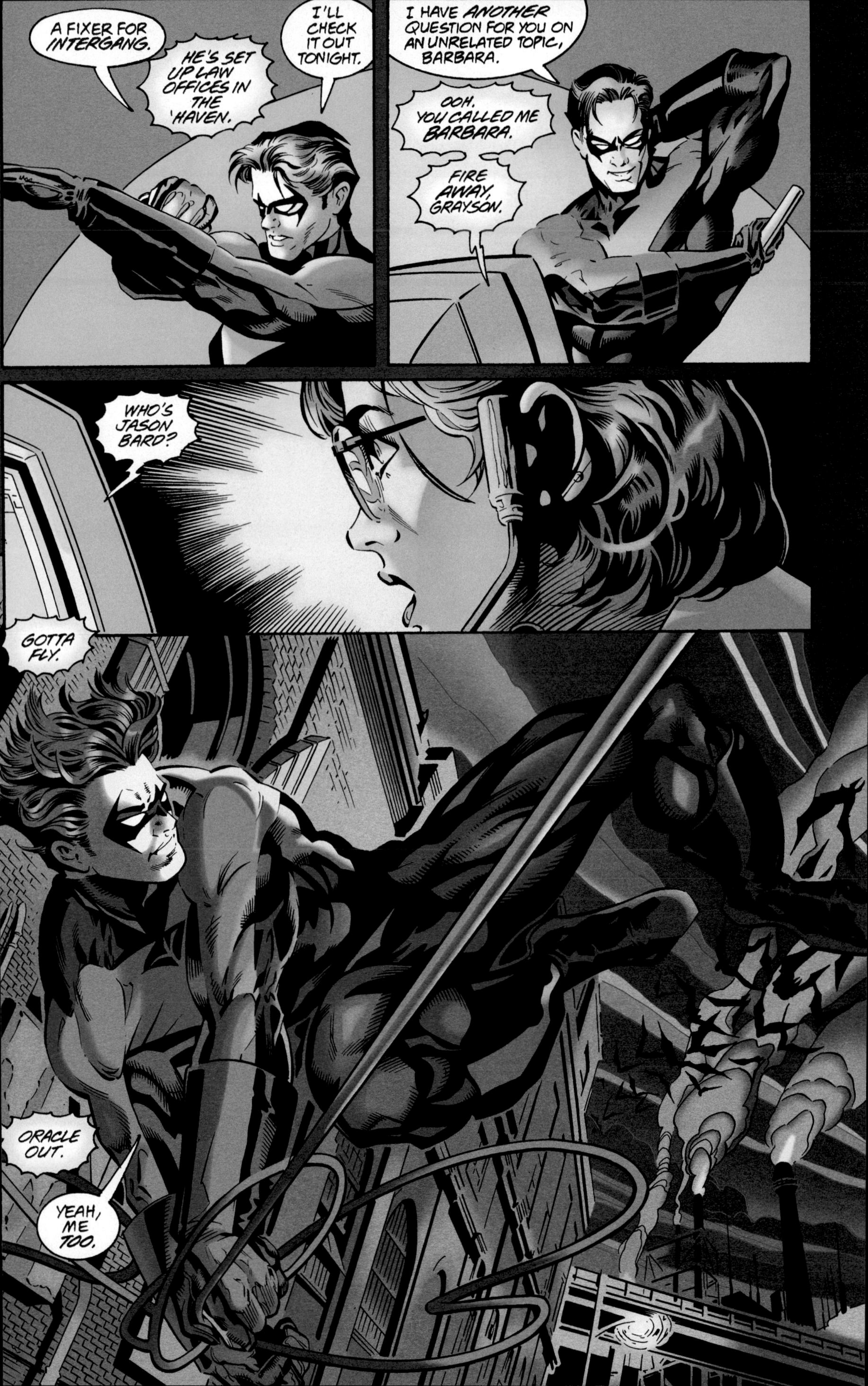
A FIXER FOR INTERGANG.
HE'S SET UP LAW OFFICES IN THE 'HAVEN.
I'LL CHECK IT OUT TONIGHT.
I HAVE ANOTHER QUESTION FOR YOU ON AN UNRELATED TOPIC, BARBARA.
OOH. YOU CALLED ME BARBARA.
FIRE AWAY, GRAYSON.
WHO'S JASON BARD?
GOTTA FLY.
ORACLE OUT.
YEAH, ME TOO.

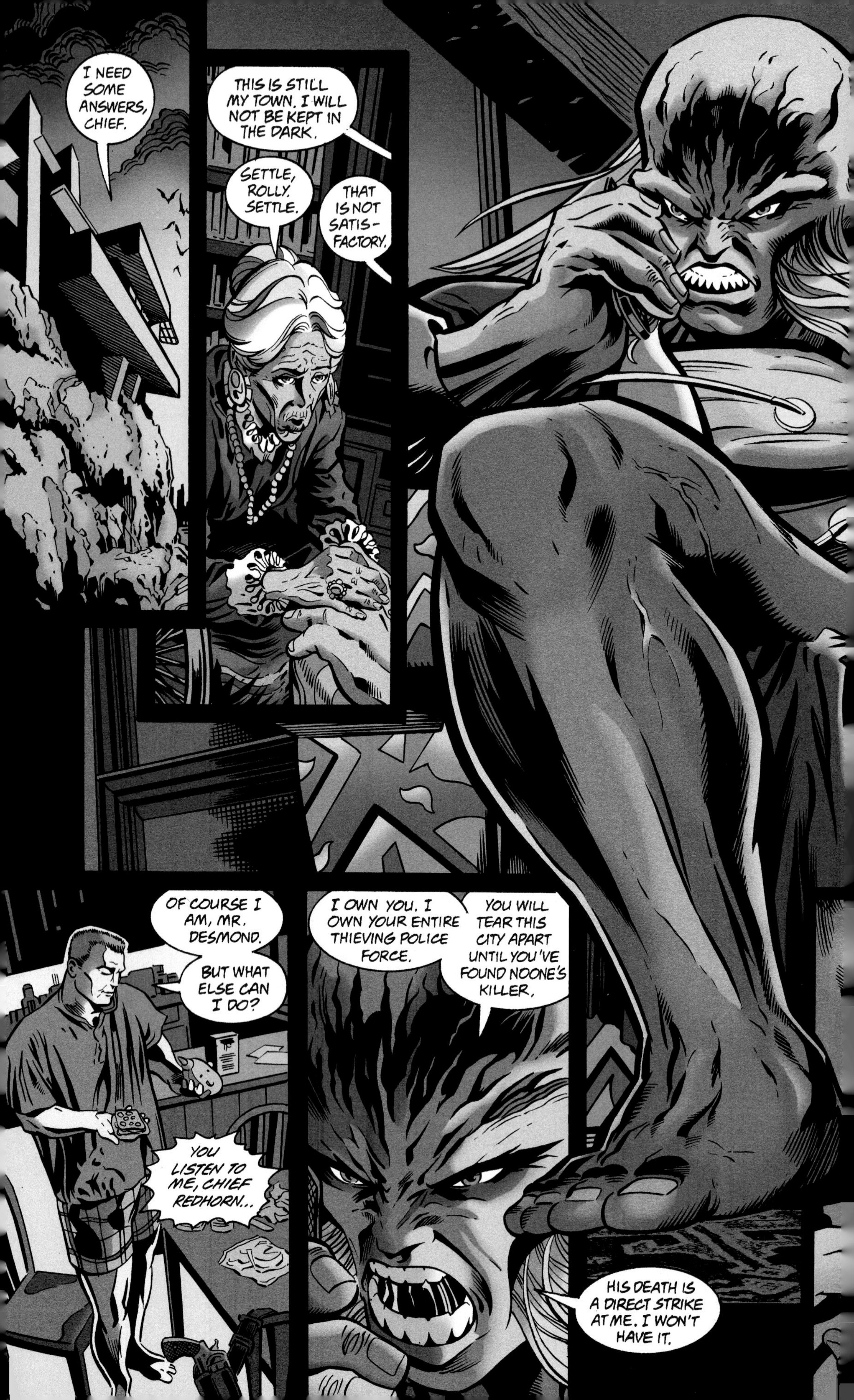
I NEED SOME ANSWERS, CHIEF.
THIS IS STILL MY TOWN. I WILL NOT BE KEPT IN THE DARK.
SETTLE, ROLLY. SETTLE.
THAT IS NOT SATIS-FACTORY.
OF COURSE I AM, MR. DESMOND.
BUT WHAT ELSE CAN I DO?
YOU LISTEN TO ME, CHIEF REDHORN...
I OWN YOU. I OWN YOUR ENTIRE THIEVING POLICE FORCE.
YOU WILL TEAR THIS CITY APART UNTIL YOU'VE FOUND NOONE'S KILLER.
HIS DEATH IS A DIRECT STRIKE AT ME. I WON'T HAVE IT.

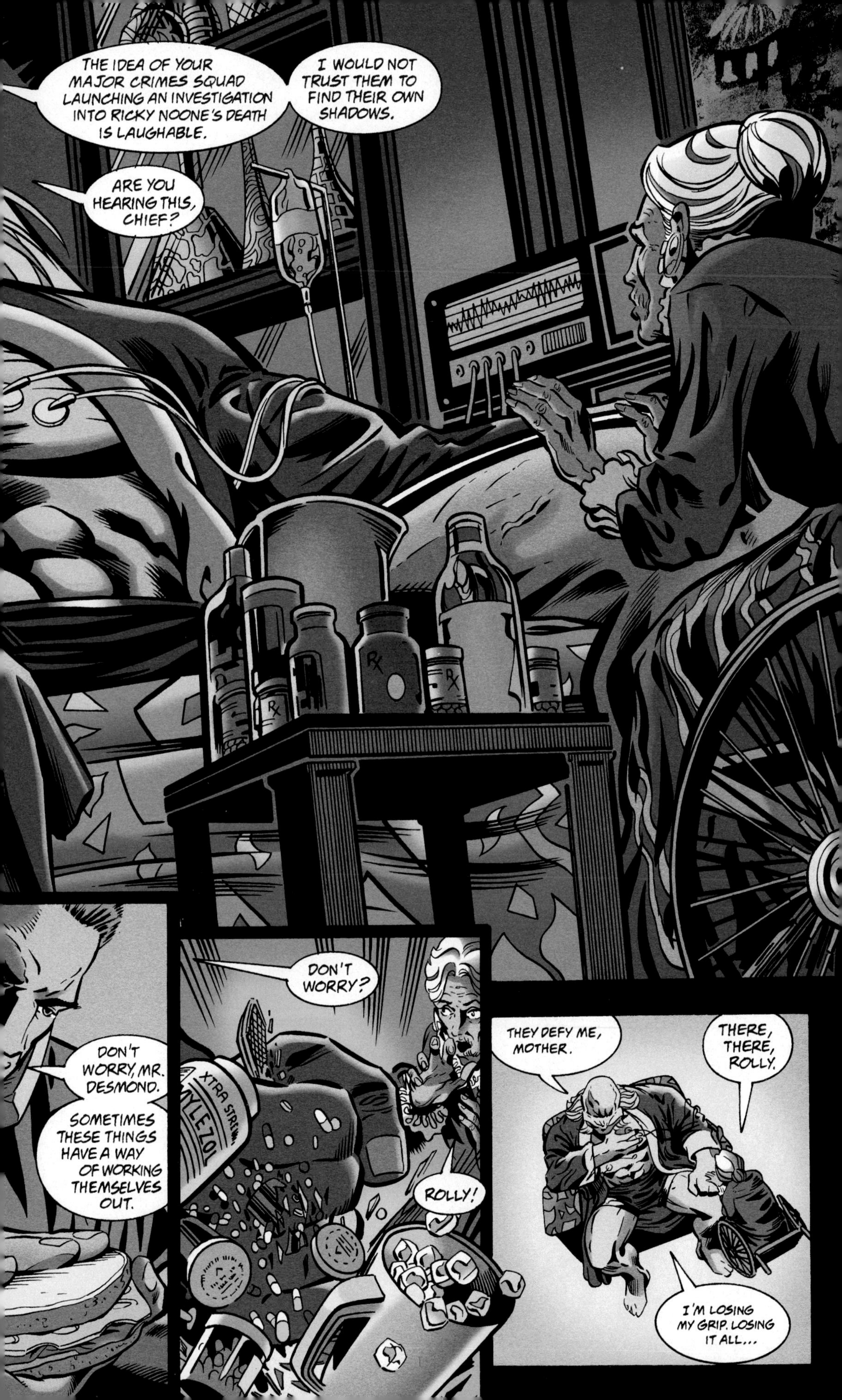
THE IDEA OF YOUR MAJOR CRIMES SQUAD LAUNCHING AN INVESTIGATION INTO RICKY NOONE'S DEATH IS LAUGHABLE.
I WOULD NOT TRUST THEM TO FIND THEIR OWN SHADOWS.
ARE YOU HEARING THIS, CHIEF?
DON'T WORRY, MR. DESMOND.
SOMETIMES THESE THINGS HAVE A WAY OF WORKING THEMSELVES OUT.
DON'T WORRY?
ROLLY!
THEY DEFY ME, MOTHER.
THERE, THERE, ROLLY.
I'M LOSING MY GRIP. LOSING IT ALL...

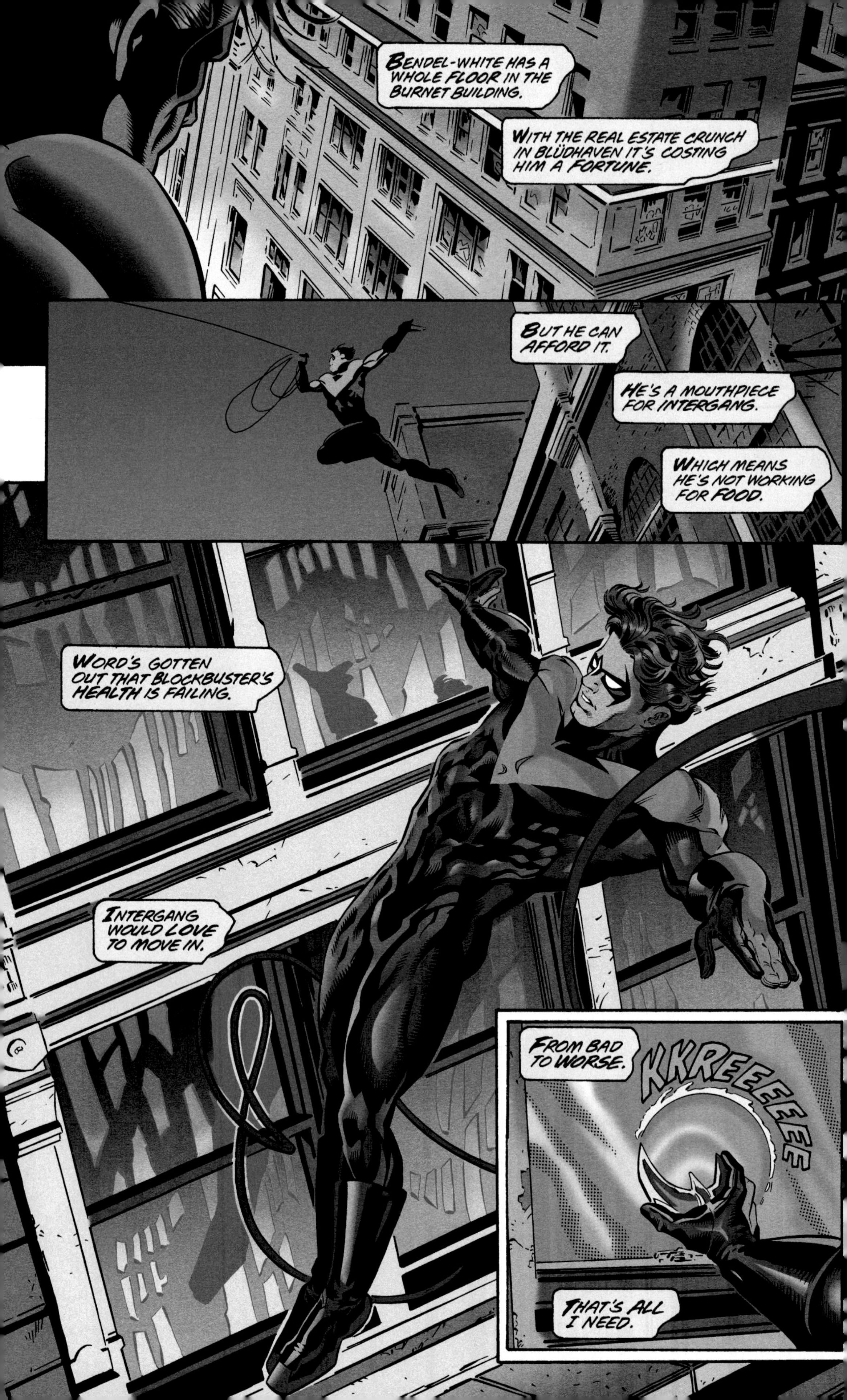
BENDEL-WHITE HAS A WHOLE FLOOR IN THE BURNET BUILDING.
WITH THE REAL ESTATE CRUNCH IN BLÜDHAVEN IT'S COSTING HIM A FORTUNE.
BUT HE CAN AFFORD IT.
HE'S A MOUTHPIECE FOR INTERGANG.
WHICH MEANS HE'S NOT WORKING FOR FOOD.
WORD'S GOTTEN OUT THAT BLOCKBUSTER'S HEALTH IS FAILING.
INTERGANG WOULD LOVE TO MOVE IN.
FROM BAD TO WORSE.
KKREEEEEEE
THAT'S ALL I NEED.

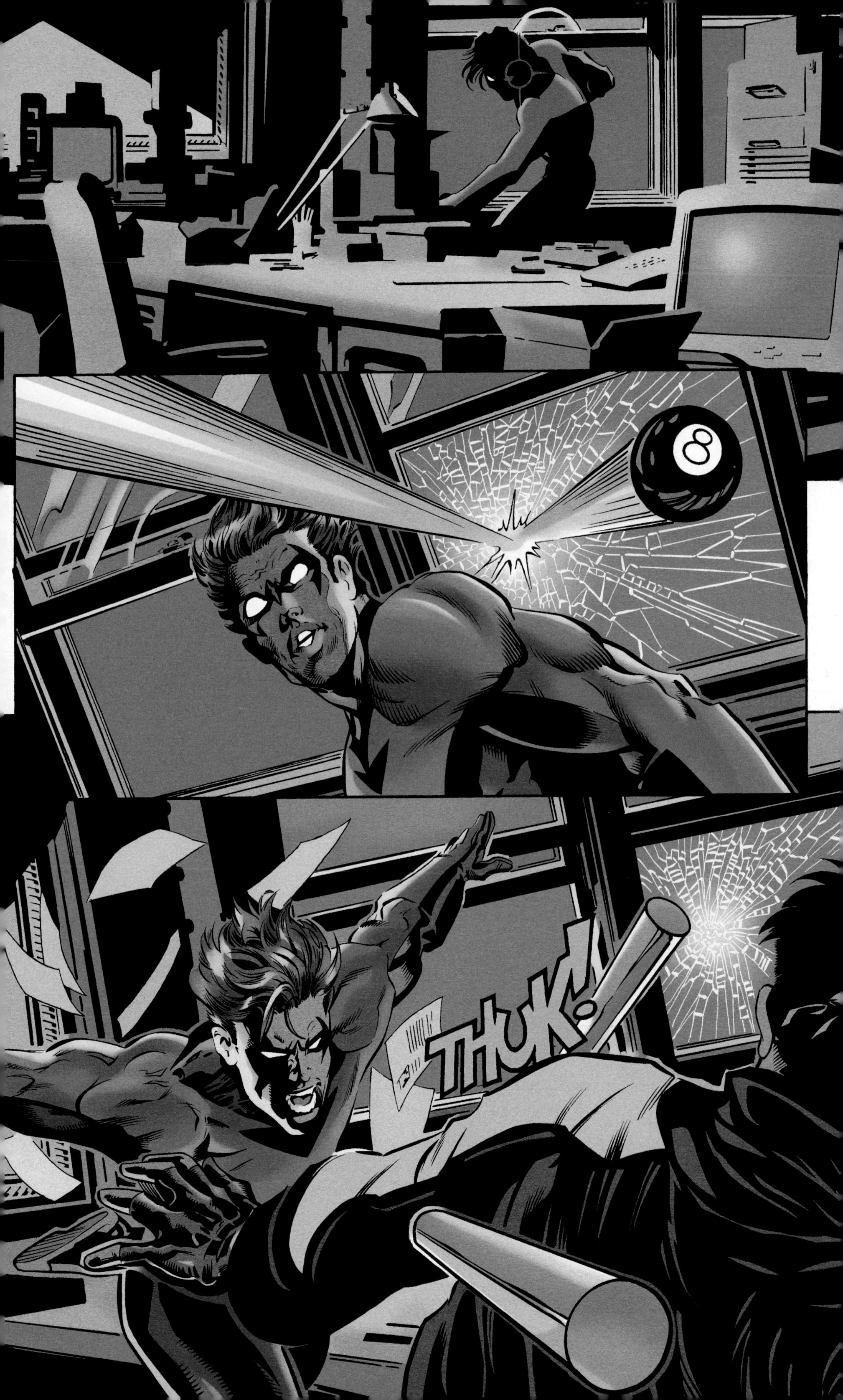
THUK!

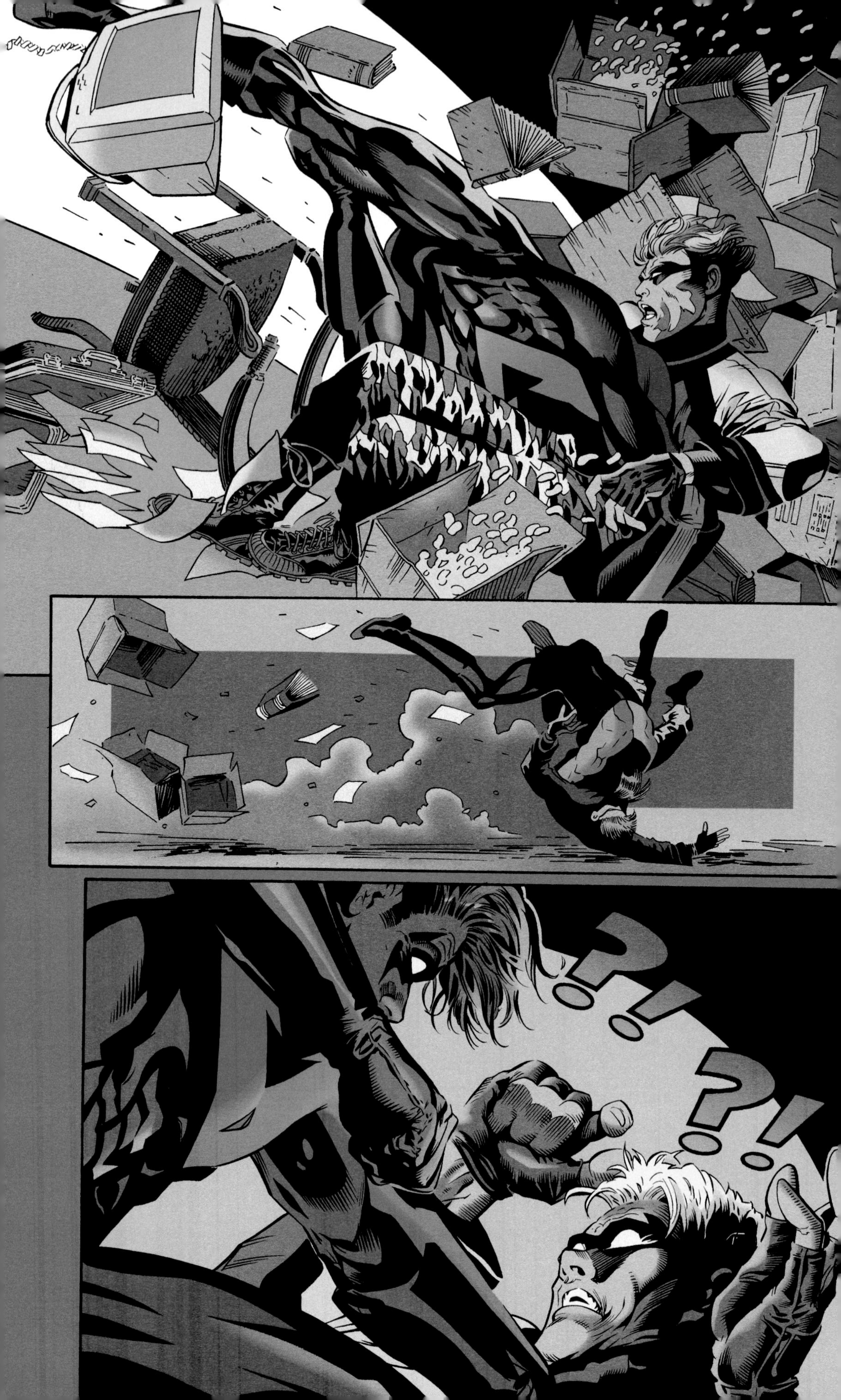
?!
?!

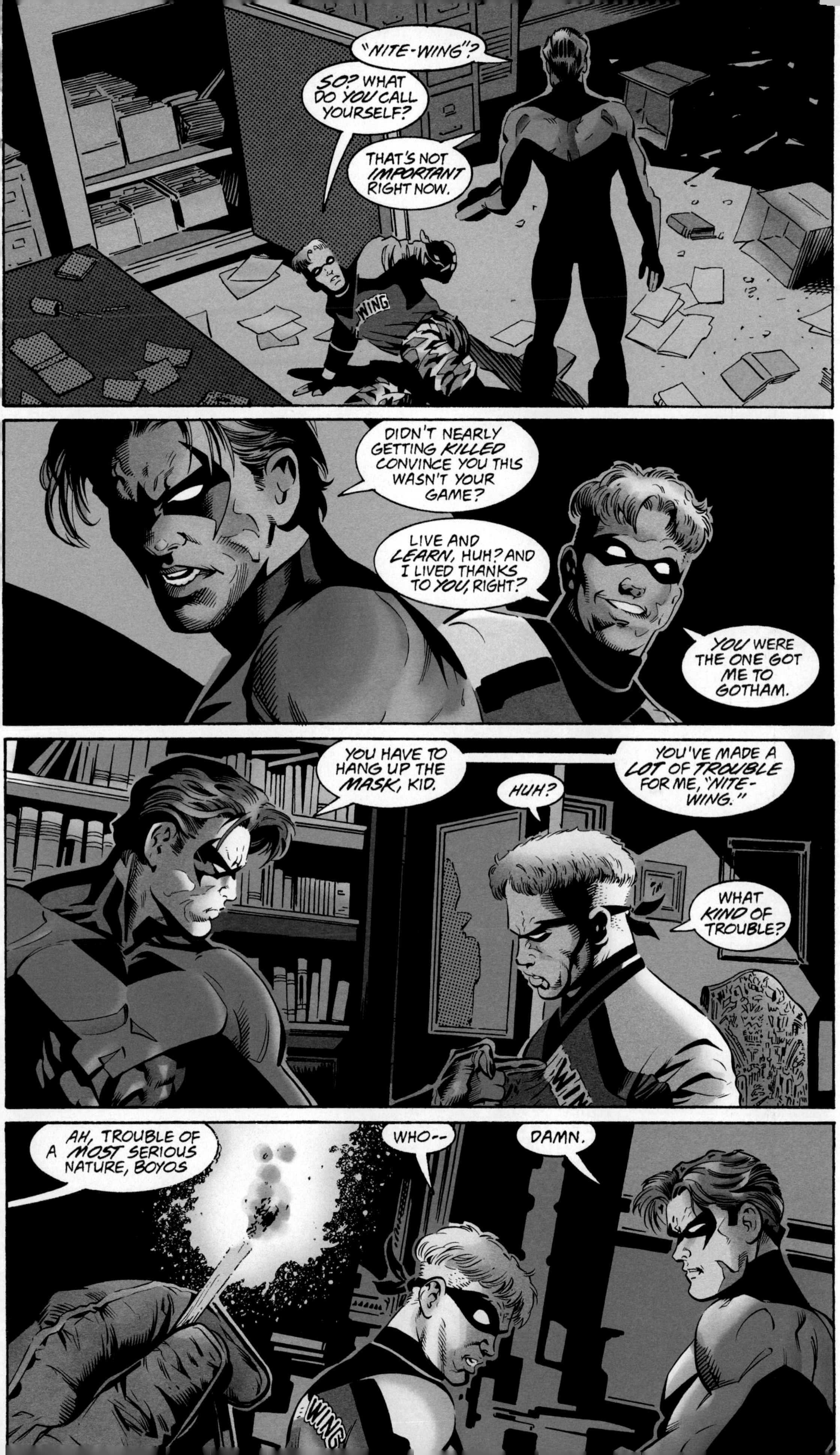
"NITE-WING"?
SO? WHAT DO YOU CALL YOURSELF?
THAT'S NOT IMPORTANT RIGHT NOW.
WING
DIDN'T NEARLY GETTING KILLED CONVINCE YOU THIS WASN'T YOUR GAME?
LIVE AND LEARN, HUH? AND I LIVED THANKS TO YOU, RIGHT?
YOU WERE THE ONE GOT ME TO GOTHAM.
YOU HAVE TO HANG UP THE MASK, KID.
HUH?
YOU'VE MADE A LOT OF TROUBLE FOR ME, "NITE-WING."
WHAT KIND OF TROUBLE?
AH, TROUBLE OF A MOST SERIOUS NATURE, BOYOS
WHO--
DAMN.
WING

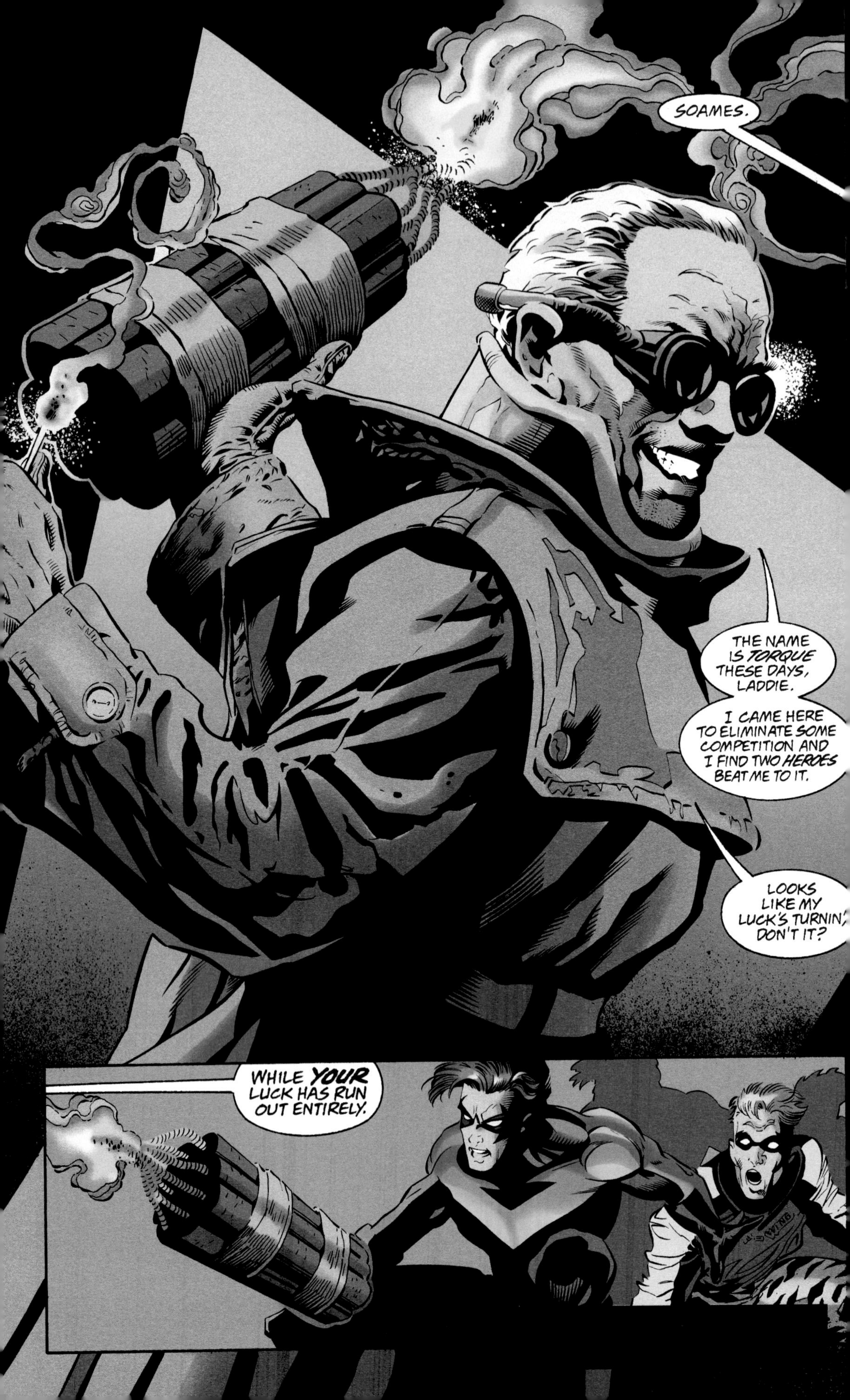
SOAMES.
THE NAME IS TORQUE THESE DAYS, LADDIE.
I CAME HERE TO ELIMINATE SOME COMPETITION AND I FIND TWO HEROES BEAT ME TO IT.
LOOKS LIKE MY LUCK'S TURNIN', DON'T IT?
WHILE YOUR LUCK HAS RUN OUT ENTIRELY.

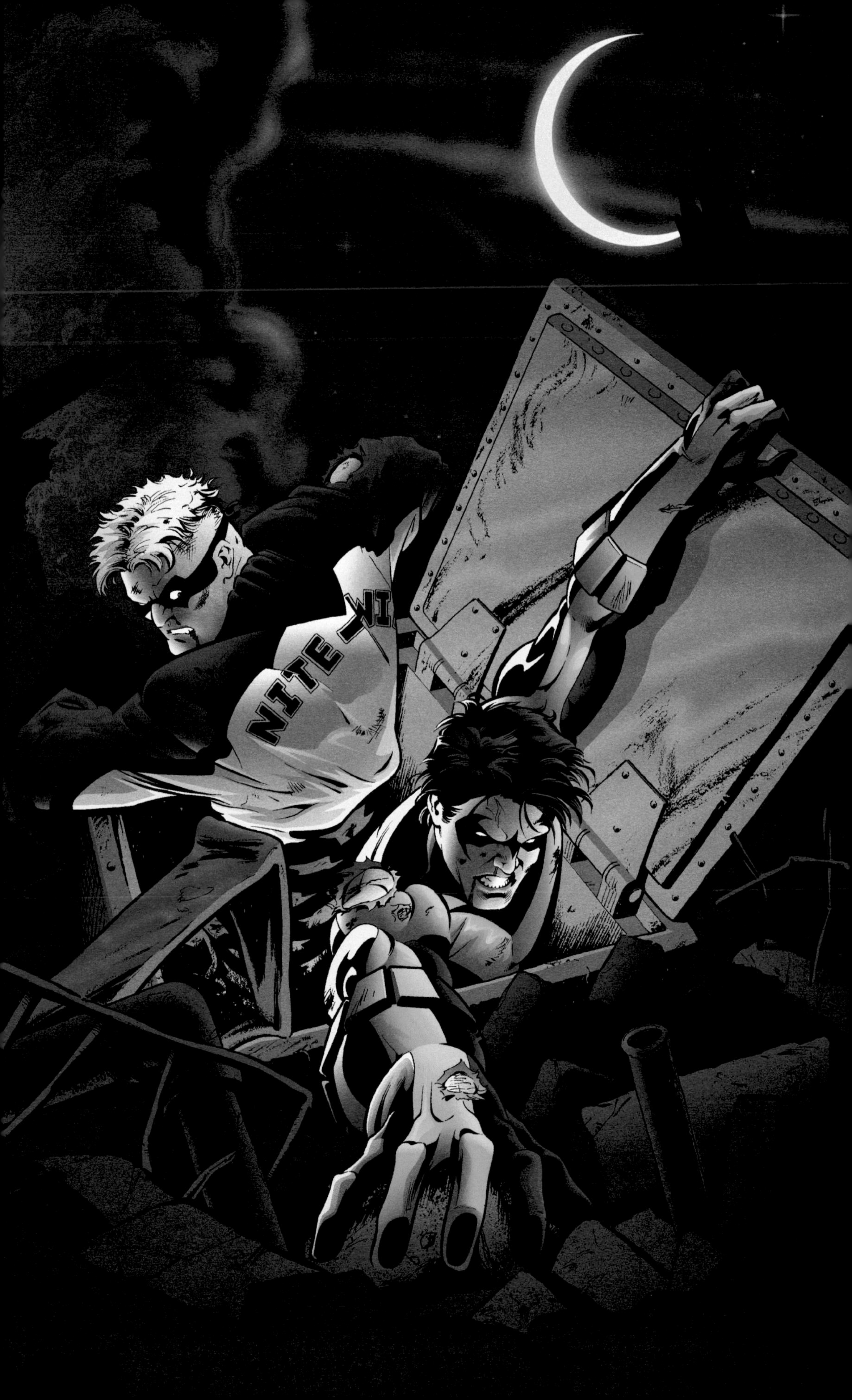
NITE

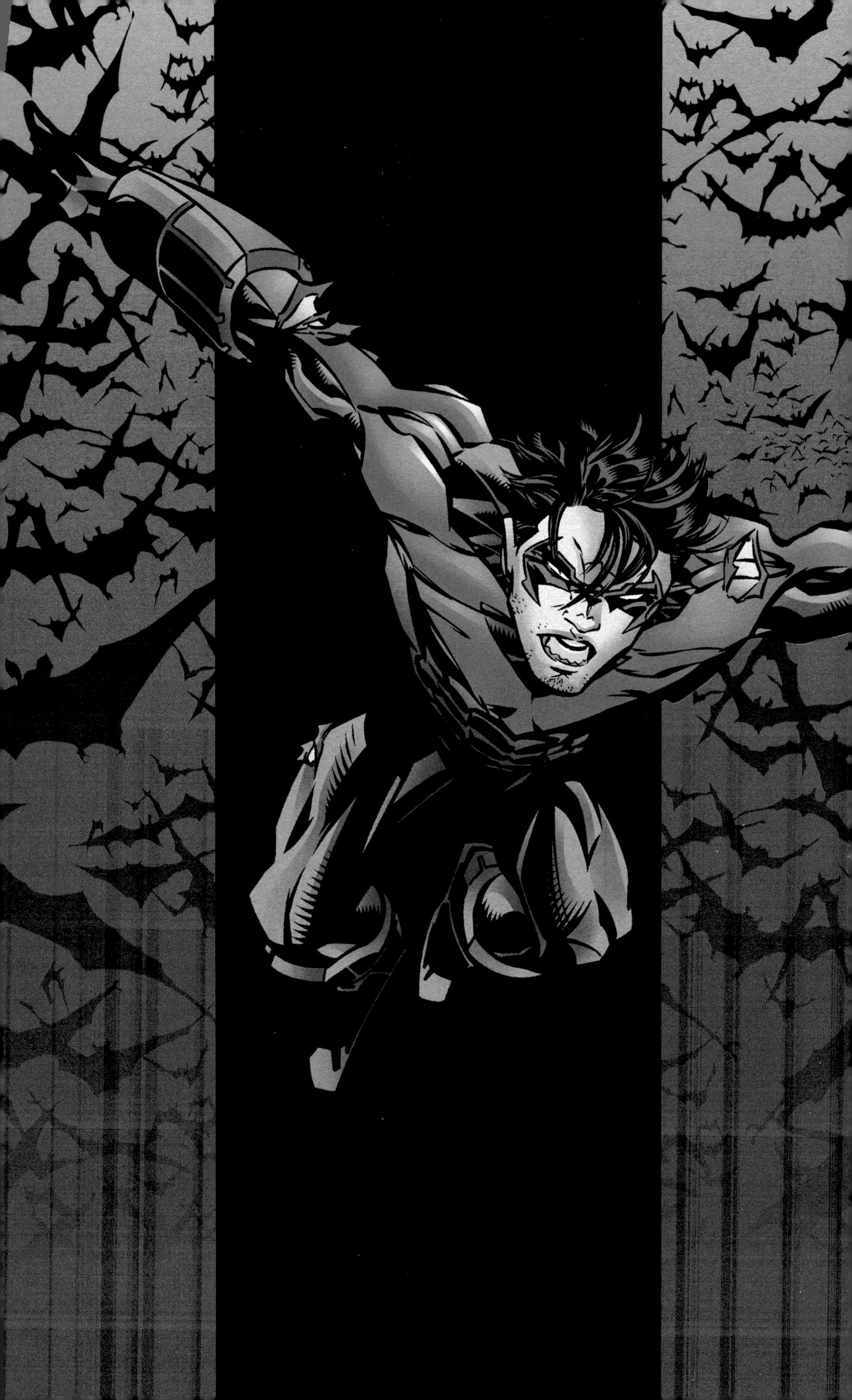

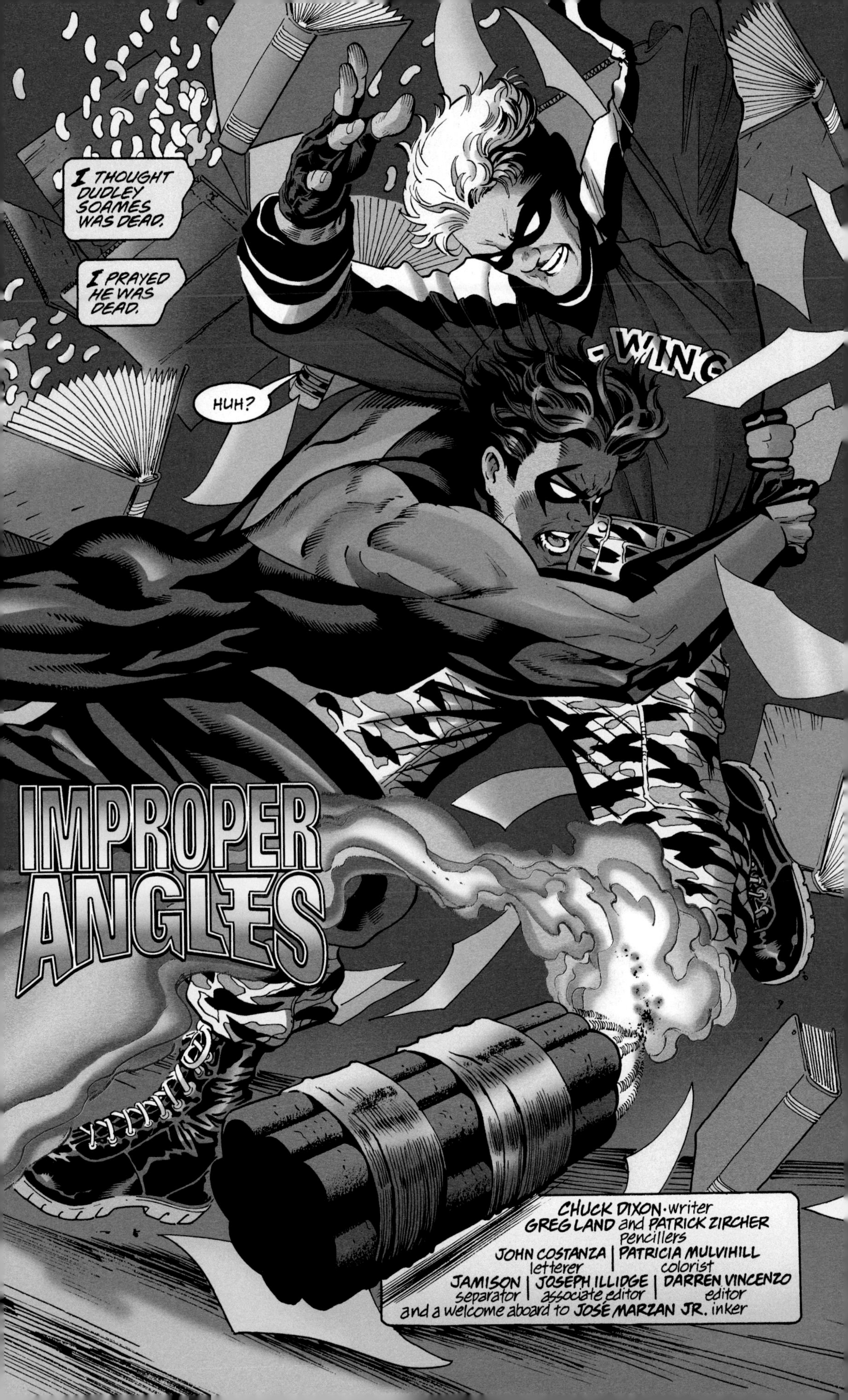

I THOUGHT DUDLEY SOAMES WAS DEAD.
I PRAYED HE WAS DEAD.
HUH?
IMPROPER ANGLES
CHUCK DIXON·writer
GREG LAND and PATRICK ZIRCHER pencillers
JOHN COSTANZA letterer | PATRICIA MULVIHILL colorist
JAMISON separator | JOSEPH ILLIDGE associate editor | DARREN VINCENZO editor
and a welcome aboard to JOSE MARZAN JR. inker

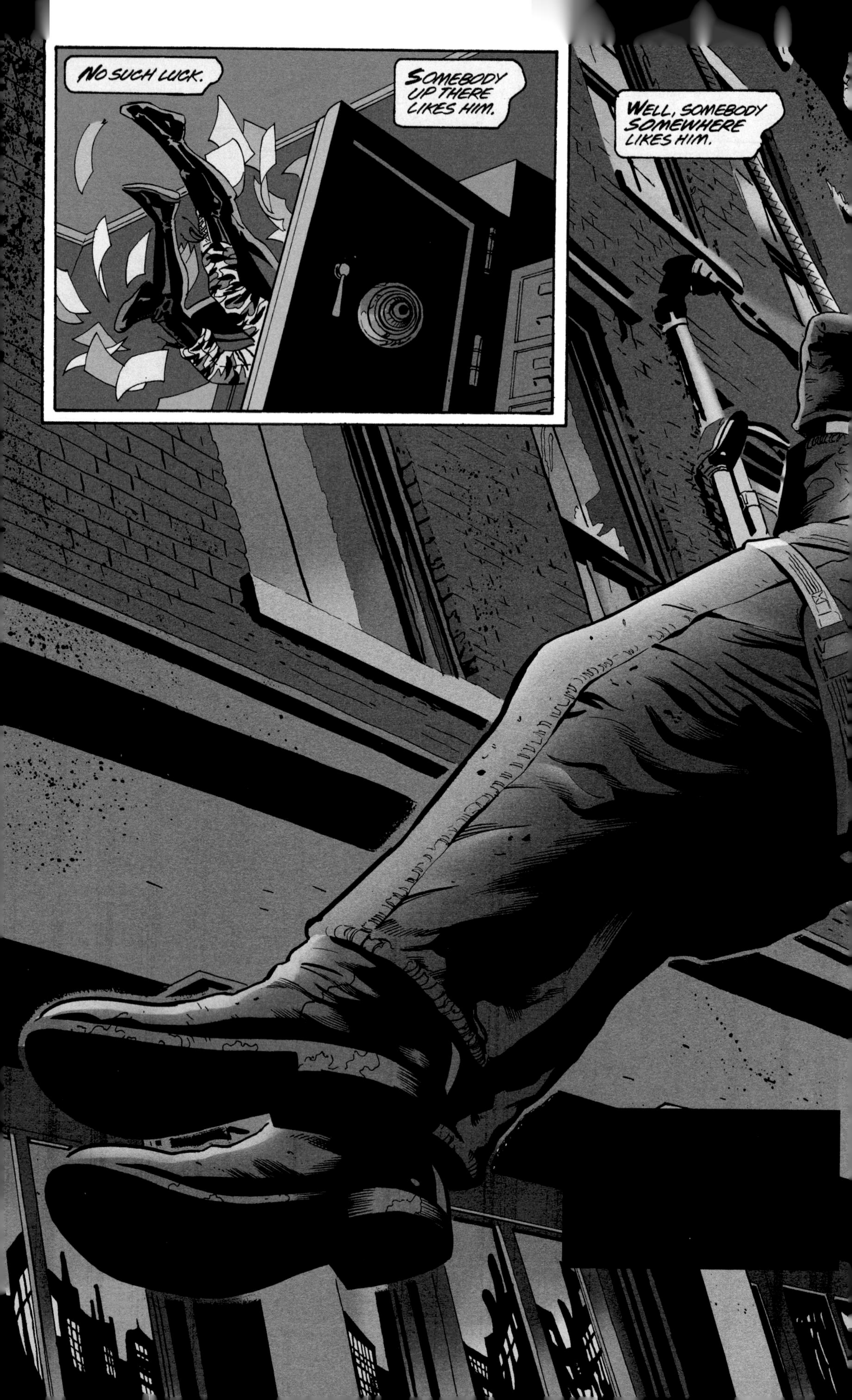
NO SUCH LUCK.
SOMEBODY UP THERE LIKES HIM.
WELL, SOMEBODY SOMEWHERE LIKES HIM.

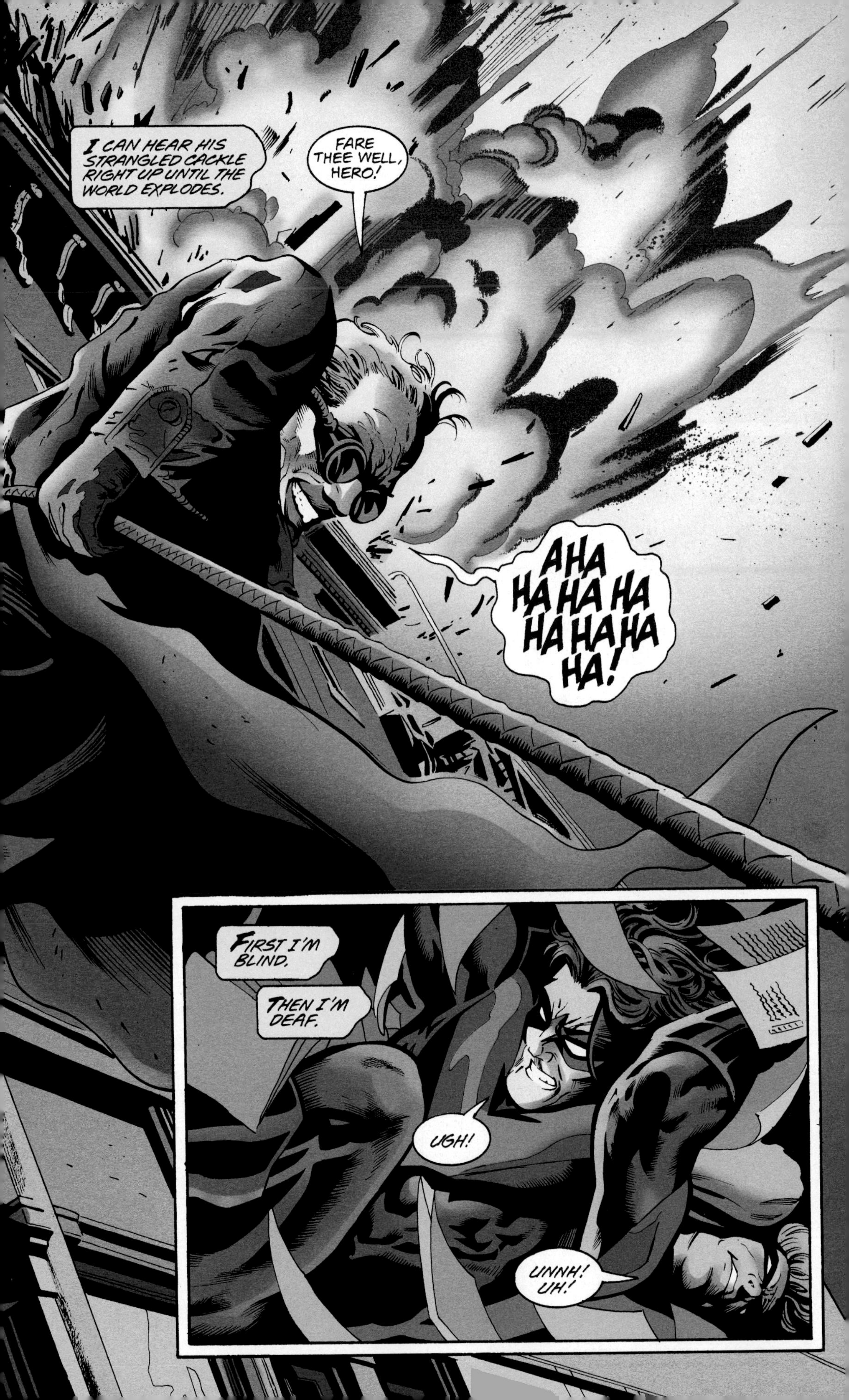
I CAN HEAR HIS STRANGLED CACKLE RIGHT UP UNTIL THE WORLD EXPLODES.
FARE THEE WELL, HERO!
AHA HA HA HA HA HA HA HA!
FIRST I'M BLIND.
THEN I'M DEAF.
UGH!
UNNH! UH!

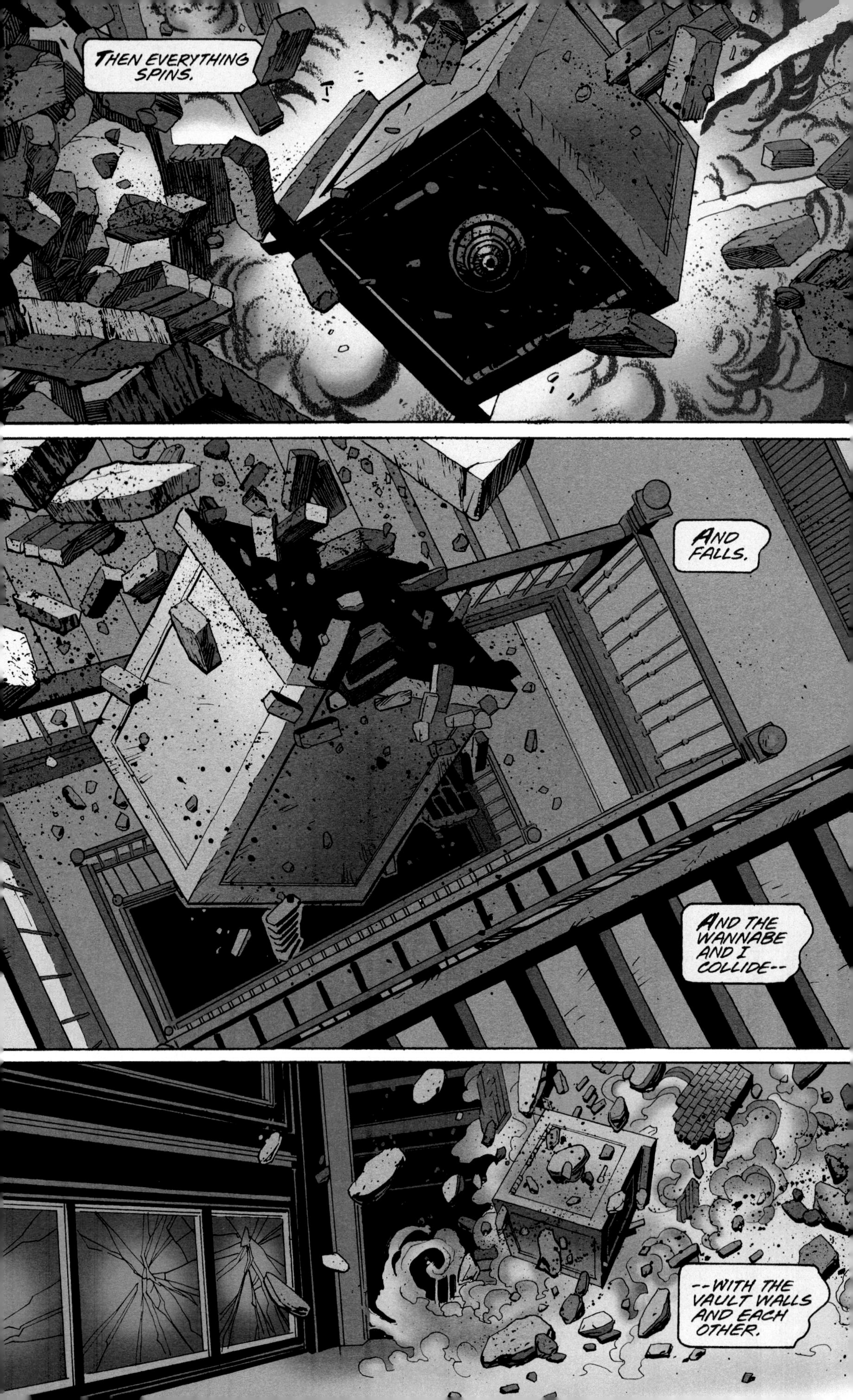
THEN EVERYTHING SPINS.
AND FALLS.
AND THE WANNABE AND I COLLIDE--
--WITH THE VAULT WALLS AND EACH OTHER.

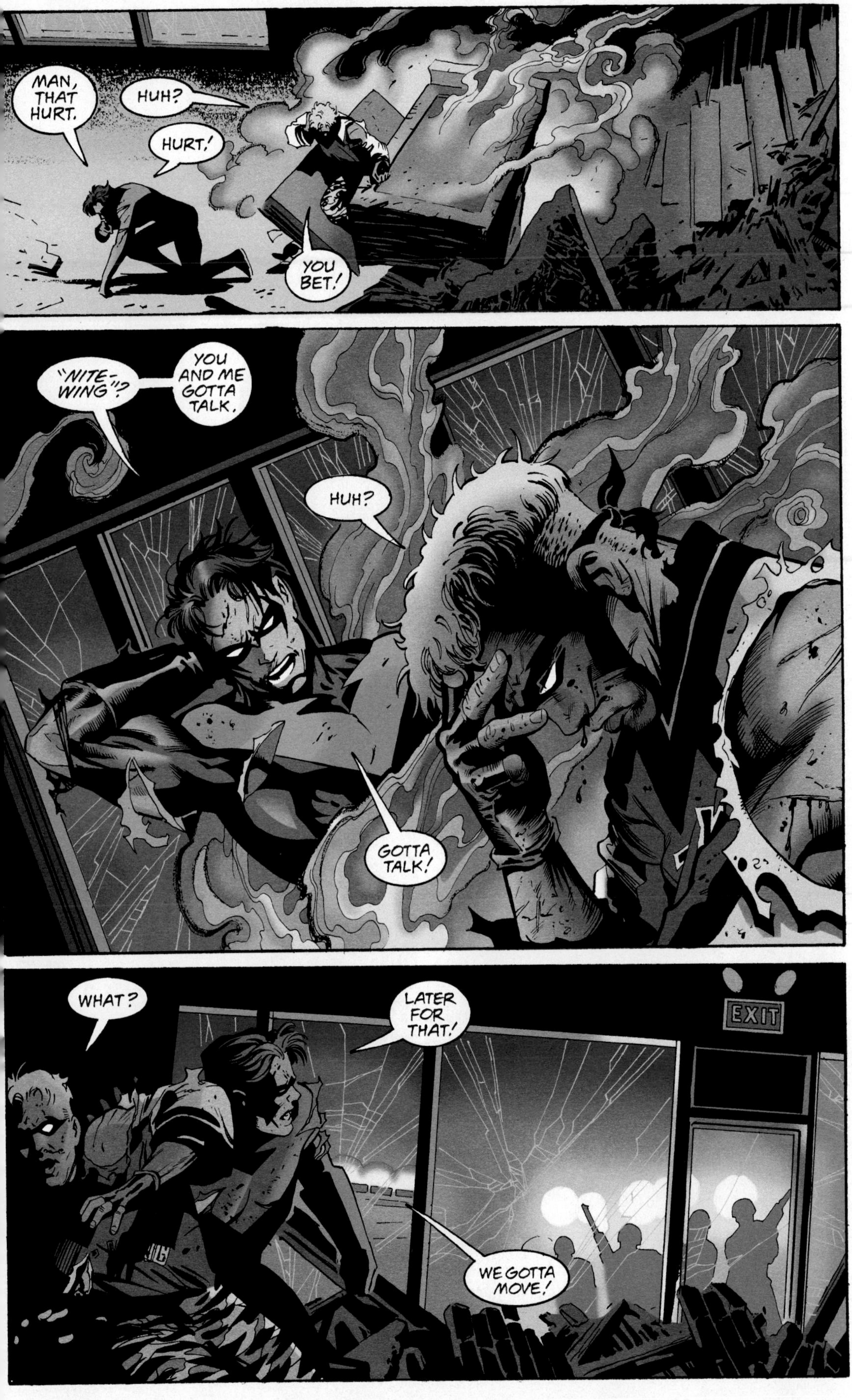
MAN, THAT HURT.
HUH?
HURT!
YOU BET!
"NITE-WING"?
YOU AND ME GOTTA TALK.
HUH?
GOTTA TALK!
WHAT?
LATER FOR THAT!
EXIT
WE GOTTA MOVE!

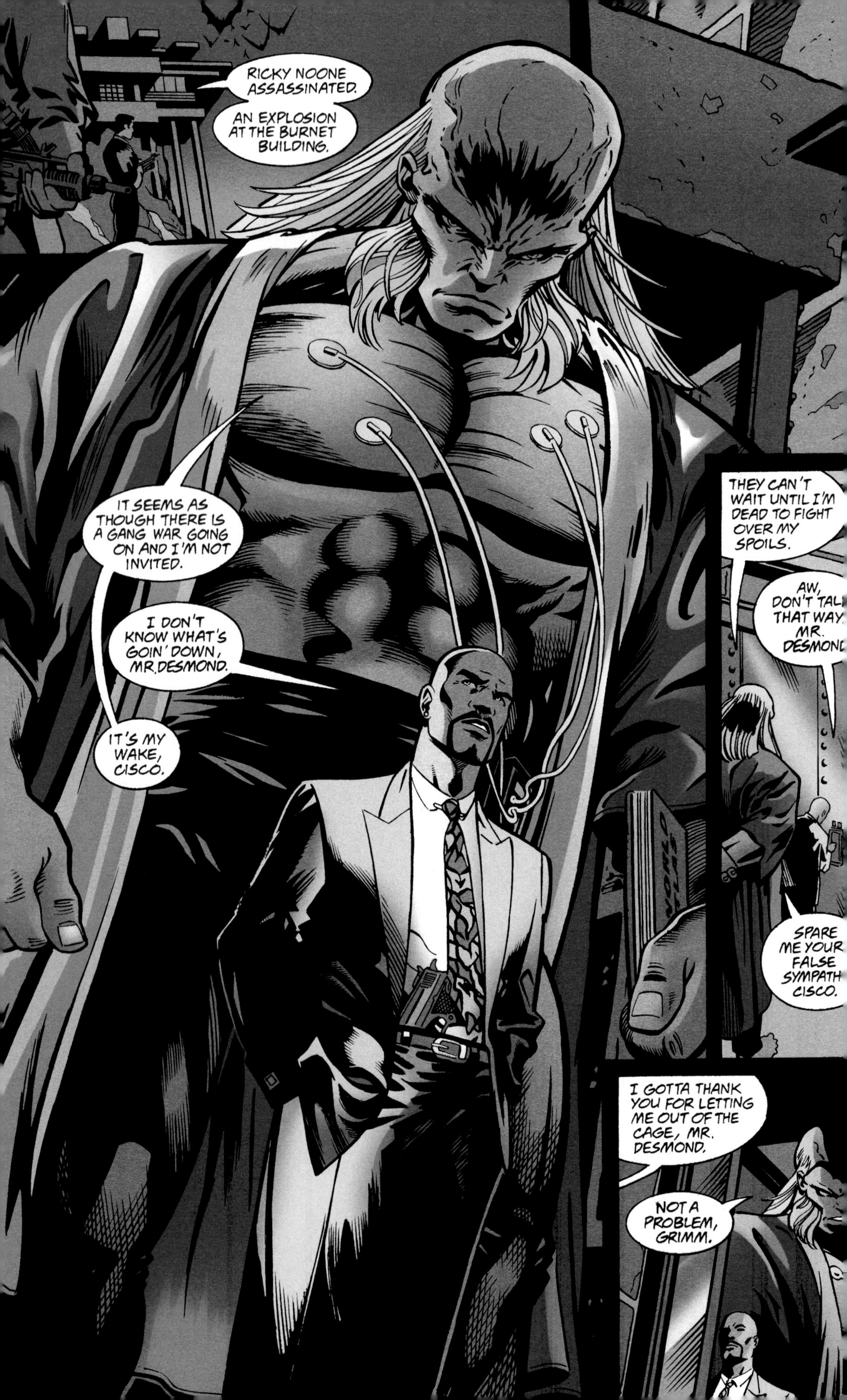
RICKY NOONE ASSASSINATED.
AN EXPLOSION AT THE BURNET BUILDING.
IT SEEMS AS THOUGH THERE IS A GANG WAR GOING ON AND I'M NOT INVITED.
I DON'T KNOW WHAT'S GOIN' DOWN, MR. DESMOND.
IT'S MY WAKE, CISCO.
THEY CAN'T WAIT UNTIL I'M DEAD TO FIGHT OVER MY SPOILS.
AW, DON'T TAL THAT WAY, MR. DESMON
SPARE ME YOUR FALSE SYMPATH CISCO.
I GOTTA THANK YOU FOR LETTING ME OUT OF THE CAGE, MR. DESMOND.
NOT A PROBLEM, GRIMM.

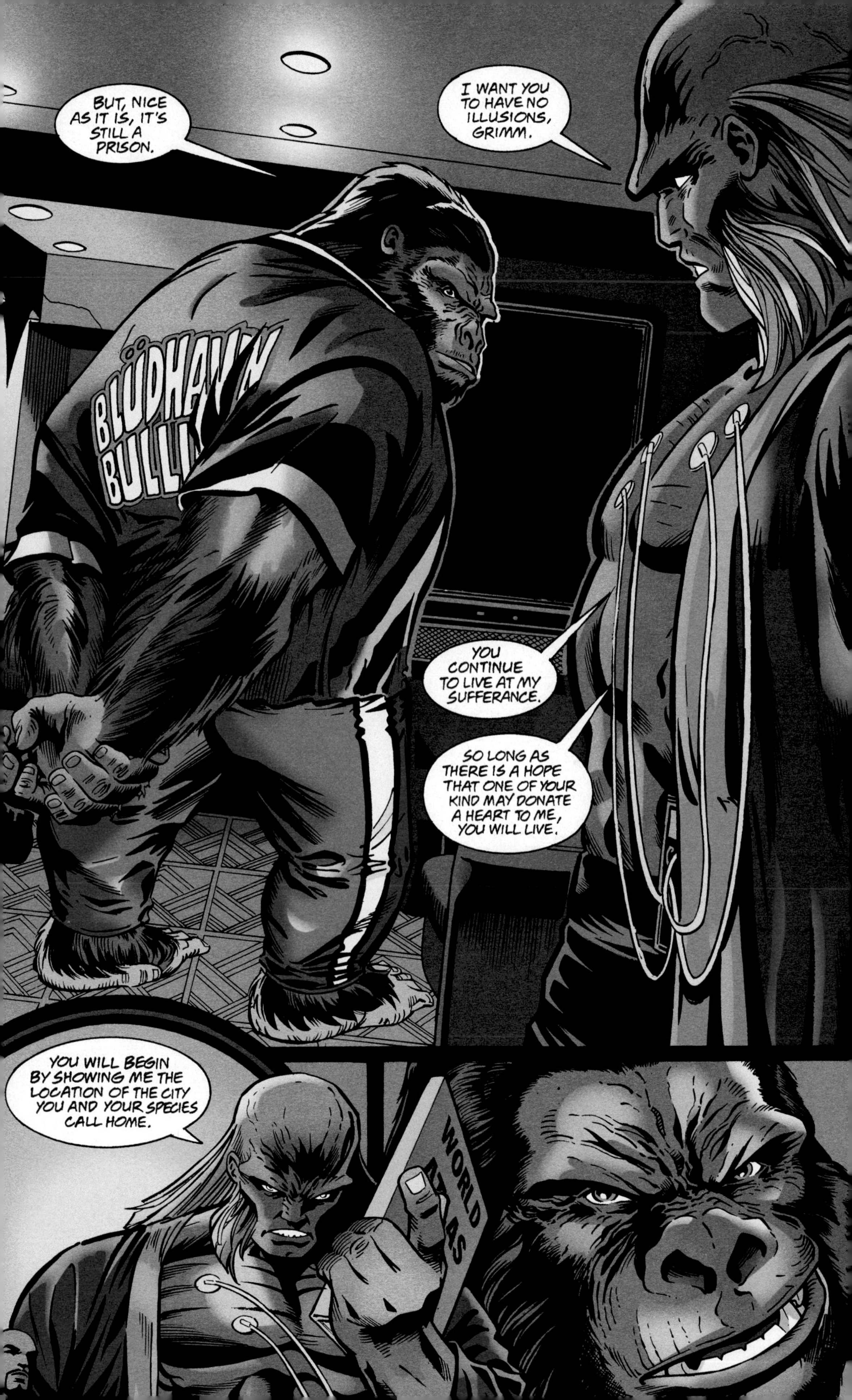
BUT, NICE AS IT IS, IT'S STILL A PRISON.
I WANT YOU TO HAVE NO ILLUSIONS, GRIMM.
YOU CONTINUE TO LIVE AT MY SUFFERANCE.
SO LONG AS THERE IS A HOPE THAT ONE OF YOUR KIND MAY DONATE A HEART TO ME, YOU WILL LIVE.
YOU WILL BEGIN BY SHOWING ME THE LOCATION OF THE CITY YOU AND YOUR SPECIES CALL HOME.
WORLD

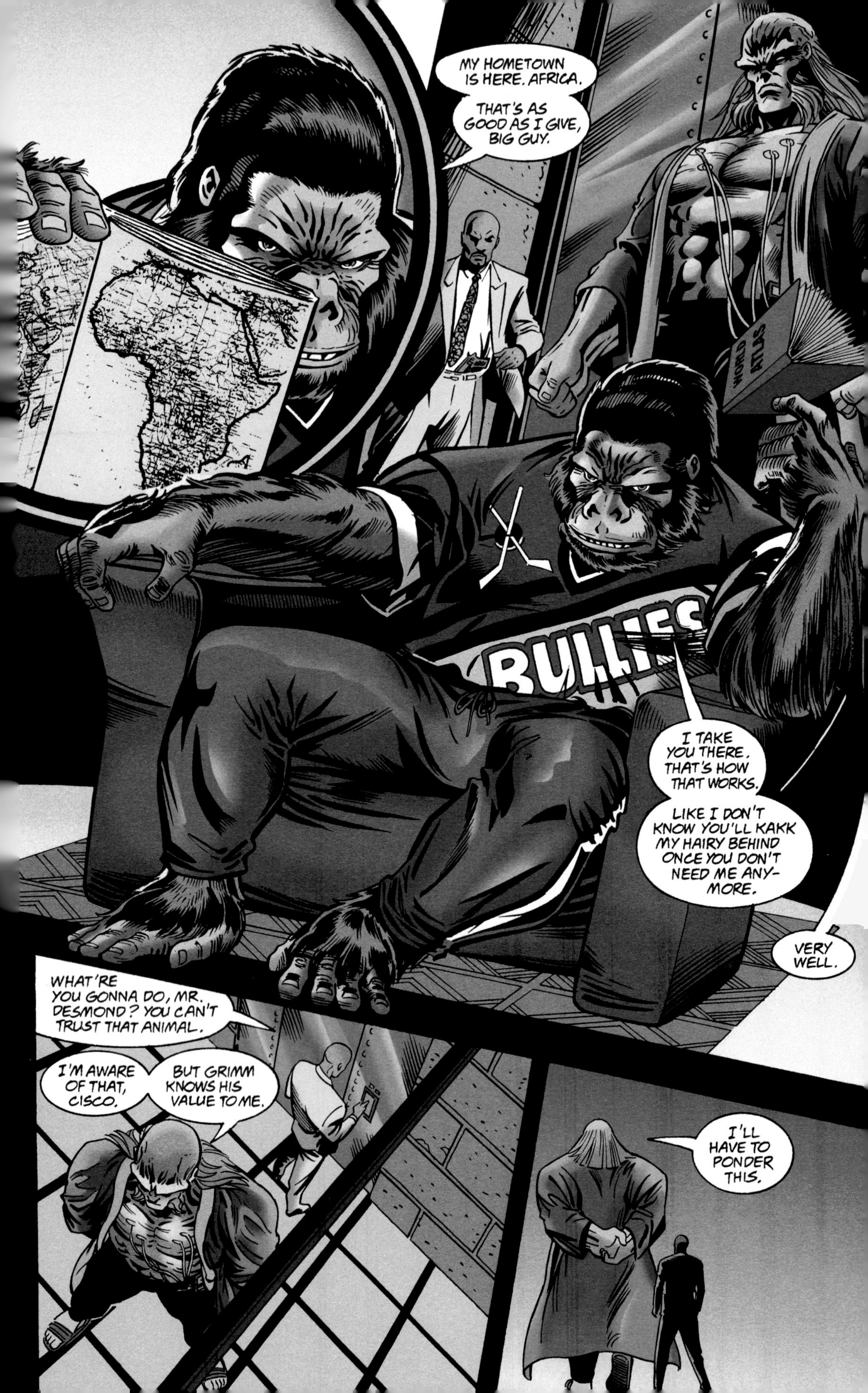
MY HOMETOWN IS HERE. AFRICA.
THAT'S AS GOOD AS I GIVE, BIG GUY.
WORLD ATLAS
BULLIES
I TAKE YOU THERE. THAT'S HOW THAT WORKS.
LIKE I DON'T KNOW YOU'LL KAKK MY HAIRY BEHIND ONCE YOU DON'T NEED ME ANY-MORE.
VERY WELL.
WHAT'RE YOU GONNA DO, MR. DESMOND? YOU CAN'T TRUST THAT ANIMAL.
I'M AWARE OF THAT, CISCO.
BUT GRIMM KNOWS HIS VALUE TO ME.
I'LL HAVE TO PONDER THIS.

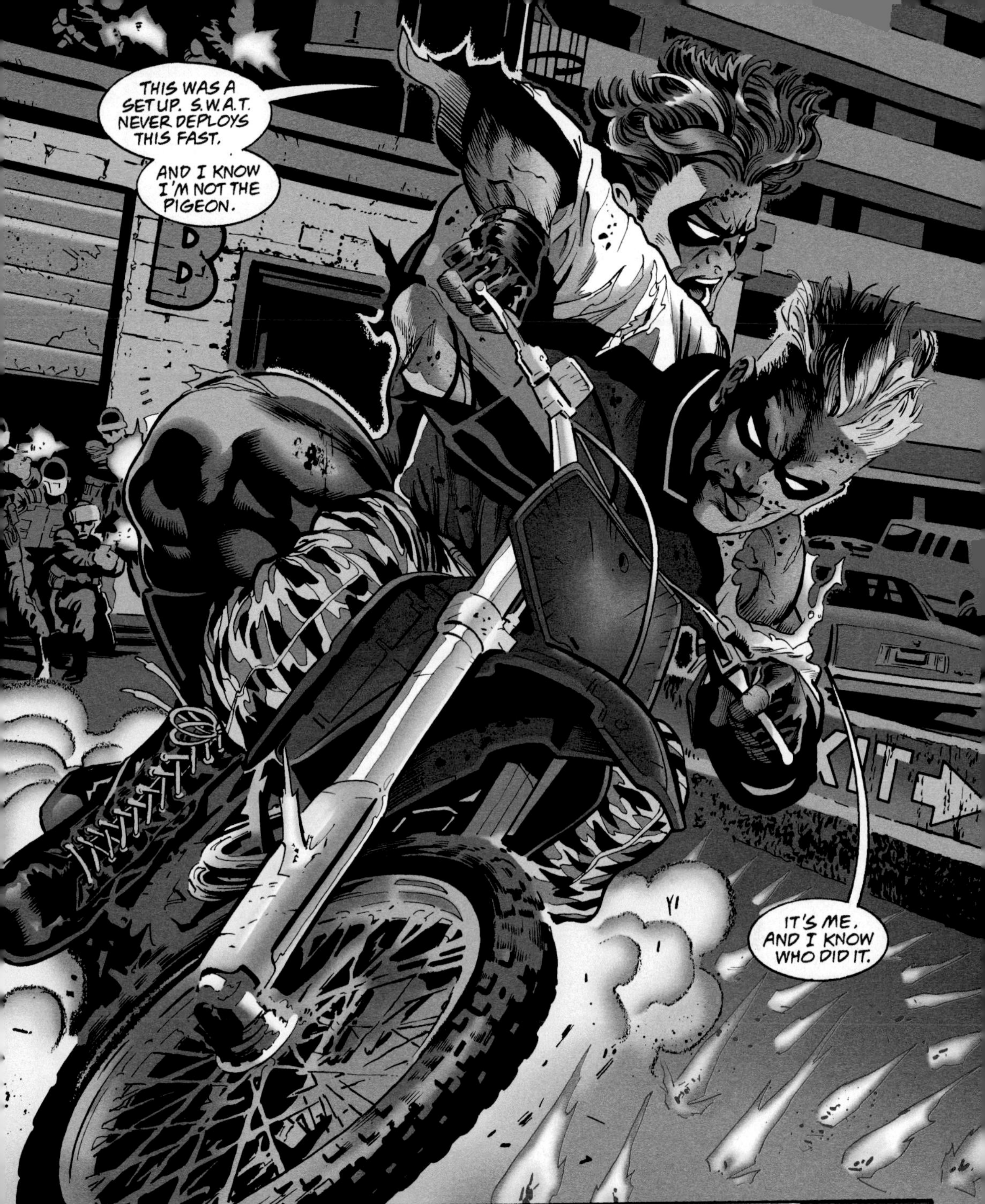
THIS WAS A SET UP. S.W.A.T. NEVER DEPLOYS THIS FAST.
AND I KNOW I'M NOT THE PIGEON.
IT'S ME. AND I KNOW WHO DID IT.
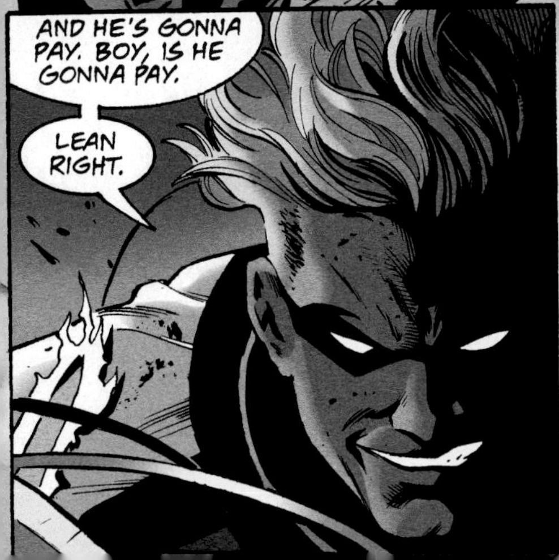
AND HE'S GONNA PAY. BOY, IS HE GONNA PAY.
LEAN RIGHT.
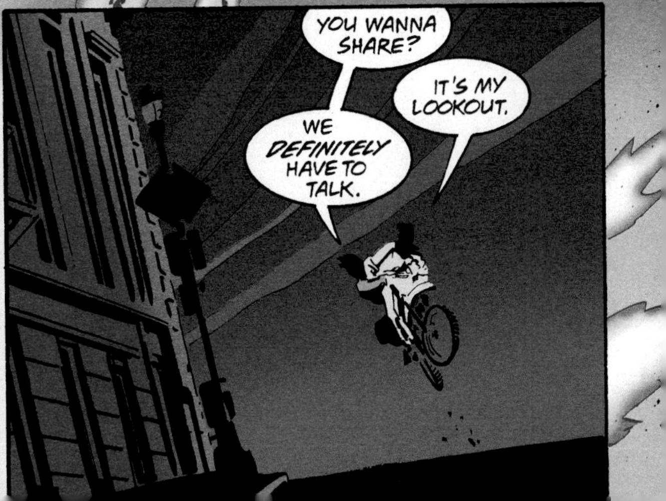
YOU WANNA SHARE?
IT'S MY LOOKOUT.
WE DEFINITELY HAVE TO TALK.

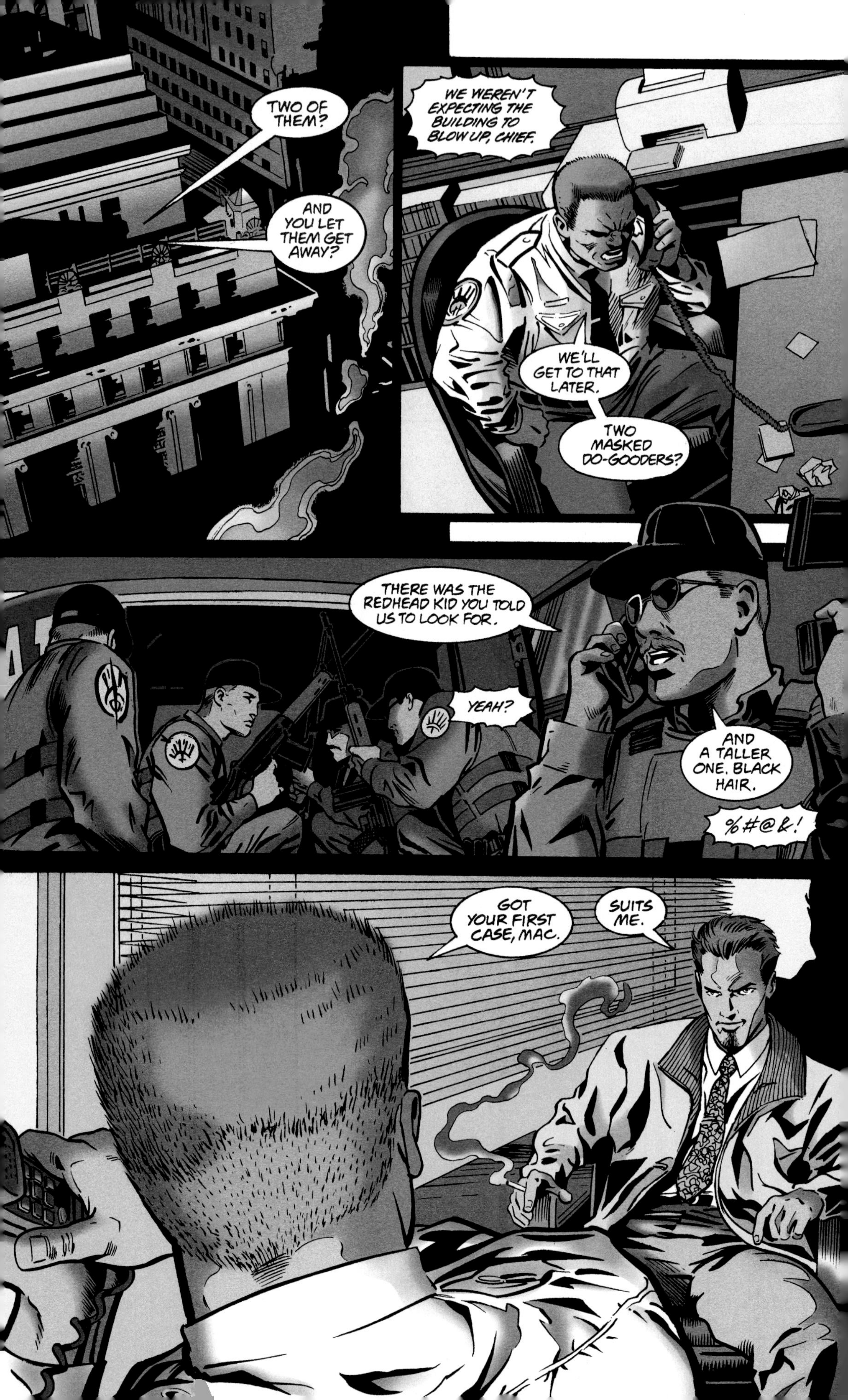
TWO OF THEM?
AND YOU LET THEM GET AWAY?
WE WEREN'T EXPECTING THE BUILDING TO BLOW UP, CHIEF.
WE'LL GET TO THAT LATER.
TWO MASKED DO-GOODERS?
THERE WAS THE REDHEAD KID YOU TOLD US TO LOOK FOR.
YEAH?
AND A TALLER ONE. BLACK HAIR.
%#@&!
GOT YOUR FIRST CASE, MAC.
SUITS ME.

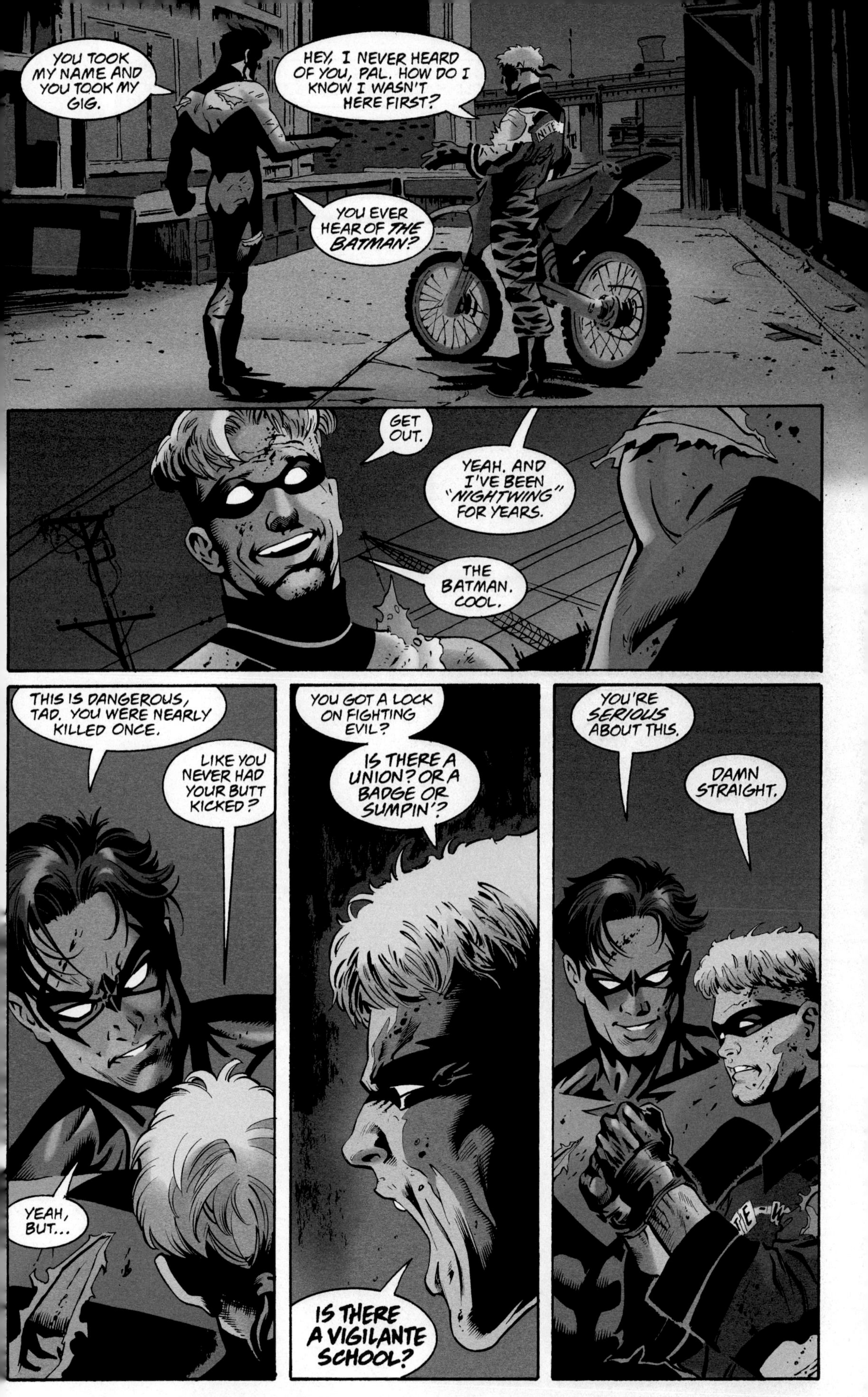
YOU TOOK MY NAME AND YOU TOOK MY GIG.
HEY, I NEVER HEARD OF YOU, PAL. HOW DO I KNOW I WASN'T HERE FIRST?
YOU EVER HEAR OF *THE BATMAN*?
GET OUT.
YEAH. AND I'VE BEEN "*NIGHTWING*" FOR YEARS.
THE BATMAN. COOL.
THIS IS DANGEROUS, TAD. YOU WERE NEARLY KILLED ONCE.
LIKE YOU NEVER HAD YOUR BUTT KICKED?
YEAH, BUT...
YOU GOT A LOCK ON FIGHTING EVIL?
IS THERE A UNION? OR A BADGE OR SUMPIN'?
IS THERE A VIGILANTE SCHOOL?
YOU'RE *SERIOUS* ABOUT THIS.
DAMN STRAIGHT.

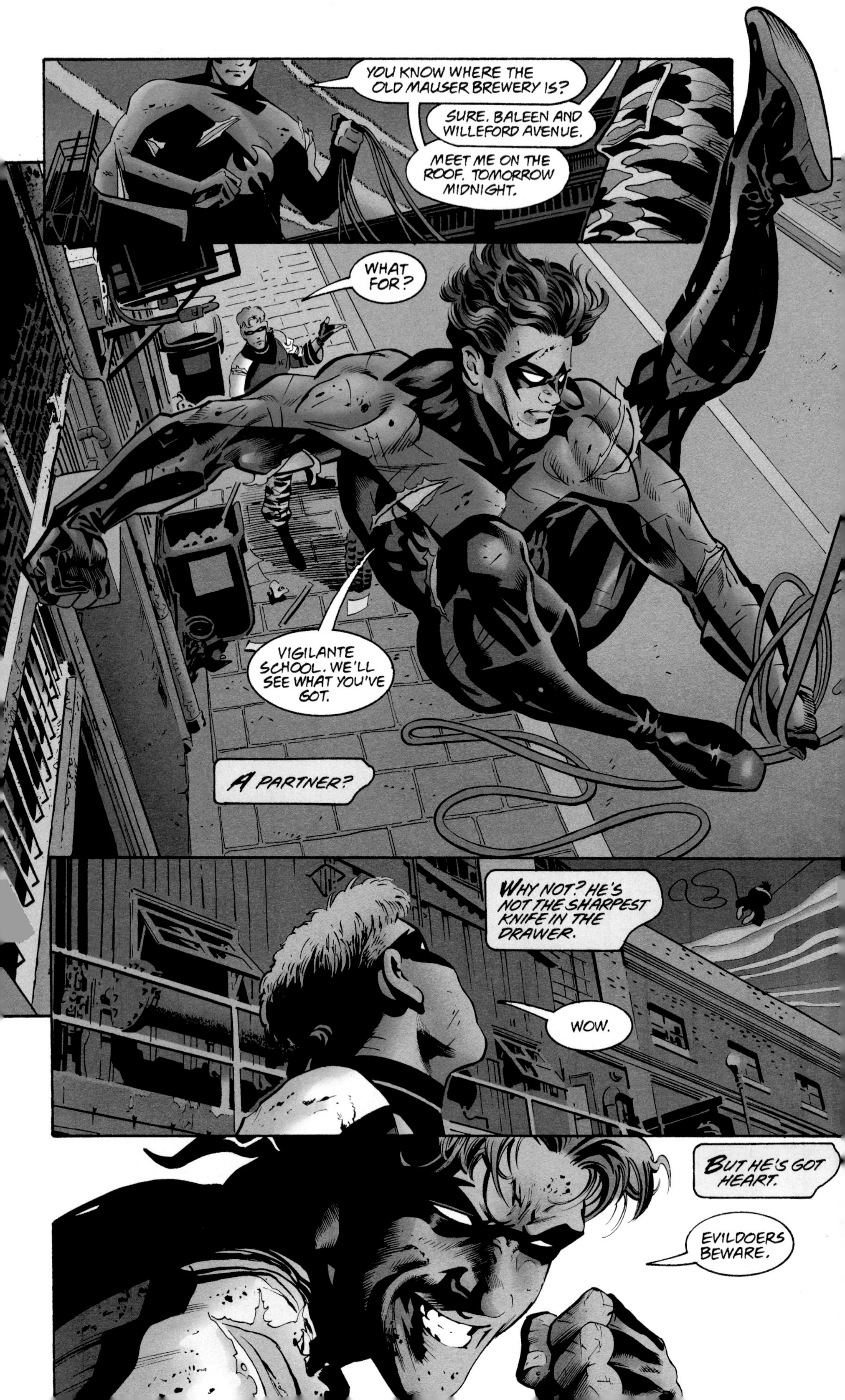
YOU KNOW WHERE THE OLD MAUSER BREWERY IS?
SURE. BALEEN AND WILLEFORD AVENUE.
MEET ME ON THE ROOF. TOMORROW MIDNIGHT.
WHAT FOR?
VIGILANTE SCHOOL. WE'LL SEE WHAT YOU'VE GOT.
A PARTNER?
WHY NOT? HE'S NOT THE SHARPEST KNIFE IN THE DRAWER.
WOW.
BUT HE'S GOT HEART.
EVILDOERS BEWARE.

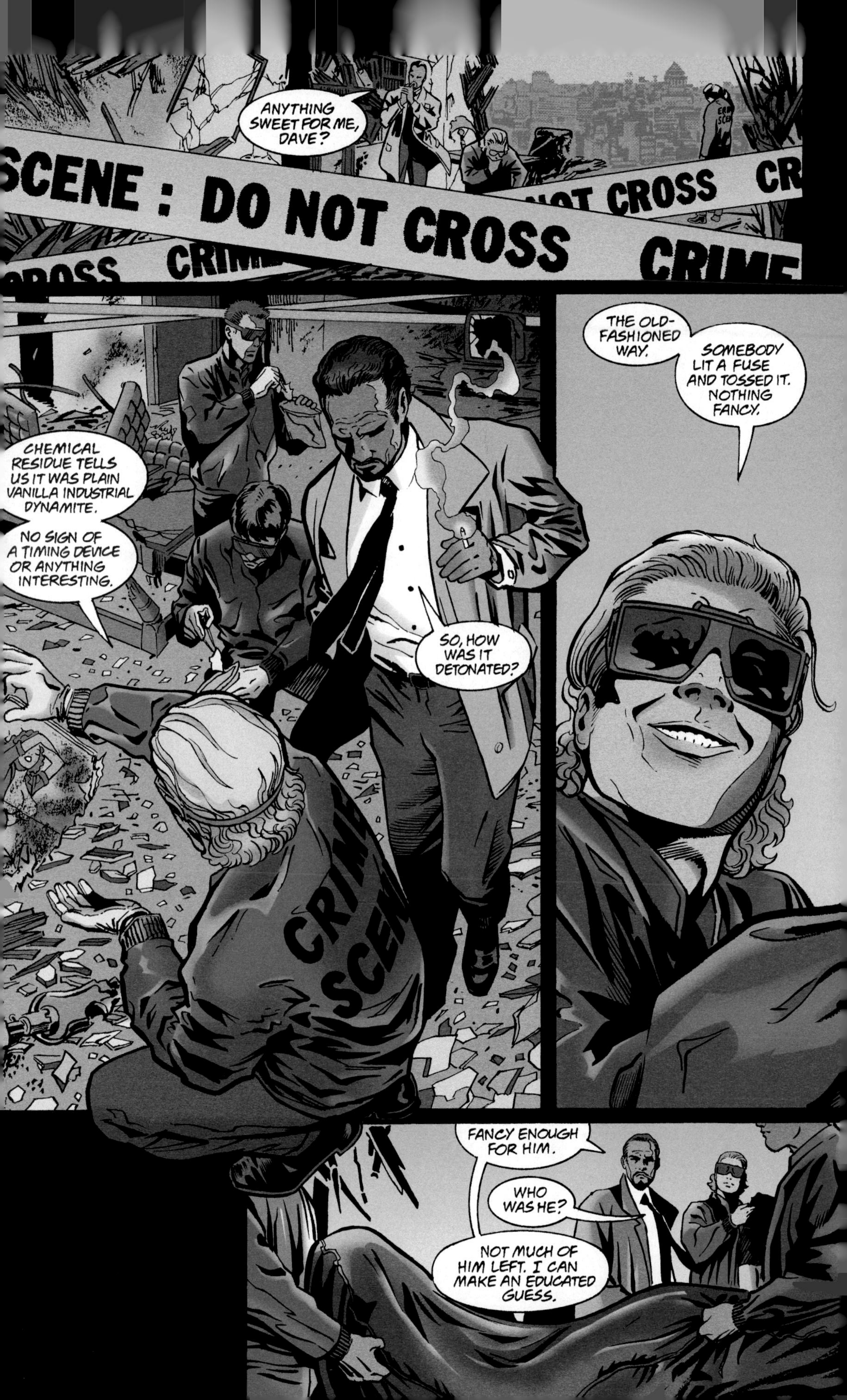
ANYTHING SWEET FOR ME, DAVE?
SCENE : DO NOT CROSS
CRIME
CHEMICAL RESIDUE TELLS US IT WAS PLAIN VANILLA INDUSTRIAL DYNAMITE.
NO SIGN OF A TIMING DEVICE OR ANYTHING INTERESTING.
SO, HOW WAS IT DETONATED?
THE OLD-FASHIONED WAY.
SOMEBODY LIT A FUSE AND TOSSED IT. NOTHING FANCY.
FANCY ENOUGH FOR HIM.
WHO WAS HE?
NOT MUCH OF HIM LEFT. I CAN MAKE AN EDUCATED GUESS.

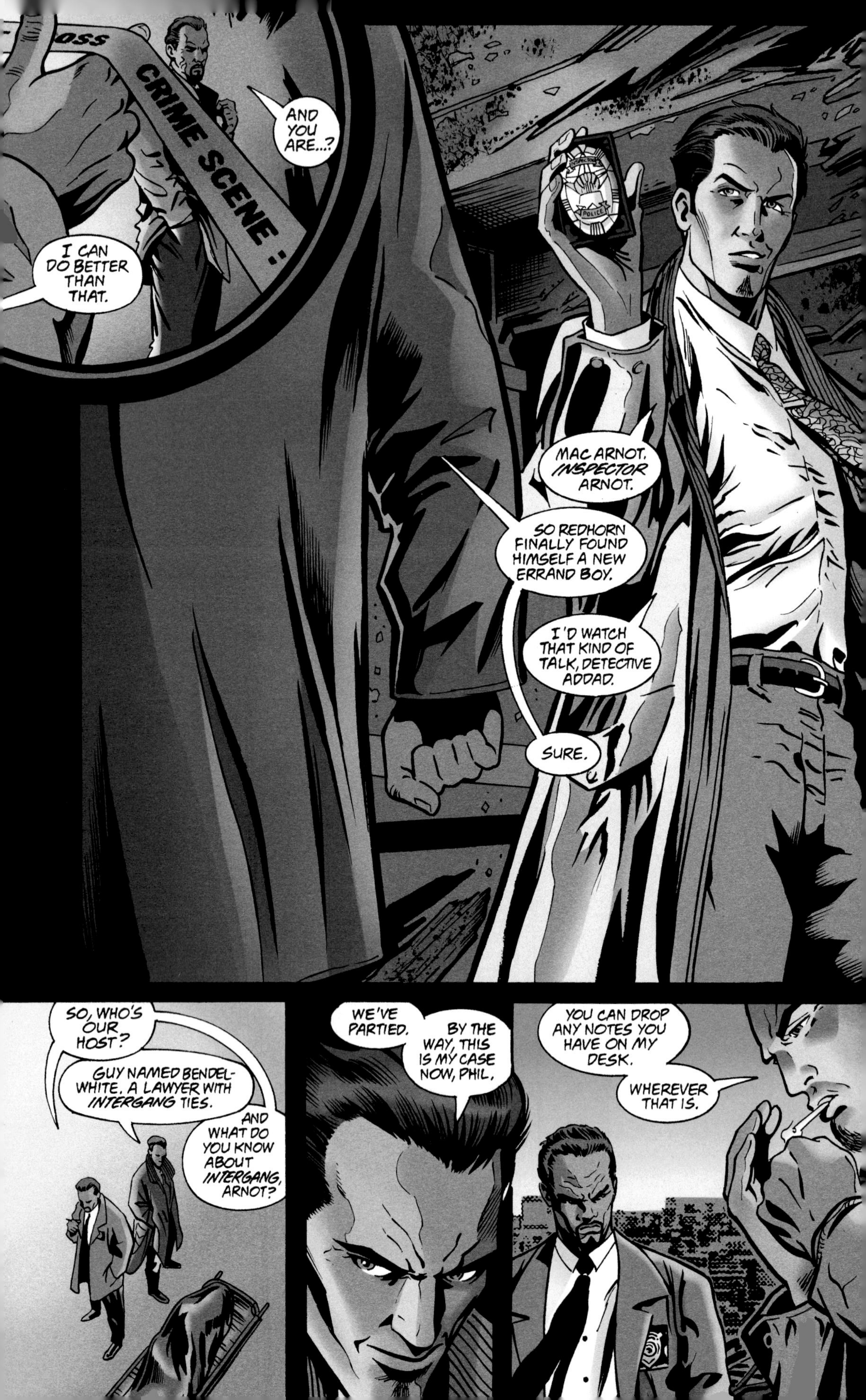
CROSS
CRIME SCENE
AND YOU ARE...?
I CAN DO BETTER THAN THAT.
POLICE
MAC ARNOT. *INSPECTOR* ARNOT.
SO REDHORN FINALLY FOUND HIMSELF A NEW ERRAND BOY.
I'D WATCH THAT KIND OF TALK, DETECTIVE ADDAD.
SURE.
SO, WHO'S OUR HOST?
GUY NAMED BENDEL-WHITE. A LAWYER WITH *INTERGANG* TIES.
AND WHAT DO YOU KNOW ABOUT *INTERGANG*, ARNOT?
WE'VE PARTIED.
BY THE WAY, THIS IS MY CASE NOW, PHIL.
YOU CAN DROP ANY NOTES YOU HAVE ON MY DESK.
WHEREVER THAT IS.

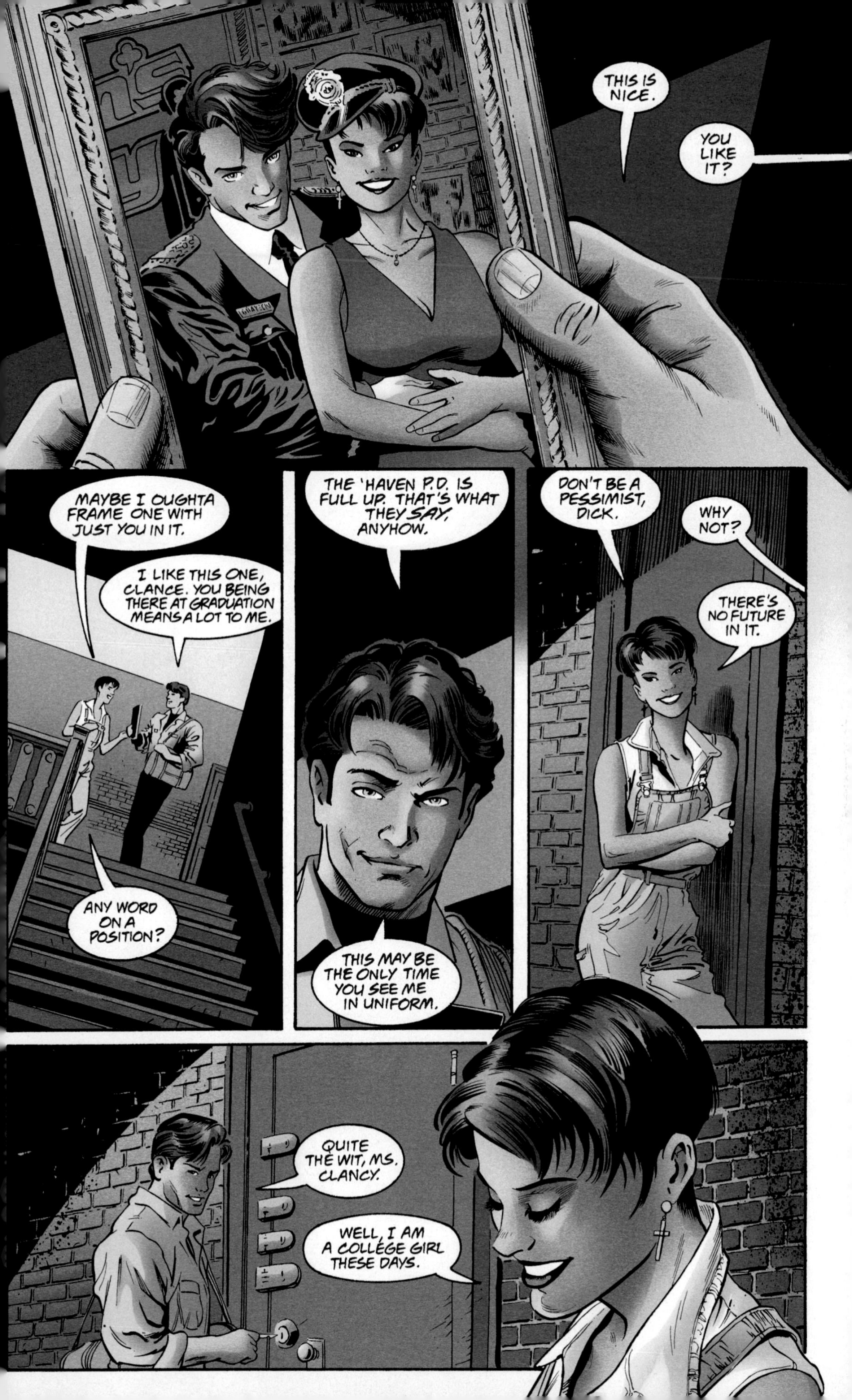
THIS IS NICE.
YOU LIKE IT?
MAYBE I OUGHTA FRAME ONE WITH JUST YOU IN IT.
I LIKE THIS ONE, CLANCE. YOU BEING THERE AT GRADUATION MEANS A LOT TO ME.
ANY WORD ON A POSITION?
THE 'HAVEN P.D. IS FULL UP. THAT'S WHAT THEY SAY, ANYHOW.
THIS MAY BE THE ONLY TIME YOU SEE ME IN UNIFORM.
DON'T BE A PESSIMIST, DICK.
WHY NOT?
THERE'S NO FUTURE IN IT.
QUITE THE WIT, MS. CLANCY.
WELL, I AM A COLLEGE GIRL THESE DAYS.

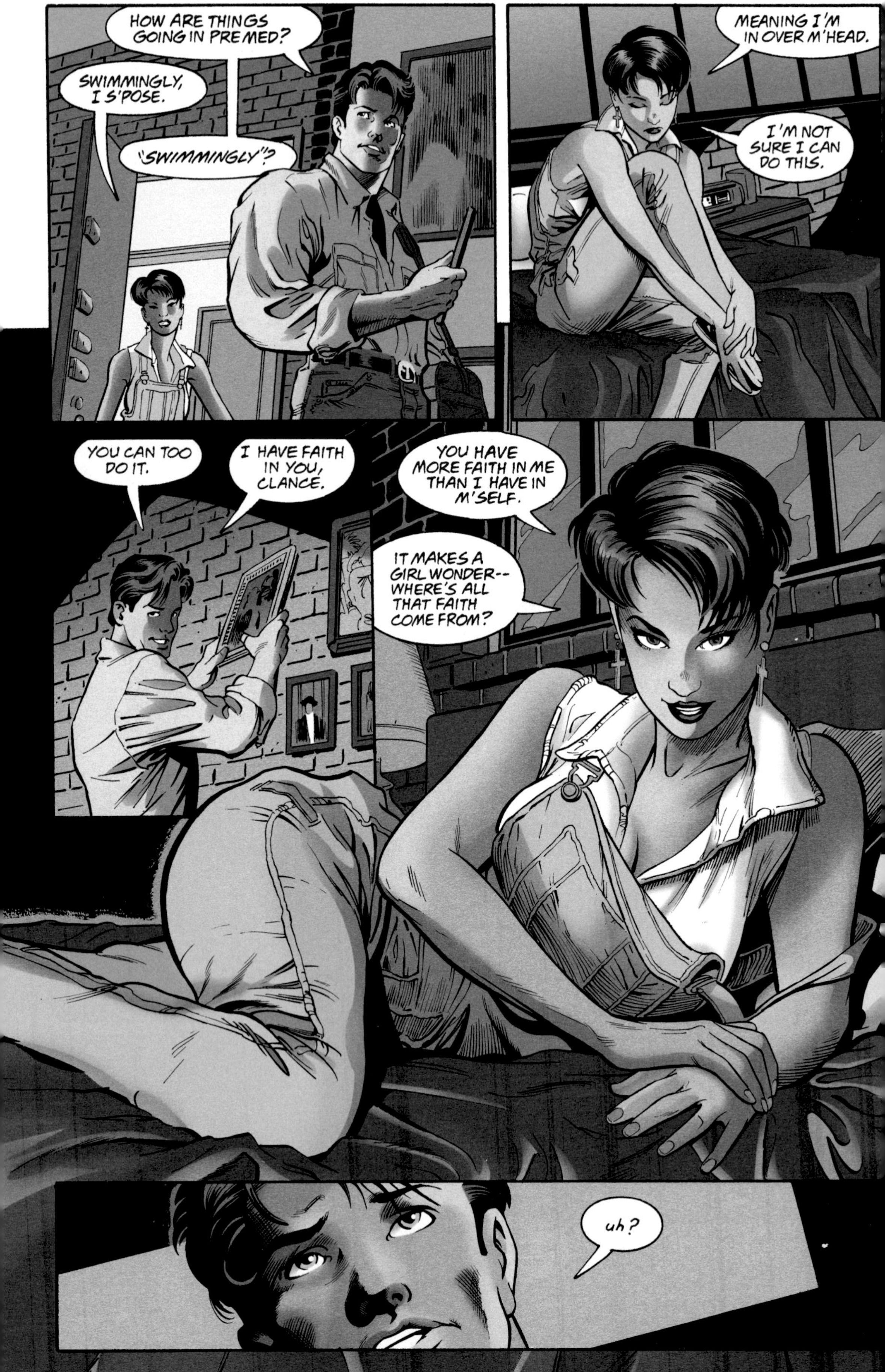
HOW ARE THINGS GOING IN PREMED?
SWIMMINGLY, I S'POSE.
"SWIMMINGLY"?
MEANING I'M IN OVER M'HEAD.
I'M NOT SURE I CAN DO THIS.
YOU CAN TOO DO IT.
I HAVE FAITH IN YOU, CLANCE.
YOU HAVE MORE FAITH IN ME THAN I HAVE IN M'SELF.
IT MAKES A GIRL WONDER-- WHERE'S ALL THAT FAITH COME FROM?
uh?

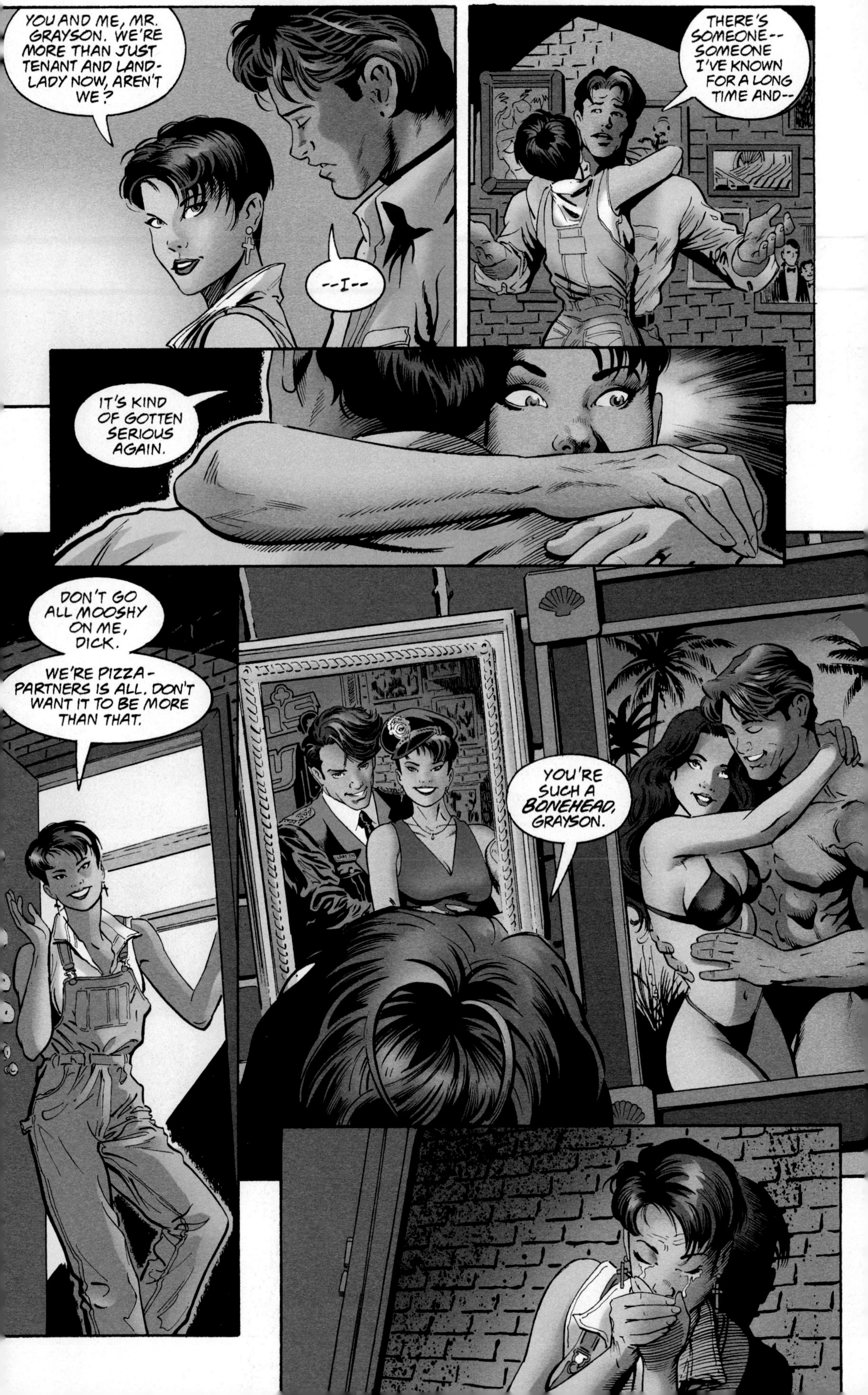
YOU AND ME, MR. GRAYSON. WE'RE MORE THAN JUST TENANT AND LAND-LADY NOW, AREN'T WE?
--I--
THERE'S SOMEONE-- SOMEONE I'VE KNOWN FOR A LONG TIME AND--
IT'S KIND OF GOTTEN SERIOUS AGAIN.
DON'T GO ALL MOOSHY ON ME, DICK.
WE'RE PIZZA-PARTNERS IS ALL. DON'T WANT IT TO BE MORE THAN THAT.
YOU'RE SUCH A BONEHEAD, GRAYSON.

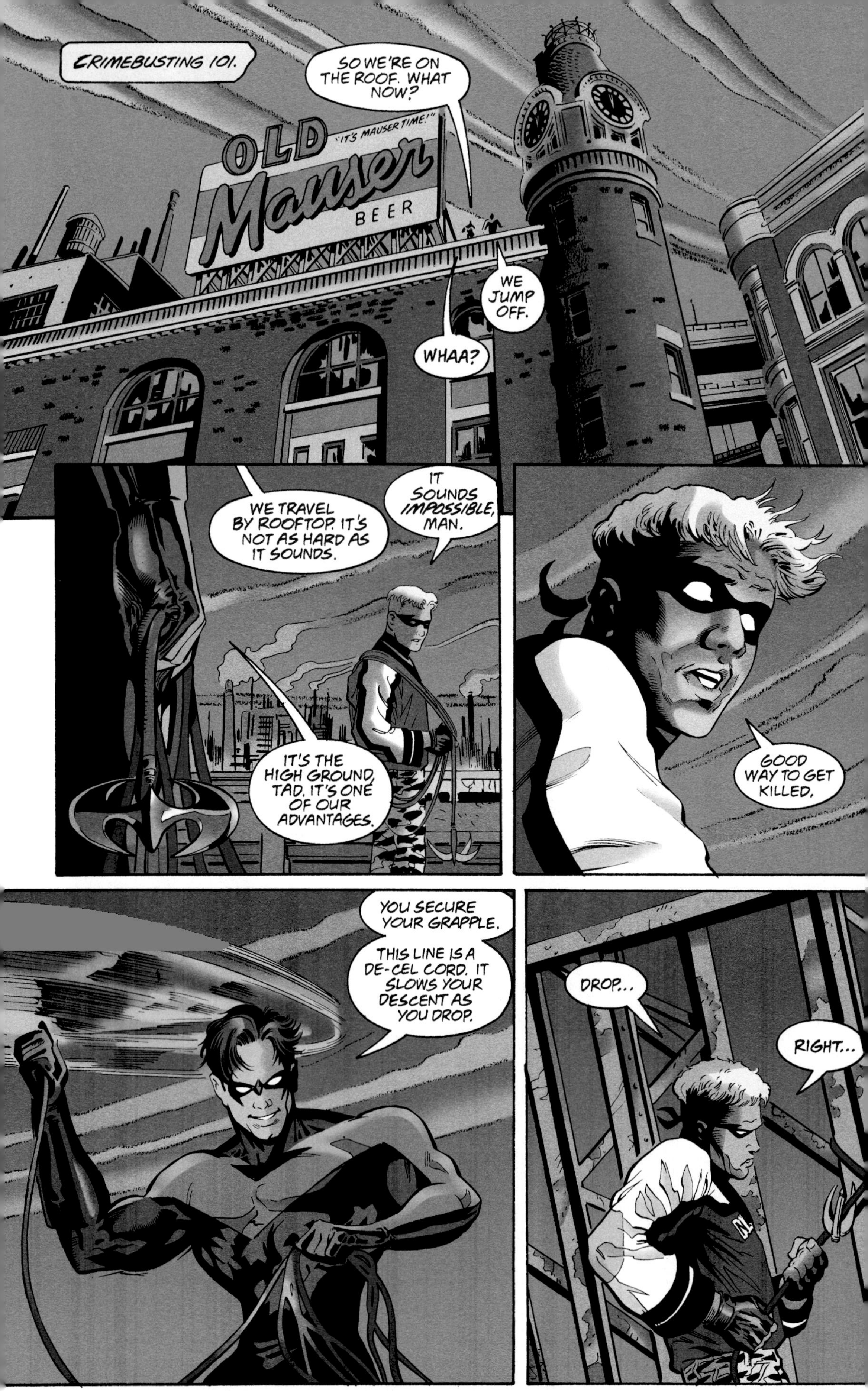
CRIMEBUSTING 101.
SO WE'RE ON THE ROOF. WHAT NOW?
OLD Mauser BEER
"IT'S MAUSER TIME!"
WE JUMP OFF.
WHAA?
WE TRAVEL BY ROOFTOP. IT'S NOT AS HARD AS IT SOUNDS.
IT SOUNDS IMPOSSIBLE, MAN.
IT'S THE HIGH GROUND, TAD. IT'S ONE OF OUR ADVANTAGES.
GOOD WAY TO GET KILLED.
YOU SECURE YOUR GRAPPLE.
THIS LINE IS A DE-CEL CORD. IT SLOWS YOUR DESCENT AS YOU DROP.
DROP...
RIGHT...

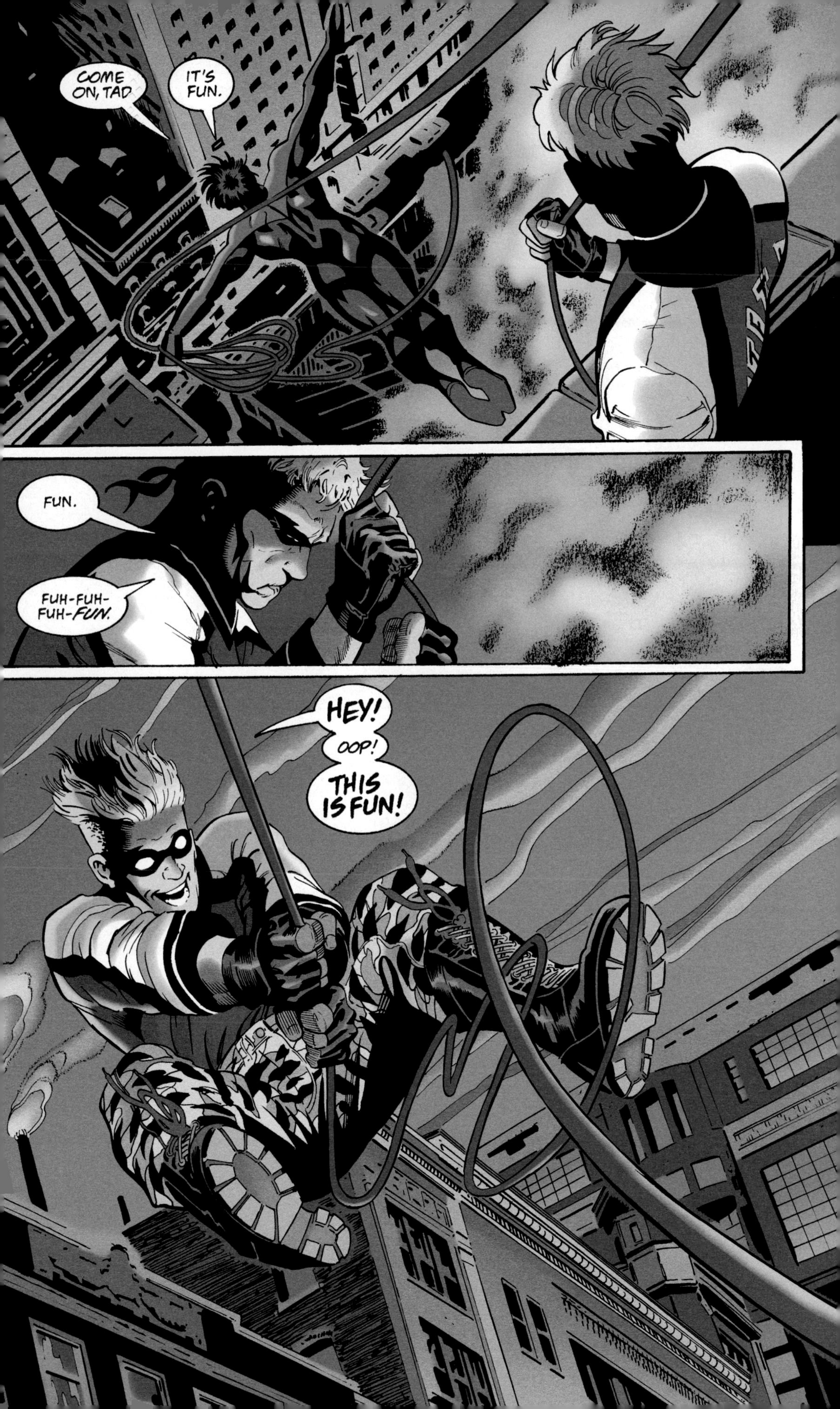
COME ON, TAD
IT'S FUN.
FUN.
FUH-FUH-FUH-*FUN*.
HEY!
OOP!
THIS IS FUN!

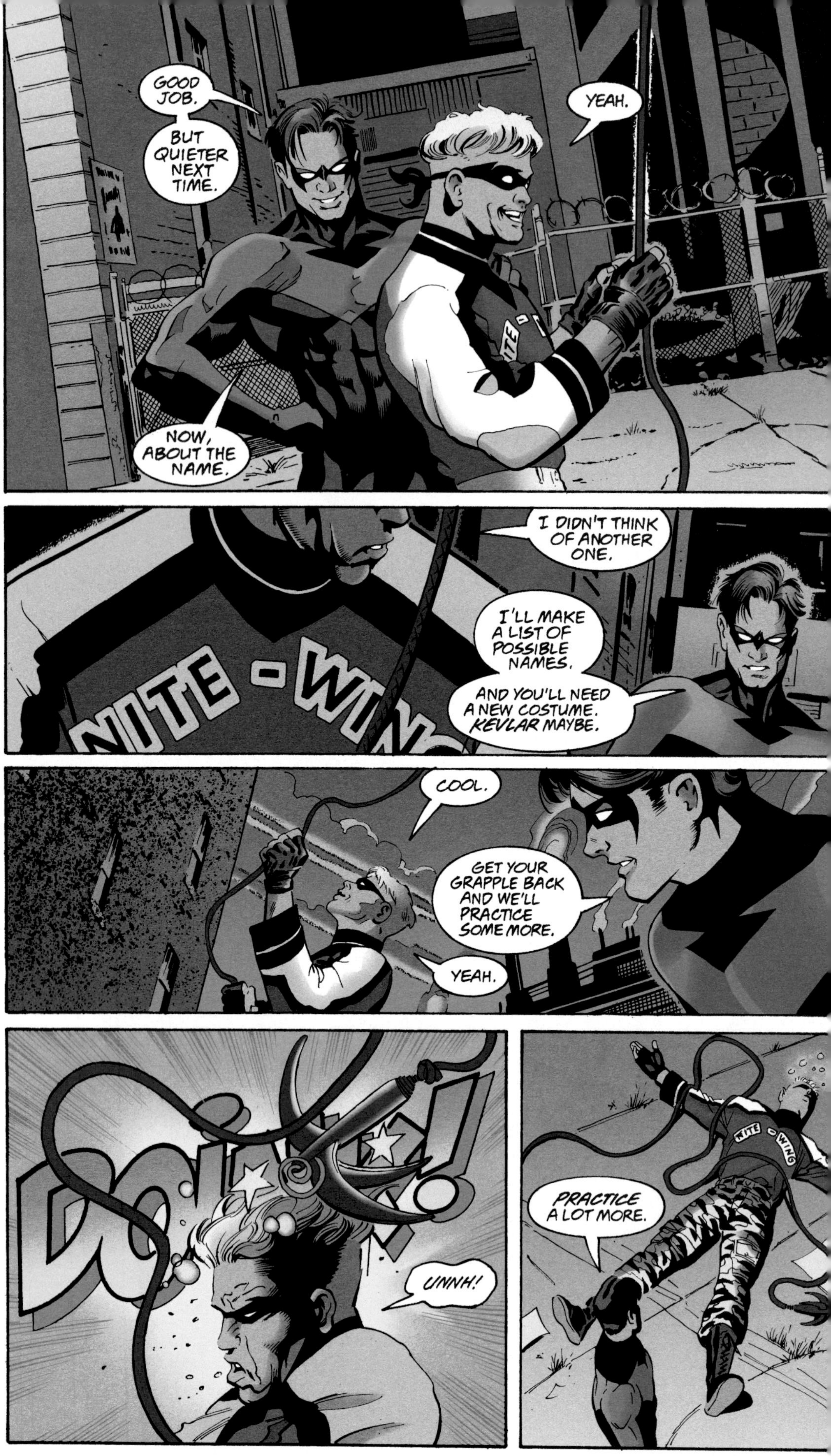
GOOD JOB.
BUT QUIETER NEXT TIME.
YEAH.
NOW, ABOUT THE NAME.
I DIDN'T THINK OF ANOTHER ONE.
I'LL MAKE A LIST OF POSSIBLE NAMES.
AND YOU'LL NEED A NEW COSTUME. *KEVLAR* MAYBE.
COOL.
GET YOUR GRAPPLE BACK AND WE'LL PRACTICE SOME MORE.
YEAH.
UNNH!
NITE - WING
PRACTICE A LOT MORE.

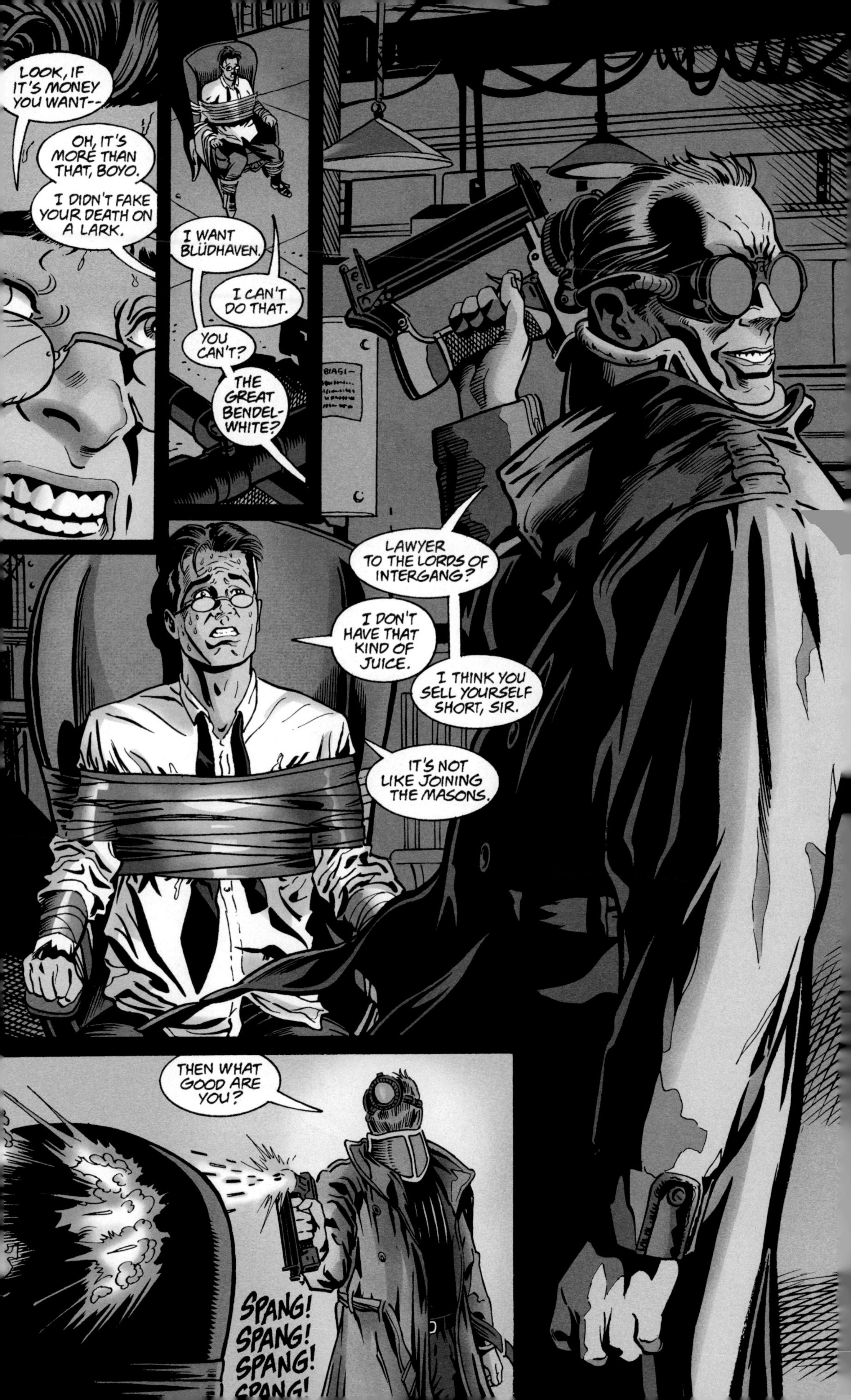
LOOK, IF IT'S MONEY YOU WANT--
OH, IT'S MORE THAN THAT, BOYO.
I DIDN'T FAKE YOUR DEATH ON A LARK.
I WANT BLÜDHAVEN.
I CAN'T DO THAT.
YOU CAN'T?
THE GREAT BENDEL-WHITE?
LAWYER TO THE LORDS OF INTERGANG?
I DON'T HAVE THAT KIND OF JUICE.
I THINK YOU SELL YOURSELF SHORT, SIR.
IT'S NOT LIKE JOINING THE MASONS.
THEN WHAT GOOD ARE YOU?
SPANG!
SPANG!
SPANG!

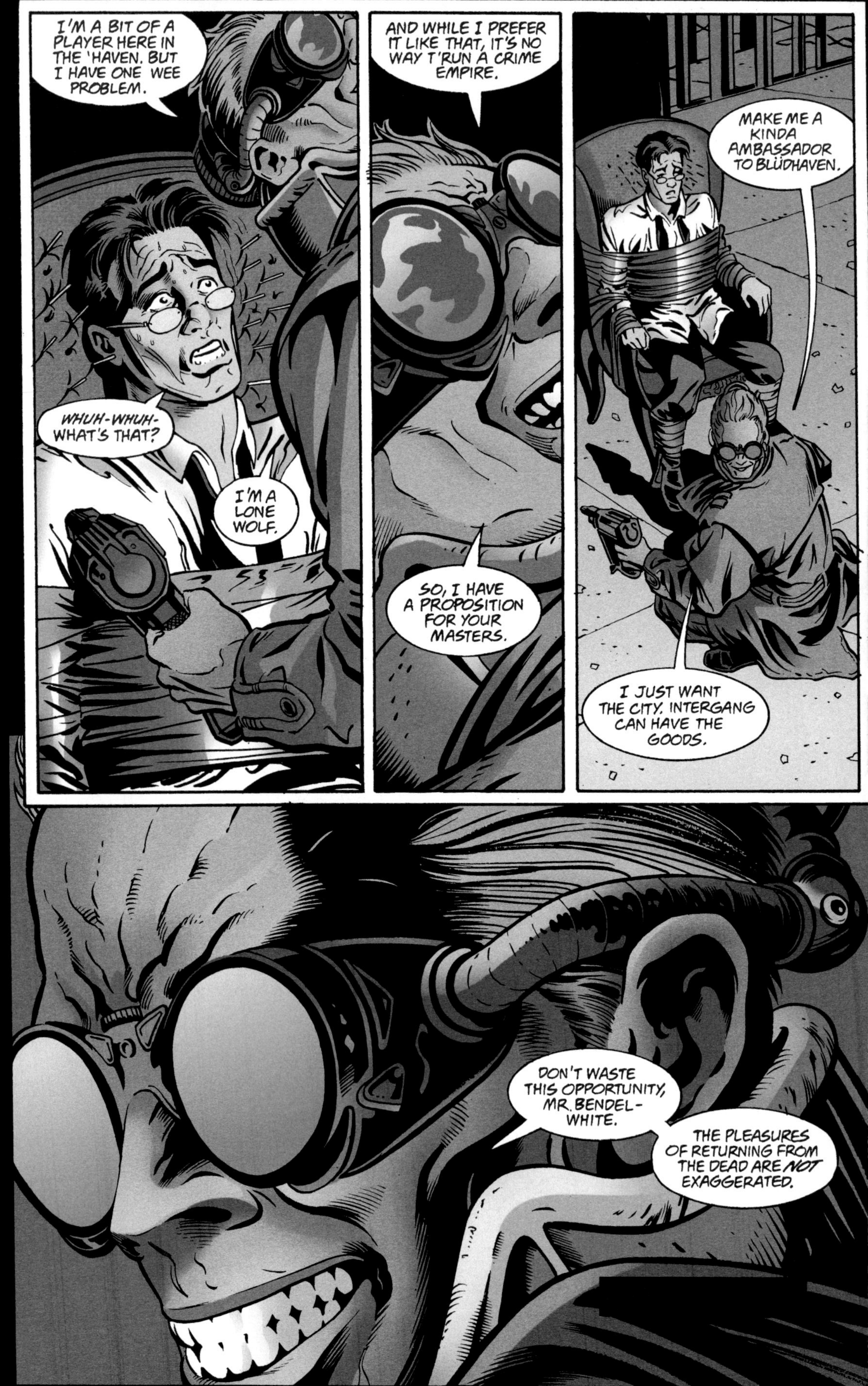
I'M A BIT OF A PLAYER HERE IN THE 'HAVEN. BUT I HAVE ONE WEE PROBLEM.
WHUH-WHUH-WHAT'S THAT?
I'M A LONE WOLF.
AND WHILE I PREFER IT LIKE THAT, IT'S NO WAY T'RUN A CRIME EMPIRE.
SO, I HAVE A PROPOSITION FOR YOUR MASTERS.
MAKE ME A KINDA AMBASSADOR TO BLÜDHAVEN.
I JUST WANT THE CITY. INTERGANG CAN HAVE THE GOODS.
DON'T WASTE THIS OPPORTUNITY, MR. BENDEL-WHITE.
THE PLEASURES OF RETURNING FROM THE DEAD ARE *NOT* EXAGGERATED.

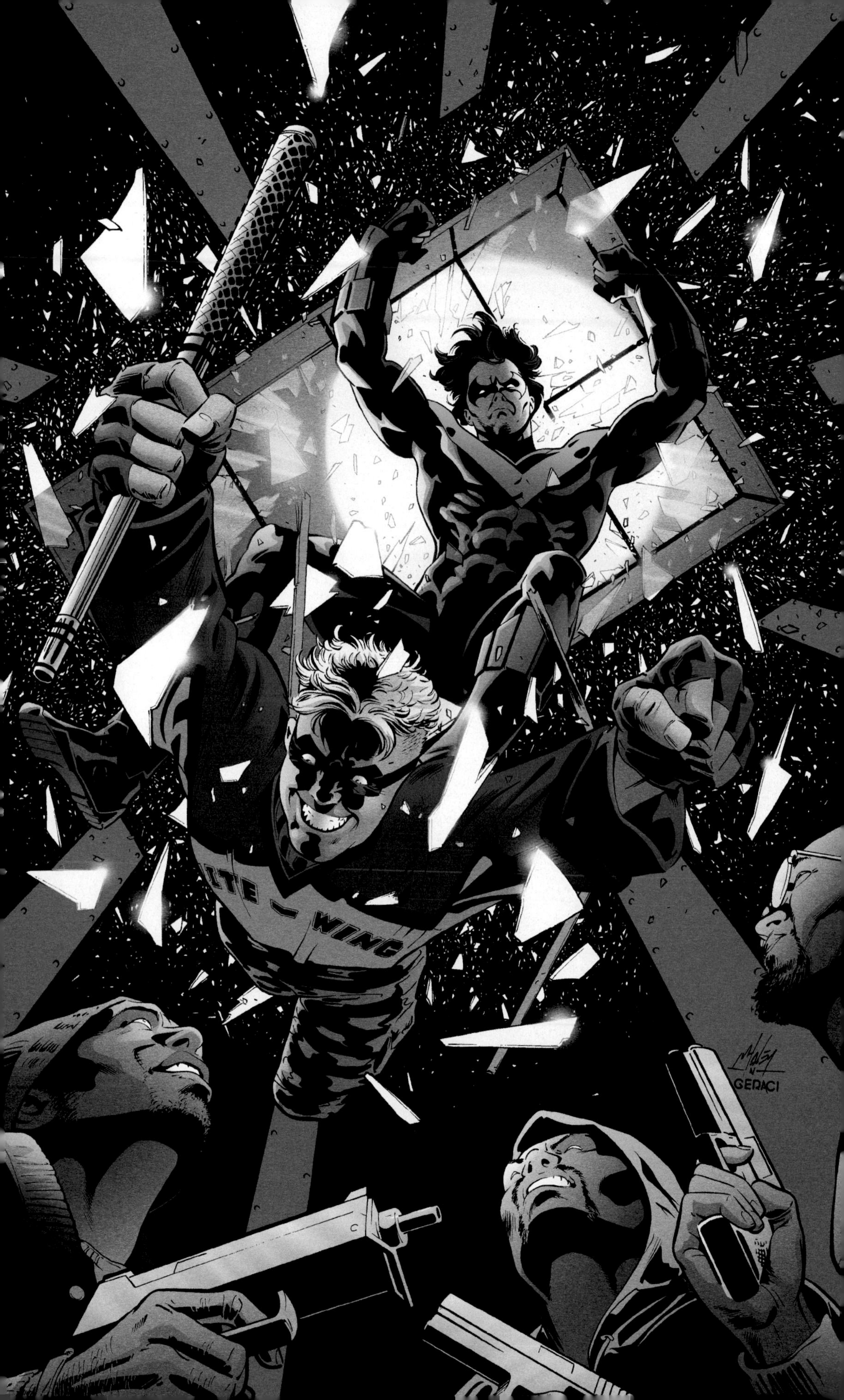
WING
GERACI

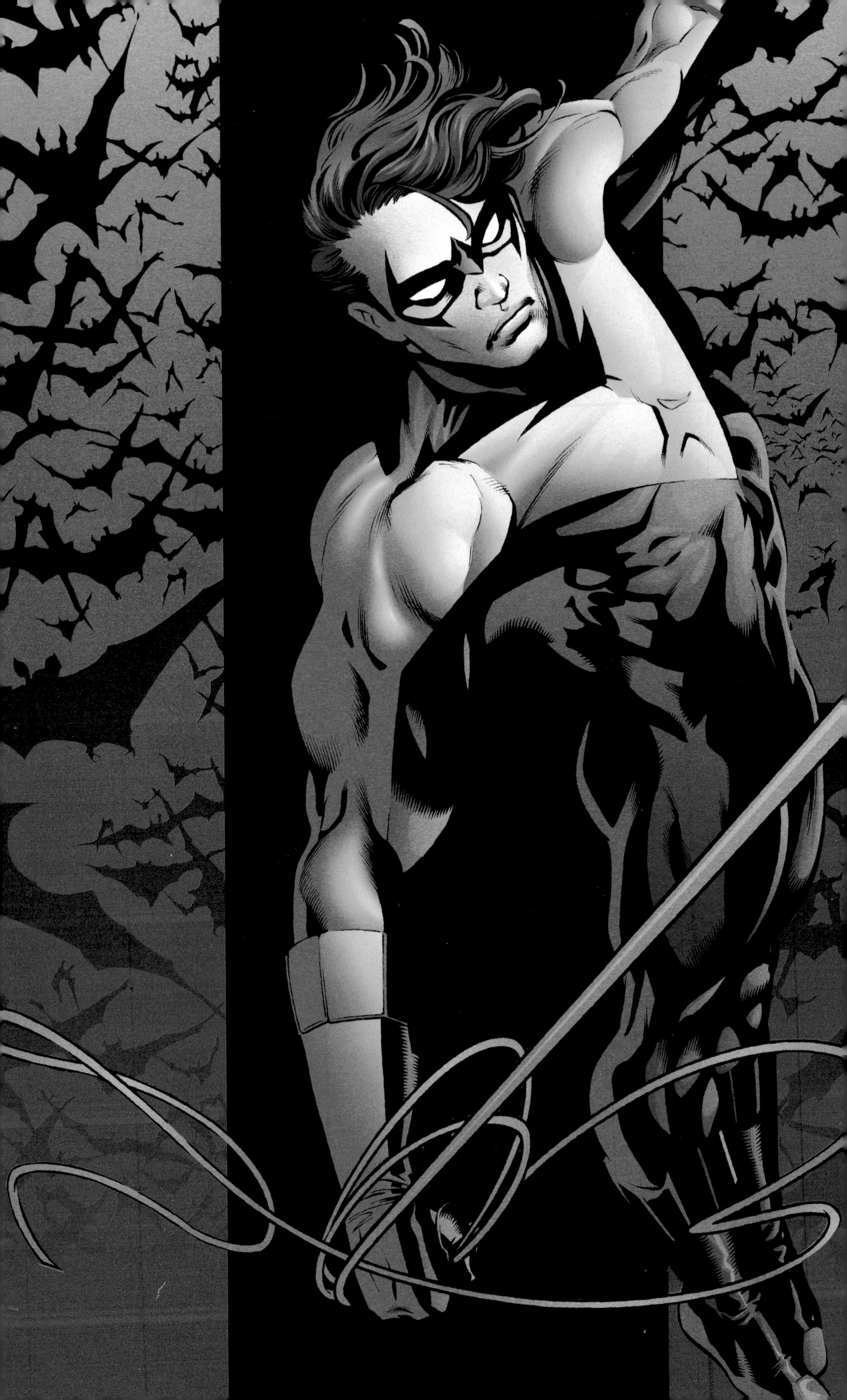

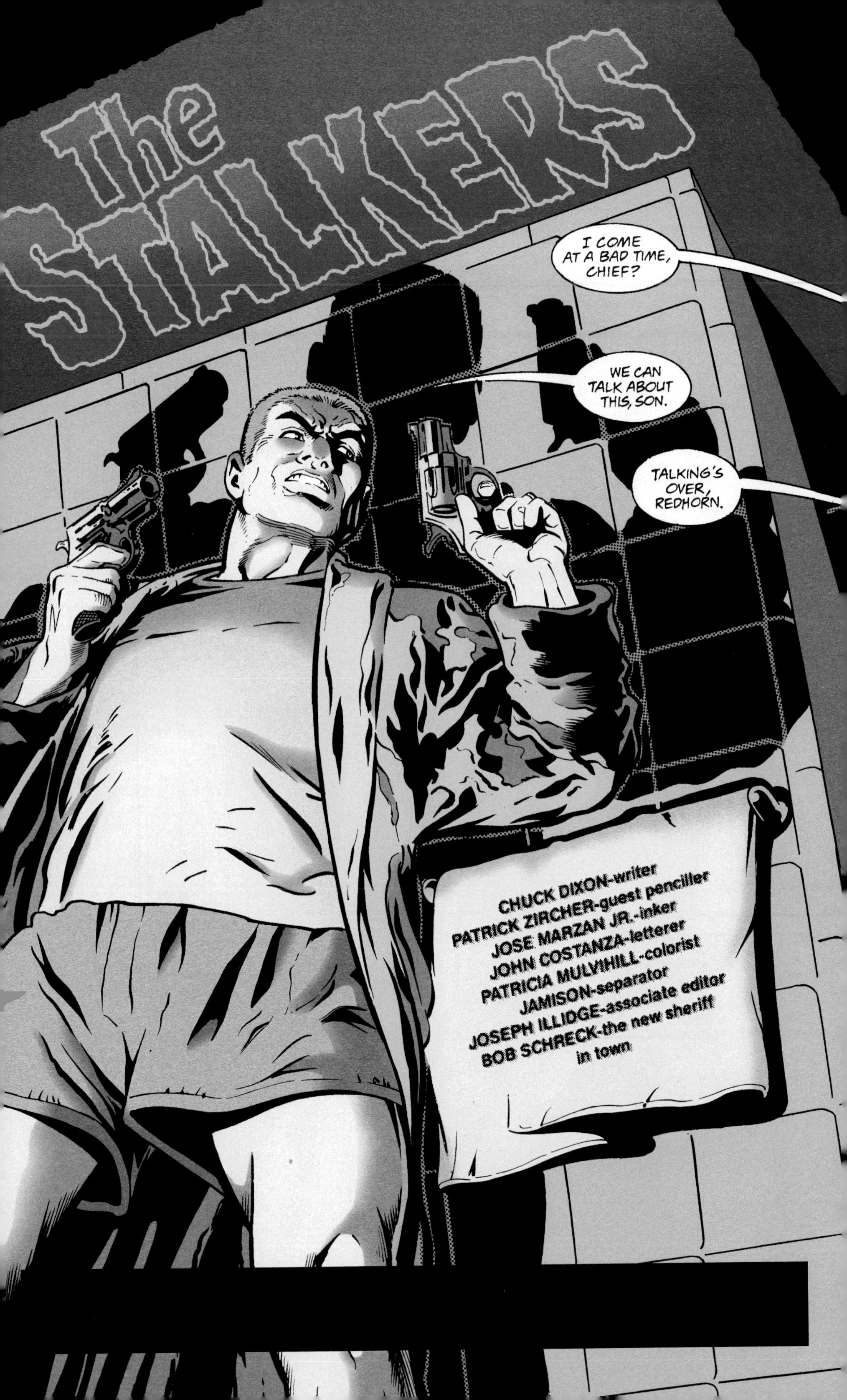

The STALKERS
I COME AT A BAD TIME, CHIEF?
WE CAN TALK ABOUT THIS, SON.
TALKING'S OVER, REDHORN.
CHUCK DIXON-writer
PATRICK ZIRCHER-guest penciller
JOSE MARZAN JR.-inker
JOHN COSTANZA-letterer
PATRICIA MULVIHILL-colorist
JAMISON-separator
JOSEPH ILLIDGE-associate editor
BOB SCHRECK-the new sheriff in town

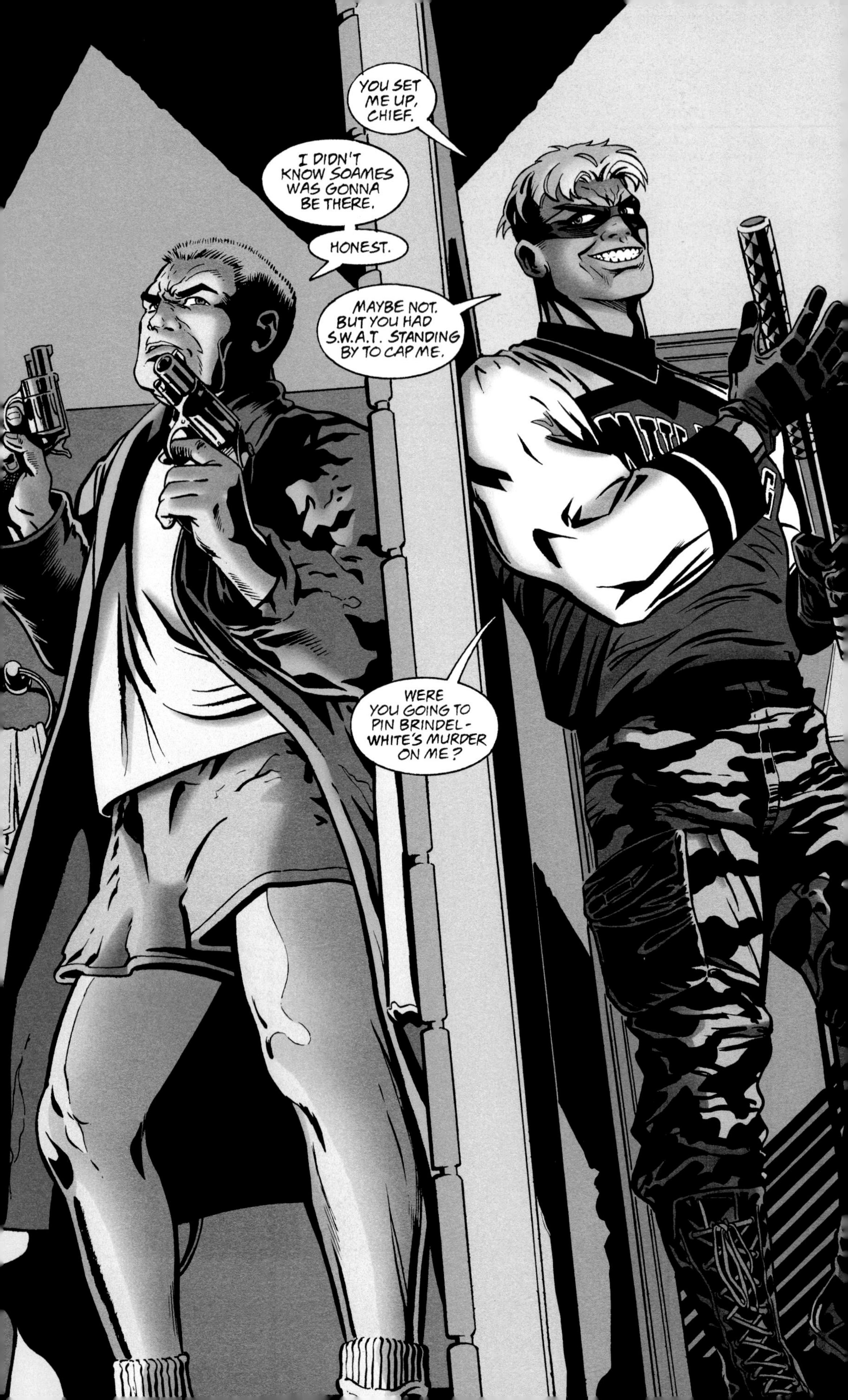
YOU SET ME UP, CHIEF.
I DIDN'T KNOW SOAMES WAS GONNA BE THERE.
HONEST.
MAYBE NOT. BUT YOU HAD S.W.A.T. STANDING BY TO CAP ME.
WERE YOU GOING TO PIN BRINDEL-WHITE'S MURDER ON ME?

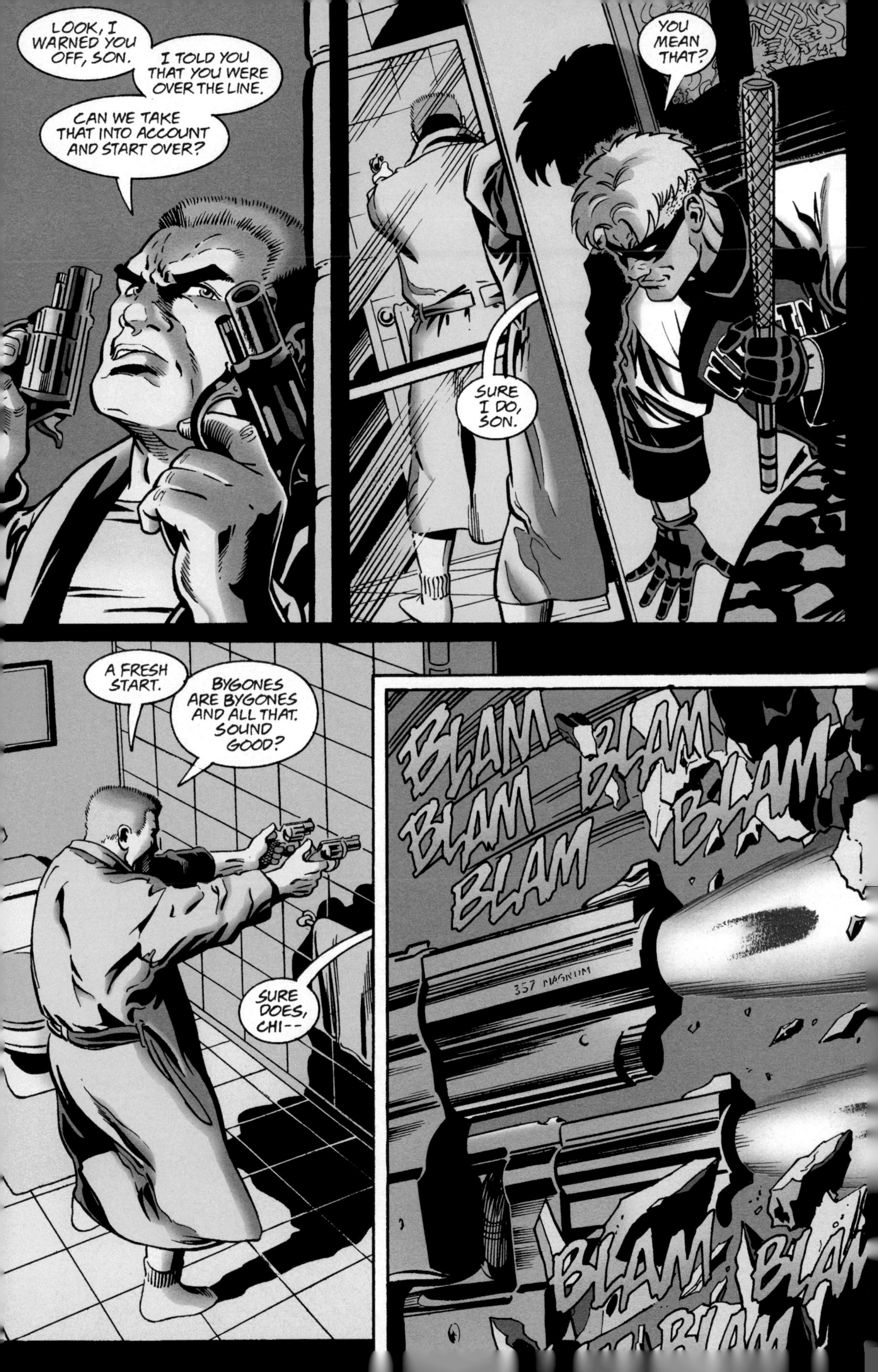
LOOK, I WARNED YOU OFF, SON.
I TOLD YOU THAT YOU WERE OVER THE LINE.
CAN WE TAKE THAT INTO ACCOUNT AND START OVER?
YOU MEAN THAT?
SURE I DO, SON.
A FRESH START.
BYGONES ARE BYGONES AND ALL THAT. SOUND GOOD?
SURE DOES, CHI--
BLAM BLAM
BLAM BLAM BLAM
BLAM BLAM
357 MAGNUM
BLAM BLAM

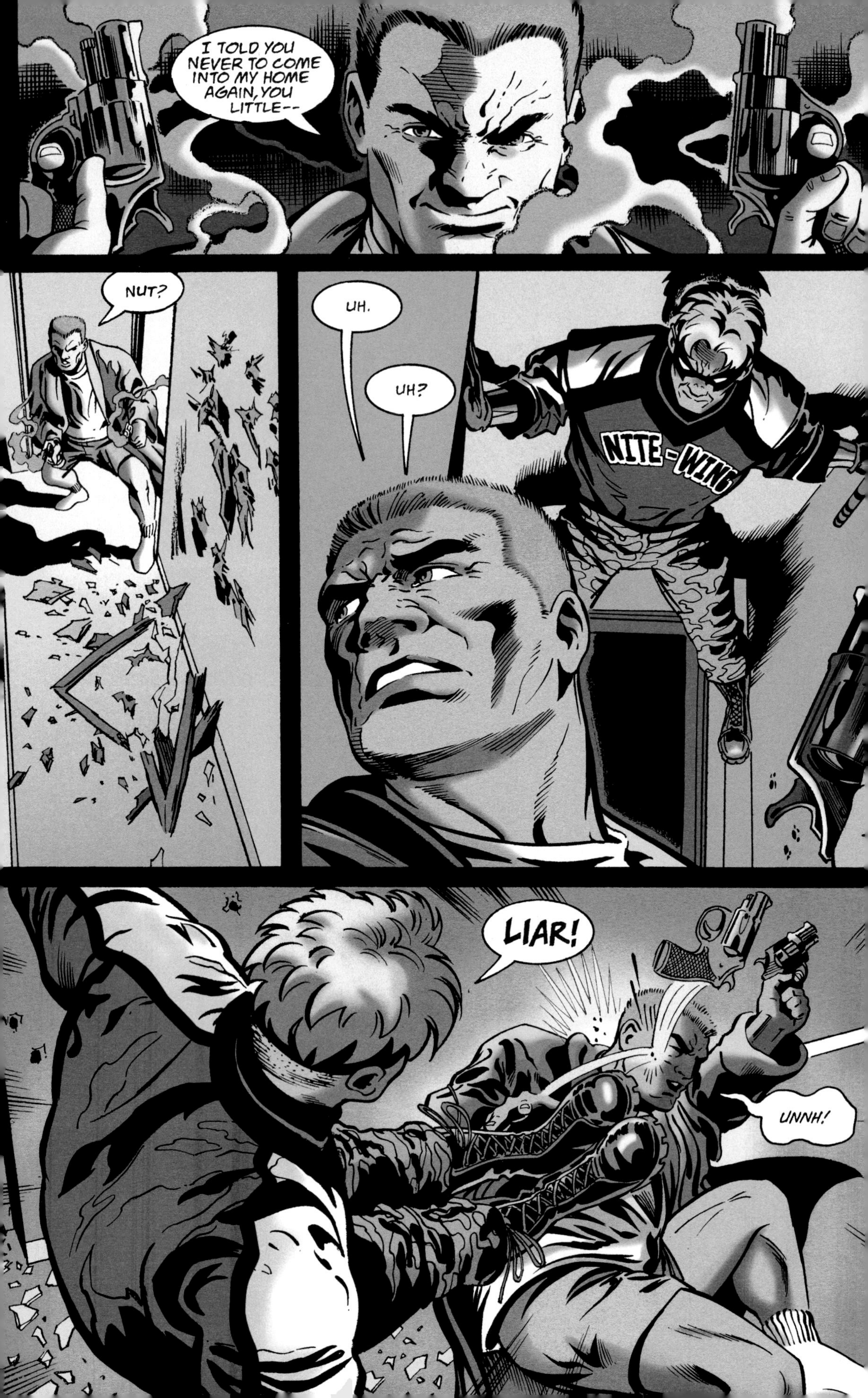
I TOLD YOU NEVER TO COME INTO MY HOME AGAIN, YOU LITTLE--
NUT?
UH.
UH?
NITE-WING
LIAR!
UNNH!

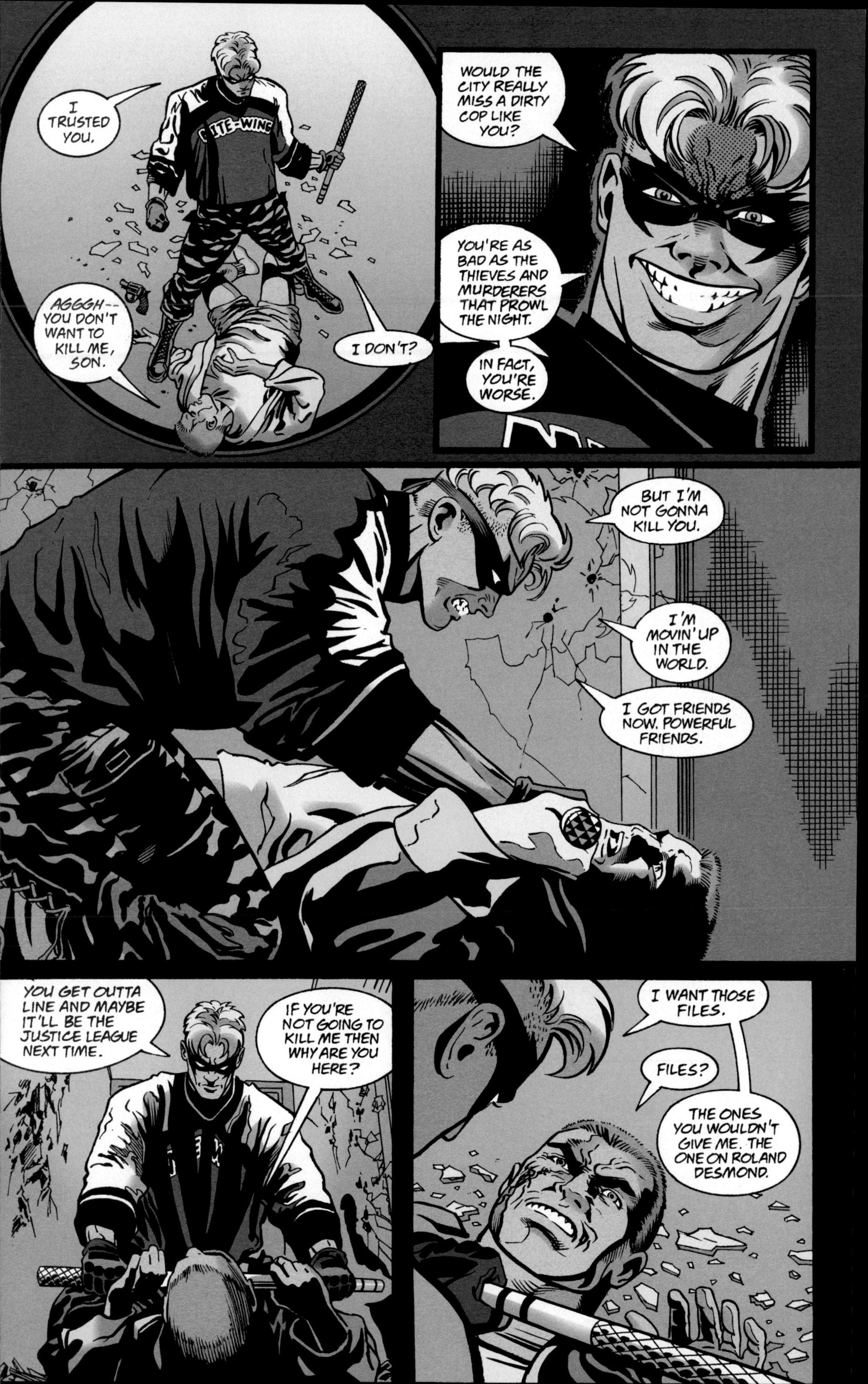
I TRUSTED YOU.
AGGGH-- YOU DON'T WANT TO KILL ME, SON.
I DON'T?
WOULD THE CITY REALLY MISS A DIRTY COP LIKE YOU?
YOU'RE AS BAD AS THE THIEVES AND MURDERERS THAT PROWL THE NIGHT.
IN FACT, YOU'RE WORSE.
BUT I'M NOT GONNA KILL YOU.
I'M MOVIN' UP IN THE WORLD.
I GOT FRIENDS NOW. POWERFUL FRIENDS.
YOU GET OUTTA LINE AND MAYBE IT'LL BE THE JUSTICE LEAGUE NEXT TIME.
IF YOU'RE NOT GOING TO KILL ME THEN WHY ARE YOU HERE?
I WANT THOSE FILES.
FILES?
THE ONES YOU WOULDN'T GIVE ME. THE ONE ON ROLAND DESMOND.

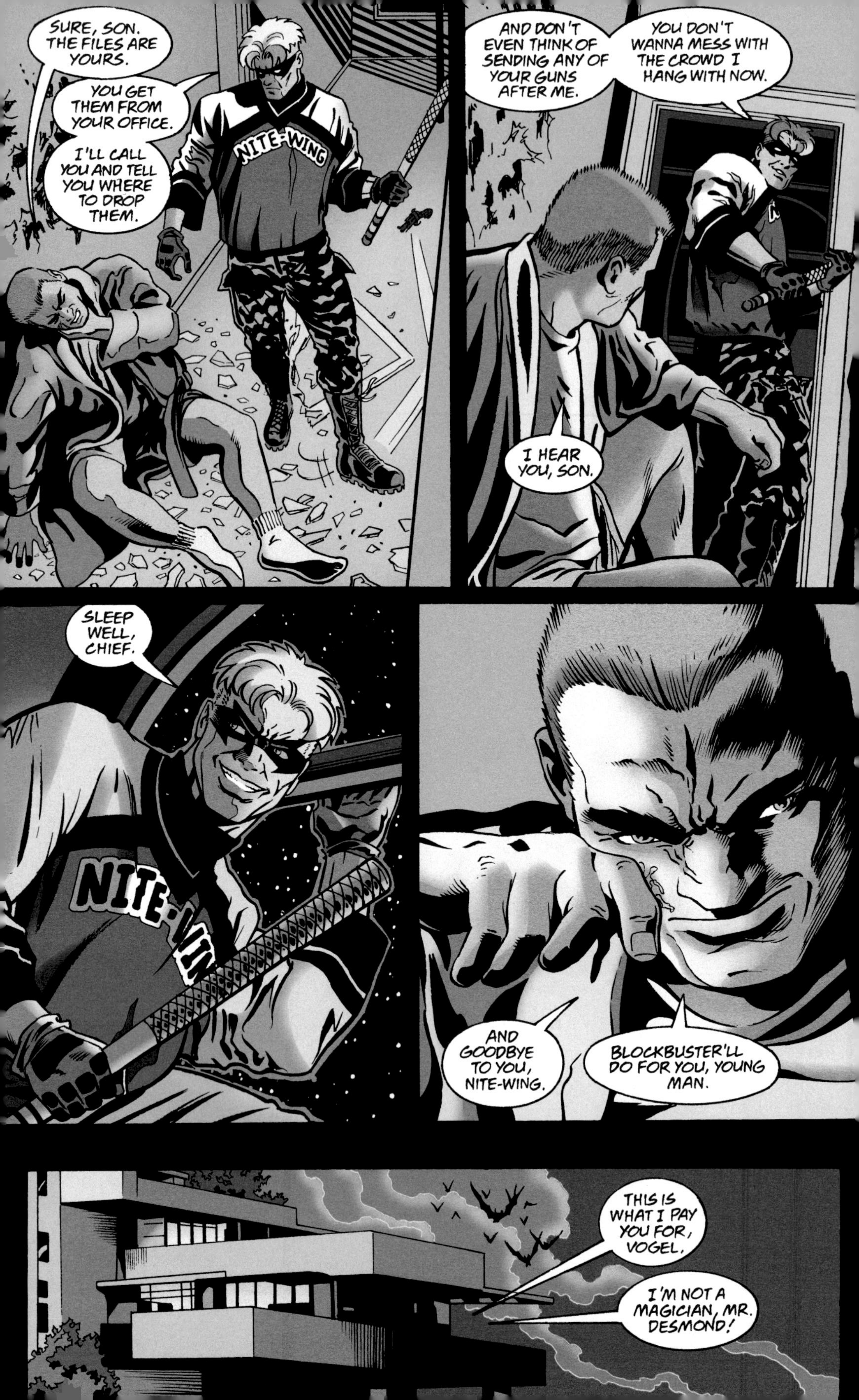
SURE, SON. THE FILES ARE YOURS.
YOU GET THEM FROM YOUR OFFICE.
I'LL CALL YOU AND TELL YOU WHERE TO DROP THEM.
AND DON'T EVEN THINK OF SENDING ANY OF YOUR GUNS AFTER ME.
YOU DON'T WANNA MESS WITH THE CROWD I HANG WITH NOW.
I HEAR YOU, SON.
NITE-WING
SLEEP WELL, CHIEF.
NITE-WING
AND GOODBYE TO YOU, NITE-WING.
BLOCKBUSTER'LL DO FOR YOU, YOUNG MAN.
THIS IS WHAT I PAY YOU FOR, VOGEL.
I'M NOT A MAGICIAN, MR. DESMOND!

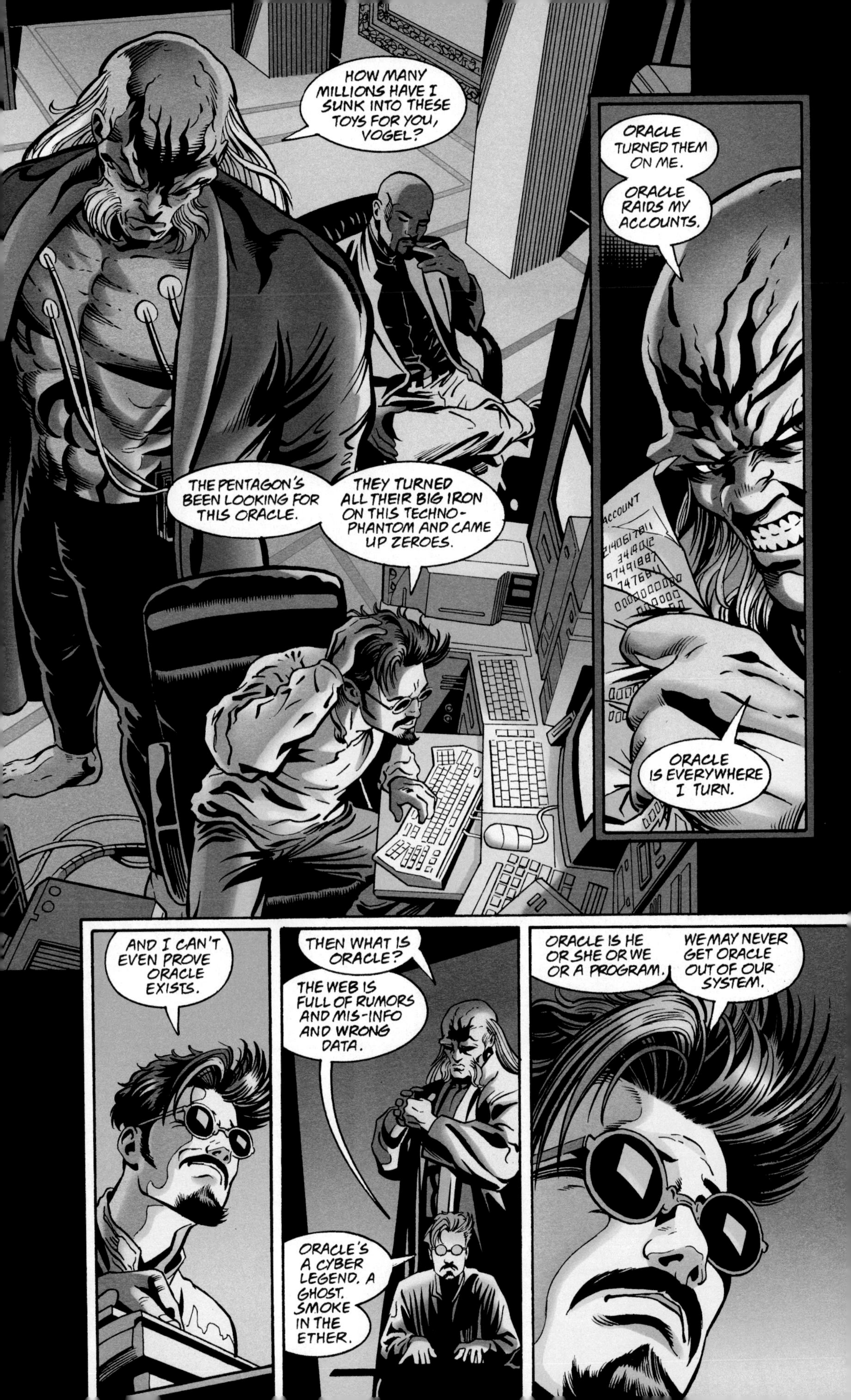
HOW MANY MILLIONS HAVE I SUNK INTO THESE TOYS FOR YOU, VOGEL?
ORACLE TURNED THEM ON ME.
ORACLE RAIDS MY ACCOUNTS.
ORACLE IS EVERYWHERE I TURN.
THE PENTAGON'S BEEN LOOKING FOR THIS ORACLE.
THEY TURNED ALL THEIR BIG IRON ON THIS TECHNO-PHANTOM AND CAME UP ZEROES.
AND I CAN'T EVEN PROVE ORACLE EXISTS.
THEN WHAT IS ORACLE?
THE WEB IS FULL OF RUMORS AND MIS-INFO AND WRONG DATA.
ORACLE'S A CYBER LEGEND. A GHOST. SMOKE IN THE ETHER.
ORACLE IS HE OR SHE OR WE OR A PROGRAM.
WE MAY NEVER GET ORACLE OUT OF OUR SYSTEM.

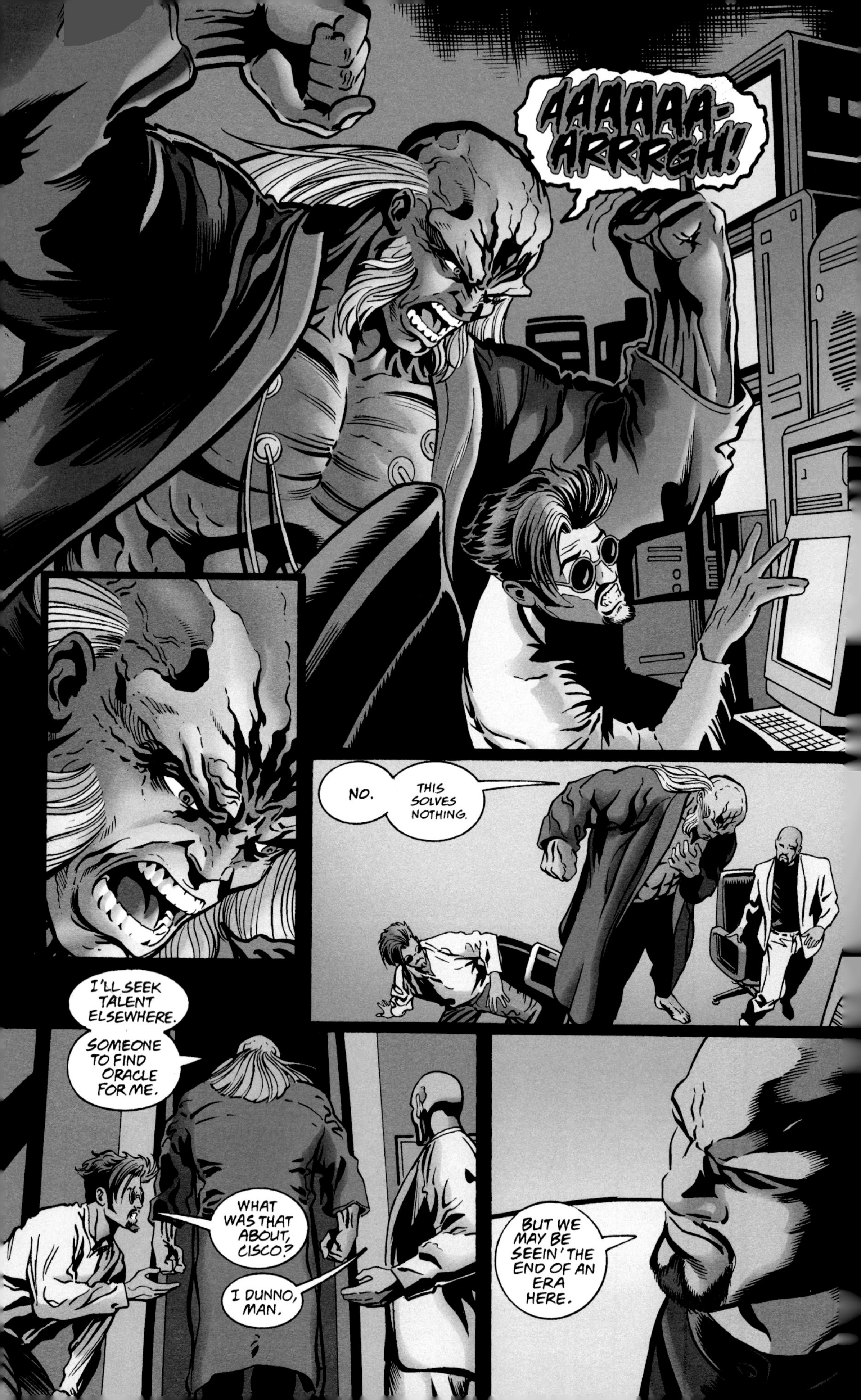
AAAAAA-ARRRGH!
NO.
THIS SOLVES NOTHING.
I'LL SEEK TALENT ELSEWHERE.
SOMEONE TO FIND ORACLE FOR ME.
WHAT WAS THAT ABOUT, CISCO?
I DUNNO, MAN.
BUT WE MAY BE SEEIN' THE END OF AN ERA HERE.

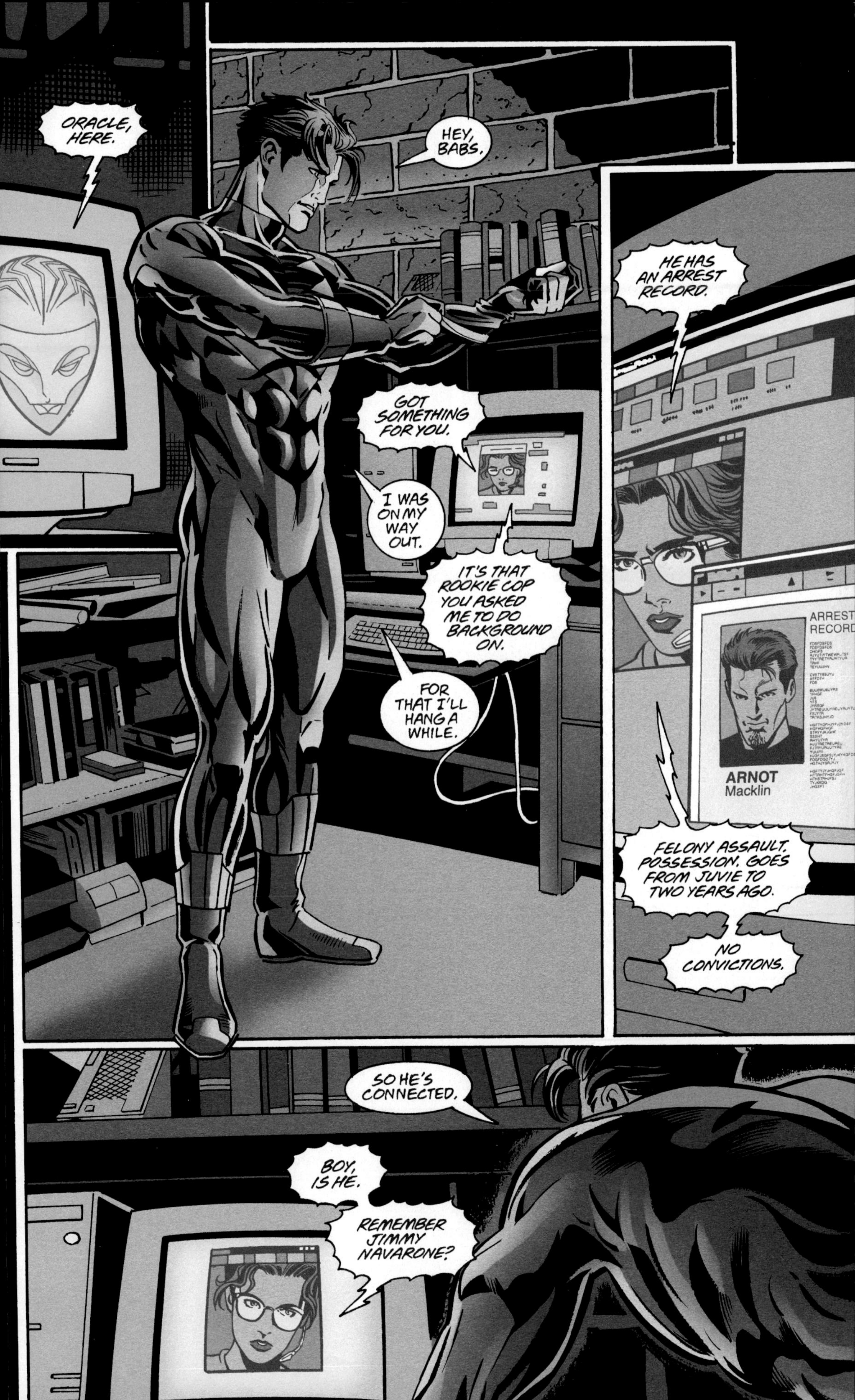
ORACLE, HERE.
HEY, BABS.
GOT SOMETHING FOR YOU.
I WAS ON MY WAY OUT.
IT'S THAT ROOKIE COP YOU ASKED ME TO DO BACKGROUND ON.
FOR THAT I'LL HANG A WHILE.
HE HAS AN ARREST RECORD.
ARREST RECORD
ARNOT
Macklin
FELONY ASSAULT. POSSESSION. GOES FROM JUVIE TO TWO YEARS AGO.
NO CONVICTIONS.
SO HE'S CONNECTED.
BOY, IS HE.
REMEMBER JIMMY NAVARONE?

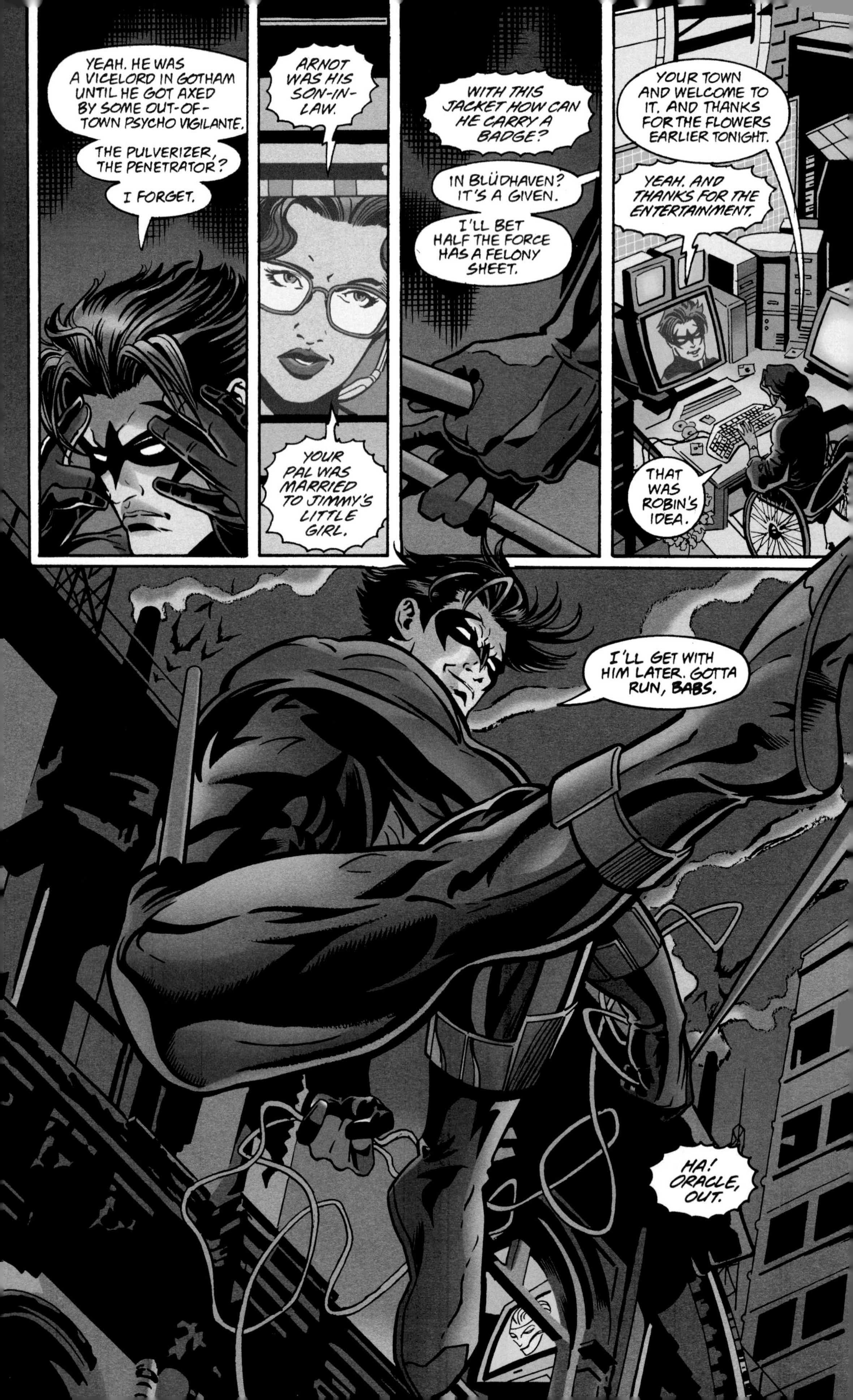
YEAH. HE WAS A VICELORD IN GOTHAM UNTIL HE GOT AXED BY SOME OUT-OF-TOWN PSYCHO VIGILANTE.
THE PULVERIZER, THE PENETRATOR?
I FORGET.
ARNOT WAS HIS SON-IN-LAW.
YOUR PAL WAS MARRIED TO JIMMY'S LITTLE GIRL.
WITH THIS JACKET HOW CAN HE CARRY A BADGE?
IN BLÜDHAVEN? IT'S A GIVEN.
I'LL BET HALF THE FORCE HAS A FELONY SHEET.
YOUR TOWN AND WELCOME TO IT. AND THANKS FOR THE FLOWERS EARLIER TONIGHT.
YEAH. AND THANKS FOR THE ENTERTAINMENT.
THAT WAS ROBIN'S IDEA.
I'LL GET WITH HIM LATER. GOTTA RUN, BABS.
HA! ORACLE, OUT.

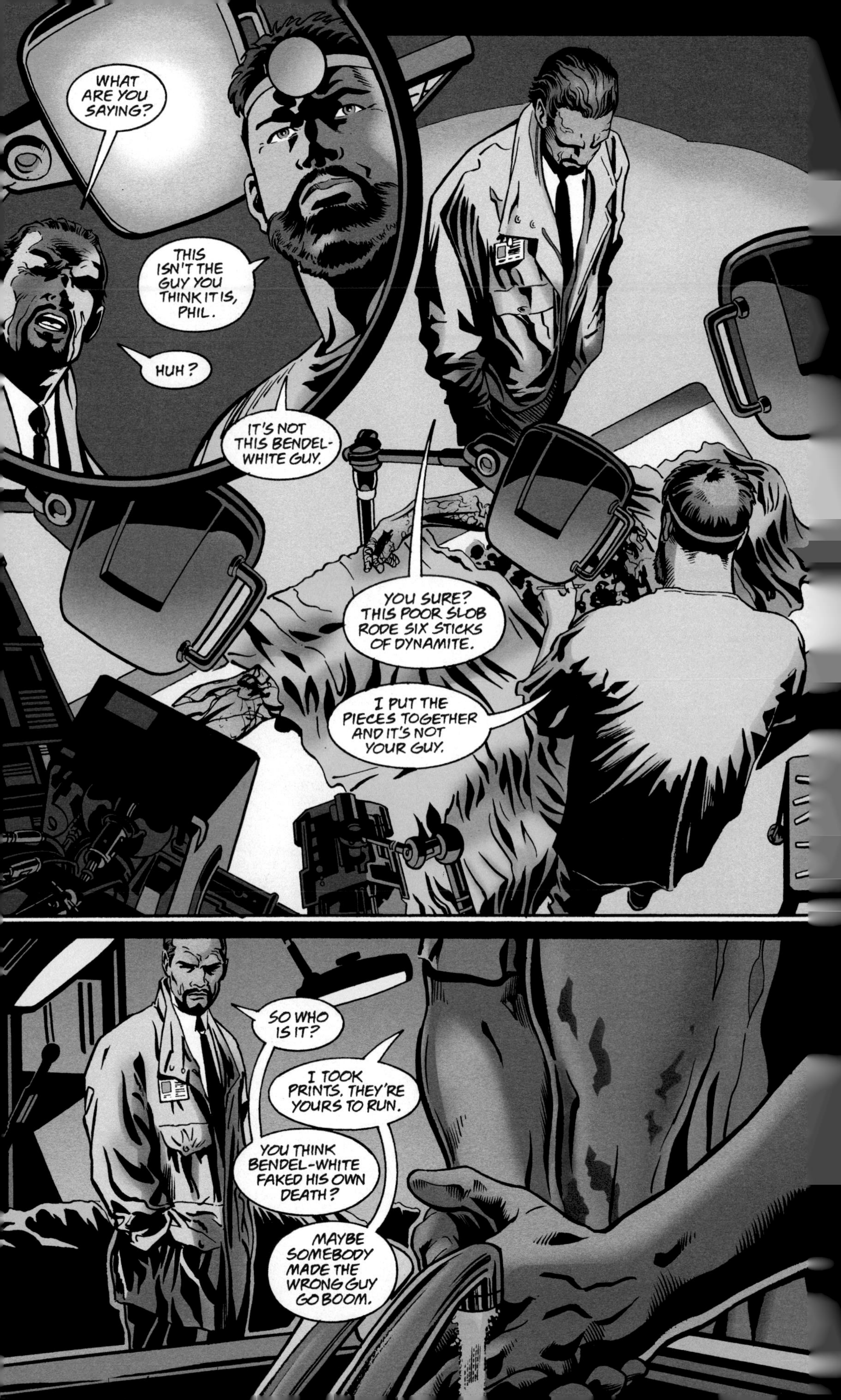
WHAT ARE YOU SAYING?
THIS ISN'T THE GUY YOU THINK IT IS, PHIL.
HUH?
IT'S NOT THIS BENDEL-WHITE GUY.
YOU SURE? THIS POOR SLOB RODE SIX STICKS OF DYNAMITE.
I PUT THE PIECES TOGETHER AND IT'S NOT YOUR GUY.
SO WHO IS IT?
I TOOK PRINTS. THEY'RE YOURS TO RUN.
YOU THINK BENDEL-WHITE FAKED HIS OWN DEATH?
MAYBE SOMEBODY MADE THE WRONG GUY GO BOOM.

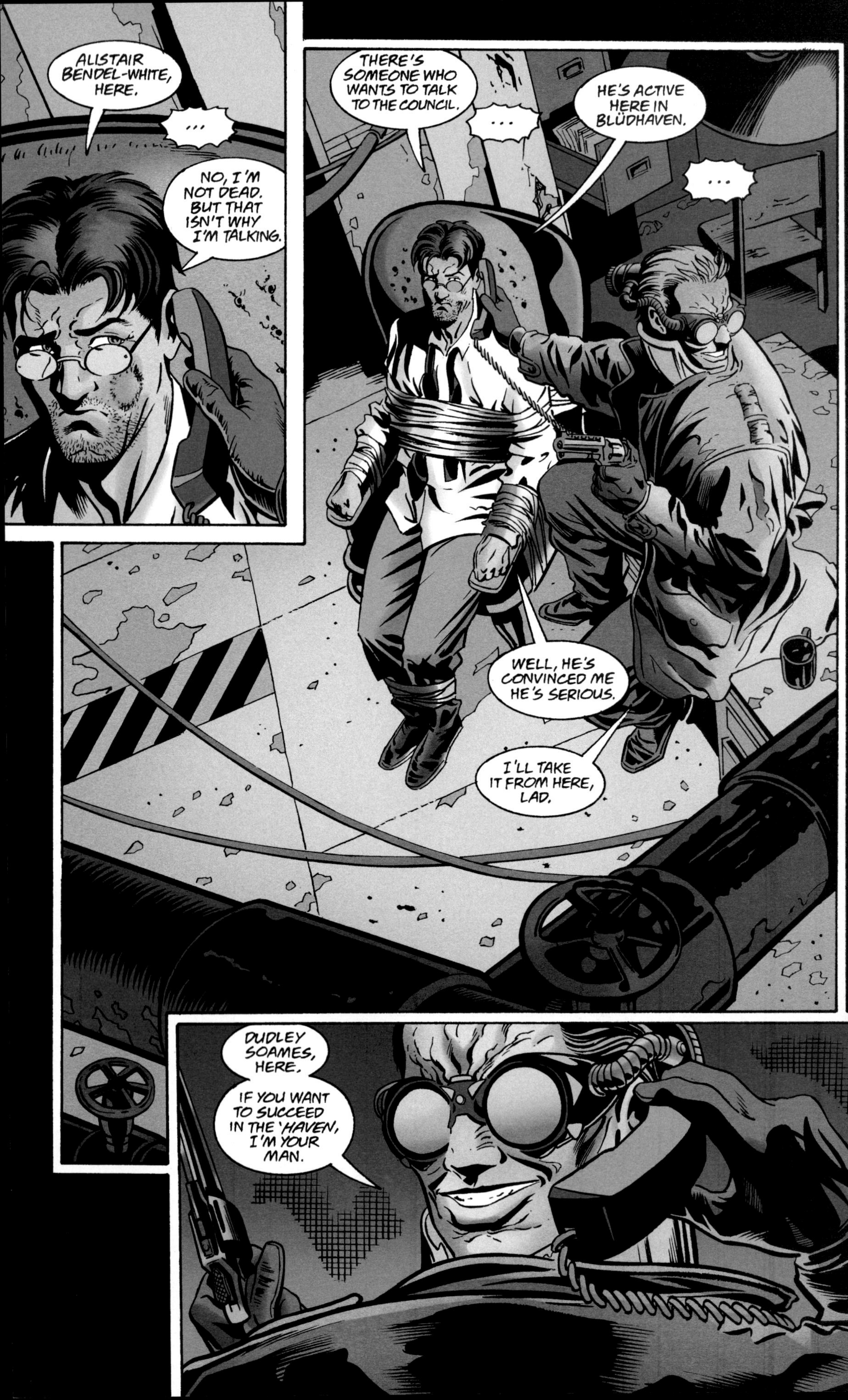
ALISTAIR BENDEL-WHITE, HERE.
...
NO, I'M NOT DEAD. BUT THAT ISN'T WHY I'M TALKING.
THERE'S SOMEONE WHO WANTS TO TALK TO THE COUNCIL.
...
HE'S ACTIVE HERE IN BLÜDHAVEN.
...
WELL, HE'S CONVINCED ME HE'S SERIOUS.
I'LL TAKE IT FROM HERE, LAD.
DUDLEY SOAMES, HERE.
IF YOU WANT TO SUCCEED IN THE 'HAVEN, I'M YOUR MAN.

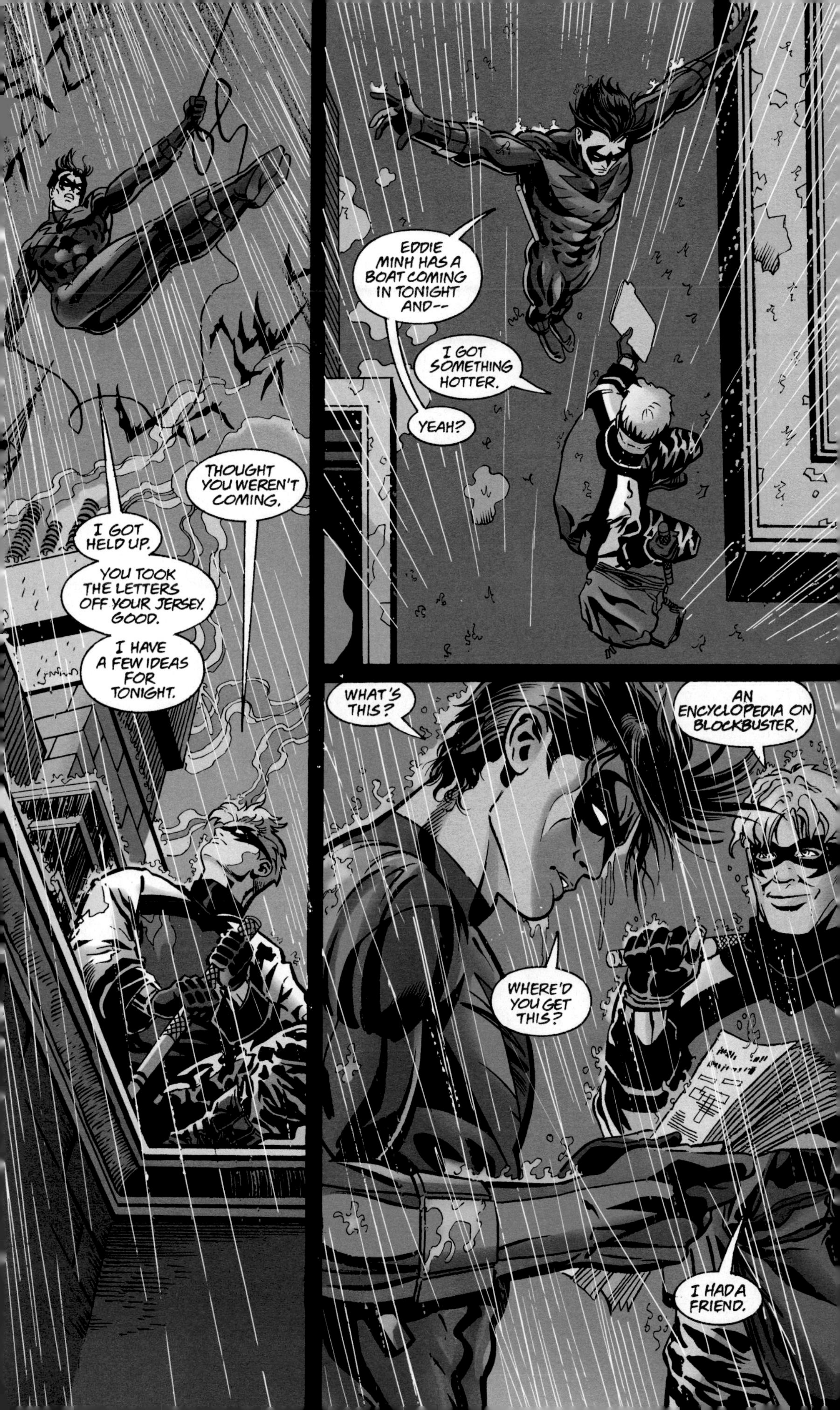
THOUGHT YOU WEREN'T COMING.
I GOT HELD UP.
YOU TOOK THE LETTERS OFF YOUR JERSEY. GOOD.
I HAVE A FEW IDEAS FOR TONIGHT.
EDDIE MINH HAS A BOAT COMING IN TONIGHT AND--
I GOT SOMETHING HOTTER.
YEAH?
WHAT'S THIS?
AN ENCYCLOPEDIA ON BLOCKBUSTER.
WHERE'D YOU GET THIS?
I HAD A FRIEND.

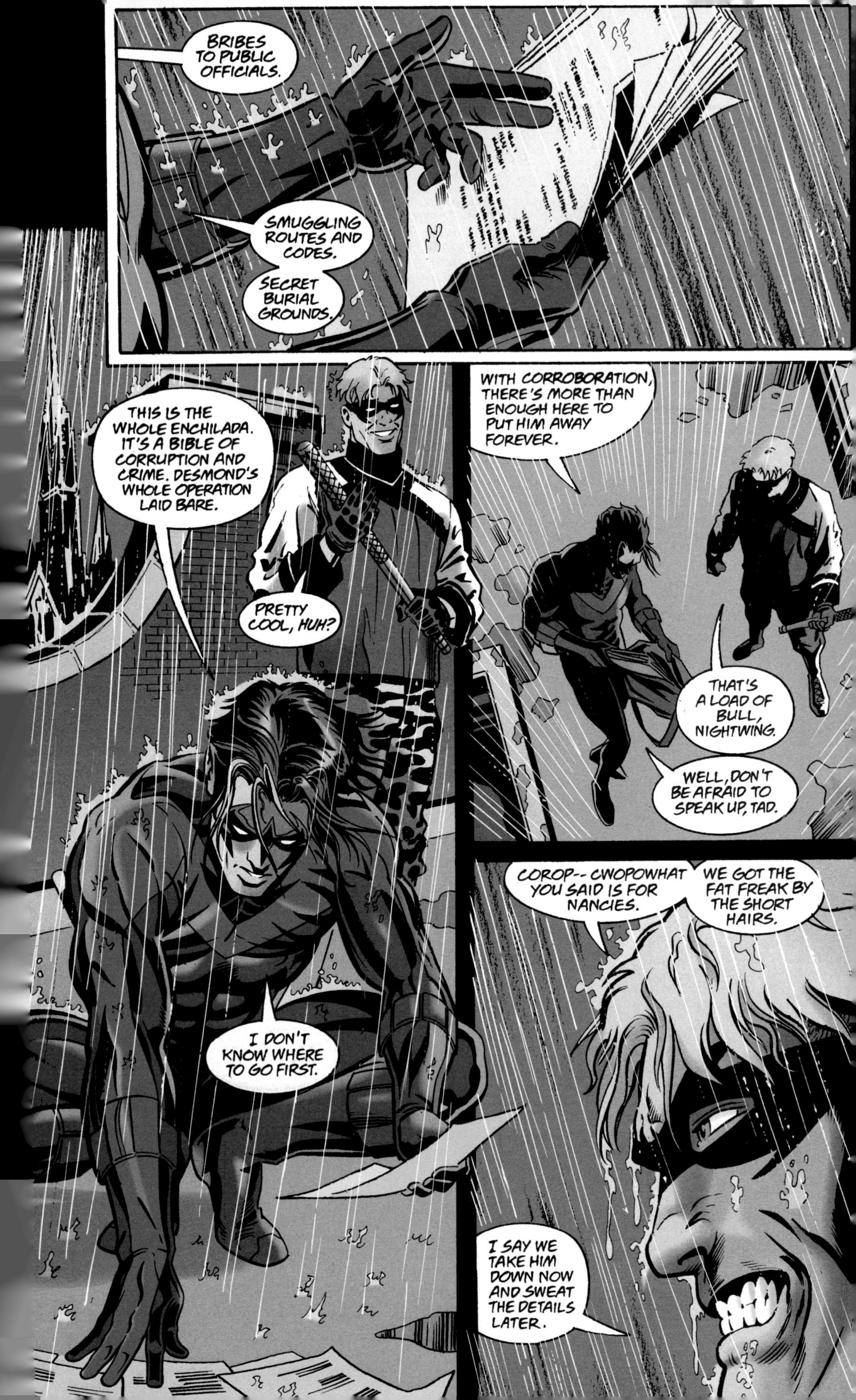
BRIBES TO PUBLIC OFFICIALS.
SMUGGLING ROUTES AND CODES.
SECRET BURIAL GROUNDS.
THIS IS THE WHOLE ENCHILADA. IT'S A BIBLE OF CORRUPTION AND CRIME. DESMOND'S WHOLE OPERATION LAID BARE.
PRETTY COOL, HUH?
I DON'T KNOW WHERE TO GO FIRST.
WITH CORROBORATION, THERE'S MORE THAN ENOUGH HERE TO PUT HIM AWAY FOREVER.
THAT'S A LOAD OF BULL, NIGHTWING.
WELL, DON'T BE AFRAID TO SPEAK UP, TAD.
COROP-- CWOPOWHAT YOU SAID IS FOR NANCIES.
WE GOT THE FAT FREAK BY THE SHORT HAIRS.
I SAY WE TAKE HIM DOWN NOW AND SWEAT THE DETAILS LATER.

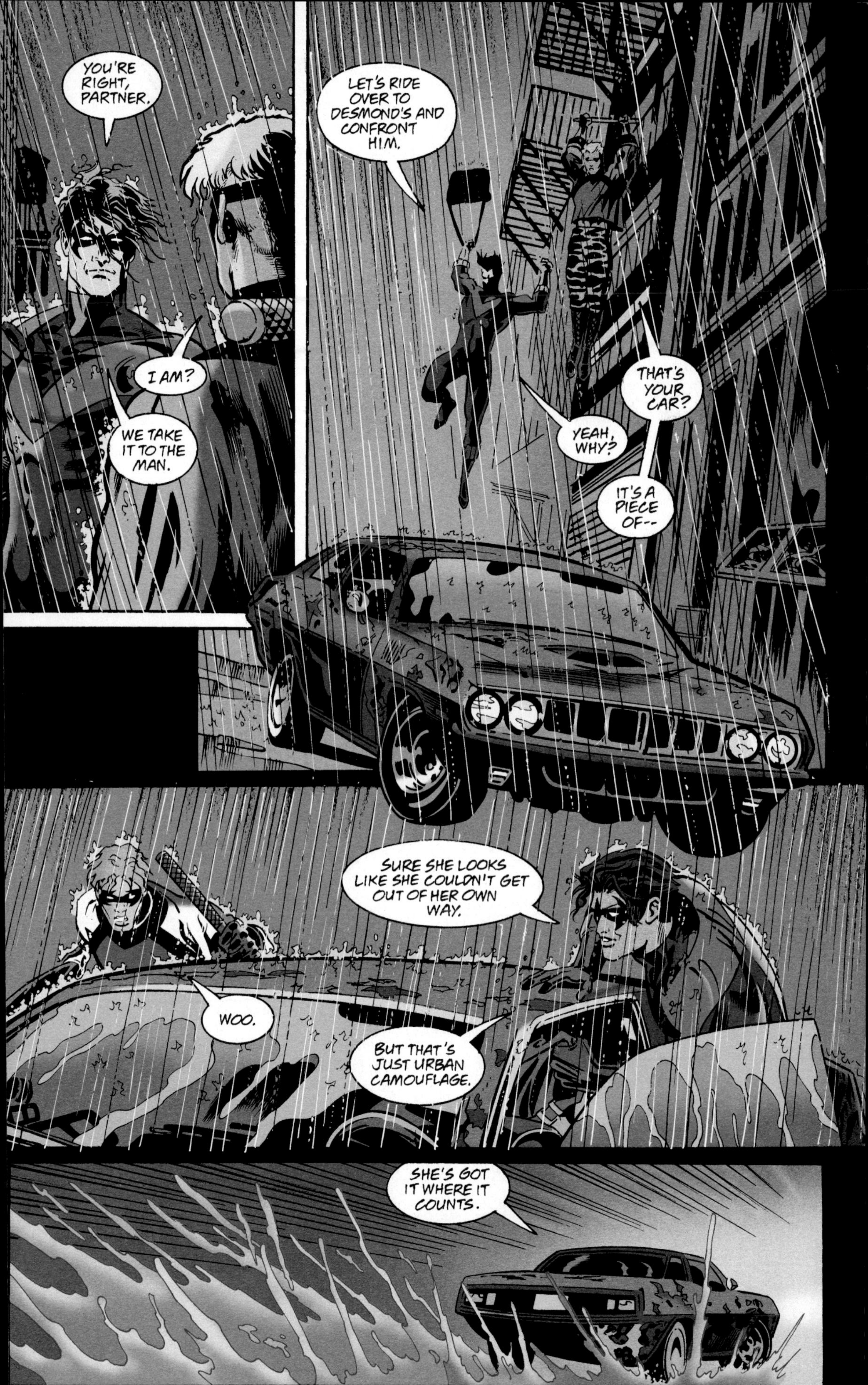
YOU'RE RIGHT, PARTNER.
I AM?
WE TAKE IT TO THE MAN.
LET'S RIDE OVER TO DESMOND'S AND CONFRONT HIM.
THAT'S YOUR CAR?
YEAH, WHY?
IT'S A PIECE OF--
SURE SHE LOOKS LIKE SHE COULDN'T GET OUT OF HER OWN WAY.
WOO.
BUT THAT'S JUST URBAN CAMOUFLAGE.
SHE'S GOT IT WHERE IT COUNTS.

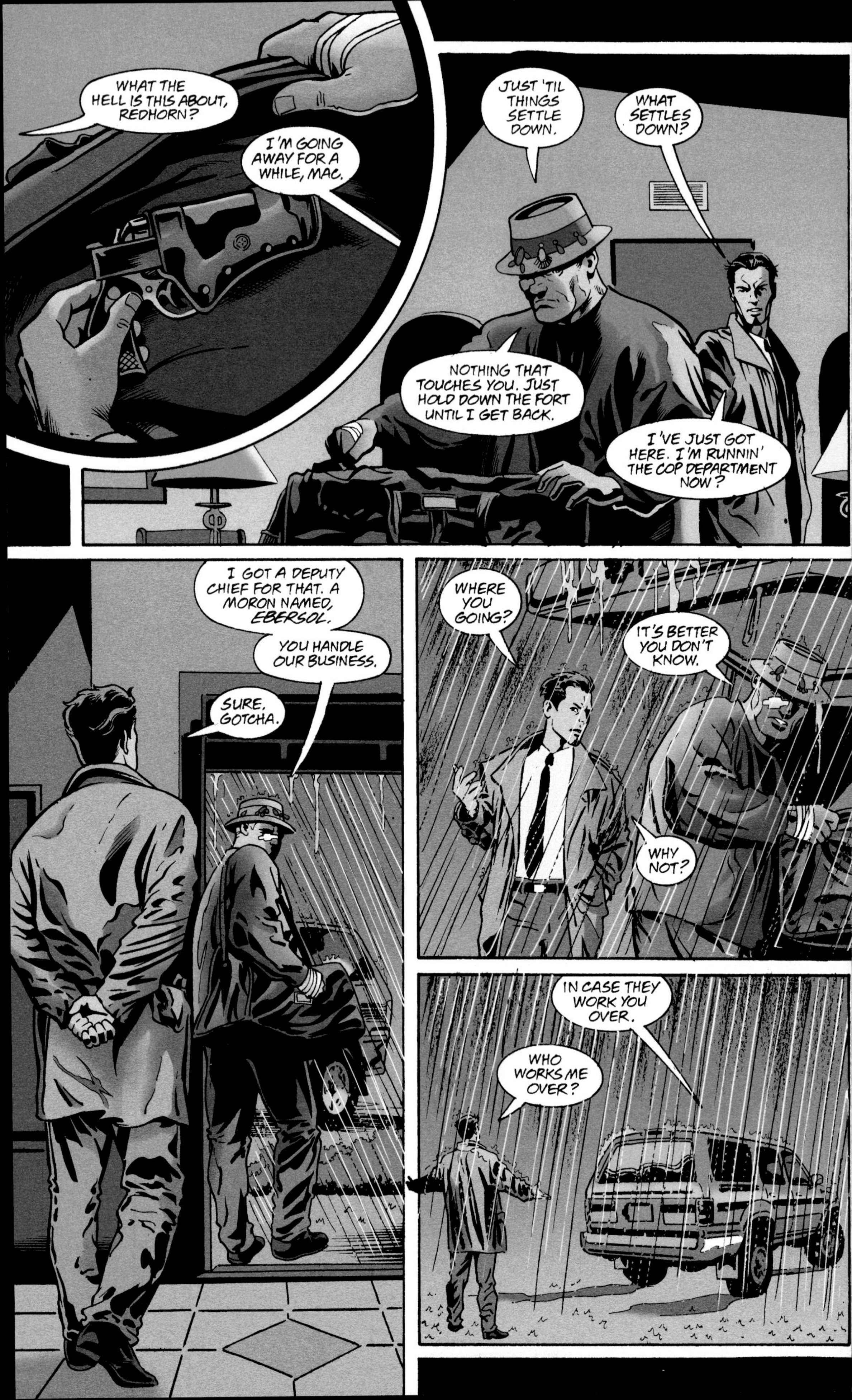
WHAT THE HELL IS THIS ABOUT, REDHORN?
I'M GOING AWAY FOR A WHILE, MAC.
JUST 'TIL THINGS SETTLE DOWN.
WHAT SETTLES DOWN?
NOTHING THAT TOUCHES YOU. JUST HOLD DOWN THE FORT UNTIL I GET BACK.
I'VE JUST GOT HERE. I'M RUNNIN' THE COP DEPARTMENT NOW?
I GOT A DEPUTY CHIEF FOR THAT. A MORON NAMED, EBERSOL.
YOU HANDLE OUR BUSINESS.
SURE, GOTCHA.
WHERE YOU GOING?
IT'S BETTER YOU DON'T KNOW.
WHY NOT?
IN CASE THEY WORK YOU OVER.
WHO WORKS ME OVER?

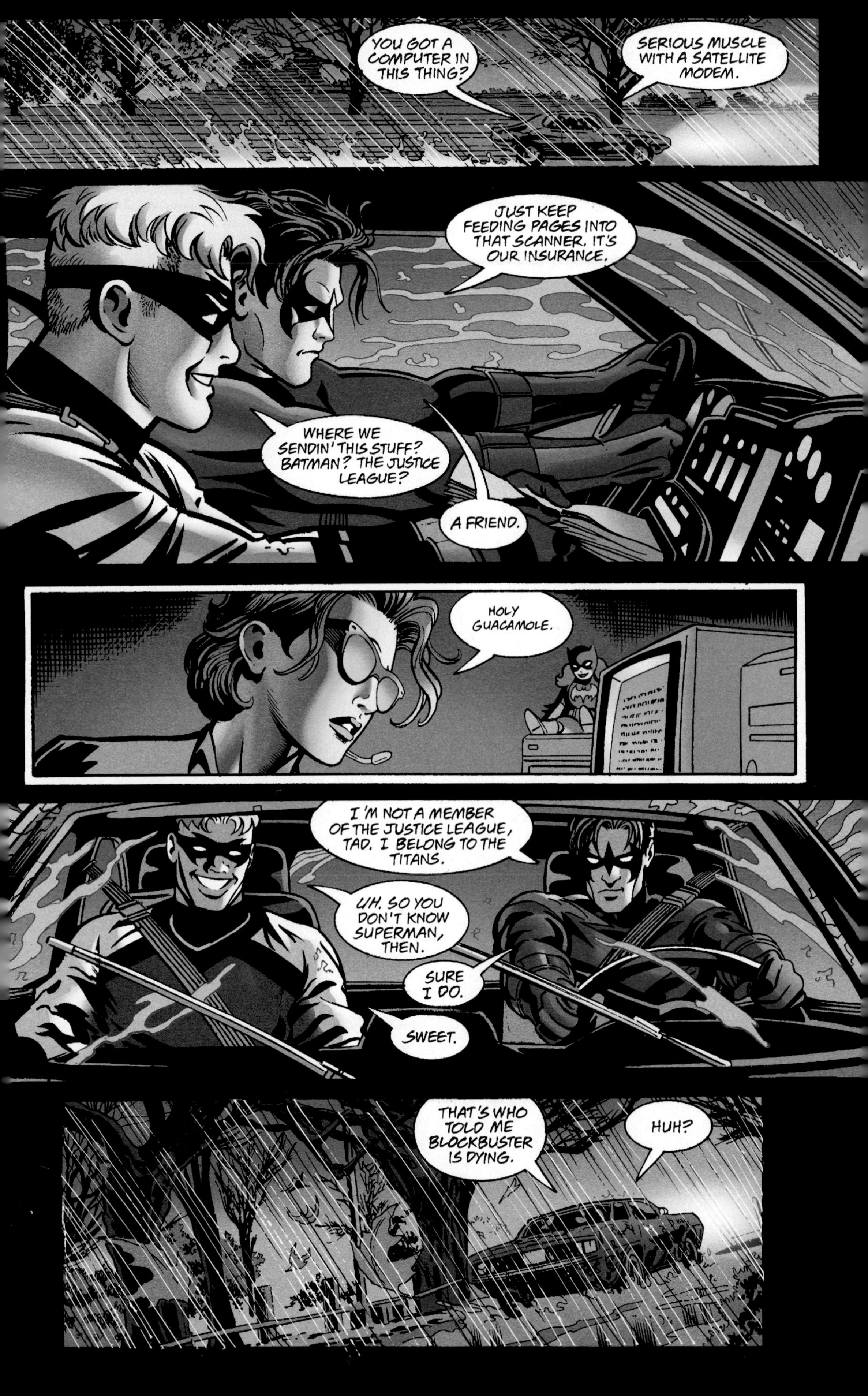

YOU GOT A COMPUTER IN THIS THING?
SERIOUS MUSCLE WITH A SATELLITE MODEM.
JUST KEEP FEEDING PAGES INTO THAT SCANNER. IT'S OUR INSURANCE.
WHERE WE SENDIN' THIS STUFF? BATMAN? THE JUSTICE LEAGUE?
A FRIEND.
HOLY GUACAMOLE.
I'M NOT A MEMBER OF THE JUSTICE LEAGUE, TAD. I BELONG TO THE TITANS.
UH. SO YOU DON'T KNOW SUPERMAN, THEN.
SURE I DO.
SWEET.
THAT'S WHO TOLD ME BLOCKBUSTER IS DYING.
HUH?

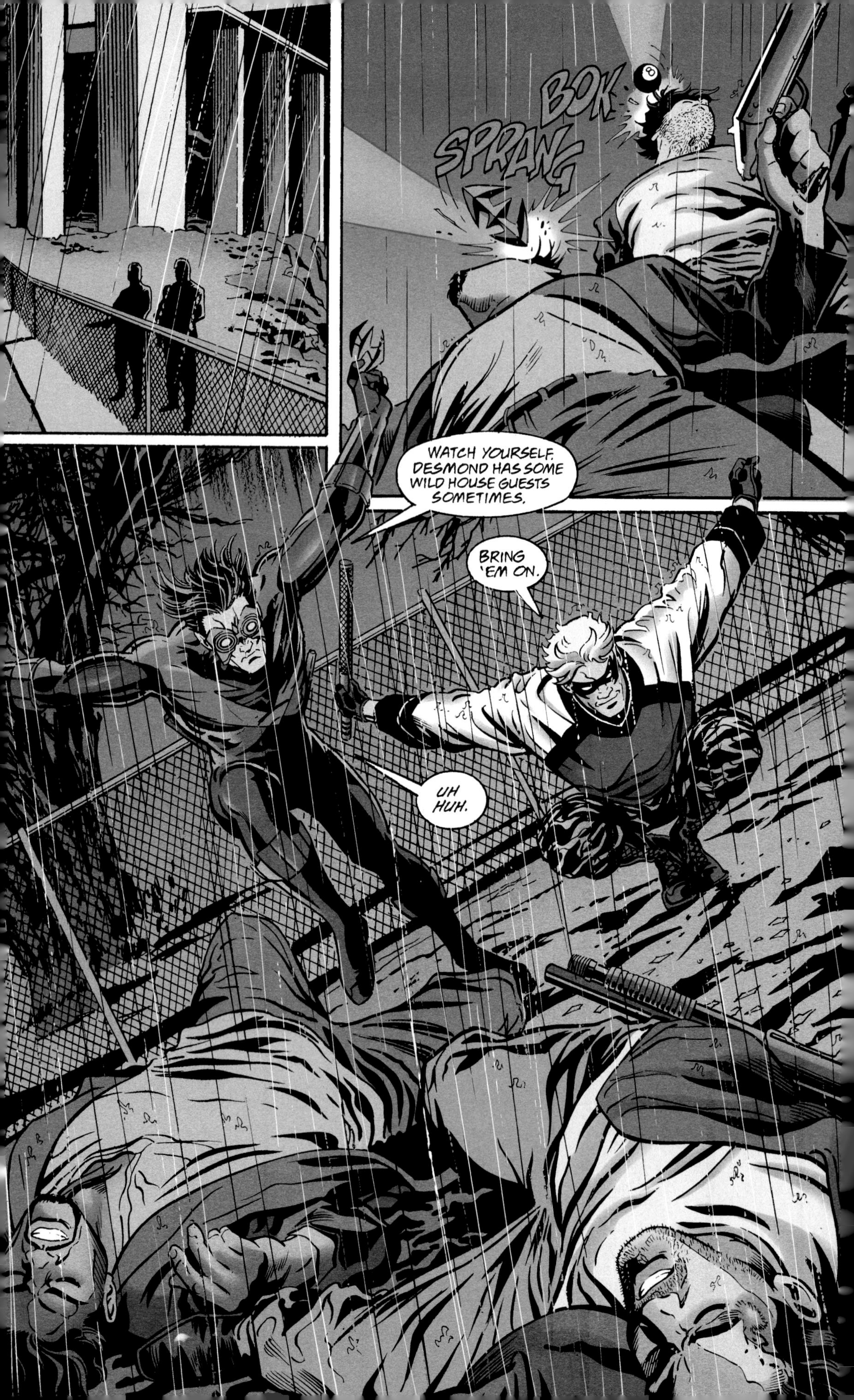
BOK
SPRANG
WATCH YOURSELF. DESMOND HAS SOME WILD HOUSE GUESTS SOMETIMES.
BRING 'EM ON.
UH HUH.

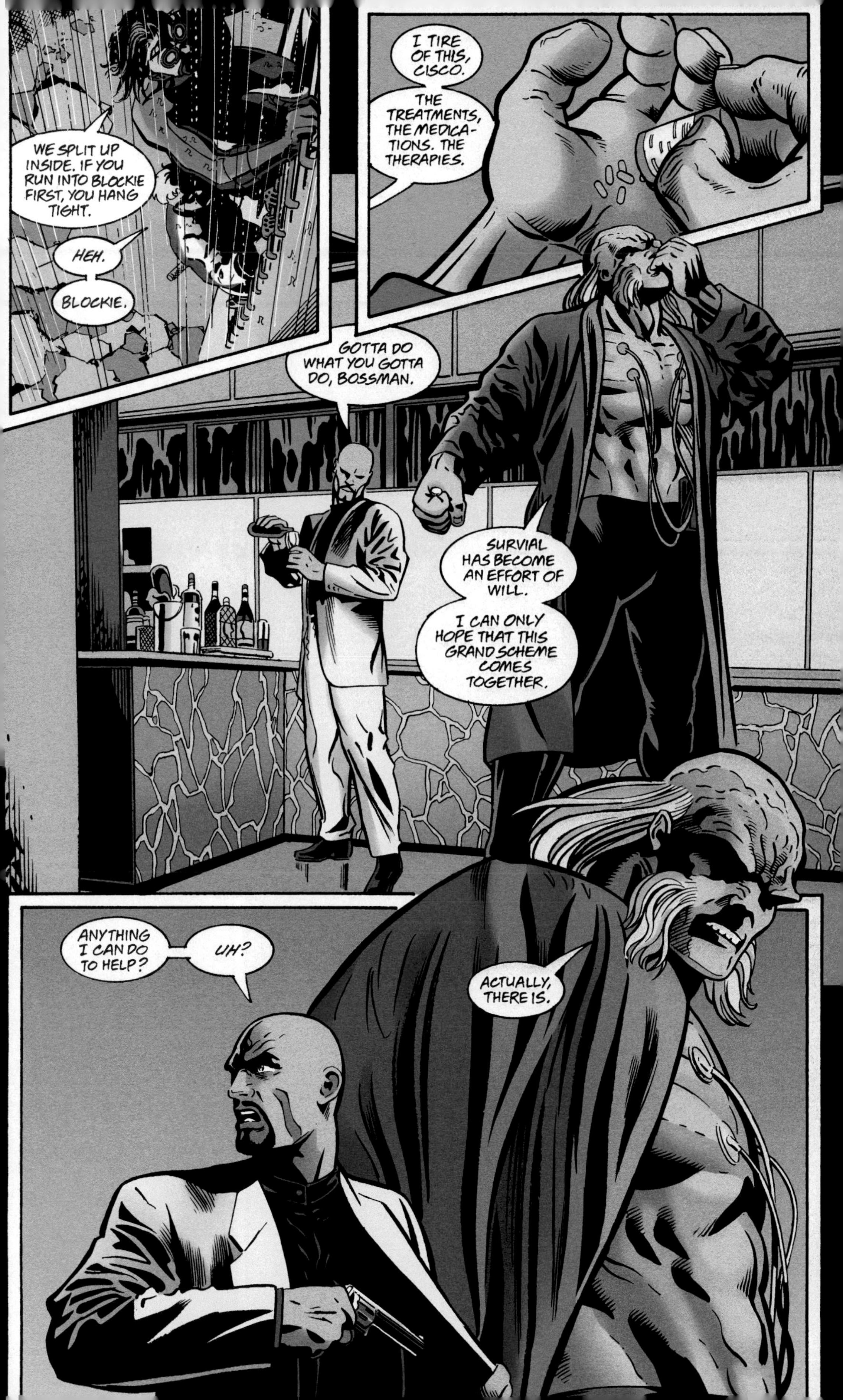
WE SPLIT UP INSIDE. IF YOU RUN INTO BLOCKIE FIRST, YOU HANG TIGHT.
HEH.
BLOCKIE.
I TIRE OF THIS, CISCO.
THE TREATMENTS, THE MEDICA-TIONS. THE THERAPIES.
GOTTA DO WHAT YOU GOTTA DO, BOSSMAN.
SURVIAL HAS BECOME AN EFFORT OF WILL.
I CAN ONLY HOPE THAT THIS GRAND SCHEME COMES TOGETHER.
ANYTHING I CAN DO TO HELP?
UH?
ACTUALLY, THERE IS.

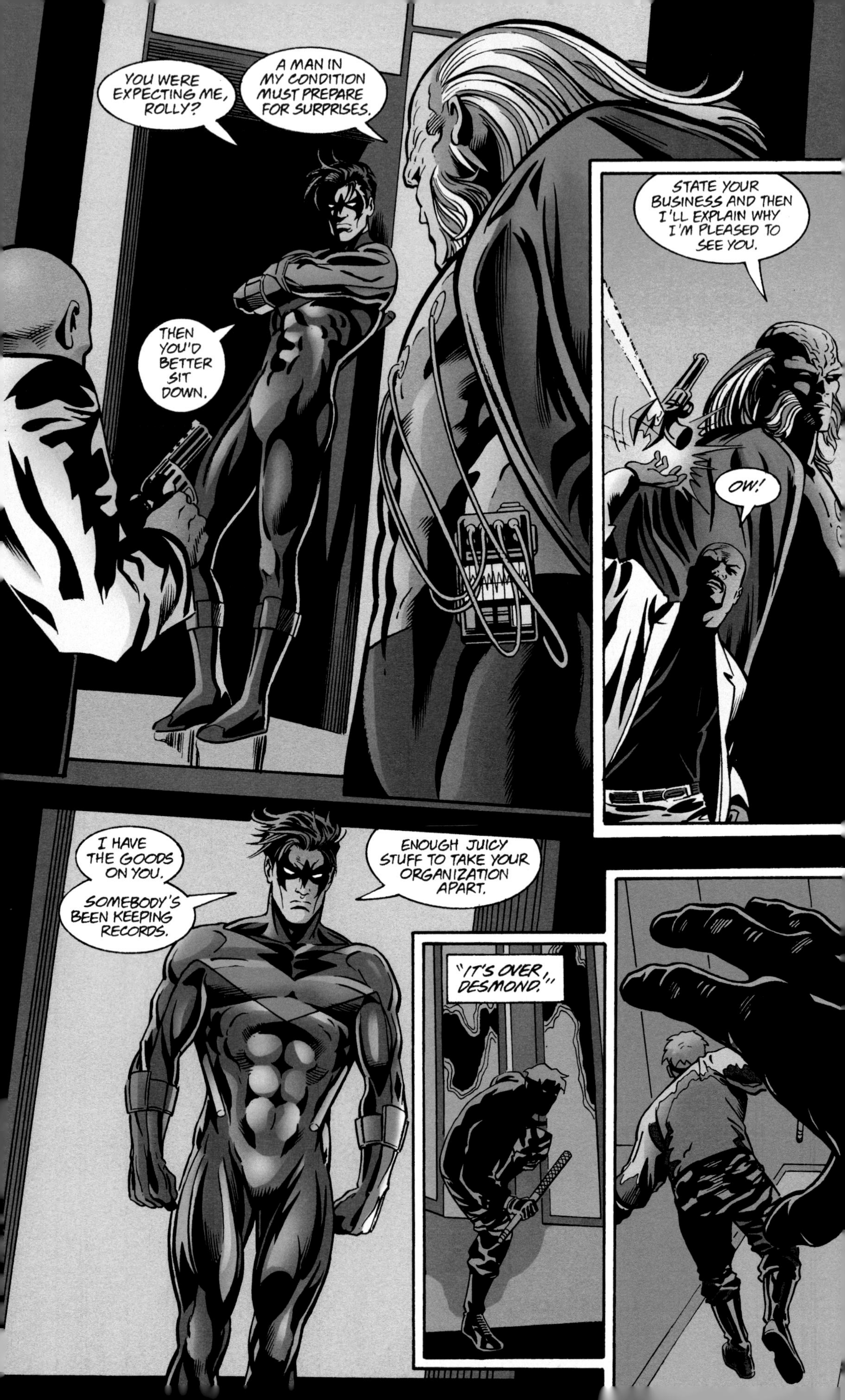
YOU WERE EXPECTING ME, ROLLY?
A MAN IN MY CONDITION MUST PREPARE FOR SURPRISES.
THEN YOU'D BETTER SIT DOWN.
STATE YOUR BUSINESS AND THEN I'LL EXPLAIN WHY I'M PLEASED TO SEE YOU.
OW!
I HAVE THE GOODS ON YOU.
SOMEBODY'S BEEN KEEPING RECORDS.
ENOUGH JUICY STUFF TO TAKE YOUR ORGANIZATION APART.
"IT'S OVER, DESMOND."

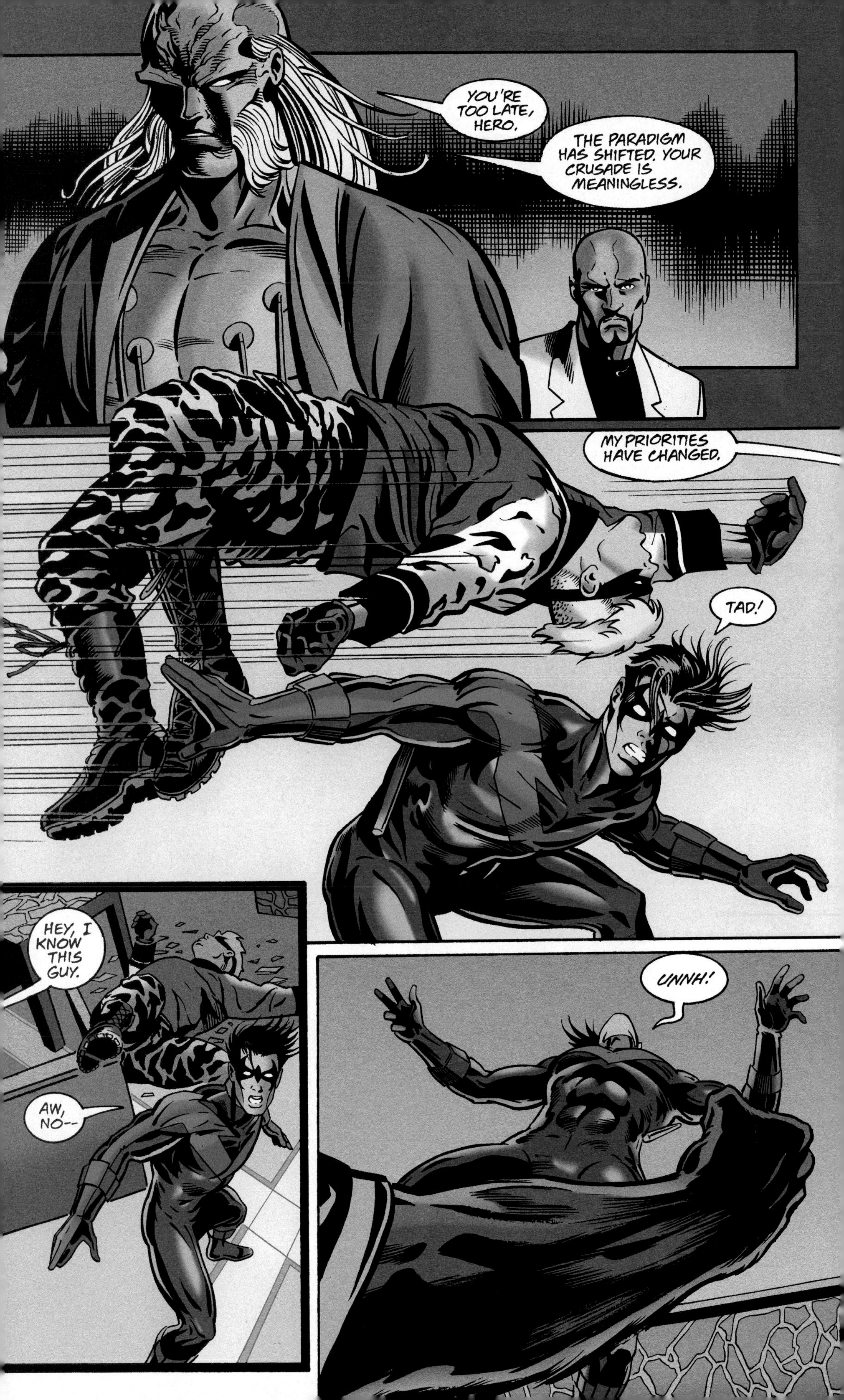
YOU'RE TOO LATE, HERO.
THE PARADIGM HAS SHIFTED. YOUR CRUSADE IS MEANINGLESS.
MY PRIORITIES HAVE CHANGED.
TAD!
HEY, I KNOW THIS GUY.
AW, NO--
UNNH!

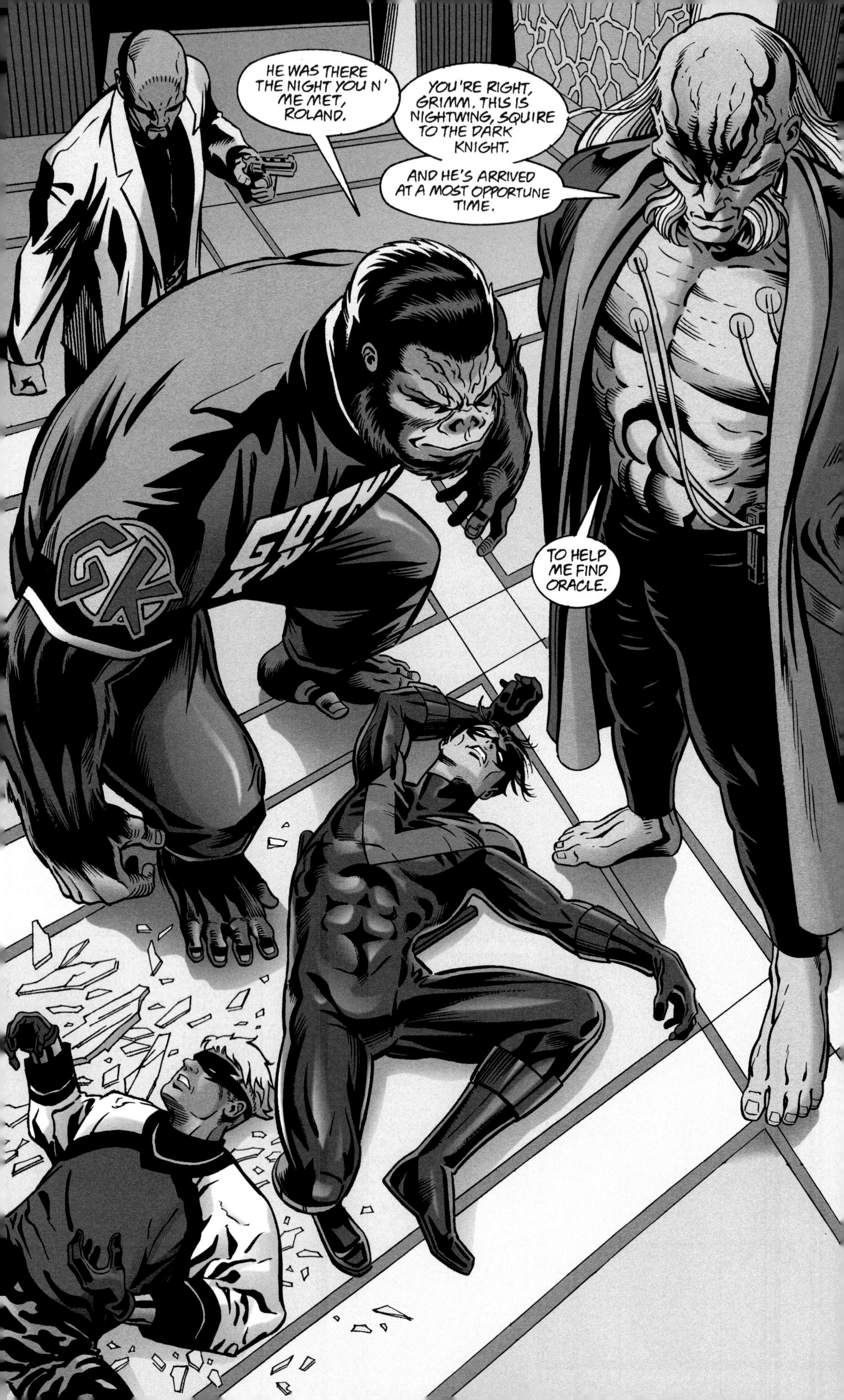
HE WAS THERE THE NIGHT YOU N' ME MET, ROLAND.
YOU'RE RIGHT, GRIMM. THIS IS NIGHTWING, SQUIRE TO THE DARK KNIGHT.
AND HE'S ARRIVED AT A MOST OPPORTUNE TIME.
TO HELP ME FIND ORACLE.

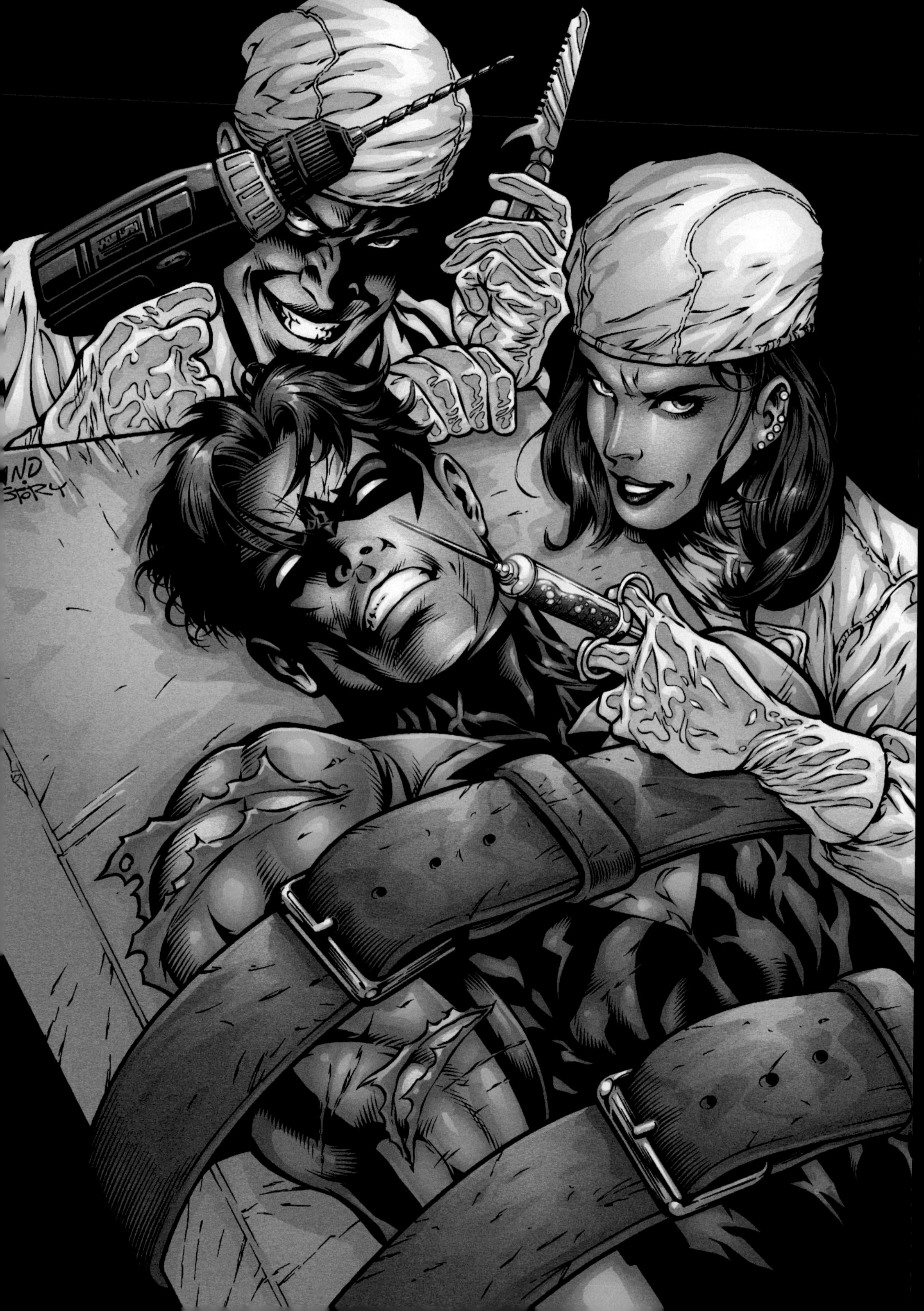

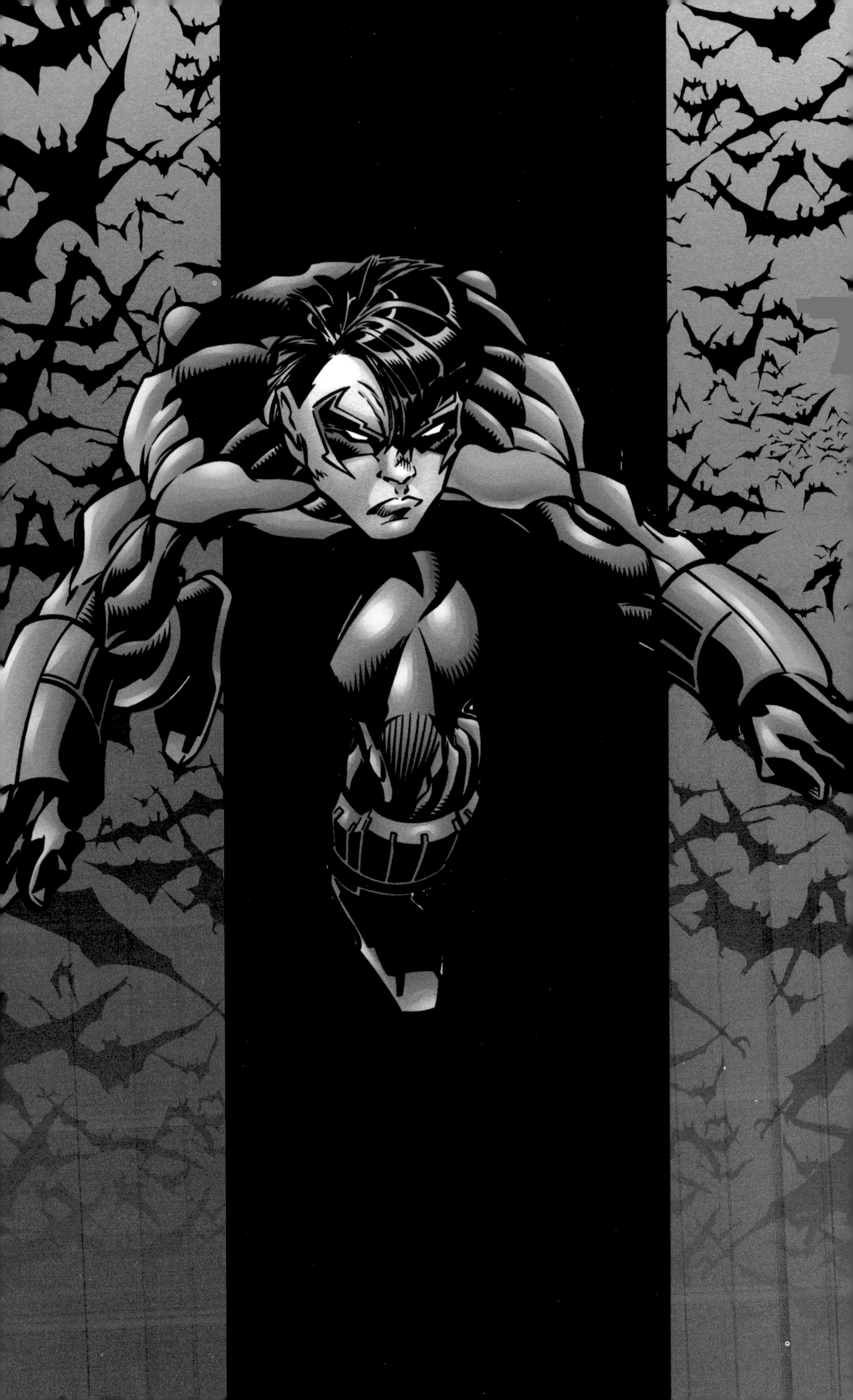

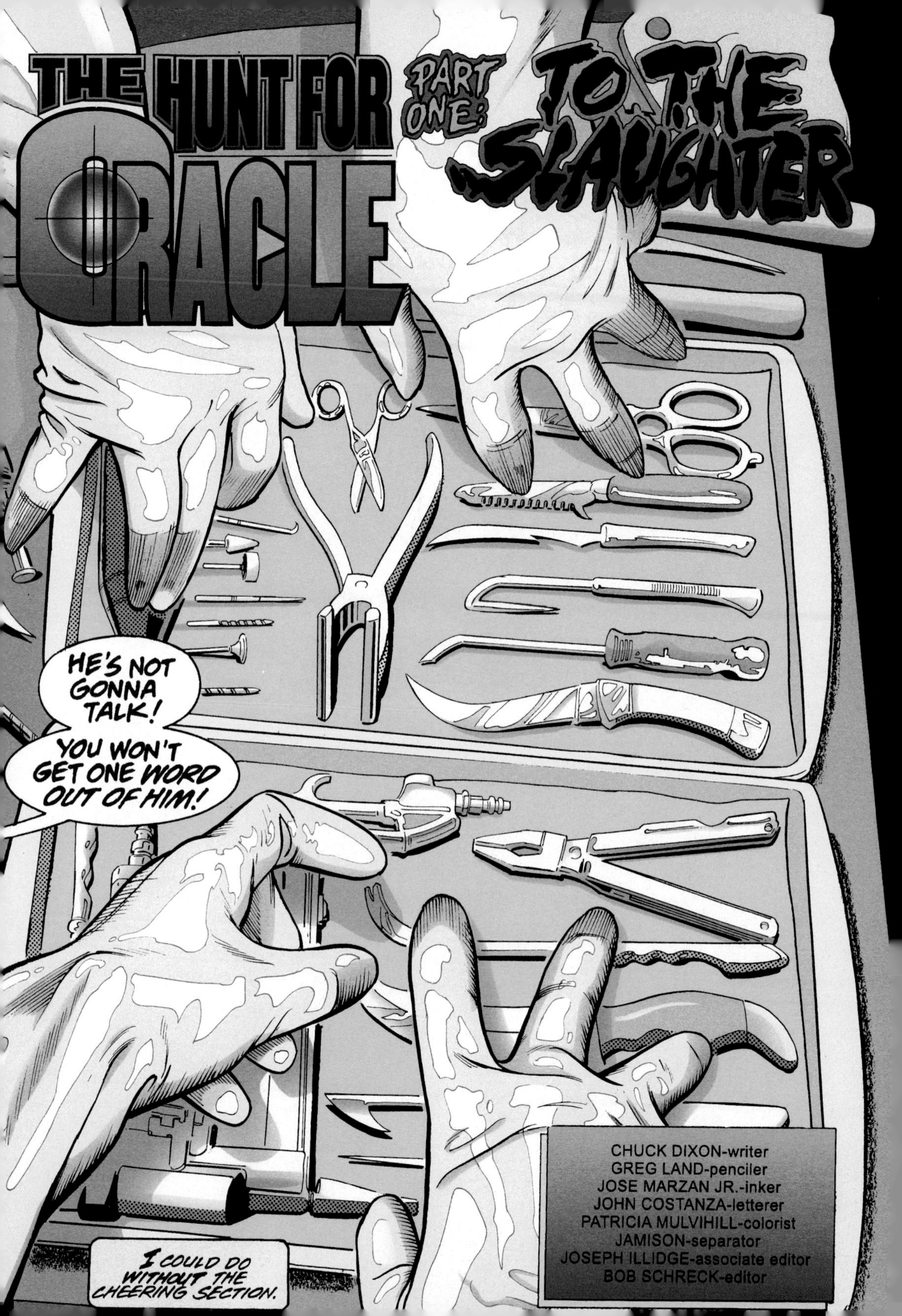
THE HUNT FOR ORACLE
PART ONE: TO THE SLAUGHTER
HE'S NOT GONNA TALK!
YOU WON'T GET ONE WORD OUT OF HIM!
I COULD DO WITHOUT THE CHEERING SECTION.
CHUCK DIXON-writer
GREG LAND-penciler
JOSE MARZAN JR.-inker
JOHN COSTANZA-letterer
PATRICIA MULVIHILL-colorist
JAMISON-separator
JOSEPH ILLIDGE-associate editor
BOB SCHRECK-editor

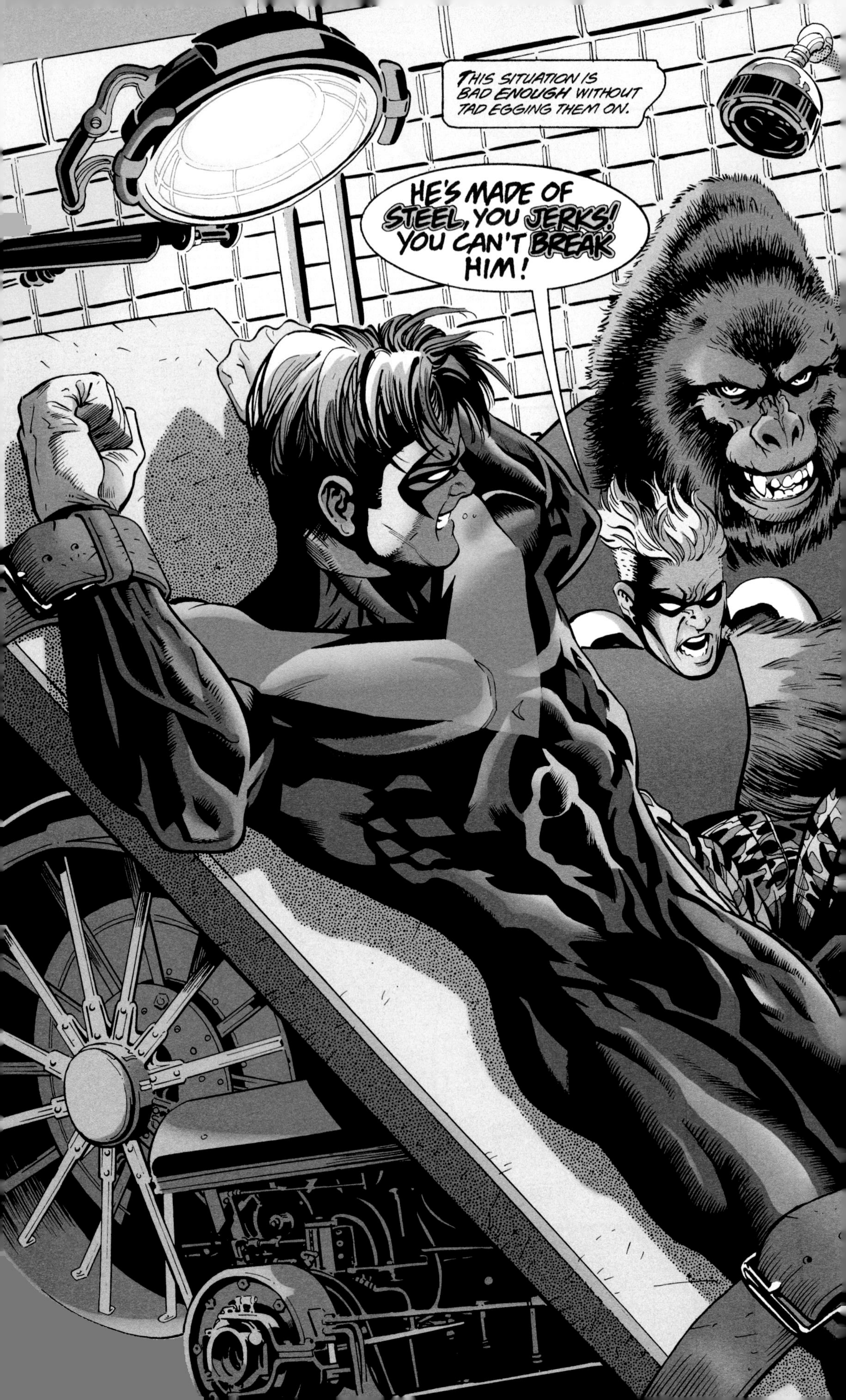
THIS SITUATION IS BAD ENOUGH WITHOUT TAD EGGING THEM ON.
HE'S MADE OF STEEL, YOU JERKS! YOU CAN'T BREAK HIM!

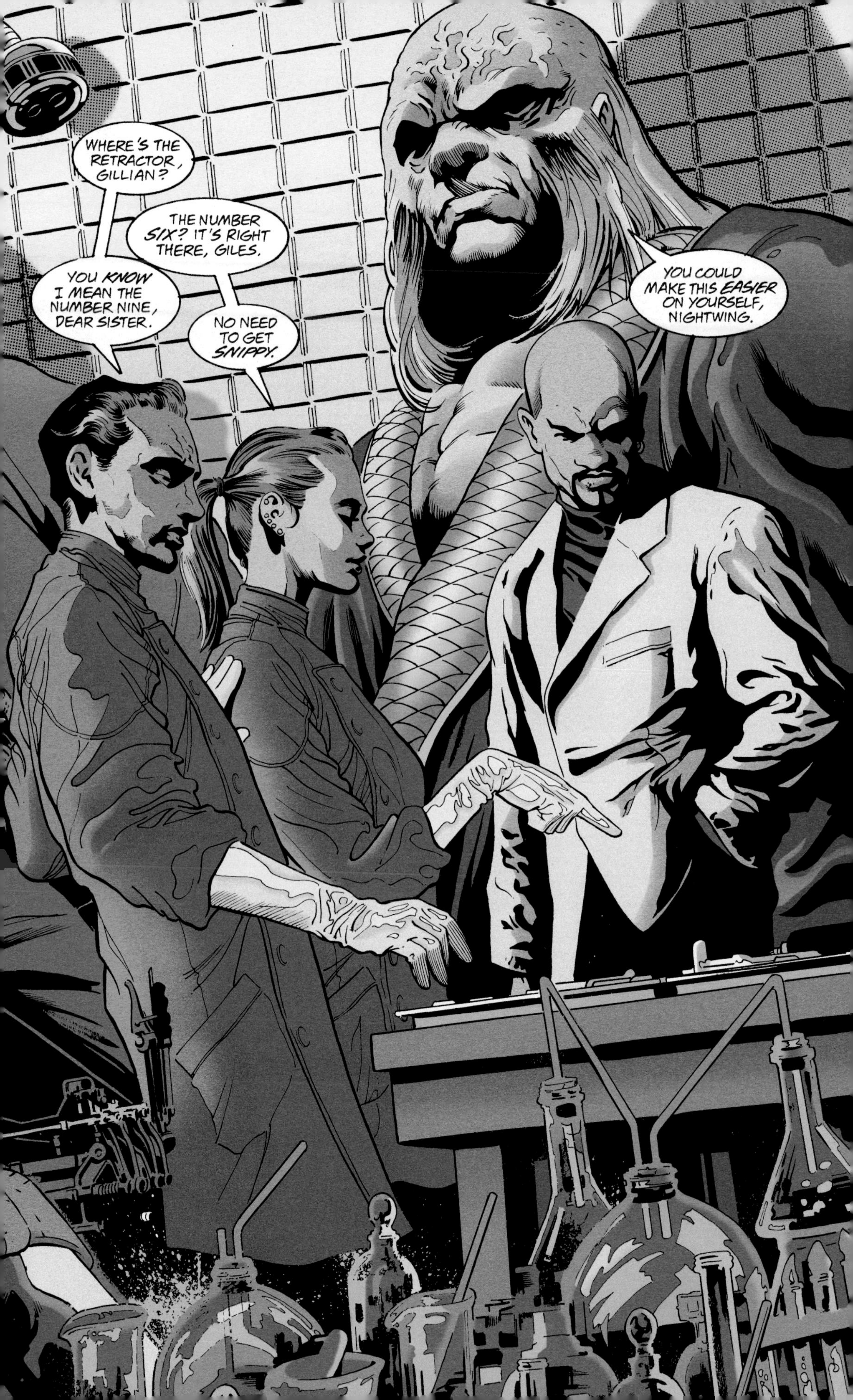
WHERE'S THE RETRACTOR, GILLIAN?
THE NUMBER SIX? IT'S RIGHT THERE, GILES.
YOU KNOW I MEAN THE NUMBER NINE, DEAR SISTER.
NO NEED TO GET SNIPPY.
YOU COULD MAKE THIS EASIER ON YOURSELF, NIGHTWING.

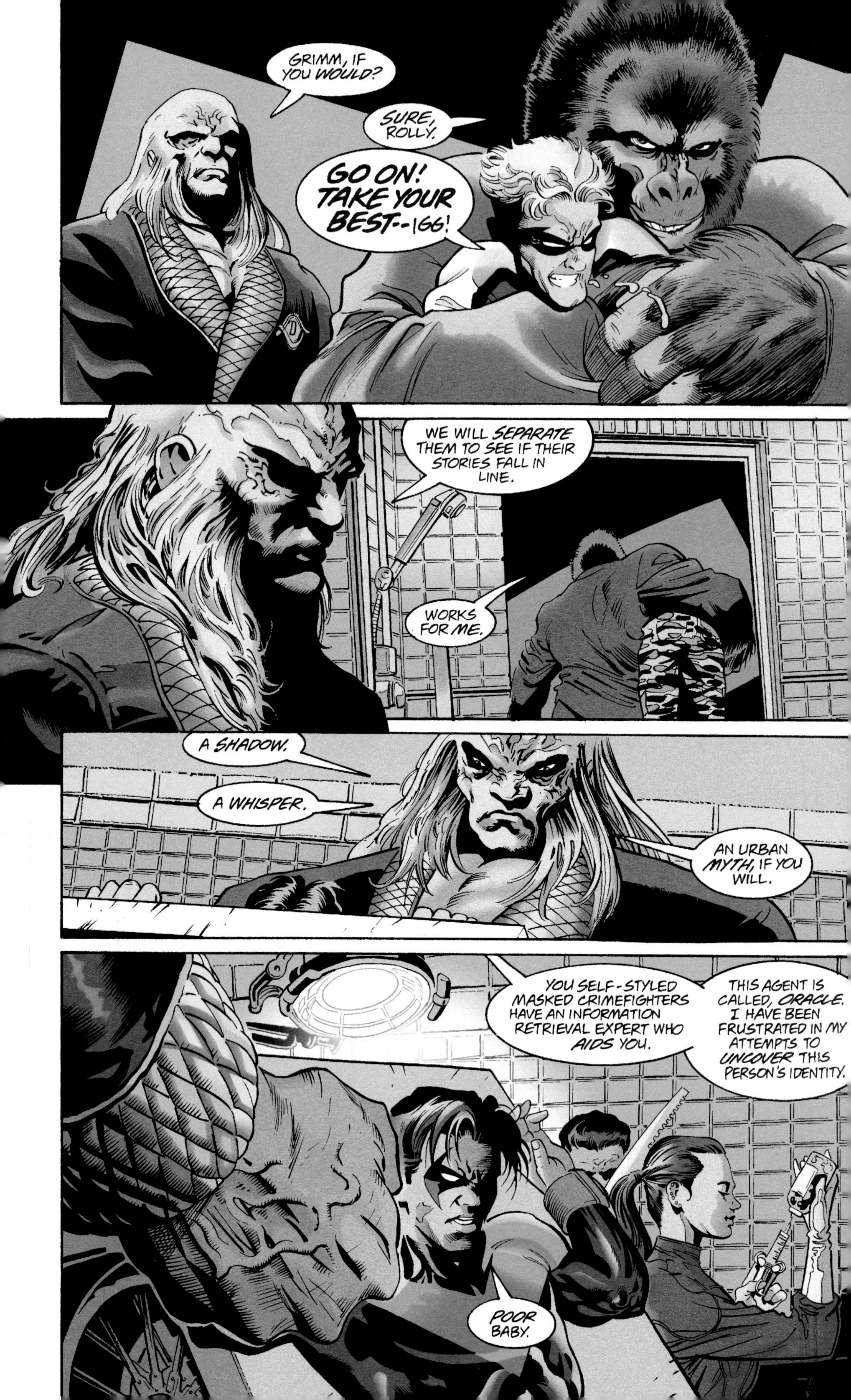
GRIMM, IF YOU WOULD?
SURE, ROLLY.
GO ON! TAKE YOUR BEST--IGG!
WE WILL SEPARATE THEM TO SEE IF THEIR STORIES FALL IN LINE.
WORKS FOR ME.
A SHADOW.
A WHISPER.
AN URBAN MYTH, IF YOU WILL.
YOU SELF-STYLED MASKED CRIMEFIGHTERS HAVE AN INFORMATION RETRIEVAL EXPERT WHO AIDS YOU.
THIS AGENT IS CALLED, ORACLE. I HAVE BEEN FRUSTRATED IN MY ATTEMPTS TO UNCOVER THIS PERSON'S IDENTITY.
POOR BABY.

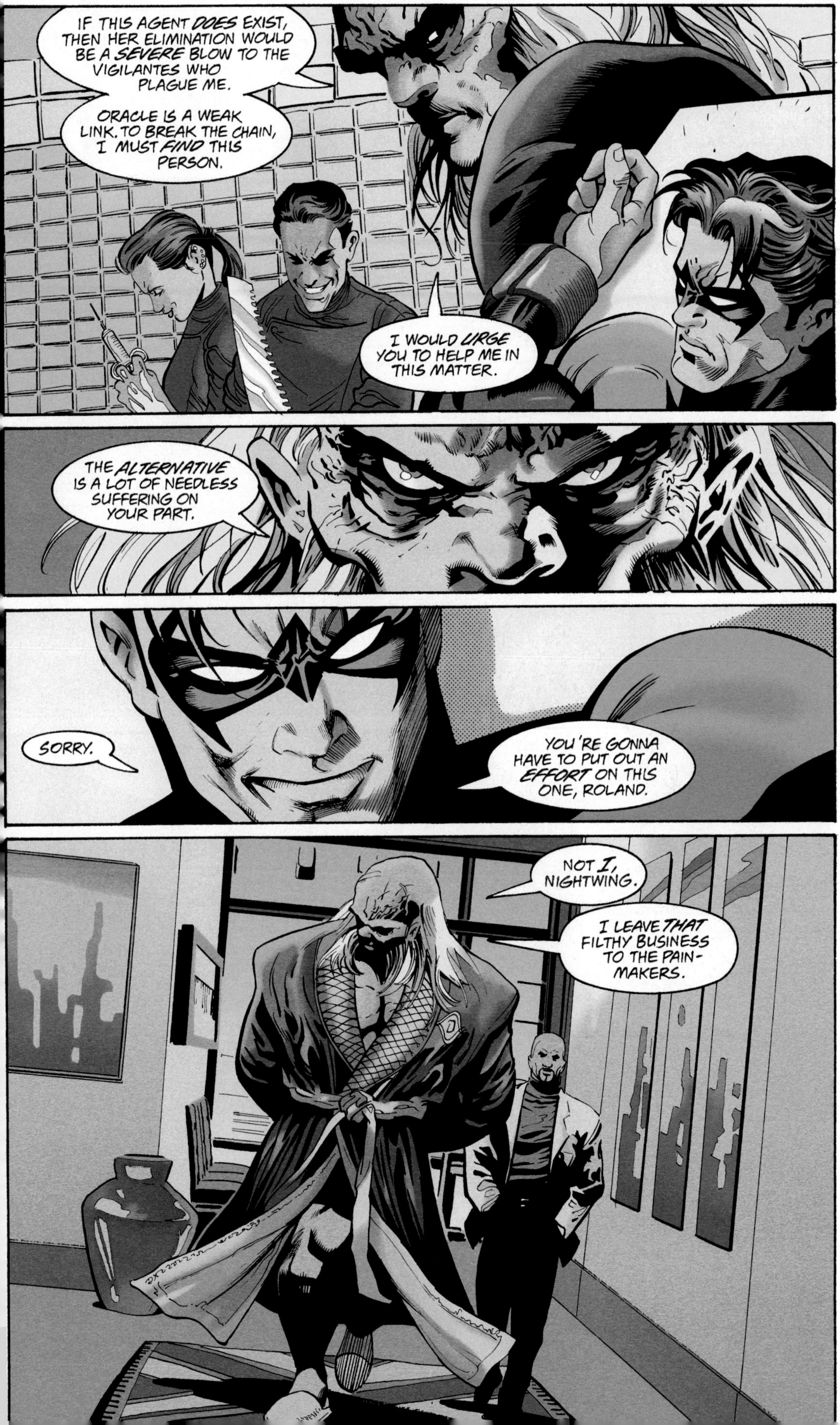
IF THIS AGENT DOES EXIST, THEN HER ELIMINATION WOULD BE A SEVERE BLOW TO THE VIGILANTES WHO PLAGUE ME.
ORACLE IS A WEAK LINK. TO BREAK THE CHAIN, I MUST FIND THIS PERSON.
I WOULD URGE YOU TO HELP ME IN THIS MATTER.
THE ALTERNATIVE IS A LOT OF NEEDLESS SUFFERING ON YOUR PART.
SORRY.
YOU'RE GONNA HAVE TO PUT OUT AN EFFORT ON THIS ONE, ROLAND.
NOT I, NIGHTWING.
I LEAVE THAT FILTHY BUSINESS TO THE PAIN-MAKERS.

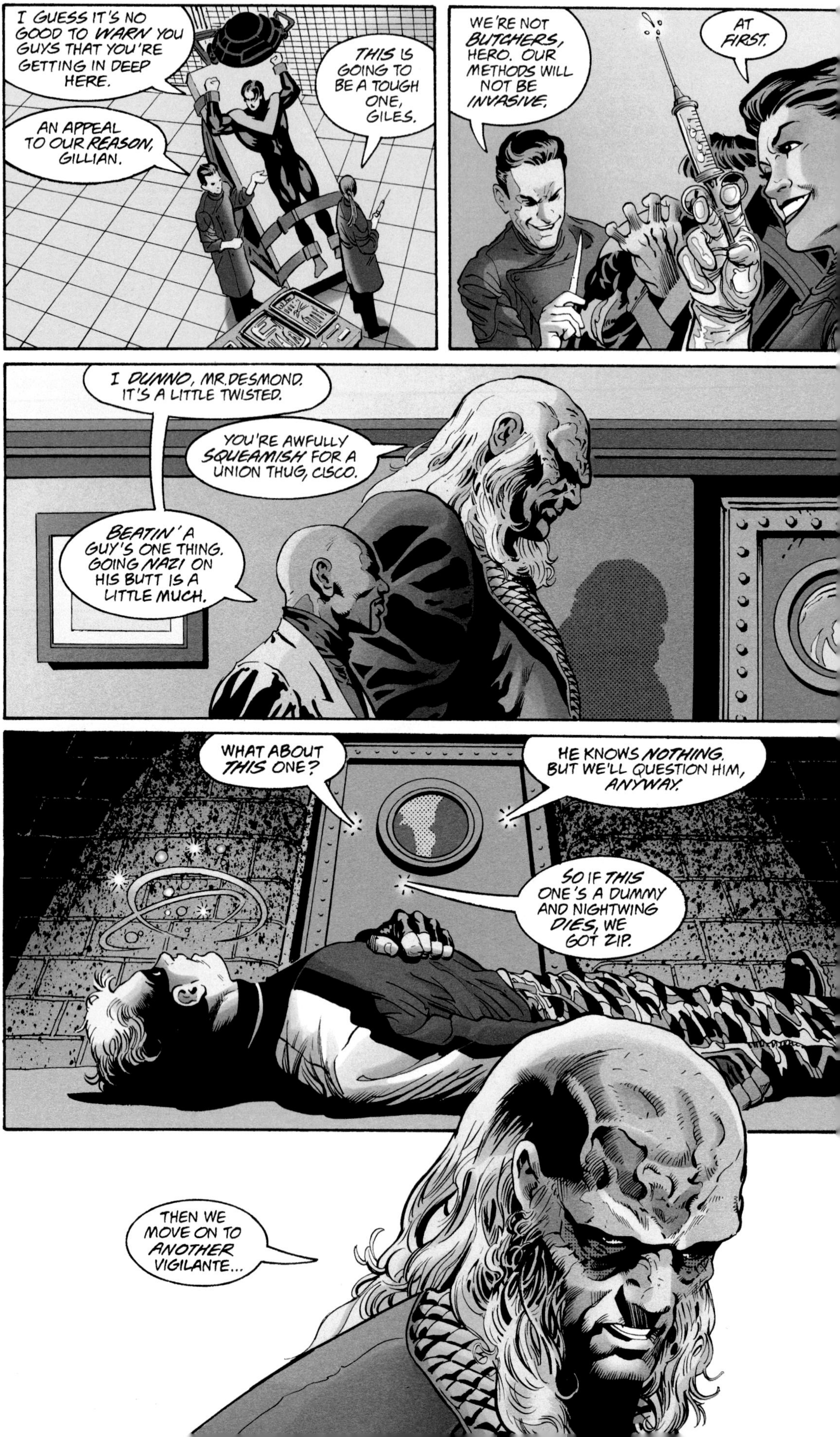

I GUESS IT'S NO GOOD TO WARN YOU GUYS THAT YOU'RE GETTING IN DEEP HERE.
AN APPEAL TO OUR REASON, GILLIAN.
THIS IS GOING TO BE A TOUGH ONE, GILES.
WE'RE NOT BUTCHERS, HERO. OUR METHODS WILL NOT BE INVASIVE.
AT FIRST.
I DUNNO, MR. DESMOND. IT'S A LITTLE TWISTED.
YOU'RE AWFULLY SQUEAMISH FOR A UNION THUG, CISCO.
BEATIN' A GUY'S ONE THING. GOING NAZI ON HIS BUTT IS A LITTLE MUCH.
WHAT ABOUT THIS ONE?
HE KNOWS NOTHING. BUT WE'LL QUESTION HIM, ANYWAY.
SO IF THIS ONE'S A DUMMY AND NIGHTWING DIES, WE GOT ZIP.
THEN WE MOVE ON TO ANOTHER VIGILANTE...

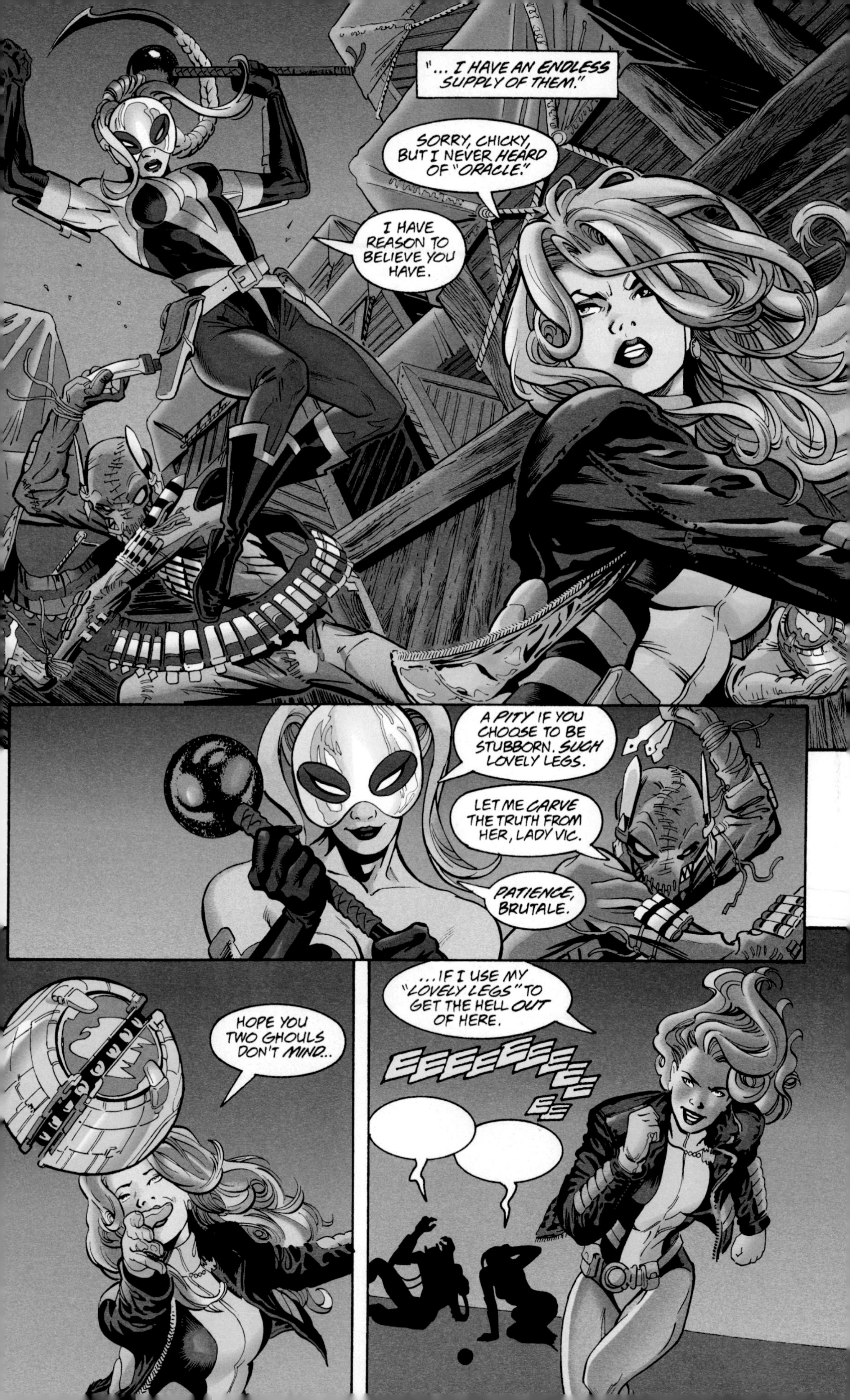
"... I HAVE AN ENDLESS SUPPLY OF THEM."
SORRY, CHICKY, BUT I NEVER HEARD OF "ORACLE."
I HAVE REASON TO BELIEVE YOU HAVE.
A PITY IF YOU CHOOSE TO BE STUBBORN. SUCH LOVELY LEGS.
LET ME CARVE THE TRUTH FROM HER, LADY VIC.
PATIENCE, BRUTALE.
HOPE YOU TWO GHOULS DON'T MIND...
...IF I USE MY "LOVELY LEGS" TO GET THE HELL OUT OF HERE.
EEEEEEEEEEEEE

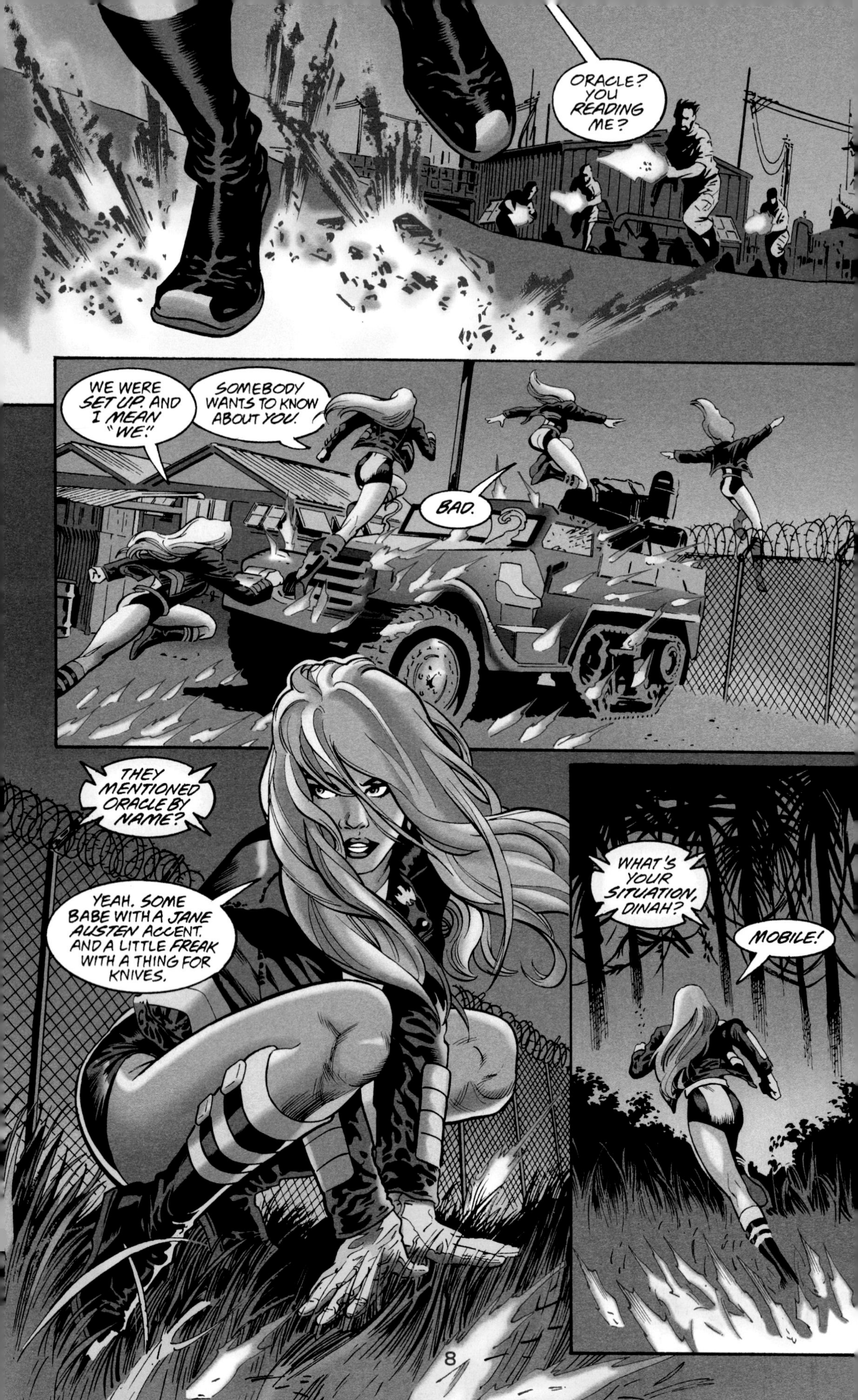
ORACLE? YOU READING ME?
WE WERE SET UP. AND I MEAN "WE."
SOMEBODY WANTS TO KNOW ABOUT YOU.
BAD.
THEY MENTIONED ORACLE BY NAME?
YEAH. SOME BABE WITH A JANE AUSTEN ACCENT. AND A LITTLE FREAK WITH A THING FOR KNIVES.
WHAT'S YOUR SITUATION, DINAH?
MOBILE!

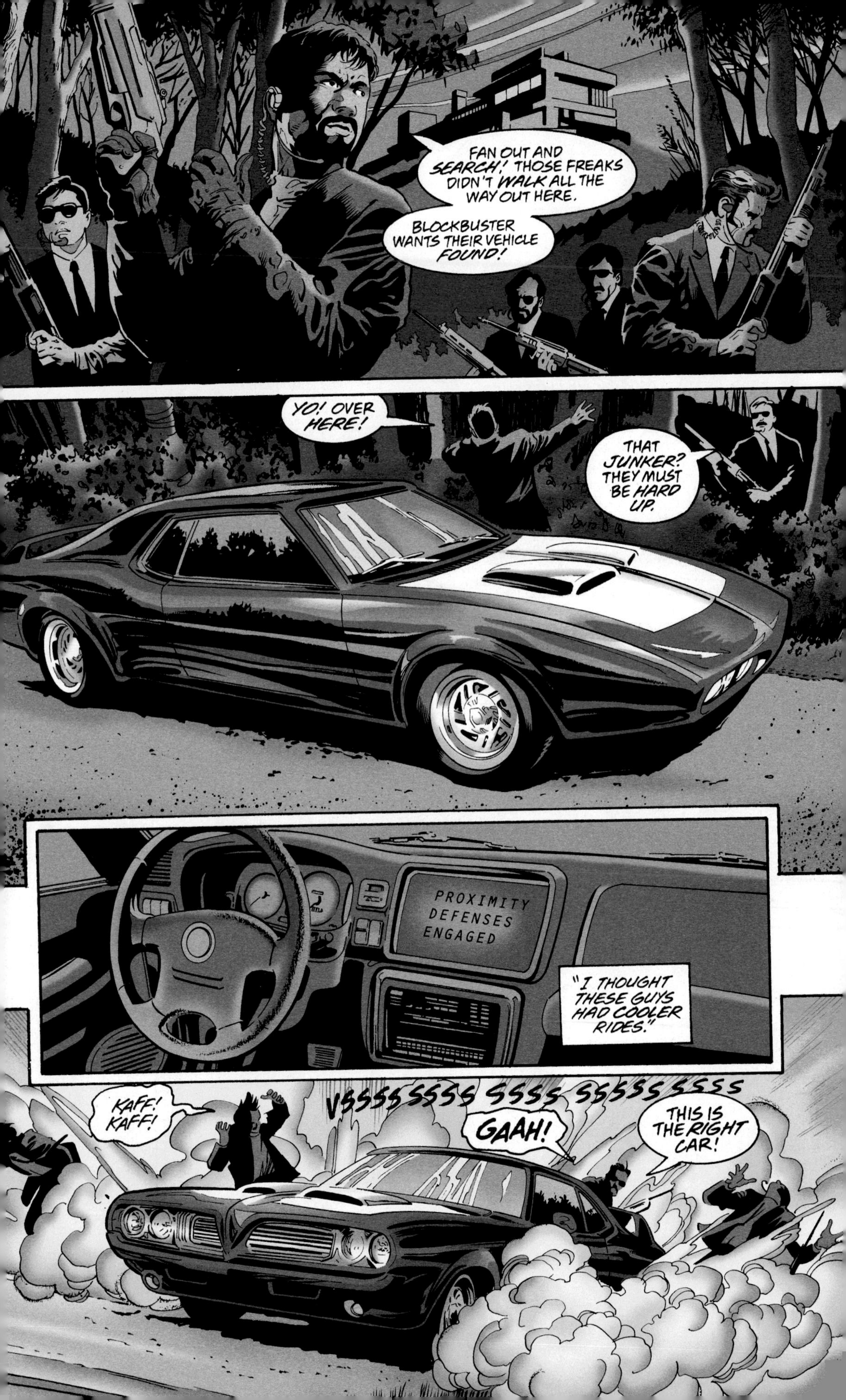
FAN OUT AND SEARCH! THOSE FREAKS DIDN'T WALK ALL THE WAY OUT HERE.
BLOCKBUSTER WANTS THEIR VEHICLE FOUND!
YO! OVER HERE!
THAT JUNKER? THEY MUST BE HARD UP.
PROXIMITY DEFENSES ENGAGED
"I THOUGHT THESE GUYS HAD COOLER RIDES."
KAFF! KAFF!
VSSSSSSSSS SSSS SSSSS SSSSS
GAAH!
THIS IS THE RIGHT CAR!

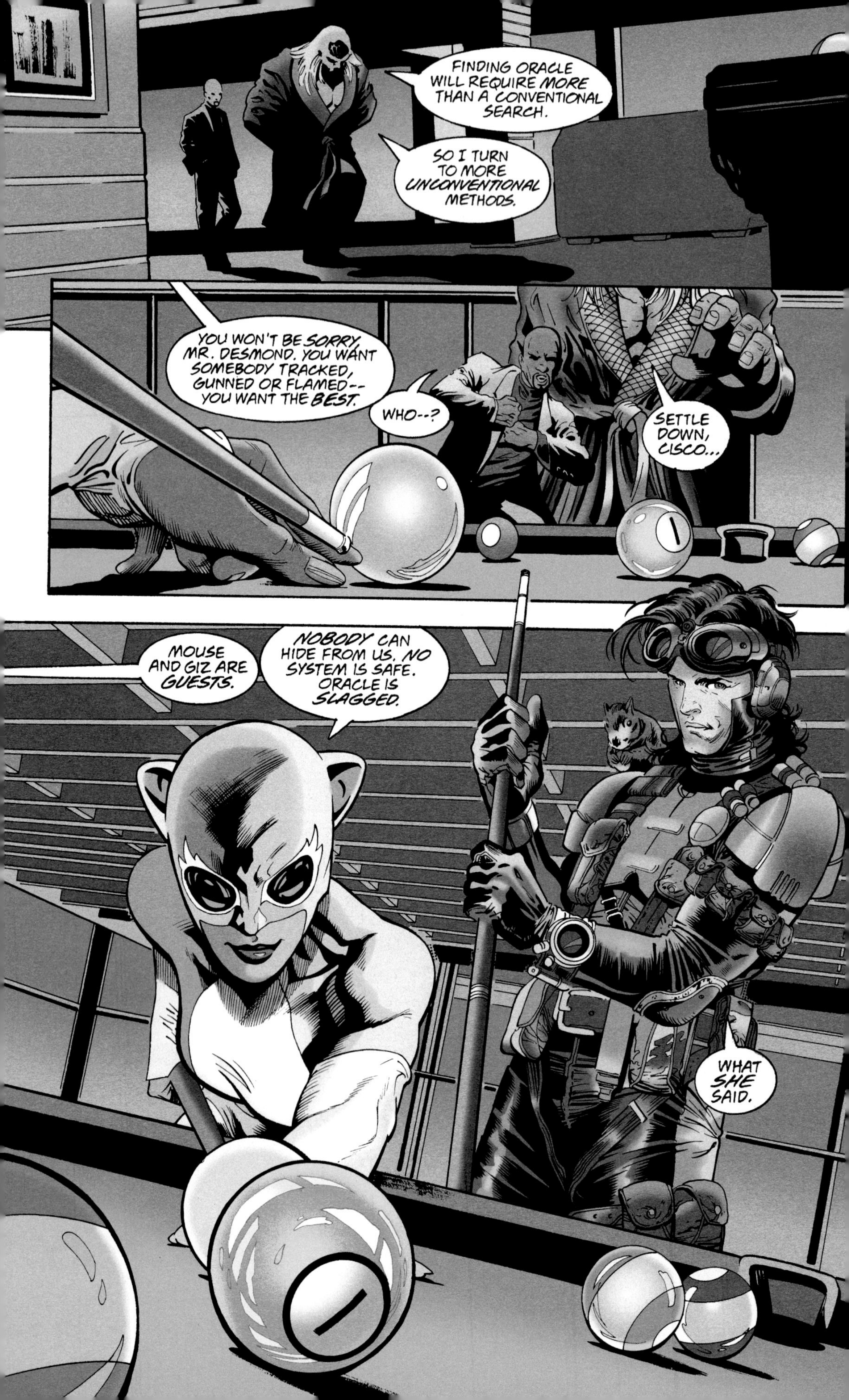
FINDING ORACLE WILL REQUIRE MORE THAN A CONVENTIONAL SEARCH.
SO I TURN TO MORE UNCONVENTIONAL METHODS.
YOU WON'T BE SORRY, MR. DESMOND. YOU WANT SOMEBODY TRACKED, GUNNED OR FLAMED-- YOU WANT THE BEST.
WHO--?
SETTLE DOWN, CISCO...
MOUSE AND GIZ ARE GUESTS.
NOBODY CAN HIDE FROM US. NO SYSTEM IS SAFE. ORACLE IS SLAGGED.
WHAT SHE SAID.

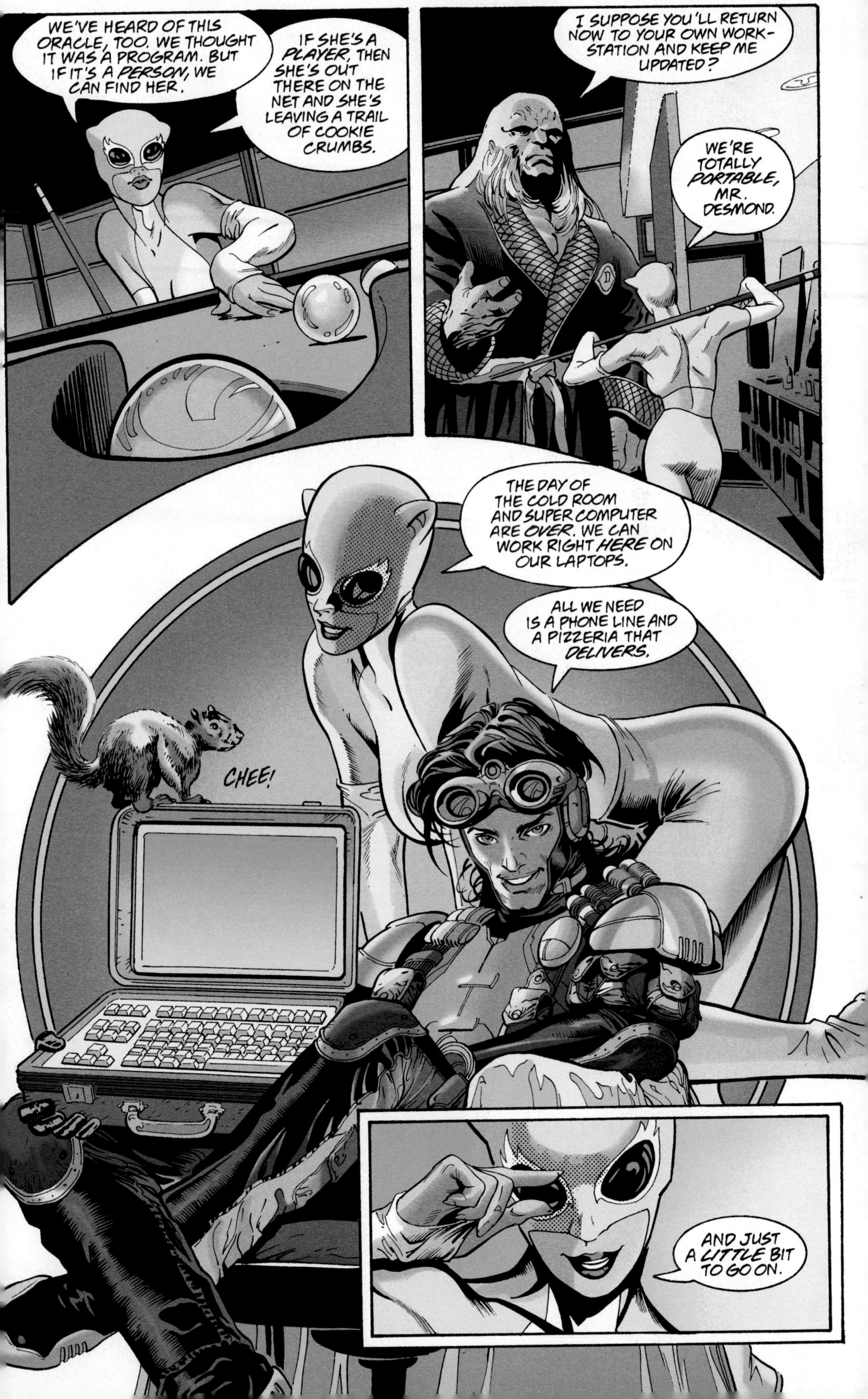
WE'VE HEARD OF THIS ORACLE, TOO. WE THOUGHT IT WAS A PROGRAM. BUT IF IT'S A PERSON, WE CAN FIND HER.
IF SHE'S A PLAYER, THEN SHE'S OUT THERE ON THE NET AND SHE'S LEAVING A TRAIL OF COOKIE CRUMBS.
I SUPPOSE YOU'LL RETURN NOW TO YOUR OWN WORK-STATION AND KEEP ME UPDATED?
WE'RE TOTALLY PORTABLE, MR. DESMOND.
THE DAY OF THE COLD ROOM AND SUPER COMPUTER ARE OVER. WE CAN WORK RIGHT HERE ON OUR LAPTOPS.
ALL WE NEED IS A PHONE LINE AND A PIZZERIA THAT DELIVERS.
CHEE!
AND JUST A LITTLE BIT TO GO ON.

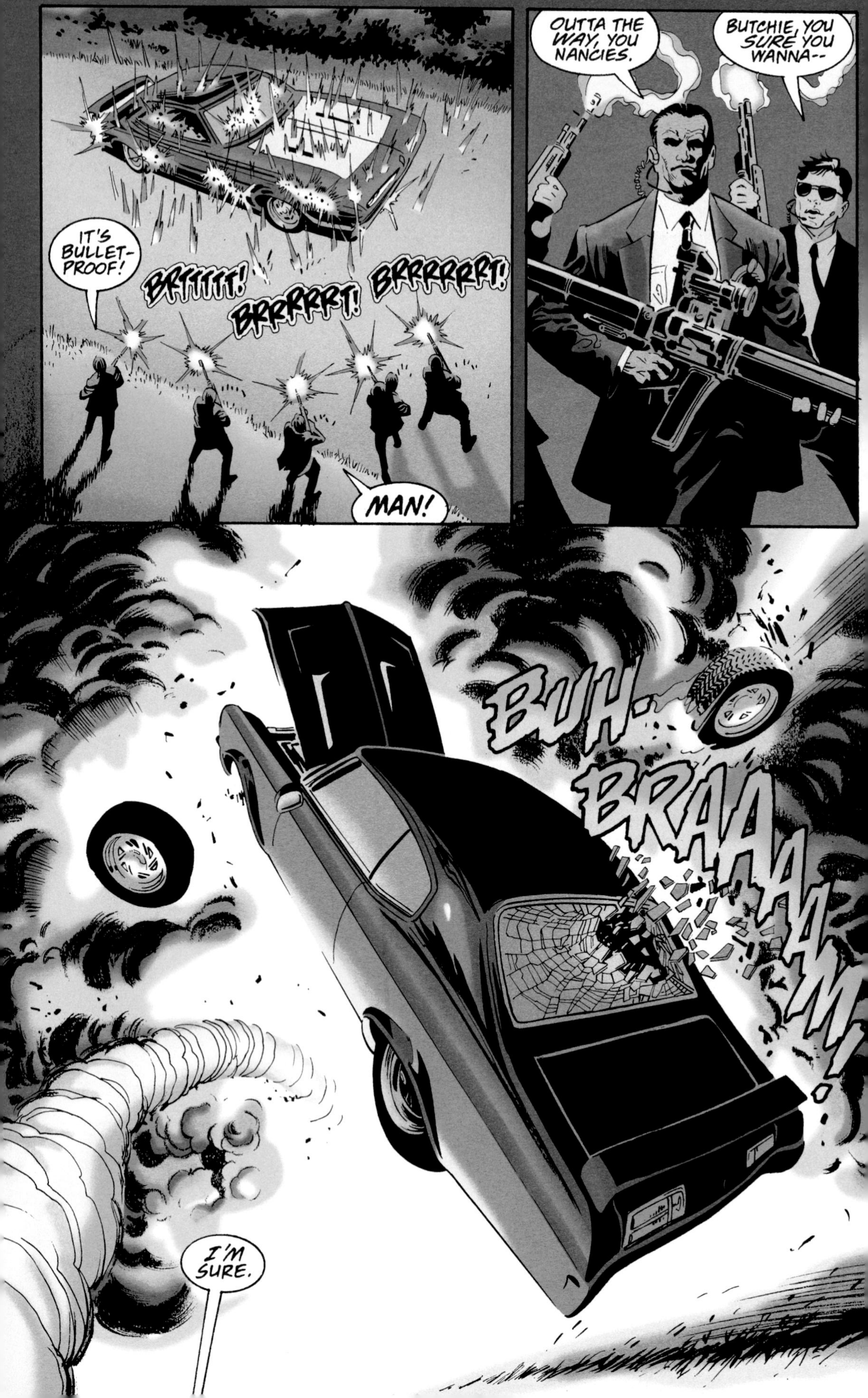

IT'S BULLET-PROOF!
BRTTTTT!
BRRRRRT!
BRRRRRRT!
MAN!
OUTTA THE WAY, YOU NANCIES.
BUTCHIE, YOU SURE YOU WANNA--
BUH-BRAAAAM!
I'M SURE.

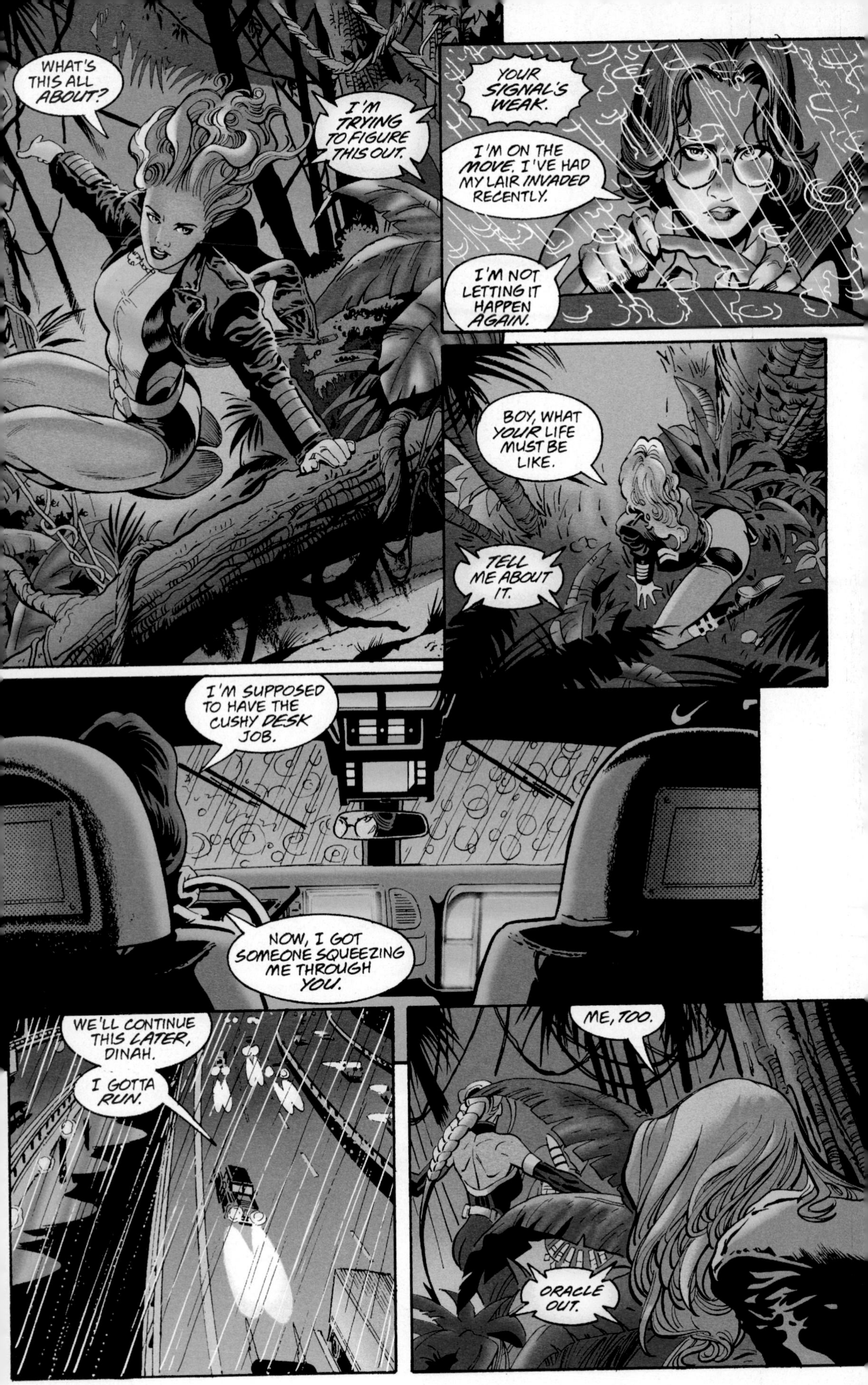
WHAT'S THIS ALL ABOUT?
I'M TRYING TO FIGURE THIS OUT.
YOUR SIGNAL'S WEAK.
I'M ON THE MOVE. I'VE HAD MY LAIR INVADED RECENTLY.
I'M NOT LETTING IT HAPPEN AGAIN.
BOY, WHAT YOUR LIFE MUST BE LIKE.
TELL ME ABOUT IT.
I'M SUPPOSED TO HAVE THE CUSHY DESK JOB.
NOW, I GOT SOMEONE SQUEEZING ME THROUGH YOU.
WE'LL CONTINUE THIS LATER, DINAH.
I GOTTA RUN.
ME, TOO.
ORACLE OUT.

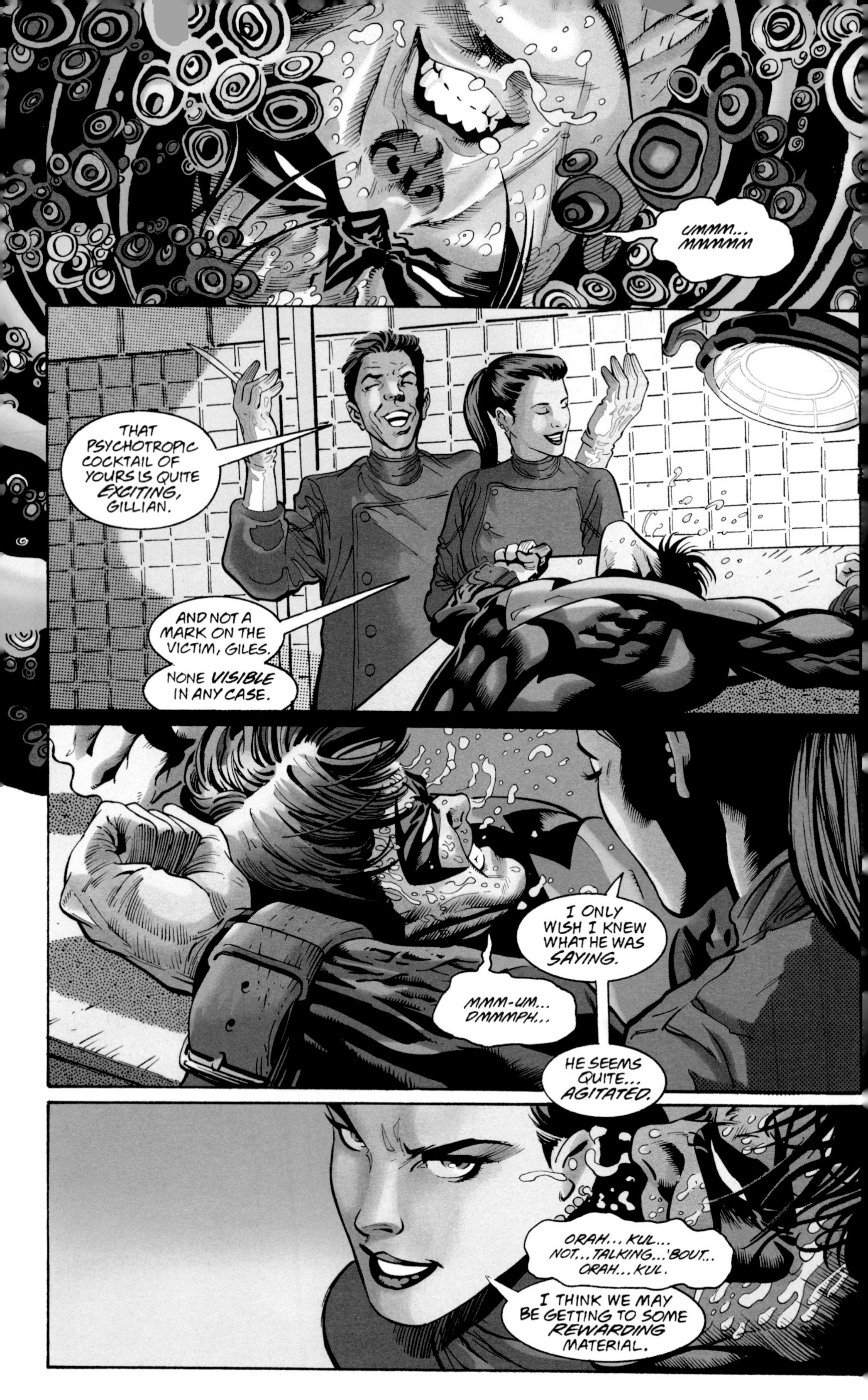
UMMM... MMMMM
THAT PSYCHOTROPIC COCKTAIL OF YOURS IS QUITE EXCITING, GILLIAN.
AND NOT A MARK ON THE VICTIM, GILES.
NONE VISIBLE IN ANY CASE.
I ONLY WISH I KNEW WHAT HE WAS SAYING.
MMM-UM... DMMMPH...
HE SEEMS QUITE... AGITATED.
ORAH... KUL... NOT... TALKING... 'BOUT... ORAH... KUL.
I THINK WE MAY BE GETTING TO SOME REWARDING MATERIAL.

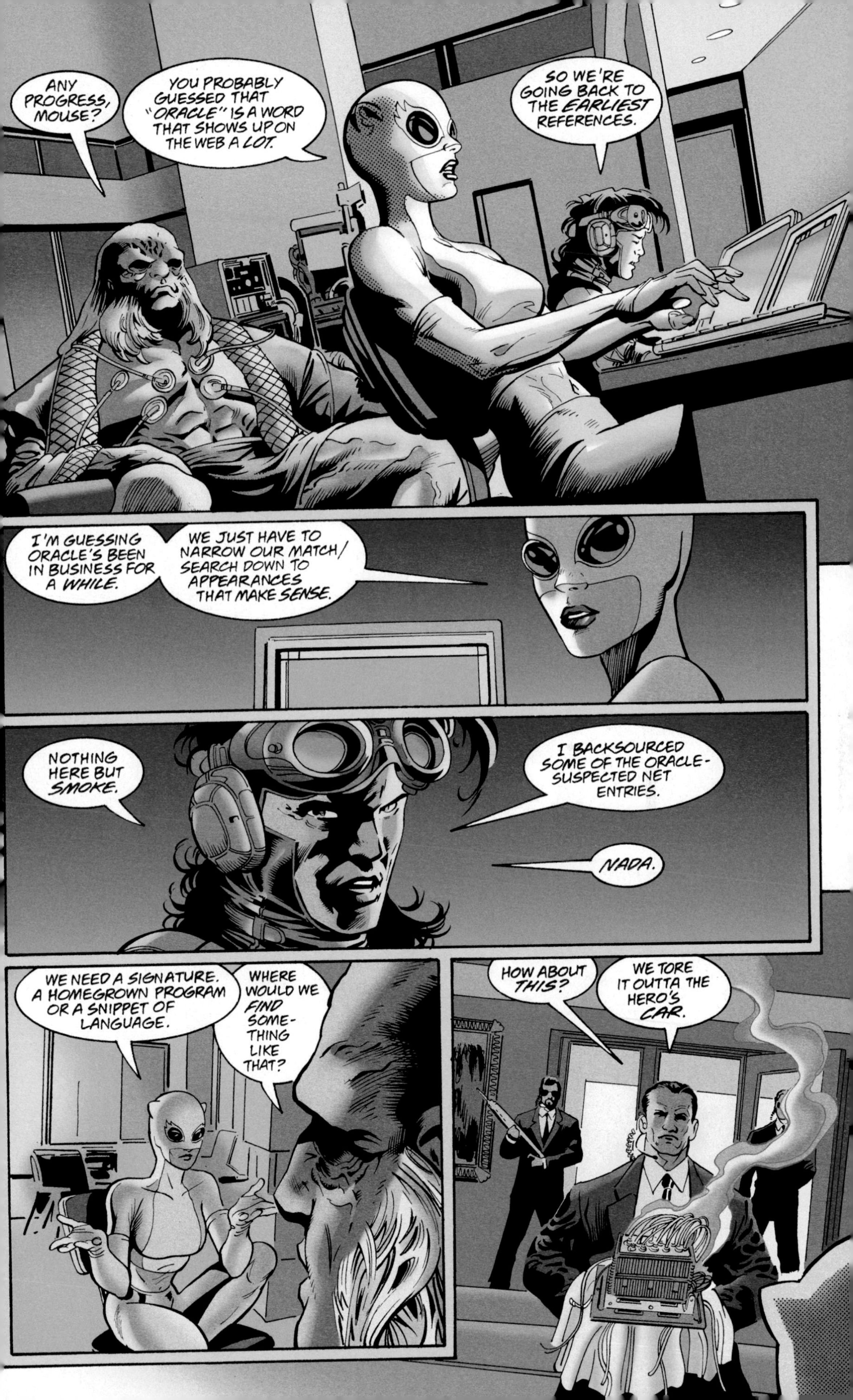
ANY PROGRESS, MOUSE?
YOU PROBABLY GUESSED THAT "ORACLE" IS A WORD THAT SHOWS UP ON THE WEB A LOT.
SO WE'RE GOING BACK TO THE EARLIEST REFERENCES.
I'M GUESSING ORACLE'S BEEN IN BUSINESS FOR A WHILE.
WE JUST HAVE TO NARROW OUR MATCH/ SEARCH DOWN TO APPEARANCES THAT MAKE SENSE.
NOTHING HERE BUT SMOKE.
I BACKSOURCED SOME OF THE ORACLE-SUSPECTED NET ENTRIES.
NADA.
WE NEED A SIGNATURE. A HOMEGROWN PROGRAM OR A SNIPPET OF LANGUAGE.
WHERE WOULD WE FIND SOME-THING LIKE THAT?
HOW ABOUT THIS?
WE TORE IT OUTTA THE HERO'S CAR.

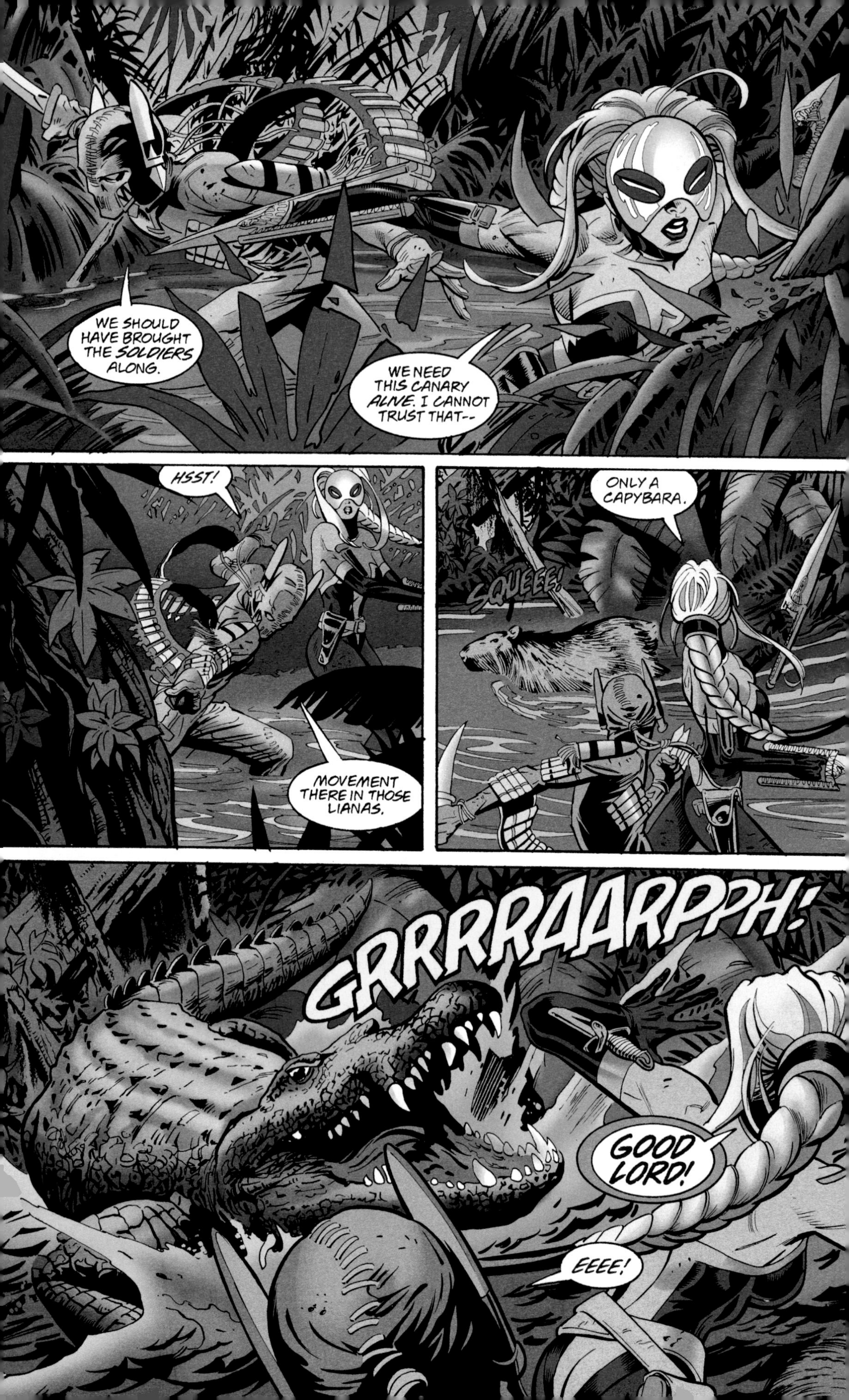
WE SHOULD HAVE BROUGHT THE SOLDIERS ALONG.
WE NEED THIS CANARY ALIVE. I CANNOT TRUST THAT--
HSST!
MOVEMENT THERE IN THOSE LIANAS.
ONLY A CAPYBARA.
SQUEEE!
GRRRRAARPPH!
GOOD LORD!
EEEE!

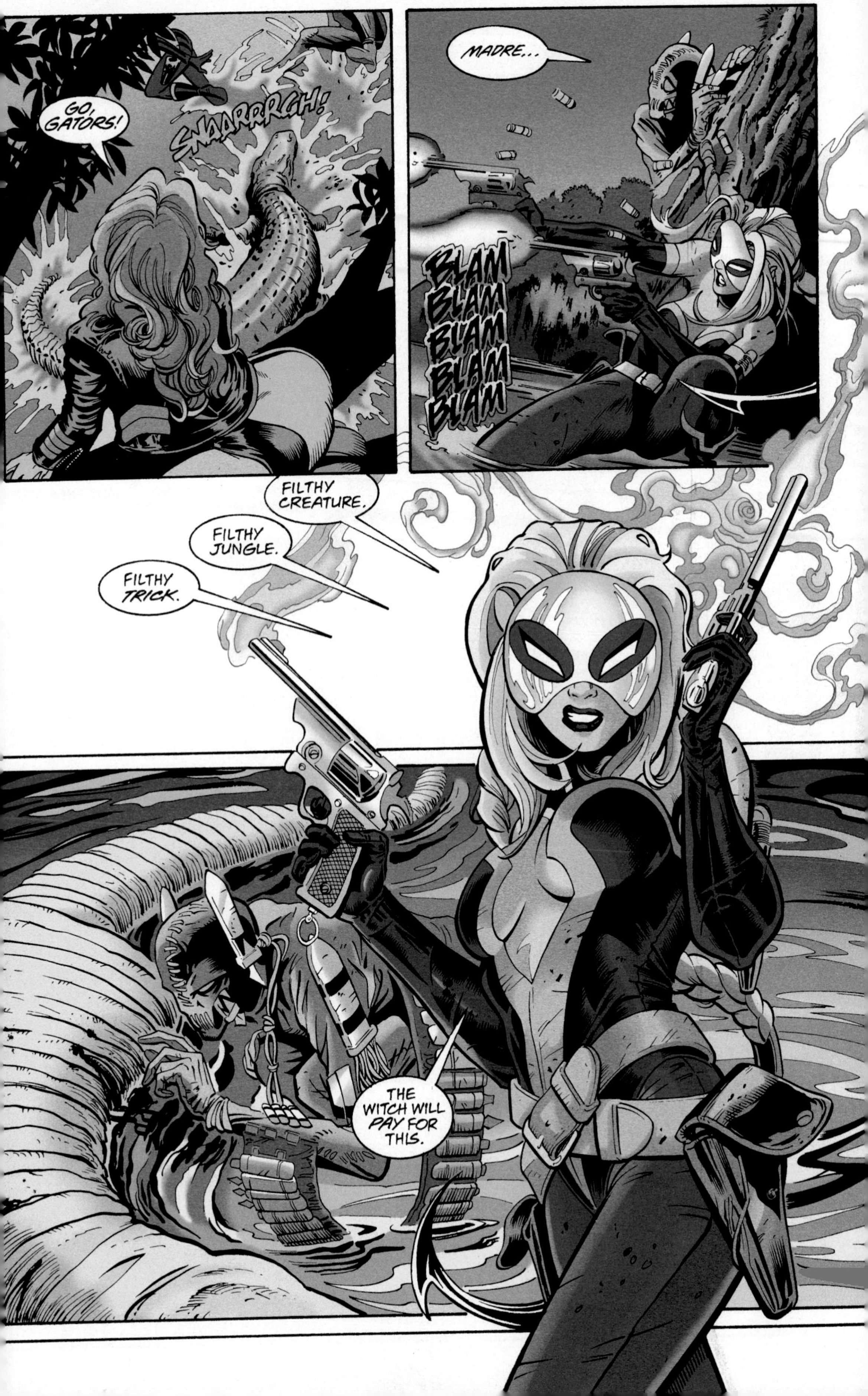
GO, GATORS!
SNAARRRGH!
MADRE...
BLAM BLAM BLAM BLAM BLAM BLAM
FILTHY CREATURE.
FILTHY JUNGLE.
FILTHY TRICK.
THE WITCH WILL PAY FOR THIS.

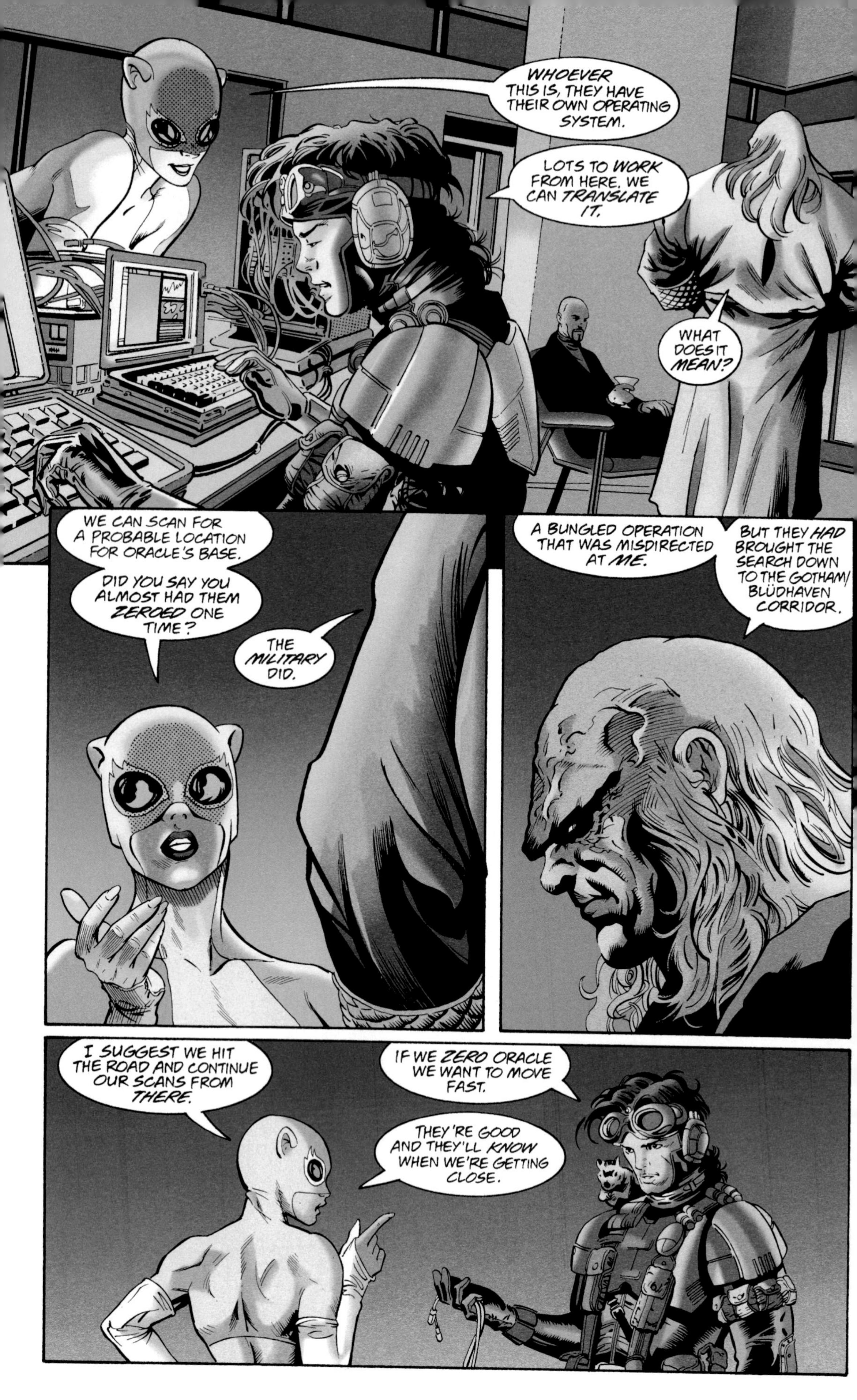
WHOEVER THIS IS, THEY HAVE THEIR OWN OPERATING SYSTEM.
LOTS TO WORK FROM HERE. WE CAN TRANSLATE IT.
WHAT DOES IT MEAN?
WE CAN SCAN FOR A PROBABLE LOCATION FOR ORACLE'S BASE.
DID YOU SAY YOU ALMOST HAD THEM ZEROED ONE TIME?
THE MILITARY DID.
A BUNGLED OPERATION THAT WAS MISDIRECTED AT ME.
BUT THEY HAD BROUGHT THE SEARCH DOWN TO THE GOTHAM/ BLÜDHAVEN CORRIDOR.
I SUGGEST WE HIT THE ROAD AND CONTINUE OUR SCANS FROM THERE.
IF WE ZERO ORACLE WE WANT TO MOVE FAST.
THEY'RE GOOD AND THEY'LL KNOW WHEN WE'RE GETTING CLOSE.

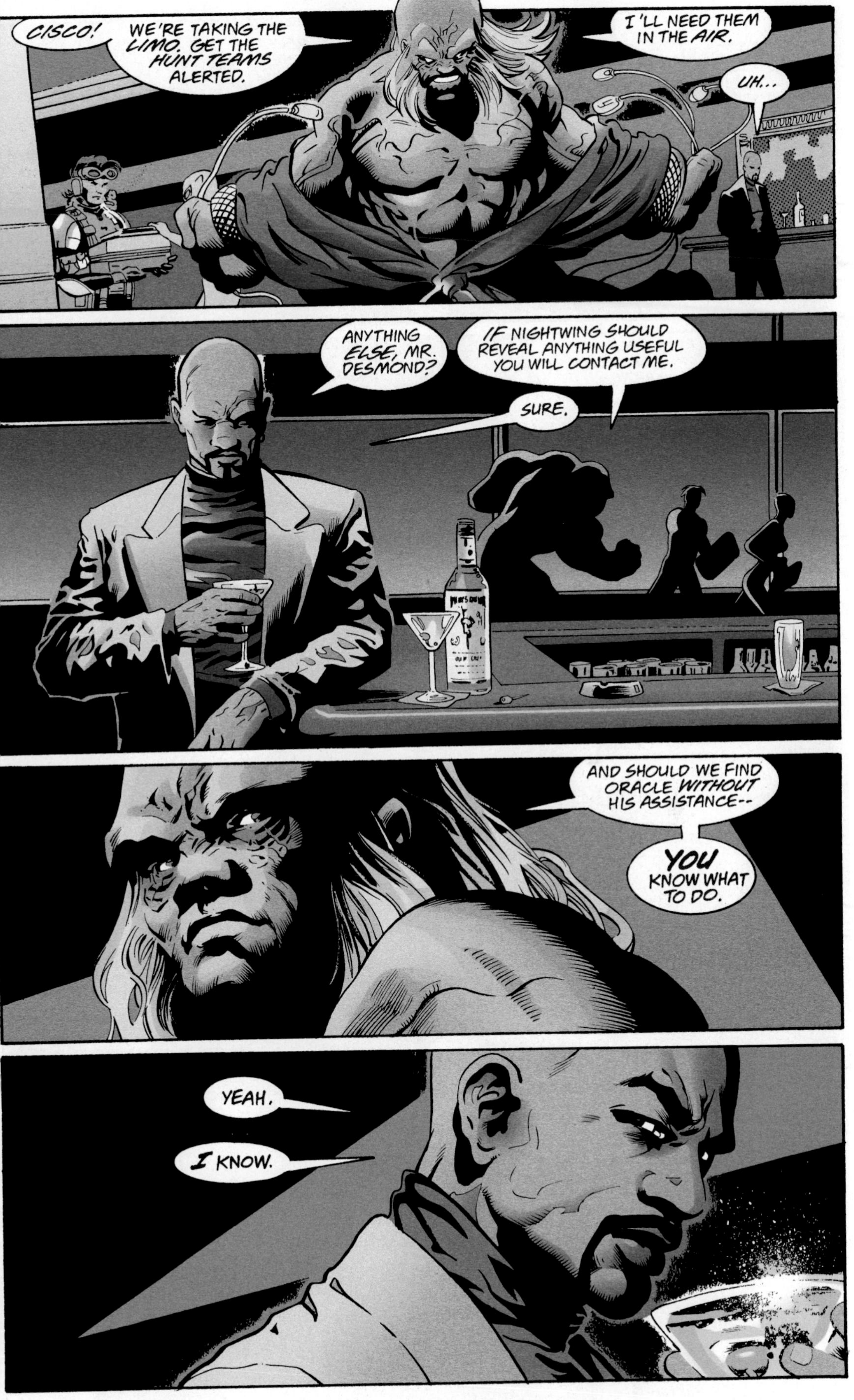

CISCO!
WE'RE TAKING THE LIMO. GET THE HUNT TEAMS ALERTED.
I'LL NEED THEM IN THE AIR.
UH...
ANYTHING ELSE, MR. DESMOND?
IF NIGHTWING SHOULD REVEAL ANYTHING USEFUL YOU WILL CONTACT ME.
SURE.
AND SHOULD WE FIND ORACLE WITHOUT HIS ASSISTANCE--
YOU KNOW WHAT TO DO.
YEAH.
I KNOW.

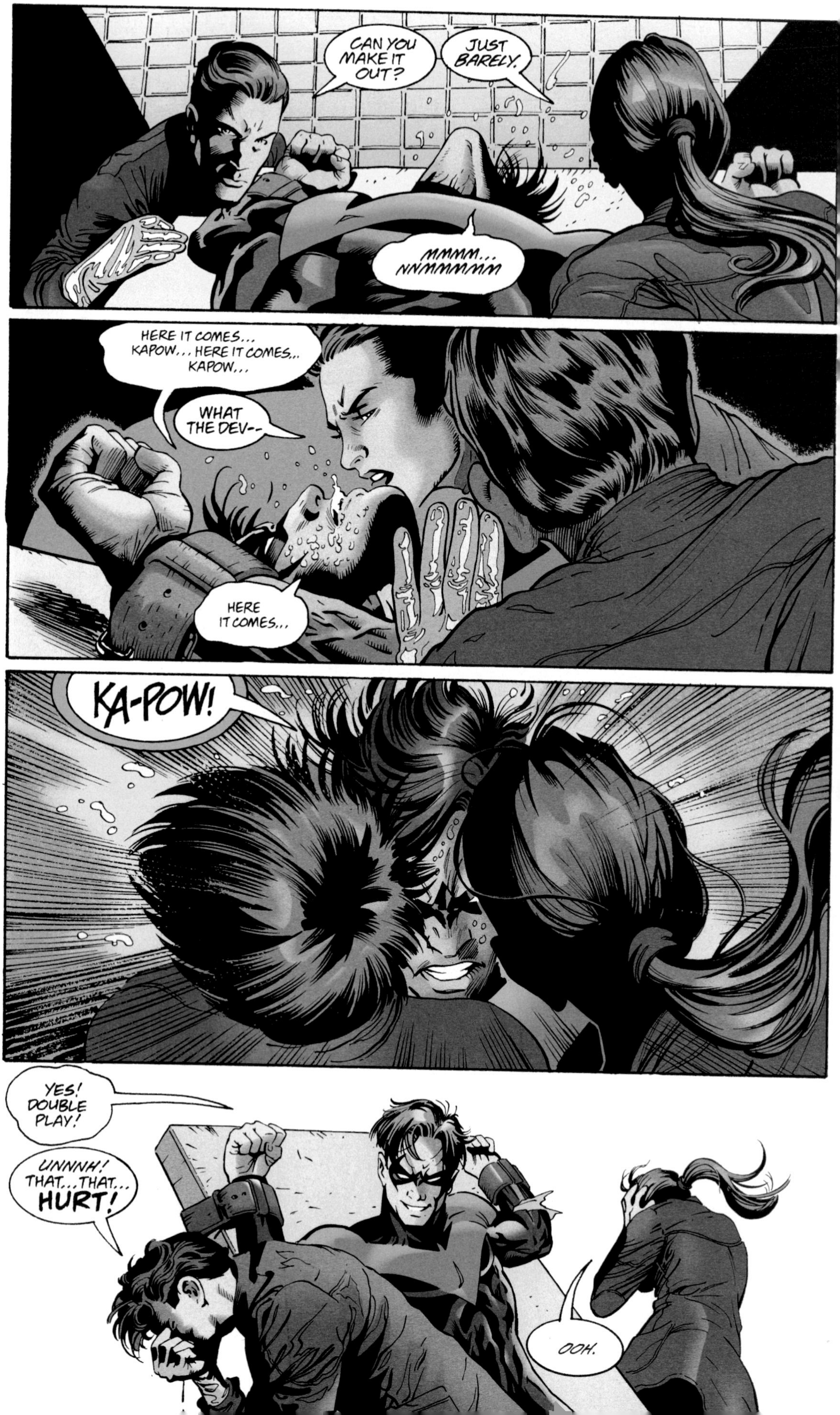
CAN YOU MAKE IT OUT?
JUST BARELY.
MMMM... NNMMMMMM
HERE IT COMES... KAPOW... HERE IT COMES... KAPOW...
WHAT THE DEV--
HERE IT COMES...
KA-POW!
YES! DOUBLE PLAY!
UNNNH! THAT...THAT... HURT!
OOH.

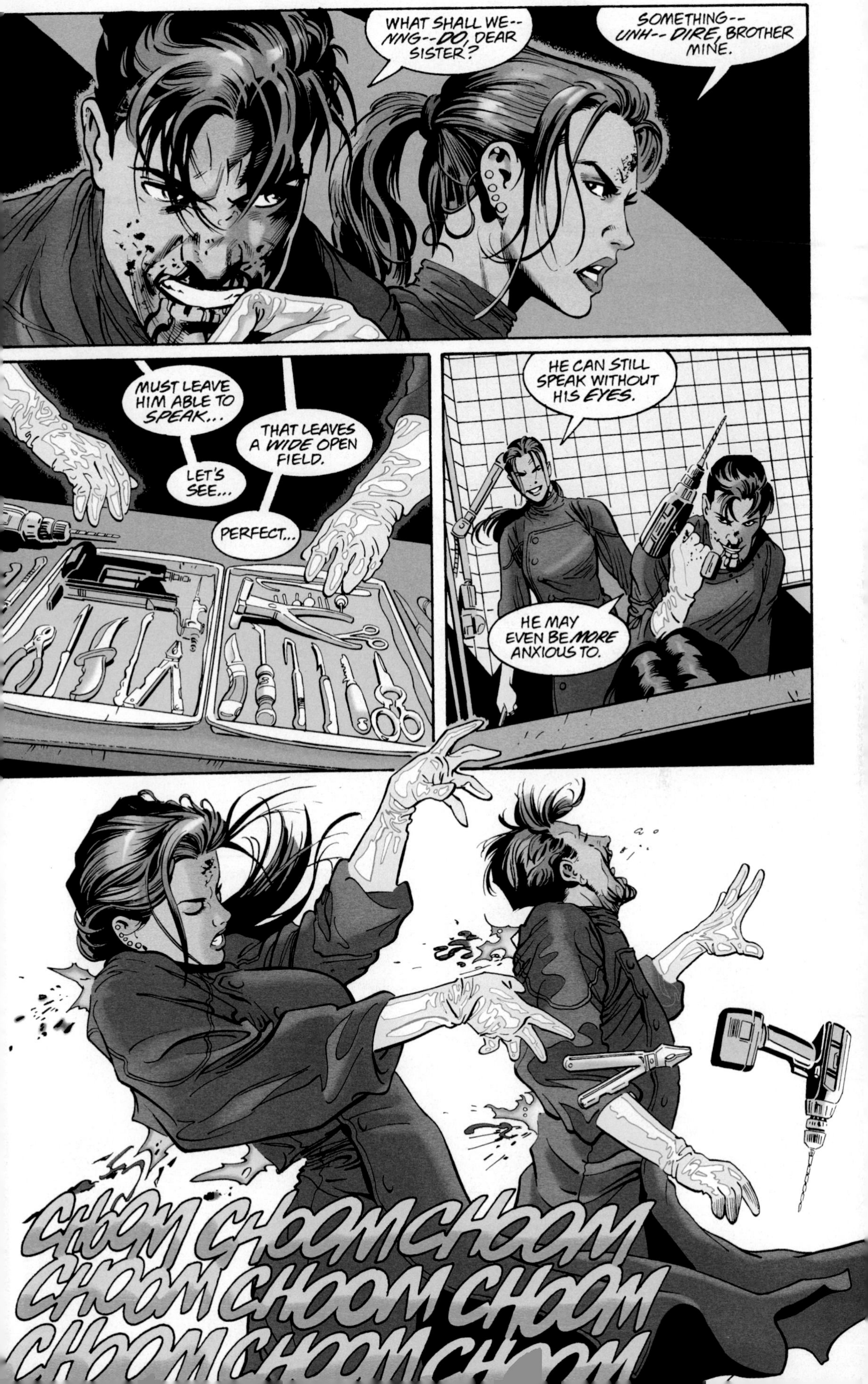

WHAT SHALL WE--
NNG--DO, DEAR SISTER?
SOMETHING--
UNH--DIRE, BROTHER MINE.
MUST LEAVE HIM ABLE TO SPEAK...
LET'S SEE...
THAT LEAVES A WIDE OPEN FIELD.
PERFECT...
HE CAN STILL SPEAK WITHOUT HIS EYES.
HE MAY EVEN BE MORE ANXIOUS TO.
CHOOM CHOOM CHOOM
CHOOM CHOOM CHOOM
CHOOM CHOOM CHOOM

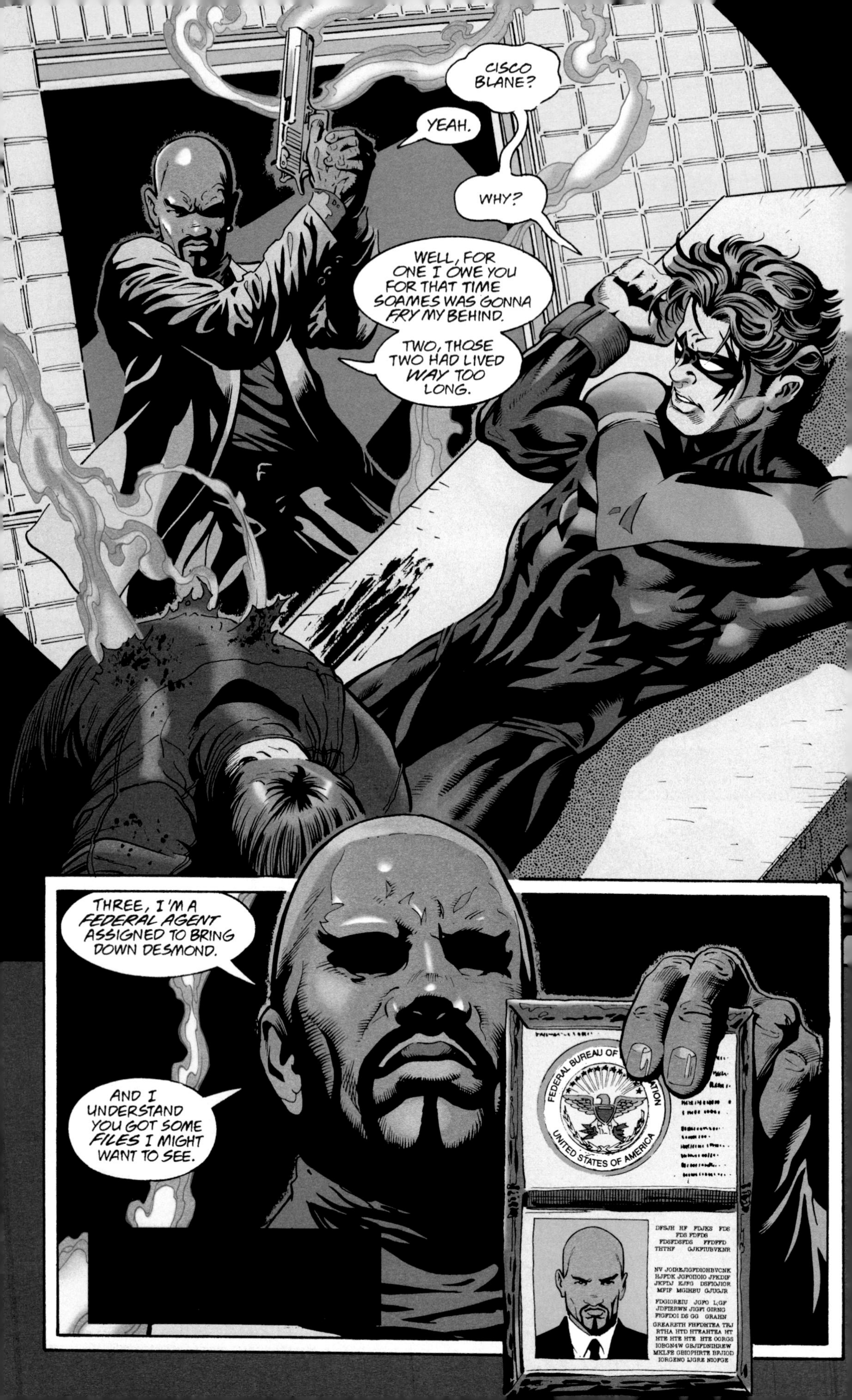
CISCO BLANE?
YEAH.
WHY?
WELL, FOR ONE I OWE YOU FOR THAT TIME SOAMES WAS GONNA *FRY* MY BEHIND.
TWO, THOSE TWO HAD LIVED *WAY* TOO LONG.
THREE, I'M A *FEDERAL AGENT* ASSIGNED TO BRING DOWN DESMOND.
AND I UNDERSTAND YOU GOT SOME *FILES* I MIGHT WANT TO SEE.
UNITED STATES OF AMERICA
[redacted]

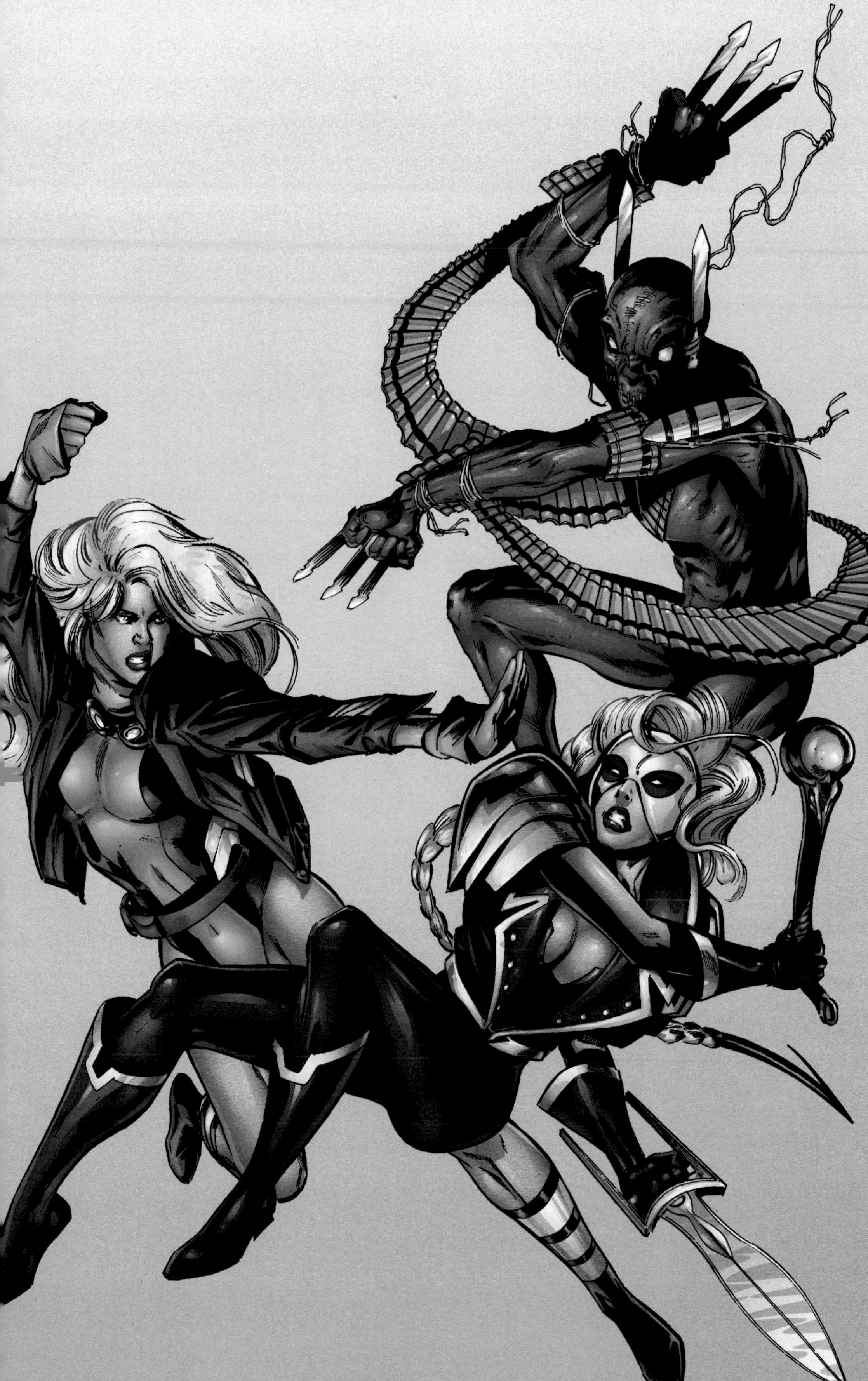

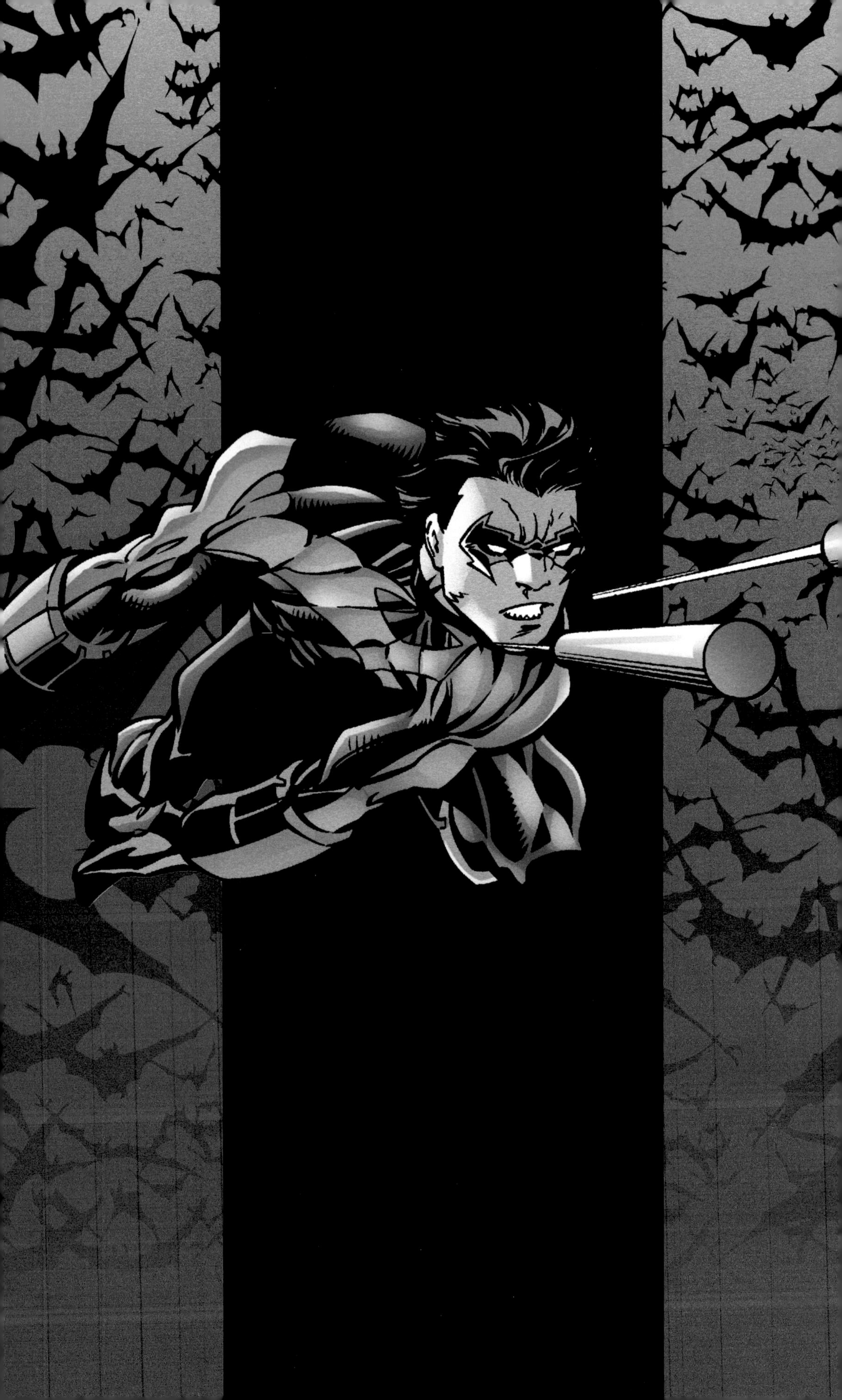

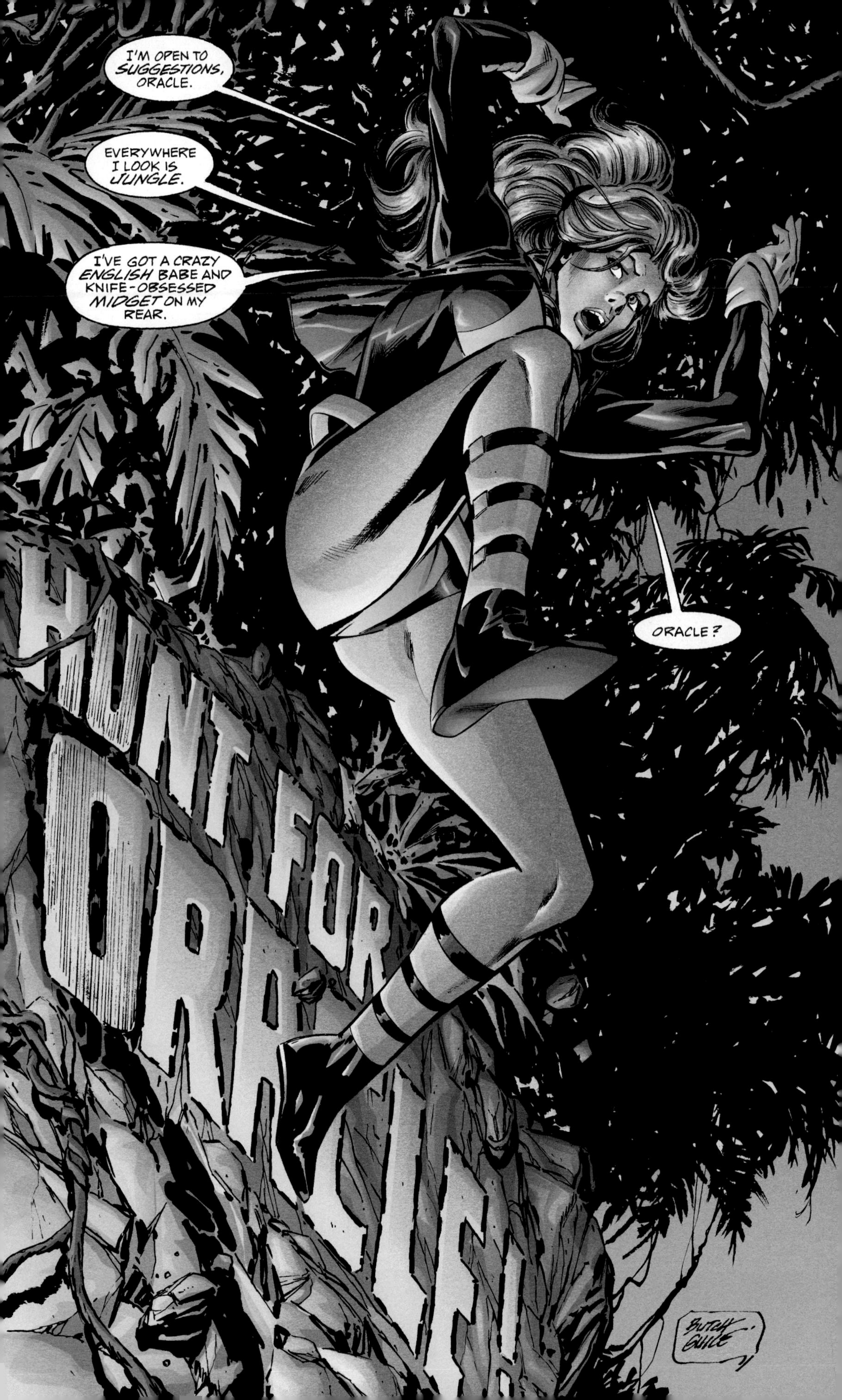
I'M OPEN TO SUGGESTIONS, ORACLE.
EVERYWHERE I LOOK IS JUNGLE.
I'VE GOT A CRAZY ENGLISH BABE AND KNIFE-OBSESSED MIDGET ON MY REAR.
ORACLE?
HUNT FOR ORACLE
BUTCH GUICE

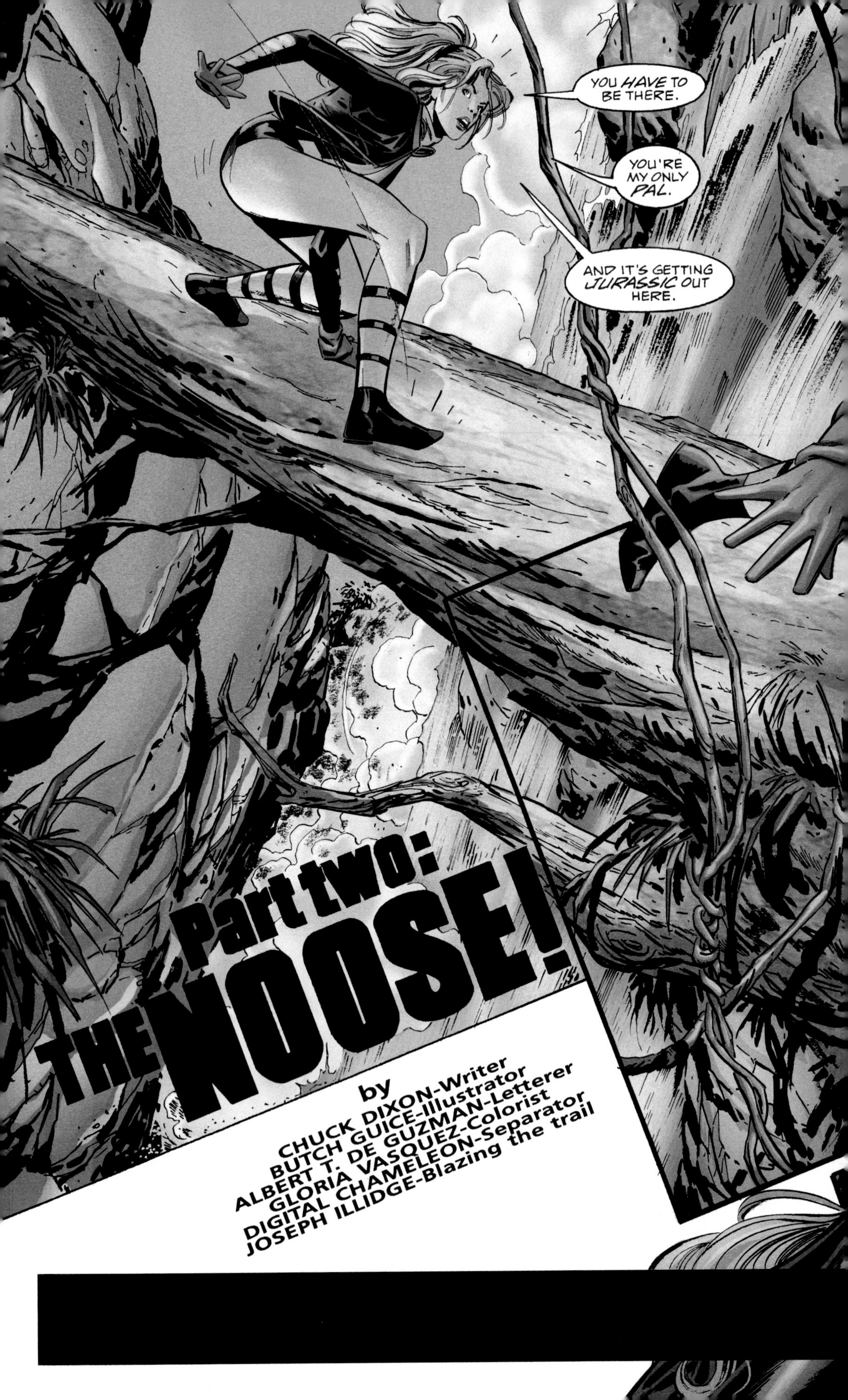

YOU HAVE TO BE THERE.
YOU'RE MY ONLY PAL.
AND IT'S GETTING JURASSIC OUT HERE.
Part two: THE NOOSE!
by
CHUCK DIXON-Writer
BUTCH GUICE-Illustrator
ALBERT T. DE GUZMAN-Letterer
GLORIA VASQUEZ-Colorist
DIGITAL CHAMELEON-Separator
JOSEPH ILLIDGE-Blazing the trail

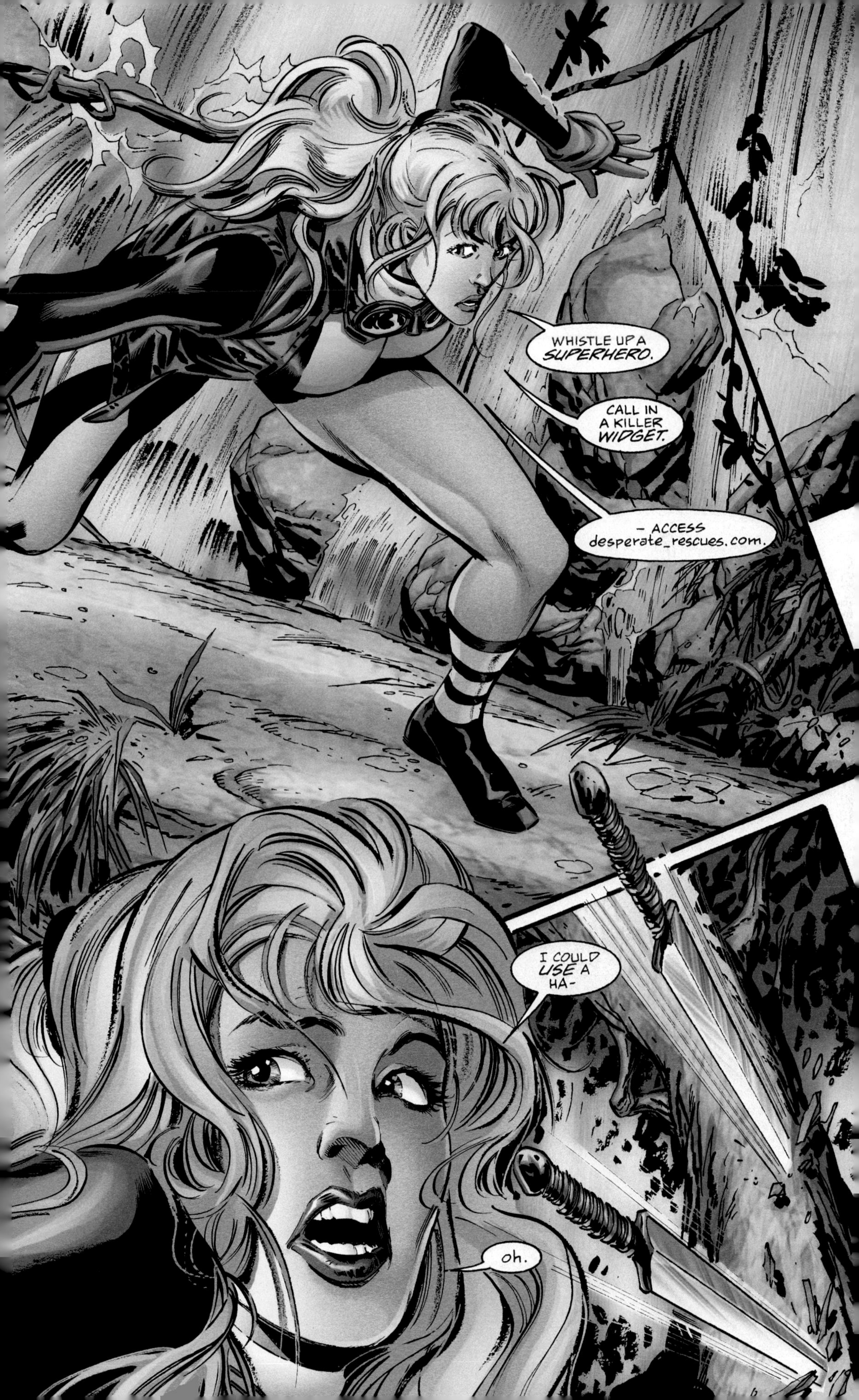
WHISTLE UP A SUPERHERO.
CALL IN A KILLER WIDGET.
- ACCESS desperate_rescues.com.
I COULD USE A HA-
oh.

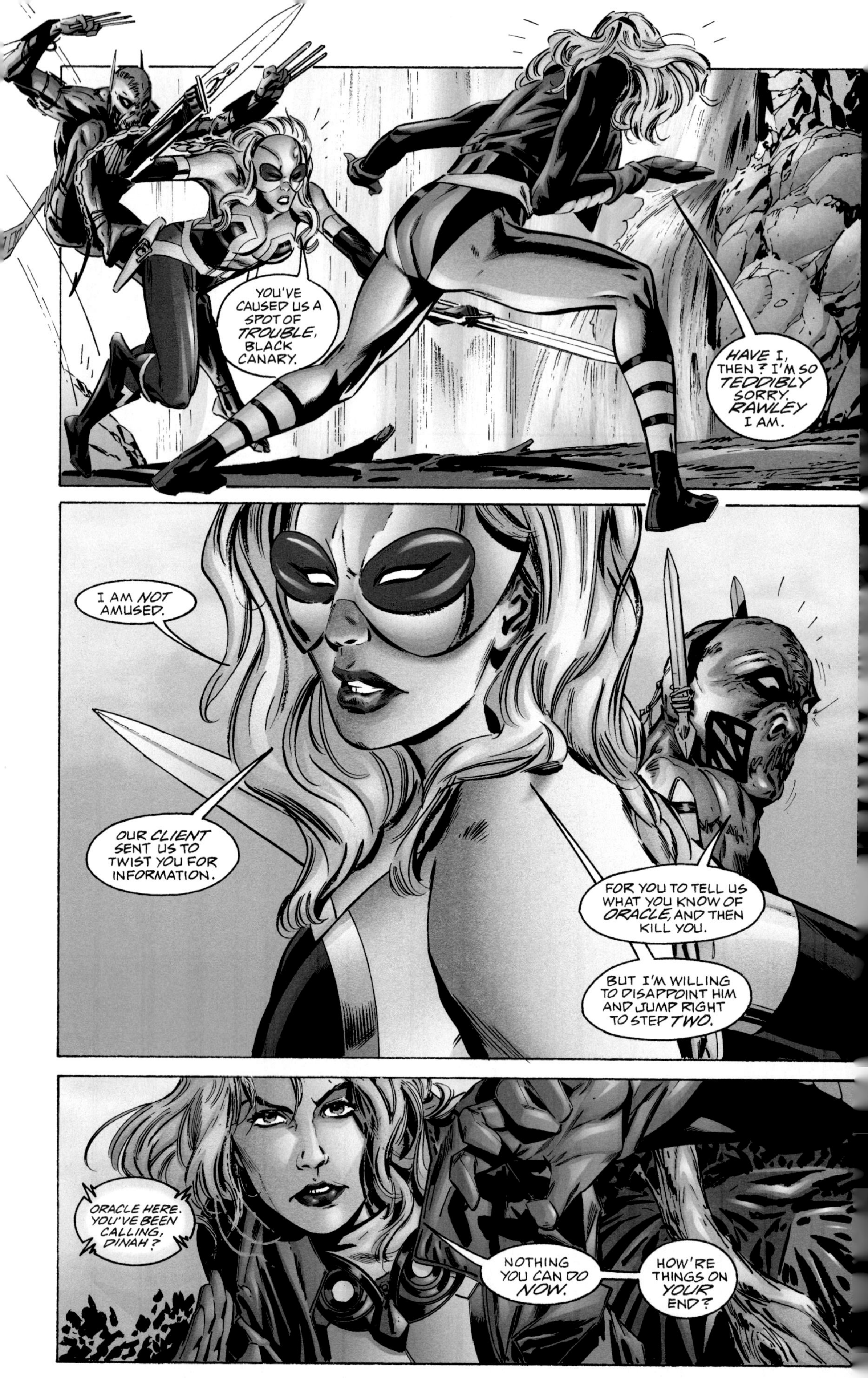
YOU'VE CAUSED US A SPOT OF TROUBLE, BLACK CANARY.
HAVE I, THEN? I'M SO TEDDIBLY SORRY. RAWLEY I AM.
I AM NOT AMUSED.
OUR CLIENT SENT US TO TWIST YOU FOR INFORMATION.
FOR YOU TO TELL US WHAT YOU KNOW OF ORACLE, AND THEN KILL YOU.
BUT I'M WILLING TO DISAPPOINT HIM AND JUMP RIGHT TO STEP TWO.
ORACLE HERE. YOU'VE BEEN CALLING, DINAH?
NOTHING YOU CAN DO NOW.
HOW'RE THINGS ON YOUR END?

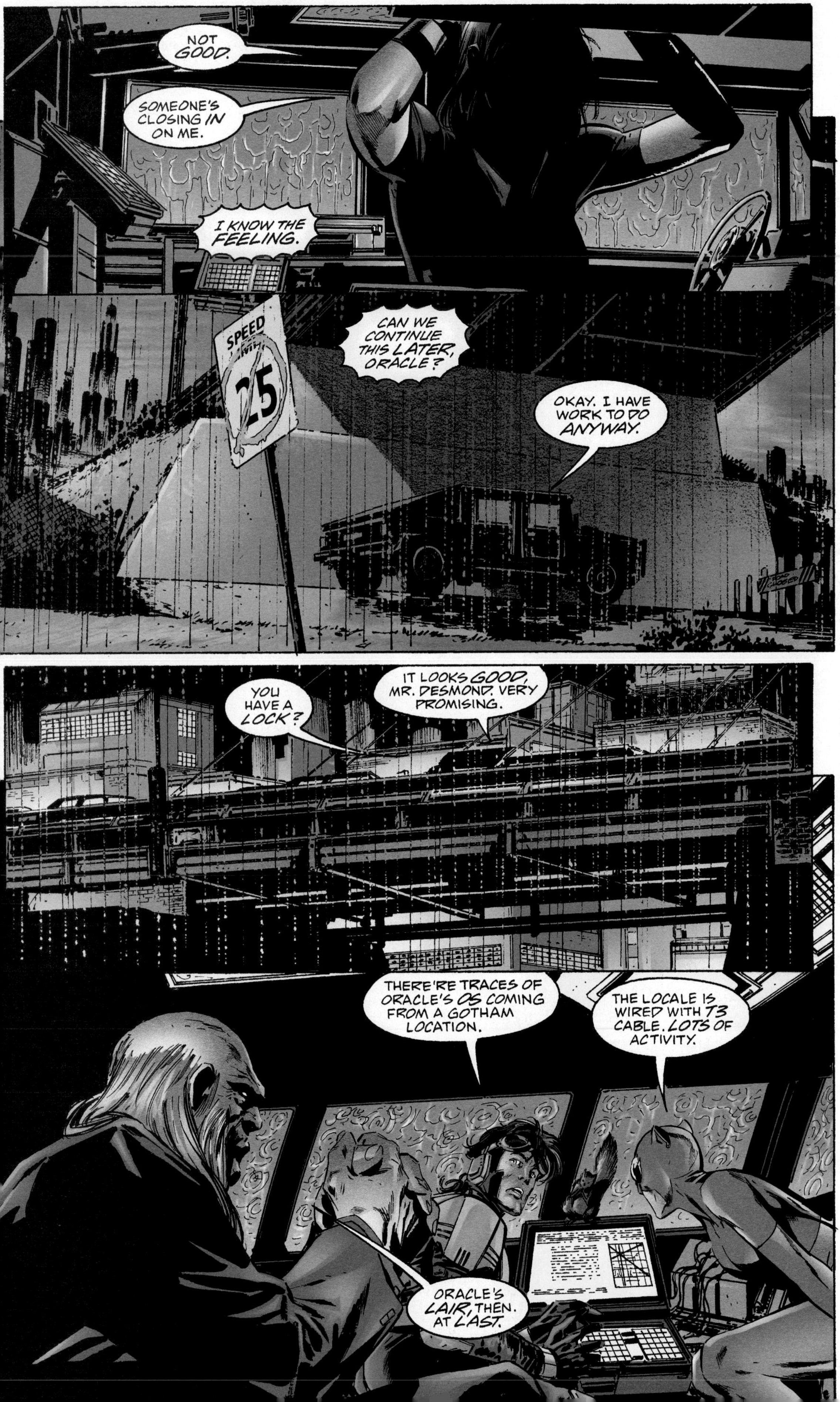
NOT GOOD.
SOMEONE'S CLOSING IN ON ME.
I KNOW THE FEELING.
SPEED
25
CAN WE CONTINUE THIS LATER, ORACLE?
OKAY. I HAVE WORK TO DO ANYWAY.
YOU HAVE A LOCK?
IT LOOKS GOOD, MR. DESMOND. VERY PROMISING.
THERE'RE TRACES OF ORACLE'S OS COMING FROM A GOTHAM LOCATION.
THE LOCALE IS WIRED WITH T3 CABLE. LOTS OF ACTIVITY.
ORACLE'S LAIR, THEN. AT LAST.

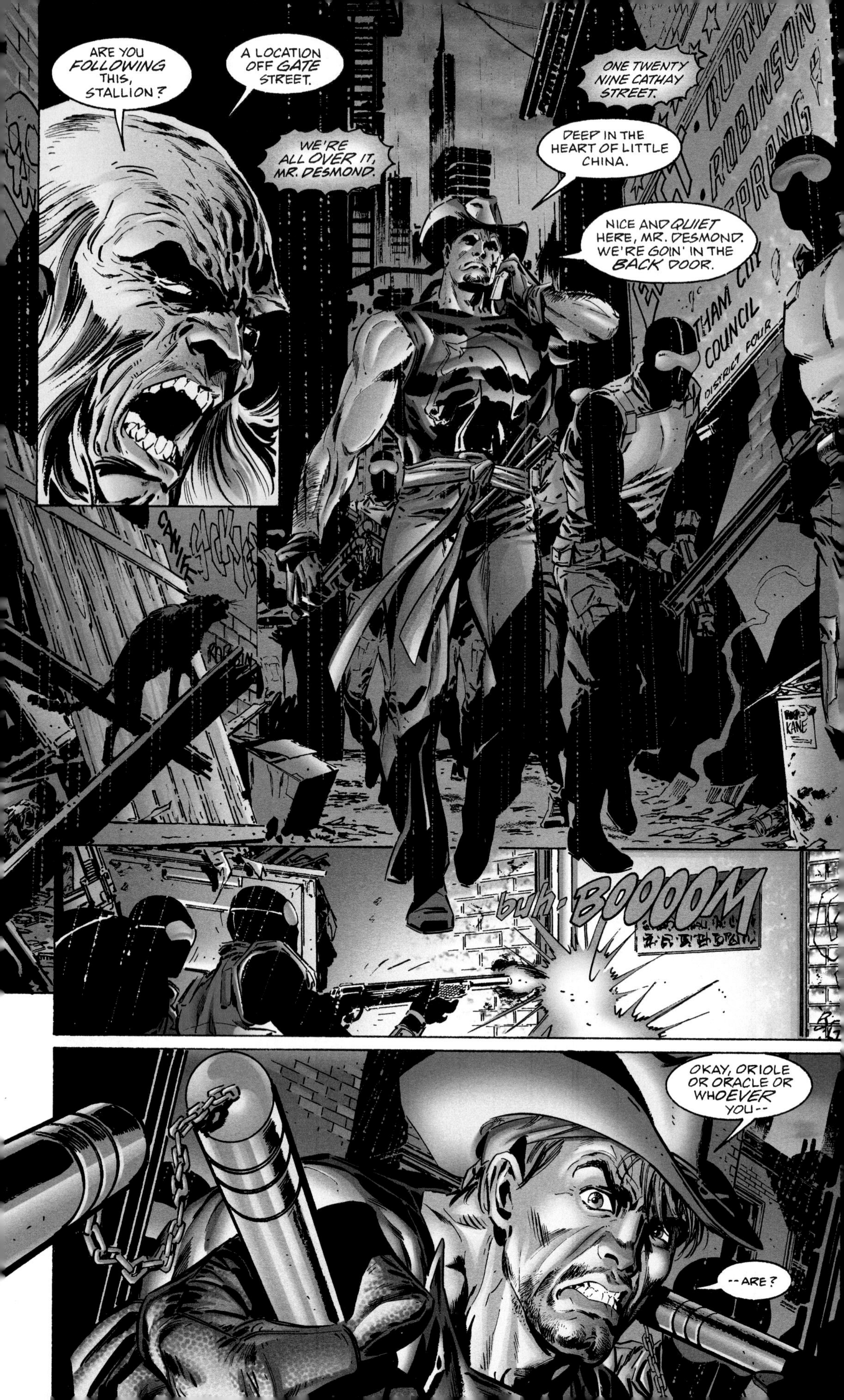
ARE YOU FOLLOWING THIS, STALLION?
A LOCATION OFF GATE STREET.
WE'RE ALL OVER IT, MR. DESMOND.
ONE TWENTY NINE CATHAY STREET.
DEEP IN THE HEART OF LITTLE CHINA.
NICE AND QUIET HERE, MR. DESMOND. WE'RE GOIN' IN THE BACK DOOR.
GOTHAM CITY COUNCIL DISTRICT FOUR
ROBINSON
KANE
buh-BOOOOM
OKAY, ORIOLE OR ORACLE OR WHOEVER YOU--
--ARE?

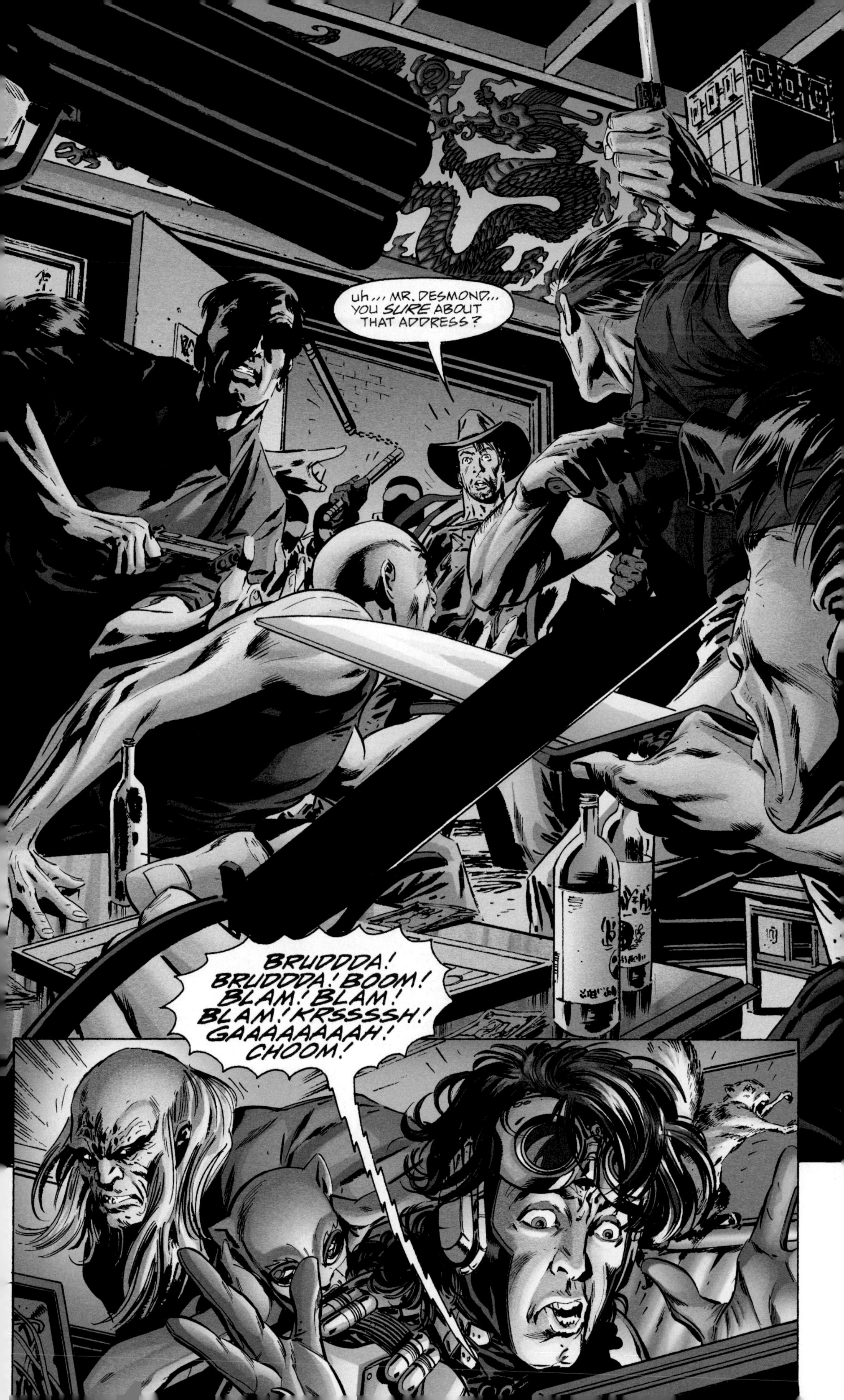
uh... MR. DESMOND... YOU SURE ABOUT THAT ADDRESS?
BRUDDDA! BRUDDDA! BOOM! BLAM! BLAM! BLAM! KRSSSSH! GAAAAAAAAH! CHOOM!

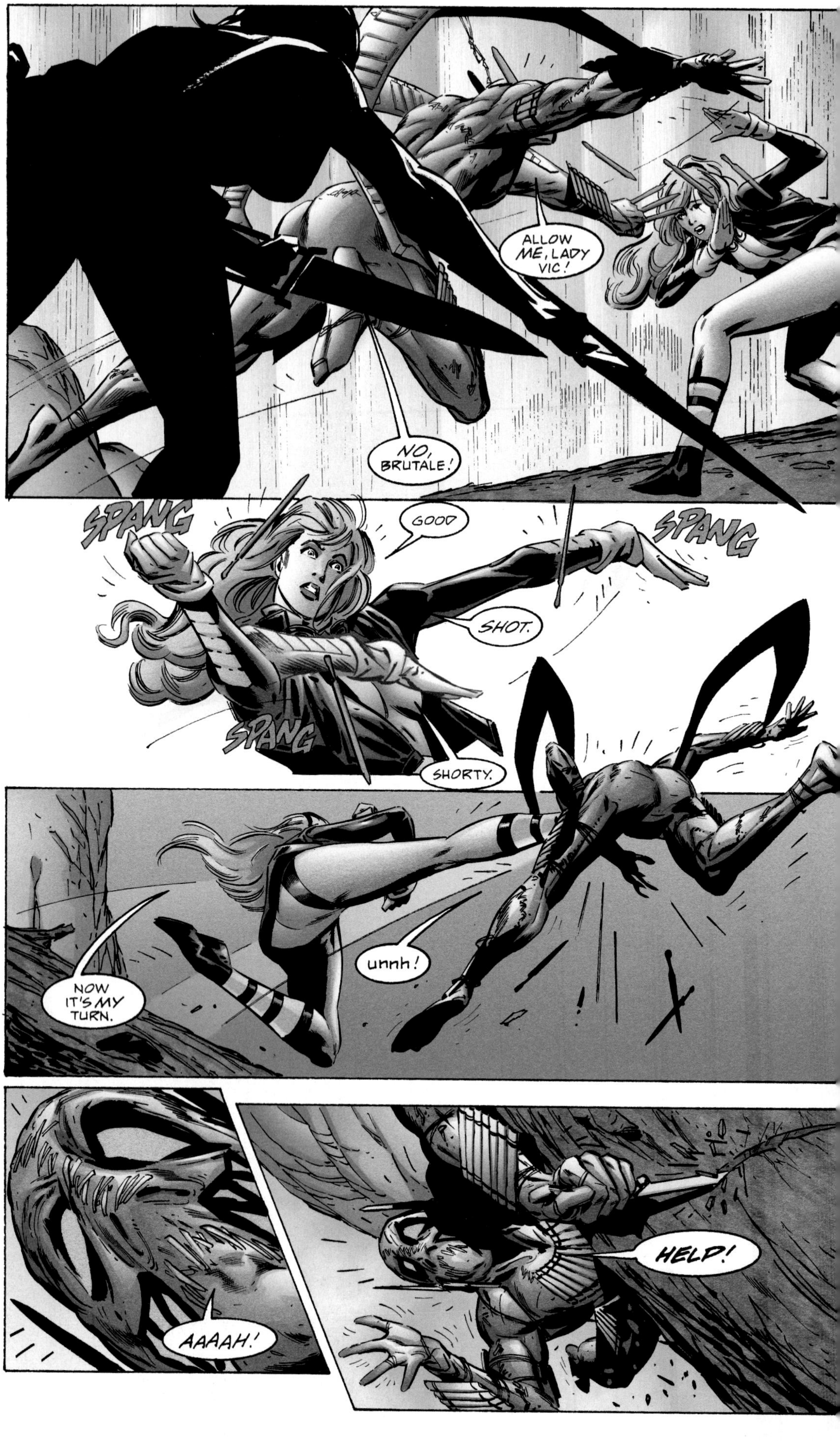
ALLOW ME, LADY VIC!
NO, BRUTALE!
SPANG
GOOD
SPANG
SHOT.
SPANG
SHORTY.
NOW IT'S MY TURN.
unnh!
AAAAH!
HELP!

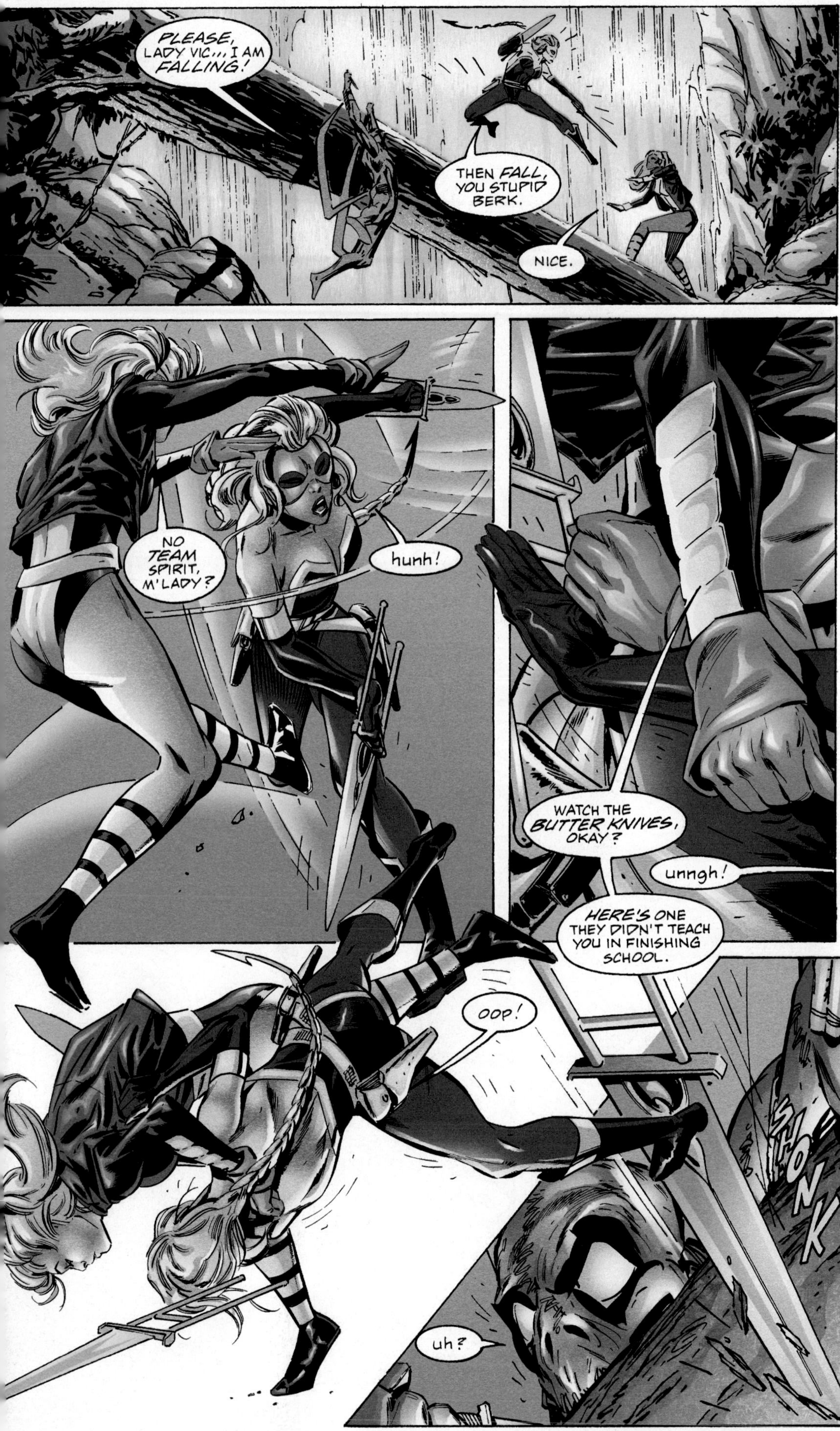
PLEASE, LADY VIC... I AM FALLING!
THEN FALL, YOU STUPID BERK.
NICE.
NO TEAM SPIRIT, M'LADY?
hunh!
WATCH THE BUTTER KNIVES, OKAY?
unngh!
HERE'S ONE THEY DIDN'T TEACH YOU IN FINISHING SCHOOL.
oop!
SHONK
uh?

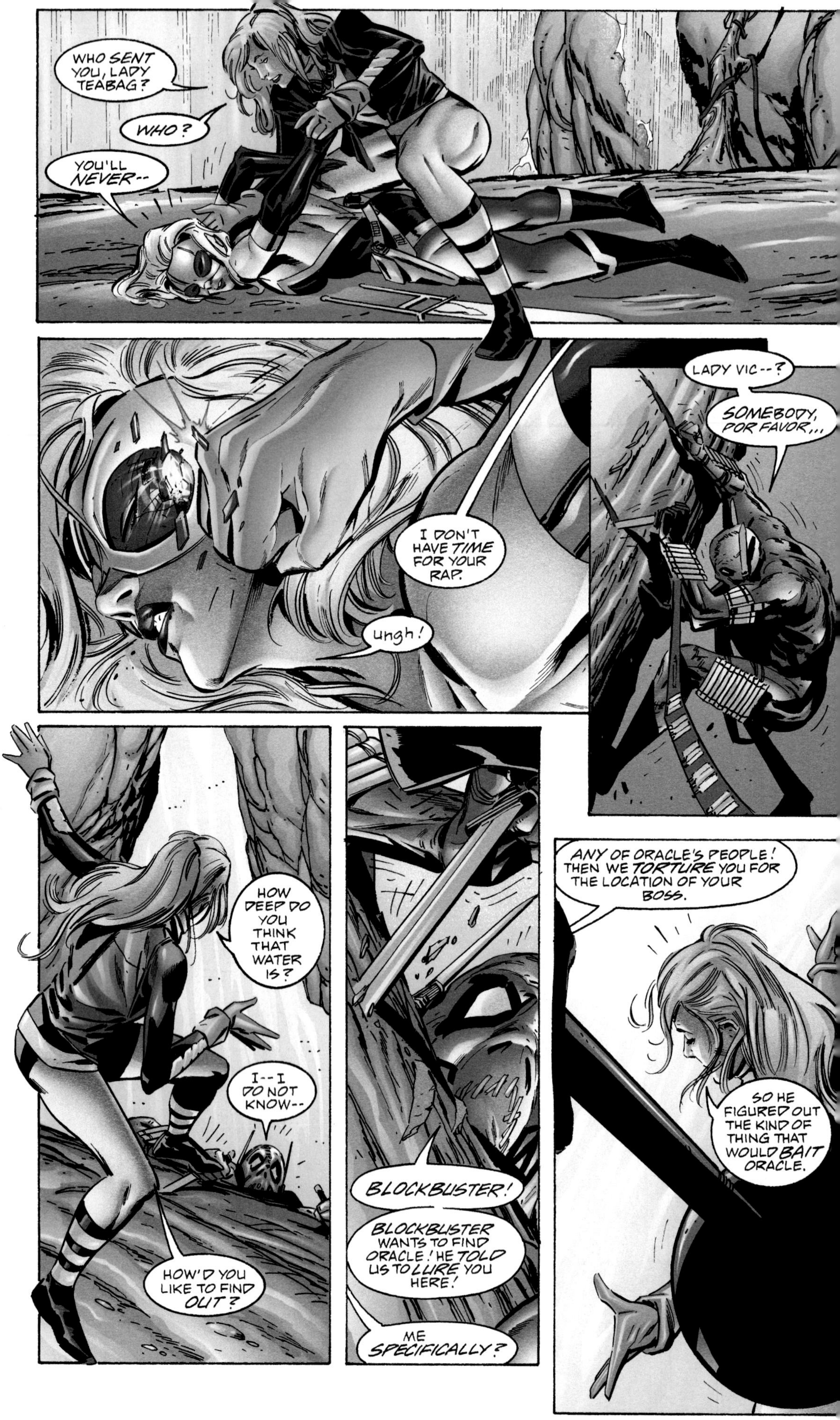
WHO SENT YOU, LADY TEABAG?
WHO?
YOU'LL NEVER--
I DON'T HAVE TIME FOR YOUR RAP.
unGH!
LADY VIC--?
SOMEBODY, POR FAVOR...
HOW DEEP DO YOU THINK THAT WATER IS?
I--I DO NOT KNOW--
HOW'D YOU LIKE TO FIND OUT?
BLOCKBUSTER!
BLOCKBUSTER WANTS TO FIND ORACLE! HE TOLD US TO LURE YOU HERE!
ME SPECIFICALLY?
ANY OF ORACLE'S PEOPLE! THEN WE TORTURE YOU FOR THE LOCATION OF YOUR BOSS.
SO HE FIGURED OUT THE KIND OF THING THAT WOULD BAIT ORACLE.

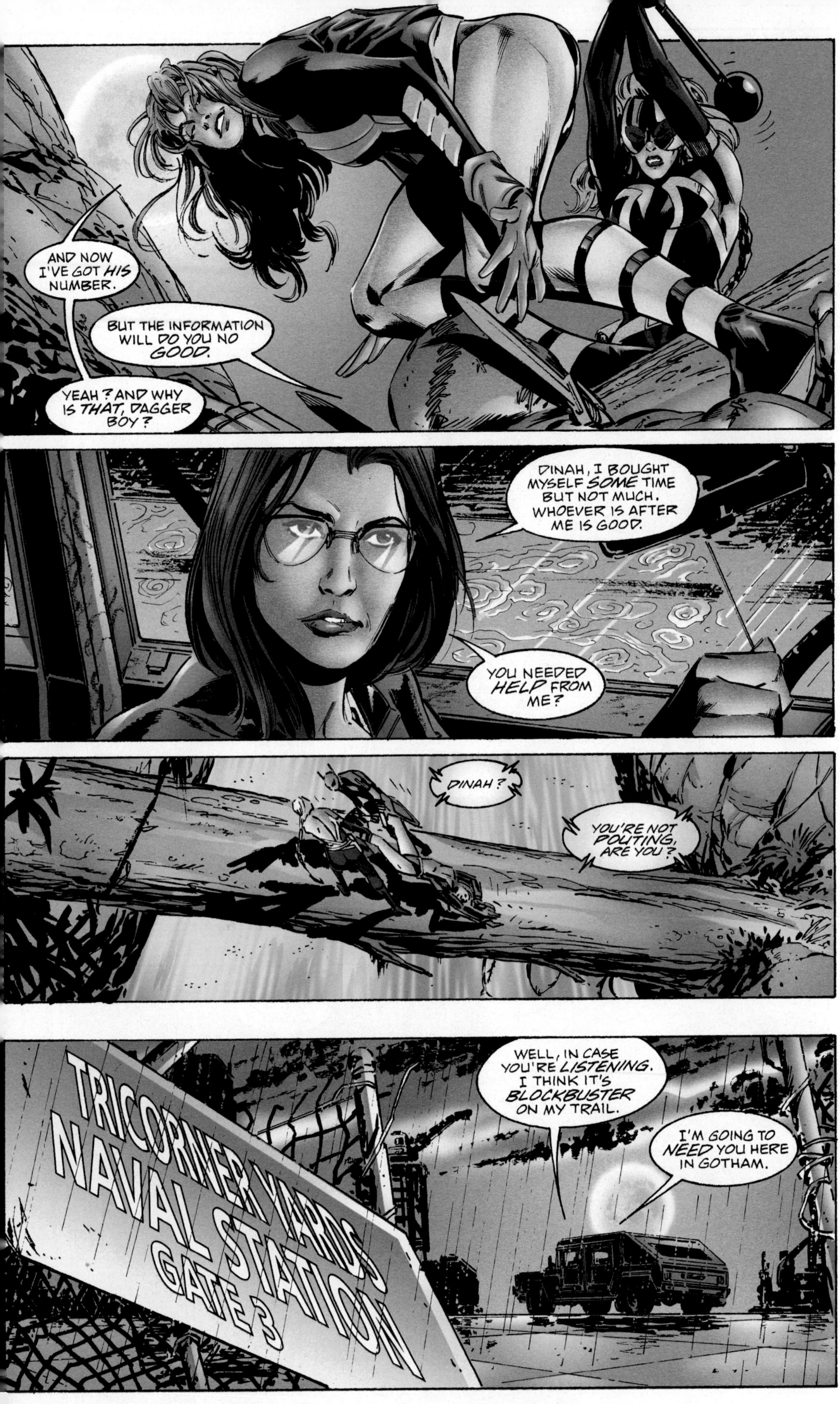
AND NOW I'VE GOT HIS NUMBER.
BUT THE INFORMATION WILL DO YOU NO GOOD.
YEAH? AND WHY IS THAT, DAGGER BOY?
DINAH, I BOUGHT MYSELF SOME TIME BUT NOT MUCH. WHOEVER IS AFTER ME IS GOOD.
YOU NEEDED HELP FROM ME?
DINAH?
YOU'RE NOT POUTING, ARE YOU?
TRICORNER YARDS NAVAL STATION GATE 3
WELL, IN CASE YOU'RE LISTENING. I THINK IT'S BLOCKBUSTER ON MY TRAIL.
I'M GOING TO NEED YOU HERE IN GOTHAM.

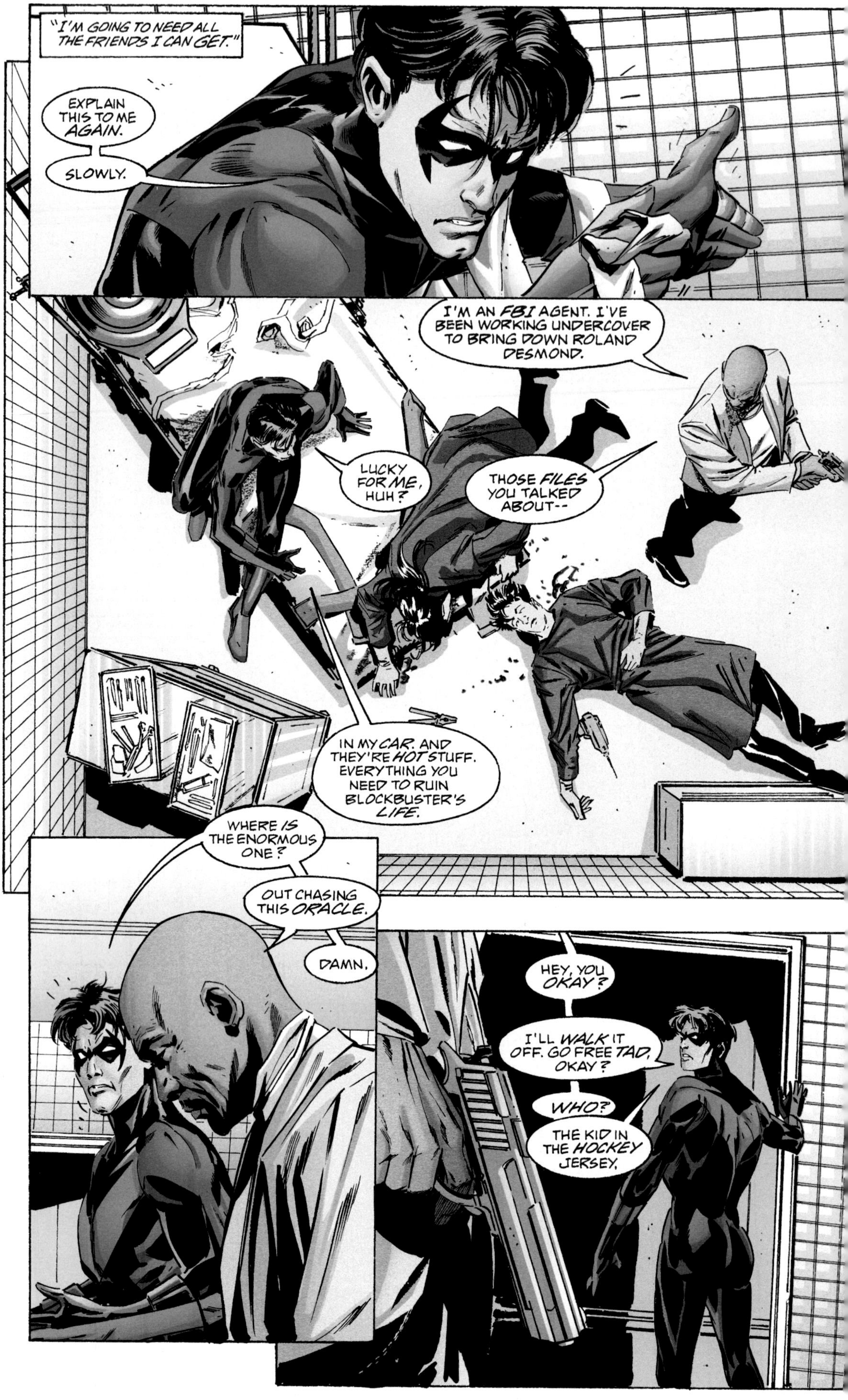
"I'M GOING TO NEED ALL THE FRIENDS I CAN GET."
EXPLAIN THIS TO ME AGAIN.
SLOWLY.
I'M AN FBI AGENT. I'VE BEEN WORKING UNDERCOVER TO BRING DOWN ROLAND DESMOND.
LUCKY FOR ME, HUH?
THOSE FILES YOU TALKED ABOUT--
IN MY CAR. AND THEY'RE HOT STUFF. EVERYTHING YOU NEED TO RUIN BLOCKBUSTER'S LIFE.
WHERE IS THE ENORMOUS ONE?
OUT CHASING THIS ORACLE.
DAMN.
HEY, YOU OKAY?
I'LL WALK IT OFF. GO FREE TAD, OKAY?
WHO?
THE KID IN THE HOCKEY JERSEY.

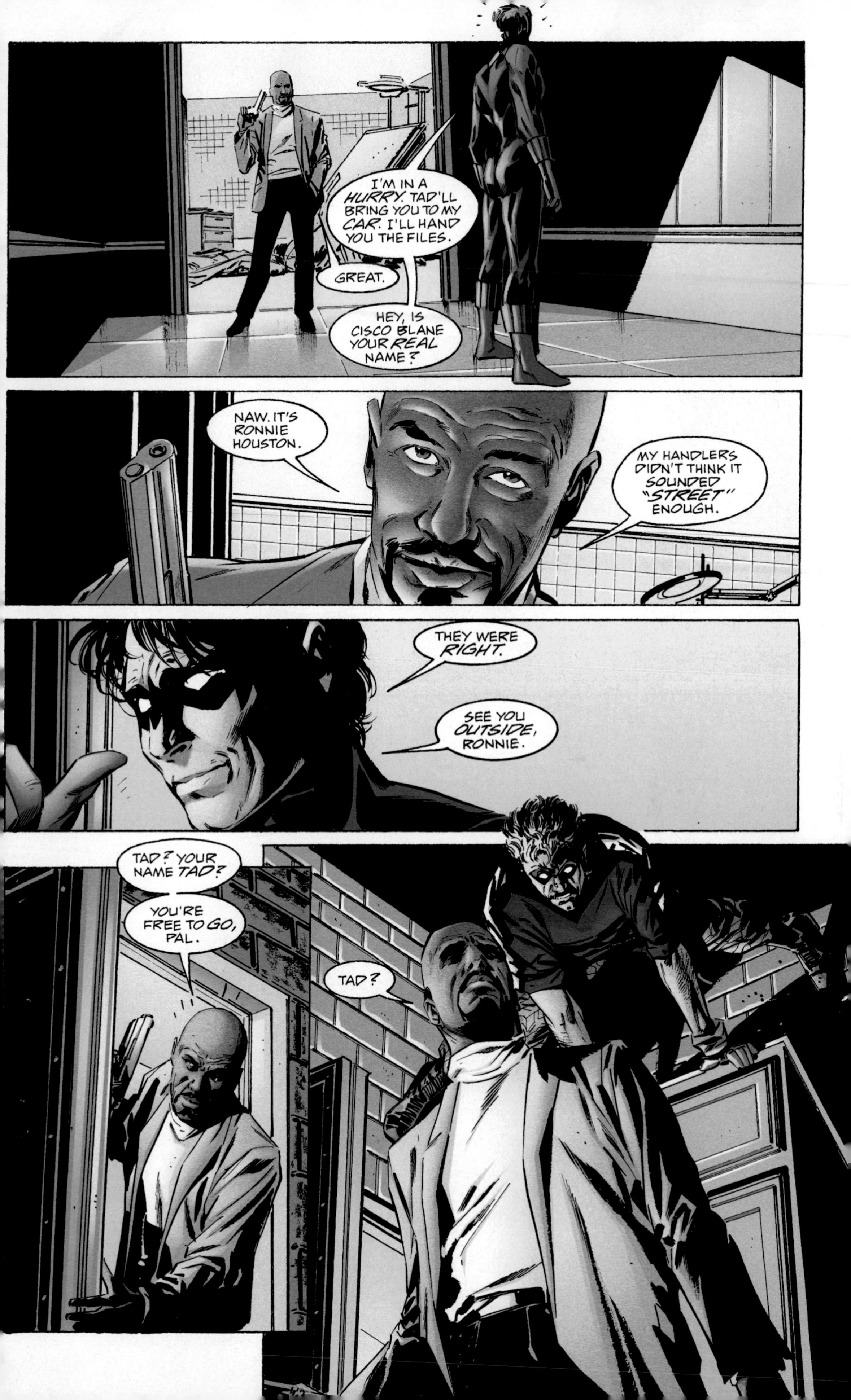
I'M IN A HURRY. TAD'LL BRING YOU TO MY CAR. I'LL HAND YOU THE FILES.
GREAT.
HEY, IS CISCO BLANE YOUR REAL NAME?
NAW. IT'S RONNIE HOUSTON.
MY HANDLERS DIDN'T THINK IT SOUNDED "STREET" ENOUGH.
THEY WERE RIGHT.
SEE YOU OUTSIDE, RONNIE.
TAD? YOUR NAME TAD?
YOU'RE FREE TO GO, PAL.
TAD?

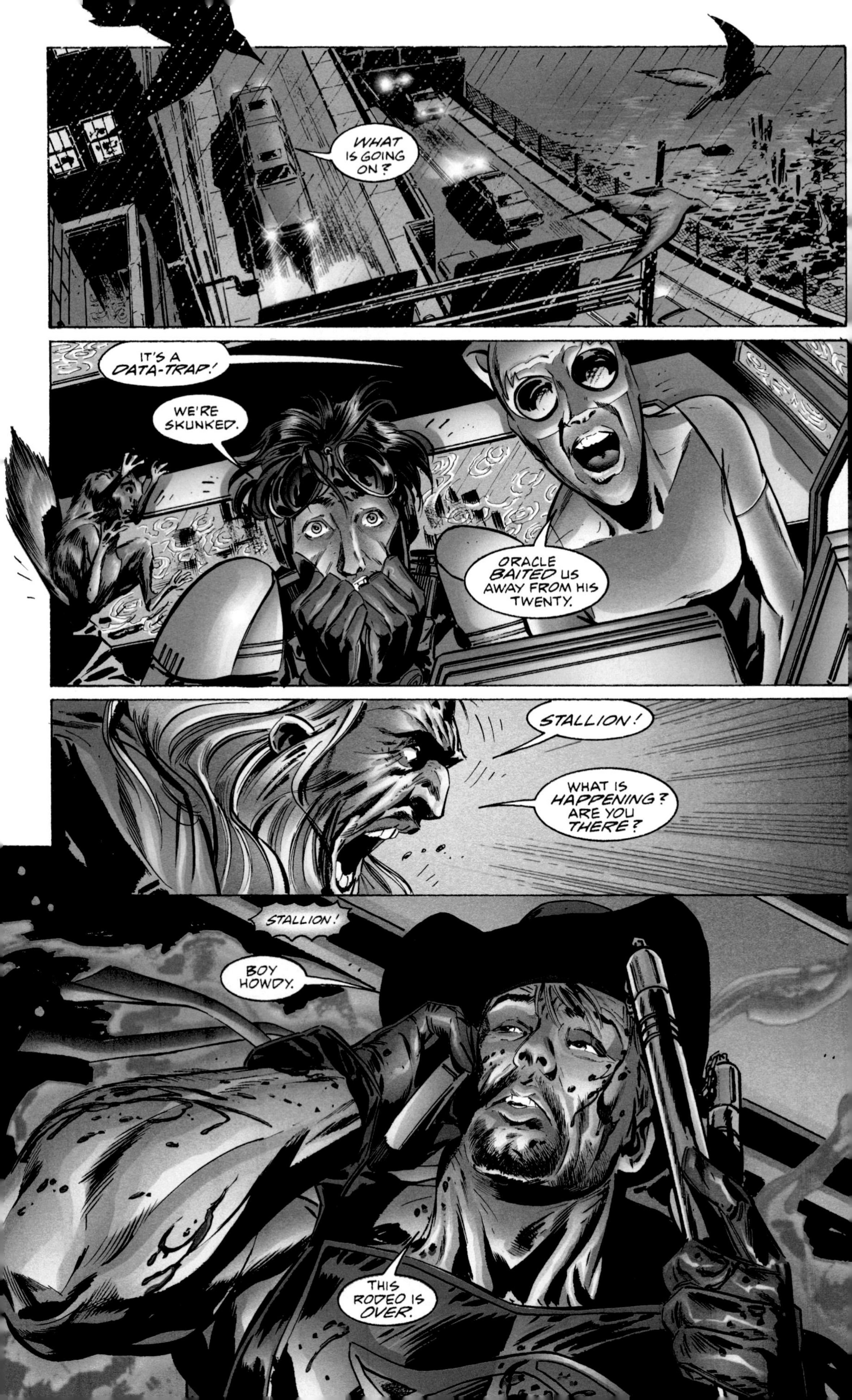
WHAT IS GOING ON?
IT'S A DATA-TRAP!
WE'RE SKUNKED.
ORACLE BAITED US AWAY FROM HIS TWENTY.
STALLION!
WHAT IS HAPPENING? ARE YOU THERE?
STALLION!
BOY HOWDY.
THIS RODEO IS OVER.

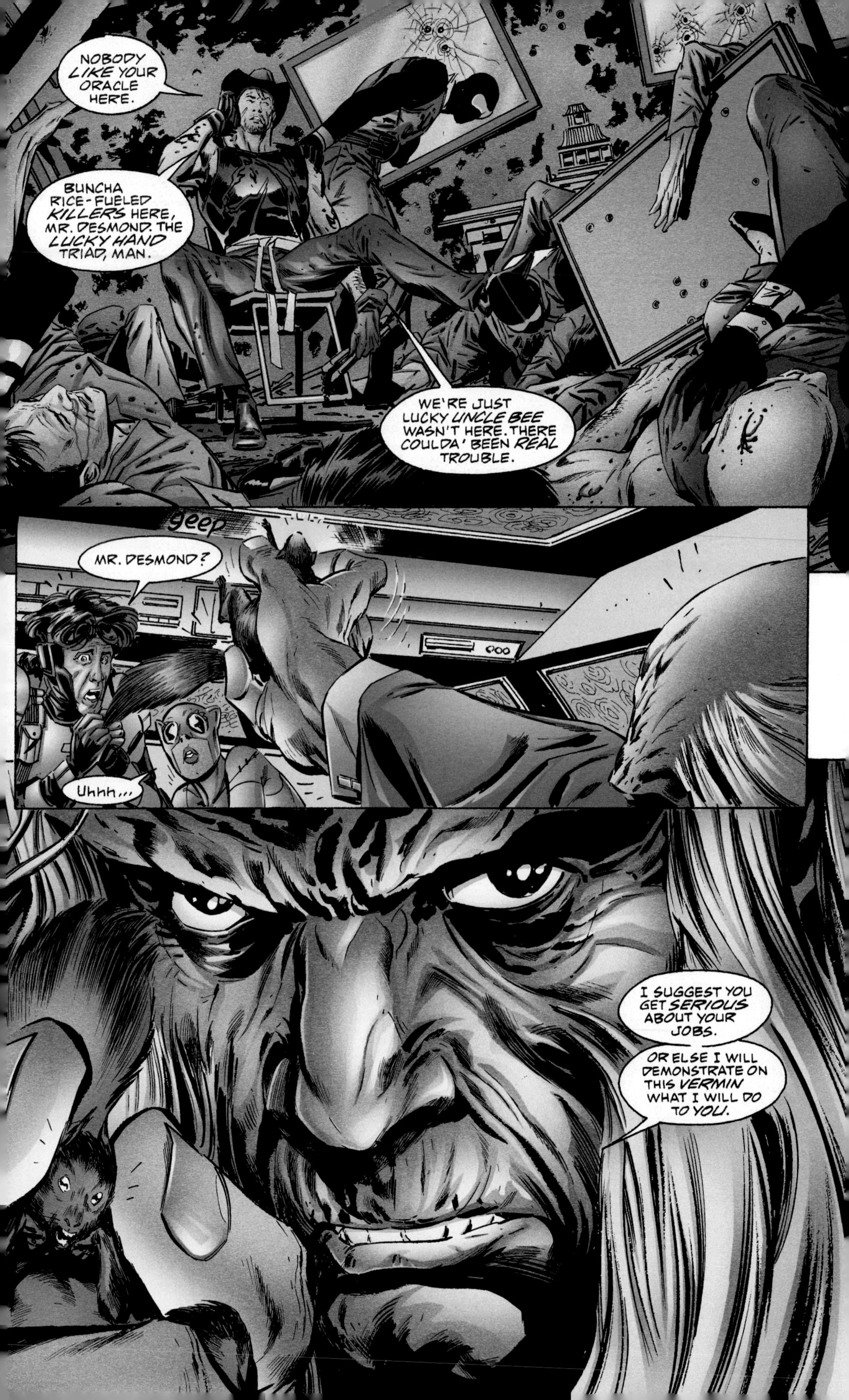
NOBODY LIKE YOUR ORACLE HERE.
BUNCHA RICE-FUELED KILLERS HERE, MR. DESMOND. THE LUCKY HAND TRIAD, MAN.
WE'RE JUST LUCKY UNCLE BEE WASN'T HERE. THERE COULDA' BEEN REAL TROUBLE.
geep
MR. DESMOND?
Uhhh...
I SUGGEST YOU GET SERIOUS ABOUT YOUR JOBS.
OR ELSE I WILL DEMONSTRATE ON THIS VERMIN WHAT I WILL DO TO YOU.

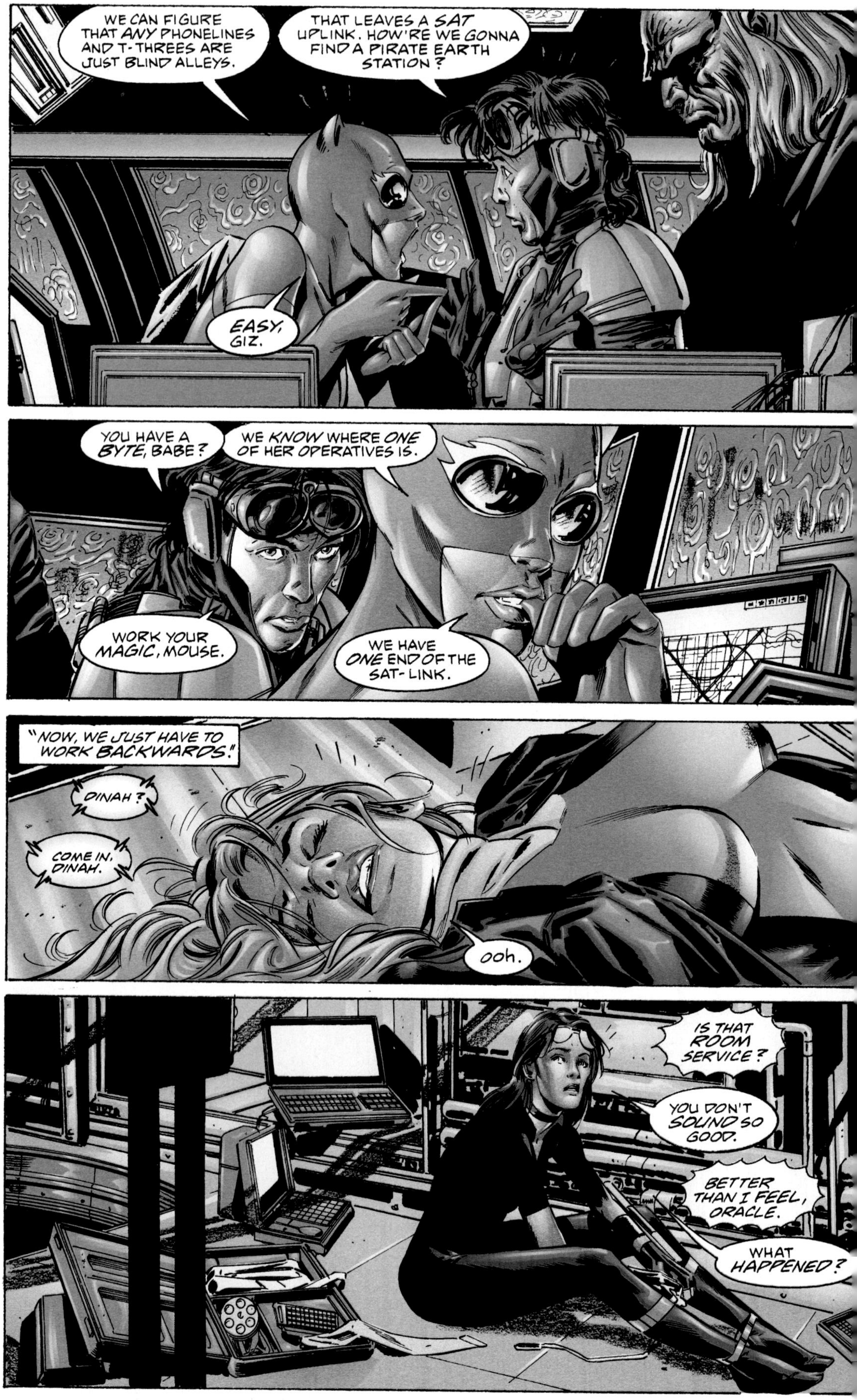

WE CAN FIGURE THAT ANY PHONELINES AND T-THREES ARE JUST BLIND ALLEYS.
THAT LEAVES A SAT UPLINK. HOW'RE WE GONNA FIND A PIRATE EARTH STATION?
EASY, GIZ.
YOU HAVE A BYTE, BABE?
WE KNOW WHERE ONE OF HER OPERATIVES IS.
WORK YOUR MAGIC, MOUSE.
WE HAVE ONE END OF THE SAT-LINK.
"NOW, WE JUST HAVE TO WORK BACKWARDS."
DINAH?
COME IN, DINAH.
ooh.
IS THAT ROOM SERVICE?
YOU DON'T SOUND SO GOOD.
BETTER THAN I FEEL, ORACLE.
WHAT HAPPENED?

I GOT SUCKER-PUNCHED BY SOME CHICK CALLING HERSELF *LADY VIC.*

THAT CINCHES IT.

IT *DOES?* CINCHES *WHAT?*

IT'S *BLOCKBUSTER.* LADY VIC IS ONE OF HIS FIRST CHOICES FOR MURDER.

WELL, THEY'RE *LOOKING* FOR YOU.

FOR ORACLE BY NAME?

I THINK THAT'S ALL THEY KNOW. LIKE YOU'RE AN URBAN *LEGEND* OR SOMETHING.

I'M GOING TO BREAK A RULE HERE.

HOW SOON CAN YOU GET BACK TO GOTHAM?

TO MY PLACE?

MY PLACE. WELL, MY *VACATION* HOME, ANYWAY.

YOU THINK THEY'LL *FIND* YOU, ORACLE?

I MIGHT HAVE TO LET THEM FIND ME.

HUH?

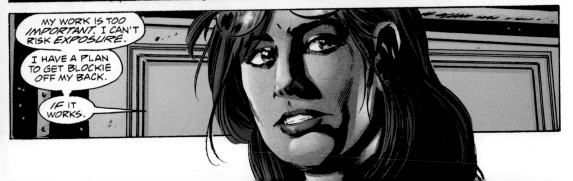

MY WORK IS TOO *IMPORTANT.* I CAN'T RISK *EXPOSURE.*

I HAVE A PLAN TO GET BLOCKIE OFF MY BACK.

IF IT WORKS.

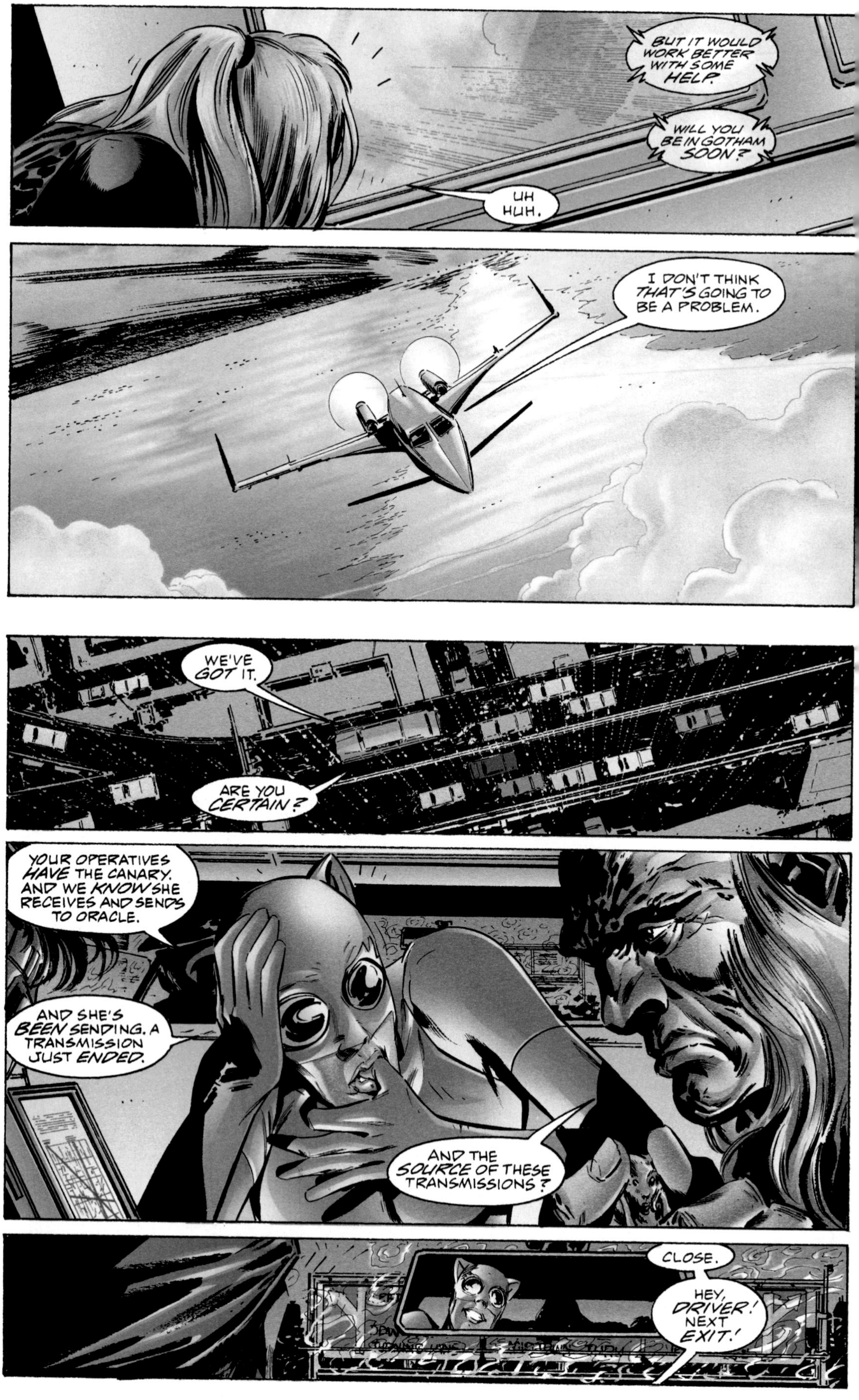
BUT IT WOULD WORK BETTER WITH SOME HELP.
WILL YOU BE IN GOTHAM SOON?
UH HUH.
I DON'T THINK THAT'S GOING TO BE A PROBLEM.
WE'VE GOT IT.
ARE YOU CERTAIN?
YOUR OPERATIVES HAVE THE CANARY. AND WE KNOW SHE RECEIVES AND SENDS TO ORACLE.
AND SHE'S BEEN SENDING. A TRANSMISSION JUST ENDED.
AND THE SOURCE OF THESE TRANSMISSIONS?
CLOSE.
HEY, DRIVER! NEXT EXIT!

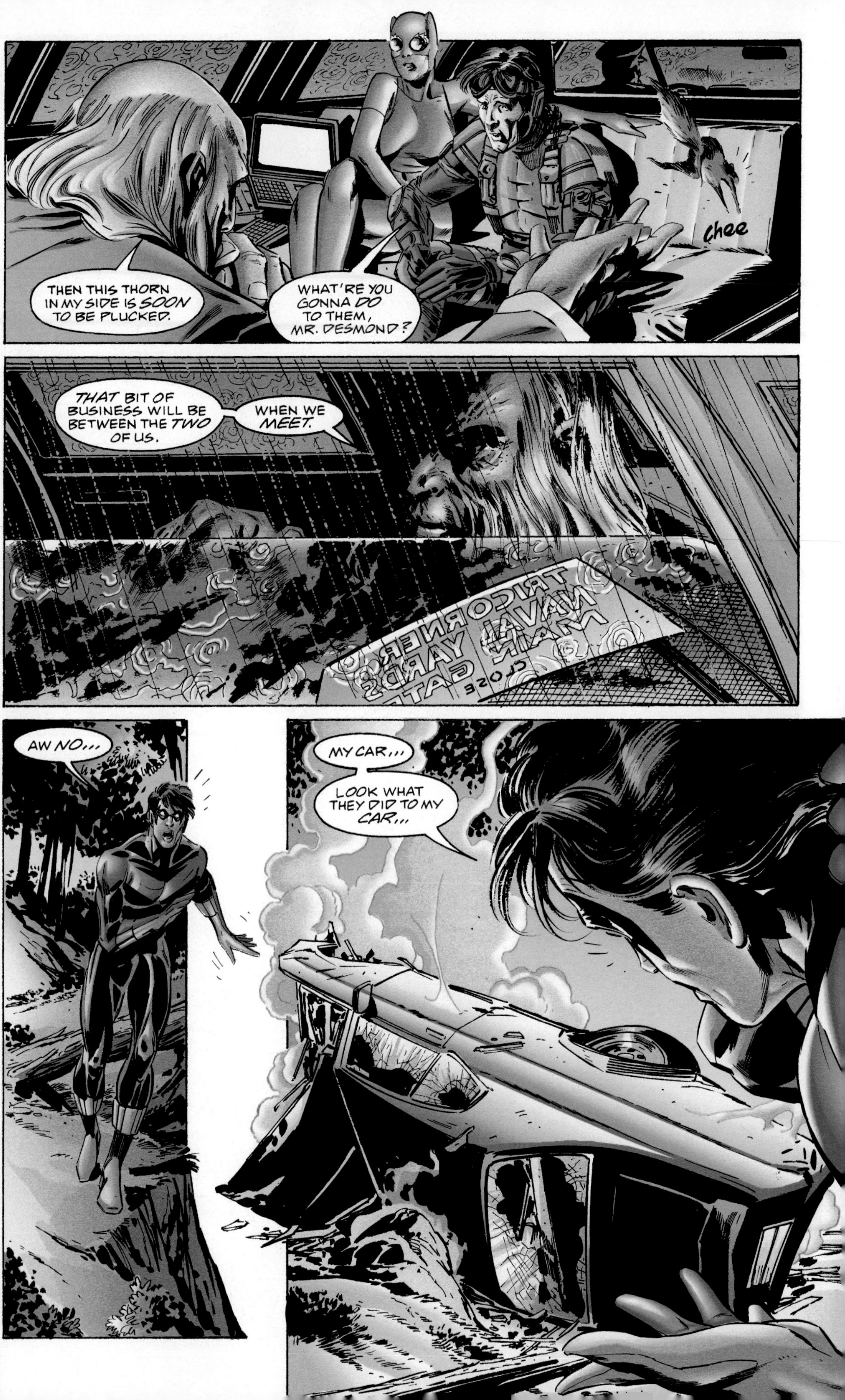
chee
THEN THIS THORN IN MY SIDE IS SOON TO BE PLUCKED.
WHAT'RE YOU GONNA DO TO THEM, MR. DESMOND?
THAT BIT OF BUSINESS WILL BE BETWEEN THE TWO OF US.
WHEN WE MEET.
TRICORNER NAVAL YARDS MAIN GATE
CLOSE
AW NO...
MY CAR...
LOOK WHAT THEY DID TO MY CAR...

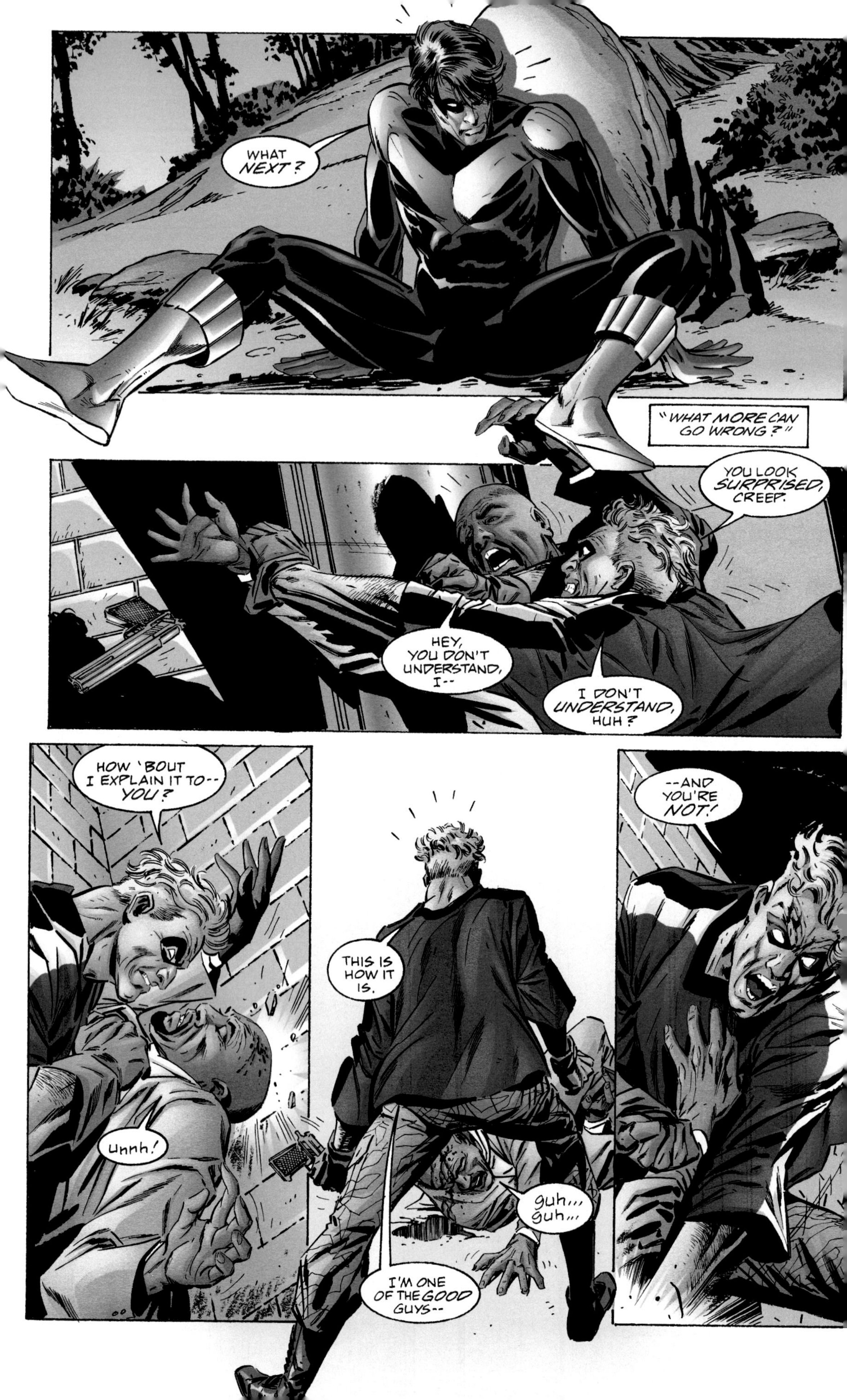
WHAT NEXT?
"WHAT MORE CAN GO WRONG?"
YOU LOOK SURPRISED, CREEP.
HEY, YOU DON'T UNDERSTAND, I--
I DON'T UNDERSTAND, HUH?
HOW 'BOUT I EXPLAIN IT TO--YOU?
unnh!
THIS IS HOW IT IS.
guh... guh...
I'M ONE OF THE GOOD GUYS--
--AND YOU'RE NOT!

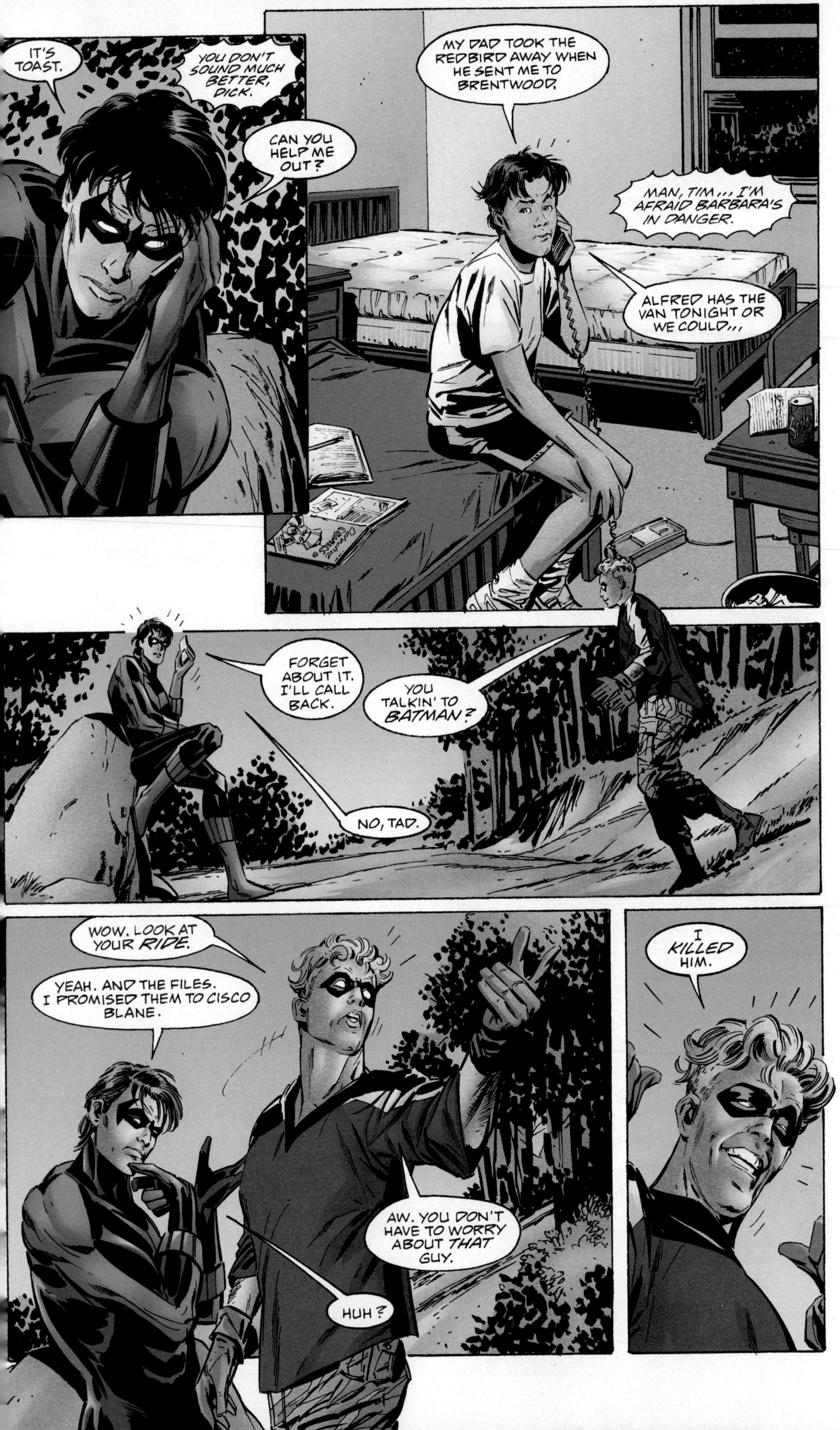
IT'S TOAST.
YOU DON'T SOUND MUCH BETTER, DICK.
CAN YOU HELP ME OUT?
MY DAD TOOK THE REDBIRD AWAY WHEN HE SENT ME TO BRENTWOOD.
MAN, TIM... I'M AFRAID BARBARA'S IN DANGER.
ALFRED HAS THE VAN TONIGHT OR WE COULD...
FORGET ABOUT IT. I'LL CALL BACK.
YOU TALKIN' TO BATMAN?
NO, TAD.
WOW. LOOK AT YOUR RIDE.
YEAH. AND THE FILES. I PROMISED THEM TO CISCO BLANE.
AW. YOU DON'T HAVE TO WORRY ABOUT THAT GUY.
HUH?
I KILLED HIM.

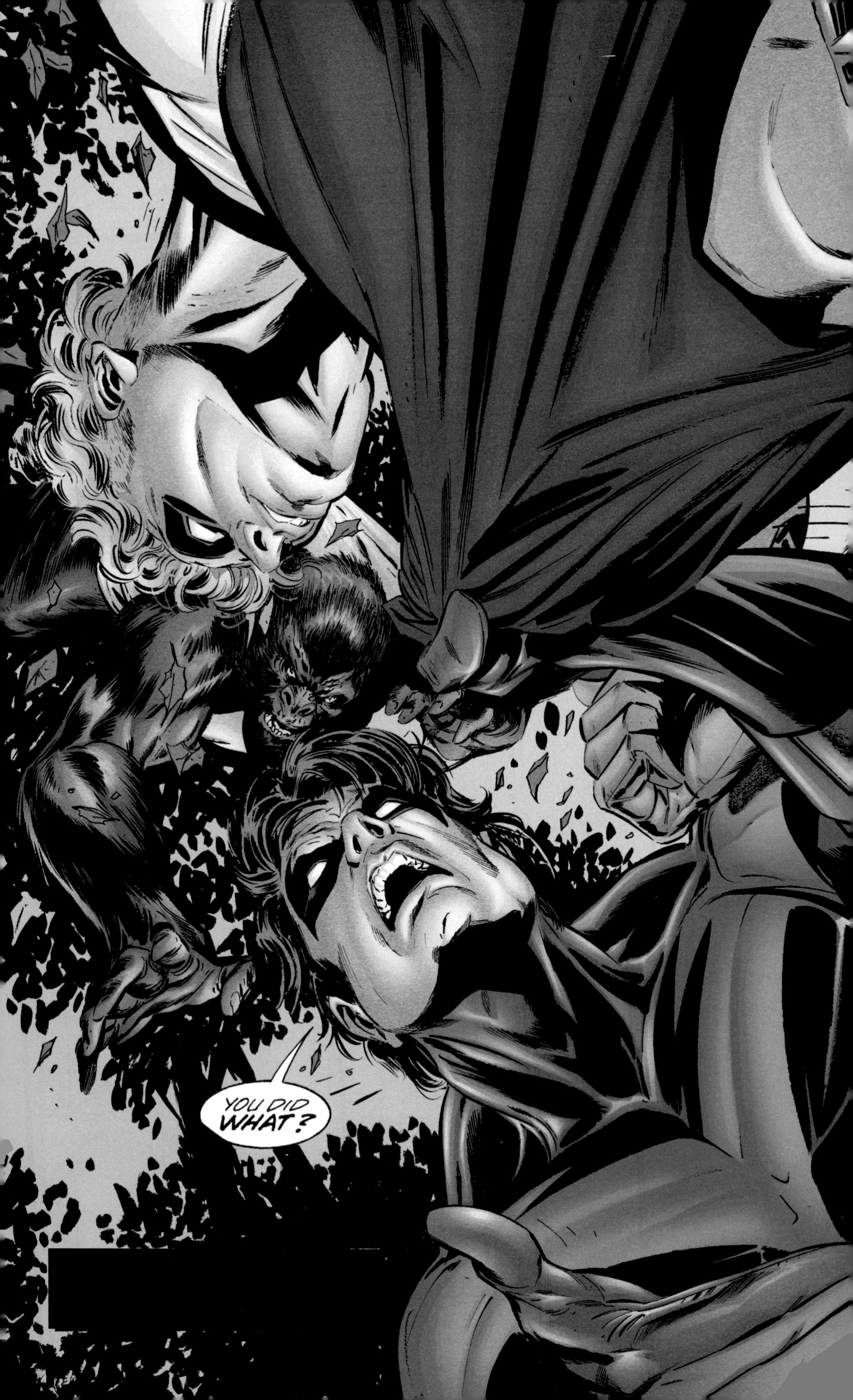
YOU DID WHAT?

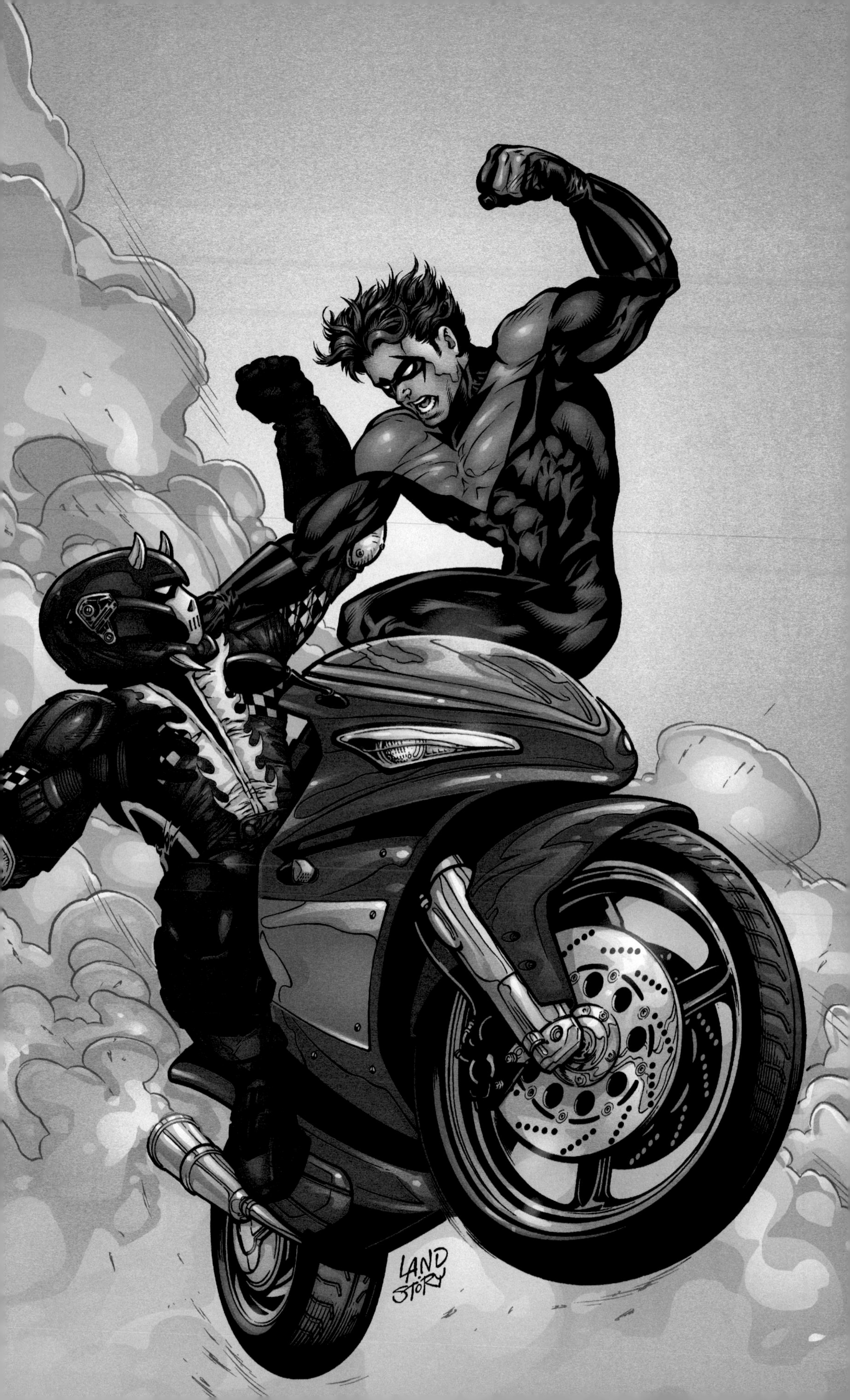
LAND
STORY

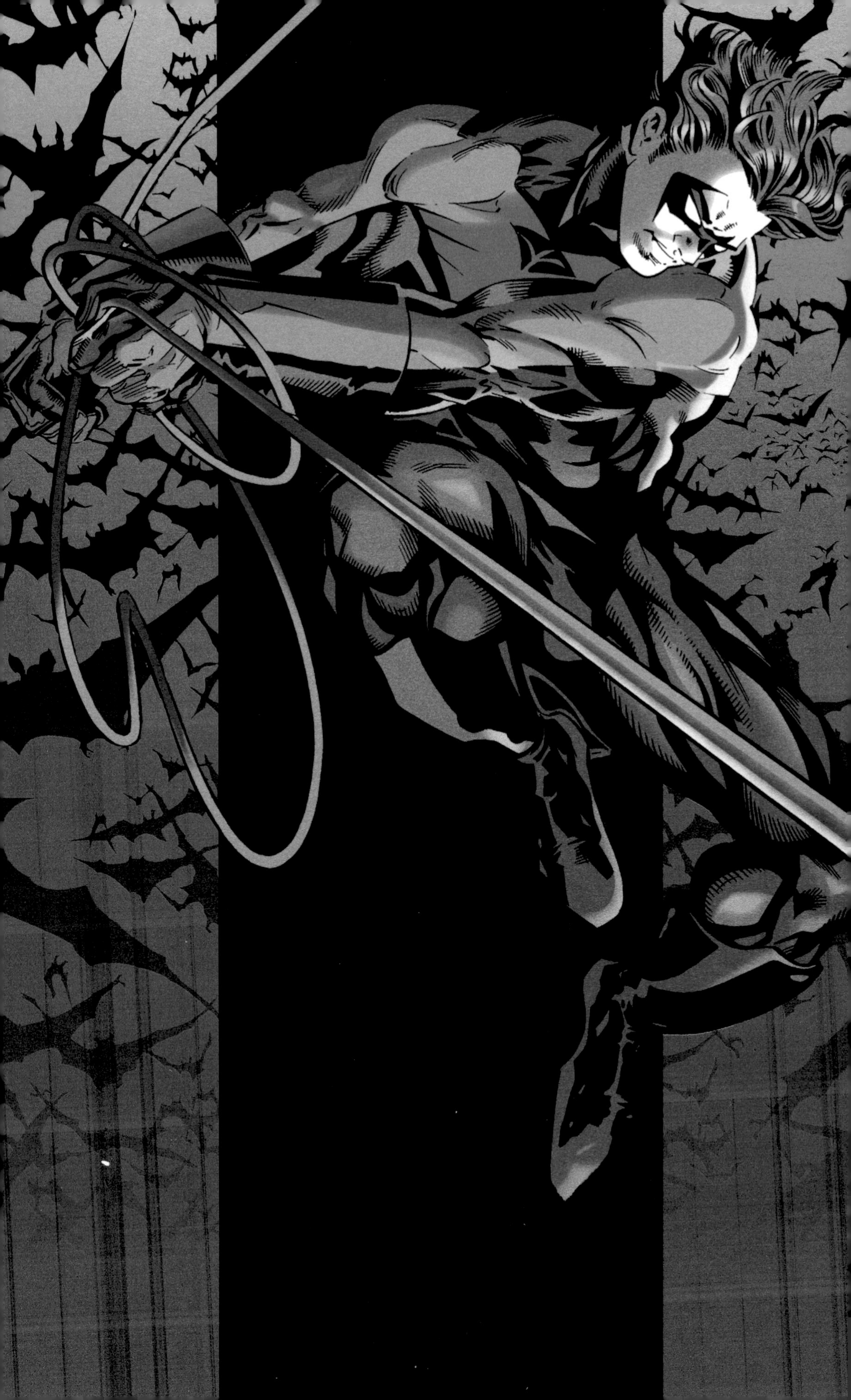

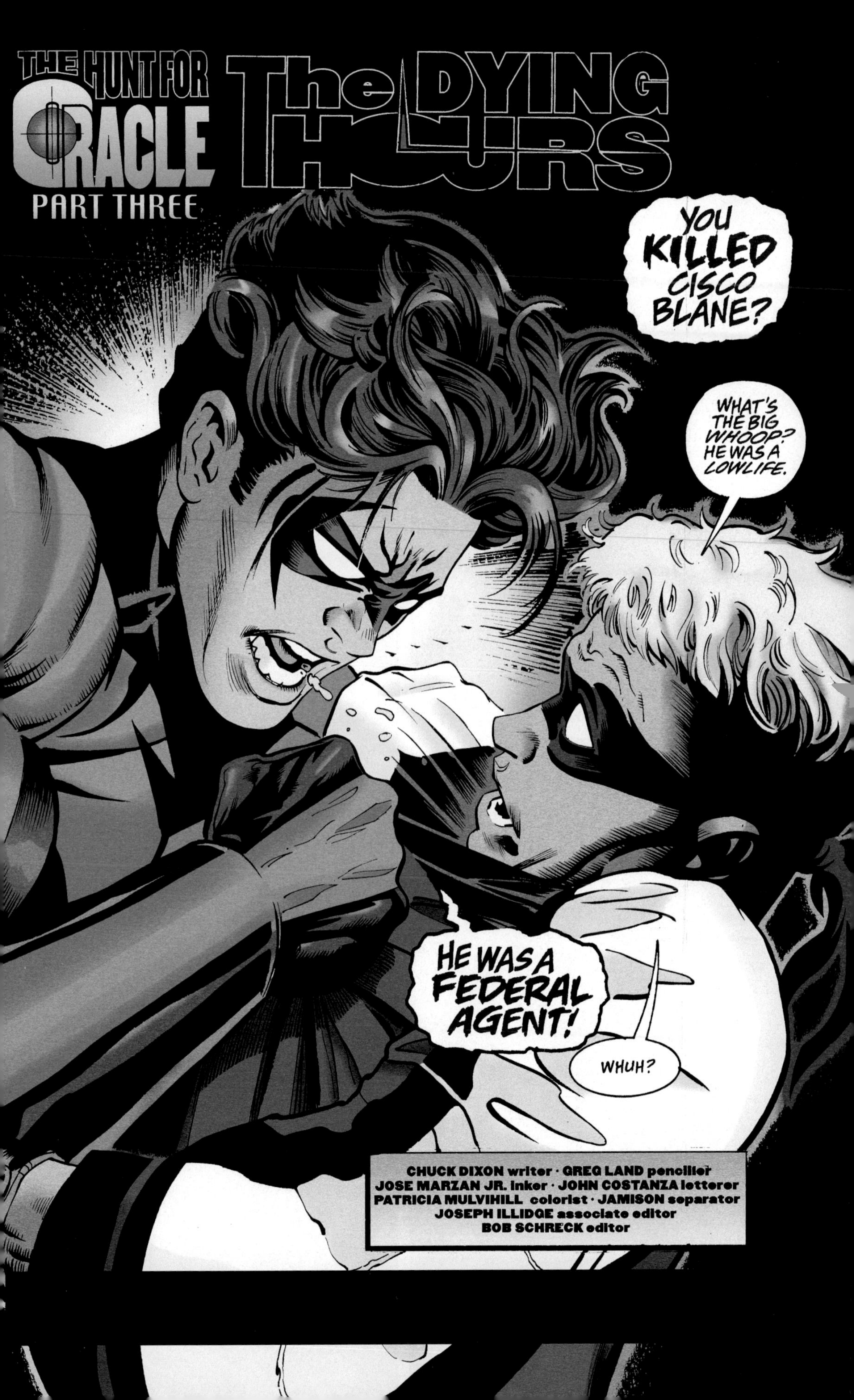
THE HUNT FOR ORACLE
PART THREE
The DYING HOURS
YOU KILLED CISCO BLANE?
WHAT'S THE BIG WHOOP? HE WAS A LOWLIFE.
HE WAS A FEDERAL AGENT!
WHUH?
CHUCK DIXON writer · GREG LAND penciller
JOSE MARZAN JR. inker · JOHN COSTANZA letterer
PATRICIA MULVIHILL colorist · JAMISON separator
JOSEPH ILLIDGE associate editor
BOB SCHRECK editor

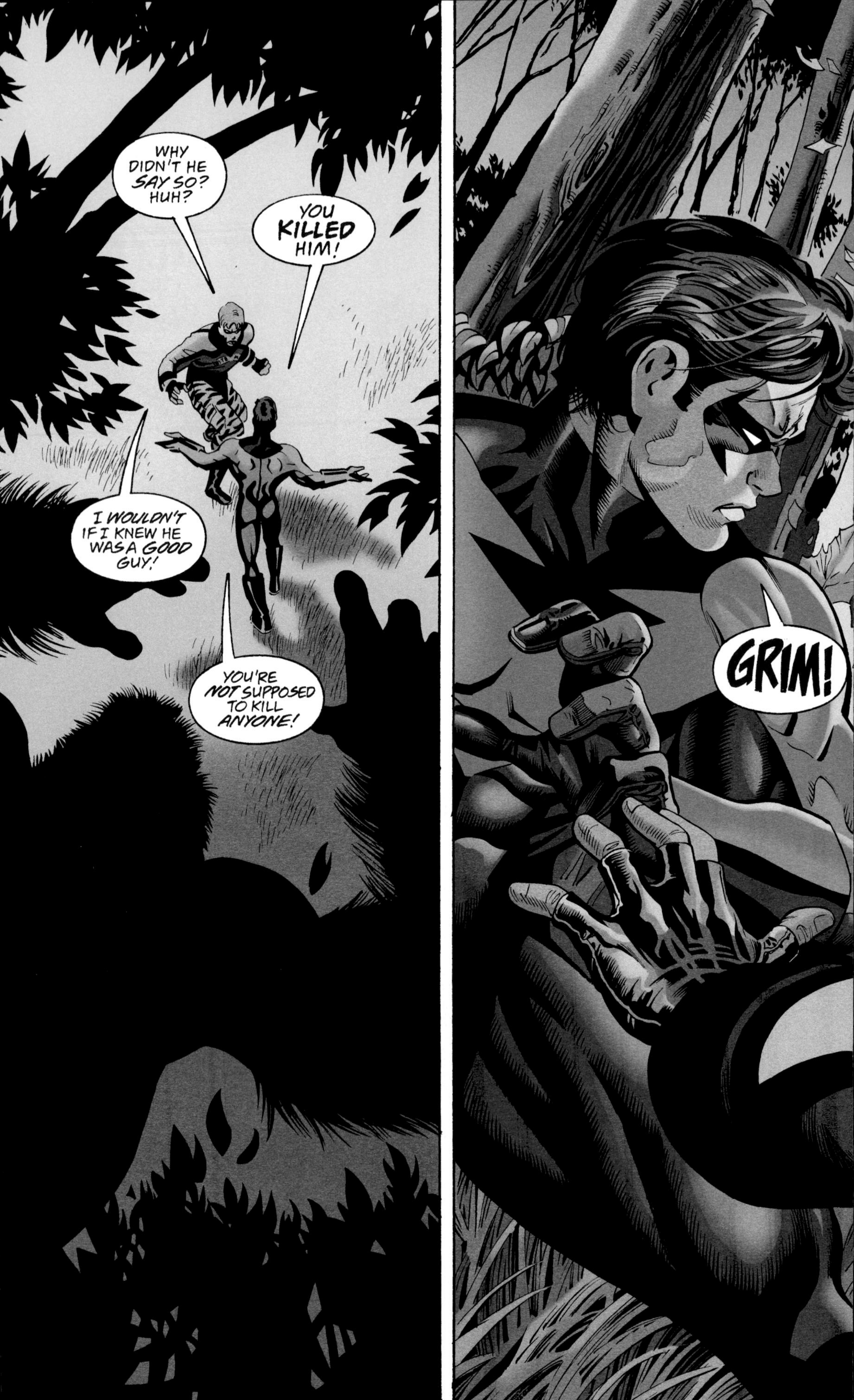
WHY DIDN'T HE SAY SO? HUH?
YOU KILLED HIM!
I WOULDN'T IF I KNEW HE WAS A GOOD GUY!
YOU'RE NOT SUPPOSED TO KILL ANYONE!
GRIM!

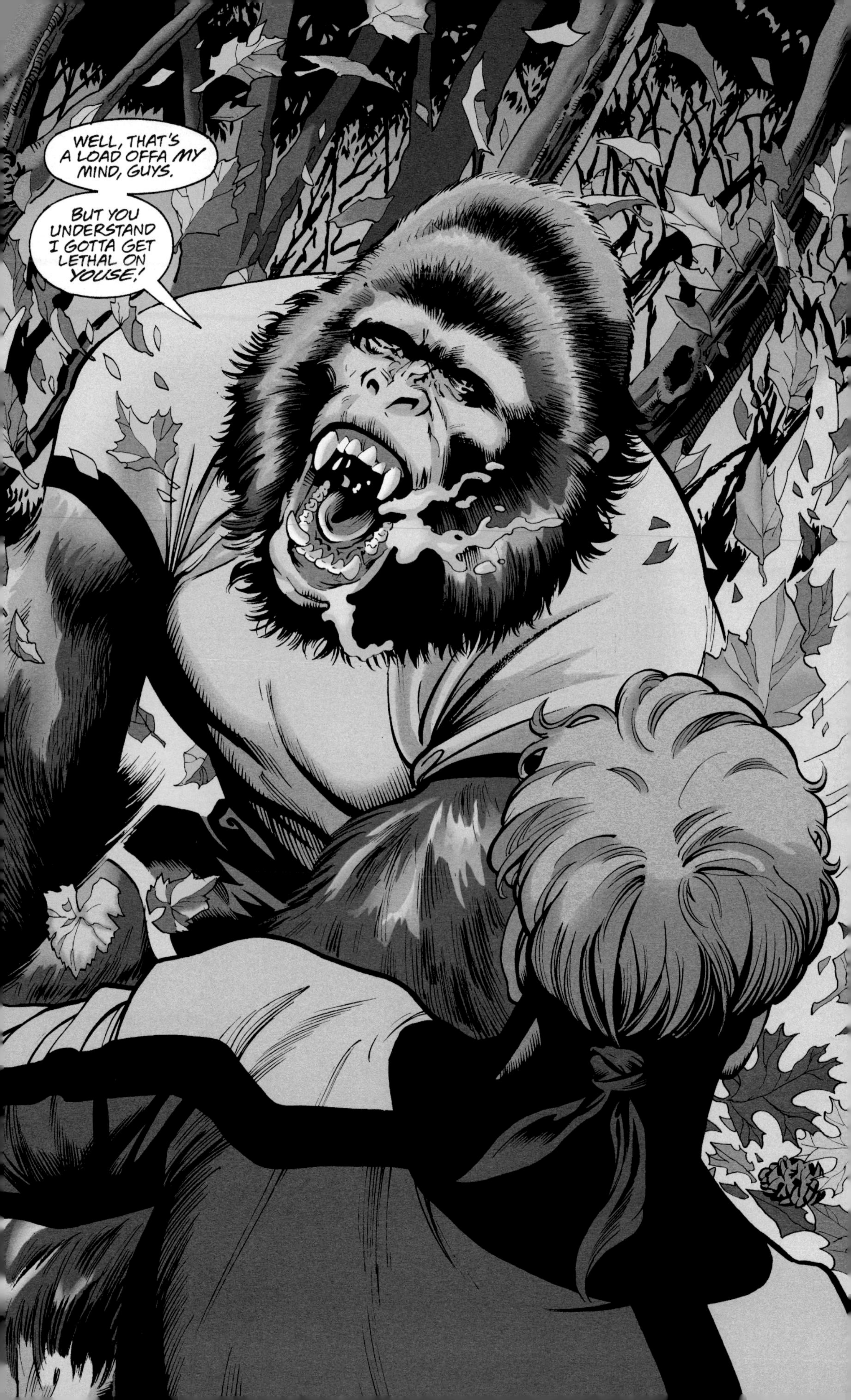
WELL, THAT'S A LOAD OFFA MY MIND, GUYS.
BUT YOU UNDERSTAND I GOTTA GET LETHAL ON YOUSE!

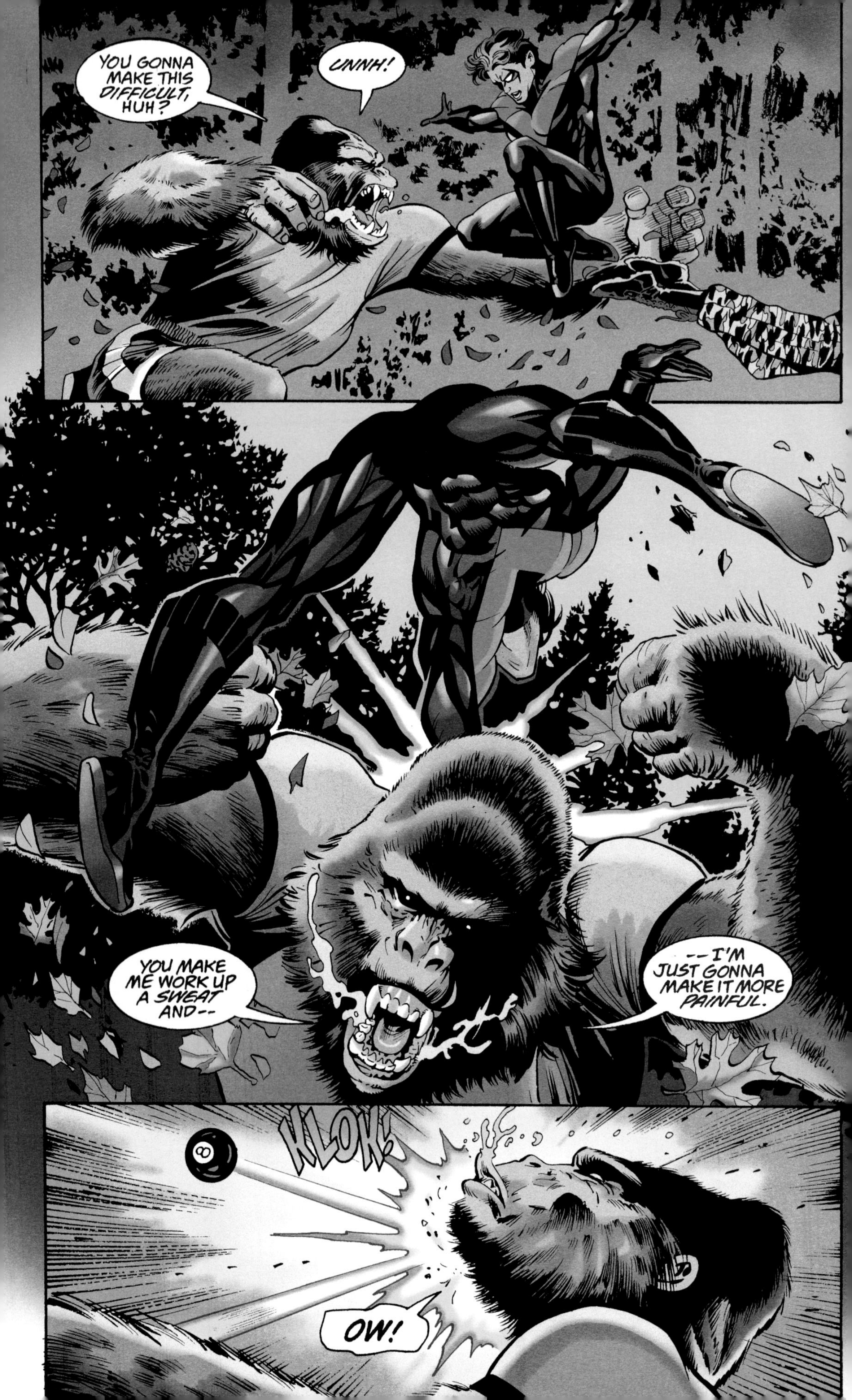
YOU GONNA MAKE THIS DIFFICULT, HUH?
UNNH!
YOU MAKE ME WORK UP A SWEAT AND--
--I'M JUST GONNA MAKE IT MORE PAINFUL.
KLOK!
OW!

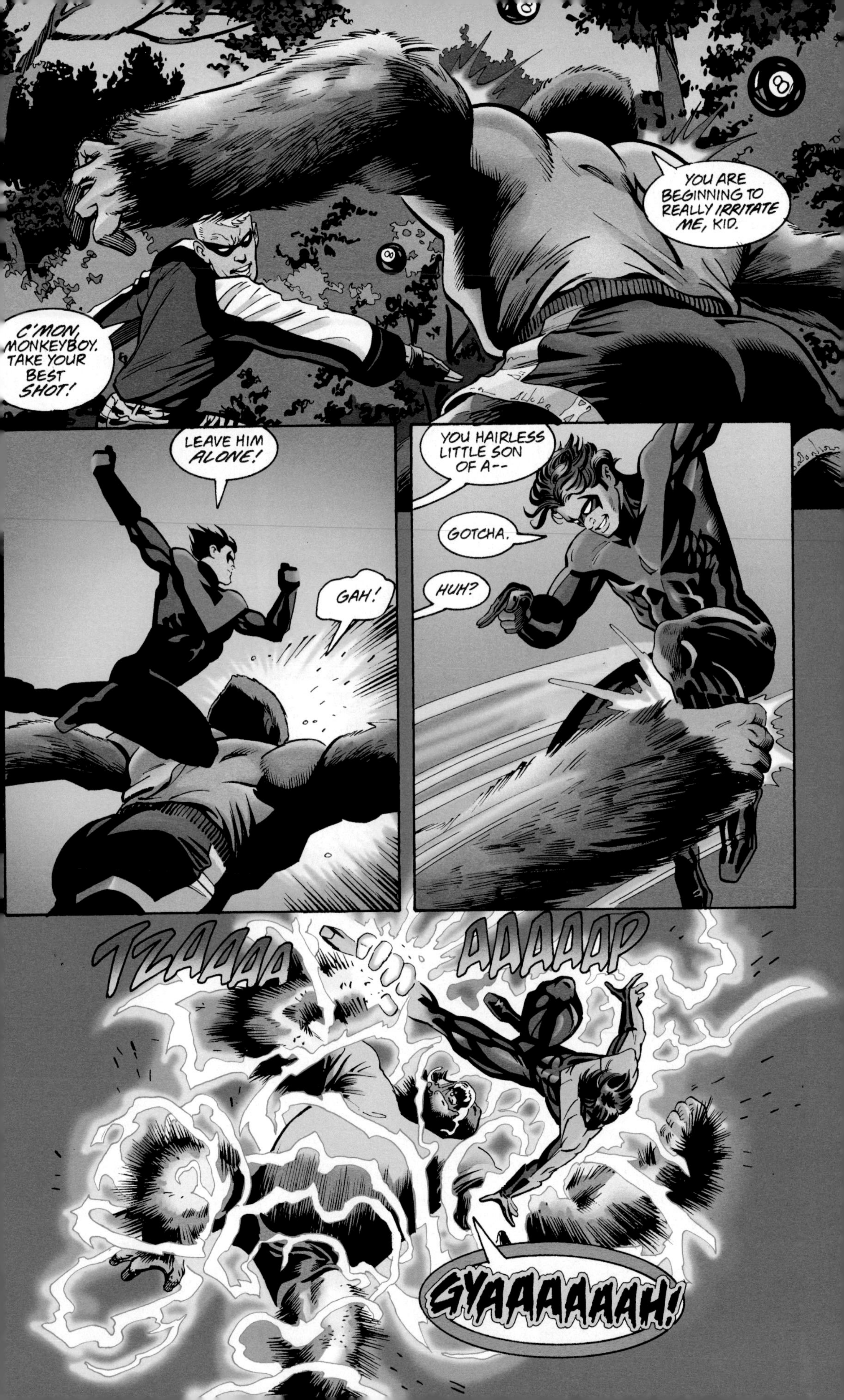
YOU ARE BEGINNING TO REALLY IRRITATE ME, KID.
C'MON, MONKEYBOY. TAKE YOUR BEST SHOT!
LEAVE HIM ALONE!
GAH!
YOU HAIRLESS LITTLE SON OF A--
GOTCHA.
HUH?
TZAAAA
AAAAAP
GYAAAAAAAH!

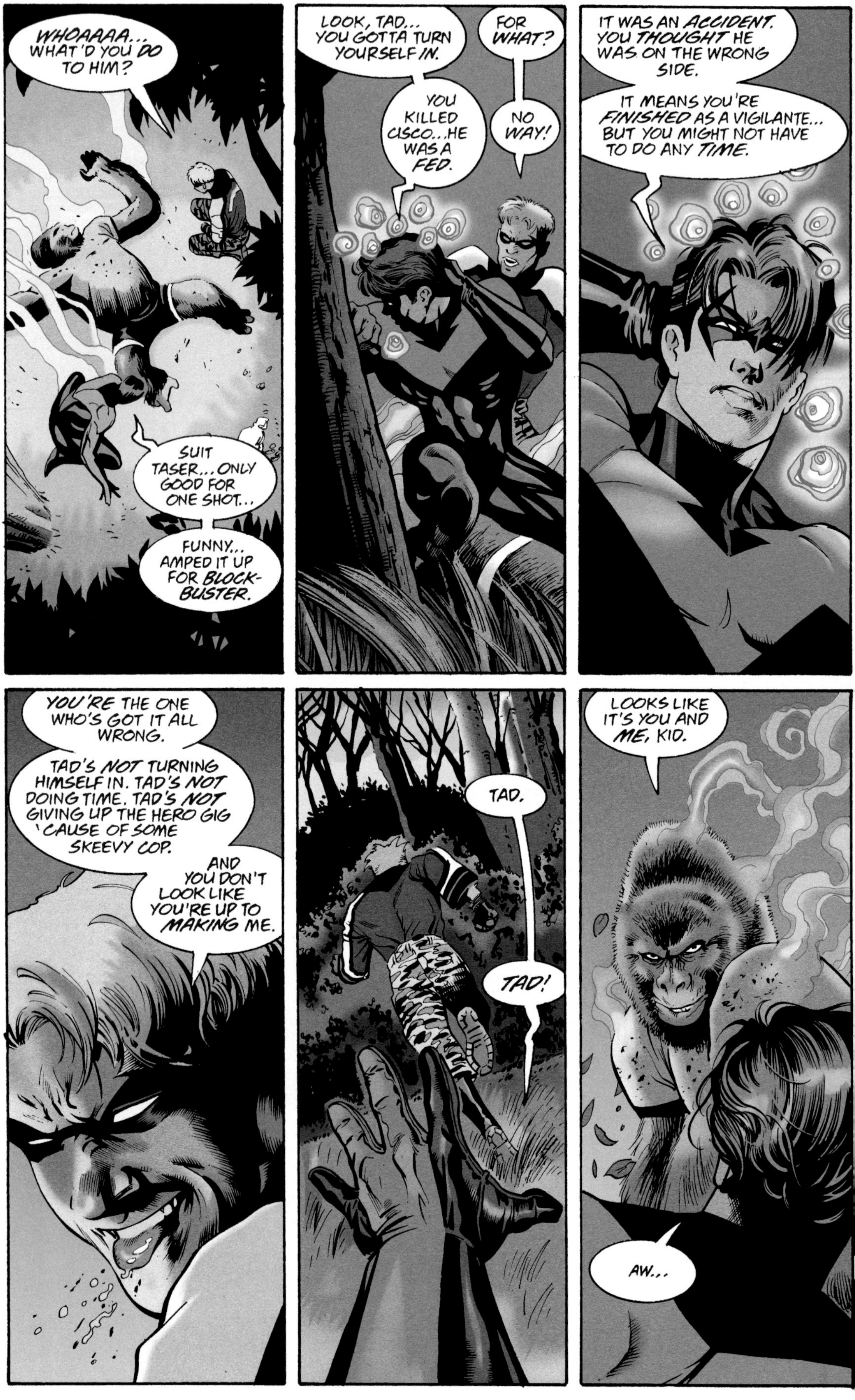
WHOAAAA... WHAT'D YOU DO TO HIM?
SUIT TASER... ONLY GOOD FOR ONE SHOT...
FUNNY... AMPED IT UP FOR BLOCK-BUSTER.
LOOK, TAD... YOU GOTTA TURN YOURSELF IN.
FOR WHAT?
YOU KILLED CISCO... HE WAS A FED.
NO WAY!
IT WAS AN ACCIDENT. YOU THOUGHT HE WAS ON THE WRONG SIDE.
IT MEANS YOU'RE FINISHED AS A VIGILANTE... BUT YOU MIGHT NOT HAVE TO DO ANY TIME.
YOU'RE THE ONE WHO'S GOT IT ALL WRONG.
TAD'S NOT TURNING HIMSELF IN. TAD'S NOT DOING TIME. TAD'S NOT GIVING UP THE HERO GIG 'CAUSE OF SOME SKEEVY COP.
AND YOU DON'T LOOK LIKE YOU'RE UP TO MAKING ME.
TAD.
TAD!
LOOKS LIKE IT'S YOU AND ME, KID.
AW...

I DISLIKE PLAYING MY HAND LIKE THIS.

I NEED MORE *RELIABLE* INFORMATION. I *CANNOT* CONTINUE SENDING MY STRIKE TEAMS ON WILD GOOSE CHASES.

MOUSE HAS IT *HAMMERED*, MR. DESMOND.

SHE READS CODE AT *LIGHTSPEED*, SIR.

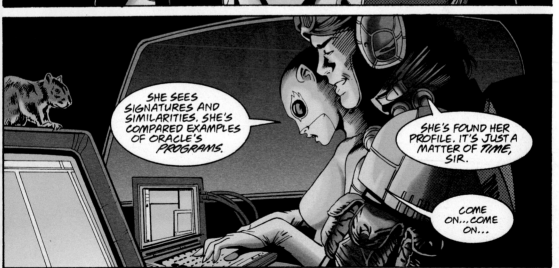

SHE SEES SIGNATURES AND SIMILARITIES. SHE'S COMPARED EXAMPLES OF ORACLE'S *PROGRAMS*.

SHE'S FOUND HER PROFILE. IT'S JUST A MATTER OF *TIME*, SIR.

COME ON... COME ON...

YOU HEAR THAT, BABY? DON'T SCREW UP.

I HEAR AND *OBEY*.

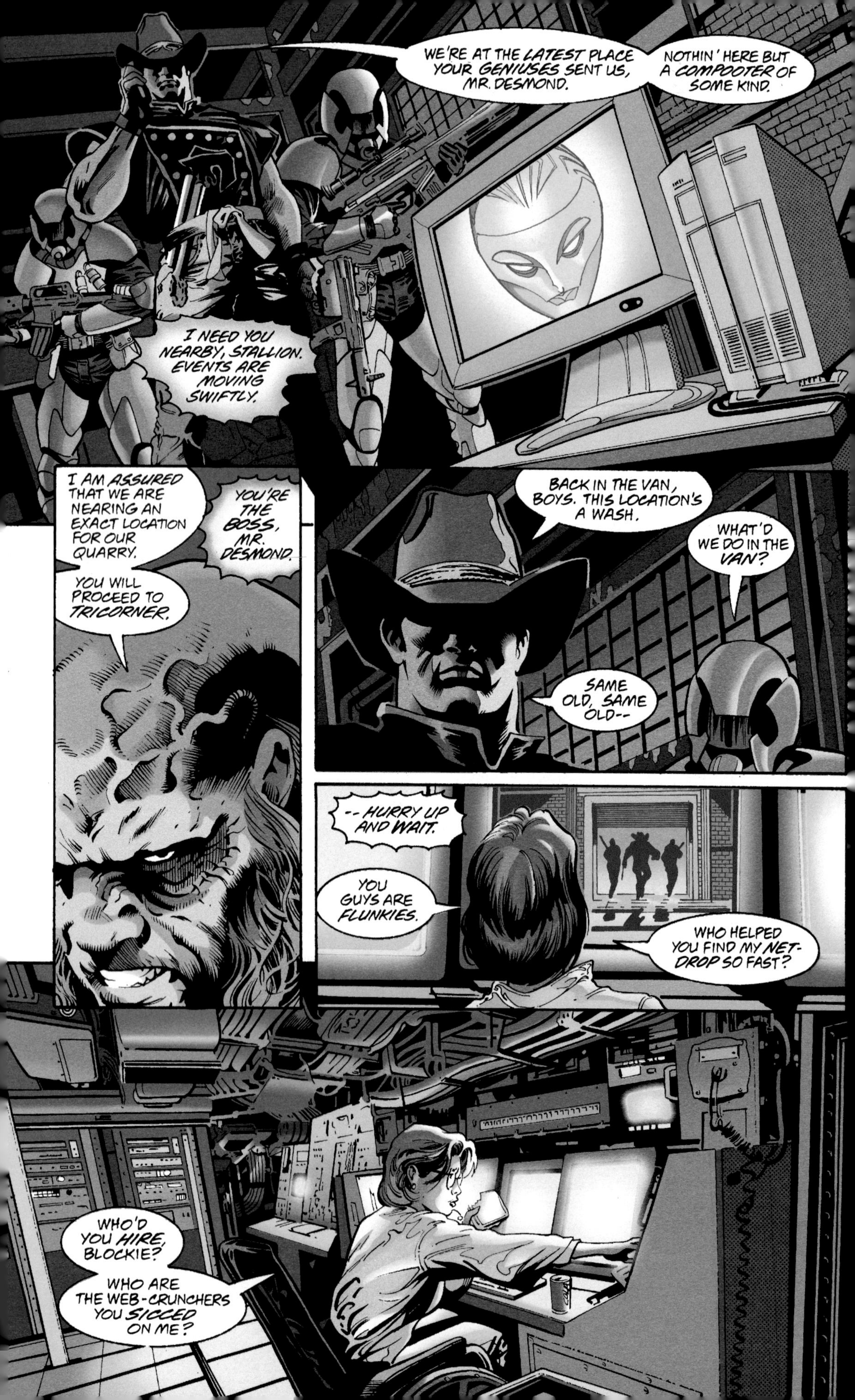
WE'RE AT THE LATEST PLACE YOUR GENIUSES SENT US, MR. DESMOND.
NOTHIN' HERE BUT A COMPOOTER OF SOME KIND.
I NEED YOU NEARBY, STALLION. EVENTS ARE MOVING SWIFTLY.
I AM ASSURED THAT WE ARE NEARING AN EXACT LOCATION FOR OUR QUARRY.
YOU WILL PROCEED TO TRICORNER.
YOU'RE THE BOSS, MR. DESMOND.
BACK IN THE VAN, BOYS. THIS LOCATION'S A WASH.
WHAT'D WE DO IN THE VAN?
SAME OLD, SAME OLD--
--HURRY UP AND WAIT.
YOU GUYS ARE FLUNKIES.
WHO HELPED YOU FIND MY NET-DROP SO FAST?
WHO'D YOU HIRE, BLOCKIE?
WHO ARE THE WEB-CRUNCHERS YOU SICCED ON ME?

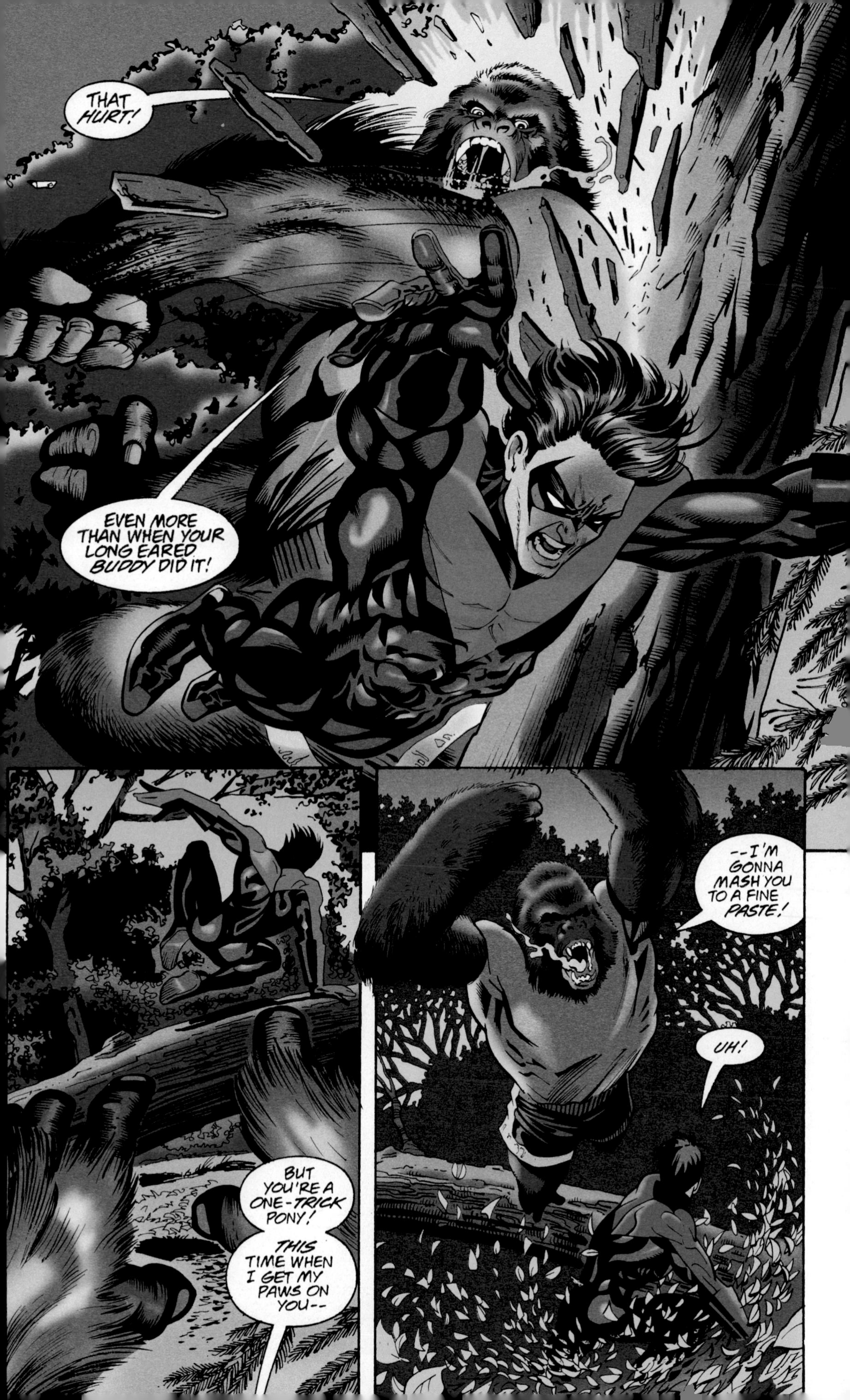
THAT *HURT!*
EVEN MORE THAN WHEN YOUR LONG EARED *BUDDY* DID IT!
BUT YOU'RE A ONE-*TRICK* PONY!
THIS TIME WHEN I GET MY PAWS ON YOU--
--I'M GONNA MASH YOU TO A FINE *PASTE!*
UH!

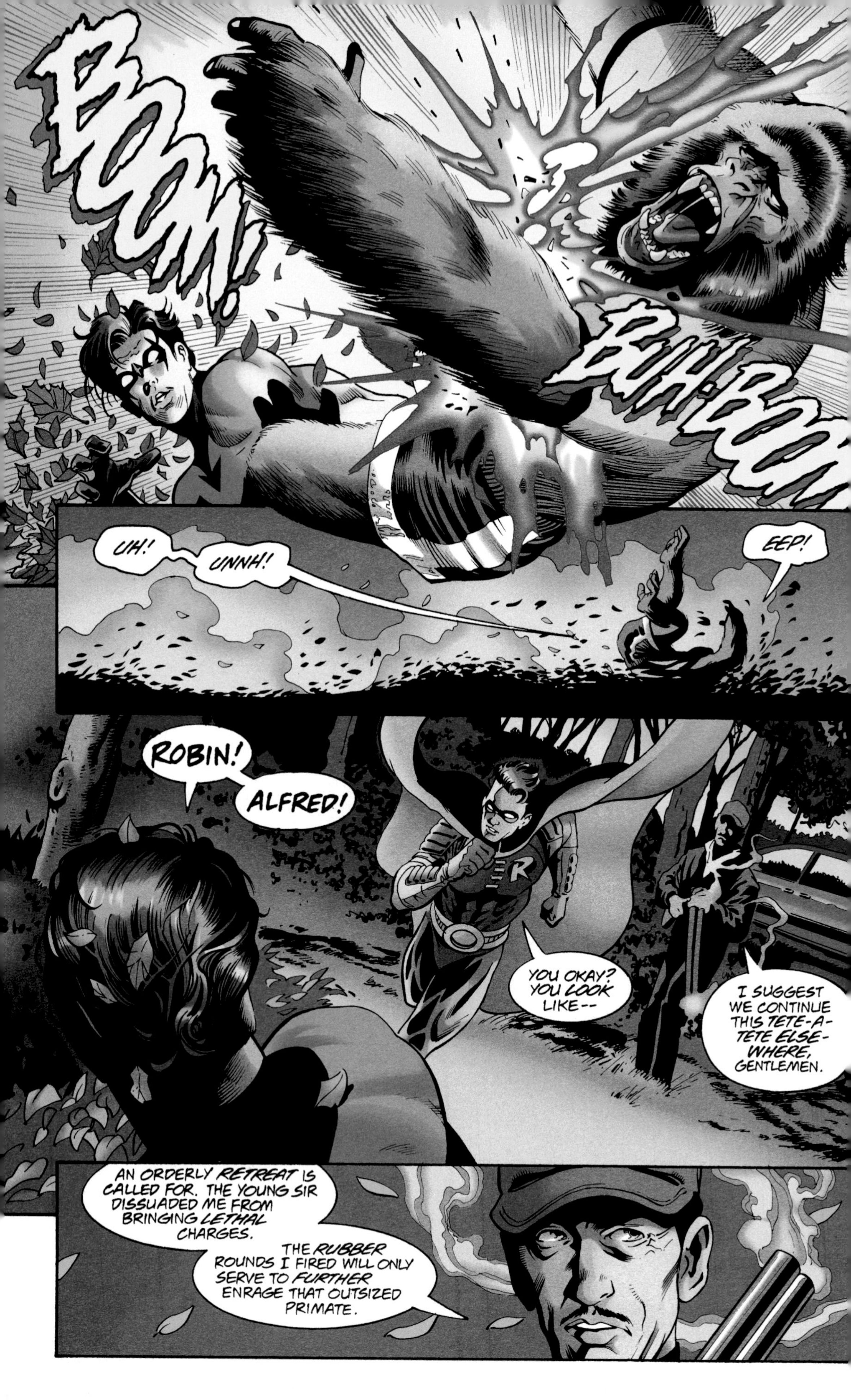
BOOM!
BLHOOM!
UH!
UNNH!
EEP!
ROBIN!
ALFRED!
YOU OKAY? YOU LOOK LIKE--
I SUGGEST WE CONTINUE THIS TETE-A-TETE ELSE-WHERE, GENTLEMEN.
AN ORDERLY RETREAT IS CALLED FOR. THE YOUNG SIR DISSUADED ME FROM BRINGING LETHAL CHARGES.
THE RUBBER ROUNDS I FIRED WILL ONLY SERVE TO FURTHER ENRAGE THAT OUTSIZED PRIMATE.

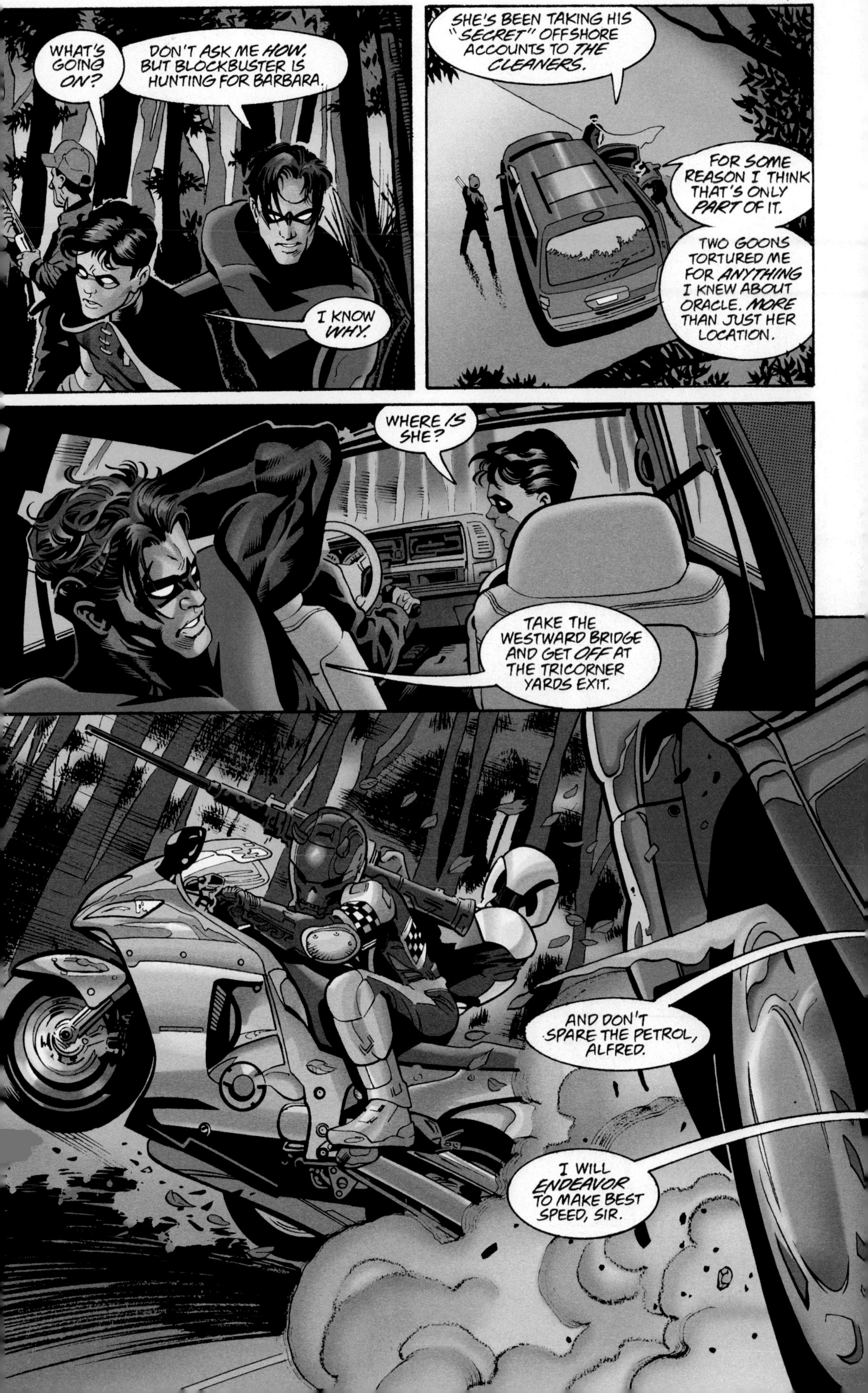
WHAT'S GOING ON?
DON'T ASK ME HOW, BUT BLOCKBUSTER IS HUNTING FOR BARBARA.
I KNOW WHY.
SHE'S BEEN TAKING HIS "SECRET" OFFSHORE ACCOUNTS TO THE CLEANERS.
FOR SOME REASON I THINK THAT'S ONLY PART OF IT.
TWO GOONS TORTURED ME FOR ANYTHING I KNEW ABOUT ORACLE. MORE THAN JUST HER LOCATION.
WHERE IS SHE?
TAKE THE WESTWARD BRIDGE AND GET OFF AT THE TRICORNER YARDS EXIT.
AND DON'T SPARE THE PETROL, ALFRED.
I WILL ENDEAVOR TO MAKE BEST SPEED, SIR.

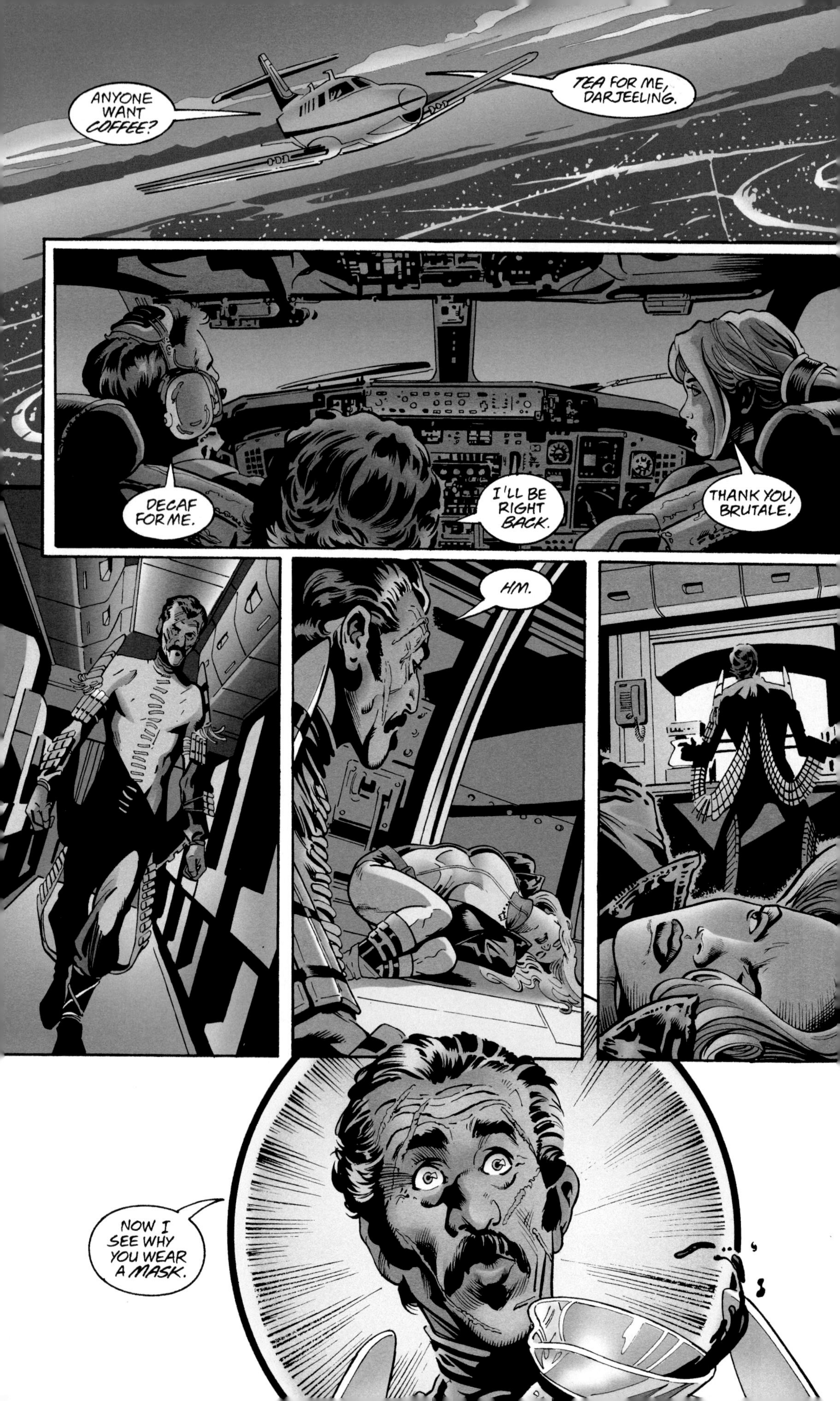
ANYONE WANT COFFEE?
TEA FOR ME, DARJEELING.
DECAF FOR ME.
I'LL BE RIGHT BACK.
THANK YOU, BRUTALE.
HM.
NOW I SEE WHY YOU WEAR A MASK.

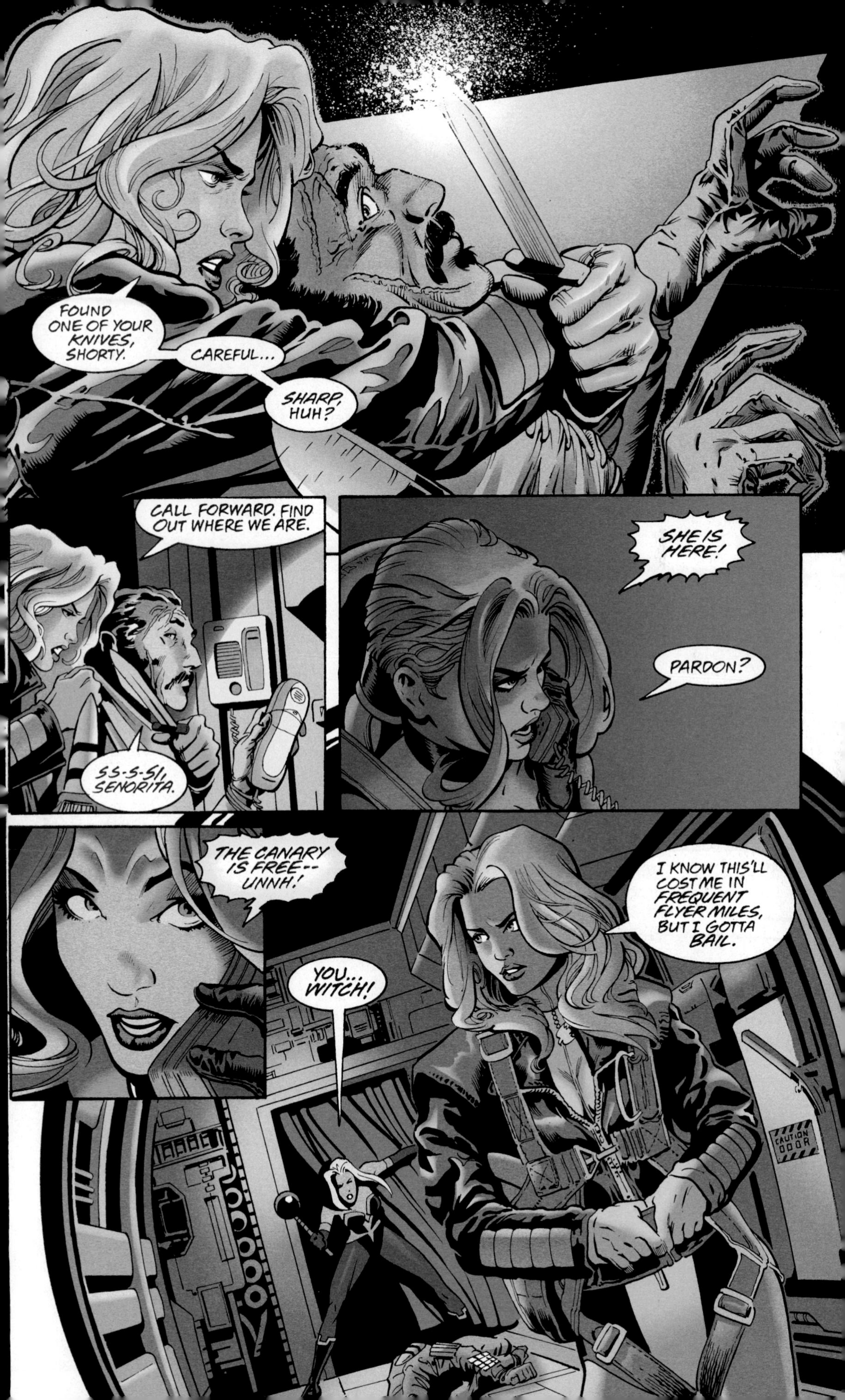
FOUND ONE OF YOUR KNIVES, SHORTY.
CAREFUL...
SHARP, HUH?
CALL FORWARD. FIND OUT WHERE WE ARE.
S-S-S-SI, SENORITA.
SHE IS HERE!
PARDON?
THE CANARY IS FREE-- UNNH!
I KNOW THIS'LL COST ME IN FREQUENT FLYER MILES, BUT I GOTTA BAIL.
YOU... WITCH!
CAUTION DOOR

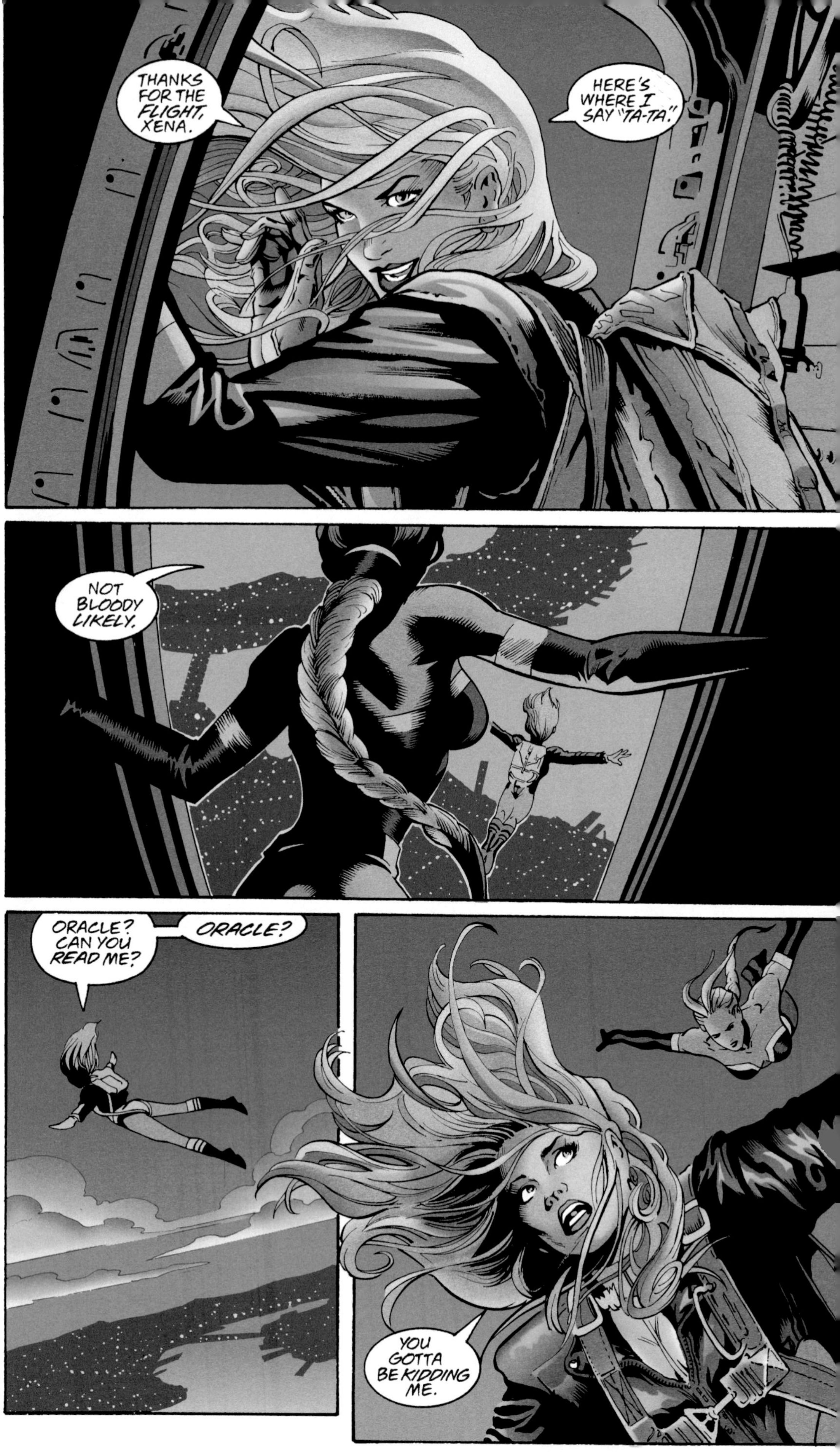
THANKS FOR THE FLIGHT, XENA.
HERE'S WHERE I SAY "TA-TA."
NOT BLOODY LIKELY.
ORACLE? CAN YOU READ ME?
ORACLE?
YOU GOTTA BE KIDDING ME.

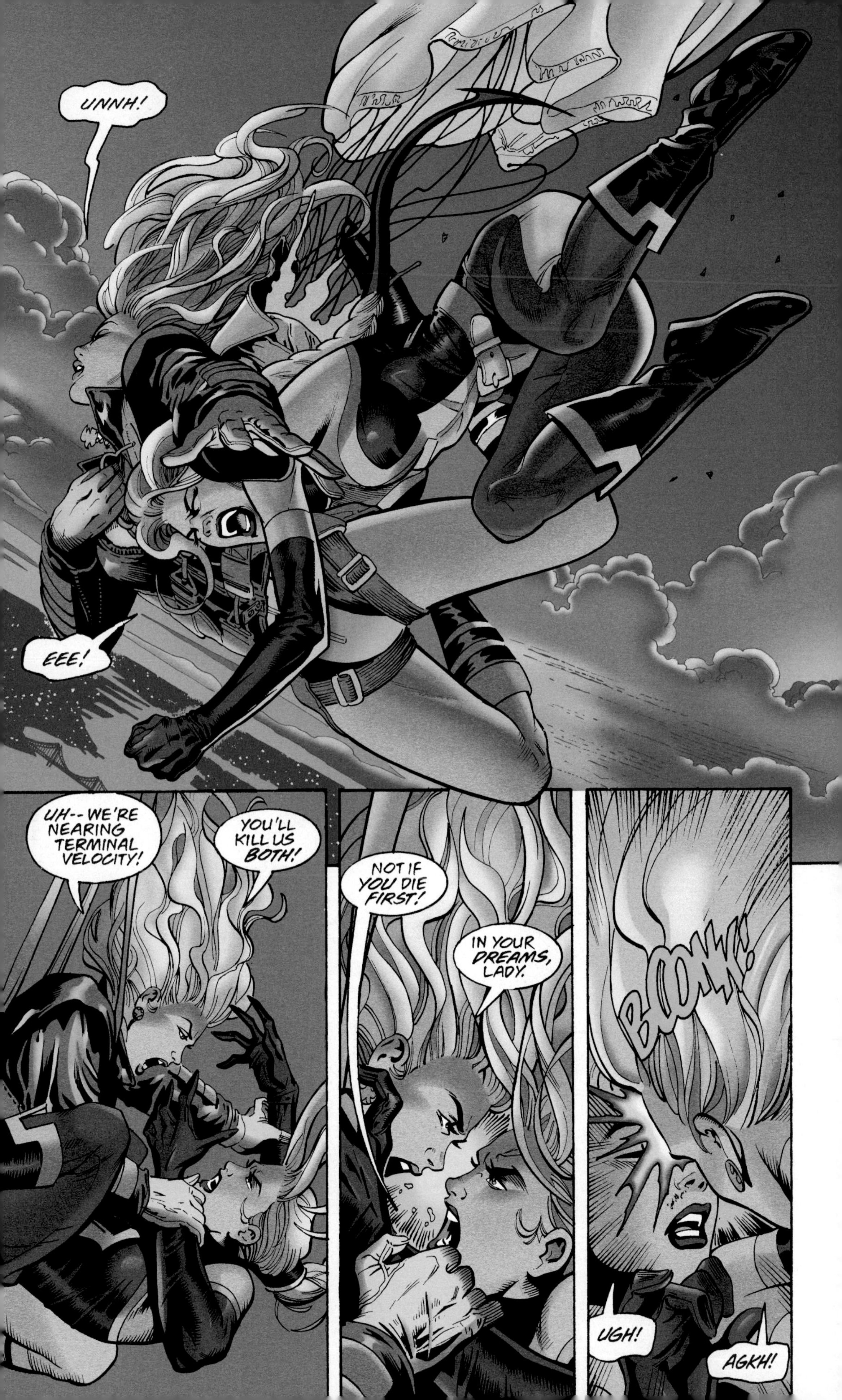
UNNH!
EEE!
UH-- WE'RE NEARING TERMINAL VELOCITY!
YOU'LL KILL US BOTH!
NOT IF YOU DIE FIRST!
IN YOUR DREAMS, LADY.
BOONK!
UGH!
AGKH!

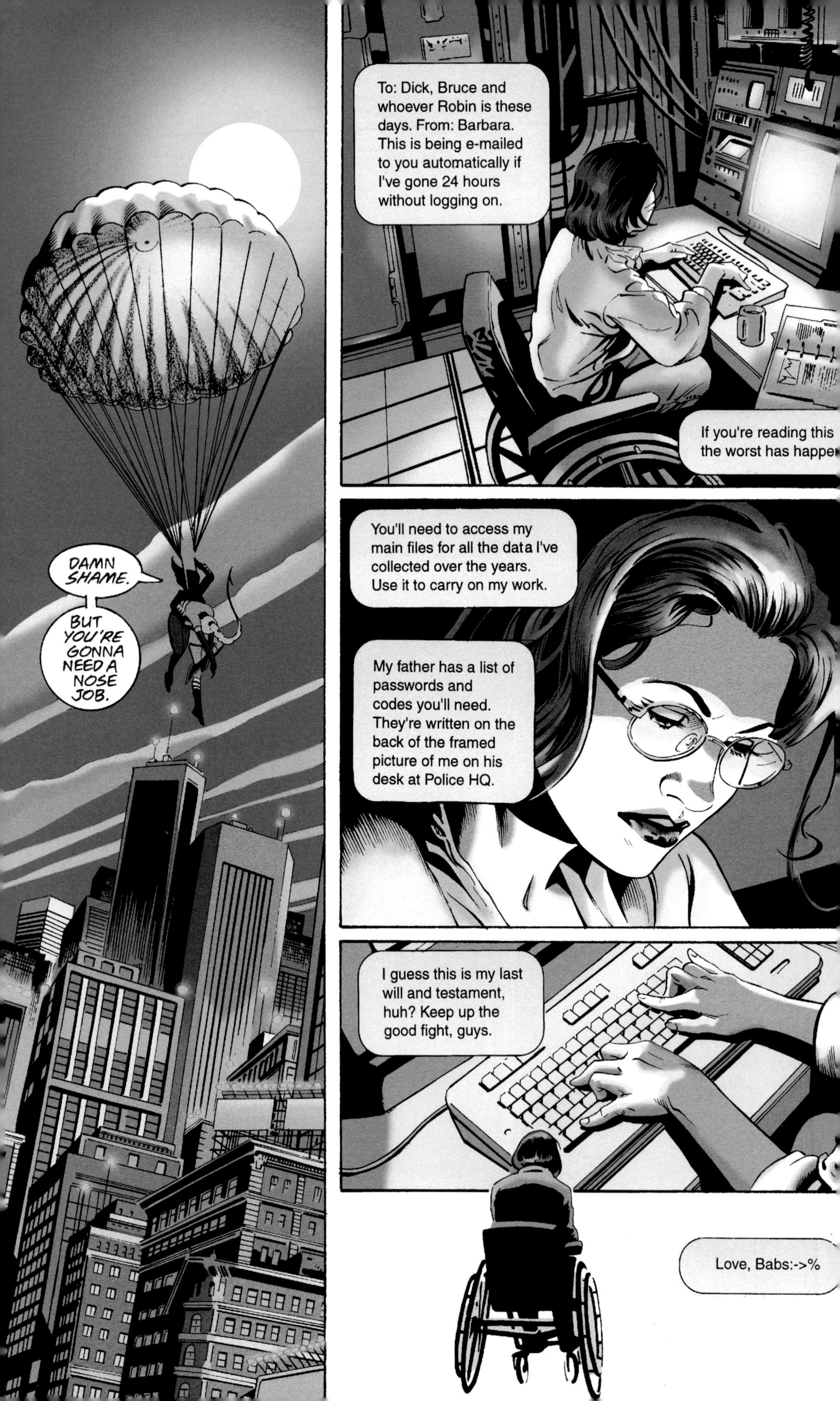
DAMN SHAME.
BUT YOU'RE GONNA NEED A NOSE JOB.
To: Dick, Bruce and whoever Robin is these days. From: Barbara. This is being e-mailed to you automatically if I've gone 24 hours without logging on.
If you're reading this the worst has happe
You'll need to access my main files for all the data I've collected over the years. Use it to carry on my work.
My father has a list of passwords and codes you'll need. They're written on the back of the framed picture of me on his desk at Police HQ.
I guess this is my last will and testament, huh? Keep up the good fight, guys.
Love, Babs:->%

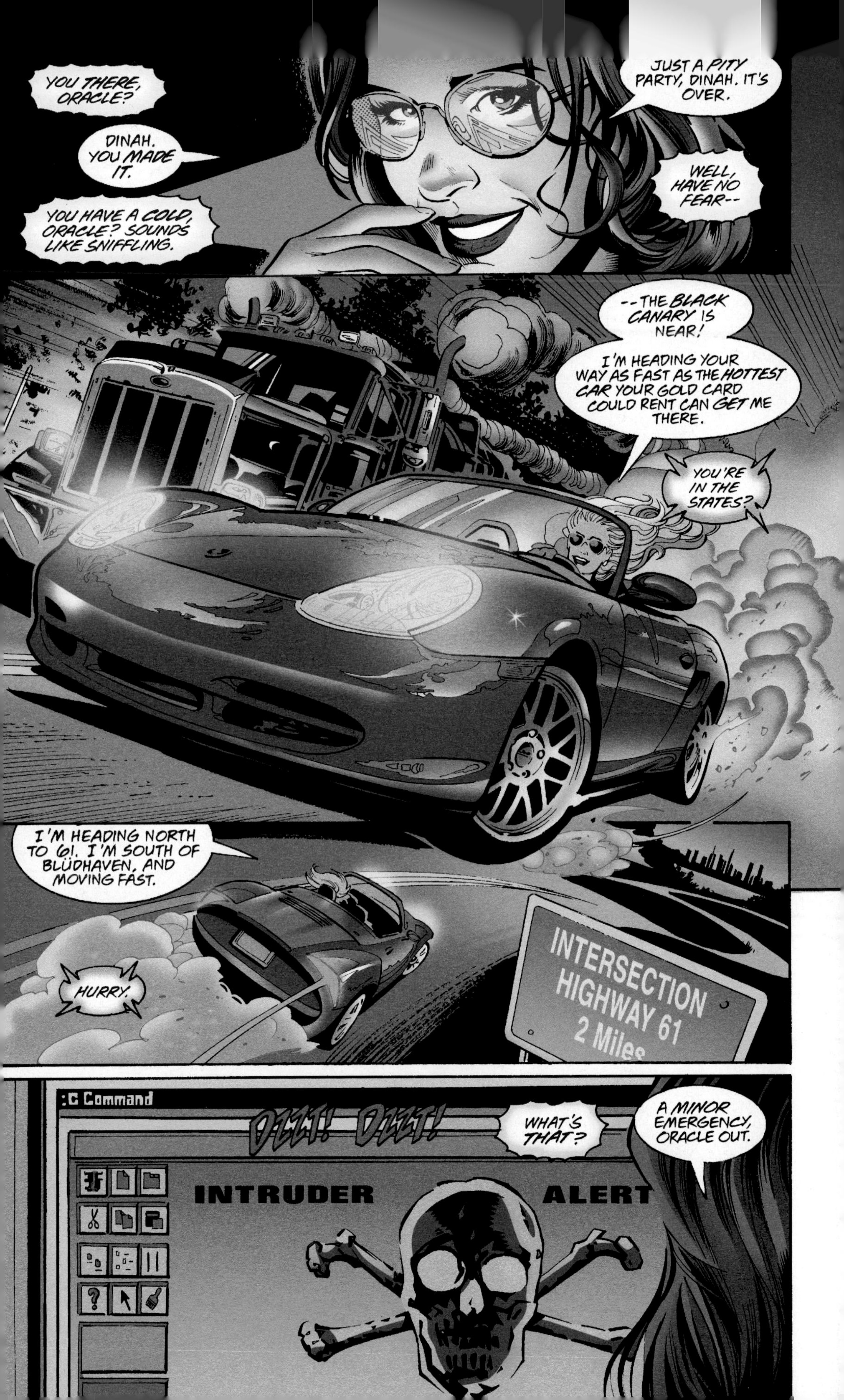
YOU THERE, ORACLE?
DINAH. YOU MADE IT.
YOU HAVE A COLD, ORACLE? SOUNDS LIKE SNIFFLING.
JUST A PITY PARTY, DINAH. IT'S OVER.
WELL, HAVE NO FEAR--
--THE BLACK CANARY IS NEAR!
I'M HEADING YOUR WAY AS FAST AS THE HOTTEST CAR YOUR GOLD CARD COULD RENT CAN GET ME THERE.
YOU'RE IN THE STATES?
I'M HEADING NORTH TO 61. I'M SOUTH OF BLÜDHAVEN, AND MOVING FAST.
HURRY.
INTERSECTION HIGHWAY 61 2 Miles
:C Command
DZZT! DZZT!
WHAT'S THAT?
A MINOR EMERGENCY, ORACLE OUT.
INTRUDER ALERT

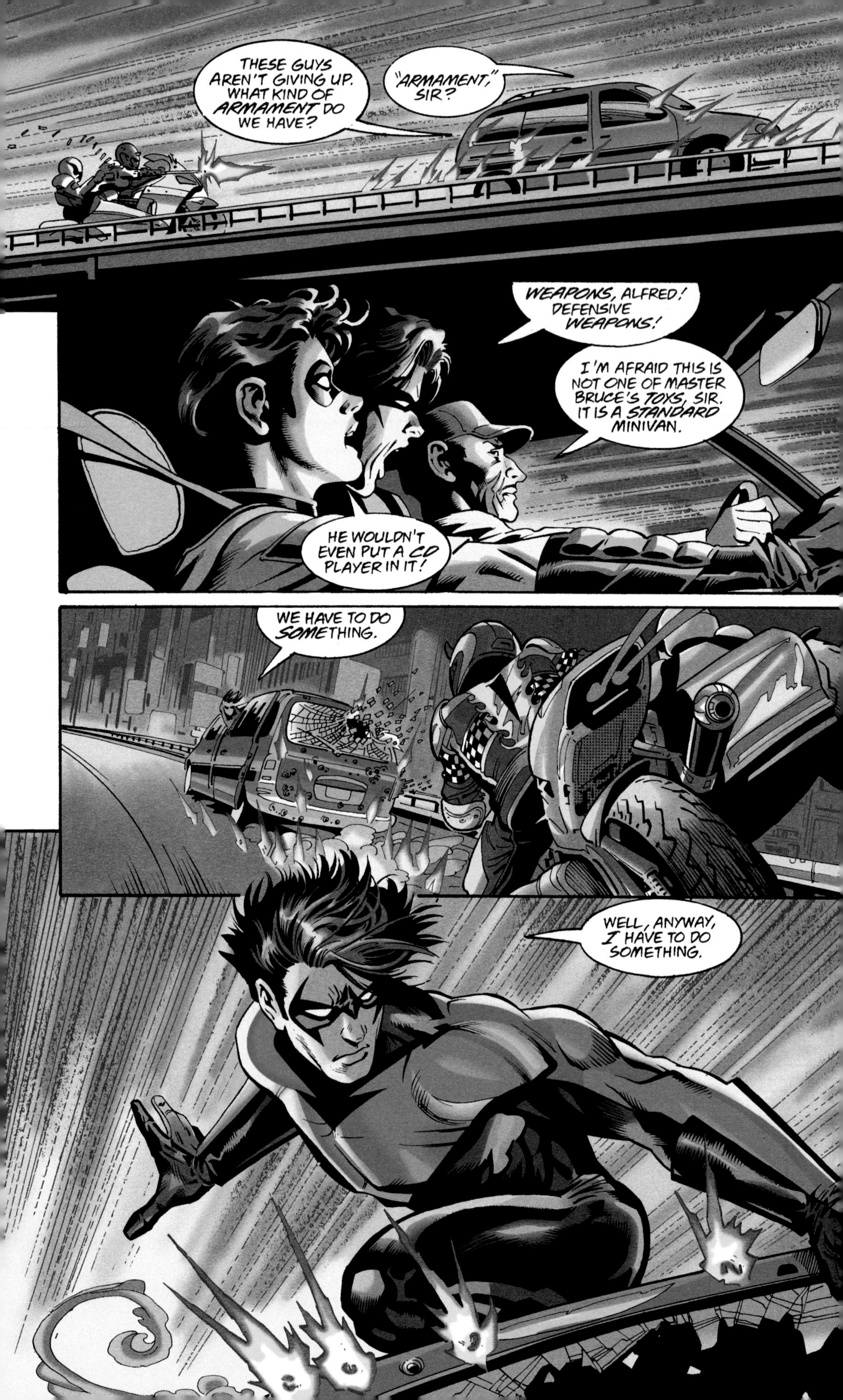
THESE GUYS AREN'T GIVING UP. WHAT KIND OF ARMAMENT DO WE HAVE?
"ARMAMENT," SIR?
WEAPONS, ALFRED! DEFENSIVE WEAPONS!
I'M AFRAID THIS IS NOT ONE OF MASTER BRUCE'S TOYS, SIR. IT IS A STANDARD MINIVAN.
HE WOULDN'T EVEN PUT A CD PLAYER IN IT!
WE HAVE TO DO SOMETHING.
WELL, ANYWAY, I HAVE TO DO SOMETHING.

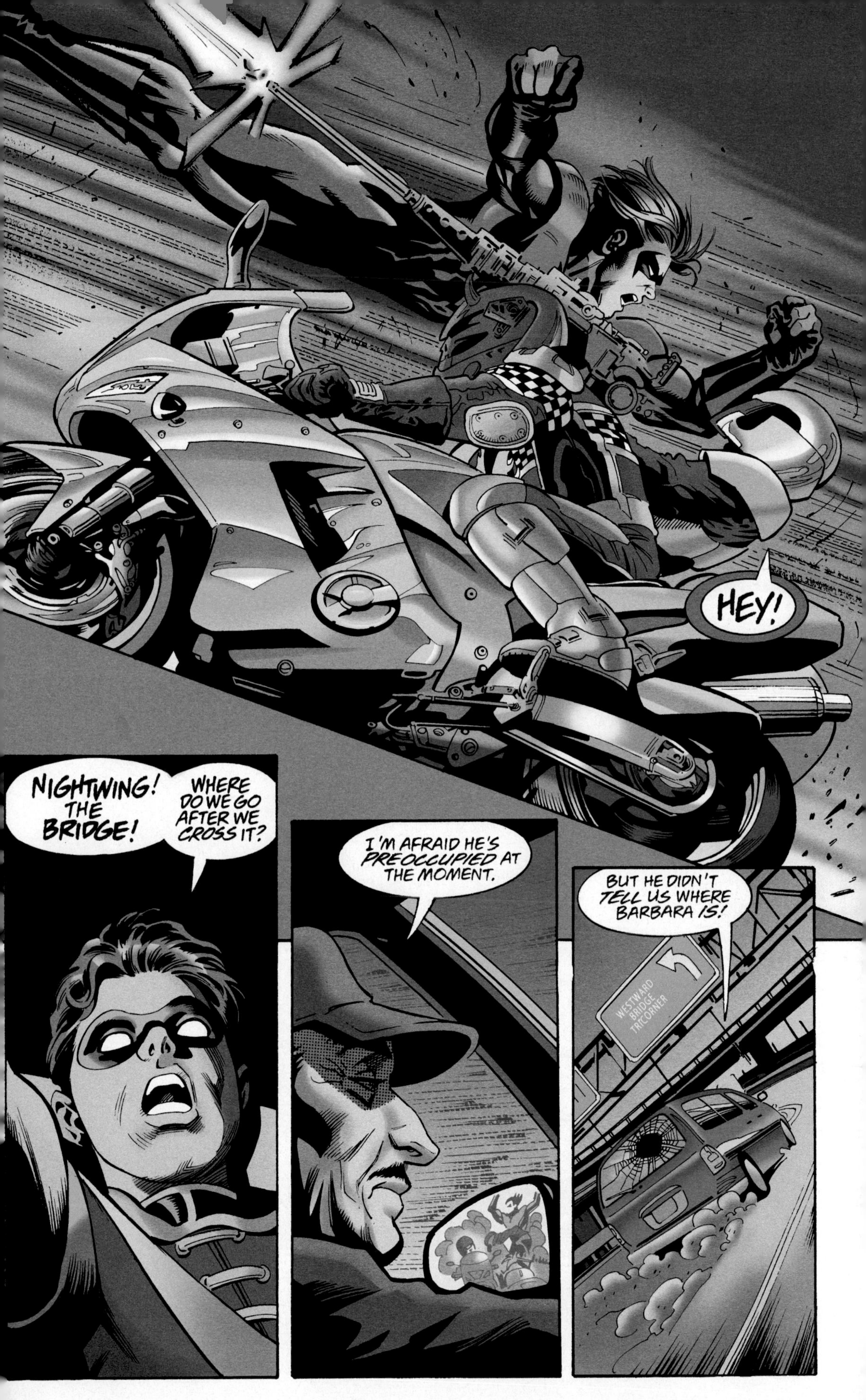
HEY!
NIGHTWING! THE BRIDGE!
WHERE DO WE GO AFTER WE CROSS IT?
I'M AFRAID HE'S PREOCCUPIED AT THE MOMENT.
BUT HE DIDN'T TELL US WHERE BARBARA IS!
WESTWARD BRIDGE TRICORNER

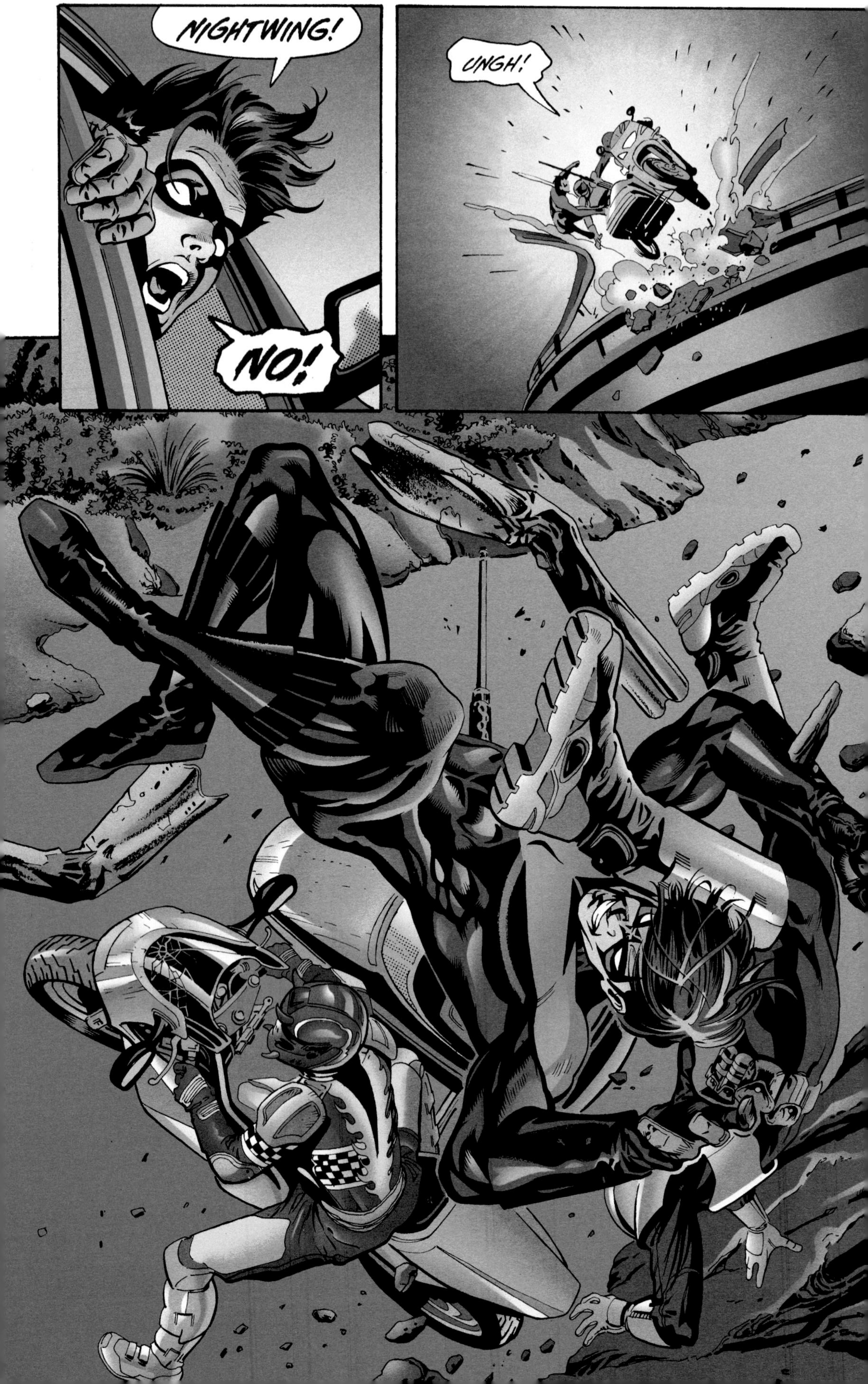
NIGHTWING!
NO!
UNGH!

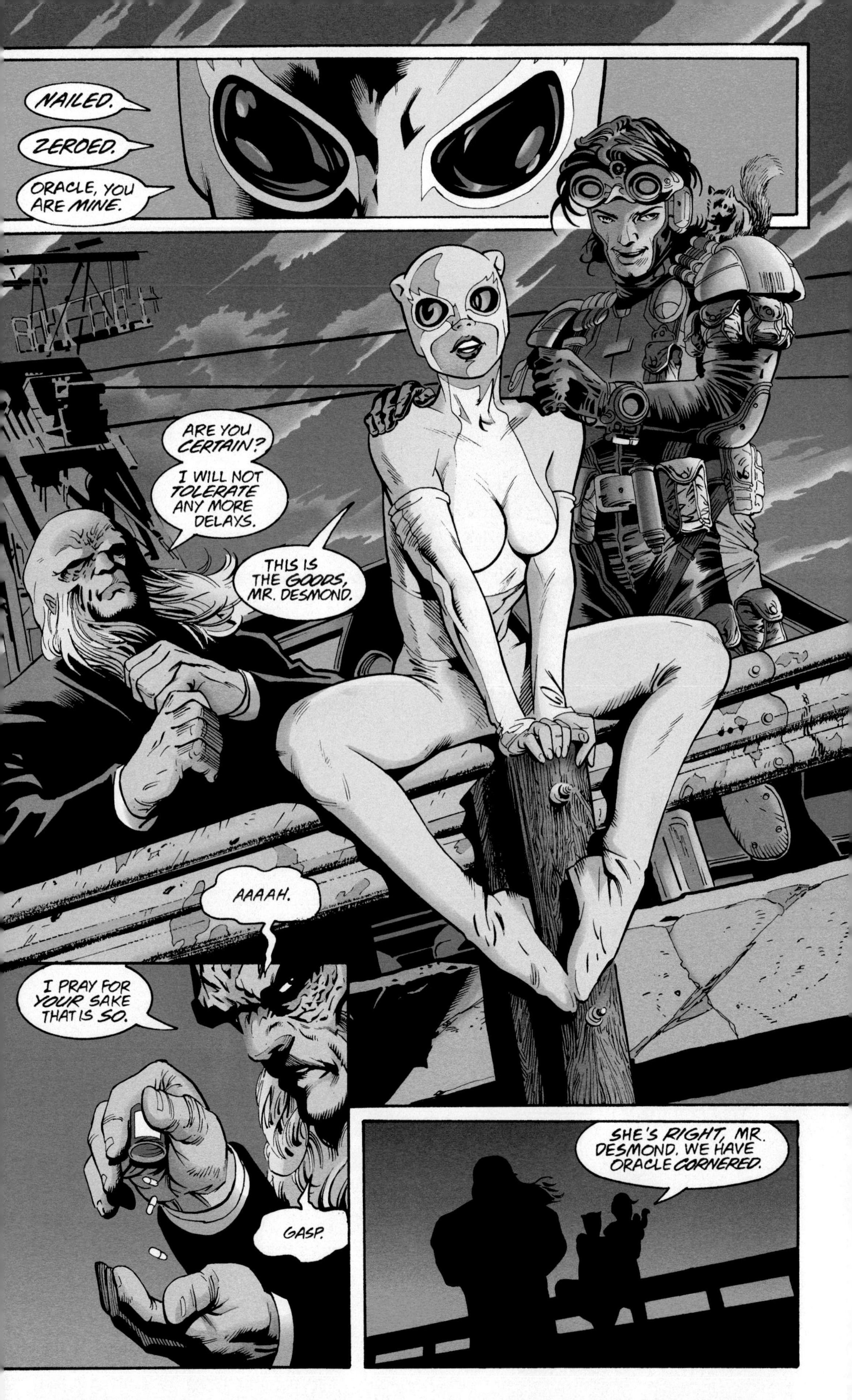
NAILED.
ZEROED.
ORACLE, YOU ARE MINE.
ARE YOU CERTAIN?
I WILL NOT TOLERATE ANY MORE DELAYS.
THIS IS THE GOODS, MR. DESMOND.
AAAAH.
I PRAY FOR YOUR SAKE THAT IS SO.
GASP.
SHE'S RIGHT, MR. DESMOND. WE HAVE ORACLE CORNERED.

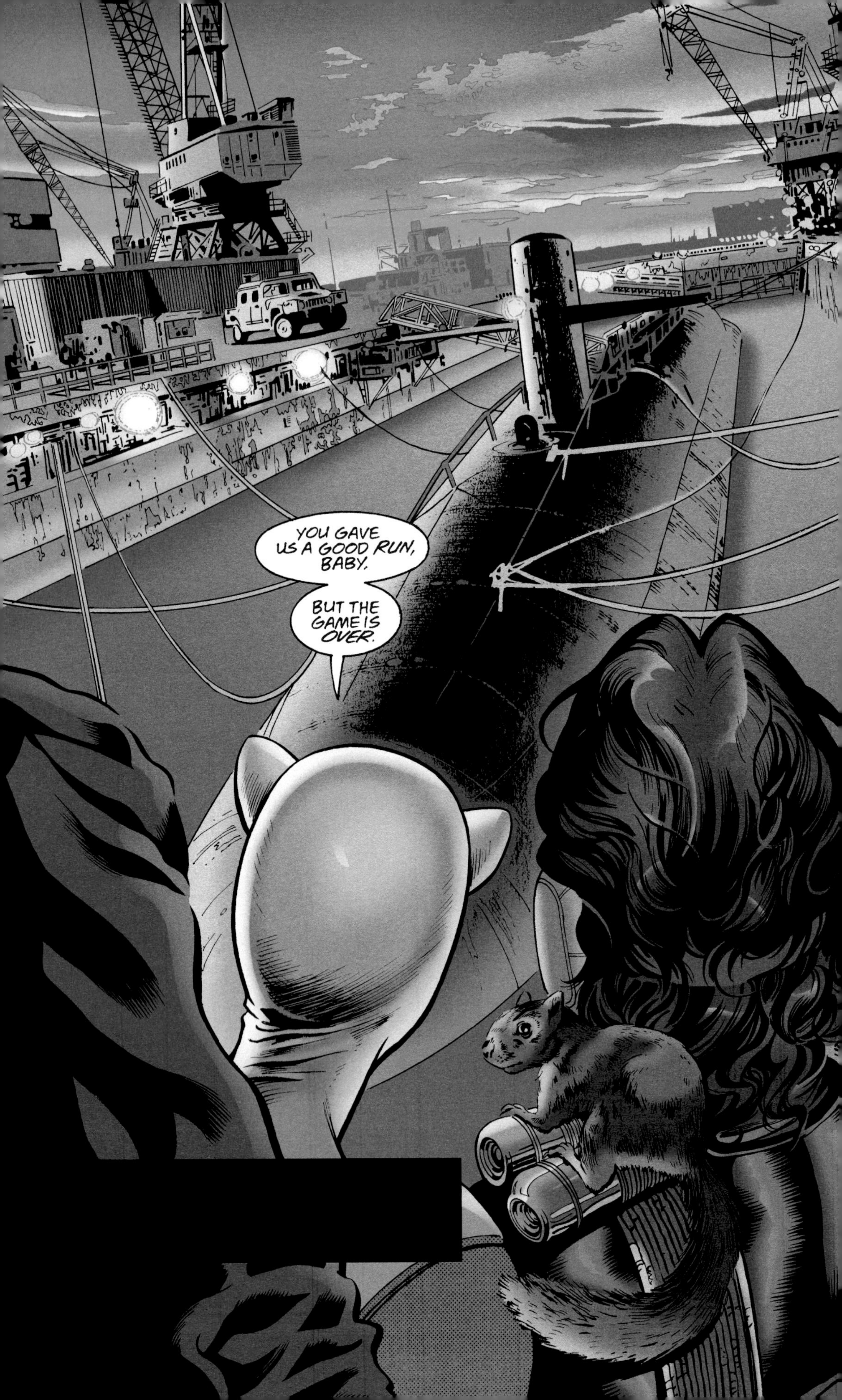
YOU GAVE US A GOOD RUN, BABY.
BUT THE GAME IS OVER.
[redacted]

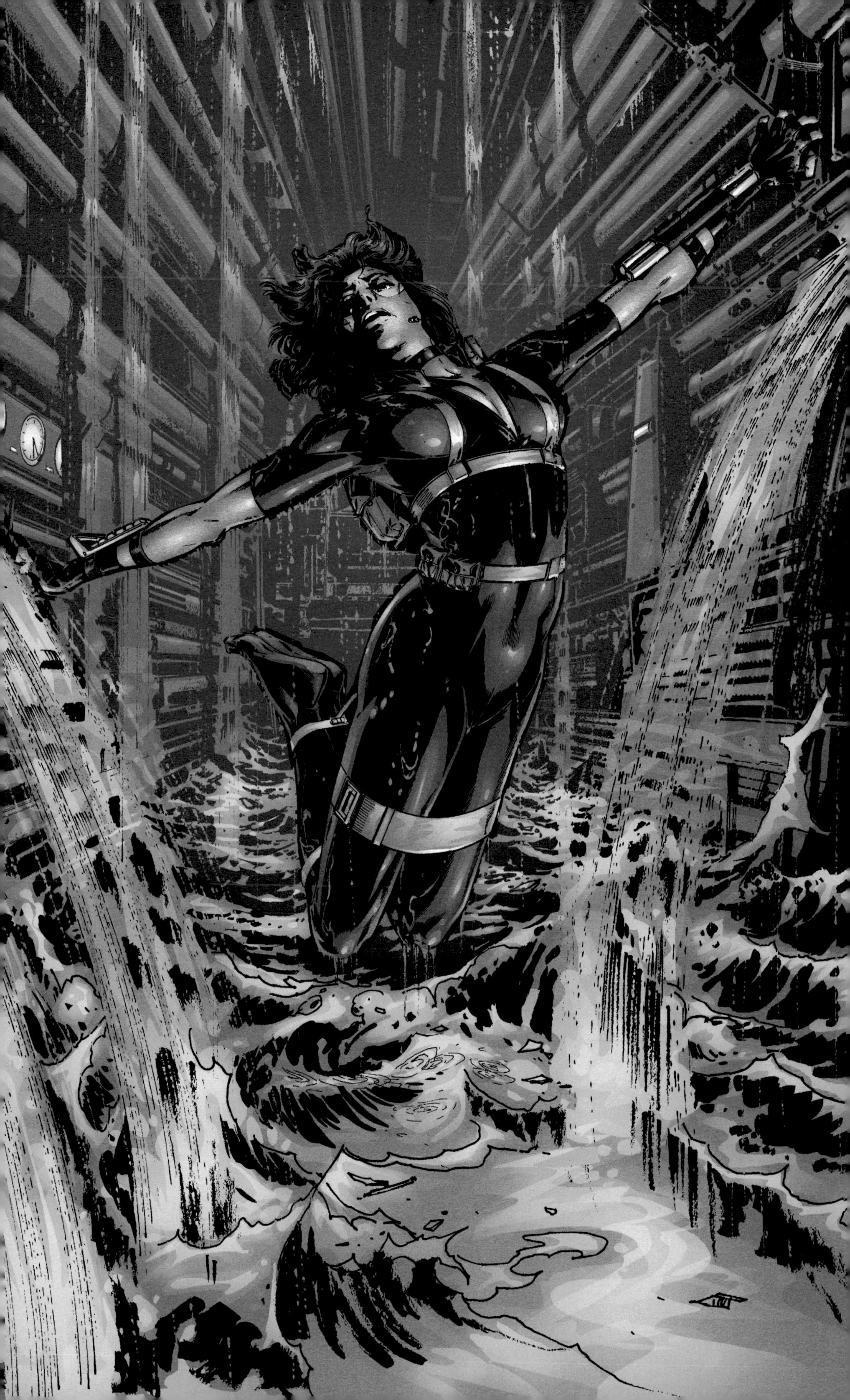

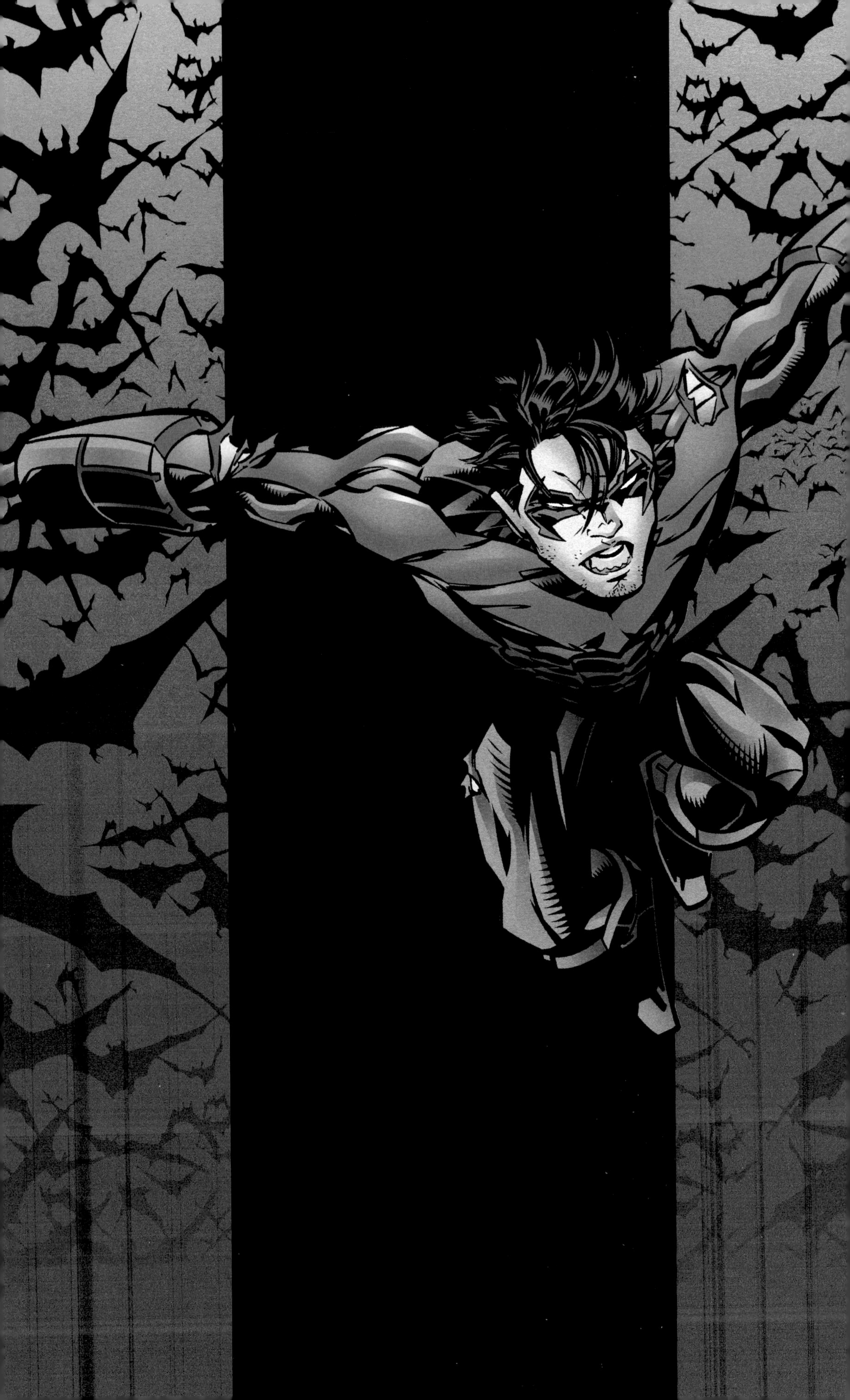

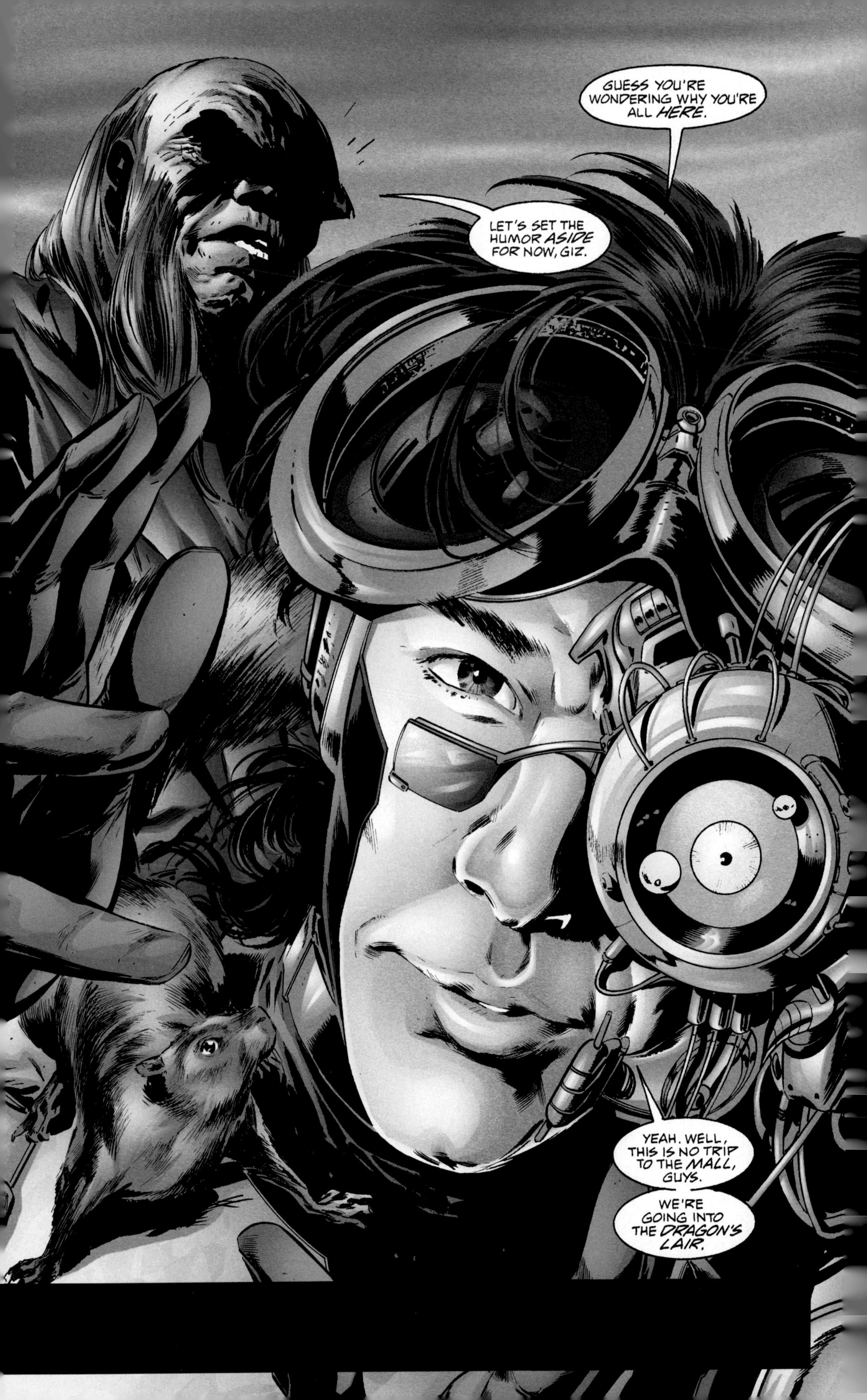
GUESS YOU'RE WONDERING WHY YOU'RE ALL HERE.
LET'S SET THE HUMOR ASIDE FOR NOW, GIZ.
YEAH. WELL, THIS IS NO TRIP TO THE MALL, GUYS.
WE'RE GOING INTO THE DRAGON'S LAIR.

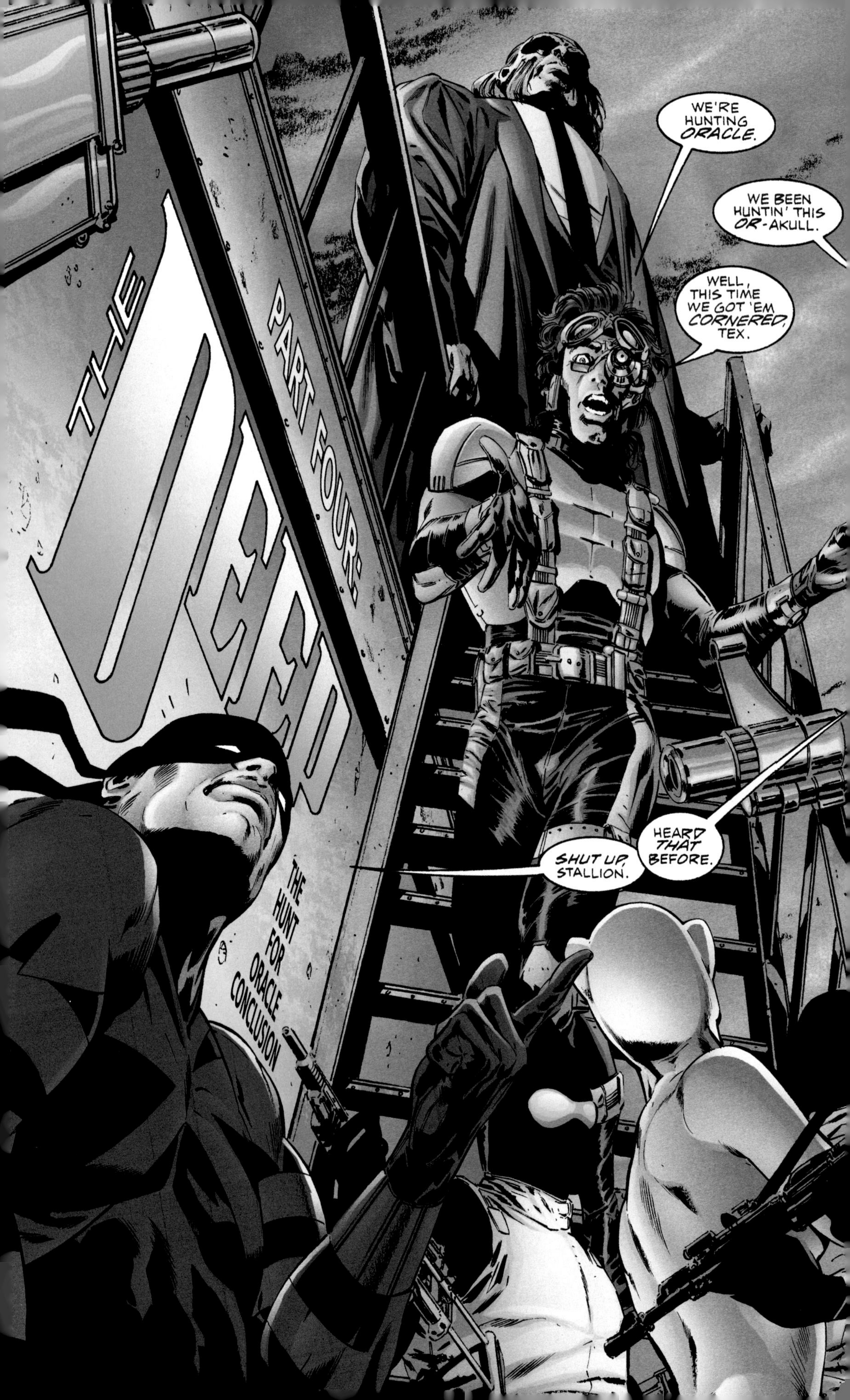
WE'RE HUNTING ORACLE.
WE BEEN HUNTIN' THIS OR-AKULL.
WELL, THIS TIME WE GOT 'EM CORNERED, TEX.
HEARD THAT BEFORE.
SHUT UP, STALLION.
THE END
PART FOUR:
THE HUNT FOR ORACLE CONCLUSION

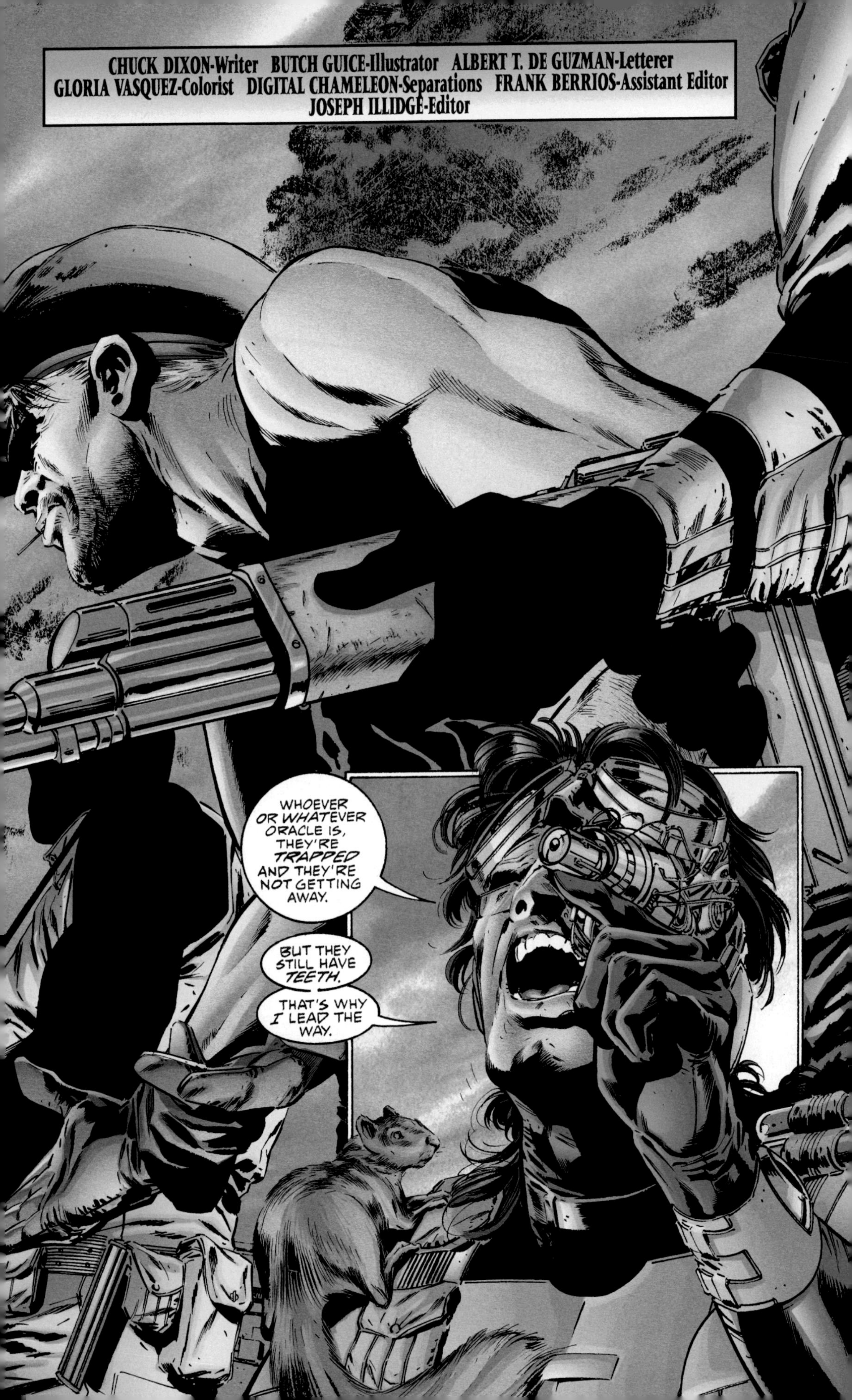
CHUCK DIXON-Writer BUTCH GUICE-Illustrator ALBERT T. DE GUZMAN-Letterer
GLORIA VASQUEZ-Colorist DIGITAL CHAMELEON-Separations FRANK BERRIOS-Assistant Editor
JOSEPH ILLIDGE-Editor
WHOEVER OR *WHATEVER* ORACLE IS, THEY'RE *TRAPPED* AND THEY'RE NOT GETTING AWAY.
BUT THEY STILL HAVE *TEETH.*
THAT'S WHY *I* LEAD THE WAY.

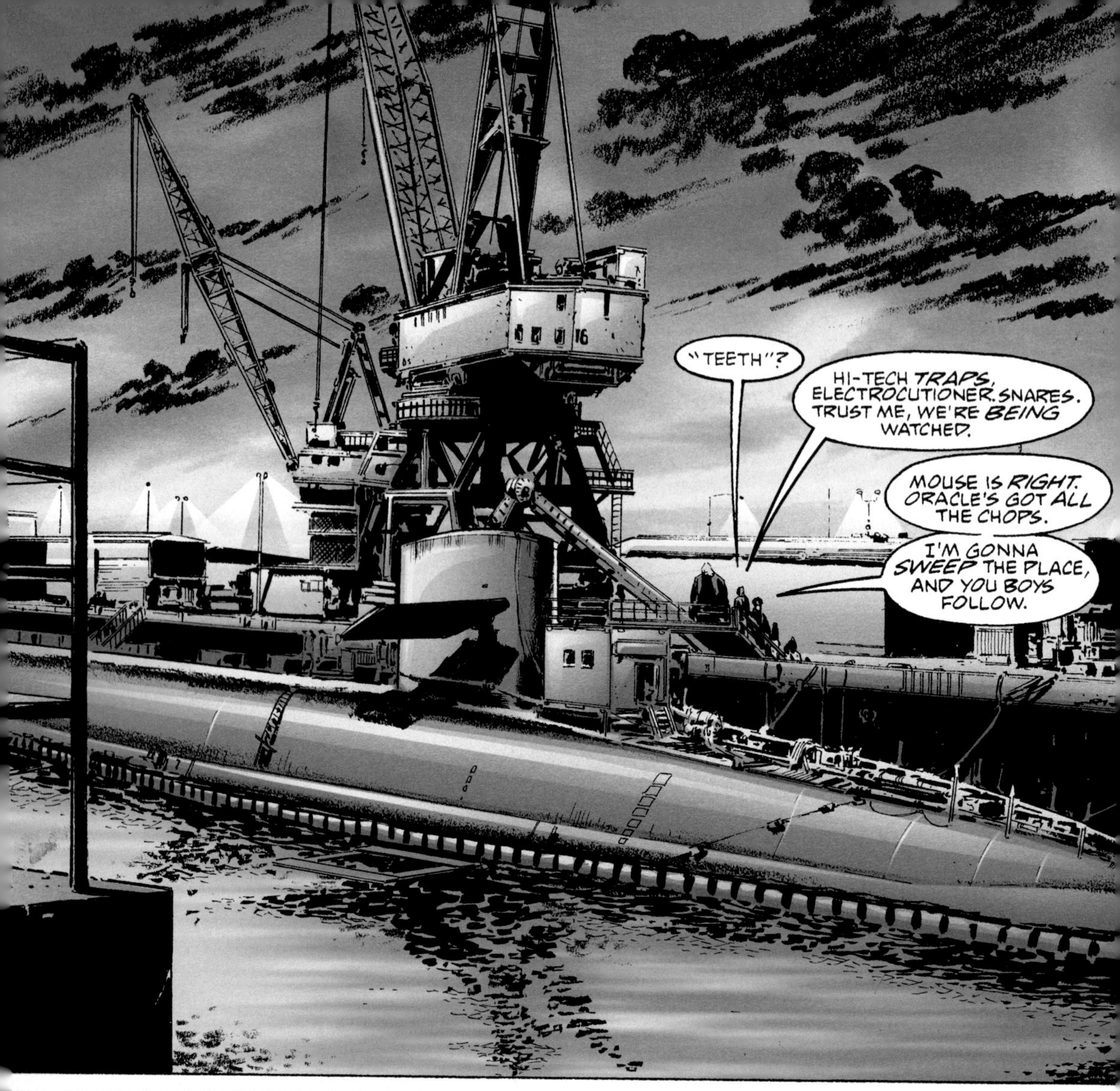
"TEETH"?
HI-TECH TRAPS, ELECTROCUTIONER SNARES. TRUST ME, WE'RE BEING WATCHED.
MOUSE IS RIGHT. ORACLE'S GOT ALL THE CHOPS.
I'M GONNA SWEEP THE PLACE, AND YOU BOYS FOLLOW.

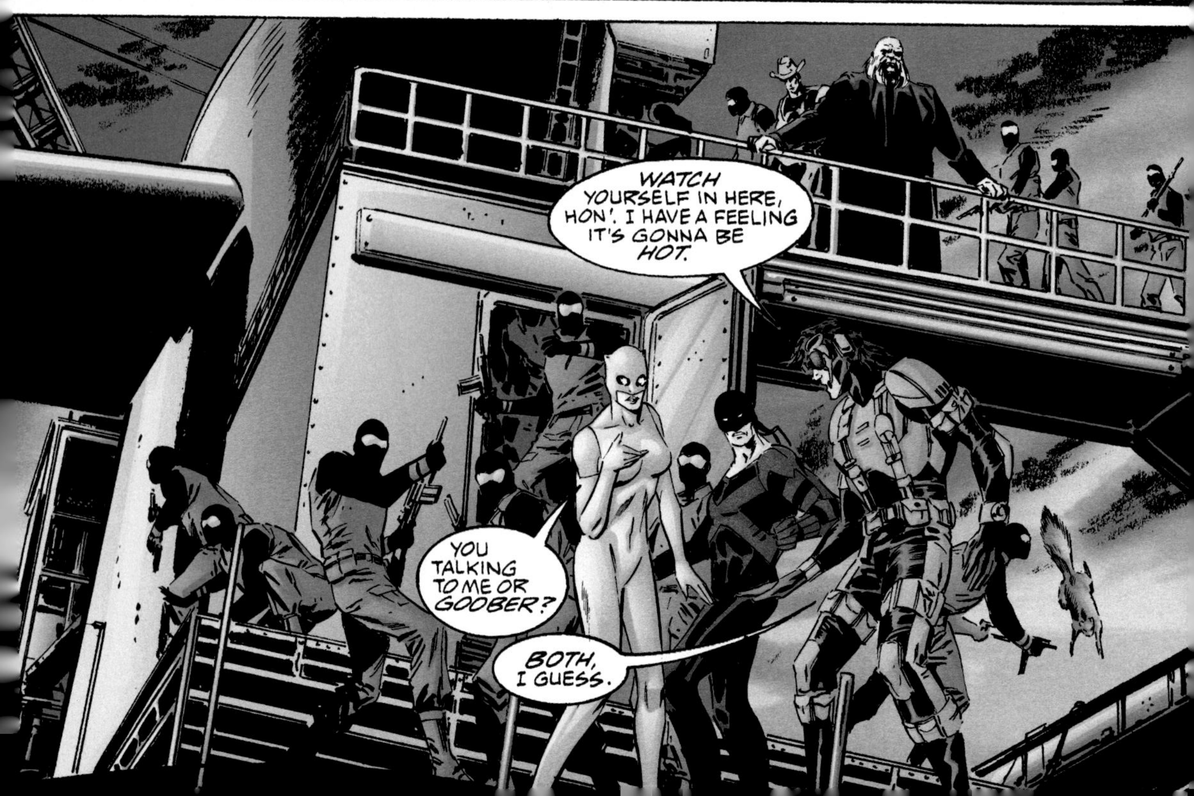
WATCH YOURSELF IN HERE, HON'. I HAVE A FEELING IT'S GONNA BE HOT.
YOU TALKING TO ME OR GOOBER?
BOTH, I GUESS.

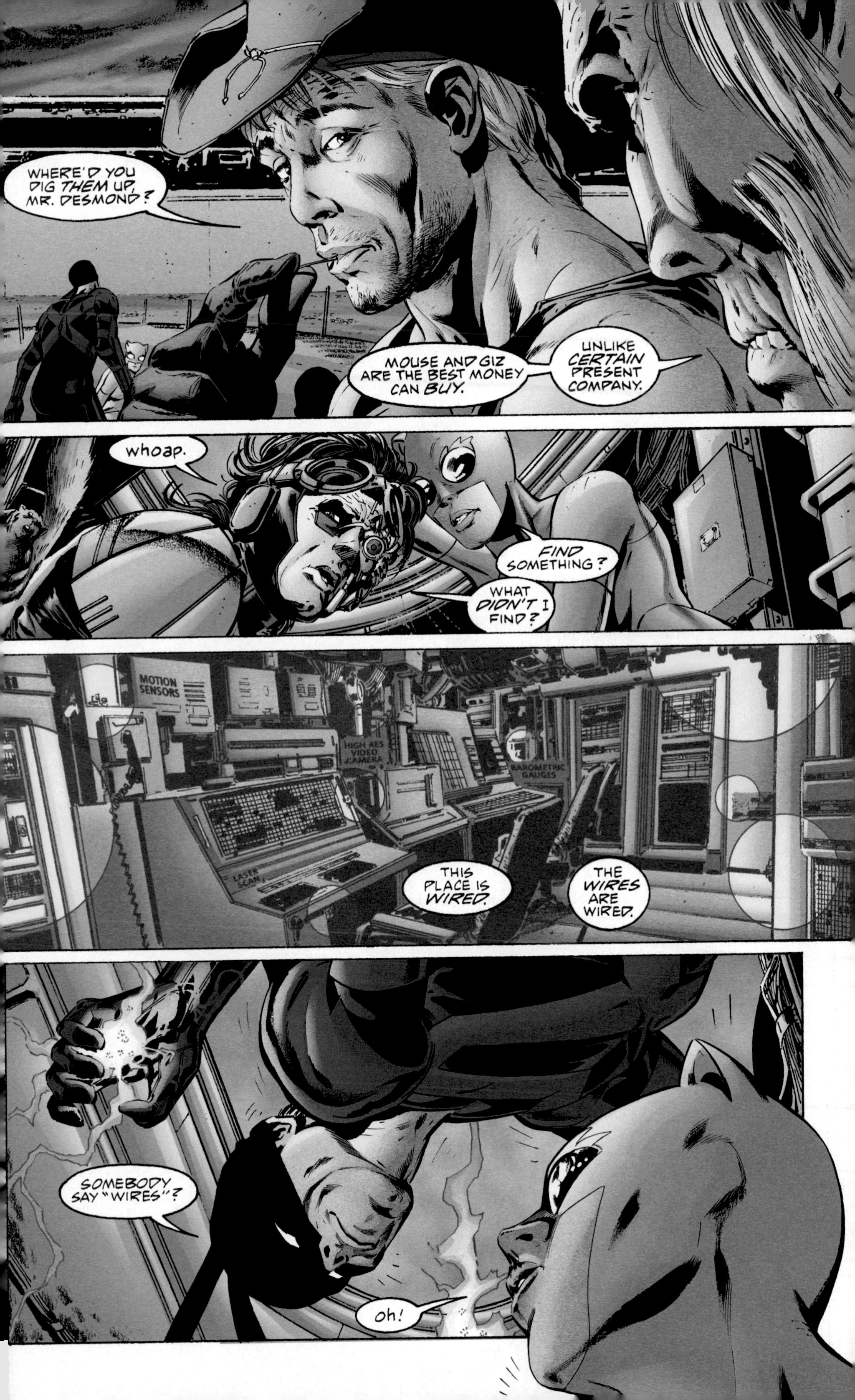
WHERE'D YOU DIG THEM UP, MR. DESMOND?
MOUSE AND GIZ ARE THE BEST MONEY CAN BUY.
UNLIKE CERTAIN PRESENT COMPANY.
whoap.
FIND SOMETHING?
WHAT DIDN'T I FIND?
MOTION SENSORS
HIGH RES VIDEO CAMERA
BAROMETRIC GAUGES
LASER SCAN
THIS PLACE IS WIRED.
THE WIRES ARE WIRED.
SOMEBODY SAY "WIRES"?
oh!

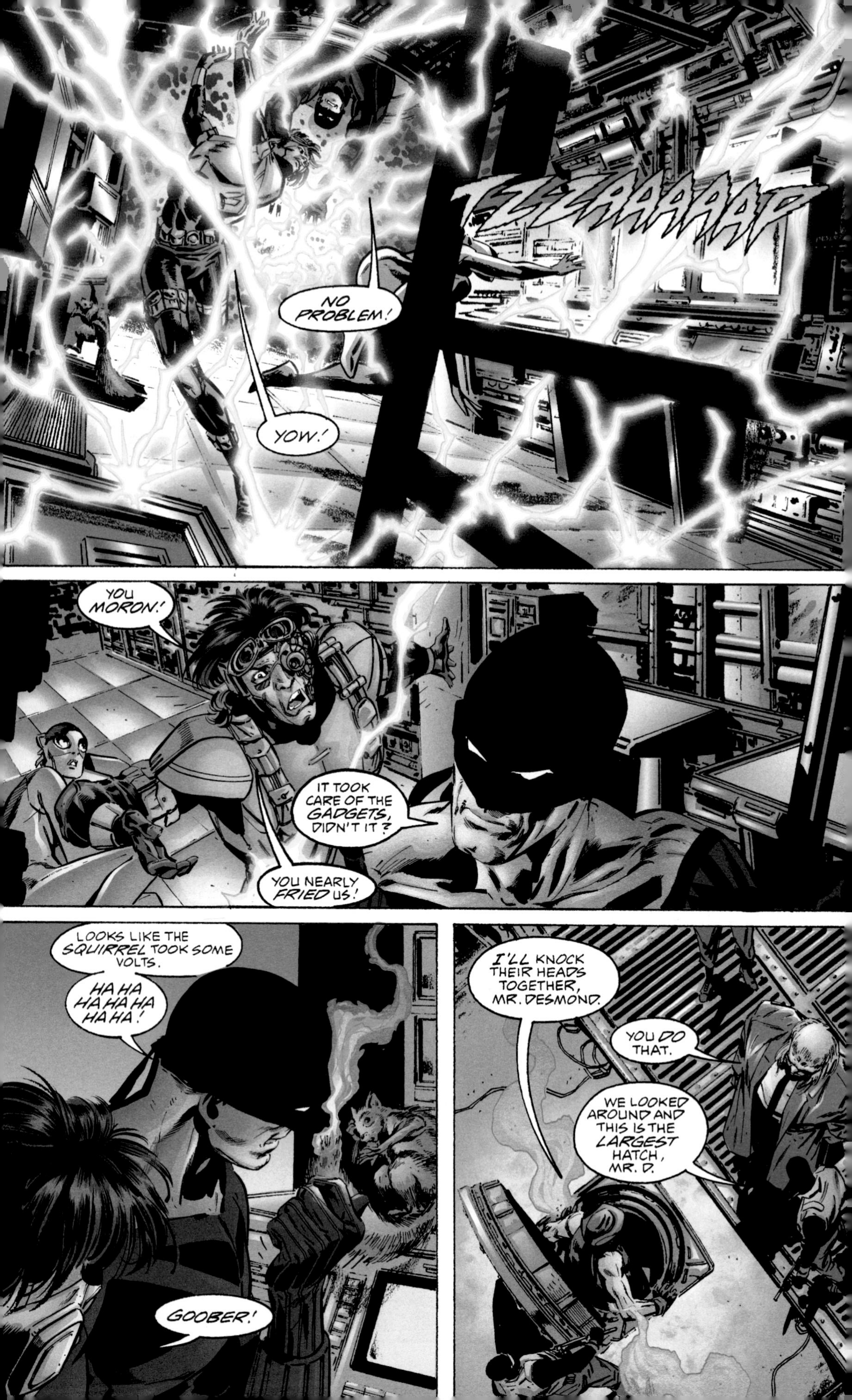
TZZZAAAAAAP
NO PROBLEM!
YOW!
YOU MORON!
IT TOOK CARE OF THE GADGETS, DIDN'T IT?
YOU NEARLY FRIED US!
LOOKS LIKE THE SQUIRREL TOOK SOME VOLTS.
HA HA HA HA HA HA HA HA!
GOOBER!
I'LL KNOCK THEIR HEADS TOGETHER, MR. DESMOND.
YOU DO THAT.
WE LOOKED AROUND AND THIS IS THE LARGEST HATCH, MR. D.

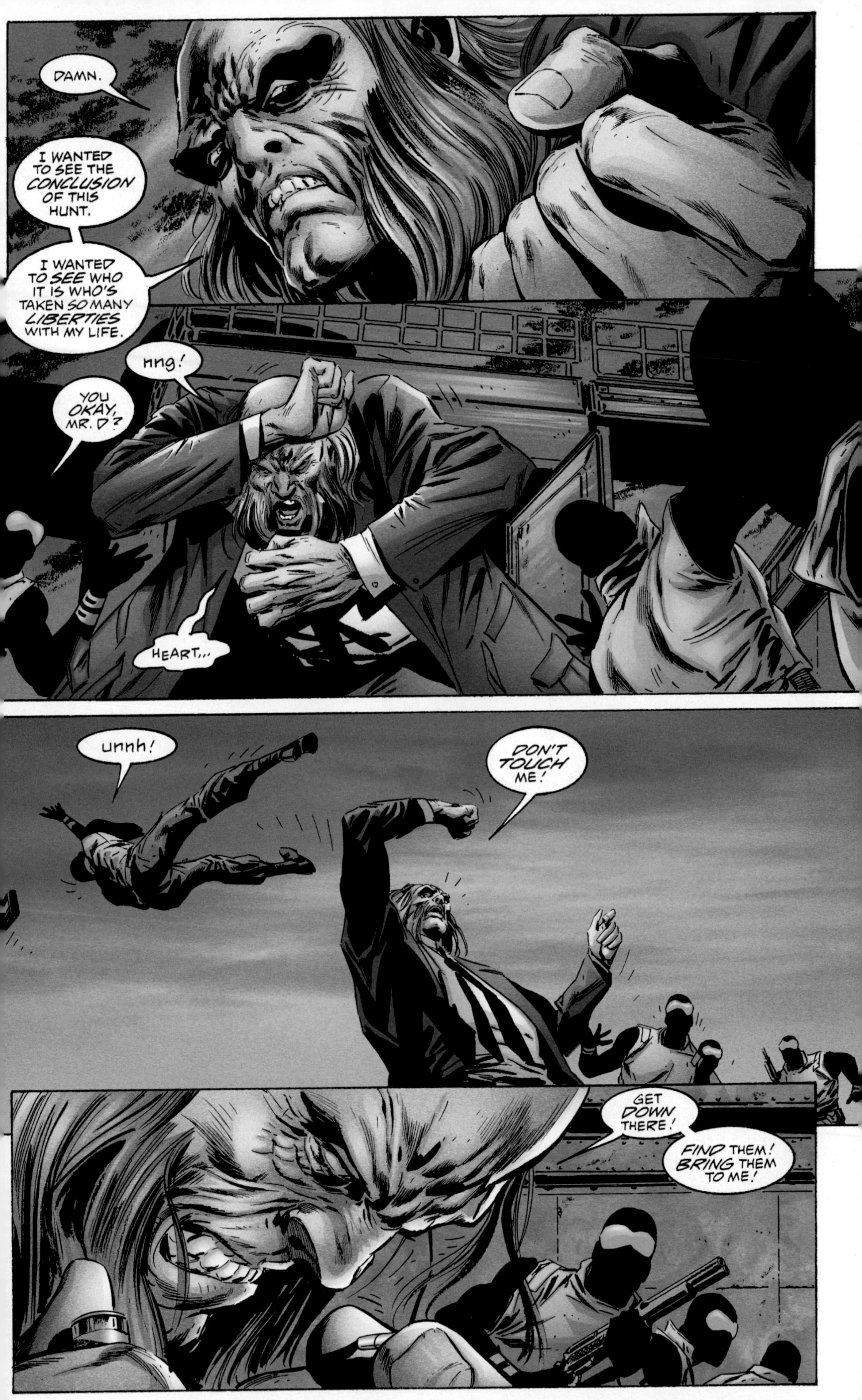
DAMN.
I WANTED TO SEE THE CONCLUSION OF THIS HUNT.
I WANTED TO SEE WHO IT IS WHO'S TAKEN SO MANY LIBERTIES WITH MY LIFE.
nng!
YOU OKAY, MR. D?
HEART...
unnh!
DON'T TOUCH ME!
GET DOWN THERE!
FIND THEM! BRING THEM TO ME!

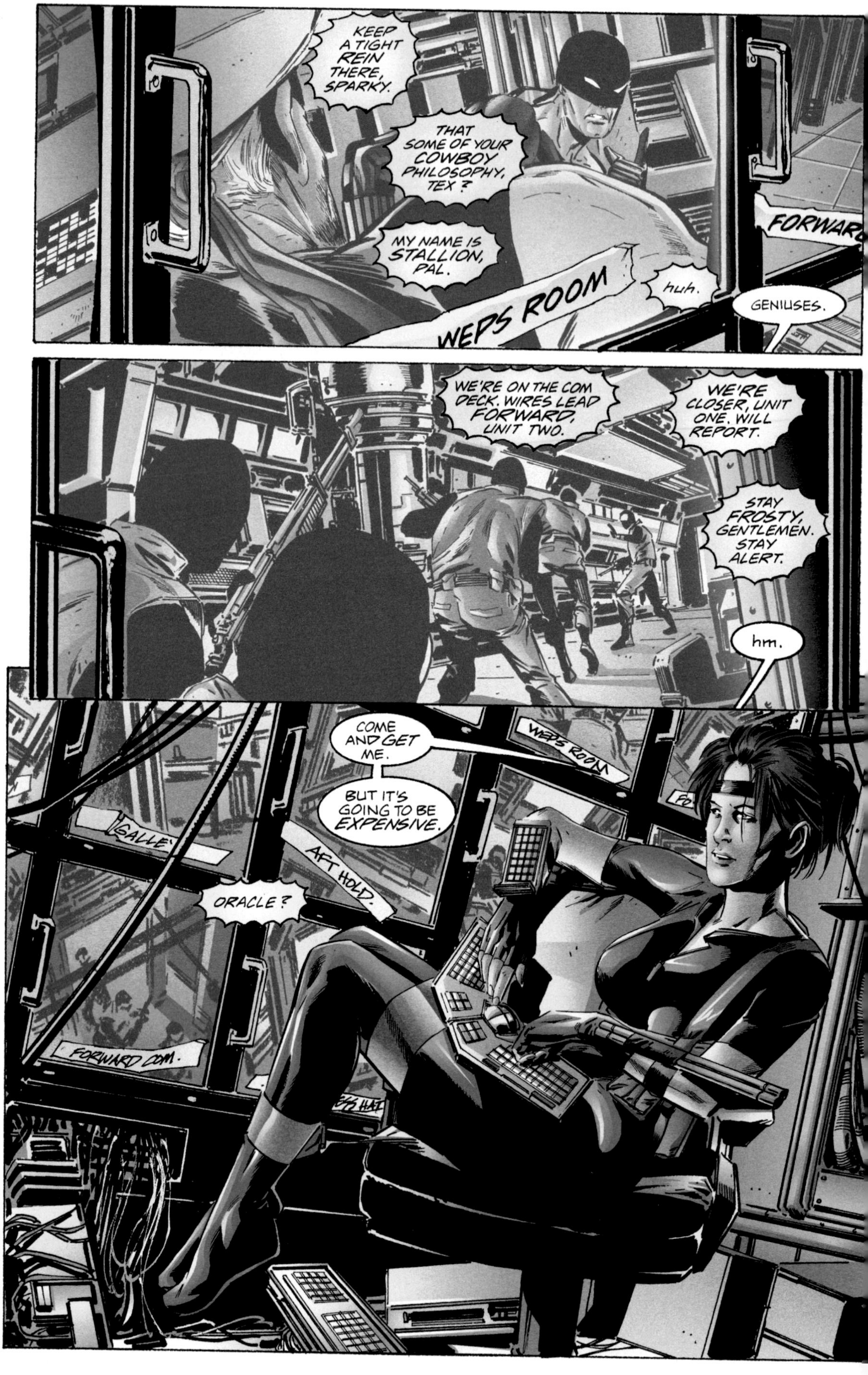
KEEP A TIGHT REIN THERE, SPARKY.
THAT SOME OF YOUR COWBOY PHILOSOPHY, TEX?
MY NAME IS STALLION, PAL.
huh.
WEPS ROOM
FORWARD
GENIUSES.
WE'RE ON THE COM DECK. WIRES LEAD FORWARD, UNIT TWO.
WE'RE CLOSER, UNIT ONE. WILL REPORT.
STAY FROSTY, GENTLEMEN. STAY ALERT.
hm.
COME AND GET ME.
BUT IT'S GOING TO BE EXPENSIVE.
WEPS ROOM
AFT HOLD
ORACLE?
FORWARD COM.

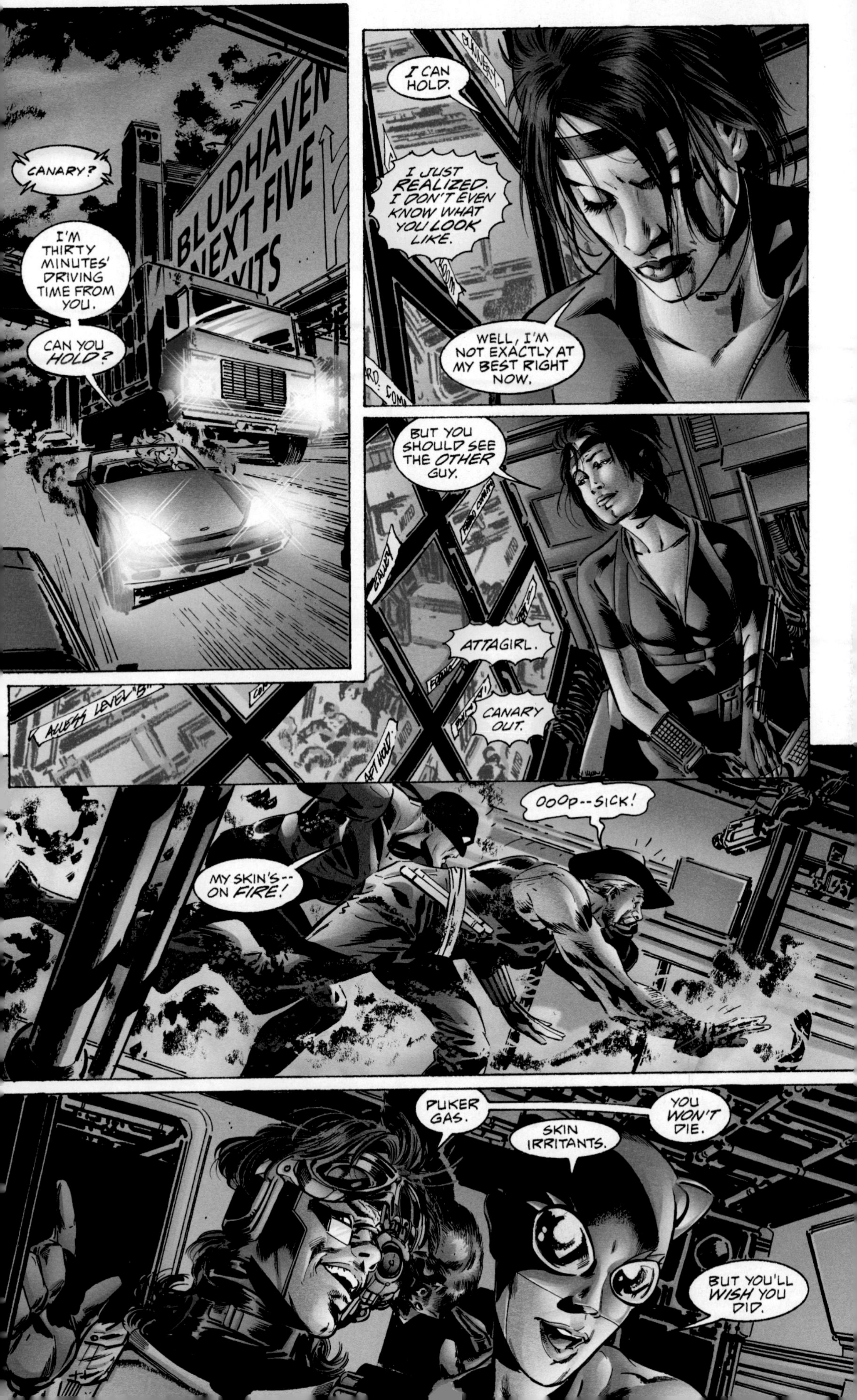
BLUDHAVEN NEXT FIVE EXITS
CANARY?
I'M THIRTY MINUTES' DRIVING TIME FROM YOU.
CAN YOU HOLD?
I CAN HOLD.
I JUST REALIZED. I DON'T EVEN KNOW WHAT YOU LOOK LIKE.
WELL, I'M NOT EXACTLY AT MY BEST RIGHT NOW.
BUT YOU SHOULD SEE THE OTHER GUY.
ATTAGIRL.
CANARY OUT.
OOOP--SICK!
MY SKIN'S--ON FIRE!
PUKER GAS.
SKIN IRRITANTS.
YOU WON'T DIE.
BUT YOU'LL WISH YOU DID.

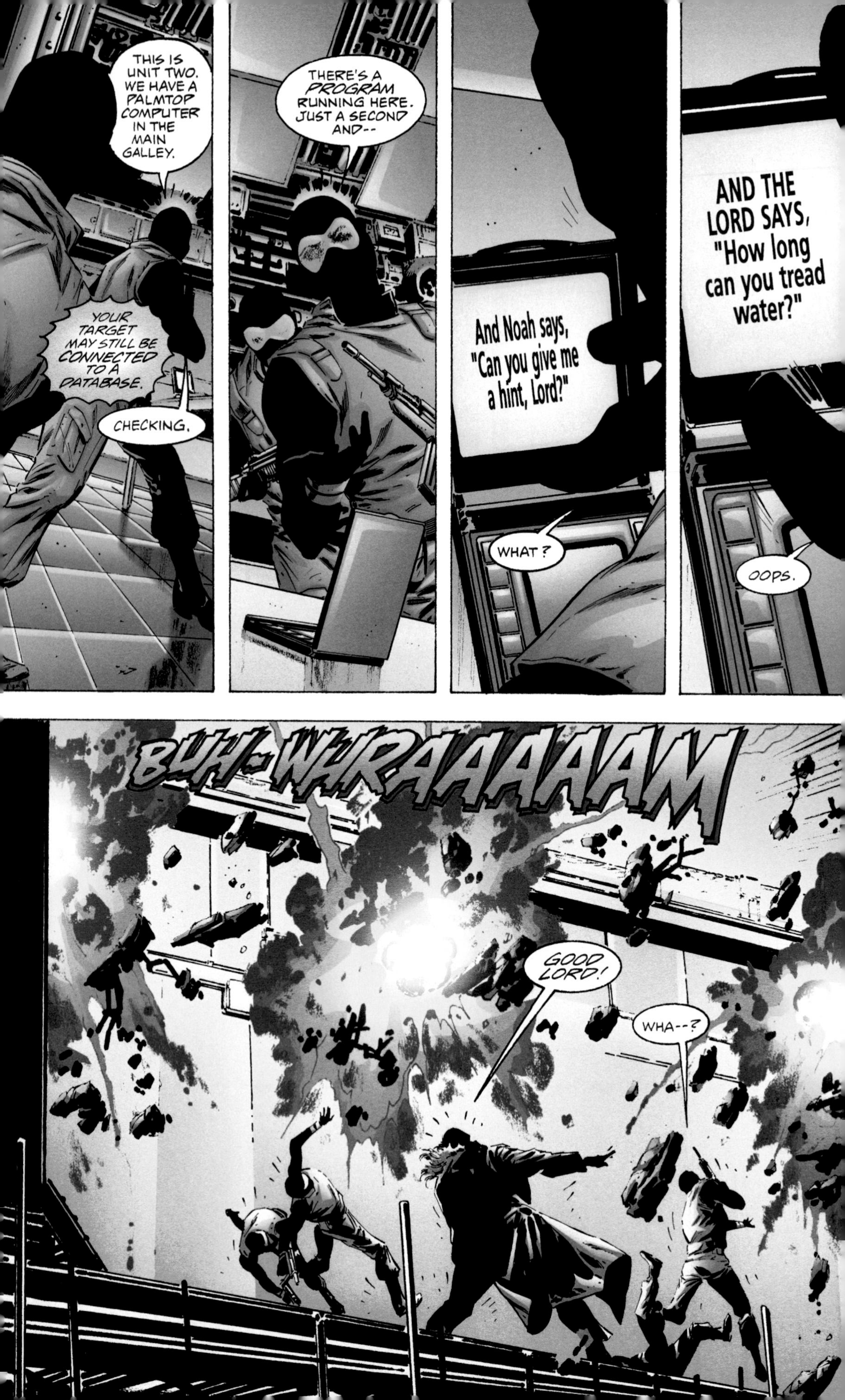
THIS IS UNIT TWO. WE HAVE A PALMTOP COMPUTER IN THE MAIN GALLEY.
YOUR TARGET MAY STILL BE CONNECTED TO A DATABASE.
CHECKING.
THERE'S A PROGRAM RUNNING HERE. JUST A SECOND AND--
And Noah says, "Can you give me a hint, Lord?"
WHAT?
AND THE LORD SAYS, "How long can you tread water?"
OOPS.
BUH-WHRAAAAAAM
GOOD LORD!
WHA--?

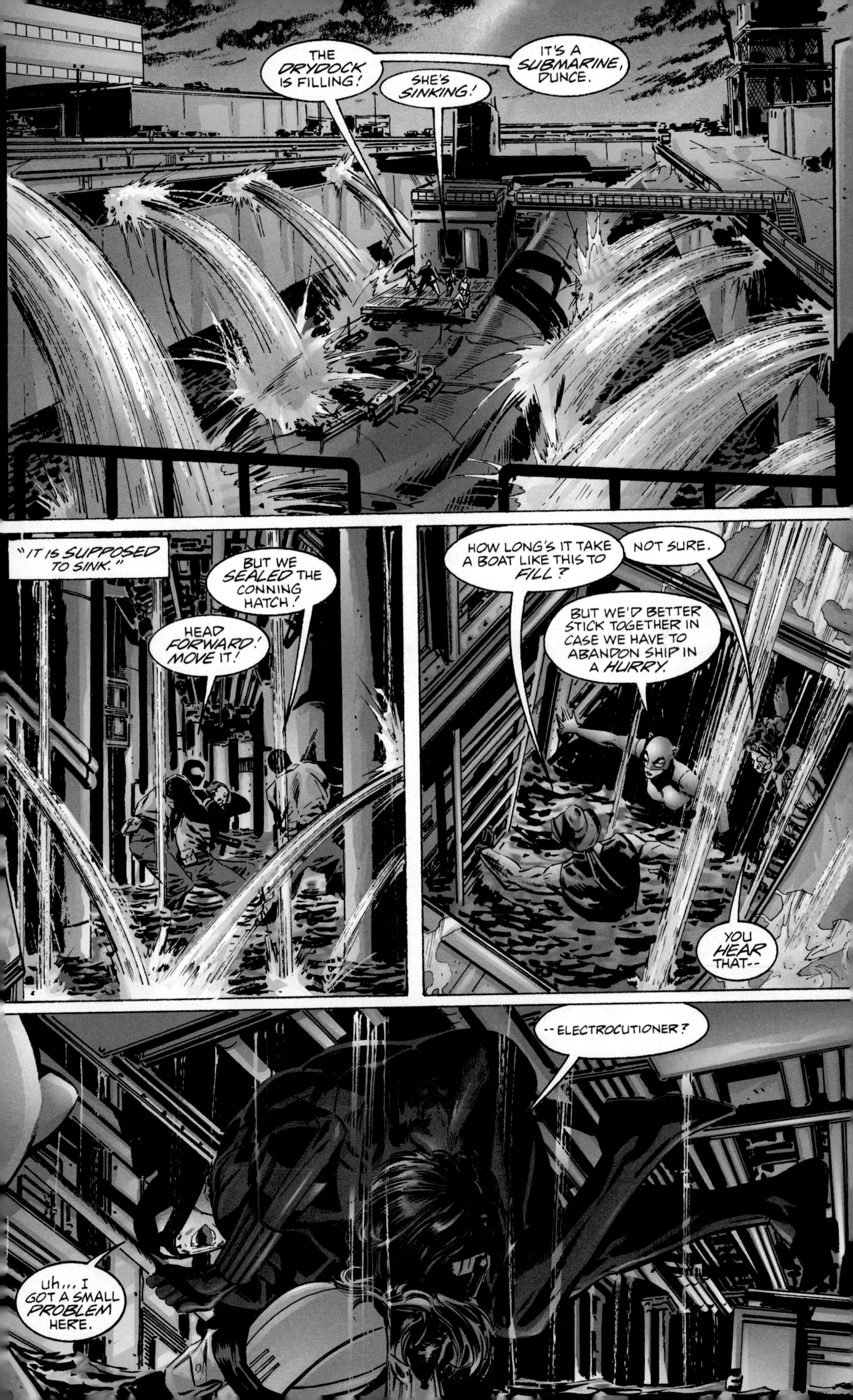
THE DRYDOCK IS FILLING!
SHE'S SINKING!
IT'S A SUBMARINE, DUNCE.
"IT IS SUPPOSED TO SINK."
BUT WE SEALED THE CONNING HATCH!
HEAD FORWARD! MOVE IT!
HOW LONG'S IT TAKE A BOAT LIKE THIS TO FILL?
NOT SURE.
BUT WE'D BETTER STICK TOGETHER IN CASE WE HAVE TO ABANDON SHIP IN A HURRY.
YOU HEAR THAT--
--ELECTROCUTIONER?
uh... I GOT A SMALL PROBLEM HERE.

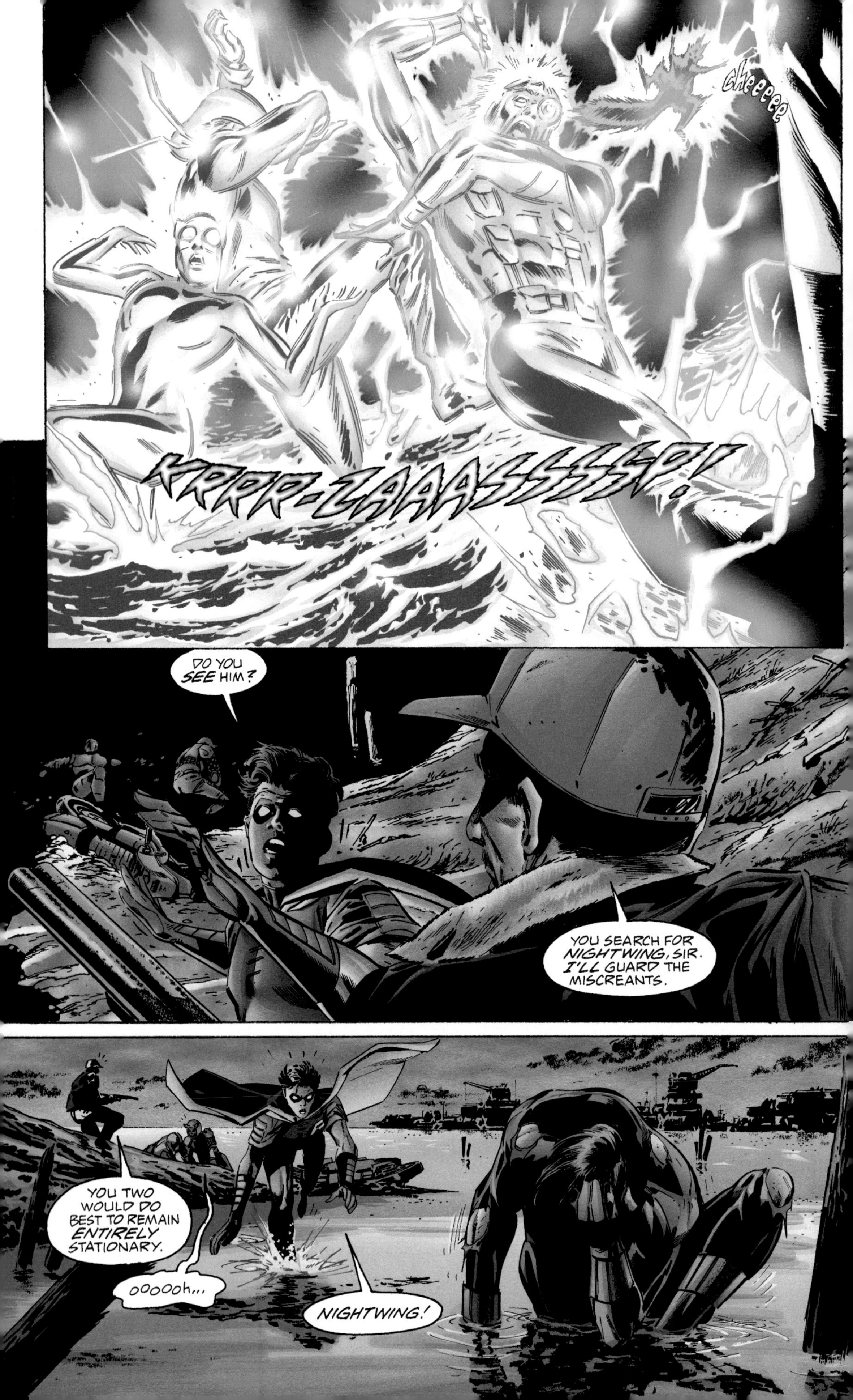
cheeeee
KRRR-ZAAASSSSP!
DO YOU SEE HIM?
YOU SEARCH FOR NIGHTWING, SIR. I'LL GUARD THE MISCREANTS.
!!
YOU TWO WOULD DO BEST TO REMAIN ENTIRELY STATIONARY.
ooooh...
NIGHTWING!

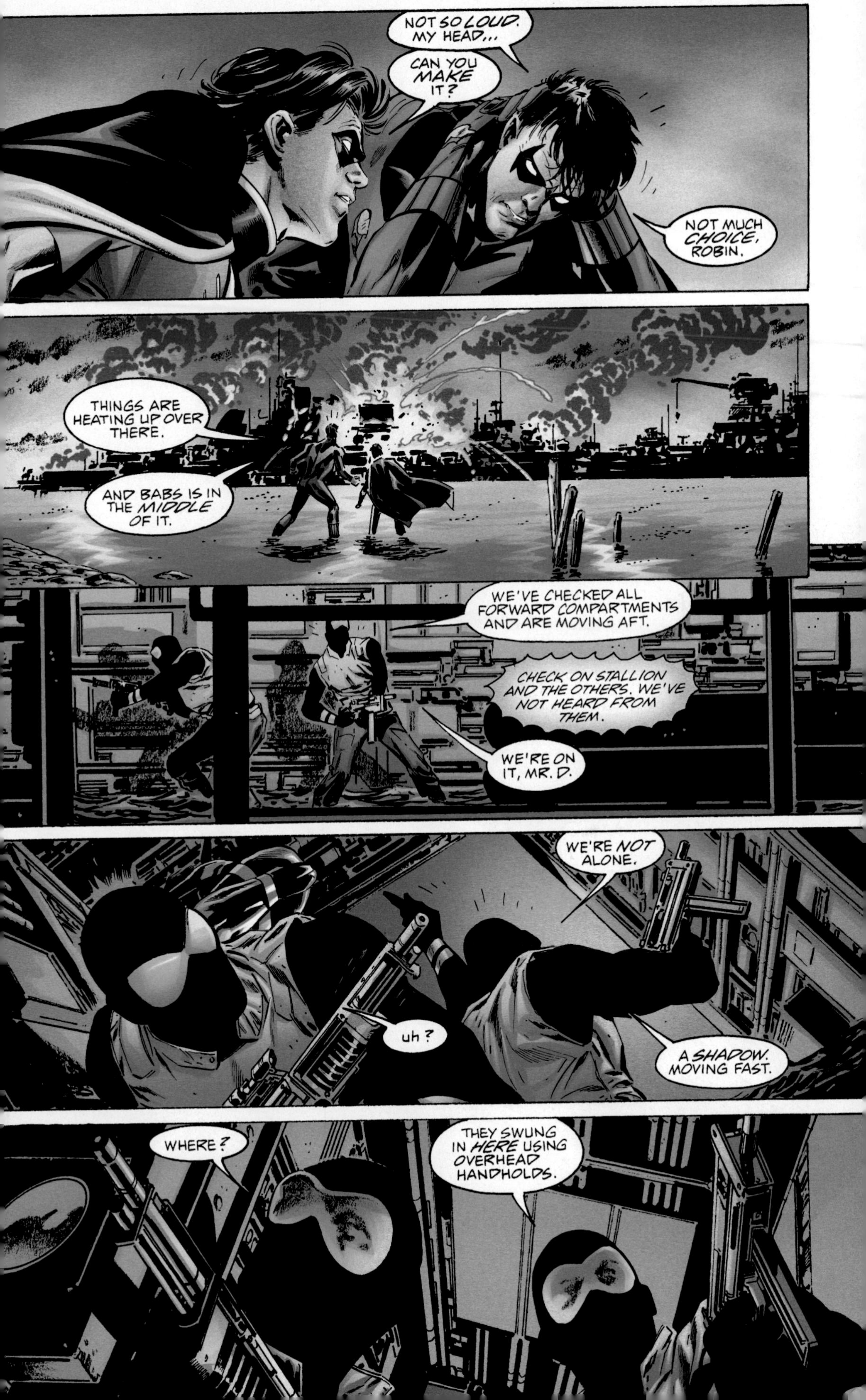
NOT SO LOUD. MY HEAD...
CAN YOU MAKE IT?
NOT MUCH CHOICE, ROBIN.
THINGS ARE HEATING UP OVER THERE.
AND BABS IS IN THE MIDDLE OF IT.
WE'VE CHECKED ALL FORWARD COMPARTMENTS AND ARE MOVING AFT.
CHECK ON STALLION AND THE OTHERS. WE'VE NOT HEARD FROM THEM.
WE'RE ON IT, MR. D.
WE'RE NOT ALONE.
uh?
A SHADOW. MOVING FAST.
WHERE?
THEY SWUNG IN HERE USING OVERHEAD HANDHOLDS.

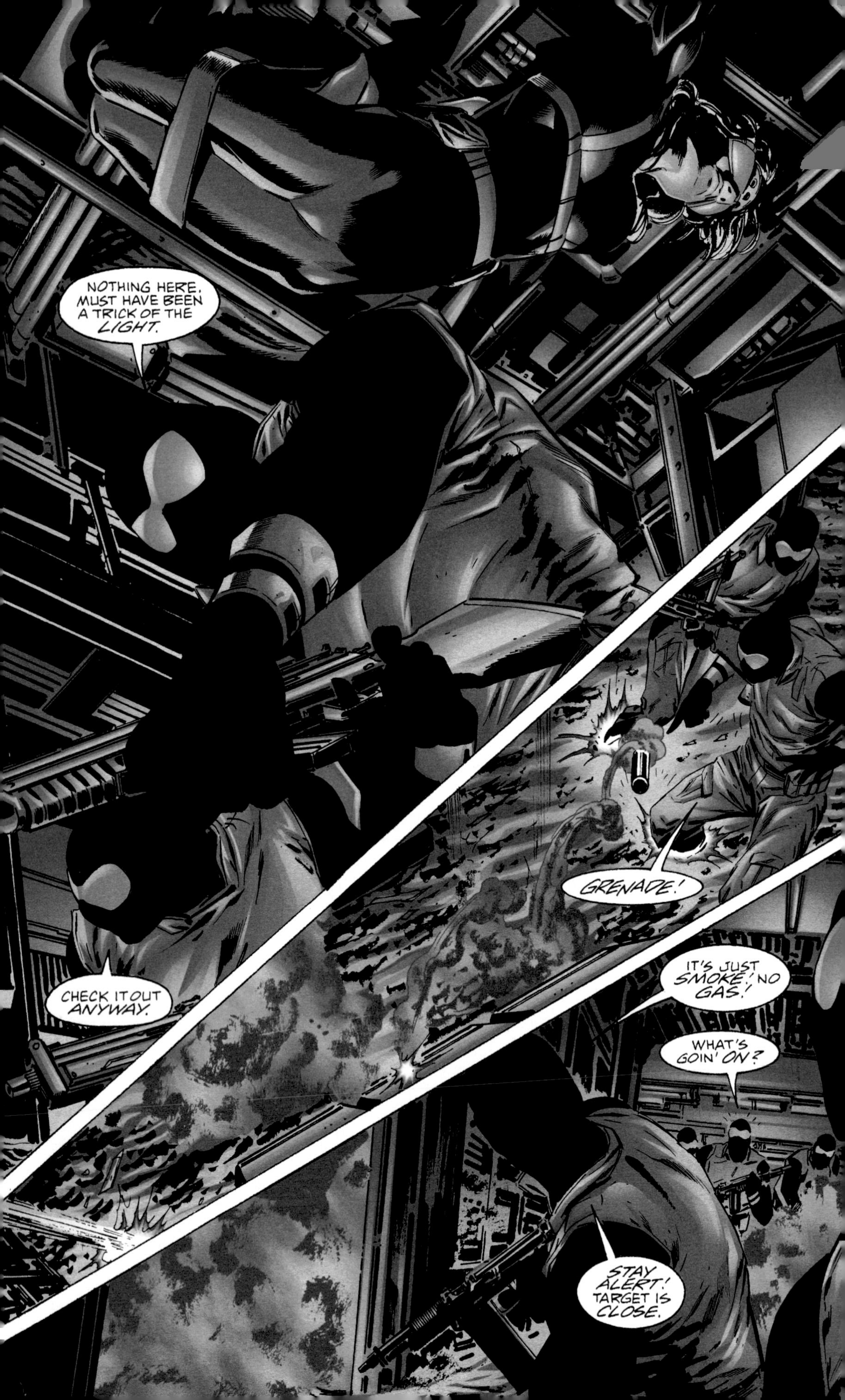
NOTHING HERE. MUST HAVE BEEN A TRICK OF THE LIGHT.
CHECK IT OUT ANYWAY.
GRENADE!
IT'S JUST SMOKE! NO GAS!
WHAT'S GOIN' ON?
STAY ALERT! TARGET IS CLOSE.

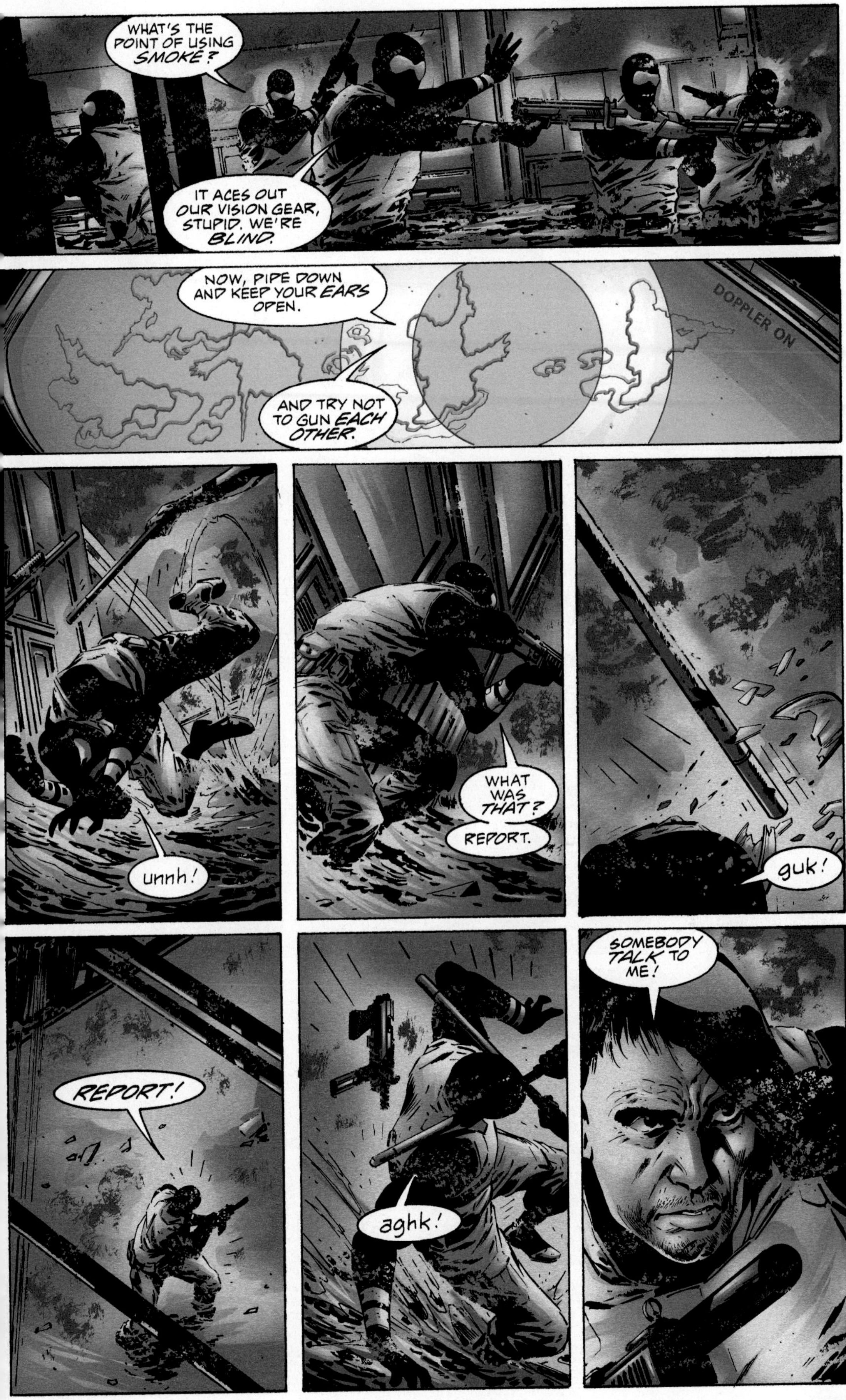
WHAT'S THE POINT OF USING SMOKE?
IT ACES OUT OUR VISION GEAR, STUPID. WE'RE BLIND.
DOPPLER ON
NOW, PIPE DOWN AND KEEP YOUR EARS OPEN.
AND TRY NOT TO GUN EACH OTHER.
unnh!
WHAT WAS THAT?
REPORT.
guk!
REPORT!
aghk!
SOMEBODY TALK TO ME!

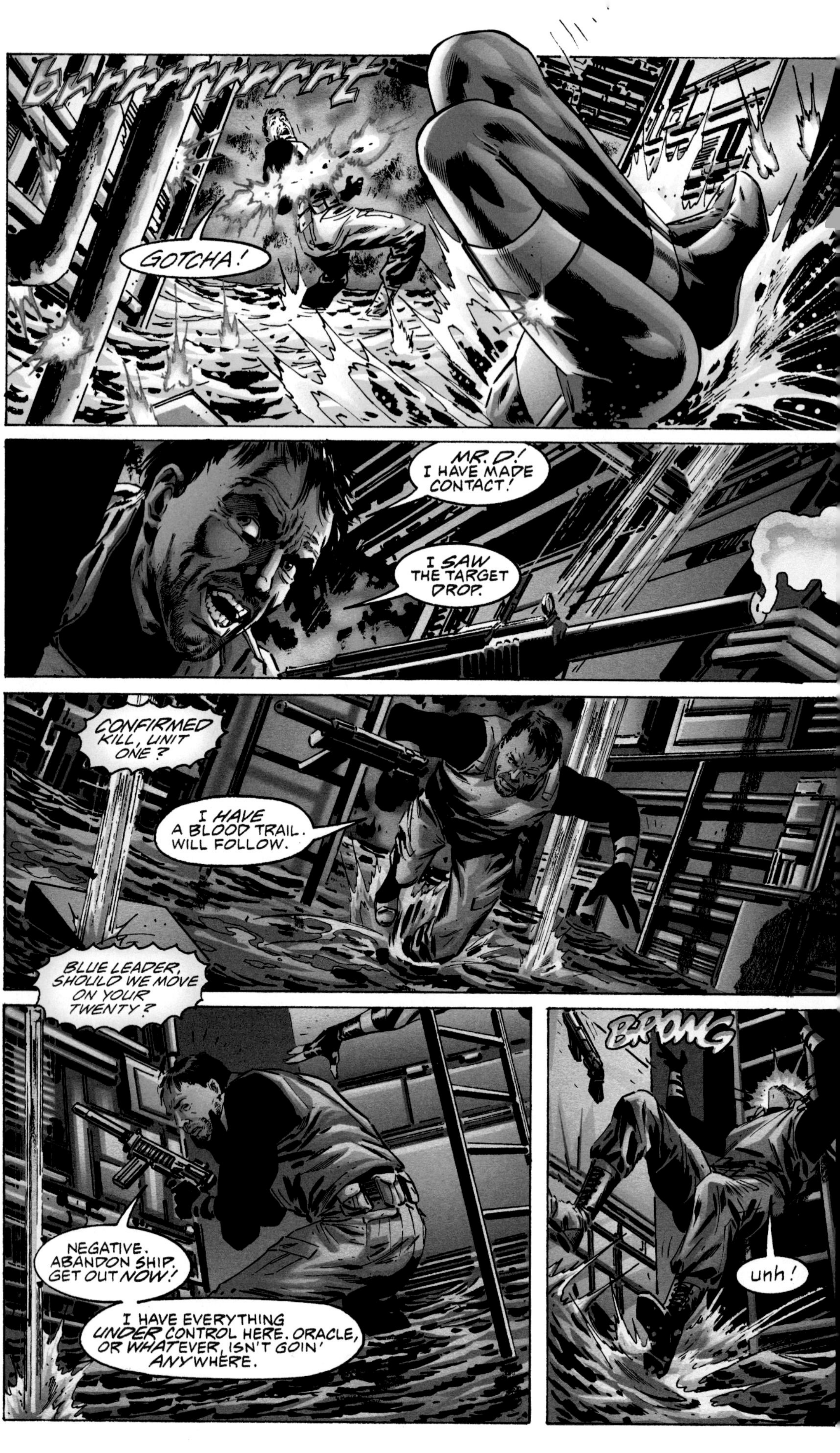
brrrrrrrrrrt
GOTCHA!
MR. D! I HAVE MADE CONTACT!
I SAW THE TARGET DROP.
CONFIRMED KILL, UNIT ONE?
I HAVE A BLOOD TRAIL. WILL FOLLOW.
BLUE LEADER, SHOULD WE MOVE ON YOUR TWENTY?
NEGATIVE. ABANDON SHIP. GET OUT NOW!
I HAVE EVERYTHING UNDER CONTROL HERE. ORACLE, OR WHATEVER, ISN'T GOIN' ANYWHERE.
BRONG
unh!

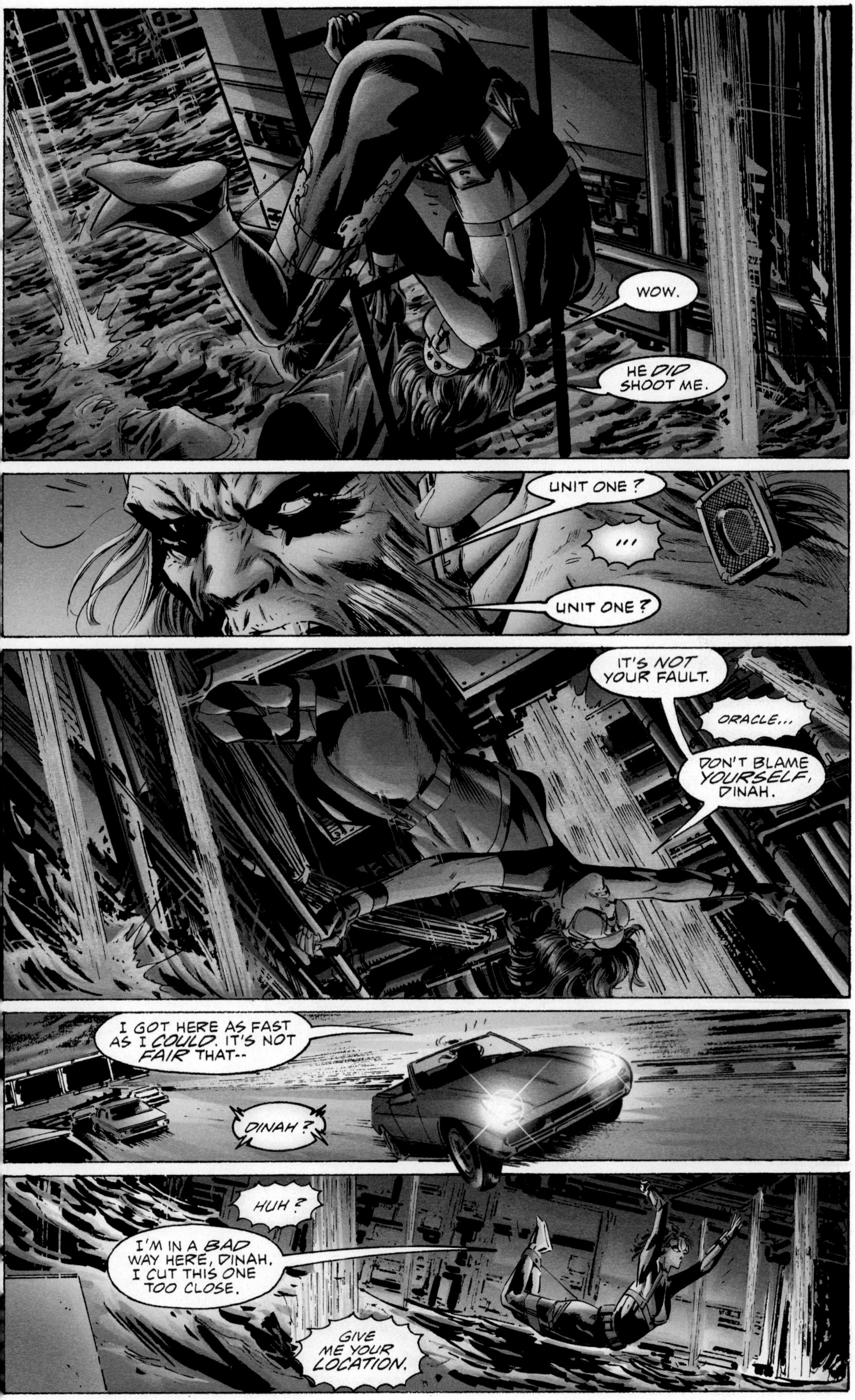
WOW.
HE DID SHOOT ME.
UNIT ONE?
...
UNIT ONE?
IT'S NOT YOUR FAULT.
ORACLE...
DON'T BLAME YOURSELF, DINAH.
I GOT HERE AS FAST AS I COULD. IT'S NOT FAIR THAT--
DINAH?
HUH?
I'M IN A BAD WAY HERE, DINAH. I CUT THIS ONE TOO CLOSE.
GIVE ME YOUR LOCATION.

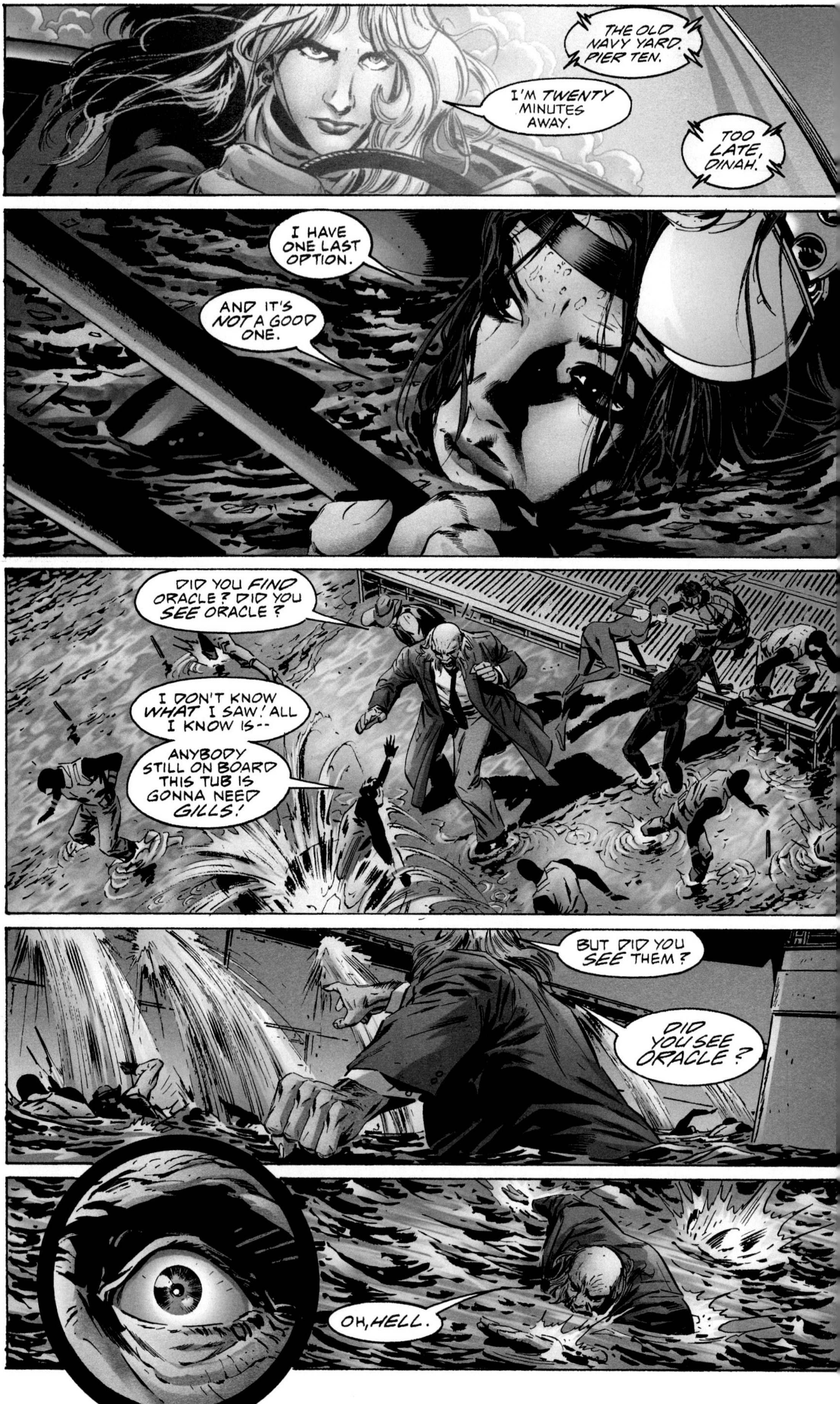
THE OLD NAVY YARD. PIER TEN.
I'M TWENTY MINUTES AWAY.
TOO LATE, DINAH.
I HAVE ONE LAST OPTION.
AND IT'S NOT A GOOD ONE.
DID YOU FIND ORACLE? DID YOU SEE ORACLE?
I DON'T KNOW WHAT I SAW! ALL I KNOW IS--
ANYBODY STILL ON BOARD THIS TUB IS GONNA NEED GILLS!
BUT DID YOU SEE THEM?
DID YOU SEE ORACLE?
OH, HELL.

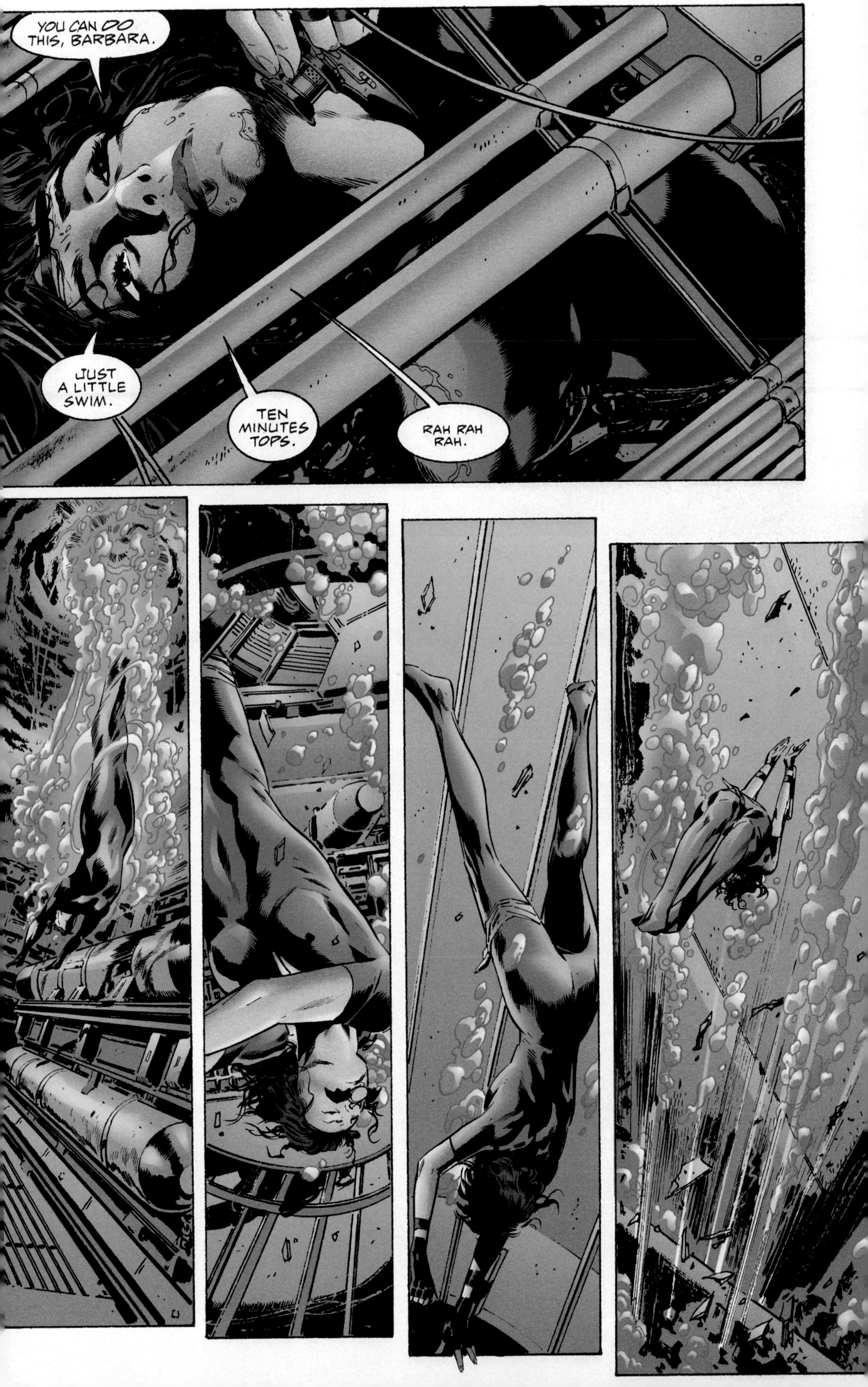
YOU CAN DO THIS, BARBARA.
JUST A LITTLE SWIM.
TEN MINUTES TOPS.
RAH RAH RAH.

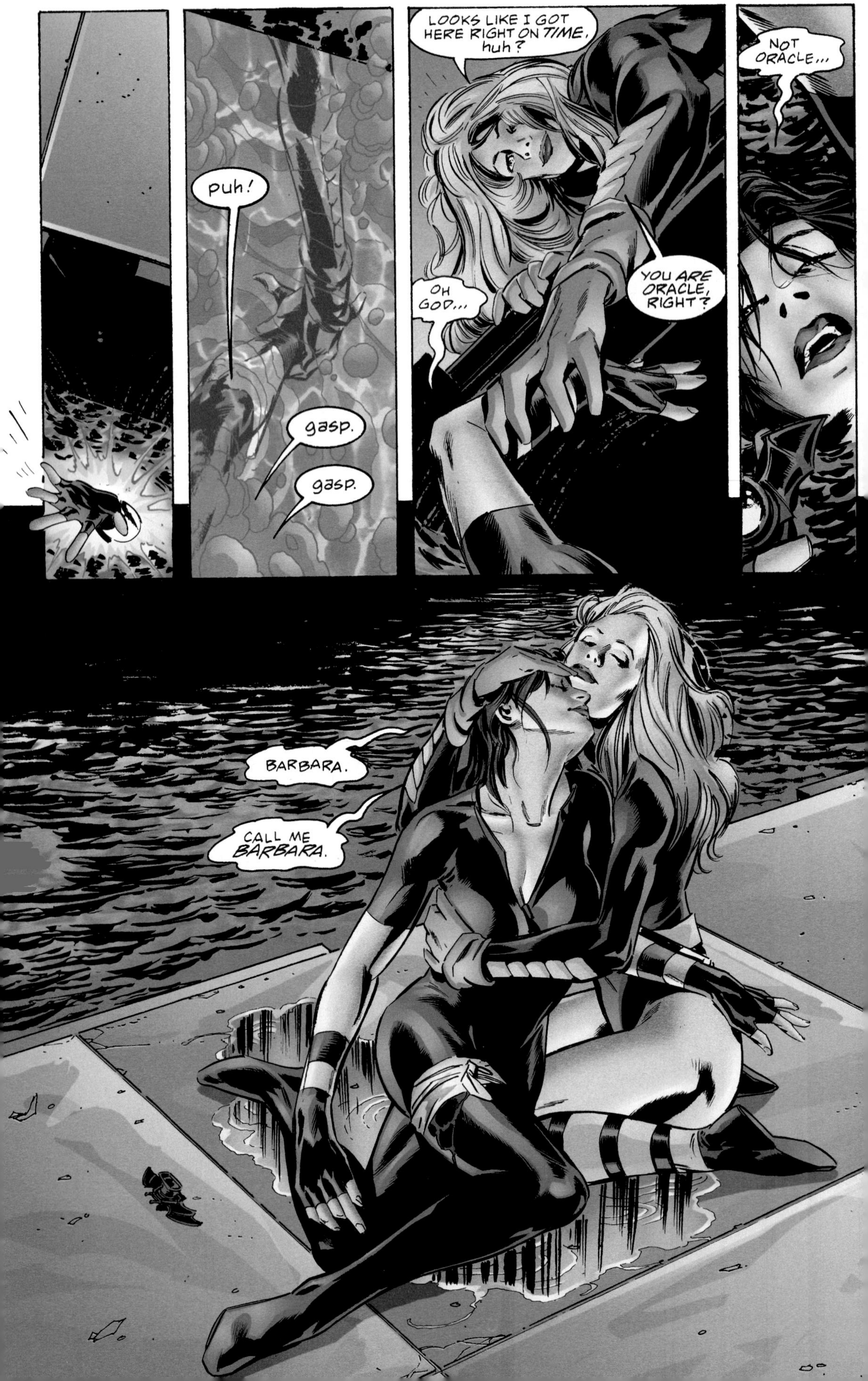
puh!
gasp.
gasp.
LOOKS LIKE I GOT HERE RIGHT ON TIME, huh?
OH GOD...
YOU ARE ORACLE, RIGHT?
NOT ORACLE...
BARBARA.
CALL ME BARBARA.

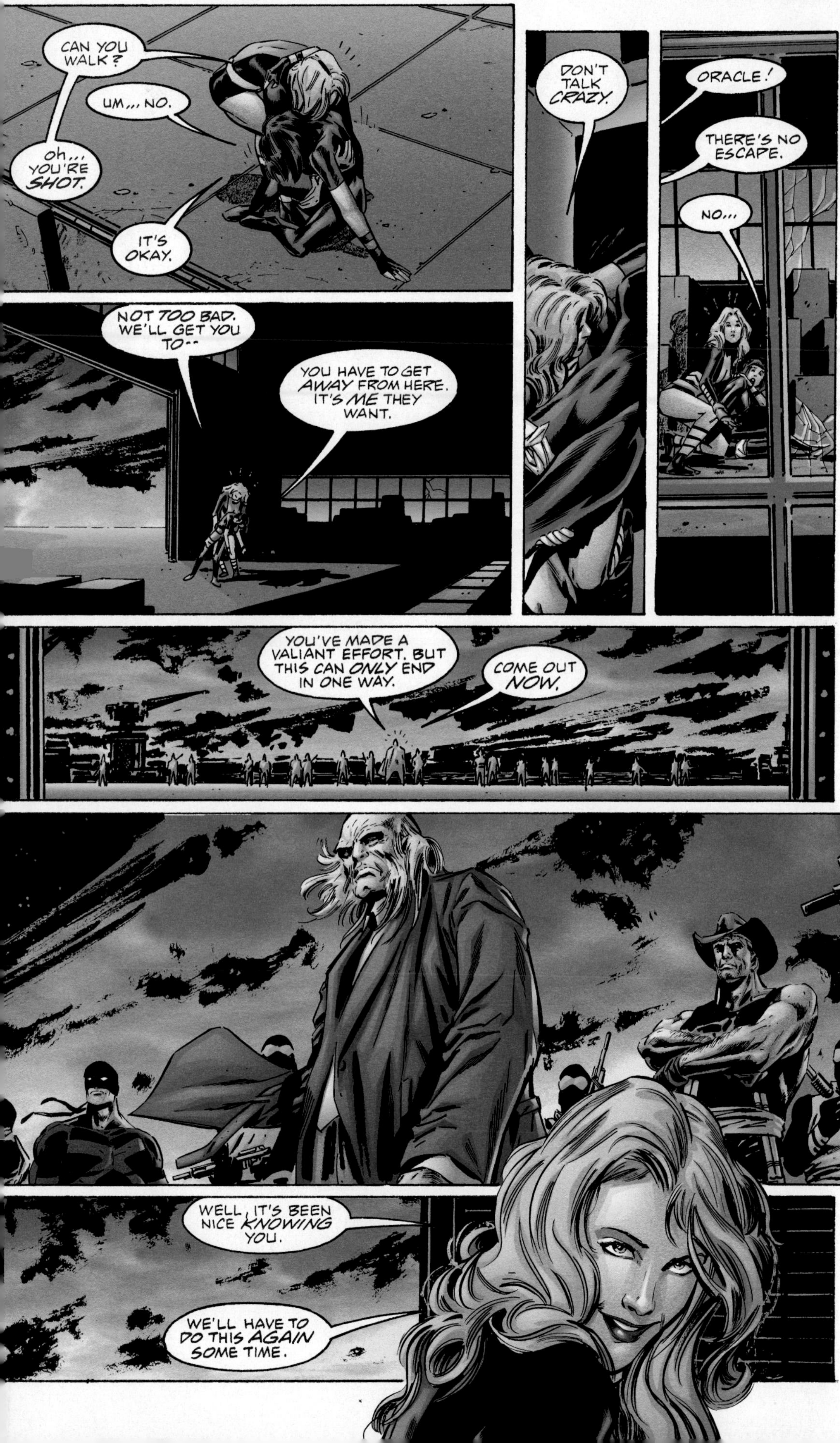
CAN YOU WALK?
UM... NO.
oh... YOU'RE SHOT.
IT'S OKAY.
NOT TOO BAD. WE'LL GET YOU TO--
YOU HAVE TO GET AWAY FROM HERE. IT'S ME THEY WANT.
DON'T TALK CRAZY.
ORACLE!
THERE'S NO ESCAPE.
NO...
YOU'VE MADE A VALIANT EFFORT. BUT THIS CAN ONLY END IN ONE WAY.
COME OUT NOW.
WELL, IT'S BEEN NICE KNOWING YOU.
WE'LL HAVE TO DO THIS AGAIN SOME TIME.

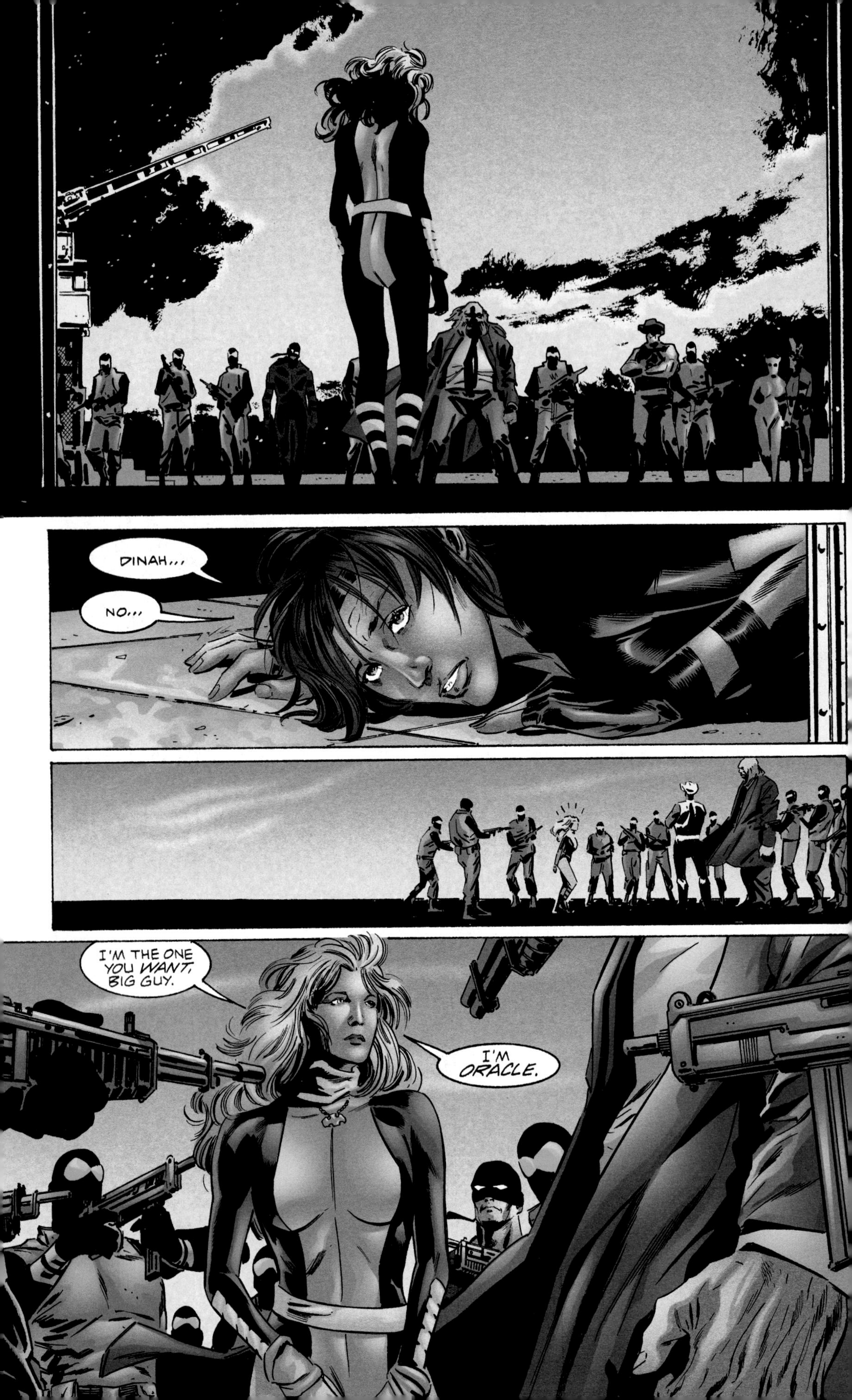
DINAH...
NO...
I'M THE ONE YOU WANT, BIG GUY.
I'M ORACLE.

EPILOGUE

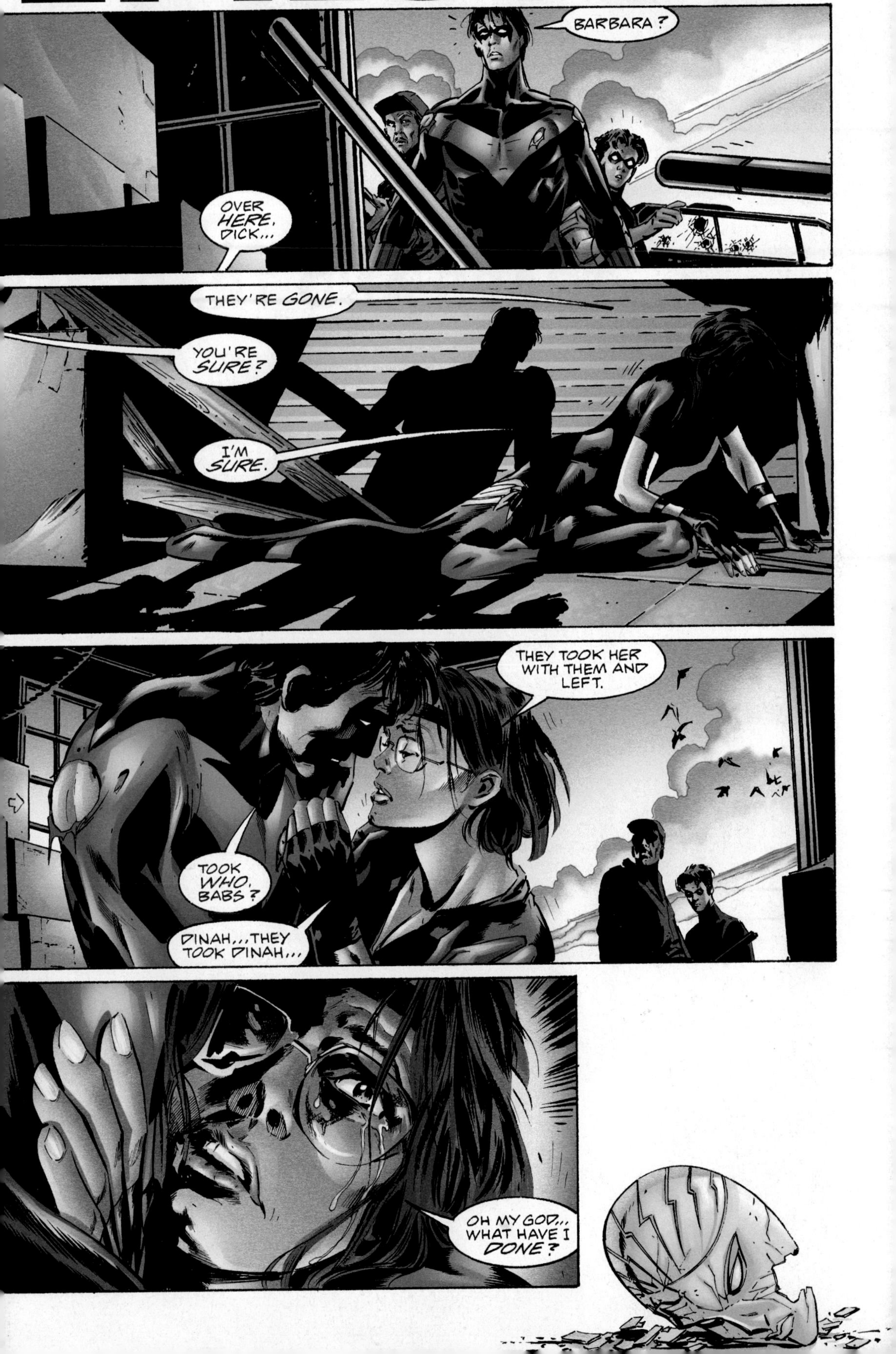
BARBARA?
OVER HERE, DICK...
THEY'RE GONE.
YOU'RE SURE?
I'M SURE.
THEY TOOK HER WITH THEM AND LEFT.
TOOK WHO, BABS?
DINAH... THEY TOOK DINAH...
OH MY GOD... WHAT HAVE I DONE?

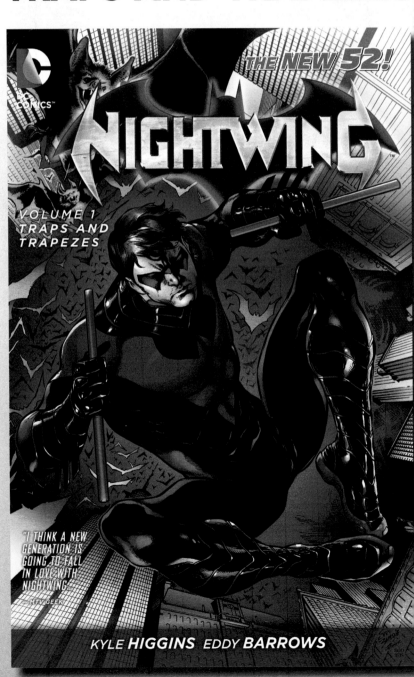